Islam and Capitalism in the Making of Modern Bahrain

Rajeswary Ampalavanar Brown

OXFORD
UNIVERSITY PRESS

OXFORD
UNIVERSITY PRESS

Great Clarendon Street, Oxford, OX2 6DP,
United Kingdom

Oxford University Press is a department of the University of Oxford.
It furthers the University's objective of excellence in research, scholarship,
and education by publishing worldwide. Oxford is a registered trade mark of
Oxford University Press in the UK and in certain other countries

Published in the United States of America by Oxford University Press
198 Madison Avenue, New York, NY 10016, United States of America

British Library Cataloguing in Publication Data
Data available

Library of Congress Control Number: 2022950878

ISBN 978–0–19–287467–2

DOI: 10.1093/oso/9780192874672.001.0001

Printed and bound by
CPI Group (UK) Ltd, Croydon, CR0 4YY

For

Ada, Andrew, Alasdair, and Ian

Acknowledgements

This book began with the aim to challenge two views: that Islam had inhibited capitalist growth in the Middle East: that Shi'ism was a source of tension that invigorated the authoritarian Sunni state. In fact Shi'ism coalesced around the Mat'am, built on its historical transnational trading networks.

I was extremely fortunate in making contact with Adam Swallow and Jade Dixon at Oxford University Press, both of whom were critical in bringing this book to fruition. I will be eternally grateful for their professional support and constant encouragement through often difficult times. I was also extremely fortunate in being led through the production process by Gangaa Radjacoumar and Jennnifer Hinchliffe. Their meticulous attention to detail and their seemingly endless patience were simply remarkable.

I owe an enormous intellectual debt to many Arabic scholars who accepted me even though I am not an Arabist. Nelida Fuccaro not only inspired me but also assisted me with insights that helped me to grasp Bahrain's sovereignty and its relations with the Gulf periphery. My deepest gratitude is for Ali Akbar Busheri of Manama, an erudite scholar and a true friend. He patiently translated a majority of the relevant documents. His and his wife's understanding for the past three years have not only sustained me but have also made our meetings really good fun.

My close friend Jonathan Ercanbrack led me through the huge literature on Islamic finance with a daring interpretation of classic thinking. My review of his *The Transformation of Islamic Law in Global Financial Markets*, which appeared in *Modern Law Review* in May of 2018, transformed me. To my mild astonishment, I have become a kind of historian of Bahrain. My understanding of Syria I owe entirely to Thomas Pierret, a leading historian of that country. A highly perceptive scholar, he offered ideas that were truly provocative, drawing on history, political theory, and ethnography. I must also give a special mention to Nick Foster, whose knowledge of Islamic law, as well as friendship and advice, were invaluable.

I owe a considerable intellectual debt to my husband Ian, and to my sons Andrew and Alasdair. They are always a major source of inspiration and support. This book is dedicated to them, and to my granddaughter Ada, who talks all the time. She provides steadfast love and assurance for all of us. Her ebullient personality is always a treasure.

I was very fortunate to meet Alaa Alaabed in Kuala Lumpur. Her generosity led me to receive help from her mother in the collection of data on Bahrain's stock market. Their collective understanding of the complicated history of the capital markets was remarkable. Additionally, I was very fortunate to meet Manaf Yousuf Hamza, who gave me a copy of his excellent PhD thesis. He was also very generous in providing all the images of Bahrain, from ancient times to the present, that appear in this book. Omid Torabi assisted me with important data on corporations. I do feel sad that Alaa, Manaf, and Omid, each of whom has produced an excellent thesis, have not been able to see them published. In the 1970s, Oxford University Press had an agent stationed in Singapore who sought out theses by local scholars for publication. I was a fortunate beneficiary.

The work of Murat Cizakca on Islamic capitalism and finance greatly inspired me. Dermot Killingley read many of my chapters with remarkable care and assigned me a programme of corrections. Michael Cook read my chapter on Islamic finance, Michael Laffan my chapter on the waqf. Derek George reproduced my image for the back cover. I am most indebted to Julia Charlton of the IT Department at Royal Holloway College, who dealt patiently with my near-endless struggle with technology.

Rana Mitter was supportive and insightful right from the start of my study of Bahrain. I owe a considerable intellectual debt to Tirthankar Roy and his wide-ranging work on the modern economic history of India, and to Khairuddin and to Christian Lekon, and their work on Islam. Chris Bayly was an inspirational historian of Asia and parts of the Middle East. I think often, with great respect, of John Bastin, my graduate supervisor at the School of Oriental and African Studies, who had confidence in me and set me on the right scholarly path. I have also been fortunate to learn much from Charles Tripp, and especially from his work on the moral economy of the Middle East. During my research, I interviewed Hatim El Tahir, the Director of Deloitte in Manama. The interview was approved by the Bahrain Department of Finance; these materials were already in public circulation.

My years of research on Asia involved frequent learning from David Faure, Choi Chi Cheung, and Thomas Dubai. Justin Pierce greatly enhanced my understanding of aspects of Islamic law. In my time at the London School of Economics, first teaching and then on a Leverhulme research fellowship, I learnt much from Les Hannah, Malcolm Faulkus, and Lord Desai in understanding capitalism in all areas of the non-European world. None of the above are responsible for any errors or misjudgements here.

This book would not have been undertaken without funding from the Leverhulme Trust, under its provision of grants for retired scholars. Every effort has been made to secure necessary permissions to reproduce copyright material in this work.

Contents

List of Figures

List of Tables

List of Abbreviations

AAOIFI	Auditing and Accounting Organization for Islamic Financial Institutions
AB	Advising Bank
AFIB	Alternative Finance Investment Bond
BAPCO	Bahrain Petroleum Company
BATELCO	Bahrain Telecommications Company
BCBS	Basel Committee on Banking Supervision
BCSR	Bahrain Centre for Studies and Research
BIS	Bank for International Settlements
CAR	Capital Adequacy Requirement
CDO	Collateralized Debt Obigation
C.E.	Common Era
CIS	Collective Investment Schemes
DCR	Displaced Commercial Risk
DGS	Deposit Guarantee Scheme
DIFC	Dubai International Financial Centre
EC	European Council
EEA	European Economic Area
ESUA	Exchange in Satisfaction and User Agreements
EU	European Union
FSA	Financial Services Authority
FSCS	Financial Services Compensation Scheme
FSMA	Financial Services and Markets Act 2000
GCC	Gulf Cooperation Council
HMRC	Her Majesty's Revenue and Customs
HPP	Home Purchase Plan
IAB	International Accounting Board
IAH	Investment Account Holders
IB	Issuing Bank
IBB	Islamic Bank of Britain
ICC	International Chamber of Commerce
ICTA	Income and Corporations Tax Act
IDB	Islamic Development Bank
IDR	Issuer Default Rating
IFI	Islamic Financial Institution
IFRS	International Financial Reporting Standards
IFSB	Islamic Financial Services Board
IFSL	International Financial Services London
IIC	Islamic Investment Company

IIFM	International Islamic Financial Market
IILM	International Islamic Liquidity Management Centre
IIRA	International Islamic Ratings Agency
IMF	International Monetary Fund
INCOTERMS	International Commercial Terms
IOSCO	International Organization of Securities Commissions
LIBOR	London Interbank Overnight Rate
LIF	Law of Islamic Finance
LMC	Liquidity Management Centre
LRD	Land Registration Department
LSE	London Stock Exchange
MENA	Middle East and North Africa
MLIF	Municipal Law of Islamic Finance
NS&I	National Savings & Investment
OECD	Organization for Economic Cooperation and Development
OIC	Organization of the Islamic Conference
PFLB	Popular Front for the Liberation of Bahrain
PLS	Profit and loss sharing
PRA	Prudential Regulatory Authority
PSIA	Profit-sharing and investment account
RAO	Regulated Activities Order
SDLT	Stamp Duty Land Tax
SPL	Sanghi Polyesters Ltd.
SPV	Special Purpose Vehicle
SSB	Sharia Supervisory Board
TCF	Treating Customers Fairly
TID	The Investment Dar
TII	The International Investor
TNC	Transnational Corporation
UAE	United Arab Emirates
UK	United Kingdom
UNCITRAL	United Nations Commission on International Trade Law
US	United States
VAT	Value Added Tax
WTO	World Trade Organization

1

Introduction

In the Shadow of Ethical Capitalism—The State, Law, Oil, and the Economic Transformation of Bahrain

Bahrain, the small island nation situated in a bay on the south-western coast of the Persian Gulf, experienced a series of quite remarkable economic transformations during the twentieth century. From the seventeenth century, pearling had been the economic mainstay of Bahrain, indeed of coastal peoples throughout the Gulf.[1] By the 1930s, however, pearling had faded, and was replaced as the mainstay of the Bahrain economy by the extraction of crude oil. But oil production in turn faded, as Bahrain's reserves declined by the 1970s, and the country underwent a third economic transformation. In recent decades, Bahrain has created a highly innovative financial sector to serve Bahrain's oil-rich neighbours, a powerful hub of Islamic finance. In this it has been assisted by the huge inflow of oil wealth from the Gulf producers, revenues that have driven the urbanization, industrialization (notably in aluminium and cement), and financial expansion of Bahrain. From the final decades of the twentieth century, oil capital has transformed Bahrain's economy.

This book is concerned principally with that most recent economic transformation, and, in particular, with the emergence of Bahrain as a major centre of Islamic finance. It is therefore much concerned with the details, the mechanics, of economic and financial change. But the book attempts to go much further than that, to explore the social, religious, and political contexts in which that transformation took place, indeed its social, religious, and political impacts. Thus, the creation of a powerful capacity in Islamic finance clearly has a crucial religious context in the need to secure compliance with Shari'ah law. Or again, a vastly growing financial sector, as well as rapid urbanization and industrial expansion, clearly had substantial demographic implications—as indeed had the prosperity of the pearling and

[1] Robert A. Carter, *Sea of Pearls: Seven Thousand Years of the Industry that Shaped the Gulf* (London: Arabian Publishing, 2012).

Islam and Capitalism in the Making of Modern Bahrain. Rajeswary Ampalavanar Brown, Oxford University Press.
© Rajeswary Ampalavanar Brown (2023). DOI: 10.1093/oso/9780192874672.003.0001

then the oil economies in earlier times—for territorially small Bahrain had always been highly dependent on immigrant labour and immigrant skills. And finally, economic transformation—whether from pearling to oil or from oil to Islamic finance—inevitably brought social and political tensions. It is the exploration of those contexts and impacts that drive this book. First, however, it is essential to provide detail on Bahrain's economic, social, and political history, for that history has had a long reach and profoundly shapes modern Bahrain. That historical account is the major concern of this first chapter.

The Evolution of the State

The coastal settlements in the Persian Gulf had long been populated by migrants and merchants, living and trading under local tribal rulers.[2] In the fifteenth century, the islands of Bahrain were ruled by the Al-Jabr family from Najd, with powerful links to Hormuz under Portuguese rule. By the eighteenth century, the Al-Madkhur family from Oman governed Bahrain as a dependency of Iran. In 1783, Utub tribes from the Arabian Peninsula occupied these islands and this ended Iranian power. Subsequently, within the Utub confederation, the Al-Khalifah family became identified with an increasingly important British presence. There soon evolved a modern state under the British. These political changes took place alongside a vibrant commercial culture, a booming trade in Gulf pearls and then, in the twentieth century, the exploitation of oil. Until the last decades of the nineteenth century, British interests in Bahrain were mainly economic and Manama was the commercial centre. By agreements in 1880 and in 1892, Bahrain became an informal British colony. British interference in the affairs of Bahrain then intensified, creating a power struggle between the Al-Khalifah rulers and the British. An important legacy of this contest was the creation of Manama as a powerful mercantile city under British control.

From the 1820s, British influence had become increasingly strong, as the Al-Sabah, Al-Khalifah, and Al-Maktum families established themselves in Kuwait, Bahrain, and Dubai, respectively, as protégées of the Government of

[2] W. Floor, *The Persian Gulf: A Political and Economic History of Five Port Cities, 1500–1730* (Washington, DC: Mage, 2006);Nelida Fuccaro, *Histories of City and State in the Persian Gulf: Manama since 1800* (Cambridge: Cambridge University Press, 2009); Nelida Fuccaro, 'Mapping the Transnational Community: Persians and the Space of the City in Bahrain, c.1869–1937', in *Transnational Connections in the Arab Gulf*, edited by Madawi al-Rasheed (London: Routledge, 2005); Fuad I. Khuri, *Tribe and State in Bahrain: The Transformation of Social and Political Authority in an Arab State* (Chicago, IL: Chicago University Press, 1980).

India.[3] In 1869, Britain imposed an Al-Khalifah as ruler in Bahrain, Shaikh Isa Bin Ali, to bring to an end inter-tribal disputes. Until 1923, the regions of Bahrain were allocated among leading members of the Al-Khalifah family, each having the power to impose taxes and to evolve a distinctive administration. This disadvantaged indigenous groups such as the Bahranah, who were Shia Arabs, and whose lands were appropriated by the Al-Khalifah family. After an uprising in 1922, the British intervened in the following year to remove Shaikh Isa Bin Ali and replace him with his son, Shaikh Hamad Bin Isa.[4]

The period from 1926 to 1957 saw the transformation of Bahrain into a modern state, led by the British Advisor, Charles Belgrave. Under Belgrave's administration, Bahrain's ruling family advanced its status and privileges. Belgrave allocated one-third of oil income to the ruler and reserved all centres of power to the Al-Khalifah family. It relied on oil wealth. With independence in 1971, a constitutional monarchy emerged, with an elected national assembly from 1973. But power and wealth remained firmly concentrated in the ruling family. It controlled most of the land in Bahrain.[5]

Cities are crucial for securing stable political structures, notably for tribal groups seeking to dominate competing tribes, immigrants, and diverse religious groups.[6] Fuccaro notes the weakness of tribal cohesion within urban settings. Ibn Khaldun, too, has emphasized the loss of Al 'asabiyyah, of tribal solidarity, in the urban setting. That said, the building of political and economic institutions reflected ambitions for state creation, contingent on international links within the Middle East. Manama achieved economic and political importance through its Shia merchants, while Muharraq was dominated by Sunnis and by the Al-Khalifah family, which had close ties with the British presence in the region, critical for the rise of a stable state. In the nineteenth century, the development of the tribal towns of Muharraq, Budaya, and Hidd was linked to coastal trade and the pearl trade in particular. This eased the pressure on agricultural land as merchant-seafarers were concentrated in the urban centres. The new tribal-mercantile 'associational

[3] Nelida Fuccaro, 'Pearl Towns and Early Oil Cities: Migration and Integration in the Arab Coast of the Persian Gulf', in *Migration and the Making of Urban Modernity in the Ottoman Empire and Beyond*, edited by Ulrike Freitag, Malte Fuhrmann, Nora Lafi, and Florian Riedler (London: Routledge, 2010), pp. 99–100.
[4] T. T. Farah, *Protection and Politics in Bahrain 1869–1915* (Beirut: The American University of Beirut, 1985); Khuri, *Tribe and State in Bahrain*; A. B. Kemball, 'Statistical and Miscellaneous Information Connected with the Possessions, Revenues, Families of the Ruler of Bahrain', *Bombay Selections*, vol. 24, p. 291.
[5] M. Herb, *All in the Family: Absolutism, Revolution, and Liberal Prospects in the Middle East Monarchies* (New York: Suny Press, 1998).
[6] Nelida Fuccaro, 'Understanding the Urban History of Bahrain', *Critique: Critical Middle Eastern Studies*, vol. 17 (2000), p. 51.

economy' played a major role in financing the pearl trade, later moving with ease into the oil industry. Many areas of Muharraq, Budaya, and Hidd had tribal names that declared their kinship-based organization.[7] Thus Muharraq became a marker for Sunni tribal authority. This marked the decline of Bahrain's Shi'a community, and the weakening of its religious institution, Bilad Al-Qadim. In the twentieth century, the growth of Manama as the centre of British commercial operations led Shi'as to protect their Islamic traditions through the Waqf and Ma'tam. In 1832, Manama had a population of around 25,000, which included non-tribal Shi'a, Iranians, and Arabs from Al-Ahsa', Al-Qatif, and Basra. The Sunni population was fragmented and included Arab tribes from coastal areas surrounding Bahrain, slave families, and 550 Utub.[8] Manama, with its considerable British presence, soon became the new political capital, with a municipal government under close British supervision. The establishment of the municipality (Al-baladiyyah Al-Manama) in 1919 was a significant move by the British in transferring regional autonomy to Shi'as, in that it preserved moderate Shi'ism and leadership as well as Ja'fari jurisprudence within the community. The establishment of the municipality in 1919 built local power by creating socio-economic spaces independent of the ruling family that had secured control through a relative of the Amir. The municipality also acquired control over the provision of electricity, roads, markets, gardens, cemeteries, and the police. It became a powerful autonomous institution supported by taxes on water, houses, and commercial premises. A special tax was levied on customs duties until 1929, when it was replaced by a monthly government subsidy.[9]

The British perceived the decentralized, patrimonial, coercive system of tribal estates under the control of the monarchy as being detrimental to administration and to the protection of important communities, both Bahraini and non-Bahraini. Manama had a high proportion of Indians, Iranians, and immigrants from the Arabian Peninsula. In 1905, Britain acquired direct jurisdiction over these groups and created a legal structure that gave non-Bahrainis representation on the municipal council. Four out of the eight members of the council belonged to Bahrain's foreign communities and were direct appointments by the British political agent. This increased the communities' influence and reinforced Bahrain's cosmopolitan culture. The Al-baladiyyah Al-Manama thus had an important role in modernizing the

---

[7] Fuccaro, 'Understanding the Urban History of Bahrain', p. 55.

[8] John George Lorimer, *The Gazetteer of the Persian Gulf, Oman and Central Arabia* (Calcutta: Office of the Superintendent Government Printing, 1908; republished by Farnborough: Gregg International, 1970), vol. 2, p. 1160.

[9] 'Municipal Proclamations, 1929–1950', India Office Records R/15/2/1250 and R/15/2/1218, cited in Fuccaro, 'Understanding the Urban History of Bahrain', pp. 57–9.

state, by providing a municipal structure with independent power.[10] Similar structures were established for Muharraq in 1927, Hidd in 1945, Rifa' in 1951, and Sitra and Jidd Hafs in 1958. These advances were funded by the discovery of oil in the 1930s. After Bahrain gained independence in 1971, Al-baladiyyah and Makhatira came under a newly created Ministry of Housing and Agriculture. The entire territory of the islands was organized into eight municipal districts: Manama, Muharraq, Jidd Hafs, Northern Area, Al-Budayya', Central Area, Sitra, and Rifa'. The districts, urban and rural, were integrated into a centralized political system.[11]

The British-established municipalities created serious tensions with the tribal identities of the Al-Khalifah monarchy. On the one hand, it was feared that the municipalities were symbolic of Bahrain's submission to the British. On the other, the municipalities could be seen as securing the modernization of Bahrain and as closing the Shi'a–Sunni divide and the urban–rural division.[12] Fuccaro has demonstrated that urbanization contributed to the fragmentation of Bahrain's political culture and social fabric. As early as 1904, Lorimer[13] had shown the exploitation of rural Shi'a by urban-dominated Sunni tribal groups. Also evident was the absence of a tribal kinship ideology among Shi'ite, which hampered the creation of a sustainable political leadership. The Sunni–Shi'a divide and the widening urban–rural division arose from rapid urbanization. Between 1941 and 1981, the urban population grew from 56 per cent to 81 per cent of the total population. In fact, as early as 1959, only 5 per cent of the labour force was engaged in agriculture.[14] This urban growth was focused on Manama, Hidd, and Rifa, and on housing towns such as Isa Town and Hamad Town. Rural society was isolated and suffered marked economic deprivation, while the new towns increased sectarian tensions, especially after the 1979 Iranian Revolution and as the poor Shi'a religious networks expressed opposition to the state. The Shi'a identified poverty with state oppression.

With the expansion of Manama from the early nineteenth century, the rich merchants there established increasing ties with its administrative elite. By the 1930s, Manama had been transformed from tribal rule to municipal administration. Charles Belgrave, the British Advisor to the ruler between

---

[10] R. L. Hill, 'Baladiyya-Arab East', *Encyclopedia of Islam*, 2nd ed., vol. 1, 1976.

[11] Fuccaro, 'Understanding the Urban History of Bahrain', p. 59.

[12] M. G. Rumaihi, *Bahrain: Social and Political Change Since the First World War* (London: Bowker, 1976).

[13] John Lloyd Lorimer, *The Gazetteer of the Persian Gulf, Oman, and Central Arabia*. Calcutta: Office of the Superintendent Government Printing, 1908, vol. 2, pp. 237-41, 622.

[14] Nelida Fuccaro, 'Understanding the Urban History of Bahrain', p. 61; Bahrain: Ministry of State for Cabinet Affairs, Directorate of Statistics, The Population of Bahrain: Trends and Prospects (January 1979), pp. 79–80.

1926 and 1957, reformed state institutions and administrative and financial procedures.[15] This led to extensive land reclamation along the northern and eastern coast of Manama, and the redirection of economic and financial interests towards the sea and away from rural Bahrain. There would be no coherent rural administration until the creation of the Makhatira Office in the 1950s.

For over two centuries, Manama has been the major centre for Bahrain's merchant community, with close ties to the ruling elite. The expansion of trade conducted by Indian and Iranian merchants, each with strong links to the local aristocracy, was secured by the fact that those foreign merchants enjoyed British protection.[16] The strong foreign presence in Manama led to a renaissance of religious institutions such as the Ma'tam, Ja'fari courts, clubs, schools, and trade unions in both rural and urban areas. Religious ceremonies such as Ashura performed by the Ma'tam became institutionalized in Manama, strengthening the social and religious identities of the Shi'a majority. The Ma'tam and the Ashura ritual also became instruments for airing grievances against the Sunni state. In 1892, the Ma'tam Al-Ajam Al Kabir embraced substantial numbers of Iranian immigrants in Ajam, Laki, and Kanu. In 1895, the Ma'tam Al-'Ahsa'iyyin at Muharraq also had substantial numbers of immigrants. 'New nationalist slogans, class divisions and ideas of social progress were closely intertwined with old patronage politics, quarter solidarities, manifestations of religious devotion and religious organizations.'[17] There were two important and interdependent dimensions of the city and region that shaped the religious and legal autonomy, as well as the socio-economic power, of the Shi'a. First was the emergence of a formal British protectorate and the modernization of state and administration, for this involved the creation of local government, a centre of power in the municipality. The new municipal power that embraced the mercantile community, assumed responsibility for legislation and taxation. Thus, in the 1920s, the municipality acted as the main source of legislation, in parallel with the customs administration and the Department of Land Registration. However, to reduce the excessive and often corrupt ambitions of Shaykh Hamad, in 1929–30 Charles Belgrave dismantled the municipal regime headed by the regent. The Majlis (tribal council) was dissolved and Shaykh 'Abdallah, Hamad's brother, was appointed the new head. This marked a shift in power from the municipality to the administration led by Belgrave. With the

---

[15] Fuccaro, 'Understanding the Urban History of Bahrain', pp. 71–2.
[16] Fuccaro, 'Understanding the Urban History of Bahrain', p. 73; Fuccaro, *Histories of City and State*, pp. 73–111.
[17] Fuccaro, *Histories of City and State*, p. 225.

decline of the pearl industry followed by the depression of the 1930s, popular discontent rose, with land possession, and specifically a sharp increase in illegal landlords, a significant issue. Shi'ite land ownership was at stake.[18] Defining land possession and regulating transfers in land use required technical legal competence. But this was often difficult to achieve in a period of political volatility and substantial economic change.

The creation of the Department of Land Registration (LRD) in 1925 was followed in 1926 with the establishment of two Waqf departments.[19] However, the law considered all unregistered plots of land as belonging to the state and this created problems for the Waqf and for the LRD. The Waqf Directorate had to apply to the courts to claim ownership of land and to government departments for building and water supply permits. Most of the Waqf land, acquired through inheritance, was not registered, and therefore was open to being taken over by the state. Even in the 1990s, claims by the Ja'fari Waqf's in Bahrain's courts for the registration of properties accounted for 30 per cent of cases relating to property.[20] Earlier, in 1926, Charles Belgrave, who feared increasing disorder as a result of the proliferation of illegal landlords, sought to enforce the registration of mortgages and to provide legal protection for vulnerable residents in both the rural districts and in Manama. A proclamation in December 1927 required the registration of land. A further proclamation in May 1930 introduced registration fees, while a third proclamation in August 1932 laid down the procedures for acquiring mortgages. Finally, legislation in 1940 established the legal requirements to confirm ownership of land, and these have remained in force.[21] The 1973 Constitution also sought to provide protection for land ownership. The National Charter of 2001 emphasized that private ownership is inviolable, and that private land could be appropriated by the state only for public purpose. At the same time, the Civil Law of September 2001 declared that all unregistered land belongs to the state. In fact, inherited Shi'ite lands were vulnerable to seizure, not only by the state but also by private interests.[22] The Acquisition and Compensation Law of 1970 gave the right to take over land only to the state. However, BAPCO and ALBA acquired oil-bearing land from the Ministry of

---

[18] Fuccaro, *Histories of City and State*, pp. 125–6.

[19] References in British Library, India Office Records (IOR) 23/6/1923 and IOR 18/7/1927.

[20] Manaf Yousuf Hamza, 'Land Registration in Bahrain: its Past, Present and Future within an Integrated GIS Environment' (PhD dissertation, University of East London, 2003), p. 41.

[21] References in IOR 15/2/1940.

[22] This abuse of the Acquisition and Compensation Law of 1970 is recorded in the Bahrain media: *Al-Ayam*, 22 July 2002, 12 January 2003, 15 March 2003; *Akhbar–Alkhaleej*, 18 July 2002; *Al-Wasat*, 10 March 2003.

Oil and BATELCO from the Ministry of Works. Here the LRD had no control over land transactions. A further complicating issue concerned the right of non-Bahrainis (Arabs, Iranians, Indians, and Europeans) to own land. The Nationality Law and the Land Ownership Proclamation issued in 1937 had withdrawn from foreign nationalities the right to own land in Bahrain and had given the state the authority to seize their properties. But with the establishment of the GCC in May 1981, GCC citizens acquired the right to own property in Bahrain. Other nationalities could own property only in specific areas.

It is important to relate this account of the legal position of land in Bahrain to Sunni and Shi'ite laws governing Waqf land, the mosques, graveyards, shops, residential buildings, gardens, and open lands. Shi'a religious courts dealt with the law relating to personal status, that included the ownership of land and immovable property. The Shi'a courts were thus involved in dispute settlement. Shi'ites concentrated more on the Ma'tam than on the Waqf as it was a distinct institution and was less vulnerable to seizure by the state.[23] Rising political and religious authority and increasing cosmopolitanism led to the inclusion of Shari'ah law and customary law alongside Indian criminal and civil law in the courts of the British protectorate.

It would be appropriate now to consider urbanization and socio-economic change in Muharraq before returning to consider Manama and its socio-economic evolution, shaped to a large degree by oil. The growth of Muharraq on the north-eastern island of Bahrain led to its emergence as the capital of the Al-Khalifah administration. It also accommodated a majority of the Utub groups who arrived from the late eighteenth century. By 1905, there were 2800 Utub in Muharraq out of a total population of around 20,000.[24] However, Muharraq lost influence from 1905 and the Al-Khalifah administration moved to Sakhir in the 1920s, although it remained part of the tribal hinterland surrounding Manama. The powerful pearling tribes of Muharraq, including Al-Jalahimah and Al-Ibn 'Ali, owned a large number of ships and they financed the industry. Their wealth reinforced relations with the ruling aristocracy, although they formed a close urban community. It was their tribal solidarity, as opposed to sectarian sentiment, which articulated the urban hierarchies of royalty and merchants.[25] The distance between them and the poor Shi'a agriculturalists was clear. Lorimer classed them as a 'race' as

---

[23] Fuccaro, *Histories of City and State*, pp. 16–17, 219; Fuccaro, 'Understanding the Urban History of Bahrain', p. 78.
[24] Lorimer, *The Gazetteer of the Persian Gulf*, vol. 2, p. 1270.
[25] Fuccaro, *Histories of City and State*, pp. 26, 29.

opposed to a 'tribe'.[26] The distinct character of Shi'ite villages included allotments with canals and water wells. This differential power and hierarchy, built on economic specialization and sectarian affiliation, was evident in the fact that tribal aristocrats resided in the oldest quarters of Muharraq, while Shi'a artisans and Hawala merchants formed their own enclaves.[27] This pattern of separation persisted into the 1960s.

In contrast, Manama had a mixed population and developed diverse clusters of immigrants. Its merchants were of mixed backgrounds and the wealthy elite included Sunni, Shi'a, and Hawala Arabs from southern Iran, along with Persians and Indians. These communities were socially and politically outside the tribal structure, and they exploited the international ambitions and competitiveness of the city. This fed into the urbanization of Manama, creating new centres of economic power, driven by the oil industry from the 1950s and Islamic finance from the 1970s. The tribal identity of the Al-Khalifah family and their ties to select business elites meant that Shi'ite clerics sought unity through rituals (as in Ashura) and in Ma'tam congregations to secure their power and social visibility. The importance of the Ma'tam led Busheri and Kazeruni, powerful Shi'a families, to bring 30 per cent of the Persian population of Dashti under their protection in Manama, providing stronger links to religious and political structures.[28] Some Manama Shi'a leaders did create social and political connections in rural Manama. The Ibn Rajabs acquired land in their ancestral village of Bilad Al-Qadim.[29] These merchants also invested in property of Manama for reasons of political prestige. Religious buildings in Manama demonstrated mercantile power. They were symbols of wealth connected to charities, that is to the Waqf and Ma'tam. Abd Al-'Aziz Lutf' Ali Khunji, a merchant from Lingah, sponsored the large mosque in the suq and was a prominent local philanthropist. He also established several mosques for destitute Persian and Baluchi immigrants in poor districts of Manama. Shi'a concentrated on the Ma'tam and, by 1913, Manama had 13 Ma'tam buildings, creating communal enclaves of piety and philanthropy.[30] The early sponsors of these charities were pearl merchants, landowners, even artisans, petty traders, Shi'ite fishermen, and labourers. After the collapse of pearling in the late 1920s, these endowments came under the scrutiny of the religious courts and were integrated into the modern administration. But community

---

[26] Lorimer, *The Gazetteer of the Persian Gulf*, vol. 2, pp. 237–41.
[27] Lorimer, *The Gazetteer of the Persian Gulf*, vol. 2, pp. 1269–71.
[28] Interview with Ali Akbar Busheri, 2 August 2015.
[29] Minutes by Political Agent Bahrain, 21 January 1938, IOR R/15/2/151.
[30] Fuccaro, *Histories of City and State*, pp. 105–10.

Ma'tams (Ma'tim) still remained, financed by individual contributions from elite merchants. After 1939, the Ma'tam also became associated with diverse professionals.

Another significant development was the acquisition of property in Muharraq by Sunni Persian notables, specifically in Al-Hidd and the two Al-Rifa towns which already had a Sunni majority. These became powerful, cohesive districts with clear ethnic sectarian personalities, providing Bahrain with a stable socio-economic structure. In urban Manama, the Al-Khalifah administration, with its ties to India, Qatar, Iran, and the Saudi Emirs of central Arabia, created a powerful clique. The merchants, both Shi'a and Sunni, were dependent on the Al-Khalifah administration in both their long-distance and transit trade and in order to exploit the opportunities brought by oil. There were important differences between Manama and Muharraq. The advantages of Manama included its strong civic identity and the British presence, which loosened the grip of the Bahrain rulers. It had strong connections to the maritime economy and yet possessed spatial proximity to rural Bahrain. Its merchants acted as brokers between the Al-Khalifah family and Bahrain's external economy.[31] The unique socio-economic and political structure of Manama made it distinctive, even after Bahrain's union with the Gulf states within the GCC in 1981.

The extraction of oil interacted with the political order and social institutions of Bahrain in distinctive ways, quite different from Kuwait, the UAE, and Saudi Arabia. Urbanization, modernization, state centralization, and the in-migration of workers from Pakistan, India, and the Philippines are central themes in the narrative of Bahrain's oil economy. Earlier, the centres of the pearling industry had attracted merchants from India, Iran, and East Africa, and had created secure commercial communities in Manama. These immigrant merchants were a powerful economic force and were not subject to state control: they became liable for customs duties only after 1869. The Indian and Persian merchants carved out powerful positions as horse dealers and in commodity trade, notably trade in foodstuffs. A close relationship emerged between the immigrant merchants and the indigenous rulers.

The immigrants to Bahrain in the early nineteenth century carried British Indian certificates issued by the British in India. In 1860, the law in India was codified and subsequently the Indian legal code was extended to the Gulf.[32] After the First World War, this extra-territorial jurisdiction was clarified by orders-in-council decrees that transformed the principalities in the Gulf

---

[31] Fuccaro, *Histories of City and State*, pp. 9–14.
[32] Husain M. Al-Baharna, *British Extra-Territorial Jurisdiction in the Gulf 1913–1971* (Slough: Archive Editions, 1998), pp. 1–51.

into imperial protectorates. By the interwar period, Bahrain was attracting migrants from Persia, East Africa, Egypt, and Iraq, although the majority still came from India. By 1923, British agents in Manama were operating a modern customs administration, which required traders to confirm their nationality. The use of registration of nationality for, in effect, surveillance was opposed by Shi'a and Sunni clerics who feared it would fragment the transnational community. Nationality papers became subject to intense scrutiny, in particular the papers of pearl divers and labourers from Najd and Iran, who were regarded as major instigators of urban unrest. When the British authorities initiated the reform of tribal administration in the 1920s, it aroused opposition from the Al-Khalifah aristocracy, who argued that Persian immigrants were foreigners benefiting from the British protectorate.[33] The Bahrain Nationality and Property Law of 1937 targeted the Persians, encouraging them to abandon their links with Persia. The subjects of Al-Khalifah, including Arab Persians, were now given Bahraini citizenship. At issue was the ownership of land and property. The 1937 Bahrain Nationality and Property Law sought to transform wealthy Persians into loyal citizens. This alerted immigrants to the need to acquire land to secure their legal position. The nationality laws now led to an increase in the issue of official permits, although a large number of Persians who held no official passport were imprisoned. The emphasis on ownership of property and on nationality replaced traditional loyalties and increased the cosmopolitan nature of Bahrain. However, rural Bahrain was still home to more Shi'ites, a reminder of the earlier in-migration of Persians. Oil had made obsolete the existing network structures, a development associated with in-migration from Asia, Persia, and the Gulf states, with an emphasis on religious identity and the regional economies. This development was contingent on international linkages, both commercial and political.

The immigrants included not only merchants and labourers but also Sunni and Shi'a ulama from Najd and Iraq, escaping the puritanical Wahhabi regime established by the Al-Sa'ud family in central Arabia and the new orthodoxy promoted by the Hamidian regime in southern Iraq.[34] Thus, ulama, merchants, and migrant workers all sought a new beginning in Bahrain. The Gulf's seafaring and migrating culture had underscored Bahrain's cosmopolitan character. The most successful maritime empire was that of the

---

[33] British Resident Bushehr to Foreign Department, Government of India, 17 December 1904, IOR L/P&S/1081; Fuccaro, *Histories of City and State*, chapter 5.

[34] Selim Deringil, 'The Struggle against Shi'ism in Hamidian Iraq: A Study in Ottoman Counter-Propaganda', *Die Welt des Islams* (Leiden: Brill, New Series, 1990), pp. 45–62.

Al-Qawasim in the UAE from the eighteenth century.[35] The Indian merchants included Hindu moneylenders. The Ismaili Shi'a sect was particularly
powerful and from the 1830s the British favoured Persian merchants. Wealthy
Indian merchants congregated in syndicates protected by British law and
traded in food, textiles, and pearls. Slaves were brought from East Africa and
Baluchistan, even after emancipation. The urban centre, shaped by diverse
immigration, retained strong family and religious networks.[36]

Bahrain's competitive advantage over its Gulf neighbours derived from the
in-migration of merchants and its specialization in the pearl industry and
in transnational trade. After the discovery of oil in the early 1930s, new centres of economic power emerged in Manama, and subsequently underpinned
Bahrain's rise as a major hub of Islamic finance. Granovetter has emphasized the 'strong embeddedness' of regional business networks woven into
economic specialisms.[37]

The in-migration of merchants reinforced identity politics, as merchant
families from across the Middle East emphasized their tribal, family, and
religious connections in the port towns and in their transnational networks.
The Al-Shirawis, Ashis, Kanoos, Al-Gurg, and the Al-Muwayyad are prominent examples.[38] Tribal patronage was closely identified with the state and
the ruling aristocracies, whose alliances with tribal leaders, merchants, and
militias were vital in maintaining the stability of the state. The aristocracies
cemented their power through political and economic alliances and moulded
the political infrastructure of urban society. Clusters of Indian and Persian
merchants managed Manama. In contrast, the pearling industry had earlier attracted numerous tribes, villagers, and agriculturalists. At the turn of
the twentieth century, Shi'a from the agricultural regions of Bahrain and Al-
Ahsa' had moved to Manama, but they were transient and moved from port
to port. In contrast, the Arab, Persian, Indian, and Jewish merchant families
built links with other migrant groups and created institutions separate from
the existing tribal administration—modern schools, mosques, synagogues,
Hindu temples, Husayniyyahs (temple for commemorating life and martyrdom of Shii imam Husayn) for the celebration of Ashura, and even Majlises
used for the distribution of food to the poor. Their close connections with the
British and the Saudi family of central Arabia were reasons for the strength

[35] Nelida Fuccaro, 'Pearl Towns and Early Oil Cities', pp. 99–116.
[36] Fuccaro, 'Pearl Towns and Early Oil Cities'; Fuccaro, 'Mapping the Transnational Community',
pp. 39–58.
[37] M. Granovetter, 'Problems of Explanation in Economic Sociology', in *Networks and Organizations:
Structure, Form and Action*, edited by N. Nohria and R. Eccles (Cambridge, MA: Harvard University Press,
1992), p. 5.
[38] Fuccaro, 'Pearl Towns and Early Oil Cities', pp. 99–116.

of Shi'ism in Bahrain. In contrast, labour migrants suffered social isolation, spatial segregation, and political marginalization. The shanty towns outside the inner cities clung to ethnic solidarities and outside Manama they were populated mainly by Persians. The ancient Persian Shi'a families had ancestral links with greater Bahrain, a formidable historical legacy. The emphasis on tribal ancestry boosted the development of a local Shi'ite movement. In Manama, the Kanoo family, one of the richest in the Gulf, claimed to have come from southern Iraq and Iran in the eighteenth century.[39]

The interactions of immigrant and indigenous religious, cultural, political, legal, and bureaucratic tenets produced a social and political cosmopolitanism in Bahrain distinct in the Gulf, reinforced with the arrival of oil. Bahrain was unique in the individuality of its laws and institutions, and this not only shaped its modernity but also curbed Shi'ite sectarianism. The Shi'ites maintained institutions such as the Ma'tam and their public Ashura ceremonies, and rarely pursued sectarian extremes.

Another crucial feature of Bahrain's urban development was the emergence of voluntary associations that reinforced patron–client structures, especially in Manama. This was a key factor in shaping in-migration into Bahrain. The associations, particularly the Waqf and Ma'tam of the Shi'ites, achieved religious autonomy, independent Ja'fari courts, and a role in local politics. A variety of circumstances created Shi'ite stability in Bahrain, in contrast to a descent into sectarian violence, notably in Syria.[40]

The municipal administration shaped the economy and business.[41] The merchant class exploited the municipality of Manama, created in 1919, to establish patronage networks with the royal family. Business provided institutional platforms for the distribution of civic assistance, jobs, food, and funds for Ashura ceremonies. The municipal councils assumed responsibility for public health, as well as compliance with building regulations and the maintenance of public areas. Administrative structures brought political affiliations, notably with the Al-Khalifah family. Patronage became crucial in elections to municipal councils. Only property owners were entitled to vote.[42] The creation of the municipality secured the power of the ruling family, although it also limited the potential excesses of an authoritarian state.

---

[39] Fuccaro, *Histories of City and State*, chapter 3; Khalid M. Kanoo, *The House of Kanoo: A Century of an Arabian Family Business* (London: London Centre of Arabian Studies, 1997), p. 1.

[40] See Thomas Pierret, *Religion and State in Syria: Sunni Ulama from Coup to Revolution* (Cambridge: Cambridge University Press, 2013).

[41] Fuccaro, 'Pearl Towns and Early Oil Cities', pp. 99–116.

[42] Fuccaro, 'Pearl Towns and Early Oil Cities', pp. 100–8; electoral lists and minutes of local meetings for 1927–29 (IOR 15/2/1923 and 1218]; 1934–45 (IOR R/15/2/1921 to 1931); 1946–50 (IOR R/15/2/1932).

In 1945, Charles Belgrave initiated Manama's waterfront renewal. That development was implemented in stages through land reclamation. Belgrave's remarkable creation was Bab Al-Bahrayn, which he designed in 1945 as the seat of government.[43] This was part of a complex that was built in front of the harbour after 1939. That rectangular building was conceived as the gateway to modern Bahrain, said to resemble the Gateway to India, built by the British in Bombay between 1913 and 1924. The Bab Al-Bahrayn building fused British colonial public architecture with distinct Arab features in the balustrades and doors. The development of Manama's waterfront from the 1950s was clearly a response to the needs of the oil industry. Manama's new warehouses were the largest in the Gulf, serving Bahrain as well as the oil companies in Qatar and Saudi Arabia and the international firms that had now begun to establish branches in Bahrain.[44] Government investment in customs and excise facilities, offices, and in modern technology, ambitious projects to expand the export–import economy, led to further development of the waterfront on the northeast coast. The islands surrounding Bahrain were connected by new causeways and bridges, while new airport facilities consolidated Bahrain's position as a major air-transport hub. British withdrawal in 1971 led to further redesigning of the north waterfront. Among the new prestige projects were the Bahrain Financial Harbour in Manama in the 1990s, followed by the Shaikh Khalifa bin Salman Port at Hidd in 2003. The reclamation of Bandar Al Seef as a district of Al-Busaytin district of Muharraq in 1992 aroused protests from fishermen and villagers, particularly the Shi'ites. Heavy infrastructural investment, often involving land grabs by the state and private developers, seriously affected poor villagers. While the urban centres became drawn into global trends of consumerism and leisure, an area that is increasingly wealthy, the rural areas were increasingly impoverished.[45] The transformation of urban life after the discovery of oil in the early 1930s, and then much later the creation of Bahrain as a hub of Islamic finance, was striking, although urbanization was also marked by pronounced socio-economic inequalities. Alongside rising consumerism and leisure, there were camps for foreign labourers employed in the oil industry. Manama's rising culture of consumerism was marked by retail outlets, cinemas, and leisure. Fuccaro notes the suburban city of Awali, a secluded,

---

[43] Charles D. Belgrave, *Personal Diaries, 1926–57* (Exeter: University of Exeter, Arab World Documentation Unit; Charles D. Belgrave, *Personal Column* (London: Hutchinson, 1960).

[44] Fuccaro, *Histories of City and State*, pp. 193–4.

[45] Nelida Fuccaro, 'Shaping the Urban Life of Oil in Bahrain: Consumerism, Leisure and Public Communication in Manama and in the Oil Camps 1932–1960s', *Comparative Studies of South Asia, Africa, and the Middle East*, vol. 33, no. 1 (2013): pp. 59–74.

opulent company town built by BAPCO in the desert in 1937.[46] Awali was a complex of modern foreign influences. It was the base of BAPCO from its origins as an American oil company established by Standard Oil of California in 1929. In 1936, BAPCO was registered as a subsidiary of Caltex, the powerful California Texas Oil Corporation.[47] Awali was a fascinating juxtaposition of American modernity and the British Raj, built on the political residency in Al-Jufayr district from 1947.[48] The majority of the employees of the American oil company were British. By the mid-1950s, Awali emerged as a community of some two thousand British expatriates.[49] Awali was protected by BAPCO's security force, headed by former members of the Palestine police. The Indian and Persian workers lived in bunk homes, in contrast to the luxury residences of the white employees.[50] One writer characterizes Awali as 'a mixture of the holiday camp and the army [barracks], with hints of a new satellite town predominant as the number of wives and families increases ... It is common criticism to call oil camps suburban ... People in oil camps have no city.'[51] The spatial, gender, and ethnic divisions in the oil industry were often disguised by the attributes of the modern city but the city could not completely hide resentment against the dominance exercised by the Western corporations and the extravagance of the royal family. Activist eruptions never hit Awali as they did Manama in the 1950s and mid-1960s, the latter provoked by the royal family's indulgent use of the Awali Club and BAPCO's exclusive beach resort. High profits in the oil industry secured an authoritarian ruling family. The oil industry was divisive, securing an authoritarian supremacy underpinned by the harsh treatment of its foreign workers.[52]

Fearing opposition from nationalists and from local governments, as was occurring in Iran, Kuwait, and Saudi Arabia, BAPCO brought in social welfare and healthcare programmes, increased business opportunities for local entrepreneurs, and improved transport and housing. Petrol stations became an emblem of modernization. BAPCO also brought advances in radio, cinema, and printing, facilitating company propaganda and advertising. The

---

[46] Fuccaro, 'Shaping the Urban Life of Oil in Bahrain', p. 59.

[47] Bahrain Petroleum Company, *The BAPCO Story* (Manama, n.d.).

[48] Roderic Owen, *The Golden Bubble: Arabian Gulf Documentary* (London: Collins, 1957), pp. 44–7.

[49] John Gornall, 'Some Memories of BAPCO', typescript, Awali, Bahrain, May 1965, p. 12; *The Bahrain Petroleum Company Ltd, Annual Report, 1956*; *Annual Report to the Ruler of Bahrain by the Bahrain Petroleum Company Ltd, 1954*, p. 17; H. V. Mapp, *Leave Well Alone! Where Oil Shapes Dynasties and Destinies* (Southend: Prittle Brook, 1994), pp. 84, 132; Fuccaro, 'Shaping the Urban Life of Oil in Bahrain', p. 67.

[50] Mapp, *Leave Well Alone!*, pp. 101–2, 191–2.

[51] Owen, *The Golden Bubble*, p. 134.

[52] 'Report of the BAPCO Work Stoppage and the General Troubles in Bahrain', 13 March 1965, Busheri Archive, Manama. Details of the 1965 disturbances are in The National Archives (TNA) FO 371/179788 to 199790.

theme was prosperity and modernity. The Awali housewife was portrayed shopping while the husband was a contented worker. The education projects raised the literacy rate. The image was that of exorbitant youth consumption and leisure. But the inequalities between urban and rural, between Sunnis and impoverished rural Shi'ites were not faced, creating severe problems for the future. Shi'ism in Bahrain continued to provide an ideology for rural resistance to state power. In contrast, in Saudi Arabia, Kuwait, Iran, and Iraq, absolutism remained entrenched.[53] In Bahrain, American and British influences dominated, with expatriate oil interests creating close links to the Al-Khalifah family, nurturing what Manama's youth perceived as a corrupt regal authoritarianism. BAPCO made serious efforts to promote a more positive image through weekly magazines, the cinema, and other forms of media promoting Westernized lifestyles.

Manama in the 1950s and 1960s was a young urban society, an urban society reflecting the youth culture of the West, a 'mechanical' town of cinemas, cars, radios, and aeroplanes.[54] But there was also subversive politics, notably during the nationalist disturbances of 1953–57 and the student demonstrations of the mid-1960s. Bahrain's youth, while soaking up the consumer culture funded by oil, also showed contempt for its social evils. Manama's youth was highly critical of the exploitation of labour, both indigenous and foreign, by American oil companies supported by the Al-Khalifah family. Youth protest followed the new ideologies of nationalism, Ba'thism, and communism. The grassroots organizations that rose in the 1950s represented two prominent groups, a young commercial class empowered by oil wealth, and professionals with modern education involved in the state bureaucracy.[55] There was no contradiction between consumer hedonism and political activism. Education and increased literacy in English and Arabic nurtured the nationalist movement. An independent Arabic press fuelled political activism. The *Sawt Al-Bahrain*, with connections to Al-Ha'yah, published between 1950 and 1954, and the weekly *Al-Qafilah*, published between 1953 and 1956 and with a circulation of four to five thousand, generated political ideas among the lower urban classes. Radio also fed the greater public understanding of political ideologies. Oil wealth increased the popularity of cinema and of youth clubs funded by local entrepreneurs. A prominent example was the Ahali cinema owned by Ibrahim Muhammad Al-Zayyani,

---

[53] Frank Trentmann, 'Beyond Consumerism: New Historical Perspectives on Consumption', *Journal of Contemporary History*, vol. 39, no. 3 (2004): pp. 383–4; Fuccaro, 'Mapping the Transnational Community', pp. 39–58.

[54] Owen, *The Golden Bubble*, p. 55; Fuccaro, 'Shaping the Urban Life of Oil in Bahrain', p. 61.

[55] Fuccaro, *Histories of City and State*, pp. 173–86, 227–8.

a descendant of a powerful pearl-merchant dynasty. The Cinama 'al-Lu'lu, the Pearl Cinema, was part of the Al-Qusaybis family business empire. The Al-Qusaybis were from the Arabian Peninsula and had built their business interests in the oil era.[56] Manama's five cinemas offered films in Arabic and Hindi, musicals, dramas, historical epics, and comedies. That consumerism fed Bahrain's cosmopolitanism, with enticing romantic, exotic, and luxurious settings and images. The cinema also brought to the viewing public advertisements for exotic foods and foreign goods, challenging social and political conservatism, while between the early 1930s and the late 1950s, the youth clubs combined ideologies of political resistance with social interaction. Bringing together culture, education and sports, the youth clubs provided drive for a progressive nationalist movement. By the 1950s, the government and BAPCO were promoting sport, not only in clubs but also in schools, as an instrument for moral education.

The links between youth culture, consumerism, and political mobilization saw the transformation of Manama from a local into a major international commercial centre. The combination of oil wealth, a modern business culture, technological advance, and trade in consumer goods triggered a commercial revolution in Manama. Its own entrepreneurs dominated until the oil boom in the Gulf states and the decline in Bahrain's own oil resources in the 1970s. The rise in population, including foreign residents, expanded the trade in new commodities in Manama after the collapse of the pearl industry. Local merchants acted as agents for foreign firms, marketing consumer goods and modern services in the oil-rich economies of the region, particularly in the eastern province of Saudi Arabia. There arose a major import trade in luxury cars and in office equipment and furniture from India and Europe as well as from Japan. By the 1950s, with no significant local industry, the import trade remained central to economic growth in Manama. Manama's traditional commercial culture became intertwined with foreign suppliers, using new technologies in sales and distribution. In the 1950s and 1960s, the Arabic press became the main vehicle for advertising international brands as important for social prestige, a concept particularly popular in Saudi Arabia.[57] Sheaffer fountain pens, certainly a prestige item, were advertised in Bahrain in the context of the consumption of pearls and carpets, sold in Bahrain's luxury stores. James Belgrave, the son of Charles Belgrave, orchestrated the

[56] Fuccaro, 'Shaping the Urban Life of Oil in Bahrain', p. 63.
[57] Fuccaro, 'Shaping the Urban Life of Oil in Bahrain', p. 66; Relli Schechter, 'Global Conservatism: How Marketing Articulated a Neotraditional Saudi Arabian Society during the First Oil Boom, c.1974–1984', *Journal of Macromarketing*, vol. 31, no. 4 (2011), p. 31.

image of Manama as the hub of the Persian Gulf, although this was more a public relations strategy than an advertising campaign.[58]

British and American firms saw Manama as the centre of the regional oil economy. The British Overseas Airways Corporation, BOAC, added Manama as a destination in 1932. Gulf Aviation was established in 1950 as a private company by ex-RAF pilot, Freddie Bosworth, and offered services to all Gulf destinations. Travel agencies catering for these two airlines were owned and managed by the Kanoo and Al-Qusaybi families. By the 1960s, both families had strong interests in construction, consumer goods, in supplying the oilfields, and in shipping. Kanoo's travel agency had branches in Awali, BAPCO's company town, and in Abqaiq, Al-Khubar, and Ras Tannurah in the oil-rich east coast of Saudi Arabia. The Al-Qusaybi travel agency consolidated its hold on Gulf Aviation as it acted as the agent for Saudi Arabia Airlines and Kuwaiti Airways, established as national carriers in 1946 and 1954 respectively.[59]

Popular Protest in Bahrain from 1900: Challenges to Religion, the Economy, and Patronage

In the early decades of the twentieth century, political passions in Bahrain were moderated by communal ties, the patronage of elites both tribal and mercantile, and by regional cohesion. The pearl boom further defused popular discontent, while the Waqf and Ma'tam afforded Shi'ites avenues for expressing grievance against tribal government. However, the end of the pearl boom and the emergence of the oil economy from the beginning of the 1930s coincided with the closer integration of Bahrain with her Gulf neighbours and the creation of a more organized tribal state and society dominated by Sunnis, with less flexible ethnic identities. There was now fertile terrain for social and political disorder, as the disadvantaged rural and urban regions of Bahrain sought new opportunities after the pearl boom. Protest and disorder in Bahrain can be interpreted as representing collective public devotion by Shi'ites, seen in the celebration of Muharram (the first month of the Islamic calendar) and Ashura (marking the death of Imam Husayn), organized by the

---

[58] J. H. D. Belgrave, *Welcome to Bahrain*, 3rd ed. (London: Augustan Press, 1957), pp. 1, 4, 7, 13, 17, 22 and 177: J. H. D. Belgrave, *Welcome to Bahrain*, 5th ed. (London: Augustan Press, 1965).
[59] Fuccaro, 'Shaping the Urban Life of Oil in Bahrain', p. 68. For modernity and the late consumer society in Egypt, see Relli Schechter, 'Reading Advertisements in Colonial/Development Context: Cigarettes Advertising and Identity Politics in Egypt *c*.1919–1939', *Journal of Social History*, vol. 39, no. 2 (2005), pp. 483–4; Kanoo, *The House of Kanoo*.

Shia Ma'tams. The rituals of chest-beating and self-mutilation, and the the-atrical representation of the Karbala can be seen as the expression of political and sectarian grievances in public. Further they were a form of collective bar-gaining by urban Shi'ites aligned with the rural poor. Finally, they expressed anger at the violation of the 'moral economy' of Shi'ism.

Perhaps, too, there is a Bahrain parallel to the European narrative of worker resistance to harsh economic and social conditions in periods of great change.[60] The Bahrain experience in the decline in the pearl industry and in the expansion of the highly capital-intensive oil industry can be read through the perspective of E. P. Thompson's analysis of riots as a complex form of direct popular action. The Western ideal of 'social contract' is evident in the direct action pursued by Shi'ites in Bahrain, who formed a high pro-portion of Bahrain's disadvantaged agriculturalists.[61] Moreover, Juan Cole has argued that riots erupt when local solidarities are disrupted by changes in the global political economy—as in Bahrain with the ending of the pearl boom in the 1920s and then the widening of economic inequalities as the oil industry rose to prominence.[62] With the decline of pearling and the rise of the oil industry, Bahrain's political and economic landscape was domi-nated by the seizure of land from rural Shi'ites to create the infrastructure for the oil industry. That dispossession and resulting poverty drove much of the protest. Oil posed a serious threat to spatial autonomy, threatening Shi'ites trapped in rural poverty. Through the ferocity of the Muharram and Ashura rituals and ceremonies, state authority was challenged. And Bahrain's pearl divers, boat owners, and occasional migrants poured into Manama, ignit-ing inter-communal conflict and threatening Bahrain's authoritarian state.[63] Riotous politics was thus a response to the tensions created by the different stages of Bahrain's integration into the global capitalist economy, dominated by oil. And violent clashes in Bahrain in 1953, along communal, religious, ethnic, and racial lines, expressed deep resentment against the Sunni state.

---

[60] Eric J. Hobsbawm, 'Machine Breakers', in *Uncommon People: Resistance, Rebellion and Jazz* (London: Abacus, 1952), pp. 6–22; Eric J. Hobsbawm, *Worlds of Labour: Further Studies in the History of Labour* (London: Weidenfeld and Nicolson, 1984); Eric J. Hobsbawm, *Primitive Rebels* (Manchester: Manchester University Press, 1984).

[61] E. P. Thompson, 'The Moral Economy of the English Crowd in the Eighteenth Century', *Past and Present*, vol. 50, no. 1 (1971), pp. 76–136; Ervand Abrahamian, 'The Crowd in Iranian Politics 1905–1953', *Past and Present*, vol. 41, no. 1 (1968), pp. 184–210.

[62] Juan Ricardo I. Cole, 'Of Crowds and Empires: Afro Asian Riots and European Expansion 1857–1882', in *States of Violence*, edited by Fernando Coronil and Julie Skurski (Ann Arbor, MI: University of Michigan Press, 2006), pp. 269–306. See also Juan R. I. Cole, *Sacred Space and Holy War: The Politics and History of Shi'ite Islam* (London: I. B. Tauris, 2002).

[63] Edmund Burke, 'Towards a History of Urban Collective Action in the Middle East: Continuities and Change 1750–1980', in *Etat, ville et mouvements sociaux au Magreb et au Moyen-Orient/Urban Crises and Social Movements in the Middle East*, edited by Kenneth Brown, Bernard Hourcade, Michele Jole, Claude Liauzu, Peter Sluglett, and Sami Zubalda (Paris: L'Harmattan, 1989), pp. 45–8.

Within these protests, it is important to note, solidarities among the workforce, both in the pearl industry and later in the oil industry, created powerful cross-sectarian political organizations.

Class inequalities often corresponded with sectarian fault lines. Shi'ites accounted for 70 per cent of the population, while the ruling house and its allies were Sunni. Shi'a felt they were denied government jobs and resources and that they were the focus of repression. Sunni Al-'Utub dominance of Bahrain exposed Shi'ites to discrimination. However, to a degree, Shi'ites in Bahrain were protected by local structures and mercantile networks. The merchant networks and often elusive municipal government under the British protectorate weakened the authority of the Al-Khalifah aristocracy. In fact, it was only with the rise of the oil economy from the 1950s, and Bahrain's closer links to oil-wealthy Gulf neighbours, that the coercive power exercised by the Al-Khalifah family increased.

Outbreaks of disorder were often random, as in a 1904 conflict between Persians and the Al-Khalifah governor of Manama, when Persian shops and homes were sacked. Such violent incidents tended to be sudden and sporadic. The attacks on the Persians by the Al-Khalifah governor and his supporters arose from their fear that British agents were providing protection to the Persians. The British tended to view the tribal areas as volatile and seditious and therefore intervened.[64] British protection increased after 1923, and urban groups, such as the Baharna community, which rallied to the British, posed a serious challenge to the ruling family. Another disturbing development was the increasing presence of migrant groups, tribesmen, dock workers, seasonal labourers, and pearl divers from Najd, looking for loot but aligning with the Sunni elites. Persians and other restless elements were dragged in to provide muscle for disorder.

In this early period, Muharraq was the centre of Bahrain's Arab government while Manama was the centre for foreigners, the municipality (Baladiyyah), and British influence. Ironically, Arab tribal nationalism was reinforced by British reform of local government, for the municipality was seen as a stronghold of foreign interests. British agents and the Baladiyyah were tarnished as foreign. Arab tribal nationalism also portrayed the Persians as foreign, and as a threat to Arab Bahrain. That antagonism was aggravated by the decline of the pearling industry and the subsequent weakening of the ties between the ruling aristocracy and Sunni and Shi'ite pearl merchants. Bahrain had long practised a moderate Shi'ism but this was now being threatened by the demise of pearling and the erosion of mercantile power. This

---

[64] Fuccaro, *Histories of City and State*, pp. 153–4.

brought with it the potential for communal, ethnic, religious, class, and mercantile conflict. Riots in Manama and Muharraq in 1926 weakened the ties between the pearl divers and the merchant and political elites but strengthened class identity. The disappearance of the old social and economic order of divers and merchants marked a crucial stage in the transition to state centralization and increasing inequalities. The protests were met by harsh punishments from an increasingly authoritarian state.[65]

It would be useful here to pause to consider how Shi'ism in Bahrain was moderate, not only because it held to the philosophy of Twelver Shi'ism but also because it drew on folk Shi'ism with its diverse Shi'ite traditions. Notable here was the fact that the Baharna, Shi'ite Arabs indigenous to Bahrain but economically disadvantaged, comprised half of the Shi'i population in Bahrain. The Ajam are of Iranian descent and are relatively wealthy. In Bahrain, Safavids created a set of religious institutions, including religious judges to supervise the judicial system.[66] The building of mosques and training of ulamas contributed to a moderate form of religious practice, matched with the sacrificial elements of original Shi'ism. Bahrain's Shi'ites created informal networks associated with religious institutions, the mosques and Ma'tams, and maintained a decentralized structure with intimacy between members that made infiltration by the state difficult. That structure, autonomous from the state and independent in the collection of revenues, provides 'organizational opportunity'.[67] This rich interplay of local social structures and economic conditions with regional dynasties was reinforced by the adoption of the less radical Twelver Shi'ism that was less threatening to Sunnis in Bahrain.

The rise of the European mercantile empires, including the Portuguese and the British, had a direct impact on Shi'ism. The adoption of Twelver Shi'ism, considered less radical, faced less opposition from Sunni leaders.[68] In the 1860s, in a population of 70,000, five-sixths of the inhabitants of Manama were Shi'ites. Their moderation and resilience were reflected in their ability to accommodate the constant immigration of Sunnis, although ultimately the Sunnis challenged their economic position. However, Sunni ruling circles suspected that Bahrain's Shi'ites were susceptible to Iranian influence and manipulation. In the 1990s some of the more radical Bahraini Shi'ites had connections to Iran but most came from the more conservative school

---

[65] Fuccaro, *Histories of City and State*, pp. 162–3.
[66] Juan Cole, *Sacred Space and Holy War*, pp. 44–5.
[67] Charles Kurzman, 'Organizational Opportunity and Social Movement Mobilization: A Comparative Analysis of Four Religious Movements', *Mobilization*, vol. 3, no. 1(1998), pp. 23–49.
[68] Cole, *Sacred Space and Holy War*, pp. 56–7.

of jurisprudence, the Akhbari. For Shi'ites in Bahrain, the Ma'tam and the rituals and public processions for Muharram and Ashura have provided stability.

Following the demise of pearling and with the rise of the oil industry, the Shi'ites used the performance of Ashura and Muharram rituals to consolidate their political and social identities, despite waning financial support from Shi'ite merchants. In the 1950s, Muharram was marked by political dissent. The mourning houses did not possess architectural or artistic elegance, or even express the strong tribal ethos of Shi'ite saints. They only 'mirrored the cultural and political divisions between Persians and Arabs'.[69] The rituals were used to express disenchantment with government and the sense of oppression and injustice. The Muharram festivities also symbolized the emancipation of Manama from Muharraq, the state capital. The rituals sought to underplay sectarian divisions, and this was also reflected in the creation of separate Sunni–Shi'ite courts, a gesture of accommodation towards Ja'fari jurisprudence. In addition, in 1925 the Ma'tams were integrated into an institutional network, and from 1927 the endowments came under the control of the Department of Shi'i Pious Foundation.

These developments created strong labour solidarity, uniting oil workers, professionals, and government employees. With the rise of oil, class identity was strengthened in the workforce while mercantile patronage within the Ma'tam was eroded. Throughout the 1930s, 1940s, and 1950s, community leaders and leading merchants were reconciled to youth populist movements, while progressive elites introduced new inter-sectarian institutions tinged with Arab nationalism. These decades also saw growing resentment against the British protectorate. Thus, the Ma'tam Al-Shab, which attracted many Persian employees of the Bahrain Petroleum Company, held subversive political ideas, including resentment against the Pahlavi regime. But sectarian violence during the Muharram procession in 1953, in which oil workers were core participants, led to the realization that consensus between Sunnis and Shi'ites was crucial. Charles Belgrave sought to confront this disorder through municipal councillors and the Sunni and Shi'ite elites. But Fuccaro sees here the emergence of nationalists who appealed directly to the populace in opposing sectarian divisions, urban conservatism, and imperialist encroachment.[70] 'These enlightened leaders were to guide the masses into a new public arena as rational and modern subjects', engaging with Rahman

---

[69] Fuccaro, *Histories of City and State*, p. 166.
[70] Fuccaro, *Histories of City and State*, p. 171.

Al-Bakir's plea against sectarianism.[71] Al-Bakir created the High Executive Committee, a populist organization based in Manama, which, by 1956, had emerged as the first political association to be recognized by the government. The force of oil set youth in motion, although restrained to a degree by Al-Bakir. The end of the municipality and the dissolution of the Majlis councils in 1951 undermined the old merchant classes and their power, while young Arab activists with nationalist passion organized popular militant movements with strong anti-British sentiment.

In the 1950s, a proliferation of leisure associations also served to increase political mobilization. But it was journalism above all that promoted Arabism as a progressive ideology. It fought for justice for workers, in particular local workers, resenting the fact that by 1956, 41 per cent of the manual labour employed in the oil industry and in construction was foreign. By the late 1950s, BAPCO and the government sought to 'nationalize' and 'Arabize' the workforce to appease the nationalists.[72] Ironically, this led to a flood of labour from the Gulf states. The media criticized allegiance to tradition, community, sects, kinship ties, and patronage networks as disruptive of the nation's historic homogeneity. It saw tribal loyalty to the Al-Khalifah ruling family, that family's relations with the British, and the politics of patronage surrounding the municipal council in Manama as driving sectarian divisions.[73]

The Al-Ha'yah organization, created in 1954, involved a further attempt by young nationalists to revolutionize the political landscape, linking rural and urban areas and attracting merchants suffering from the collapse of the pearl industry. Youthful nationalists held that labour relations were central in challenging the government and foreign interests in the oil sector. The first labour union was established in 1955 under the sponsorship of Al-Ha'yah. It had 6,000 members from BAPCO and the government service, and it pushed for reform of the labour laws. Also important was the creation of cross-sectarian cooperative institutions, including a compensation bureau and insurance unit for drivers.[74] This was the work of youthful nationalists with close class and religious links. BAPCO workers also attracted impoverished youths from the outskirts of Manama. Mosques, Ma'tams, and their religious celebrations

---

[71] Fuccaro, *Histories of City and State*, p. 172, and al-Bakir's autobiography, *Abd al-Rahman, Min al-Bahrayn ila al-manfa* (Beirut: Dar al Kuniz al-Arabiyyah, 2nd ed., 2002), pp. 49–62.

[72] W. A. Beiling, 'Recent Developments in Labor Relations in Bahrayn', *Middle East Journal*, vol. 13, no. 2 (1959), pp. 156–69; D. Finnie, 'Recruitment and Training of Labor: The Middle East Oil Industry', *Middle East Journal*, vol. 12, no. 2 (1958), pp. 127–43; Fahim I. Qubain, 'Social Classes and Tensions in Bahrain', *Middle East Journal*, vol. 9, no. 3 (1955), pp. 269–80.

[73] *Sawt al-Bahrayn: Majallah Adabiyyah wa Ijtima 'iyyah* (Beirut: al-Mu'assasah al-'Arabiyyah li al-Dirasat wa al-Nashr, 4 vols., 2003), vol. 1, p. 1369; Fuccaro, *Histories of City and State*, p. 180; Khuri, *Tribe and State in Bahrain*, pp. 198–9.

[74] Fuccaro, *Histories of City and State*, pp. 180–1.

were drawn into the Al-Ha'yah movement. Islam took on a unifying role in the economic and political struggle.[75] It also captured a new form of 'egalitarianism, [the] participatory and cross-confessional character of the movement'.[76] Al-Ha'yah used the distribution of leaflets and bulletins to spread its message. It organized political rallies against the removal of the poor from their land because of reclamation for infrastructure projects and for the oil industry. These protests were directed at British power and foreign capital, in a transition from 'old fashioned riots' to nationalist demonstration.[77]

'The potential for political dissidence embedded in Shi'i political culture and ritual resurfaced under the shadow of the new nationalist rhetoric. Many of the young, the unemployed and disaffected used the Muharram celebrations to mobilize against the government, the supporters of the Arabist secular line promoted by Al-Bakir and in some cases, even against the old notable class—and inflamed by Ma'tam preachers started a righteous revolution against the Al-Khalifah, Belgrave, British imperialism and the urban reactionaries.'[78] The rising protest was clearly evident in the Ma'tam Al-Qassab, Hajj'Abbas, Al-Madan, and Ras Rumman, each of which was drawn into nationalist dissent. But the protests under Al-Ha'yah were increasingly undermined by sectarian divisions within the nationalist movement, and by November 1956 it had collapsed, in part also because of an external crisis, the second Arab–Israeli war and the British occupation of the Suez Canal. Moreover, the British protectorate now permitted the government to create a national security structure that inhibited the activities of clubs and political associations.[79] The demise of Al-Ha'yah can also be attributed to the ideology of Arabism, which alienated Persian Shi'is. The secular Arabism of Al-Bakir triggered the emergence of conflicting ideologies, and Shi'i factions within the movement formed a splinter group called the National Pact before the dissolution of Al-Ha'yah.[80] Despite the movement's decline, Al-Ha'yah members were recruited into the bureaucracy and acquired political influence and wealth. The nationalist elites were now in association with the government and the state absorbed the ideological apparatus of Arabism. With the nationalist upheaval, left-wing politics surfaced briefly in the underground movement of the Iranian Communist Party (Tudeh) in the early 1950s. The 1950s also witnessed rising racism against Indian labour and also against Jews.

---

[75] Khuri, *Tribe and State in Bahrain*, pp. 203–4, 210.
[76] Fuccaro, *Histories of City and State*, p. 182.
[77] R. A. Read, 'Report on Strikes and Riots in Bahrain', 12 March 1956, TNA, FO 371/120545.
[78] Fuccaro, *Histories of City and State*, p. 184.
[79] Khuri, *Tribe and State in Bahrain*, p. 104.
[80] Fuccaro, *Histories of City and State*, pp. 186, 188.

In the 1950s, oil reshaped politics and public life through nationalist movements, political rallies, strikes, demonstrations, and the religious processions of Muharram and Ashura, thereby diminishing the role of the pearling mercantile elite and notables. The tension between rapid socio-economic change driven by oil and the conservatism of the process of nation-building was in time to see the emergence of an increasingly authoritarian state. Urbanization and land reclamation drove rural Shi'ites into economic decline and into protest politics. The Al-Khalifah autocracy then reinforced its control, drawing on its growing economic power, which it shared to a degree with Bahrain's increasingly global business lineages, including the Kanoos.

The tensions between Shi'a and Sunni and the frequent protests by Shi'ites was driven in part by the deprivation suffered by Shi'as in rural Bahrain, particularly during the oil era. The principal aim of the British reform of land rights from the 1920s had been to protect Shi'a agriculturalists. When Belgrave arrived in 1927, it was apparent that the often-arbitrary custom that determined land ownership, and in particular the structure of ownership under the Waqf and Ma'tam, had increased the authority of the Al-Khalifah family and their Sunni allies. In 1929, the land claimed by the royal household covered more than three-quarters of Bahrain's productive land, and included vast tracts around Manama. The family controlled the most productive land in northern Bahrain, with Shaykh Hamad's brother, Shaykh Muhammad ibn Isa, becoming the largest owner of rural land in the 1930s. Since Shi'as were the majority of agriculturalists in Bahrain, this created serious sectarian resentment.[81] Rising population and growing oil wealth among urban residents created fear among the Shi'a that their land was under threat. Tabu (land registration) had, to a degree, preserved the claims of villagers over uncultivated land and hence made that land accessible for the poor. Tabu also allowed village committees to re-draw the boundaries of plots to avert a land crisis for the poor. But these protective measures were eroded by the rise of oil and by the increase in land reclamation by the state.

The isolation (both economically and spatially) of Shi'a rural hamlets from Manama, with its oil wealth, global corporations, and leisure facilities for rich city youth, fuelled communal hostilities. The Shi'a majority clearly saw the growing disparities of wealth and power, particularly after the surge in oil capital from Saudi Arabia and Kuwait in the 1980s and 1990s. With increasing poverty and decay, rural Shi'a moved into the oil and service sectors. But they retained their village links, at least until the 1950s.[82] Thus in the 1940s, young

---

[81] Belgrave to Political Agent, Bahrain, 19 November 1931, IOR R/15/2/807; Fuccaro, *Histories of City and State*, p. 215; Khuri, *Tribe and State in Bahrain*, pp. 101–7.
[82] Fuccaro, *Histories of City and State*, pp. 216–17.

Shi'a had returned to their villages to create more Ma'tams based upon family ties. These Ma'tams were later instrumental in the organization of riot politics, and their religious work provided emotional and economic support for the mobilization of rural labour against the state in the 1950s. The rural response to nationalist agitation was influenced by the political sympathies of the traditional rural leaders, especially those who controlled the Ma'tam. The moderate form of Shi'ism in Bahrain, compared to Syria and Lebanon, can be explained by the fact that 'Arab nationalism had left the sectarian and traditionalist outlook of Bahrain's rural society comparatively untouched'.[83] However, as argued earlier, Bahrain's moderate Shi'ism is a legacy of Twelver Shi'ism (embellished by intellectual clerics), of Bahrain's trading history, and of the institutions of the Waqf and Ma'tam which permeated society and politics. Juan Cole explains Bahrain's moderation in terms of the tenacity of its Shi'ite culture, despite repeated Sunni tribal invasions. In the 1860s, in Bahrain's total population of 70,000, all the agriculturalists and five-sixths of the inhabitants of Manama were Shi'ites.[84]

Moderate political attitudes and the Shi'ites' strong religious devotion led them to tolerate the land seizures being carried out by the ruling family, which contributed to the contraction of Bahrain's agricultural economy from the 1950s. By 1959, only 5 per cent of the labour force in Jidd Hafs and Sitrah, two hamlets which flourished as satellites of Manama, were employed in agriculture.[85] Yet it was not rural workers who mobilized against the government in the 1950s but urban labour activists and nationalists in Manama. The unprecedented power of the state was evident in accelerating urbanization, while agriculturalists, who suffered increasing deprivation, maintained their commitment to the land and rural economy. It was not the absence from rural society of aggressive Arab nationalism that restricted Bahrain's agricultural communities to silent protest but rather their respect for their clerics. Shi'i clerics did lament the loss of land and the demise of the agricultural economy in their opposition to the 'alien' tribal regime of Al-Khalifah. Title deeds provided some security to elements of Manama's floating communities

---

[83] Minutes by W. J. Adams, 18 September 1958, TNA FO 371/132531; Fuccaro, *Histories of City and State*, p. 218.

[84] William Gifford Palgrave, *Narrative of a Year's Journey through Central and Eastern Arabia, 1862–1863*, 2 vols. (London: Macmillan, 1865, reproduced by Gregg Publishing, 1969), vol. 2, pp. 201–15; Juan R. Cole, 'Rival Empires of Trade and Immami Shi'ism in Eastern Arabia, 1300–1800', *International Journal of Middle East Studies*, vol. 19, no. 3 (1987), pp. 177–204; Juan R. Cole, *Roots of North India: Shi'ism in Iran and Iraq: Religion and State in Awadh, 1722–1859* (Berkeley, CA: University of California Press, 1980); Cole, *Sacred Space and Holy War*.

[85] Fuccaro, *Histories of City and State*, pp. 217–18. See also Ministry of State for Cabinet Affairs, Directorate of Statistics, Bahrain, The Population of Bahrain: Trends and Prospects, January 1979, pp. 84–5.

in shanty towns, but the Al-Khalifah usurped rural land, increasing the distress of rural Shi'ites. By the 1980s, rural communities were suffering further losses, as land was appropriated for prestigious waterfront projects in Manama and for housing projects for the new middle classes. There was substantial unrest in the mid-1990s, involving disaffected young men with few employment opportunities. In time, the opposition made advances in formal politics. Thus, in the 2006 municipal elections, of the 10 successful candidates, seven were from Al-Wifaq, a Shi'a political organization, reflecting in part the Islamization of Bahrain's formal politics.[86]

In Bahrain, it was charismatic ulama who sustained Shi'ite power and provided the resistance to an authoritarian state. The Shi'ites in Bahrain are of diverse ethnic and social communities. The Al-Baharna, the earliest migrants, are of Persian descent while the Arab Shi'ites are from the Al-Ahsa province of Saudi Arabia. The ulama, providing core leadership, possessed legal expertise, and their knowledge of Shi'ite law, history, and tradition facilitated their emergence as a powerful political force, with the potential to be independent from the state. However, the Shi'ite ethnic cleavages have been intensified by class divisions, as the mercantile Shi'ites and those in the bureaucracy have created powerful ties with the Sunni ruling family.[87] This division played an important role in the later protest movements largely driven by economic grievance.[88]

In the aftermath of the first Gulf War (1990–91), a secular, cross-sectarian opposition movement attempted to restore the National Assembly and to remove the state of emergency introduced in 1975.[89] This movement, dominated by intellectuals, frustrated merchant elites, and bureaucrats, produced a series of petitions, circulated among the people and then submitted to the government. The response by the state was subtle repression.[90] That, in turn, increased the power of the ulama through the Ma'tams.[91] Around four hundred Ma'tams used social, political, and educational meetings to drive resistance to the state. They mobilized the Khums (trust funds) to support

---

[86] Fuccaro, *Histories of City and State*, pp. 230–1.

[87] Fred H. Lawson, *Bahrain: the Modernization of Autocracy* (Boulder, CO: Westview Press, 1989), p. 5. Fred H. Lawson, 'Repertoires of Contention in Contemporary Bahrain', in *Islamic Activism: A Social Movement Theory Approach*, edited by Quintan Wiktorowicz (Bloomington, IN: Indiana University Press, 2004), pp. 89–111.

[88] Rabi Uzi and Joseph Kostiner, 'The Shi'is in Bahrain: Class and Religious Protest', in *Minorities and the State in the Arab World*, edited by Ofra Bengio and Gabriel Ben-Dor (Boulder, CO: Lynne Rienner, 1999), pp. 171–88.

[89] Lawson, 'Repertoires of Contention in Contemporary Bahrain', pp. 96–7.

[90] Brian P. Maynard, 'The Role of the Ulama in Shi'ite Social Movements: Bahrain, Lebanon and Iraq' (MA thesis, Main National Security Affairs, Naval Postgraduate School, 2005), pp. 43–4.

[91] Luayy Bahri, 'The Socio-Economic Foundations of the Shi'ite Opposition in Bahrain', *Mediterranean Quarterly*, vol. 11, no. 3 (2000), pp. 129–43.

the poor, thereby exposing the state's abandonment of welfare programmes for vulnerable Shi'ites. This strategy bridged the divide between the Shi'ite elites and the rural poor. The Ma'tams gave the ulama power and influence. It is important to note that the ulama attracted both Sunni and Shi'ite. They organized their own demonstrations but also gained control of other protests. One powerful advantage for the Shi'ite clerics was that the Sunni ulama were subsumed in the authoritarian state, and thus their reputation was less that of scholars and more that of adjuncts of the state. The Shi'ites, in contrast, had legal and societal autonomy. The authority of the Shi'ite ulama was a function of their religious-legal learning, independent of the state. The ulama remained the senior religious official for the municipality. Through the mosque and Ma'tam, the ulama provided welfare for the vulnerable, the disabled, and the poor. They also acted as judges on points of religious law. They accepted a limited role in political activism while protecting religion and culture from internal and external threats. The Bahraini Shi'ites were cautious about the Iranian revolution, only drawing on it occasionally to drive religious activism.[92]

Although the ulama were quietist in seeking remedies for grievances, in the early 1990s there was an eruption of social resistance. Principally this was the result of increasing economic distress, arising from the actions of the Al-Khalifah administration in land reclamation—the creation of prestige projects involved the seizure of land from the Shi'ites—and the in-migration of foreign labour, which led to substantial unemployment among Shi'ite youth. In the early 1990s the administration favoured major firms by subsidizing the construction of prestige projects such as Western-style shopping centres and luxurious flats: small local enterprises received no state subsidies. Subsidies were also provided for tourism and light industry, forcing up the recruitment of foreign labour. Shi'ites employed in heavy industry suffered shrinking wages or even dismissal. Further displacement occurred among Bahraini women who had entered the workforce only in the 1980s but were now dismissed because of fears within government over the rise of Islamist politics. This further increased unemployment among poor Shi'ites. In 1994, the arrest of prominent Shi'ite ulama added to the anger among unemployed

---

[92] Maynard, 'The Role of the Ulama in Shi'ite Social Movements', pp. 17–18; Moojan Momen, *An Introduction to Shi'i Islam: The History and Doctrines of Twelver Shi'ism* (New Haven, CT: Yale University Press, 1985), pp. 191–2. For criticism of the Iranian clerics, see also Joseph Eliash, 'Misconceptions Regarding the Juridical Status of the Iranian "Ulama"', *International Journal of Middle East Studies*, vol. 10, no. 1 (1979), p. 21. See also Linda S. Walbridge, 'Introduction: Shi'ism and Authority', in *The Most Learned of the Shi'a: The Institution of the Marja' Taqlid*, edited by Linda S. Walbridge (New York: Oxford University Press, 2001), pp. 5–6; Said Amir Arjomand, *The Turban for the Crown* (New York: Oxford University Press, 1988), pp. 92–3.

Shi'ites, resulting in mass protests.[93] The failure of the state to implement the legislative reforms promised under the 1973 constitution reinforced the Shi'ite sense of abandonment.

The constitution of 1973 provided for a National Assembly consisting of 44 members: 30 were elected (the franchise was limited to men) and 14 were royal appointees. The 1973 general election was the only election held under that constitution because it was abrogated by Shaikh Isa in 1975. He was angered by the National Assembly's refusal to accept a security bill that severely restricted civil liberties. In August 1975, he suspended the constitution and dissolved the assembly. These acts became a rallying point for the opposition. Bahrain was governed under emergency laws from 1975 to 2002. Shi'ites held five ministries in the mid-1970s but not those for security or foreign affairs, which were held by members of the ruling elite.[94]

The establishment of the Consultative Council in 1992 was an attempt by the administration to appease the advocates of democratic reform. The Council had 40 members (many had served in the National Assembly), but it had no legislative power and its debates were never made public. Shi'ites held 21 of the 40 seats, and their presence gave greater opportunities for the raising of Shi'ite grievances. In 1994, there were violent protests, triggered by repression, rising unemployment among Shi'ites, and disappointment with the slow pace of political reform. The 1994 protests were precipitated by the circulation of an open letter to the Emir, seeking the return of the National Assembly. The petition had attracted 22,000 signatures.[95] The leaders of the petition were mainly Shi'ite ulama. But the protests only encouraged the Emir to resist. He was angered by physical attacks on affluent tourist zones and later the destruction of Saudi-owned cars. However, the key grievance remained the seizure of land by well-connected business. In 2007, fishermen in Malakiyya village protested against a cousin of the king who had appropriated the land on the seafront and thereby denied the fishermen their livelihood. This protest led to police brutality. Particularly serious were the battles between the youth of the village and the riot police. The King intervened and forced the cousin to abandon the land he had seized.[96] In Sitra, a coastal town, a land reclamation

[93] Maynard, 'The Role of the Ulama in Shi'ite Social Movements', p. 77.

[94] J. E. Peterson, *The Arab Gulf States: Steps Towards Political Participation* (New York: Praeger, 1988), pp. 76–7, 133; Uzi and Kostiner, 'The Shi'is in Bahrain', pp. 171–88, 133, 173. A critical reading on political resistance in the Middle East is Charles Tripp, *The Power and the People: Paths of Resistance in the Middle East* (Cambridge: Cambridge University Press, 2013).

[95] Joe Stork, 'Bahrain Crisis Worsens', *Middle East Report*, no. 204 (July–September 1997), pp. 33–5.

[96] Land reclamation and seizures by the royal family and their associated merchant cliques are discussed in Fuad Al-Ansari, 'Public Open Space on the Transforming Urban Waterfront of Bahrain: The Case of Manama City' (PhD thesis, Newcastle University, 2009), chapters 7–9.

had been ordered by the Ministry of Defence. But the local residents resisted, although the authorities ultimately pushed through the reclamation.

A charity marathon in 1994 involved significant ulama participation. The government's response was to deport Shaikh Ali Salman Al Buladi. This was followed by the arrest of Shaikh Abd Al-Amir Al Jamri, the leader of the Bahrain Islamic Freedom Movement and a former member of the National Assembly. In 1995, the government sought to negotiate secretly with Shaikh Al Jamri, Abd Al Wahab Hussain, Shaikh Khalil Sultan, and Hasan Mushaima. The talks were conducted by Ian Henderson, head of Bahrain's Intelligence Service. But it was the Shi'ite ulama, with their considerable resources and effective organizational structures, that compelled the state to respond, as seen in King Hamad's reforms in 2002.

On succeeding his father in 1999 and becoming King in 2002, Shaikh Hamad bin Isa Al-Khalifah sought a return to constitutional rule, under a National Action Charter, in order to avoid a recurrence of the 1990s protests and rioting. The charter stipulated the creation of two chambers, one through elections (in which women had the vote) and the second through appointees. This was too ambiguous for the opposition. King Hamad then sought a compromise with the ulama. He instituted an elected lower chamber with legislative powers while the upper house would have merely an advisory role. This was accepted by the main opposition groups and the National Action Charter was confirmed in a referendum with 98.4 per cent in favour. Seeking further to placate the opposition, the King abolished some repressive security laws, released political prisoners, and invited exiles to return and set up political parties and newspapers. But at that point King Hamad promulgated the 2002 Constitution. This led to a boycott of parliamentary elections by the four main political groups: Al-Wifaq, the most popular Shia grouping; the National Democratic Action Party, a large leftist group; Islamic Action, a marginal Shia group; and the National Democratic Rally Society, a marginal Arab nationalist grouping. The sectarian groups in Bahrain, until then engaged in episodic protest, became a major movement seeking change in existing structures of power.[97] This was a serious challenge to the more authoritarian state being built by King Hamad: the upper house, the Shura Council, had 40 members, each appointed by the King, while the lower house, the Chamber of Deputies, had 40 elected members, elected on a four-year term. The Shura Council included Jewish, Christian, and female legislators to emphasize diversity but in fact it drew attention away from the 'divide and

[97] Michel Foucault, *Power/Knowledge: Selected Interviews and Other Writings 1972–1977*, translated and edited by Colin Gordon and Leo Marshall (New York: Pantheon Books, 1980), pp. 78–107; Tripp, *The Power and the People*, pp. 106–17.

rule' approach of the government. The Speaker of the House was from the Shura Council and was ratified by the King. The strengthening of an authoritarian legislature was accompanied by a division between the civil law courts and the Shari'ah courts, with a clear demarcation of their jurisdictional powers. Judges of middle and lower courts were appointed by the Prime Minister, again a member of the royal household.

Although Shi'a power is attributed to the fact that between 60 and 70 per cent of the population of Bahrain is Shi'a, that domination has been eroded by the state granting nationality to immigrants, all, presumably, Sunni. From 2001 to 2007, each year on average 9,000 citizens of Sunni heritage were created. In addition, Hamad granted citizenship to third-generation stateless Persians.[98]

Since independence in 1971, the Al-Khalifah family has held an almost complete monopoly on power, while making small concessions to limited democracy. In challenging this authoritarianism, the ulama sought the restoration of the National Assembly. This demand was secular.[99] The appeal to moderates is a key factor in the movement's success, in contrast to the failure of militant Shi'ism in the 1980s. That extremism perished because of fears of splitting the Shi'ite community—Persian versus Arab ethnicity, moderate versus radical. In addition, a key difference between the Bahraini protests and those in Lebanon and Iraq was the former's focus on international opinion.[100] Bahrainis sought international support. The US Navy's Fifth Fleet headquarters in Manama had a major impact on the protests for democracy. The Al-Khalifah regime occasionally sought to tarnish the opposition with claims that it was an Iranian proxy with ambitions to establish an Islamic state.

The Structure of the Book

The next chapter explores the importance of the Waqf and Ma'tam in Bahrain, institutionalized in law and land. These two institutions were a central element in the growth of Islamic finance that led in time to the establishment of Bahrain as the financial hub of the Gulf. Moreover, to a degree the Waqf and Ma'tam protected land from appropriation by the state by placing it within the Shari'ah legal code. Chapter 3 focuses on the rise of Islamic banking in Bahrain in recent decades. Islamic finance in Bahrain draws on capital

---

[98] Justin Gengler, *Group Conflict and Political Mobilization in Bahrain and the Arab Gulf: Rethinking the Rentier State* (Bloomington, IN: Indiana University Press, 2015), pp. 43–8, 96, 154–5, 176.

[99] Bahri, 'The Socio-Economic Foundations of the Shi'ite Opposition in Bahrain', p. 130.

[100] Maynard, 'The Role of the Ulama in Shi'ite Social Movements', p. 58.

flows from the oil-rich Gulf states which have made it possible for Bahrain to emerge as a major hub of Islamic finance, next in importance only to Malaysia. Moreover, Bahrain's colonial past has encouraged a market liberalization of the role of Shari'ah governed by English common law, a process that has involved subtle but important shifts in the interpretation of Shari'ah. Commercial disputes in Bahrain are now commonly resolved in local municipal and English courts. That adaptability has encouraged Bahrain's experiments with innovative financial instruments, and that, in turn, has led to the growth of off-shore banking. Substantial capital inflows from Bahrain's oil-rich Gulf neighbours have also sustained activity on Bahrain's stock exchange in recent decades, the focus of Chapter 4. Private ownership in listed companies is limited, as the state is the major investor in Bahrain's stock market. Concerns have been raised over the stock market's procedures with respect to asset pricing, commercial arbitration, and the involvement of political and legal interests, notably commercial banks and state-owned corporations, in bankruptcy and liquidation. Chapter 5 examines the relationship between the state and the stock market through oil wealth. The power of the Bahrain state grew with the power of oil, particularly from the early 1970s. High oil prices in the 2000s further heightened the state's position in the economy, especially in the drive towards diversification away from oil and in the reform of labour markets aimed at reducing the dependence on foreign labour and increasing the essential skills of local labour. It is often argued that Bahrain's authoritarian state survives through its access to oil wealth and its co-option of business elites. But Bahrain is unique in the Middle East, in that the state is responsive to secular institutions and to political pressures through the law.

Following on, Chapter 6 examines the impact of the 2008 Global Financial Crisis on the Bahrain economy. The oil price boom and the consequent major inflows of capital from the oil-rich Gulf states from the 1990s fuelled Bahrain's remarkable growth and economic diversification, although weaknesses remained. In particular, the corporate sector, riding the credit boom, was clearly vulnerable to a significant downturn. During the 2008 Global Financial Crisis, the banks retained profits and were a major source of liquidity for the stock market. But Bahrain did not escape the impact of the 2008 financial crisis entirely, and it was a firm reminder of the vulnerability of global Bahrain to external financial crises. The Arab Spring of 2011, the focus of Chapter 7, provided a further warning to the authorities, a warning that the inequalities and deprivation arising from rapid economic change could fuel substantial protests against the established order, protests sufficiently severe as to lead to intervention by Saudi forces. In recent decades, Bahrain's provision in education, health services, and in the physical infrastructure has expanded considerably, largely financed by the off-shore financial sector, itself driven by the capital inflows from the oil-rich Gulf neighbours. However, that growth masks increasing socio-economic inequalities, deprivation, and an increasing alienation against the Al-Khalifah family and its associated mercantile elites, many of whom are Shi'ite. Deprivation has been particularly pronounced among the urban middle-class youth, who have faced poor educational opportunities and then unemployment, and among farmers and fishermen, facing loss of land and reduced access to fishing waters as a consequence of Bahrain's aggressive land reclamation and economic diversification. In short, rapid economic growth, economic diversification, and urbanization have greatly increased inequalities within the Sunni-dominated state.

Chapter 8 explores the Bahrain state in detail, focusing on its relations with local capital. A major component in the Bahrain economy is a group of prominent business families, in some cases dating back to the seventeenth century. The families have not challenged the present-day state-owned corporations. Rather, the state, employing sovereign wealth funds and its commercial agencies, formed cartels with the compliant merchant class. This is evident in the petrochemical corporations (producing and refining oil), real estate developers, telecommunications corporations, and the banks. In broad terms, the separation between private and public control is vague, as the political ruling families are often major shareholders in Bahrain's corporations. Moreover, cross-border mergers and listing on foreign stock markets provide important forms of internationalization. Foreign investment into Bahrain brought with it liberal economic behaviour, especially in aluminium production, cement production, oil refining, food processing, water, electric power, telecommunications, and transport, in particular air transport. Chapter 9 examines in more detail Bahrain's transnational trading networks, a central element in its powerful corporate sector.

Chapter 10 examines labour regimes, migration, and productivity. The state's initiatives, especially industrial diversification away from oil, have substantially altered Bahrain's labour structure and recruitment in recent decades. In particular, the government has sought to regulate the employment of expatriates, while training locals for positions in telecommunications, electronics, and technology. The public sector may have performed even more poorly than the private sector. Government subsidies in the public sector led local employees to remain in inefficient positions and to resist opportunities to acquire new skills and to move into more competitive sectors. Chapter 11 considers in detail Bahrain's recent substantial diversification away from oil and towards industrial production. And Chapter 12 focuses on Bahrain's measures to challenge climate change, measures taken in the context of powerful market forces. Without doubt, Bahrain faces a long-term threat to the huge oil wealth that has been crucial in financing its modern economic transformation, a threat from the pressures to reduce world dependence on fossil fuels.

The concluding chapter, Chapter 13, explores the character of capitalism in modern Bahrain. It especially draws out the ways in which it has accommodated the demands of Shari'ah, and in this, counters the oft-repeated assertion that Islam is inimical to economic modernization. Much of the recent literature on the politics and economy of the Middle East has focused on an alleged decline compared to the advance of Europe from the seventeenth century. For example, Timur Kuran persists in identifying legal obstacles rooted in Islamic law as the cause of the decline.[101] My position is that 'the decline' in the Middle East countries has been greatly exaggerated, indeed that recent decades have seen substantial growth, particularly in Islamic finance and in industrialization, an impressive globalization in both sectors. Moreover, merchant families of the seventeenth century, notably the Safar and Kanoo, have retained and indeed expanded their power. It is unlikely that Arab entrepreneurs could have matched the achievements of the Europeans over the past three centuries. But that is not decline, for it also obscures the historical achievements of the Arabian peninsula, since 1600 in, for example, pearling and in an expansive Indian Ocean trade in food and silk, built in part on commercial contracts with the Europeans. The alleged constraining influence of Shari'ah on capitalism—and the Weberian connection of Protestant ethics to the spirit of capitalism, alluding to the alleged aversion of Shari'ah to capitalist innovation—can no longer be sustained. An important adjustment of Shari'ah involves Hiyal, a legal device that avoids strict observance of Shari'ah law. At the present time, Islamic finance uses Hiyal to defend its modern practices and to achieve aims forbidden by Shari'ah.[102] This exploration of capitalism in Bahrain also engages with Justin Gengler's work on the rentier state in Bahrain and the Gulf. I see Bahrain not as a rentier state, because the ruling monarchy had wealth and wealth autonomy, while merchants, too, had independence through their historical trading status and maintained their global ambitions in heavy industry and trade.

---

[101] Timur Kuran, *The Long Divergence: How Islamic Law Held Back the Middle East* (Princeton, NJ: Princeton University Press, 2011).

[102] Patricia Crone, *Meccan Trade and the Rise of Islam* (Oxford: Basil Blackwell, 1987). Jonathan Ercanbrack, *The Transformation of Islamic Law in Global Financial Markets* (Cambridge: Cambridge University Press, 2015), chapter 3, 'Islamic Commercial Doctrine and Classical Commercial Transactions', pp. 50–86; Frank E. Vogel, 'The Contract Law of Islam and of Arab Middle East', in *International Encyclopedia of Comparative Law* (Leiden: Brill), vol. VII (2006), chapter 7, pp. 1–162; Satoe Horii, 'Reconsideration of Legal Devices (Hiyal) in Islamic Jurisprudence: The Hanafis and their "Exits" (Makharij)', *Islamic Law and Society*, vol. 9, no. 3 (2002), pp. 312–57.

The conclusion ends with a brief examination of economic and financial change in Dubai, which has recently emerged as a potential challenger to Bahrain as a major financial hub. The comparison provides yet further insight into Bahrain's distinctive economic and financial transformation in modern times.

2

Land, Waqf, Ma'tam, and the Moral Economy

The waqf is a charitable endowment and remains widespread throughout the ummah (community).[1] The concept of the waqf as an Islamic institution orig-inates not in the Quran. Its origin is derived from the sayings of the Prophet Mohammed.[2] The ma'tam, a congregation or house of mourning, is Shiite. Historically, it provided a vehicle that facilitated pious acts of charity and is often divided into two types.[3] The first provides for the maintenance of the descendants of the waqf founder (waqf dhurri) and is referred to as a private or family waqf. The second is dedicated to public utilities (waqf khayri) or public waqf. The latter type of waqf served a socio-economic purpose, and is often described as 'philanthropic waqf', as its predominant aim is to support the poorer segments of society through the endowment.[4] These types of waqf often contributed to the establishment of an infrastructure of services that were otherwise missing or poorly executed, such as education, research, pub-lic libraries, healthcare, village wells, boreholes, and other community needs. They also served wider societal needs such as the provision of dams and land for roads and bridges.[5]

---

[1] For example, in Egypt in 1942 it was thought that waqf land constituted 11.5 per cent of all pri-vate agricultural land. Gabriel Baer, *Studies in the Social History of Modern Egypt* (Chicago, IL: Chicago University Press, 1969); Murat Cizakca, 'Awqaf in History and Its Implications for Modern Islamic Eco-nomics', *Islamic Economic Studies*, vol. 6, no. 1 (1998); David S. Powers, 'The Islamic Family Endowment [waqf]', *Vanderbilt Journal of Transitional Law*, vol. 32, no. 4 (1999), pp. 1167–90.

[2] On the origins of waqf generally see S. Heyneman, *Islam and Social Policy* (Nashville, TN: Vander-bildt University Press, 2004); Alastair Hudson, *Great Debates in Equity and Trusts* (Basingstoke: Palgrave Macmillan Education, 2014); Simon Gardner, *An Introduction to the Law of Trusts* (Oxford: Oxford University Press, 2011). For discussion on the early foundations of waqf, see M. Gil, 'The Earliest Waqf Foundations', *Journal of Near Eastern Studies*, vol. 57, no. 2 (1998), pp. 125–40. The origins of the waqf are detailed in the hadith (3:895), describing Umar bin Al Khattab being advised by the Prophet Mohammed to bequeath land 'as an endowment and to give its fruits as charity': Jane Harrigan and Hamed El Said, *Economic Liberalization, Social Capital and Islamic Welfare Provision* (Basingstoke: Palgrave Macmillan, 2009).

[3] R. Peters, 'Waqf in Classical Islamic Law', in *The Encyclopaedia of Islam*, edited by P. J. Bearman, T. H. Bianquis, C. E. Bosworth, E. van Donzel, W. P. Heinrichs (Leiden: Brill, 2000), pp. 59–63.

[4] Although it was not a particular requirement of a public endowment, there is no requirement that only the poor could benefit from the waqf. This is different in other forms of Islamic charity such as zakat.

[5] See D. Pioppi, 'From Religious Charity to the Welfare State and Back: The Case of Islamic Endowments (waqfs) Revival in Egypt', EU Working Papers, RCAS No. 2004/34.

Islam and Capitalism in the Making of Modern Bahrain. Rajeswary Ampalavanar Brown, Oxford University Press.
© Rajeswary Ampalavanar Brown (2023). DOI: 10.1093/oso/9780192874672.003.0002

This is a study of the economic evolution of the waqf which, institutionalized in law and land, assisted the renaissance of Islamic finance and the creation of Bahrain as the financial hub of the Gulf states. Bahrain, which struggles for an identity between the oil-wealthy Gulf countries and the disturbing Saudi Arabian and Iranian encroachments, exemplifies Hodgson's assertion that the waqf became the primary 'vehicle for financing Islam as a society'.[6] In the contemporary Middle East, Islamic philanthropy has become a vital tool in state control, as in Syria: and in the tension between Sunni Islam and Shiism, it offers an opportunity to escape a hostile state.[7] Fyzee Asaf considered the waqf as a form of internal colonizing of Mohammedan law, a religious contract that was fundamental for an Islamic moral economy.[8]

The creation of Bahrain as a centre of Islamic finance was made possible by oil capital flows and the establishment of modern financial instruments. At the same time, it is clear that an Islamic moral economy survives through a culturally distinct Islamic finance. The mediation in a market free of riba (interest), maisir (gambling), and ambiguity (gharar) is not only central to the financial market but is also closely involved in the financing of charitable endowments (waqf, ma'tam), consolidating assets in land and property, while building financial and political power on local, regional, and trans-regional bases.

While legal institutions and practices assisted in the transition to a competitive system, Islamic finance had separate players: the government, the private market sector, and the non-profit sector. The political and administrative thrust of Islamic finance raised crucial questions with respect to the role of the central bank, whether there should be a dual (Islamic and non-Islamic) banking system, and the appropriate tax structure. For Bahrain, the financial infrastructure, developed through centuries of international trade and transfers of money through Sunni and Shi'i religious sites from India to Najaf, was now buttressed by the political power of the Al-Khalifah family and the rise of Islamic finance from 1970, providing Bahrain with a vital context, encircled as it was by wealthy Sunni neighbours. With membership of the United Nations, the Arab League, and the GCC in 1981, and a fine-grained institutionalization of Sunni power, Shia identity remained strong, particularly through Shia philanthropy encapsulated in the waqf and ma'tam.

---

[6] Marshall G. S. Hodgson, *The Venture of Islam: Conscience and History in a World Civilization*, vol. 2 (Chicago, IL: Chicago University Press, 1974), p. 124.

[7] Thomas Pierret, *Religion and State in Syria: The Sunni Ulama from Coup to Revolution* (Cambridge: Cambridge University Press, 2013), pp. 96, 221.

[8] Asaf Ali Asghar Fyzee, *Outlines of Muhammadan Law* (New Delhi: Oxford University Press, 5th ed., 2008), p. 274.

In Bahrain, the Ajam claimed to have been the first to organize the 'Ashura processions outside the ma'tam in the surrounding streets according to a practice they imported from Iran'.[9] Many powerful Shia merchants of cosmopolitan Manama and Muharraq evolved close ties to the Al-Khalifah family, particularly after the reforms of the 1920s that involved the abolition of the feudal system. In an era of turbulent political change, the Shia waqf and ma'tam, tapping flows of international capital from religious sources, shaped the Shia moral economy with social responsibilities and expectations.[10]

A complicating feature in the evolution of the waqf and ma'tam was the conflict between Shari'ah and civil law. Owners of waqf lands, feeling secure because of the traditional rules of perpetuity as well as the Shari'ah rules preserving family inheritance, often failed to register their lands. However, a 1927 proclamation allocated ownership through registration. Further proclamations in 1930, 1932, and 1941 introduced land transactions within six months, implemented through the civil courts. A trust is an English legal concept and is not recognized in civil law, as civil law does not permit the division of ownership. Within a trust there are three interests: that of the trustee, who acquires legal title but only temporarily; that of the beneficiary who acquires equitable title; and that of the person to whom ownership passes upon the termination of the trust. This division was derived from the estate concept in England, as ownership was vested in the king. Also, the theory of tenure determined the distribution of lands throughout the kingdom. Tenure and duties of tenants as opposed to ownership and the rights and duties of owners differentiates the common law from the civil law.[11] Ownership is not strictly a concept of private property law in the common law tradition.

However, in civil law, ownership is a concept opposed to fragmentation. Transfer of ownership must take place in full or not at all. Thus, a functional segregation between legal and equitable title, or between beneficial and security title, does not prevail. Property in the civil law tradition derives from the Justinian Code. The French Revolution emphasized the Roman tradition by eliminating divided property rights, which carried the tarnished reputation of feudalism. Hence the number of restricted property rights was curtailed. It is clear that the trust does not fit within any limited type of divided property

[9] Laurence Louer, *Transnational Shia Politics: Religious and Political Networks in the Gulf* (London: Hurst, 2011), p. 143.
[10] References in IOR/15/2/1219; 23/6/1923–18/7/1927; Siraj Sait and Hilary Lim, *Land, Law and Islam: Property and Human Rights in the Muslim World* (London: Zed Books, 2006), pp. 147–73.
[11] John Henry Merryman, 'Ownership and Estate (Variations on a Theme by Lawson)', *Tulane Law Review*, vol. 48 (1974), pp. 916, 927, 940, 941; Henry Hansman and Ugo Mattei, 'The Functions of Trust law: A Comparative Legal and Economic Analysis', *New York University Law Review*, vol. 73 (1998), pp. 434, 442.

rights recognized by civil law: it is simply not permissible. The Islamic waqf is considered to be the originator of the English common law trust.[12] The waqf is held in perpetuity, no longer by the founder or by another person, only by the charity as the owner of the waqf is God. Similar to the trust, legal and beneficial title to the property is separated. Ownership and utility were never combined in the same person at the same time. However, Bahrain often found English law rather than Shari'ah to be more useful in international commercial contracts because it possesses greater legal accuracy and certainty.

After 1971, an authoritarian Sunni-dominated state in Bahrain was absorbing lands to accelerate economic growth. The fact that owners had not registered their lands empowered the authoritarian state. Contract law, rent and leasehold law, and the old proclamations relating to waqf were now covered by the Civil Law of September 2001. The law claimed that its principles derived from Islamic law, but the Government also provided political justification for its land reforms by securing cooperation from Sunni and Shia Councils. The threat to Ja'fari and Sunni waqf was severe. It was particularly serious for the Ja'fari waqf which, by the 1990s, owned 30 per cent of awqaf land.[13]

In this contested domain of state, Islamic finance, Shari'ah, and leadership of the mutawalli, it was also the free flow of capital that sustained the moral economy. Islamic taxes such as Khums and Zakat provided liquidity, much of it derived from the free flow of oil wealth.[14] The ideological and political momentum in Islamic finance was also seen in Iran after the 1979 Revolution, where a distinct configuration of state religious banking evolved between economic centralization and local social and religious autonomy through the ma'tam, cash waqf, hawala, and religious institutions. In Iran, Islamic finance had worked out a modus vivendi with the state.[15]

---

[12] Monica M. Gaudiosi, 'The Influence of the Islamic Law of WAQF on the Development of Trust in England: The Case of Merton College', *University of Pennsylvania Law Review*, vol. 136 (1988), p. 1231; Paul Stibbard, David Russell, and Blake Bromley, 'Understanding the Waqf in the World of the Trust', *Trust and Trustees*, vol. 18 (2012), pp. 785, 786.

[13] Manaf Yousuf Hamza, 'Land Registration in Bahrain: its Past, Present and Future within an Integrated GIS Environment', PhD dissertation, University of East London, 2003, p. 41.

[14] In Malaysia, the other major centre, Islamic finance flourished as a protected financial institution with state contracts for building airports and roads and assisting rapid economic growth. The Islamic portfolio of lending had maturity and flexibility, being risk averse but also bloated by religious dues such as zakat, sadaqqa, and state-sponsored Hajj funds and the savings of the pious, while planning of state investment was undertaken by the state's Khazanah Nasional Berhad (Investment Trust).

[15] Farhad Nili, 'Iran: Islamic Banking and Finance', in *The Islamic Finance Handbook: A Practitioner's Guide to the Global Markets*, edited by Sasikala Thiagaraja, Andrew Morgan, Andrew Tebbutt, and Geraldine Chan (Singapore: Wiley, 2014), pp. 175–212. For Singapore, see Rajeswary Ampalavanar Brown, 'Islamic Endowments and the Land Economy in Singapore: The Genesis of an Ethical Capitalism, 1830–2007', *South East Asia Research*, vol. 16, no. 3 (2008), pp. 343–404. And for Thailand, Rajeswary Ampalavanar Brown, *Islam in Modern Thailand: Faith, Philanthropy, and Politics* (London: Routledge, 2014).

This chapter seeks to locate the specific case of the state in Bahrain that transitioned from a form of quasi-colonial Shari'ah, a form of Anglo-Mohammadan law, to one in which a hegemonic Sunni minority would coexist with a majority Shi'i underclass. Questions of land and its development have been critical. And sites of religious significance have emerged as a source of regional development and autonomy, in particular in the city of Manama. Shari'ah and waqf and ma'tam administration has then been an important means of reconciling conflicts within civil society.

In her excellent study of Manama, Nelida Fuccaro details the role of religious institutions, in particular the ma'tam, in influencing political power. While the Sunni religious establishment is sustained by the Al-Khalifah tribal ethos, the Shi'i clerical lineages flourished through Ashura rituals and ma'tam congregations. The reputation of Shi'i religious leaders Ahmad ibn Sayyid al-Alwai and Abd al-Ali ibn Rajab rested on lineages dating back to 1602. These powerful elites persist to the present as powerful community leaders, the Bushehris, with a strong power base in al-Mukharaqah, al-Hammam, and Bu Sirrah. The Ibn Rajab family was linked to the Al-Khalifah family and served as agents for the British India Steam Navigation Company between 1873 and 1889. Such bonds of patronage were also sustained through Shi'i networks in the Middle East.[16] By the 1920s, the roles of entrepreneur, landowner, and patron of waqf and ma'tam had become underpinned by close relationships with the ruling aristocracy. Manama Shi'i leaders also established ties with the rural population, as when Ibn Rajab emphasized ties to the ancestral village of Bilad al-Qadim.

Ma'tam buildings are synonymous with public Ashura ceremonies, sponsored by pearl merchants in the 1920s and more recently by powerful merchants trading notably in varieties of wood as well as in pearls. A 'dual spatial hierarchy of markets, and residential areas mapped fairly accurately the Sunni–Shi'i political divide'.[17] While the flamboyant self-mutilation and violent flagellation reinforced Shi'i tradition, celebrations of Ashura were symbolic of Shi'i autonomous power. The mercantile power of Shi'i is

See also Charles Tripp, *Islam and the Moral Economy: The Challenge of Capitalism* (Cambridge: Cambridge University Press, 2006); Nelida Fuccaro, *Histories of City and State in the Persian Gulf: Manama since 1800* (Cambridge: Cambridge University Press, 2009); Nelida Fuccaro, 'Mapping the Transnational Community: Persians and the Space of the City in Bahrain, *c.*1869–1937', in *Transnational Connections in the Arab Gulf*, edited by Madawi al-Rasheed (London: Routledge, 2005), pp. 39–58; Fuad I. Khuri, *Tribe and State in Bahrain: The Transformation of Social and Political Authority in an Arab State* (Chicago, IL: Chicago University Press, 1980). Much of this analysis of current issues has benefited from discussions with Justin Pierce of the Law Department, Lund University, and Nelida Fuccaro of SOAS and now at New York University.
[16] Fuccaro, *Histories of City and State*, pp. 99–100.
[17] Fuccaro, *Histories of City and State*, p. 111.

emphasized in the waqf, ma'tam, and Ashura rituals, a continuity of power from pearl trading to oil refining to global Islamic finance.

The Flexibility of the Waqf

Given the flexibility of the waqf, it became a widely used financial tool throughout the Muslim world, employed by the wealthy and the political elite, not only for the provision of pious acts of public benefit but also for the protection of wealth.[18] Many commentators have further argued that the waqf had a pivotal role to play in Islamic society, not just socially but also economically, especially in rural economies dominated largely by agriculture. Villages and communities often became reliant on waqf to provide services such as access to water for irrigation. Awqaf functioned in a manner that had, at its core, the relief of the poor and were not designed to become vehicles of profit-making or enrichment. The 'social good' element, as Cizakca points out, arose largely out of the economic failings and underdevelopment of the Middle East.[19]

The nature of waqf and more importantly the role that it plays within Muslim societies has provoked disagreement between scholars in recent times.[20] Some suggest that by its very nature it must be viewed as a tool of 'social good', that it contributes positively to the needs of the people, and that given the provision of places of worship, schools, research environments, and in some cases medical or care facilities, it cannot be read in any other way.[21] But many see the waqf as a restrictive institution, a tool through which land is tied to limited uses and causes such land to be locked into the Shari'ah,

[18] See Roger Owen, *The Middle East in the World Economy 1800–1914* (London: I. B. Tauris, 1981); Brown, 'Islamic Endowments and the Land Economy in Singapore'.
[19] Murat Cizakca, *A History of Philanthropic Foundations: The Islamic World from the Seventh Century to the Present* (Istanbul: Bogazici University Press, 2000).
[20] For the roles of the waqf and the state, and the relationship between the two, see 'Abdullahi Ahmed An-Na'im, *Islam and the Secular State: Negotiating the Future of Shari'a* (Cambridge, MA: Harvard University Press, 2009), particularly pp. 79–84. See also M. Kahf, 'Towards the Revival of Awqaf: A Few Fiqhi Issues to Reconsider', Paper presented at the Harvard Forum of Islamic Finance and Economics 1999; M. A. Sadique, 'Development of Dormant Waqf Properties: Application of Traditional and Contemporary Modes of Financing', *International Islamic University of Malaysia Law Journal*, vol. 18 (2010), p. 75; Timur Kuran, 'Why the Middle East is Economically Underdeveloped: Historical Mechanisms of Institutional Stagnation', *Journal of Economic Perspectives*, vol. 18 (2004); J. A. Goldstone, 'Islam, Development and the Middle East: A Comment on Timur Kuran', in *Institutional Barriers to Economic Change: Cases Considered* (Washington, DC: USAID, 2003); Timur Kuran, *The Scale of Entrepreneurship in Middle Eastern History: Inhibitive Roles of Islamic Institutions*, Economic Research Initiatives at Duke, Working Paper No. 10 (2008); Timur Kuran, 'Legal Roots of Authoritarian Rule in the Middle East: Civic Legacies of the Islamic Waqf', *American Journal of Comparative Law*, vol. 64, no. 2 (2016).
[21] See G. Makdisi, *Islamic Institutions of Learning in Islam and the West* (Edinburgh: Edinburgh University Press, 1981).

making reinvestment and rejuvenation difficult. Other scholars see Islamic capitalism within the waqf.[22]

Following colonization and the growth of the independent state, in many Islamic countries the dominant view of the waqf focused on the harmful effect of tying up land and protecting wealth.[23] This has led to state involvement in the waqf and specifically waqf property.[24] Many countries, including Bahrain, through aggressive or systematic programmes of land appropriation, sought to put land to better use or pursued land distribution programmes following appropriation.[25] More than this, waqf land that was subject to a public purpose or in some way served the community was not incorporated under the authority of the waqf boards and consequently fell under the control of the state.

The controversial argument here is that Islam suppressed capitalist growth. Kuran argues that the waqf inhibits Islamic entrepreneurship because of 'enforced allocational restrictions—barred the pooling of resources—institutional creativity—limits flexibility and innovation'. This is echoed by Gabriel Baer who argues that the Egyptian waqf created a concentration of land within a tiny elite, causing immiseration through the high rents charged to tenants.[26]

This study of Bahrain seeks to describe a vibrant economic and financial structure, a moral economy with low risk, and one that uses Islamic precepts to underpin a secure form of capitalism. The pioneers of this argument are Barbara Metcalf and Jurgen Habermas.[27] Kuran's pessimism is enforced by the absence of local studies to underpin his work, an absence

---

[22] Jürgen Habermas, *The Structural Transformation of the Public Sphere: Inquiry into a Category of Bourgeois Society* (Cambridge: Polity Press, 1992); Nadir Ozbek, 'Philanthropic Activity, Ottoman Patriotism and the Hamidian Regime 1876–1909', *International Journal of Middle Eastern Studies*, vol. 37 (2005), pp. 59–81; Aharon Layish, 'The Muslim Waqf in Israel', *Hamizrah Hehadash: The New East, Quarterly of the Israel Oriental Society*, vol. XV, no. 1–2 (1965), pp. 38–56.

[23] This led to a number of countries limiting or abandoning private or family waqf, for example Yemen, Egypt, and Algeria.

[24] Some commentators also suggest that both public and private waqf were subject to abuse and maladministration, which ultimately contributed to the decline of the waqf as an institution.

[25] As examples, see land reclamation programmes in Syria, Turkey, Tunis, Egypt, and Algeria.Mehran Kamrava (ed.), *Gateways to the World: Port Cities in the Persian Gulf* (London: Hurst, 2016); Alvin J. Cottrell et al., *The Persian Gulf States: A General Survey* (Baltimore, MD: Johns Hopkins University Press, 1980); Mandeel Fa'eq Juma, 'Planning Regulations for the Traditional Arab–Islamic Built Environment in Bahrain', MA dissertation, University of Newcastle, 1992; Fuad I. Khuri, *From Village to Suburb: Order and Change in Greater Beirut* (Chicago, IL: University of Chicago Press, 1975); Pierret, *Religion and State in Syria*; Khuri, *Tribe and State in Bahrain*; Anthony D. King, *Colonial Urban Development: Culture, Social Power and Environment* (London: Routledge and Kegan Paul, 1976).

[26] Kuran, *The Scale of Entrepreneurship in Middle Eastern History*; Kuran, 'Why the Middle East is Economically Undeveloped', p. 3. Gabriel Baer, *Studies in the Social History of Modern Egypt*, pp. 81–3. Cizakca, *A History of Philanthropic Foundations*.

[27] Barbara Daly Metcalf, *Making Muslim Space in North America and Europe: Comparative Studies in Muslim Societies* (Berkeley, CA: University of California Press, 1992), p. xii; Habermas, The Structural Transformation of the Public Sphere.

of empirical and statistical evidence. For example, rent-seeking attitudes that inhabit entrepreneurship, a key Kuran theme, is not evident in Bahrain, as oil wealth funds state capitalism, aligned with Shi'i and Sunni merchant interests. However, there is serious poverty among the Shi'i in rural areas, as the state focused on the urban centres and on global expansion through Islamic finance. The state's global ambitions are very clear.

Between 2001 and 2007, Bahrain's REITs (Real Estate Investment Trusts), listed on the stock exchange, coordinated with Singapore's MUIS (Majlis Ugama Islam Singapore, the Muslim Religious Council of Singapore), and the Warees Investment Company, and collaborated with Temasek, a Singapore state investment group, in financial and land development projects in Singapore among the Hadrami merchant elite. The Gulf investors were conventional but also included Islamic banks and Islamic mutual funds. From 2001, REITS, with sovereign wealth funds, could invest in Singapore land development projects.[28] The investment was highly leveraged and risk was offset by rising oil prices. The Bahrain government-linked companies in the Gulf do not publish information on their acquisitions in Asia, the Middle East, and Europe. Many rural parts of Bahrain are neglected while lucrative land projects in Singapore, Africa, and Europe are pursued. Even when development projects in Bahrain's rural areas were being undertaken in the late 1990s, there were deleterious consequences for Shia waqf and ma'tam lands and for employment because of the state's appropriation of land. Consequently, there were Shi'i protests and uprisings from the 1960s, through the Arab Spring of 2011, and into 2017. These are analysed in chapters 9 and 11, which focuses on land appropriation by the state and rising labour in-migration from South Asia.

The controlled resistance by Bahrain's majority Shi'i community contrasts with Syria where charities, that had flourished from the 1920s within a liberal economic system, and where the state had preserved a 'flexible system of legislation … and then ushered in the Renaissance of Islamic Knowledge', were cruelly disrupted in 1958 when a restrictive legal system was imposed as a result of Syria's union with Nasser's Egypt. Syria's secession from the Arab Union in 1961 allowed for a brief return to liberalism. But then the Ba'thist coup of 1963 destroyed legal structures and led to the creation of state-led charities and unions. By the 1980s the independent charities had

---

[28] Annual Reports, Warees Investments, May 2008; MUIS and Warees Investment Reports, 2001–06; Singapore, Temasek Holdings Annual Report, 2006–07; Brown, 'Islamic Endowments and the Land Economy in Singapore'; Mahmoud A. El Gamal, *Islamic Finance, Law, Economics and Practice* (Cambridge: Cambridge University Press, 2006), pp. 126, 131, 132, 199.

been transformed into 'social care bureaux', under the firm control of an authoritarian state.[29]

But my central argument here is that Islamic law and institutions are flexible and that the waqf in particular has the potential to participate in sustainable forms of global capitalism. It promotes access to finance and property. The cash waqf is fuelled by moneylending and remittances from traders, harnessing local and transnational Islamic assets and institutions such as FinTech to emerge as global financiers. FinTech is highly innovative in the creation of autonomous block-chain smart contracts and the employment of complex algorithms, and it provides access to international expertise. The spread of cryptocurrencies, along with access to artificial intelligence, peer-to-peer lending, crowdfunding, and mobile payment systems are all part of this rapid innovation. The digitalization of Islamic trade finance, via blockchain and other technologies, is market driven, while ethical financial instruments such as murabahah, mudarabah, musharakah, and kafalah guarantee contracts are used.[30] This enables the GCC to diversify its oil dependent economy through advances in technology in international trade and finance. It also encourages the emergence of soft-law systems and new modes of state and non-state regulation.[31] In short, to see Islamic financial institutions as fundamentally backward is to ignore the mighty technological advance that has taken place.[32]

Shaping Land Ownership and Regional Power within Charities

Land ownership and use in Bahrain remains a source of tension between the various interests in the Kingdom.[33] The tension arises in two forms, the first being the extent to which the state, and until recently, by extension, the ruling

---

[29] Thomas Pierret, 'The Charitable Sector in Syria under the Ba'th: The Irrelevance of Law', unpublished paper.

[30] Kafalah is a contract guarantee that provides assurance in terms of performance and value when the transaction carries substantial risk.

[31] Jonathan Ercanbrack, *The Digital Revolution and Transformation of Global Trade: The Islamic Financial Paradox* (Oxford: Oxford University Press, forthcoming).

[32] Mohamed Hazik and Hassnian Ali, *Blockchain, Fintech and Islamic Finance* (Berlin: Walter de Gruyter, 2019) focuses on the wide range of FinTech technologies that are now well established, including artificial intelligence, big data block-chain, and machine learning, and explores their impact on the Islamic finance industry. See also Imtiaz Mohammad Sifat and Azhar Mohamad, 'Revisiting Fiat Regime's Attainability of Shari'ah Objectives and Possible Futuristic Alternatives', *Journal of Muslim Minority Affairs*, vol. 38, no. 1 (2018), which explores the use of cryptocurrencies in Islamic finance to realize Islam's higher objectives (maqasid al-shari'ah).

[33] The report of the Bahrain Independent Commission of Inquiry into the protests from February 2011 identified the lack of affordable housing and long waiting lists as one of the reasons for the unrest.

family, has acquired land and retained ownership.[34] Accusations were often made against the ruling family that it had embarked on a programme of land appropriation, in effect denying Shi'ite access to land.[35] As a further point, land registered to the state is then leased to private contractors, to the exclusion of the general population.[36] Second, the underdevelopment of Shi'i waqf and the use of the law to restrict investment in, and development of, property often meant that land is being used as a tool of oppression by the ruling family against the Shi'i. The difficulties associated with waqf in Bahrain are therefore historically evident.

It is accepted that the laws of waqf pertaining to the perpetuity and ownership of property form the main obstacle to the development and regeneration of the waqf land. For the purpose of this chapter, 'perpetuity' is taken to be the requirement that, once a property is dedicated, it remains waqf forever. In the same way, the conditions stipulated by the founder tie the property's use to the originating condition. As a result, waqf that is said to be made for only a limited period of time is void. The nature of waqf lends itself more to the donation of real property than to other objects, although there have been waqf of livestock, books, and other similar items. The question of ownership is also a matter of debate amongst scholars. However, it is generally accepted that ownership does not rest with the management or the beneficiaries (with notable exceptions, for example among the Maliki, one of the four Sunni schools of law). This makes it potentially difficult to deal with waqf property, although in limited circumstances there can be judicial involvement to alter the use of the property where it is no longer relevant, or to settle disputes as to its use. This is a particularly interesting question where land is endowed to a legal person. A voluntary giving of property permits the founder to stipulate the purpose and management of the waqf, which must not be altered.

---

[34] The ruling family was criticized in the 1970s for undertaking a systematic 'land grab' in Bahrain which had resulted in it being the largest landowner in the kingdom. Middle East Report no. 40, 6 May 2005, p. 9 draws attention to the fact that tens of thousands of poor Shi'ites are forced to live in cramped and poor quarters, while the royal family owns more land than it uses, as well as most prime real estate. For further discussion on the land ownership of the ruling family, see Eric Hooglund, 'Bahrain', in *Persian Gulf States: Country Studies*, edited by Helen C. Metz (Washington, DC: U.S. Government Printing Office, 1994), p. 123; Khuri, *Tribe and State in Bahrain*, pp. 35–41.

[35] In addition, there exists the presumption that land acquisition is motivated by the wish to attract foreign investment and tourism. This is associated with the role of Bahrain from the 1980s as a hub of Islamic finance and a need for economic diversification away from dependence on oil capital flows from GCC neighbours. A number of recent large-scale investments have centred around these priorities, even though they involved land reclamation. However, it should be pointed out that four new townships, totalling 250,000 new homes, such as the North Bahrain New Towns scheme, have been created.

[36] The issue has been raised in the Bahrain parliament and has resulted in heated debate: see http://gulfnews.com/news/gulf/bahrain/bahrain-parliament-wants-solution-to-land-reclamation-issue-1.567052; see also http://www.thenational.ae/news/world/middle-east/bahraini-public-lands-sold-and-rented-to-private-investors.

This is on condition that the purpose is in compliance with the Shari'ah. Traditionally any revenues generated by the waqf had to be used exclusively for its original purpose or in a way stipulated by the founder. In other words, in an attempt to protect the waqf property, the law had the opposite effect and often left the land derelict and failing to meet its charitable purpose.[37]

In many ways, the private waqf in Bahrain was evidence of the 'locking out' of property for the wealthy, as Timur Kuran asserts.[38] However this is a complex issue. In Bahrain, the rise of Islamic finance that is often Shari'ah compliant and the rise of the waqf as a force for social justice and economic growth for Shi'ites, meant that the majority of waqf and ma'tam were held by Shi'ites. Their preservation, and in particular increasing empowerment of Shi'i women through ma'tam, emerged as crucial priorities, although the dynamics of this could be obscured by the state's economic ambitions, particularly with the oil capital flows after 1971 and the urgent drive to improve infrastructure. The waqf's perpetuity and descendent inheritance produces a large number of actual or potential beneficiaries with a claim to some part of the land. This inevitably leads to disagreement over its use and the investment of funds generated under a specific waqf. In Bahrain, the lack of state involvement in the regulation of private waqf and the duality of the administrative system of land ownership, on the one hand, and the Shari'ah on the other, has made the development of some urban land almost impossible, and this has had a damaging impact on the local economy. As Mustapha Ben Hamouche points out, it has led to building degradation and at times complete abandonment of land and property, due to the lack of consensus between beneficiaries.[39] In Muharraq, the demolition of buildings belonging to the royal family in order to construct a cultural centre was highly controversial. Also the Seyadi Masjed was renovated within the waqf property.[40]

Manama, too, saw important renovations and loss of awqaf, which is clearly evident in aerial photographs taken in 1930, 1939, and after 1971. In 2001, the

---

[37] As a result, there have, in recent times, been proposals from prominent scholars and jurists that the waqf as an institution is in need of reform. For some, for example Monzer Kahf, the waqf is a useful tool for socio-economic development and the empowerment of the third sector but it needs revivification as a modern institution: it should not be forgotten but reformed. M. Kahf, 'Financing and Development of Awaqf Property', available at www.monzer.kahf.com

[38] Kuran, *The Scale of Entrepreneurship in Middle Eastern History*.

[39] Mustapha Ben Hamouche, 'Manama: The Metamorphosis of a Gulf City', in *The Evolving Arab City: Tradition, Modernity and Urban Development*, edited by Yasser Elsheshtawy (London: Routledge, 2008), pp. 196–208.

[40] The Siyadi Masjed in Muharraq, built in 1910, is located at the Shaykh ISA Home. Abdullah bin Isa Siyadi was a rich pearl merchant in Muharraq. It is a Sunni mosque and the renovation was carried out by the Department of Archaeology. Private Collection, Busheri Archive, Manama. Photos and narratives, provided by Ali Akbar Busheri in 2015–18.

Housing and Urban Development Committee (HUDC) delineated heritage areas in Muharraq and Manama but this led to serious dislocation of Shia communities, as some of the heritage area was rural and populated by poor Shi'ite agriculturalists who had earlier lost their livelihood from the pearl industry.

The cadastral database of July 2002 shows that, out of a total of 183,000 parcels of waqf, 1989 were Ja'fari waqf, 7,378 were state waqf, and only 564 were Sunni waqf.[41] Ninety per cent of the old villages around Manama, Muharraq, Hidd, and Rifa contain Shi'i waqf, which are mainly vast areas of wasteland with derelict buildings.[42] These areas lack capital for redevelopment and are also constrained by the Islamic rule of perpetuity pertaining to waqf lands. The developed and wealthy waqf in Manama and Muharraq are owned by Sunni Muslims with connections to the Al-Khalifah family.[43] The deplorable state of waqf land and properties in the old villages, and the divergence between the Sunni and Shi'i sects, is compounded by the reluctance of the predominantly Sunni state administration to intervene in Shi'i strongholds.

The Shi'ites, an already disadvantaged religious group, living under a privileged, wealthy Sunni aristocracy in Bahrain, a city state with a serious shortage of land, failed to incorporate Shi'i waqf assets in redevelopment projects.[44] Consequently, the Shi'i charities in Bahrain have become key actors in the protests for the creation of a civil society. Prior to the 1930s, the Shi'i charities enjoyed considerable autonomy. But with the discovery of oil, the private institutions of waqf and ma'tam, with their vast land assets, were open to exploitation by the state, which was building oil pipelines, refineries, and related installations. Shi'i ma'tam, and waqf were highly vulnerable. Registration of these charities became essential. Sunni and Shi'i registered the waqf and took on more formal responsibilities for their management.

The Land Registration Directorate, established in 1924, dealt largely with land disputes. The first land law was introduced in 1924, with further legislation in 1936 and 1971 to meet advances in the economy. A new law in 2006 forbade transfers of land to private ownership, which can infringe the

---

[41] The Gazette and Land Registration Department, Monthly Statistics, 1980–2009.

[42] Ministry of Housing and Municipalities, 1989–2009.

[43] Hamza, 'Land Registration in Bahrain', table 5.2, p. 44.

[44] For a comparison with Singapore, see Brown, 'Islamic Endowments and the Land Economy in Singapore'. In Singapore, entrepreneurial performance and wealth accumulation are often linked to cultural flexibility, as many Singapore Hadramis remain integrated with major business figures in Hadhramaut and Saudi Arabia. See also Rajeswary Ampalavanar Brown, 'Capitalism and Islam: Arab Business Groups and Capital Flows in South East Asia', in *Remaking Management: Between Global and Local*, edited by Chris Smith, Brendan McSweeney, and Robert Fitzgerald (Cambridge: Cambridge University Press, 2008); and Brown, *Islam in Modern Thailand*.

rules relating to waqf land.[45] But the land laws remained weak, with loopholes in regulation and overlapping jurisdictions in planning bodies. The rise of municipal power protected public spaces, restricting the usurpation of Shia land.[46]

The expansion of the charities sector continued unabated, as is evident in Table 2.1, showing the growth of the awqaf between 1980 and 2000. The growth in registrations illustrates the subjugation of the waqf through royal gifts of trust lands to courtiers, and other manoeuvres to retain state control after 1971. The Shi'ite response was to evade the subjugation by focusing on ma'tam rather than the Shi'ite waqf.[47] Shi'ite ma'tam also became public sites of religious and community identity for female Shi'i groups. Men used ma'tam for political activity while women initiated secular education, and also grappled with legal, social, and health issues. Thus, by the 1990s, literacy rates for men soared to 87 per cent and for women, a reputable 75 per cent. By 2001, it was 88.6 per cent for men and 83.6 per cent for women.[48]

State involvement in land ownership and particularly in waqf came about in Bahrain through the formation of a state institution responsible for waqf property. This arose for a number of reasons, from colonization, to restrictive Shari'ah principles, the abuse of waqf at the hands of the nazir [manager], to the rise of the modern state and the use of land registration and regulation. In late 1926, the management of waqf property remained in the hands of the nazir. However, following a number of high-profile frauds, including the conviction of the Sunni Qadi of Muharraq for land misappropriation, the Waqf Department was established in 1926.

Though Sunni waqf were few, the misappropriations there were frequent because of the lack of a supervisory authority. While Shi'i waqf land was under the authority of an elected board, Sunni waqf were left under the personal authority of the jurists until 1952.[49] This presented a problem for the Sunni rulers, as many waqf were formed under Shi'i ownership. But

[45] References in IOR/R/15/2/1976; IOR15/2/1980. Bahrain Government Annual Reports; The Official Gazette, Land Registration Directorate, monthly statistics and detailed statistics provided at Annex D. These reports are from 2001 to 2009.

[46] Al-Ansari, 'Public Open Space on the Transforming Urban Waterfront of Bahrain', pp. 134, 182; Sait and Lim, *Land, Law and Islam*, chapter 7.

[47] Hamza, 'Land Registration in Bahrain', pp. 24–35, 37; see also Nelida Fuccaro, 'Islam and Urban Space: Ma'tam in Bahrain before Oil', *Newsletter of the Institute for the Study of Islam in the Modern World*, no. 3 (1999), p. 12. Interviews with A. L. Shomali and Makey, directors of Sunni and Jaffari Waqf on 9 July 2002 and 23 July 2002 respectively, cited in Hamza, p. 27. Busheri Archive of Ali Akbar Busheri in Manama, 1990–2006: typed notes on waqf and ma'tam in Manama; and primary documents of ma'tam from Ministry of Justice and Islamic Affairs, collected by Akbar Busheri.

[48] Sophia Pandya, 'Women's Shi'i Ma'atim in Bahrain', *Journal of Middle East Women's Studies*, vol. 6, no. 2 (2010), p. 34. For an earlier understanding of these features, see IOR/15/2/1219 and IOR 15/2/130, dated 23 June 1923 and 18 July 1927.

[49] Khuri, *Tribe and State in Bahrain*, p. 113.

Table 2.1 Registrations of awaqf

Hajiri Year	Gregorian Year	Number of Cases	Gregorian Year	Number of Cases	Gregorian Year	Number of Cases
1346	1927–28	280	1961	1998	1996	7894
1347	1928–29	357	1962	2107	1997	8942
1348	1929–30	464	1963	2399	1998	10106
1349	1930–31	394	1964	2268	1999	9964
1350	1931–32	575	1965	2043	2000	11163
1351	1932–33	444	1966	2276	2001	13432
1352	1933–34	443	1967	2897		
1353	1934–35	537	1968	2650		
1354	1935–36	545	1969	2733		
1355	1936–37	756	1970	3171		
1356	1937–38	516	1971	3318		
1357	1938–39	710	1972	4471		
1358	1939–40	573	1973	5445		
1359	1940–41	457	1974	4801		
1360	1941–42	837	1975	5450		
1361	1942–43	923	1976	6684		
1362	1943–44	871	1977	4858		
1363	1944–45	738	1978	4478		
1364	1945–46	941	1979	3846		
1365	1946–47	750	1980	3665		
1366	1947–48	1115	1981	4407		
1367	1948–49	968	1982	4656		
1368	1949–50	923	1983	5550		
1369	1950–51	1075	1984	6623		
1370	1951–52	1045	1985	6424		
1371	1952–53	1334	1986	6394		
1372	1953–54	1235	1987	7898		
1373	1954–55	1290	1988	9570		
1374	1955–56	418	1989	9151		
	1955	1449	1990	8576		
	1956	1465	1991	7988		
	1957	1603	1992	9800		
	1958	2139	1993	10314		
	1959	2088	1994	10263		
	1960	1897	1995	8878		

Sources: Bahrain Government Annual Reports, the Official Gazette, Land Registration Department, monthly statistics; Manaf Yousuf Hamza, 'Land Registration in Bahrain: its Past, Present and Future within an Integrated GIS Environment', PhD dissertation, University of East London, 2003, p. 158.

the state sought to overcome this through the creation of waqf boards for both Sunni (entrusted to three Sunni Qadis) and Shi'i (entrusted to a Shi'i Qadi). The boards embarked on a process of registration, authentication, and management of waqf land and property. In other words, land came to be administered by semi-state boards.

There is a general requirement in Bahrain that all land must be registered and any request to build on land must be authorized through the issuance of a building permit.[50] Registration is completed on receipt from the Royal Court of a royal deed of ownership, usually processed through the Registration Department of the Survey and Registration Bureau.[51] This remains the central administrative core through which a registration certificate establishes the legal owner and designated use of the land. However, this is not necessarily the position of land subject to waqf rules, and despite land registration being introduced in the late 1920s it remains the case that not all waqf land has been registered.[52] One result is that land subject to waqf that naturally expires from lack of beneficiaries or is simply abandoned, falls into disrepair. But then all land deemed to be abandoned or without legal owner becomes the property of the king under Royal Decree Law no. 19 of 2002. The king also remains the supreme authority in allocating public lands for future use, further encouraging the belief that the state has the ability to appropriate land and use it for its own benefit.[53] Moreover, there is a programme of land reclamation in Bahrain.[54] That land, too, is state-owned, which further feeds the perception that the state controls land and therefore the construction of affordable housing, effectively controlling the ability of the economically deprived to live in the urban areas that provide employment opportunities.

Another aspect of the waqf in Bahrain that hinders the creation of permanent structures of control and power is the failure of rural Shi'i to register their awqaf lands, suggesting not indifference towards but a distrust of the Sunni state. The latter's practice of gifting lands to their associates increases such fears. Major land reclamation for development projects impinged on the waqf, both Sunni and Shi'i. Tables 2.1 and 2.2 on waqf lands show how registrations and land transactions were also affected by political instability, as in

---

[50] This falls under a number of pieces of legislation depending on the building type, although the predominant legislation is Decree Law no. 2 for 1994 and Decree Law no. 3 for 1994.

[51] This is a requirement under the Land Registration Act 1979. Chapter V, Article 48 states that registration of owned properties shall result in the issuance of title deeds. A title deed shall be executed according to the Implementing Regulations of that law. Article 1 of the Land Registration Law of 1979 states that the Land Registration Directorate shall undertake the functions of land registration.

[52] Although the Land Registration Law of 1979, chapter 6, Article 69, permits the registration of waqf through which a certificate of endowment is issued, this is possible only after being fully attested before the competent Shari'ah Court.

[53] The state also has the power to take possession of land under a 'Public Benefit Repossession', by the use of a special order which permits the Land Registry Bureau to amend the title of ownership to show the property as belonging to the Bahraini Government, although this should be read in conjunction with Article 9 of the Constitution, paragraph (c), which states 'private ownership is protected. No one shall be disposed of his property except for the public good in the cases specified and the manner stated by law and provided that the landowner is fairly compensated'. See Decree Law no. 8 for 1970 pertaining to the acquisition of lands for public purposes, amended by Decree Law no. 24 for 1975 and Decree Law 7 (1984).

[54] It is believed that the transfer of land titles by the ruling family to Sunni tribal leaders was another way of ensuring that power derived from land ownership was manipulated to the detriment of the Shia. For an overview, see Fred H. Lawson, *Bahrain: The Modernization of Autocracy* (Boulder, CO: Westview Press, 1989), p. 68.

Table 2.2 Statistics of land registry in Bahrain, 1980–2000

Type of Transaction	1980	1981	1982	1983	1984	1985	1986	1987
Grants by the Amir	330	487	568	893	1041	1146	940	1056
Individual gifts	501	492	411	521	518	595	513	613
Sale contracts	1605	2115	2341	2450	2345	2158	2081	2079
Registrations	1035	1117	901	1068	1847	1644	1650	2889
Compensations	97	85	97	97	111	120	172	140
Exchanges	14	3	11	12	11	19	33	15
Waqf	11	16	6	3	4	1	0	11
Mutual contracts	11	4	9	18	47	93	86	131
Insurance mortgages	61	88	278	416	598	469	621	595
Total Number	*3665*	*4407*	*4656*	*5550*	*6623*	*6424*	*6394*	*7898*
Mortgages discharged	0	7	34	72	101	179	298	369
Difference in properties mortgaged	61	81	244	344	497	290	323	226
Total value of properties (BD)	*23250516*	*54997985*	*111495642*	*107784949*	*88952215*	*61992415*	*64150505*	*44337503*
Concession			1					

Type of Transaction	1988	1989	1990	1991	1992	1993	1994	1995
Grants by the Amir	946	705	889	807	763	856	833	796
Individual gifts	627	583	694	668	740	748	952	792
Sale contracts	2927	3070	2946	2842	4082	4746	4307	3260
Registrations	3577	3123	2507	2192	2573	2591	2765	2257
Compensations	131	184	144	135	93	112	75	71
Exchanges	19	9	9	14	10	10	11	7
Waqf	13	44	22	11	17	24	13	13
Mutual contracts	133	101	190	109	58	27	98	311
Insurance mortgages	816	858	622	615	772	1172	1209	1371
Total number	*9570*	*9151*	*8576*	*7988*	*9800*	*10314*	*10263*	*8878*
Mortgages discharged	381	474	553	595	692	291	209	232
Difference in properties mortgaged	435	384	69	20	38	909	1000	1139
Total value of properties (BD) Concession	*64498447*	*68596747*	*65291465*	*81400711*	*117861783*	*148799024*	*137874657*	*101477742*

Continued

Table 2.2 *Continued*

Type of Transaction	1996	1997	1998	1999	2000	Total
Grants by the Amir	400	359	232	178	189	14414
Individual gifts	871	919	934	1003	987	14782
Sale contracts	2947	3217	3997	3874	4346	63735
Registrations	2202	2636	2979	3086	3581	48220
Compensations	75	39	61	52	44	2135
Exchanges	7	12	14	9	6	255
Waqf	12	13	10	16	12	272
Mutual contracts	356	378	307	305	0	2772
Insurance mortgages	1024	1369	1572	1441	1998	17965
Total number	*7894*	*8942*	*10106*	*9961*	*11163*	*168183*
Mortgages discharged	344	403	532	469	666	6901
Difference in properties mortgaged	680	966	1040	972	1332	11050
Total value of properties (BD)	*74919647*	*98057013*	*108877343*	*118873465*	*176824167*	*1913901019*
Concession						1

Source: The Official Gazette and Land Registration Department, monthly statistics: detailed statistics are provided at Annex (D).

1956 when registrations fell because of the Bahrain National Movement.[55] A decline in registrations also coincided with the Iraq–Iran war in 1980, and Iraq's invasion of Kuwait in 1990. Surprisingly, perhaps, movements in oil prices appear to have had little impact on the registration of land or in increased activity in the property market. Manaf Yousuf Hamza argues that there is no firm correlation between oil price rises and the number of properties purchased between 1980 and 2008. Perhaps the explanation lies in the fact that oil revenues are absorbed by the state. It might be added that oil price rises were usually triggered by political instability, and that *in itself* had adverse effects on investment in land.[56]

A proclamation issued in May 1930 had facilitated the speedy registration of land and ownership through the provision of fees. A further proclamation in August 1932 regulated mortgages but it was a May 1931 proclamation that had allowed these rights to be implemented in the Bahrain courts. Constitutional changes in 1973 and 2002 emphasized Islamic justice through the distribution of housing for low-income citizens.[57]

A civil law, passed in September 2001, stated that all unregistered lands belonged automatically to the state. It also designated unregistered waqf land as government property, thereby negating existing ownership. This absorption of land, together with the displacement of certain groups, led to increased religious and sectarian dominance, with the state tightening its control. Evidence of land grabs by the state are pervasive. Despite the Acquisition and Compensation Act of 1970, the municipalities could control land acquisitions, for they held budgets distinct from the central government. This prompted municipal councils to register public and private lands, ignoring ownership in waqf and ma'tam held in perpetuity and often not registered.

A further complication arose in 2002 when the Municipalities Affairs and Housing Department was integrated within the Ministry of Housing, Municipalities, and Environment, marking a seizure of power by the centre. It later became the responsibility of the Surveying and Planning Ministry. As noted, the Acquisition Law gives the right of acquisition or purchase only to the government, and major companies, including the Bahrain Petroleum Company (Bapco), ALBA (Aluminium Bahrain), and Bahrain Telecommunications, have to work through the appropriate ministry.

---

[55] Bahrain National Museum, *Miscellaneous Archives of the Municipality of Manama, 1938–1963* (Manama); 'The Gazette and Land Registration Department', in *Bahrain Monthly Statistics*, 1979–2002; Hamza, 'Land Registration in Bahrain', p. 158.

[56] Hamza, 'Land Registration in Bahrain', p. 161.

[57] Hamza, 'Land Registration in Bahrain', p. 31.

However, being outside the central core of the state, the Waqf Directorate helped to preserve the assets of the waqf and religious leadership to a considerable degree. Shi'ite leadership was vibrant and moderate, part of its appeal to the authoritarian Al-Khalifah. A rise in Shi'a exclusivism was avoided because of their integration into Bahrain's political and social fabric while preserving power through waqf and ma'tam. While an anti-government protest on 14 March 2011 was followed by repressive action by the security forces and civil defence personnel, resulting in the destruction of religious sites including historic mosques and shrines (see Figures 2.1 and 2.2), moderate Shi'ite elites provided stability.[58] A persistent and serious challenge came from the Strata Title Act introduced by royal decree in 1987, which secured the dispersal of rural waqf and ma'tam bordering on seafronts in Manama and Muharraq. To meet the growing demand for land, the government adopted projects focusing on land reclamation. Most of Manama's developed areas are on reclaimed land.[59]

Economic development through investment by Bahrain's oil-wealthy Gulf neighbours increased expatriate land ownership. During the colonial period, Britain had introduced laws to prohibit foreign ownership of land through the Nationality Law and the Land Ownership Proclamation in 1937 (which excluded Persians as well as other nationalities). But after 1970 the government gave GCC citizens legal access to property in Bahrain. Other nationalities have the same rights but are limited to certain areas.[60]

The state in Bahrain has been accused of the demolition of Islamic religious buildings used predominantly by the Shi'i community, some viewing this as the quelling of social unrest through intimidation.[61] Investigations by the Bahrain Independent Commission of Inquiry (BICI) in 2011 found that 28 Shi'i places of worship had been demolished on the orders of the state. Many were Shiite heritage institutions, such as the Sasa'a bin Sawhan Mosque in Askar, which dates from the death of Muhammad, the 400-year-old Ottoman Amir Mohammed Braighi Mosque in Aali, and the mosque of the Shia spiritual leader Sheikh Abdul Amir al-Jamri who died in 2006.[62] The destruction involved the arbitrary use of land laws pertaining to ownership

---

[58] Report of Centre for Academic Shi'a Studies, September 2014. Charles Tripp, *The Power and the People: Paths of Resistance in the Middle East* (Cambridge: Cambridge University Press, 2013).

[59] Hamza, 'Land Registration in Bahrain', pp. 38–40.

[60] References in IOR/R/15/2/1976.

[61] Various websites host photographs of the destruction, for example: http://www.mcclatchydc.com/2011/05/08/113839/while-bahrain-demolishes-mosques.html.

[62] Bahrain Center for Human Rights, Reports of 30 May 2011 and July 2011. Interview with Ali Akbar Busheri, whose photographs show clearly the destruction of waqf properties.

Figure 2.1 Shaik Khamis Mosque, built in 1559 by a prominent leader in Bahrain

Source: Courtesy of Akbar Busheri.

Figure 2.2 Bin Khalaf Mosque

and, more specifically, to the requirements for building permits. The issue is complicated by the fact that state permission is required for the rejuvenation, rebuilding, or establishment of religious buildings. Much of the destruction was built on a legal proposition stemming from Council of Ministers Decree no. 2105–05 of 2011, read in conjunction with Building Regulation Law no. 13 of 1977. The essence of this legislation is that it provides administrators with the authority to apply for a demolition order on the basis of an 'administrative violation', ultimately leading to the destruction of the property. It was argued that in a majority of the 28 demolitions, administrative violations had been committed. Despite owners or custodians having the right to appeal against the order through an administrative hearing, the buildings were demolished without that process. Where a religious structure had been authorized by the Ja'fari Waqf Board, it too was required to be notified, except where there was an immediate risk or danger to human life. This, too, had been ignored. The BICI report highlighted these failures.

The Financing of the Waqf and Ma'tam

Traditionally, the funding and revenue streams of the waqf rested on the protection of waqf property, operational financing, and the rejuvenation of the waqf.[63] The emphasis on waqf financing was not simply to enhance capital production or the expansion of the waqf. The creation of triangular relationships between the waqf, the religious group, and sometimes transnational capital illustrates the dynamism and vibrancy of the institution. Hukr, for example, is a method of financing that is seen to avoid the restraints created by perpetuity and ownership, by permitting the nazir to enter into a long lease with a third party.[64] In entering into the lease, the lessee pays to the lessor (the waqf) a lump sum up front, followed by a nominal rent for the remaining duration of the lease at times agreed between the parties. This mode of financing, while providing a mechanism through which capital is released, carries potential problems. The first is that the up-front lump sum can be eroded by management fees, resulting in the devaluation of the waqf, as the land as leased is tied to the lessee for the duration of the lease. Second, the funds are open to maladministration. Moreover, it is clear that the raising of capital in this way may not generate sufficient funds to expand the assets of the waqf or retain full use of waqf land. A contemporary consideration is that apparently there is a division between the revenue of the waqf and the waqf property itself. While the latter is bound by the rules of perpetuity (thus the inalienability of the property makes it impossible to encumber it), the same rule does not necessarily apply in respect to the waqf revenue. Put another way, in the context of hukr, the fact that there is future rent offers an avenue for capital generation, by securing a loan on the future rent income to be generated by the waqf.[65] Here it is worth adding that the tendency of awqaf in Bahrain to amass land and for managers to indulge in monopolistic

---

[63] Funding options and revenue streams have often been adapted as a result of disasters. For example, the great fires of Istanbul that destroyed large amounts of waqf property led to the permissible use of ijaratayn. The rules of perpetuity purport to ensure that the waqf operates on a long-term basis. It follows that there must be the financial tools available to balance the protection of the property with the ability to regenerate and rejuvenate. See Sadique, 'Development of Dormant Waqf Properties', pp. 18, 75.

[64] The term 'hukr' means exclusively or a monopoly. It was used in unstable economic conditions to reconcile the perpetuity clause in land ownership with the possible reallocation of the productive capacity of the land involved. It was also to foster profitable use of the land and direct proceeds to the waqf. It proved to be a valuable instrument to avert seizure of the land by the state. Interview with Ali Akbar Busheri, who gave me access to documents relating to his family waqf and ma'tam in Manama. See also Deloitte Chartered Institute for Securities and Investment, 'Islamic Finance Scalable and Sustainable Funding Source for Social Infrastructure', March 2018.

[65] This is available in limited circumstances. For further discussion, see Mohammad Tahir Sabit and Mar Iman Abdul Hamid, 'Obstacles of the Current Concept of Waqf to the Development of Waqf Properties and the Recommended Alternative', *Malaysian Journal of Real* Estate, vol. 1, no. 1 (2006).

self-interest, as exhibited in hukr, continued without hindrance until Mohsen Al Asfoor became Chairman of Bahrain's Ja'fari Awqaf in 2013. His strict focus on the development of waqf softened the grip of the mutawalli. When he presented the Ja'fari Endowments Report of 2015, its good relations with the king were clearly evident.[66]

Waqf Finance and Innovation

The aim here is to consider how the waqf and ma'tam engage with Islamic finance to shape the changing economic architecture of those charities. They had inhabited lucrative niches in trade, pearling, land, and hawala remittances through the cash waqf. They had developed partnerships within Bahrain as well as in Iran and Iraq and had sustained their core investments. The early capital flows from their diasporic links remained religious as well as financial. Here I will discuss the specific Islamic financial instruments that assisted in rejuvenating waqf land.

Ijaratayn involves a lessee paying an up-front sum that is sufficient to reconstruct or rejuvenate the land. It is paid to the lessor on the understanding that the capital will be used to reconstruct the property for the benefit of the lessee for future use. Again, this method of financing is focused on the rejuvenation of waqf property that would otherwise fall into disuse due to a lack of capital to rebuild or regenerate. The rules of perpetuity and ownership are respected in so far as the lessee obtains a right over the land only for the duration of the lease agreement, at the end of which the property in its rejuvenated condition reverts to the waqf. The difficulty with this instrument is that the upfront payment is, in essence, set against future rent income, meaning that the waqf is deprived of income for the duration of the lease. However, the up-front payment can be accompanied by a drip rental for the duration of the lease, in which case the rental will be substantially less than the market rate. But it is highly unlikely that an upfront lump sum combined with a below-market-rate rent is a commercially viable option. It depends on a number of factors, including the duration of the rental agreement and the value of the property. As with hukr, this model is focused on rejuvenation rather than on the growth of the waqf. There is also often discussion of mursad, which is a variation on the lease-based mode of finance. Under mursad, the

---

[66] Interviews with prominent Shi'ites in Manama on 25 September 2016. See also Standing Committee for Economic and Commercial Cooperation of the Organization of Islamic Cooperation (COMEC), *The Diversification of Islamic Financial Instruments: Case Study Bahrain*, edited by Alaa Alabed, 2017, pp. 168–84. The Ja'fari Waqf Directorate, an independent institution, was established in 1927.

lessee constructs property on the waqf land, the costs of which are recovered by the lessee through rent income. This model, slightly more advanced and nuanced in recent times, has been met with acceptance and in some cases has been presented as a viable option.[67]

A number of commentators have drawn attention to financial tools that are compatible with the waqf, as a result of the growth in Islamic finance. Investment instruments, as well as Shari'ah-compliant banking and finance, have now created diverse options for investment and financing. In Bahrain this presents an opportunity. An economic infrastructure and compliant financial instruments exist in Bahrain for investment in waqf. In fact, there has been a substantial increase in both Islamic finance- and waqf-compliant financial modelling. For example, in 2006 the Waqf Fund was established with the support of the Central Bank of Bahrain, and a number of Islamic financial houses provide education and training in the use and development of Shari'ah-compliant financial instruments.[68]

Therefore, the financial infrastructure exists in Bahrain to facilitate substantial investment and growth in waqf. This is particularly the case with public-based financing rather than institution-based investment. For example, istisna (contract of hire, manufacture) presents itself as a method of sale that facilitates manufacture and construction against a fixed sum payable to the manufacturer. There is also the option of certificates or bonds, known as sukuk. The structure here is based on restricted mudarabah, where an investor provides funds for a specific project in the form of mudarabah capital. The funds may be invested by a financial institution, or through public subscription by means of mudarabah certificates. The net return after the capital of the financier is restored is divided between the waqf and the investors. In practical terms, this involves the waqf management assessing the cost of the planned venture and the projected income and issuing certificates to the public through a financial service provider, where the total bond value is equal to the projected cost of the venture. In Bahrain, this presents a viable opportunity for state-backed waqf development, especially in the creation of new waqf property. Moreover, profitable waqf can invest in evolving financial instruments that will increase future income. It is clear that Islamic finance is not only complex but also heterogeneous in application and in complying with Shari'ah. This is apparent in the context of economic globalization. One also has to recognize the differences between national economies and their municipal legal adaptations of Islamic financial structures. The next section

---

[67] Islamic Fiqh Academy Jeddah, in its resolution no. 30 (5/4).
[68] COMEC, *The Diversification of Islamic Financial Instruments*, pp. 177, 180–1.

examines a number of financial instruments, each tied to a specific financial risk. With waqf and ma'tam, these financial instruments had to incorporate concepts of equality, fairness, justice, and equity, which are regarded as synonymous with Shari'ah principles. More broadly, in Bahrain the waqf had complex relations with the Sunni state, with Gulf neighbours, and with Iran. It also sought to harmonize Islamic finance with global trends while articulating differences at the local level.

Islamic Finance: From a Problem to a Solution

This section examines the use of Islamic financial instruments. It has been argued that risk sharing through mudarabah held advantages in creating wealth and encouraging vertical mobility.[69] Mudarabah and musharakah contracts are partnership arrangements with one (as in mudarabah) or more partners (as in musharakah) to provide skills and capital to a project. Any profit earned is shared in an agreed ratio and reflects return on capital but also on the effort put into the business. Equally, losses are shared on the amount of capital put in. This implies that in mudarabah, where only one party provides all the capital, the loss is borne by the sole capital provider.

An initial model of a mudarabah arrangement in 1960, discussed by Salman in his 2011 paper, showed that it was necessary to invest funds from the savings of depositors, and this was the second tier of a mudarabah arrangement.[70] The reduced risk means that corporations are less likely to go bankrupt. This provides economic stability and explains the low level of distress endured by Islamic banks in the 2008 financial crisis. However, this outcome is predicated on high levels of information and transparency in reporting revenues and costs, and also profit or loss. If information asymmetry exists between contracting parties, the prospect of moral hazard and adverse selection haunts the business, leading to higher costs and perhaps lower productivity, and a reluctance to adopt expensive technology. The less information-intensive contract is the murabahah contract, where the bank buys from the spot market in its own name, the plant, equipment, or raw materials, which are then sold to the entrepreneur on deferred payment with a marked-up price. Both mudarabah and musharakah are used in private equity investments or in asset management instruments. In the 1970s, oil-rich countries held high liquidity and could take advantage of infrastructural

---

[69] Salman Syed Ali, *Islamic Banking in the MENA Region* (Washington, DC: World Bank and Islamic Development Bank, Islamic Research and Training Institute, February 2011), pp. 1–45.
[70] Ali, *Islamic Banking in the MENA Region.*

and manufacturing growth. In retail banking, musharakah contracts are used for home mortgages. Bahrain concentrated on real estate development, with scant attention paid to the prudent allocation of capital.

Another financial instrument of 'escape' from the rigidities of Shari'ah and the state was crowdfunding. This is not seen as a permanent choice but in Bahrain the Shia diaspora had access to capital flows from Iran and this created smaller, simpler, dispersed social units.[71] Omid Torabi regards crowdfunding as the preferred model of Islamic financing for charities and civic institutions, since it conforms to the principle of risk sharing.[72] He also identifies the risks as credit risk, market risk, liquidity risk, operational risk, and legal risk. Mirakhor and Zaidi assume that crowdfunding introduces a greater scrutiny of risk. The Ijarah leasing contract is a safer model of financing, leaving musharakah as the least utilized contract.[73] There is an additional hazard in musharakah in that investors and entrepreneurs do not have the same level of information.[74] The entrepreneur is perceived to possess more information on a project than the investors.

Crowdfunding is suggested by Omid Torabi as intrinsically more beneficial to disadvantaged groups in the Islamic world, being interest-free but providing a model of profit and loss sharing. For musharakah the information asymmetry disincentive could be reduced through equity-based information crowdfunding. SMEs (small and medium-sized enterprises) struggle because of a lack of collateral, while Islamic law prevents direct borrowing. In advocating the use of crowdfunding, Omid Torabi suggests profit and loss sharing (PLS) and profit- and loss-sharing investment account (PLSIA) Shari'ah-compliant crowdfunding platforms, such as Shekra and Yomken.[75] In this way, technology, agriculture, health services, and education provide SMEs with microcredit for capital-intensive projects. Also hibah (gift) and Qard al Hasan (benevolent loans) contracts are appropriate for attracting crowdfunding. The musharakah contract with equity-based crowdfunding is operated through the issue of shares, while shared profit

---

[71] Interview with Akbar Busheri, August 2015.

[72] Omid Torabi, 'Using Reputation (Fame) to Reduce Information Asymmetry in Islamic Risk-Sharing Crowd Funding Models: A Game Theory Approach', PhD dissertation, International Centre for Education in Islamic Finance (INCEIF), 2017.

[73] N. M. Osmani and M. F. Abdullah, 'Mushrakak Mutanagisch Home Financing: A Review of Literatures and Practices of Islamic Banks in Malaysia', *International Review of Business Research Papers*, vol. 6, no. 2 (2010), pp. 272–82; Abbas Mirakhor and Iqbal Zaidi, 'Profit and Loss Sharing Contracts', in *Handbook of Islamic Banking* (Cheltenham: Edward Elgar, 2007), pp. 49–63.

[74] S. C. Myers and N. S. Majluf, 'Corporate Financing and Investment Decisions when Firms Have Information that Investors Do Not Have', *Journal of Financial Economics*, vol. 13, no. 2 (1984), pp. 187–221.

[75] Torabi, 'Using Reputation (Fame) to Reduce Information Asymmetry', p. 50; Omid Torabi and Abbas Mirakhor, *Crowdfunding with Enhanced Reputation Monitoring Mechanism (Fame)* (Oldenbourg: De Gruyter, 2020).

musharakah crowdfunding occurs within musharakah with a profit-sharing model. Then again, musharakah-shared revenue crowdfunding is linked to sukuk or musharakah. On the other hand, charities are accessing finance through donations based on hibah and Qardal al Hasan loans. Waqf and ma'tam also access debt-based crowdfunding in pure Qard al Hasan interest free loans. The charities are also offered peer-to-peer lending in compliance with Shari'ah.[76]

Crowdfunding is embedded in risk: fraud, failure, lack of liquidity, exchange rate fluctuation, and operational risk. Asymmetric information includes adverse selection of projects without appraising risk, lack of control over the borrower, or monitoring difficulties. Regulations are critical to avoid failure and perhaps secure guarantees and warranties through the state. Avoiding the risks of asymmetric information through collateral, financial intermediaries, a rigid enforcement of the law, and the purchase of insurance, reduces moral hazard.

In Egypt, crowdfunding targets medium-sized technology-driven groups such as Shekra, with distinct networks and profits distributed between shareholders and entrepreneurs. Shekra has 150 projects in technology-intensive service sectors, industry, and education. In Bahrain crowdfunding is less attractive, as the state is the major donor through oil capital flows. India, like Egypt, has crowdfunding, although venture capital is more important, attracting capital from the US and Japan.

Law: Illuminating the Boundaries between Religious Ethics and the Economics of Welfare

The law, regulations, the enforcement of arbitration, and above all the dominance of municipal legal systems meet the needs for regular funds and provide protection against adverse entrants. Therefore, Bahrain's charities, unlike the Syrian charities, have not only survived locally but have also maintained their transnational links. The municipal legal systems developed regional financial centres and operated as gateways to global financial, ethnic, and charitable communities. The surprising degree of legal consistency characteristic of the waqf and ma'tam explains why the Al-Khalifah monarchy cooperated in preserving the tightly knit religious charities, in particular those of the Shias who constitute the majority religious group in Bahrain.

---

[76] Torabi, 'Using Reputation (Fame) to Reduce Information Asymmetry', p. 52.

A complicating feature in the evolution of waqf and ma'tam was the conflict between Shari'ah and civil law. Owners of waqf lands, feeling secure with traditional rules of perpetuity as well as Shari'ah rules on preserving family inheritance, often did not register their lands. As noted earlier, they therefore faced enormous pressure from the 1927 proclamation, which allocated ownership through registration, and further proclamations in 1930, 1932, and May 1941, which allowed for the implementation of land transactions through the civil courts.

There is substantial divergence of opinion between jurisdictions over the fiqh, or the law contained in the Shari'ah with respect to economic issues. The one unanimous understanding is that the system is based on the real economy, that is, it is asset-based, as opposed to conventional finance and banking, which is debt-based.

Legal convergence is shaped in Bahrain through a colonial heritage of English common law, a civil code in 2001, and further historical legacies of jurisdictions from Egypt and Kuwait assisting the restatement of Shari'ah as the main source of legislation, although in practice it is strictly observed only in personal matters.[77] Civil law supplements commercial law in commercial matters. It can be safely argued that in the area of commercial law, the Shari'ah assumes a far lesser role than in the sphere of civil law. Saudi Arabia is an exception since there, Shari'ah is of immediate importance in the absence of statutory provisions, and sometimes despite their presence. Shari'ah has no clear function in existing commercial statutes in Oman and North Yemen, and the possibility of its stated function being exercised is very remote, except in matters of personal status associated with commercial law, as in Syria, Jordan, Qatar, Kuwait, and Bahrain. Whether a contract is of a civil or commercial nature is of great significance, for the probability of interference by Shari'ah is greater in one than the other. A contract is deemed to be of a commercial nature when concluded by contracting parties who have capacity as merchants and act for the needs of their trade. When one of the contracting parties is a merchant, Islamic fiqh (Islamic jurisprudence) is a consultative reference for judges. The constitution assisted by the supervisory framework of the Central Bank of Bahrain instructs legislators to make Shari'ah the principal source of reference. Thus, Shari'ah is one source of inspiration for legislators, provided no statutory provision and no customary law is available.

---

[77] Jonathan Ercanbrack, *The Transformation of Islamic Law in Global Financial Markets* (Cambridge: Cambridge University Press, 2015), pp. 238–62; Hassan Ali Radhi, *Judiciary and Arbitration in Bahrain* (Leiden: Kluwer Law International, 2003), pp. 75–132.

Nicholas H. D. Foster argues that Muslim states have not created a legal system based purely on Shari'ah.[78] Jonathan Ercanbrack, in his path-breaking book, *The Transformation of Islamic Law in Global Financial Markets*, asserts 'that the interaction of multiple legal systems in Bahrain provides an unequivocal demonstration that Islamic Financial Law is a process-driven legal composite, which cannot be viewed in jurisdictional isolation or as a classical Shari'ah transplant'. 'Bahrain, although sharply limiting the role of Shari'ah in its legal system, stands out as one of the early pioneers of Islamic Finance.'[79] The Bahrain industry-specific approach in its regulatory framework is captured in the use of arbitration through English courts, in the cases described in detail later. Shari'ah is limited to matters of personal status and this is exemplified by the existence of Sunni and Jaf'ari courts and Shi'i jurisprudence, while Civil Appeal Courts and the Court of Cassation provide space for dispute resolution. Bahrain is unique, too, in utilizing Shari'ah in corporate governance and providing further safeguards through the Shari'ah Supervisory Board. In order to understand the long-run entrenchment of the waqf and ma'tam in local and national environments, we have to examine the legal and financial institutions that sheltered and funded them, and therefore empowered Shi'ites and Sunnis.

Part of this legal diversity involved the widespread deployment of Talfiq (patchwork), the combining of approaches or principles from different Islamic schools of law and even drawing views from outside the four main Sunni schools. Jonathan Ercanbrack demonstrates this 'fluidity of linkages between the global and the local—a feeling of belonging, a social recognition or an ideological commonality'.[80] Legal autonomy is enshrined within the Shi'ite search for self-preservation under Sunni authoritarianism. Two earlier sections of this chapter, on crowdfunding and on Islamic law, suggested that a strong theme in Islamic philanthropy was emotion, fellow feeling,

---

[78] Nicholas H. D. Foster, 'Islamic Finance Law as an Emergent Legal System', *Arab Law Quarterly*, vol. 21, no. 170 (2007); Nicholas H. D. Foster, 'Comparative Commercial Law: Rules or Context', in *Comparative Legal Studies: A Handbook*, edited by D. Nelken and E. Orucu (Oxford: Hart Publishing, 2007); Nicholas H. D. Foster, 'Using Comparative Commercial Law in the Study of Legal Transformation: Commercial Aspects of the Early Stages of Ottoman Legal Transition', in *Islamic Law Facing the Challenges of the 21st Century*, edited by R. Shaham and A. Layish (Van Leer Jerusalem Institute, 2011), pp. 14–15, 32.

[79] Ercanbrack, *The Transformation of Islamic Law*, pp. 237–8. See also Rajeswary Ampalavanar Brown, review of Ercanbrack, 'The Transformation of Islamic Law', in *Modern Law Review*, vol. 81, no. 3 (2018), pp. 563–6.

[80] Ercanbrack, *The Transformation of Islamic Law*, pp. 340–1; Arjun Appadurai, *Modernity at Large: Cultural Dimensions of Globalization* (Minneapolis, MN: Minneapolis University Press, 2005). Note Nelken's claim that 'globalization is increasingly' uncoupling law from the state and providing a new source for legal pluralism'. David Nelken, 'Eugen Erlich, Living Law and Plural Legalities', *Theoretical Inquiries in Law*, vol. 9, no. 2 (2008), pp. 443–71.

benevolence, and a moral sensibility verging on fanaticism.[81] This is captured vividly by Jason J. Kilborn who focuses 'on treatment of and protections for debtors, whether or not engaged in business … It will reveal a deeply ambivalent and widely divided attitude toward forcing debtors to pay their debts while enjoining creditors to be patient and forgiving with respect to distressed debtors.'[82] Haider Ala Hamoudi offers a more radical perspective, asserting that 'Islamist legislative agendas in the Arab states have clearly moved beyond Islam, because of political and economic realities and in order to mobilize a base of voters who are less concerned about state mechanisms for enforcement of aspects of Shari'ah and more concerned about how their lives might be improved by state activity. Hence Islamist parties that offer agendas respecting employment, wages, private sector growth and anticorruption are certain to be more appealing to average voters, even if such platforms are not distinctively Islamic.'[83] In other words, it is the social movements in Islamic organizations that pursue campaigns to encourage the headscarf, Islamic schools, and the segregation of women in public transport. According to Hamoudi this is not part of the state's political and legislative agenda. The Egyptian Muslim Brotherhood's advocacy of a greater role for Shari'ah in 1928, and attempts in the 1980 amendment of the Egyptian Constitution to enforce Shari'ah as the sole source of law, were undermined by the use of secular law rather than Shari'ah in court decisions. Hamoudi concludes: 'Contrary to the Muslim Brotherhood's nearly century old slogan, it seems that Islam is no longer the solution': Shari'ah lacks a serious role in public affairs.[84]

Within this context of comparative law and its relevance to the study of waqf in Bahrain, I will pursue a small digression. Some academic lawyers have regarded comparative law as facilitating legislative reform and the consequent improvement of legal application. Here Nicholas D. Foster provides a nuanced analysis.[85] Zweigert and Kotz, too, in their seminal work on comparative law, assert that 'even today it is extremely doubtful whether one could draw up a logical and self-contained methodology of comparative law which

---

[81] This is reminiscent of the work on 'emotionology' by Peter Stearns and Carol Z. Stearns. 'Emotionology: the attitudes or standards that a society or a definable group within a society maintains towards basic emotions and their appropriate expression; ways that institutions reflect and encourage these attitudes in human conduct.' Peter N. Stearns and Carol Z. Stearns, 'Emotionology: Clarifying the History of Emotions and Emotional Standards', *American Historical Review*, vol. 90, no. 4 (1988), pp. 813–36.

[82] Jason J. Kilborn, 'Foundations of Forgiveness in Islamic Bankruptcy Law: Sources, Methodology, Diversity', *American Bankruptcy Law Journal*, vol. 85 (2011), pp. 323, 362.

[83] Haider Ala Hamoudi, 'Repugnancy in the Arab World', *Willamette Law Review*, vol. 48 (2012), p. 427.

[84] Haider Ala Hamoudi, 'The Death of Islamic Law', *Georgia Journal of International and Comparative Law*, vol. 38 (2010).

[85] Nicholas H. D. Foster, 'Comparative Law Research and Writing: A Guide to Newcomers to the Discipline'; and 'A Brief Introduction to Comparative Law', SOAS website 2018.

had any claim to work perfectly'.[86] They argue that functional methodology is the core of comparisons. My chapter attempts, through empirical evidence, to show how legal institutions, such as the Waqf Directorate, and Islamic leaders encounter theoretical difficulties in the application of comparative law. W. J. Kamba admits in an exploratory riposte that there are three identifiable stages involved here, a descriptive stage to appraise jurisdictions, the explanatory stage, and then an assessment of divergences and similarities before processing these legal jurisdictions.[87] I, too, am reluctant to engage too intensely in comparative law, as even in the Gulf states the waqf is grappling with the transnational development of Islamic financial law from both theoretical and empirical perspectives.

The Kuwait awqaf was established under the Ministry of Awqaf and Religious Affairs in 1993, 'with state resources utilized to promote Islamic activism'.[88] This position is radically different from that of Bahrain's charities where, unlike in Kuwait, ethical-social Islamic projects, the waqf and ma'tam, retain a considerable measure of autonomy, assisted by hybrid legal structures that reflect the interaction of pluralistic normative orderings, whether these are state law, religious law, or international financial standards. The approach here follows the advice of Gutteridge to wean research away from what he calls 'descriptive comparative law'. A more sophisticated analysis of Kuwait, with its loss of communal ties, decline of the public sphere, and loss of waqf autonomy, is captured in the thesis of Farah Al-Nakib.[89]

The Pervasive Autonomy of Shi'ism in Bahrain under the Gaze of a Sunni State

The discovery of oil in the 1930s promoted patron–client relationships between the merchant elites and the Al-Khalifah family, which saw its role as being to introduce stability. At the same time, some Shi'ites feared that the Al-Khalifah family would disrupt their links with Iran, Iraq, and elsewhere in the Middle East. However, wealthy Shia merchants used the oil revenues to construct ma'tams as religious and social places for their community. The

[86] Konrad Zweigert and H. Kotz, *An Introduction to Comparative Law*, trans. Tony Weis (Oxford: Oxford University Press, 3rd ed., 1988).

[87] W. J. Kamba, 'Comparative Law: A Theoretical Framework', *International and Comparative Law Quarterly*, vol. 23 (1974), pp. 510–12. H. C. Gutteridge, *Comparative Law: An Introduction to the Comparative Method of Legal Study and Research* (Cambridge: Cambridge University Press, 1949).

[88] Kristin Smith Diwan, *Kuwait: Finding Balance in a Maximalist Gulf* (Washington, DC: The Arab Gulf States Institute, 2018), p. 1.

[89] Farah Al-Nakib, 'Kuwait City: Urbanization, the Built Environment and the Urban Experience before and after Oil, 1786–1986', PhD thesis, University of London, 2011, pp. 235–329.

Royal family depended on these wealthy Shi'ites for loans, taxes, and customs duties, particularly with the increased flow of oil wealth. This led to the rise of an 'associational economy', that is, the dependence of the Sunni aristocracy on wealthy Shi'ites, and a less authoritarian state.[90] This helped to create a calmer Sunni Shiite identity and to strengthen regional links. It provided a fulcrum for Shi'ite power in Manama and the rural areas, although the economic disparity between urban Shias and the rural poor widened. Particularly distressing for the rural Shi'ites was the increase in land appropriation by the state for economic development and modernization. Broadly, the empowering of Shia merchants made it difficult for arbitrary rule in Bahrain to be strictly institutionalized, in contrast to elsewhere in the Middle East. British rule had also encouraged the association between rich Shi'ites and Sunni oligarchs. The appointment of Charles Belgrave in March 1926 as both judicial adviser and financial adviser to Shaikh Hamad on his private properties, led to closer ties with Shia merchants. Belgrave also gave advice to Shiite elites, while his responsibility for the judicial system drew the Shias closer with their appointment as judges to Bahrain's Shari'ah courts. In short, British rule fostered a close relationship with urban elites. Belgrave also calmed the Shia Baharna movement in the mid-1930s, not least by legislating in 1938 for the appointment of Ja'fari judges.[91] Waqf and Ma'tam provided space and autonomy for Shi'ites particularly in Manama, as Sunni elites were huddled in Muharraq.[92] The detoxification of Sunni–Shia tensions was thus enabled by Shia courts and ma'tam. Increasing autonomy for Shi'ites was enhanced by the formal recognition of the Ja'fari court and the creation of bureaucracies dedicated to Shi'ite religious hierarchies. Leadership provided by sect and Ashura rituals also helped in overcoming the divisive origins of Shi'ites from diverse parts of the Middle East. Islamic philanthropy, the waqf and ma'tam, and with it the Ja'fari madhab, provides a Shi'ite identity, similar to the Weiss assertion that the waqf in Lebanon was transformed from 'a sect in itself' to 'a sect for itself'.[93] Shi'ite autonomy, despite the diversity in historical origin, stands in contrast to the Sunnis in Bahrain, although they, too, are of diverse origin. Sunni inclusivity arises not only from their tribal background but also from bureaucratic reform undertaken from the mid-1920s to the mid-1970s.

[90] P. Cooke and K. Morgan, *The Associational Economy: Firms, Regions and Innovation* (Oxford: Oxford University Press, 1998).

[91] Legislation no. 26/1357, dated 27 October 1938, Bahrain, Ministry of State for Legal Affairs, *Collection of Laws and Proclamations*, 1977, p. 37. See also references in IOR R/15/2/176, no. 1822, CD Belgrave CD to PA, 9/12/1938.

[92] Fuccaro, *Histories of City and State.*

[93] Max Weiss, *In the Shadow of Sectarianism: Law, Shi'ism and the Making of Modern Lebanon* (Cambridge, MA: Harvard University Press, 2010), p. 134.

The increasing centralization of the Sunni state accentuated the loss of Sunni tribal identity. In contrast, although the Shi'ites were falling prey to aggressive religious fervour, religious groups both conservative and modernist aligning themselves with ideologues of left and moderate persuasion, they have never been subordinate to the state, unlike the Shi'ites in their Gulf neighbours and even in Iran.

The institutional and legal autonomy of Shi'ites, buttressed by the revenues accumulated through Khums (Shi'ite tithes) and capital flows through hawala, sustains the waqf and ma'tam.[94] The collection of Khums by the ma'tam further defended Shi'ite difference through their cemeteries. Allan Christelow argues that cemetery-related issues were a common means of focusing community autonomy and corporate identity in colonial Algeria.[95]

In August 2013, the administration of waqf property and the visibility of Ja'fari jurisprudence was further enhanced by the appointment of a new president of the Shi'ite waqf department, Shaykh Muhsin Al-Asfoor, a judge of the Shi'ite Supreme Court, a renowned moderate, and part of the Al-Asfoor religious lineage. The state also provided special aid to the Shi'ite waqf department for regeneration projects. It is clear that despite state land reclamation, oil exploration, and disputes over the state's seizure of Shi'ite villages, there was firm maintenance of Shi'ite leadership.

The ma'tam also remained strong through its Ashura rituals. The Bahrain Shi'ites rid the festival of harmful practices, referencing Shi'ite patrimony through the reformist strain. The institutionalization of power structures was further enhanced by the location of Shi'ite ma'tam and waqf within personalized clusters, in contrast to the Sunni waqf, which is often located near the bazaar. The Shi'ite waqf is also controlled through Ja'fari courts and jurisdiction.[96]

The issue of autonomy is captured in the following. The Ja'fari waqf was established in 1927 in a school in Manama, with the aim of compiling endowment properties. It was led by Sayed Adnam Sayed Alawi Al Abdul Jabbar Al Moosawi, a prominent ulama on the Sharia Judiciary and Endowments Board in 1927 and 1928. His surveys included all properties in towns and

[94] Rajeswary Ampalavanar Brown, *The Chinese and Indian Corporate Economies: A Comparative History of Their Search for Economic Renaissance and Globalization* (Abingdon: Routledge, 2017), pp. 350–65, 446–8.

[95] Allan Christelow, 'The Transformation of the Muslim Court System in Colonial Algeria: Reflections on the Concept of Autonomy', in *Islamic Law: Social and Historical Contexts*, edited by Aziz Al-Azmeh (London: Routledge, 1988), p. 226.

[96] Nelida Fuccaro, 'Understanding the Urban History of Bahrain', *Critique: Critical Middle Eastern Studies*, vol. 17 (2000), pp. 73–6, 80–1; Mahdi Abdalla A-Tajir, *Bahrain 1920–45: Britain, the Shaykh and the Administration* (London: Croom Helm, 1987), pp. 8, 80–3; Radhi, *Judiciary and Arbitration in Bahrain*, p. 18.

villages in Bahrain, and established procedures for the collection of rental income and investments. After his death in 1928, the Ja'fari Waqf Department was incorporated within the Bahrain law courts.

Between 1926 and 1957, Charles Belgrave oversaw the transfer of the administration of Shia awqaf from Qadis to elected town councils and village councils. Until 1928, the Qadis control had been strong and they were responsible for property transfers. A Sunni waqf department was set up in 1937. In 1960, the government introduced formal laws to govern waqf. A further decree in 1985 brought in additional procedures for the control of investments. In 1991, Sunni and Shi'ite Waqf Councils were established, to set budget allocations and agree membership. This increased the autonomy particularly of the Shi'ite ma'tam.[97]

As Barbara Daly Metcalf notes, without ignoring the often-high levels of deprivation, prejudice, and racism that affect many Muslims, these communities also have reserves of cultural strength, creativity, and inventiveness.[98] This is certainly true of the Shi'ites in Bahrain. More broadly, the waqf is designed to contribute to a broader 'politics of hope' for Muslim communities, particularly after the Arab Spring of 2011, and the conflict and repression that followed. The 'politics of hope' can be built around community assets and institutions able to harness local and often transnational flows of donations, endowments, and business information.

The prominent part played by Shi'ites in the uprising in 2011, and in the months leading to the Bahrain Grand Prix in April 2012, has perhaps confused our understanding of the nature of tribal power, as vested in the ruling family, the Al-Khalifah, the Shi'ites, and their religious networks. It is clear that there is no inherent opposition between the Sunnis, ruling the country, and the Shi'i. Shi'ites are the victims of discrimination, yet Sunnis have historically participated in opposition groups, as seen in 2011, when one of the initiators of the 'Roundabout' confrontation was a Sunni. Similarly, there are a number of Shi'i religious families who are very close to the ruling family, such as the Arrayedh or the Bin Rajab. The challenges came from leftists, trade unions, the college-educated young with strong affiliations to clubs, and awqaf of Shi'i. Some of the ma'tam did participate but were generally reluctant to play a political role and did not automatically sympathize with protest. Some of the most prominent awqaf and ma'tam, for example the

[97] Mohammad Taghi Razavian, 'Iranian Communities of the Persian Gulf: A Geographical Analysis', PhD thesis, University of London, 1975. See also Article 21 of the Report of V. W. Guicciardi, Personal Representative of the UN Secretary-General in Charge of Mission to Bahrain, April 1970. The report marked the renouncement by Iran of any claim to Bahrain, an important element in the autonomy of Bahrain's Shi'a community.
[98] Metcalf, *Making Muslim Space*, p. xii.

powerful Ja'fari waqf, are controlled by loyal Shi'i families. The Ja'fari waqf is extremely wealthy and cooperates with the state. The complexity of Shi'i political response is crucial.[99] Despite cross-ideological and cross-sectarian cooperation since the 1930s, the temptation for meddling in sectarian politics is clear even today in Bahrain. In March 2017, the Justice Ministry in Bahrain filed a lawsuit to dissolve the largest left-wing opposition group, on the grounds that it was a threat to security. The National Democratic Action Society was accused of violating the law and supporting terrorism and sanctioning violence. Neutral sources believe this is wholly unsubstantiated and is a prime example of Gulf states propaganda.[100] In contrast, in Syria, plans to reform the law governing charities were abandoned, with the enactment of emergency laws after the Ba'thist coup in 1963. This led to the crushing of the charity sector in Syria, with nationalization of al-Nahdat al Islamiyya and its transformation into a social care bureau.[101]

The Colonial Heritage, Law, the Al-Khalifah Monarchy, and Shi'i Leadership

Bahrain, like Kuwait, declares Shari'ah to be a prime source of jurisprudence, although secular, Western-derived civil law and modern jurisprudence are also important. Only in personal law and inheritance law is Shari'ah applied with little or no deviation. Also, customary law shapes local law. Often in Bahrain, Shari'ah is more a method than a legal statement.[102] Islamic legal foundations in Bahrain in the twentieth and twenty-first centuries were/are dedicated to pragmatism, exhibited through the Shari'ah Supervisory Board. This allowed the emergence of a hybrid legal system, not through direct reconciliation or compromise with Islamic values but by allowing legal

[99] For excellent studies of political protest in the Middle East, see Pierret, *Religion and State in Syria*; Tripp, *The Power and the People*. See also Toby Mathiesen, *Sectarian Gulf: Bahrain, Saudi Arabia and the Arab Spring that Wasn't* (Stanford, CA: Stanford University Press, 2013); Nelida Fuccaro (ed), *Violence and the City in the Modern Middle East* (Stanford, CA: Stanford University Press, 2016); Marc Valeri, 'Contentious Politics in Bahrain: Opposition Cooperation between Regime Manipulation and Youth Radicalization', in *Opposition Cooperation in the Arab World: Contentious Politics in the Time of Change*, edited by Hendrik Kraetzschmar (London: Routledge, 2012), pp. 129–49. In Bahrain, 17 mosques were affected by violence during the 2011 rising: Marc Owen Jones, *Political Repression in Bahrain* (Cambridge: Cambridge University Press, 2020).
[100] Valeri, 'Contentious Politics in Bahrain', pp. 129–49.
[101] Thomas Pierret and Kjetil Selvik, 'Limits of Authoritarian Upgrading in Syria: Private Welfare, Islamic Charities, and the Rise of the Zayd Movement', *International Journal of Middle East Studies*, vol. 41, no. 4 (2009), p. 601.
[102] See Jonathan Ercanbrack, 'The Standardization of Islamic Financial Law: Lawmaking in Modern Financial Markets', *American Journal of Comparative Law*, vol. 67, no. 4 (2019). Also Ercanbrack, *The Transformation of Islamic Law*, pp. 237–63.

disputes in Bahrain to be considered in English courts. Thus disputes in Islamic finance were, in the last resort, resolved in foreign courts according to English law. This was never the approach in Saudi Arabia where Shari'ah was fully embedded, although Saudi Arabia permitted a slight fudge involving the parallel secular law with the Nizam, which governs the corporate economy, and where jurisdiction is shaped by the Board of Grievances within the overarching presence of the Hanbali doctrine. In Bahrain, the strategic and opportunistic adaptation and harmonization of legal practice was assisted by the Shari'ah courts, where Sunni and Ja'fari courts had the power to interpret Shari'ah jurisprudence affecting waqf and ma'tam. This rise of a municipal legal system provides for local interpretation while pursuing global ambitions. The AAOIFI (Accounting and Auditing Organization for Islamic Financial Institutions) also conceded that Bahrain's interpretations were commercial necessities within Islamic legal methodology. This led Al-Asfoor, the Chairman of the Ja'fari Awqaf, to proclaim in September 2015 that Bahrain was retaining waqf autonomy without transgressing Shari'ah and was preserving harmony between Sunnis and Shi'ites.

Although interpretation of Shari'ah pertaining to waqf and ma'tam did provoke criticism from the conservatives, it was the financial guarantees on hawala, or the cash waqf, a mainstay of Shia diasporic philanthropy, that aroused the most serious opposition. This was similar to the resentment in Aceh in Indonesia that led Feener to assert that opposition was 'de-provincializing discussions of these important issues and contributing to a more global conversion dynamics of religion in contemporary societies.'[103] Bahrain was in the unique position of being able to seek harmonization of Islamic financial law through international conventions and bilateral treaties (as with Malaysia), a flexibility made possible because Shari'ah is firmly applied only in personal law.

Conclusion

In Bahrain, the waqf and ma'tam have, to a degree, protected land from appropriation by the state by placing it within the Shari'ah legal code. At the same time, Bahrain has had the flexibility to accommodate huge capital flows from oil and to secure the kingdom's emergence as the financial hub of the Gulf. In achieving this, it had the resilience to meet the challenges of a rapidly

---

[103] Michael Feener, *Sharia and Social Engineering: The Implementation of Islamic Law in Contemporary Aceh, Indonesia* (Oxford: Oxford University Press, 2013), p. 11, appendix 1.

transforming economy, from agriculture and pearling to oil production and to industrialization. Although Bahrain had limited oil reserves compared to its neighbours, it emerged as a major intermediary for oil producers and controlled huge capital flows from oil in the Gulf states. And in time it sought economic diversification and flexibility away from that oil dependence.

3

Islamic Banking in Bahrain

Religious Principles and Economic Performance

The key proposition in this chapter is that Islamic banking is not an abstract principle but is shaped by the context in which it operates. This study of Islamic finance in Bahrain focuses on its involvement in the oil capital flows from the rich Gulf states and shows how Bahrain emerged as a major hub of Islamic finance, next in importance only to Malaysia. Moreover, Bahrain's colonial past has encouraged a market liberalization of the role of Shari'ah governed by English common law. Bahrain's experiment with innovative finance has led to a growth in offshore banking and commercial dispute resolution in Bahrain's local municipal courts and overseas English courts. It is this adaptability and dynamism that has made Bahrain unique in developing innovative instruments and operations in Islamic finance.

In developing innovative financial instruments, subtle but important shifts have taken place in the interpretation of Shari'ah. This is close to the hypothesis of Laura Benton, that the search to define universal features of legal systems and legal actors appeals regularly to multiple legal authorities—an imagined geocentric solar system—and ultimately a return to faith (Shari'ah in the case of Bahrain) to account for inconsistencies.[1] The interpretation of the Shari'ah to facilitate innovation resembles the approach of behavioural economics, in which different contexts call for tailored interpretative strategies.

A further important concern of this chapter is to examine the strengths of Bahrain's Islamic banks, their adaptability and dynamism, and their closeness to resource-rich Saudi Arabia and Kuwait. This examination involves an important proposition relating to port cities as enclaves of resource-intensive countries. First, these port cities are small island economies, such as Singapore, with Malaysia as the resource-rich hinterland. Second, Jeffrey Sachs and Andrew Warner have argued that the resource-rich countries stagnated

---

[1] Laura Benton, *Law and Colonial Cultures: Legal Regimes in World History, 1400–1900* (Cambridge: Cambridge University Press, 2002), p. 8. Benton is here drawing on Roberto Mangabeira Unger, *Knowledge and Politics* (New York: Free Press, 1976).

Islam and Capitalism in the Making of Modern Bahrain. Rajeswary Ampalavanar Brown, Oxford University Press.
© Rajeswary Ampalavanar Brown (2023). DOI: 10.1093/oso/9780192874672.003.0003

after 1970 and that they missed out on export-led growth.[2] This case study of Bahrain challenges Sachs and Warner, arguing that the resource-rich hinterlands in Asia and the Middle East sustained the economic growth of small island economies and also their endogenous growth for a period after 1970. The small island economies, invigorated by this initial spurt, confidently undertook global initiatives, as Bahrain achieved with global Islamic finance.

To understand the rise of Bahrain as a major hub of Islamic finance in the Middle East, it is important to trace its historical growth within the Arabian Gulf. Ibn Khaldun has identified the first element in this growth as being tribal identity, crucial for securing political and economic networks. Also important was British colonialism, which established legal and administrative structures. There was an ethos of cosmopolitanism, in which the autonomy of Shi'ite Ja'fari jurisprudence and modern leadership reduced religious tensions.

Bahrain's oil history began in the 1930s. But as her own reserves dwindled from the 1970s, Bahrain experienced an immense inflow of oil capital from her Gulf neighbours. This led to inter-regional growth, and international banks located in Bahrain's capital, Manama, to attract oil revenues. Bahrain's cosmopolitanism facilitated the use of multiple legal inputs to mitigate the risks arising from a strict adherence to Shari'ah principles. This involved not a convergence of conventional and Islamic banking but an adroit use of local municipal and foreign courts to settle legal disputes. For the GCC countries faced with huge earnings from oil, the attraction of Bahrain was its more flexible interpretation of Shari'ah. In addition, Bahrain enabled the GCC countries to create economic initiatives in the Middle East, in North Africa, and in the West, exploiting its religious and commercial ties. For example, Saudi charities involved in infrastructural programmes in Africa sought to work through Bahrain, to circumvent their own religious conservatism. The Islamic banks and business elites were highly dependent on the Gulf monarchies. The links between the state and business were strong because the Shi'ite majority of Bahrain was regionalized in exercising power. This was reflected in the rise of Islamic charities, the waqf and ma'tam, that, while reflecting diversity between Sunni and Shi'ite, created an enduring autonomy, particularly for the Shi'ites. This is in contrast to Syria where, with the rise of the Ba'th regime from 1963, the charities came under the supervision of the state, and law became irrelevant.[3] Bahrain as a hub of Islamic finance thrived as a vital

[2] Jeffrey D. Sachs and Andrew M. Warner, 'Natural Resource Abundance and Economic Growth', Working Paper No. 5398, National Bureau of Economic Research, Cambridge, MA, 1995, pp. 1–47.
[3] Thomas Pierret, 'The Charitable Sector in Syria under the Ba'th: The Irrelevance of Law', unpublished paper; Thomas Pierret, 'State Management of Religion in Syria: The End of Indirect Rule?', in *Middle East*

source of stability and modernity in the Gulf. Its wealthy neighbours have had both a positive as well as a deleterious impact. Bahrain's dependence on Saudi Arabia and Kuwait means negotiating with corruption and opacity. And as will be discussed in a later chapter, the Souk al Manakh crisis in Kuwait in 1982 left Bahrain with huge losses.

The strength and stability of Bahrain's Islamic banks reflects in part their disciplined, if more flexible application of Shari'ah. That discipline ensures operations that are less risky than those of conventional banking. This was clear from the fact that banks from Saudi Arabia and Kuwait had to be rescued by the state during the 2008 financial crisis. Malaysian banks, too, were vulnerable. Bahrain has created a modern, sophisticated Islamic financial infrastructure, with rigorous and transparent disclosure standards and, from 2017, external audit. Corporate governance in Bahrain is rated the best in the Gulf. The World Bank Global Financial Development Database stated that Bahrain outstrips Saudi Arabia, Kuwait, and the UAE in financial success and corporate governance.[4]

But Islamic finance also has weaknesses. The poor constitute a large percentage of the depositors (because of their strong faith) but their treatment is often disadvantageous. Many are Shi'ites or foreign workers. Iran supports the poor through Qard al Hasan loans, but the figures are disappointing. In 1984, Qard al Hasan loans were 11 per cent of all loans but by 2010 this had fallen to just 6 per cent.[5]

A close comparison with conventional banks indicates the constraints imposed by Shari'ah. But in Bahrain, Shari'ah is observed more in family law than in the economic and corporate fields where there is greater flexibility. Rather, it is the high proportion of non-performing loans, lower return on assets, high operating costs, and the high asset concentration that make Islamic banks vulnerable. They are also small in size compared to conventional banks. In Bahrain, while Shari'ah boards are less prone to

Authoritarianisms: Governance, Contestation, and Regime Resilience in Syria and Iran, edited by Steven Heydemann and Reinoud Leenders (Stanford, CA: Stanford University Press, 2013), pp. 83–106.

[4] Data from World Bank Development Indicators for 2015; ICD-Thomson Reuters, *Islamic Finance Development Report 2016*, pp. 30–1; Central Bank of Bahrain, *Insurance Market Review 2015*, pp. 4, 10, 30; Committee for Economic and Commercial Cooperation of the Organization of Islamic Cooperation (COMCEC), Standing Coordination Office, *Diversification of Islamic Financial Instruments*, October 2017, prepared by Alaa Alaabed, and 'Finocracy, Bahrain', with the assistance of Irum Saba and Syed Aun Rizvi, pp. 8–9; William Bean 'The Contemporary Financial Development of Kuwait and Bahrain: A Study of Contrasts', PhD thesis, Princeton University, 1988, p. 76.

[5] Omid Torabi and Sahul Haeed bin Muhammad Ibrahim, 'Qard al-Hasan Loans in Iran', The Global University in Islamic Finance, Working Paper, Kuala Lumpur, INCEIF, 2012, p. 3. See also Farhad Nili, 'Iran: Islamic Banking and Finance', in *The Islamic Finance Handbook: A Practitioner's Guide to the Global Markets*, edited by Sasikala Thiagaraja, Andrew Morgan, Andrew Tebbutt, and Geraldine Chan (Singapore: Wiley, 2014), pp. 69, 103, 180–7, 190–1, 395–7.

insider-dealing, they are managed by ill-trained Shari'ah scholars. Regulation lacks rigour. In addition, Shari'ah boards are often funded by the banks they supervise, and this can create scepticism about the benefits of Islamic finance.

Arguing the strengths and weaknesses of Islamic banks requires detailed statistics on assets and income, the sources and uses of funds, as well as on the rate of return on the various items of the banks' portfolios. In addition, details on murabahah and other financial instruments would demonstrate the advantages of Islamic banks. Quantitative assessment of musharakah (equity finance), mudarabah (trust financing), ijarah (lease financing), murabahah (trade financing), qard al hasan (welfare loans), bay bial-thaman al-ajil (deferred payment), and istisna (progressive payments) would establish the popularity of specific instruments. There is also a distinction to be made between retail banks, wholesale banks, and investment banks in their choice of financial instruments. As the state and its associational investors are often involved in these choices, the picture can be shadowy. Nevertheless, quantitative data does provide a reasonably accurate measure of profitability and risk within Islamic banks.

From Gladiatorial Religious Maturity to Mutual Rapprochement

The instruments and practices of Islamic finance have emerged with increasing importance since the early 1960s. In Egypt in the 1960s, the Cooperative Savings Bank Mit Ghamr, providing small loans for commercial needs and coordinated savings, was a significant pioneer. In the 1960s, the Malaysian state formed the Khazanah Nasional Berhad, which coordinated savings for the Hajj pilgrims. In 1971, the Nasser Social Bank was incorporated. But it was the oil wealth created from the early 1970s that secured an extraordinary growth in Islamic banking, notably the Islamic Development Bank in Jeddah, coordinating investment in the Gulf states and in North Africa, and the Dubai Islamic Bank in the UAE, the first private Islamic bank. And in time, Islamic windows were created within conventional Western banks, tapping the talent of these banks to assist in creating Islamic financial instruments, although often modification comprises in the search for compliance to Shari'ah principles.

In the 1970s, Bahrain invited international banks to establish offshore banking units to attract oil revenues from oil-rich neighbours, notably Saudi

Arabia. These offshore units rose to 77 within 10 years.[6] Saudi development programmes stimulated growth in banking, with Islamic finance emerging dominant. Bahrain's offshore banking handled trade and construction programmes with private companies throughout the Gulf. This was accompanied by the growth of sophisticated financial tools, such that Bahrain came to challenge Malaysia and Pakistan as a centre for Islamic finance. The pre-eminence of sukuk showed that Bahrain's share was significantly high in funding infrastructural growth.

Bahrain's story is a compelling one within Islamic finance, but it was greased by abundant oil flows from Saudi Arabia and Kuwait, Bahrain's main partners. Indeed, Bahrain's emergence as the dominant hub for Islamic finance in the Gulf rested on oil wealth, although it also rested on Bahrain's long history as a trading power in the region. The flow of oil wealth into Bahrain from the 1980s, and the consequent takeover of banks, produced substantial structural changes. A flexible specialization framework emerged, with syndicated loans, club deals arranged for forward markets in diverse currencies (dollars, riyals, and regional currencies), each developed to a sophisticated international perspective. This facilitated integration within the wealthy Gulf states, endowed with an ability to overcome Shari'ah constraints by settling commercial disputes in London courts under common law.

Overseas entrants into Islamic banking and finance in Bahrain created a wide spectrum of instruments, including Islamic insurance and reinsurance, takaful and retakaful. In 2015, there were seven licensed takaful operators in Bahrain with assets totalling US$309 million. They recorded a global growth of 6.8 per cent compared to Malaysia's 23.10 per cent and Saudi Arabia's 60.7 per cent.[7] The strength of Bahrain lies in its connections with North Africa and South East Asia, in addition to the Middle East. Total market capitalization of the banking sector in Bahrain in 2013 was US$16.6 billion, and the Islamic financial sector contributed US$3.9 billion or 24 per cent. In 2012, the Central Bank of Bahrain (CBB) announced that 101 Islamic mutual funds were registered in Bahrain with total assets of US$1.7 billion and they traded through a Mutual Fund Exchange automated trading system. Two major funds were the Global GCC Islamic Fund and the IIAS Islamic MENA Fund.[8] The growth in diverse products, to a degree, disguises the political expectations of Bahrain seeking to be the financial hub of the Gulf. The argument so

---

[6] ICD-Thomson Reuters, Islamic Finance Development Report 2015.
[7] Central Bank of Bahrain, *Insurance Market Review*, pp. 4, 10, 30; COMCEC, Diversification of Islamic Financial Instruments, and 'Finocracy, Bahrain'.
[8] Deloitte Research and Analysis, *Global Impact Report*, 2012. Central Bank of Bahrain, *Financial Sector Overview*, 2015; Central Bank of Bahrain, *Financial Stability Report*, February 2017, pp. 41, 47, 49, 55.

far suggests that a significant proportion of the growth is in major state programmes. However, there is a wider political programme of concentrating on retail credit to SMEs and to waqf and ma'tam, and the use of state subsidies for these social and economic pursuits.

Islamic finance in Bahrain concentrated on retail credit to SMEs, as almost 88 per cent of businesses in Bahrain are SMEs. In addition, state corporate paternalism extended to the funding of education, health and medicine, skills training, and employment of the rural poor, the majority of whom are Shia. Working in microfinance, Ebdaa Bank and Family Bank emerged in the late 1990s. These two banks (the Ebdaa Bank was a conventional bank, and Family Bank, a Shari'ah-compliant bank) were deployed in the financing of SMEs while collaborating with Tamkeen, a project of 2006 combining economics and ethics as a vision for Bahrain's development, a vision that emphasized social responsibility on the part of business. Family Bank has further projects, including the Grameen programme which offers cheap loans to entrepreneurs based on farm and home technology projects, while Ebdaa Bank offers microfinance to farmers, women, and fishermen. In 2013, Tamkeen, in collaboration with Kuwait Finance House, introduced a range of subsidies to support the growth of SMEs. This combined a financial hierarchy of a 50 per cent subsidy incorporating murabahah finance, while Ijarah finance was directed to trade, technology, and equipment costs.[9] Such variations in funding, where a third of microfinance in 2012 was in wholesale and retail trades, while 14 per cent was in construction and 9 per cent in manufacturing, created a systematic, structural rationale behind the rather fragile combination of state support and the local charity sector. Agribusiness, too, received government aid with loans at 0 per cent interest. This survives because of an economic integration driven by the complementarity of two spheres, the state, on the one hand, and waqf and ma'tam on the other, inspired by the tenets of a moral economy. But again it should be emphasized, Bahrain's outstanding success in Islamic finance rested on the inward flow of oil wealth from Saudi Arabia.

In this way, Bahrain grew as a vibrant international financial centre. By the 1970s and 1980s, Bahrain's offshore banking units had 60–70 per cent of their business in Saudi riyals.[10] Saudi authorities, highly secretive and conservative, used Bahrain to bear the burden of the internationalization of their

[9] Hatim El-Tahir, 'Bahrain: Threads of Growth in Islamic Finance', in *The Islamic Finance Handbook: A Practitioner's Guide to the Global Markets*, edited by Sasikala Thiagaraja, Andrew Morgan, Andrew Tebbutt, and Geraldine Chan (Singapore: Wiley, 2014), p. 31.

[10] A. S. Gerakis and O. Roncesvalles, 'Bahrain's Offshore Banking Center', *Economic Development and Cultural Change*, vol. 31, no. 2 (1983), pp. 271–93.

financial infrastructure. Equally, the debacle of the 1981 financial crisis and the 1990s' suspicions of funding terrorism were concealed. Saudis remain opposed to the internationalization of the riyal. This constrained Bahrain in the 1980s because the Saudis were determined to protect the riyal. Bahrain's offshore banks, two-thirds of whose business derived from Saudi Arabia, were affected and the free transfer of riyals was restricted. Bahrain's difficulties persisted, a consequence of the Saudi Government's forward market contracts in dollars and not riyals. These constraints were also related to the wider political context, where all Saudi transactions required the approval of the Saudi Arabian Monetary Agency (SAMA). Local Saudi banks were prohibited from making foreign transactions without approval from the SAMA. The free flow of capital was a casualty.[11] The two most severe constraints on Bahrain, the Saudi regional control of Islamic finance and the collapse of Kuwait's Souk al Manakh in 1982 and the subsequent recession, drove Bahrain's expansion into Asia and Europe.

Shari'ah and Its Impact on Islamic Finance

The cornerstone of Islamic banking and finance is that it is guided by the Shari'ah. The main principles are Islam's strict rules on justice in economic exchange. Riba, predetermined interest, is forbidden because it creates unfairness for the borrower if he suffers a loss, and for the lender if inflation is high. Riba can create economic instability. Also, the borrower who has a high credit rating has access to more capital. Hence, in capitalist economies, profit and loss determine the allocation of capital, and therefore the profitability of a company determines choice. Other Shari'ah principles include avoidance of 'Maysir' (gambling); removal of 'Gharar; and participation only in 'Halal' activities. Gharar (risk/uncertainty) is when a person withholds information for personal gain. But if the risk is not serious, the financial transaction is not forbidden.

That said, there is a substantial divergence of opinion between jurisdictions concerning the fiqh or law contained in the Shari'ah with respect to economic issues. The one unanimous understanding is that the structure is based on the real economy, that is, it is asset-based, as opposed to conventional finance and banking, which is debt-based. There is still much development needed in the law, particularly in respect of fiduciaries and governance. However,

---

[11] Rodney Wilson with Abdullah Al-Salamah, Monica Malik, and Ahmed Al-Rajhi, *Economic Development in Saudi Arabia* (London: Routledge Curzon, 2004), pp. 56–74.

one must be careful not to over-regulate, to the extent of attempting to regulate ethical behaviour. Ethics need to be approached through drawing on an accumulated body of Islamic jurisprudence, which in Bahrain includes Ja'fari jurisprudence, which has been shaped by international trade and transactions over the centuries. In Bahrain, Islamic finance is innovative and profitable, and has legal means to assist in achieving moral ends, to some degree.

The impact of the constraints in Islamic finance are, first, that Islamic banks provide funds on a profit–loss-sharing basis, reflecting the value of the asset. Second, forward contracts are forbidden. This means that derivatives are affected. In addition, short-selling is prohibited, as the seller needs to own the asset being sold. Money is simply the means to facilitate trade and commerce, not an end in itself. Islamic banks are founded on the basis of sharing profit and loss. Profits are determined by who bears most risk; losses are distributed depending on shares. Ownership faces risk to the extent of its stake.

Asymmetry in information is a serious issue. For example, with shares in a company, the buyer has no additional information on takeover bids and other financial threats, what might be called insider knowledge. Gharar may not apply to business risks, but the customer is kept in the dark. There is, therefore, growing scepticism regarding the magnitude of the economic benefits of Islamic finance, even in funding Islamic charities.[12]

One well-established narrative in Islamic finance concerns the relationship between Shari'ah and the ethics and efficiency of financial institutions. An important argument in this chapter is that Islamic financial products and transactions use multiple legal inputs to mitigate the risks arising from adherence to Shari'ah. Indeed, legal disputes over commercial issues are often negotiated in English courts using English law. The legal cases of Symphony Gems, Investment Dar Company (TID), Beximco, and Dana Gas used English law to enforce Islamic financial transactions, although in the Dana Gas case the Sharjah court in the UAE did challenge its Shari'ah compliance.[13] Moreover, significant Islamic financial instruments such as sukuk are engineered to meet a particular economic objective, with intervention by bankers and Islamic scholars. In addition, national regulatory boards profile Islamic financial instruments according to necessity and economic risk.

---

[12] The IMF in 2008, when confronted with failing American banks, upheaval in the US mortgage market, and the near collapse of Irish and southern European financial institutions, hoped that oil wealth and Islamic banking would provide for recovery. But although Islamic banking has certain strengths, it was not the answer to the West's capitalist crisis.

[13] Jonathan Ercanbrack, *The Transformation of Islamic Law in Global Financial Markets* (Cambridge: Cambridge University Press, 2015), pp. 223–36; Jonathan Ercanbrack, 'Challenging Shari'ah Compliance of Islamic Finance Products: A Few Discussion Points', Working Paper for Conference on Shari'ah and Compliance of Islamic Finance, School of Oriental and African Studies, London, 22 February 2018.

These processes, as Ercanbrack demonstrates, are assisted by a range of practitioners, contributing to the flexibility of Islamic financial law particularly in Bahrain[14].

The complex relationships between Shari'ah, on the one hand, and the efficiency and ethics of Islamic financial instruments, on the other, raise a number of crucial issues. Most importantly, to what extent have Shari'ah principles been compromised in the creation of innovative financial instruments and high-performing Islamic banks in Bahrain? In brief, did Bahrain's compromise on riba (usury) in its pursuit of competitive advantage against conventional banking and its pursuit of financial pre-eminence in the Gulf, confuse the boundary between religion, business, and ethics?[15]

Strengths in Islamic Finance and Ethics

Bahrain shrewdly developed a relaxed attitude to the prohibition of riba. A low interest rate was acceptable, as Bahrain's ambition was to emerge as a global economic power mediating with wealthy neighbours. This meant that accurate market information was essential in shaping lending or mediating in capital markets. Many conventional financing products were copied and crafted into instruments which are Shari'ah compliant. In the last two decades, Islamization of conventional banking products has occurred in Bahrain through legislation and amendment. This has been a priority not in Bahrain's offshore banking but in the internal economy, to tap oil wealth from Saudi Arabia and Kuwait and avoid volatility. There has been no project to introduce new instruments of Islamic finance. Instead, the strategy has been to engineer existing conventional products, such as interest-based securities, into Shari'ah-compliant Islamic bonds, sukuk, in venture capital initiatives. This approach internalized an understanding of the spirit of Shari'ah into transactions through an undivided beneficial ownership in the underlying assets.

Government in Bahrain was interventionist rather than cautious, since the economy was being flooded with oil wealth. One source of concern was the risk involved in financial operations within Islamic banks, where they faced competition from large conventional banks. Overseas entrants offered important efficiency-enhancing financial instruments such as derivatives. But Islamic banks entered only the competitive, risky initiatives offshore.

---

[14] Ercanbrack, The Transformation of Islamic Law, pp. 198–236.
[15] Rajeswary Ampalavanar Brown, review of Ercanbrack, 'The Transformation of Islamic Law', in *Modern Law Review*, vol. 81, no. 3 (2018), pp. 563–6.

They maintained local risk-averse strategies subsidized by the state and oil capital flows. This high concentration of wealth is captured in Bahrain's Islamic banking, which accounts for 15 per cent of Islamic banking in the Gulf and is rising at a rate of 10 per cent per year. However, its deposits are short term and one assumes they are from the poor or through petro-dollars from Saudi Arabia. There are concerns that excess liquidity prevails in the Gulf area, with the result that certain banks seem to engage in compliant Islamic securities such as sukuk in order to absorb this excess liquidity. Some Islamic banks are creating interbank money markets, as in Bahrain in 2002 and in Malaysia in the 1990s. Risk management became a more sophisticated endeavour in tracing capital adequacy, not within single banks but across banks and outside the country, not just within Bahrain. It is important to recognize that Islamic finance calibrates the inevitable presence of risk, using structural information to make fine-grained judgements.

The Art of Risk Shifting within Islamic Finance

Risk sharing is at the core of the ethics of Islamic finance, where equity holders share the risks associated with investment with depositors. Alaa Alabed argues that along with participating with conventional banks came the realization within Islamic finance of the economics of ethical capitalism.[16]

Islamic banks protect themselves against crisis through risk-averse instruments that are part of an internalization of processes, as well as being propagated through Islamic ideology. But they are not innovative. Too often there are prophetic declarations of faith-led finance, while the poor, who form the majority of depositors in Islamic banks, are exploited, and the well-heeled use those savings to sustain their own consumption.

The inclination of banks to shift risk to depositors and external parties while internalizing their profits often occurred within conventional banks long before the 2008 financial crisis. A weak application of regulation and poor governance encouraged those practices. The use of state resources to rescue Islamic banks was common in Saudi Arabia and Kuwait but not in

---

[16] Alaa Alaabed, 'Risk Shifting and Islamic Banking', PhD thesis, INCEIF, the Global University of Islamic Finance, Kuala Lumpur, Malaysia, 2016. Michael Rothschild and Joseph Stiglitz, 'Equilibrium in Competitive Insurance Markets: An Essay in the Economics of Imperfect Information', *Quarterly Journal of Economics*, vol. 90, no. 4 (1976), pp. 629–49. Risk-shifting behaviour is also considered in R. C. Merton, 'An Analytic Derivation of the Cost of Deposit Insurance and Loan Guarantees: An Application of Modern Option Pricing Theory', *Journal of Banking and Finance*, vol. 1, no. 1 (1977), pp. 3–11; J. C. Duan, A. F. Moreau, and C. W. Sealy, 'Fixed-rate Deposit Insurance and Risk Shifting Behaviour at Commercial Banks', *Journal of Banking and Finance*, vol. 16, no. 7 (1992).

Bahrain.[17] Islamic finance in Bahrain sought rigour but stumbled because of actions by others within the Gulf community. Thus, within Islamic finance in Bahrain, the failure to disclose non-payment of debt, particularly by Saudi nationals, was exacerbated by weak monitoring and the slow pace of corrective action. Information asymmetry adds to this moral hazard. Another dangerous feature is the presence of short-term debt, where debt holders rarely redesign their contracts. This pattern disguises the different manner in which Shari'ah doctrines are organized in different countries. For example, Tawarruq, a sale and resale transaction used to generate cash and liquidity, is practised in Malaysia despite the ruling from the OIC Fiqh Council that it is not permitted.[18] The weakness of the regulatory institutions governing Islamic finance is covered in depth later. The AAOIFI (Accounting and Auditing Organization for Islamic Finance Institutions) and the IFSB (Islamic Financial Services Board) lack standardized compliance, although the application of Shari'ah is fairly disciplined in Bahrain, often through municipal court decisions.

Banks in Bahrain lack size, and very few are listed. Thus, pragmatism prevails in the absence of a divorce of ownership from management control. Risk-shifting incentives are influenced by bank size, capitalization, and profitability, while Islamic instruments like Mudarabah, an investment partnership, deter risk shifting. Volatile market relationships, such as stock market operations, which would further encourage risk shifting, were rather subdued in Bahrain. Bahrain's shifting of risk was lower, around 20 per cent of transactions, in comparison with other Gulf nations, and in particular with Malaysia, where the Islamic banks were less adequately capitalized than conventional banks and yet were propelled to a position of international prominence through government loans. One outcome of state support for Islamic banks in Malaysia was that the banks' dependence on the state became even more intense and risk shifting was high. In contrast, high liquidity in Bahrain through the large volume of oil flows enabled the banks to operate under a fractional reserve system where some Islamic deposits are insured through conventional deposit insurance schemes.[19] As profitability

[17] Andrew Sheng, *From Asian to Global Financial Crisis: An Asian Regulator's View of Unfettered Finance in the 1990s and 2000s* (Cambridge: Cambridge University Press, 2009).
[18] The Organization of Islamic Cooperation (OIC) was founded in 1969 and Bahrain joined in 1972. It now has 57 members and is based in Jeddah. In Tawarruq, a person buys a commodity with deferred payment then sells it to a third party for immediate cash at the spot price. The purpose is to secure cash, and the criticism is that it is similar to an interest-based product.
[19] Alaabed, 'Risk Shifting and Islamic Banking', p. 117. See also Irving Fisher, *The Works of Irving Fisher*, edited by William J. Barber et al., 14 volumes (London: Pickering and Chatto, 1996). See also Ithmaar Bank website, Mudarabah account, 5 April 2017; Al Salam Bank website, Musharakah, 9 April 2017; Central Bank of Bahrain, Financial Stability Report, February 2017.

was high, so self-discipline was lax. This averted calamity during the Global Financial Crisis of 2008.[20] Also, Bahrain reduced its risk shifting to avoid negative publicity, fearing that it would harm its ambitions to be the financial hub of the Gulf region.

Another risk for Bahrain's Islamic banks arose from their dependence on Saudi Arabia and Kuwait, for that required them to negotiate with external corruption and operate within a delocalized governance. Bahrain exhibited the usual weaknesses in its lack of financial experts and a lack of information, accentuated to a degree by its ties to Saudi Arabia where corruption was rife, and secrecy clouded all attempts to recover debt payments. There was information asymmetry in the close collaborative relationship with a powerful Saudi Arabia, a 'dependency scenario', despite the assurance that Islamic finance's strongest attribute is its risk-sharing culture.[21] Imtiaz Uddin Ahmad, challenging Seref Turen, argues that investors in the Bahrain Islamic Bank (BIB) are rewarded with high returns and reduced risk, while depositors are safeguarded.[22] In part this is due to a reconfiguration, whereby the depositors, who often deposit long-term, pay for the risk reduction enjoyed by investors. BIB also may concentrate on murabahah financing, a sale with a mark-up, which is again highly profitable with reduced risk.

In 1995 and 1996, the Beximco Pharmaceuticals Group sought working capital of $US30 million from Shamil Bank through murabahah and Ijarah (lease) transaction agreements for the purchase of specific goods. By December 1999, the Group had defaulted. An important insight provided by the Beximco case was that religious risks arise from non-compliance with Shari'ah.[23] The pattern of resource distribution and resource exploitation between depositors and investors in Islamic banks, although responsible for the reduced volatility and higher prices of the banks' shares on Bahrain's stock market, are not ultimately conducive to the competitive growth of the economies in which they operate, and the banks often depend on state and oil resources to secure their long-term survival. Thus risk-averse Islamic principles are often exploited by the powerful at the expense of poor depositors. The

---

[20] Alaabed, 'Risk Shifting and Islamic Banking', pp 70–81.

[21] The World Bank Annual Report 2015 (Washington, DC: World Bank, 2015); Abbas Mirakhor, 'Islamic Finance and Globalization: A Convergence?', Journal of Islamic Economics, Banking and Finance, vol. 3, no. 2 (2007), pp. 11–72; Abbas Mirakhor and Hossein Askari, Islam and the Path to Human and Economic Development (New York: Palgrave Macmillan, 2010); Abbas Mirakhor 'Epistemology of Finance: Misreading Smith', Islamic Finance Review, vol. 1 (2011), pp. 9–15.

[22] Seref Turen, 'Performance and Risk Analysis of Islamic Banks: The Case of Bahrain Islamic Bank', Journal of King Abdulaziz University: Islamic Economics, vol. 7 (1415/1995); comments from Imtiaz Uddin Ahmad in JKAU: Islamic Economics, vol. 10 (1418/1998), pp. 57–9.

[23] John R. Bowen, 'How Could English Courts Recognize Shariah', University of St Thomas Law Journal, no. 411 (2010). See also Ercanbrack, The Transformation of Islamic Law, pp. 227–32.

analysis below reveals the varying degrees of state engagement and paternalism in the provision of public funds to Islamic banks. This also produced high levels of unethical behaviour, as risk is absorbed by the state.

With government prompting, the volume of projects and investments will increase because of the underlying risk-averse principle. Islamic finance reduces speculation in financial markets but the secondary markets for stocks and certificates are based on profit sharing. Islamic finance can be less inflationary because the supply of money is not allowed to exceed the supply of goods. Islamic banking is less risky in terms of external shocks, liquidity risks, and insolvency risks than conventional banks, although this is difficult to substantiate because often the two systems co-exist. At the same time the need for frameworks of support for Islamic finance and for diversification into new financial products is clear.

In seeking regional expansion, it becomes apparent that Islamic finance was a double-edged sword. For example, the use of special purpose vehicles in offshore accounts and the off-the-balance-sheet nature of many transactions may disguise links to terrorism, as well as raise fears of money laundering by oil-rich Middle East states. This weakness is encouraged or facilitated by the confused structure of the regulation of Islamic banking both within Bahrain and across the MENA jurisdictions, which can involve regulation by AAOFI, IIRA, IIFM, LMC, GCIBFI, and BIBF.[24] One result was the creation of a supportive state with a policy of diversification of the economy through infrastructural projects financed by sukuk, often with an elusive Shari'ah compliance. Bahrain showed considerable skill in seeking capital in a context of weak institutional safeguards.[25]

There are several aspects of sukuk lending that should differentiate it from conventional bonds. The most important is that sukuk should not guarantee returns. Investors should not be able to expect the return of the principal plus dividends/profit without incurring the risk that they could lose. In practice, sukuk are asset-based, meaning they are structured to resemble the risk and payment profile of a conventional bond. The most important way of making

[24] AAOIFI: Accounting and Auditing Organization for Islamic Financial Institutions, established in 1990 in Bahrain as an international standard regulator for finance, providing governance and transparency. IIR: International Islamic Rating Agency, to provide rating services for Islamic financial instruments. IIFM: International Islamic Financial Market, started in 2002 in Bahrain to provide a cooperative framework for Shari'ah interpretation and to encourage the creation of a secondary market. LMC: Liquidity Management Centre, established in 2002 to facilitate the creation of Shari'ah-compliant financial products. Its main aim is the creation of an interbank money market to provide investment opportunities, short-term liquidity, tradeable instruments, and to expand the market. GCIBFI: General Council for Islamic Banks and Financial Institutions, to organize seminars and training for financial sector employees. BIBF: Bahrain Institute of Banking and Finance, to provide courses on Islamic finance.
[25] *Thomson Reuters Report* 2017, Bahrain, 'Sukuk Perceptions and Forecast Study, 2017', p. 25; Central Bank of Bahrain, *The Review*, 13 March 2015, June 2017.

this possible is to include a purchase undertaking which requires the origina-tor to buy back the sukuk asset upon default or maturity of the notes. Investors are compensated in full. A so-called true sale has not taken place, for that is contrary to Islamic commercial principles. There is no such thing as a benefi-cial sale in Islamic law, unlike English law, where a sale is outright, immediate, and allows the buyer unfettered disposition of the asset. This is not the case in almost all sukuk issuances.

AAOIFI and some Shari'ah scholars and associated organizations have identified these practices as contraventions of Shari'ah. But this rejection has fallen on deaf ears and sukuk has continued to be issued. The Dana Gas Sukuk in the UAE is a case in point.[26] It contains a purchase undertaking, making the transaction a guaranteed one. In Islamic law, profit can be obtained only through risk and ownership. If ownership and its attendant risks are not com-plete or if the risks of ownership have been passed on to the debtor (as in most Islamic financial transactions including the sukuk), the return is forbidden.

The Performance of Bahrain's Islamic Banks

According to the most recent Financial Stability Report by the Central Bank of Bahrain, in September 2016 the Capital Adequacy Ratio (CAR) for Islamic retail banks in Bahrain stood at 17.1 per cent. This compared to 19.6 per cent for their conventional counterparts and 19.1 per cent for Islamic wholesale banks.[27] The ratio of non-performing facilities (NPF) was 12.1 per cent in Islamic retail banks, as of the end of September 2016, well beyond the ratios of 4.7 per cent in conventional retail banks and 2.9 per cent in Islamic wholesale banks. Despite showing signs of improvement, Islamic retail NPF remains high. The highest ratio was recorded in the construction sector (29.4 per cent) followed by manufacturing (26.1 per cent) and commercial real estate financing (20.2 per cent).

The return on assets (ROA) for Islamic retail banks was 0.2 per cent in September 2016, which is lower than the conventional retail banks' aver-age of 1.1 per cent in the same period. The difference can be explained in part with reference to the banks' operating expenses. Operating expenses as

---

[26] Mudarabah Sukuk Issuance in 2007 in the UAE, Standard & Poor, Islamic Finance Outlook website, 2008. Gulf Finance House, based in Bahrain, issued Musharakah Sukuk through all Gulf states from July 2007 (GFH Annual Report 2007). See Standard & Poor reports and Zawya, part of Refinitiv Middle East, a website carrying regional news and intelligence (2011).
[27] All the statistics here are from Central Bank of Bahrain, *Finance Stability Report*, February 2017, pp. 4, 47, 49, 52, 53, 55. See also COMCEC, *Diversification of Islamic Financial Instruments*, pp. 68–182; ICD-Thomson Reuters, *Islamic Finance Development Report*, 2016, pp. 30–1.

a proportion of total income stood at 82.9 per cent for Islamic retail banks in September 2016, while it was only 47.5 per cent in their conventional counterparts.[28]

Bahrain's Islamic retail and wholesale banks are characterized by high asset concentration. The top recipient of Islamic retail financing in September 2016 was personal/consumer finance (23.6 per cent), followed by commercial real estate financing (15.3 per cent). Together, they accounted for 38.9 per cent of total financing extended in September 2016. Overall, real estate/construction exposure stood at 29.4 per cent in September 2016.[29]

Personal/consumer finance was the top recipient of financing from Islamic wholesale banks as well, at 21.3 per cent. It was followed by manufacturing at 19.2 per cent. Islamic wholesale banks' exposure to the real estate/construction sector was at 27.4 per cent in September 2016.[30]

Concentration renders banks vulnerable to weaknesses in the sectors being financed and increases the risk of simultaneous defaults and liquidation. But the overall verdict on the performance of Islamic banks in Bahrain and the impact of overseas entrants since the 1980s has been positive. The strategic orientations of local Islamic banks and their interaction with conventional banks increased financial innovation, and global challenges were met through strategic alliances and access to English courts. Internal control mechanisms to curb risk were retained.

It has been argued that risk sharing through Mudarabah created wealth and encouraged vertical mobility.[31] Mudarabah and Musharakah contracts are partnership arrangements with one (as in Mudarabah) or more (as in Musharakah) partners to provide skills and capital to a project. Any profit earned is shared in agreed proportions, reflecting the return on capital but also the effort put into the business. Similarly, losses are shared on the basis of the capital invested. This implies that in the case of Mudarabah, where only one party provides all the capital, the loss is borne by the sole capital provider.

An initial model of a Mudarabah arrangement in 1960, discussed by Salman Syed Ali, showed that there was the need to invest funds from the savings of depositors. This was the second tier of a Mudarabah arrangement. The reduced risk means that corporations are less likely to go bankrupt, and

---

[28] Bahrain Economic Development Board (EDB), Islamic Financial Services Industry, *Stability Report*, 2017, joint publication with World Bank.
[29] Despite increasing diversification, Islamic banks remain exposed to the risky real estate sector. Kuwait Finance House and the Financial Harbour are financed by Gulf Finance House: COMCEC, *Diversification of Islamic Financial Instruments*, p. 171.
[30] Central Bank of Bahrain, *Financial Stability Report*, February 2017, pp. 4, 49, 50, 52, 53.
[31] Salman Syed Ali, *Islamic Banking in the MENA Region*, World Bank and Islamic Development Bank, Islamic Research and Training Institute, February 2011.

this provides stability and explains the low level of distress endured by Islamic banks in the 2008 crisis. However, this strength is predicated on high levels of information and transparency in reporting revenues and costs, and also profit or loss. If information asymmetry exists between contracting parties, the prospect of moral hazard and adverse selection haunts the business, leading to higher costs and perhaps lower productivity, and a reluctance to adopt expensive technology. The less information-intensive contract is the murabahah contract, where the bank buys from the spot market in its own name the plant, equipment, or raw materials, which are then sold to the entrepreneur on deferred payment with a marked-up price.

Both Mudarabah and Musharakah are private equity investment or asset management instruments. In the 1970s, oil-rich countries had high liquidity and could freely capitalize on high growth in infrastructure and manufacturing. In retail banking, Musharakah contracts are used for home mortgages. Bahrain concentrated also on real estate development, with scant attention being paid to the prudent allocation of capital. Omid Torabi, in his innovative dissertation, regards it as the preferred model of Islamic financing since it conforms to the principle of risk sharing.[32] He identifies the risks as: credit risk, market risk, liquidity risk, operational risk, and legal risk. Mirakhor and Zaidi assume this introduces greater scrutiny of risk. The Ijarah leasing contract is a safer model of financing, leaving Musharakah as the least utilized contract.[33] There is an additional hazard in Musharakah, in that investors and entrepreneurs do not have the same level of information.[34] The entrepreneur is perceived to possess more.

The published accounts of the Islamic banks in Bahrain suggest that their disclosure standards are, in the main, rigorous and transparent. The oft-expressed anxieties of conventional financial institutions with respect to these banks' alleged operational risk, moral hazard, insolvency, cronyism, and corruption can be partly allayed through the data for risk management. Although standardization of regulation and practice within Islamic finance has been slow, the released accounts assure investors of the stability of Islamic banks. We have measures of liquidity, returns on income, as well as assets held in reserve. This data is particularly important as Islamic banking charges

[32] Omid Torabi, 'Using Reputation (Fame) to Reduce Information Asymmetry in Islamic Risk-Sharing Crowd Funding Models: A Game Theory Approach', PhD dissertation, International Centre for Education in Islamic Finance (INCEIF), 2017.

[33] N. M. Osmani and M. F. Abdullah, 'Mushrakak Mutanagisch Home Financing: A Review of Literatures and Practices of Islamic Banks in Malaysia', International Review of Business Research Papers, vol. 6, no. 2 (2010), pp. 272–82.

[34] S. C. Myers and N. S. Majluf, 'Corporate Financing and Investment Decisions when Firms Have Information that Investors Do Not Have', Journal of Financial Economics, vol. 13, no. 2 (1984); COMCEC, 'Diversification of Islamic Financial Instruments', pp. 168–82.

either low or no interest. The data for the Bahrain banks could be contrasted with the Iranian Islamic banks and the Saudi Islamic banks, which are state dominated. While profit–loss sharing is important, it is productivity and a more equitable system of returns that are more important in reducing speculation.

The inflow and outflow of petro-dollars can conceal money-laundering activities. Money laundering is particularly suspected in special purpose vehicles used in offshore accounts and are not on the balance sheets. In Bahrain, the position is complicated by Bahrain's role as the financial nexus of the oil-rich Gulf states. A further risk in Islamic finance is insider dealing, although recent scandals in American, French, and British conventional banks show that such practices are not limited to Islamic banks. Even the multiple financial regulatory bodies operating in the GCC area cannot trace and expose these practices effectively.

Commercial Pressures for Mergers and Acquisitions

Bahrain's emergence as a hub for Islamic finance was assisted by bank mergers and acquisitions. For example, in 2012, Al Salaam Bank acquired 100 per cent equity in Bahraini Saudi Bank and swiftly recorded a 95 per cent increase in net profits. First Leasing Bank merged with Ithmaar Bank to increase its paid-up capital to US$758 million. Capivest Investment Bank, Elaf Bank, and Capital Management House merged, increasing shareholder equity to US$350 million and assets to over US$400 million. These mergers increased the total assets of seven banks in this grouping to US$6.3 billion. Only through these mergers could Bahrain sustain its position, as it was restricted by its limited resources and population.[35] With rapid growth and reliance on an external resource—oil, and given the inherent instability of transient foreign banks, there were considerable risks. The 2008 crisis, though relatively mild in Bahrain, led the state to diversify the economy and integrate local resources, while pursuing foreign financial networks, alliances, and syndicates.

It is interesting to make comparisons with the performance of Islamic banks in the Sunni-dominated Gulf states of Qatar, Saudi Arabia, Kuwait,

---

[35] El-Tahir, 'Bahrain: Threads of Growth in Islamic Finance', pp. 31–2. Mergers between Islamic and conventional banks include that of Al Salam Bank Bahrain with conventional retail bank BMI Bank in February 2014 and the consolidation achieved by Elaf Bank, Capivest Investment Bank, and Capital Management House into Ibdar Bank in December 2013. Many financial institutions have located their Islamic banking business in Bahrain, for example Al Baraka Islamic Bank, Khaleeji Commercial Bank, ABC Islamic Bank, Kuwait Finance House, and Islamic Bank of Asia.

and Jordan but also the wider Middle East and North Africa region (MENA). ROE (return on equity) varied significantly, even in 2008 with the onset of the global recession. The ROE for Bahrain's Islamic banks in 2008 was 7.2 per cent, in Kuwait 8.2 per cent, Qatar 11.9 per cent, Saudi Arabia 10.7 per cent, and in Jordan 14.4 per cent. By 2009, the ROE had declined in Islamic banks partly because of the financial crisis. Bahrain and Kuwait showed negative ROE while ROE increased in Qatar. In Bahrain, the decline in ROE was because Bahrain has a large number of small Islamic banks with a relatively low capital base, and that reduces their capacity to absorb credit losses from distressed financial instruments such as murabahah and ijarah transactions. In Kuwait, the culprit is weak regulation and banks in turmoil relocating to foreign jurisdictions. Kuwait, too, had been exposed to volatility in the real estate sector. Excess liquidity through oil wealth had repercussions in Bahrain, in contrast to the UAE, which saw strong protective intervention by the state in 2009 compared to Bahrain and Kuwait.[36]

Return on assets was negative in Bahrain, −7 per cent, with −2.1 per cent in Kuwait. Only Qatar had an impressive rise to 4 per cent.[37] Asset utilization, as defined by the ratio of total investment to total assets, was high and rising between 2006 and 2008. It was at 87.6 per cent in the UAE in 2008, while the lowest ratio was in Saudi Arabia at 53.5 per cent. This high asset utilization ratio is due to profit sharing of deposit contracts between Islamic banks and depositors through Mudarabah-based accounts. Mudarabah-based deposit accounts were invested in economically secure sectors such as state infrastructure, public housing, and state industries. The asset utilization ratio increased in 2009 in most countries. Bahrain saw an increase of 73 per cent, Saudi Arabia 75.6 per cent, and the UAE 68 per cent. The rise in Bahrain and Saudi Arabia asset utilization, along with an increase in the proportion of banks' liquid assets, point to a growing demand for finance and a decisive increase in Islamic banking.[38]

The ratio of net operating income to total assets for Islamic banks varied in the MENA region between 2006 and 2009.[39] There was a sharp decline for Bahrain's Islamic banks in 2009 compared to previous years. The ability to tap and use information to maximize profits is limited, shown not least in a shortage of skilled bankers and entrepreneurs and in the slow development of hierarchical organizations to maximize profit. There is a failure of Schumpeterian and Coase economics within culturally dictated fragile

---

[36] Ali, *Islamic Banking in the MENA Region*, p. 28.
[37] Ali, *Islamic Banking in the MENA Region*, p. 29, data for 2006–09.
[38] Ali, *Islamic Banking in the MENA Region*, p. 30.
[39] Ali, *Islamic Banking in the MENA Region*, p. 30.

market economics. Saudi Arabia, too, showed poor performance despite an overflowing of oil wealth. The proportion of net operating income in total income is lowest for Bahrain and highest for Saudi Arabia. Operational expenses as a percentage of income were highest in Bahrain and lowest in Saudi Arabia. This may be due to economies of scale, given the larger size of Saudi banks as opposed to the smaller Islamic banks in Bahrain.

The Aftermath of Rising Oil Production in the Gulf

With soaring oil prices, Bahrain attracted capital for domestic economic initiatives in infrastructure and through multilateral trade deals. An increase in the price of oil, from US$30 a barrel to almost US$100 at the end of 2007, created a market boom, with real GDP growth of 6–7 per cent.[40] Despite a downturn in the 2008 financial crisis, the region still saw considerable growth in GDP. By 2013, the region's GDP totalled US$1.37 trillion. Bahrain had impressive capital and trade surpluses. In addition, international banks came in, converting the vast liquidity into new industry as well as into sophisticated financial services. One of the reasons for the greater sustainability of Bahrain's Islamic finance was its stock market. The Bahrain Bourse was invigorated by strong state and private equity activity. Ironically, all this frenzy resulted in the poor Shia communities losing land and property. This was a gradual process of disempowerment.

The emergence of a rising vibrant Islamic finance from the 1970s rested on the rise in oil revenues. But the oil price fell in the late 1980s, affecting Bahrain. Even Kuwait suffered a loss of 22 per cent in oil revenues in the 1980s.[41] The bulk of Bahrain's oil revenues, flowing in from Kuwait and Saudi Arabia, was directed into infrastructural development. In addition, Bahrain's financial interests were directed into the more lucrative offshore banking. In the mid-1970s, Bahrain invited major international banks to establish offshore banking units. Its close connections to Kuwait, however, also had adverse consequences because of the speculative frenzy surrounding the Souk al Manakh and its eventual collapse, with a loss of US$94 billion, in 1982.

The Souk collapse (considered in detail in Chapter 4) had both positive and negative influences on Bahrain's financial sector. The Bank of Bahrain

[40] Ercanbrack, *The Transformation of Islamic Law*, p. 240.
[41] Hoda Selim and Chahir Zaki, 'The Institutional Curse of Natural Resources in the Arab World', in *Understanding and Avoiding the Oil Curse in Resource-rich Arab Economies*, edited by Ibrahim Elbadawi and Hoda Selim (Cambridge: Cambridge University Press, 2016), pp. 326–42.

and Kuwait (BBK), which had concentrated shareholdings held by powerful individuals who had abused the bank's lending policies, was now, with declining oil prices, faced with a dramatic fall in net profits, from 18 per cent of total earnings in 1983 to 7 per cent of total earnings in 1984. This resulted in a fall in dividends of 35 per cent.[42] BBK bad loans originating from the Souk collapse were estimated at 85 per cent of total bad loans, and this led to the creation in 1984 of a special loan loss reserve account, into which a third of BBK earnings were deposited. BBK struggled. New capital was raised while no dividends were paid.

There was clearly a threat to Bahrain because of its central position in the Gulf as a major hub, for it was exposed to the repercussions arising from any financial distress in the region. Two of the most powerful forces affecting Islamic banks in the last two decades have been oil wealth and the associated speculative behaviour in stocks. Kuwait, receiving unprecedented amounts of oil wealth, embarked on a perilous course of unbridled speculation on the unofficial market, and the risks were aggravated by the presence of only a small number of publicly traded Kuwaiti companies on the official stock exchange. The scarcity of listed companies was a result of caution on the part of the Sheikh who feared a collapse in the economy. In addition, Kuwaiti investors were cushioned by high earnings from oil and lulled into complacency by a protective state culture, as it had rescued investors in earlier market panics in 1976 and 1977.[43]

The Souk episode stifled the creation of regional markets. The losses were located principally in subprime mortgages, and post-dated cheques were common, because associational networks that included family and co-religionists pervaded the Middle East. The Chandlerian concept of personal capitalism with highly individualistic traits does not intrude into those dense networks. The Middle East, with communal loyalties embedded in regional business networks, made loan repayment an unpredictable phenomenon. Although powerful and cohesive, they were not 'espousing virtues of district wide governance derived from deep implantation of actors in robust regional socio-cultural structures'.[44]

---

[42] Bean, 'The Contemporary Financial Development of Kuwait and Bahrain', p. 76.

[43] Central Bank of Kuwait, *The Kuwait Economy in Ten Years: Economic Report for the Period 1969–79*. See annual reports of the Central Bank of Kuwait for 1980 to 1999. See also Jill Crystal, *Oil and Politics in the Gulf: Rulers and Merchants in Kuwait and Qatar* (Cambridge: Cambridge University Press, 1995); Farah Al-Nakib, 'Kuwait City: Urbanization, the Built Environment and the Urban Experience before and after Oil, 1786–1986', PhD thesis, University of London, 2011, pp. 167–82.

[44] Andrew Popp and John Wilson, 'Business in the Regions: From "Old" Districts to "New" Clusters?', *Business in Britain in the Twentieth Century*, edited by Richard Coopey and Peter Lyth (Oxford: Oxford University Press, 2009), p. 74. See also M. Piore and C. Sabel, *The Second Industrial Divide: Possibilities for*

In contrast, Bahrain was creating a sophisticated financial infrastructure. The impact of oil wealth on the indirect as well as the direct financing of Bahrain's private sector occurred through her capital markets. The relationship between oil revenues and the emergence of Bahrain as a financial hub for the oil-rich countries of the GCC also saw rising levels of industrial investment, while simultaneously funding local development projects within the waqf and ma'tam, although only on a small scale.

Despite Bahrain's sound institutional framework, its financial deepening was weak because of spillovers from GCC crises and it was unable to contain the repercussions of the Souk al Manakh in Kuwait. Instability threatened by the high levels of private credit (almost 50 per cent in Bahrain and 60 per cent in Kuwait) caused concern and yet Bahrain remained rather sanguine.[45] Bahrain's lead in syndicated lending and cross-border banking, and its expansion into sovereign wealth funds, did include some generous social welfare programmes. But because Bahrain's population in 2011 was only 1.22 million, including foreigners, its dependence on oil revenues (85.5 per cent of total revenue in 1970, declining to 25.1 per cent in 2011) had potentially serious consequences for the economy. Ironically, Kuwait's revenues from oil rose from 43.25 per cent in 1970 to 51.3 per cent in 2011.[46] Although Bahrain achieved a diversified development into non-oil industrialization, which came to account for 75 per cent of GDP, exports were still principally of oil, though not all its own. Bahrain's hydrocarbon revenues constituted three-quarters of total revenues. But Bahrain's restructuring of the economy towards higher-growth sectors was exposing its rural areas, occupied by Shi'as, to economic decline, which fed into growing scepticism towards the Sunni state's ruthless policies. This, in turn, further intensified the state's repressive rule and led to an increase in violence and civil unrest.[47]

Offshore Banking: A More Subtle Judgement

With market liberalization and the rise in disputes over the interpretation of Shari'ah, most Islamic financial transactions were governed ultimately by

Prosperity (New York: Basic Books, 1984); C. Sabel and J. Zeitlin, 'Historical Alternatives to Mass Production: Politics, Markets and Technology in Nineteenth-century Industrialization', *Past and Present*, no. 108 (1985), pp. 133–76; U. Staber, N. Schaefer, and B. Sharma (ed), *Business Networks: Prospects for Regional Development* (Berlin: de Gruyter, 1996).

[45] Selim and Zaki, 'The Institutional Curse of Natural Resources', pp. 352–3.
[46] Selim and Zaki, 'The Institutional Curse of Natural Resources', p. 329.
[47] Selim and Zaki, 'The Institutional Curse of Natural Resources', p. 334.

English common law. This led to a growth of offshore banking. Bahrain Financial Harbour (BFH), the Dubai International Financial Centre (IFC), and the Qatar Financial Centre (QFC) were based largely in common law jurisdictions. This has facilitated innovative measures which include the abolition of rigid currency controls, the creation of private banks, new laws permitting foreign ownership of indigenous banks, and a drive to harmonize municipal law with international standards.

Increased foreign participation in Bahrain's stock market, involving both private equity and international investor activity, in particular following the 2008 financial crisis, had an impact on improving and modernizing financial regulation. This was far distant from Bahrain's initial experience with offshore banking in the 1980s, when the selection of financial products and their performance were dictated by Saudi investors, with weak governance and a speculative informal stock market in Kuwait.

The position of the Bahrain Monetary Agency (BMA) as lender of last resort is highly complicated because of the existence of 70 OBUs (Offshore Banking Units) and their acceptance of deposits from foreign banks with less regulation, alongside the 19 domestic banks. No distinction was made between foreign and domestic banks if they were incorporated in Bahrain. This could cause havoc with reserves, creating infringements of the rules of the BMA. The power of the state in such an open economy proved to be limited. Also, the Souk crisis created a sense of fragility that lingers in Bahrain, as it diminished the authority of the BMA and increased Bahrain's exposure to external economic downturns.

The adaptability and dynamism displayed by foreign and local banks when seeking collaborations can be seen in an analysis of Investcorp, the top investment banking company in Bahrain, founded in 1982. It had been established to purchase companies in the West and in the Gulf, in particular in Saudi Arabia, and to sell shares to wealthy Arabs. Links to foreign investment grew by 25 per cent by 1986, with profits at US$15.2 million in the same year. Assets rose from US$259.5 million in 1985 to US$418 million in 1986. Investcorp sought more funds, estimated at US$50 million for three years, from major lenders. Although most of its clients are from the Gulf, it has over 175 corporate investments in the USA, Europe, the Middle East, and Africa. In 2009, it secured US$1 billion in US hedge fund mandates.[48] It also had credit management assets of over US$11 billion, managed through London, New York, and Singapore.

[48] *Annual Report of Investcorp*, 2010.

Regulation: The Quest for Institutional Underpinnings and the Resultant Errors

Flawed regulatory frameworks made structural improvements in Islamic finance more difficult. The Shari'ah boards were not only riddled with insider dealings but ceded power to ill-trained Shari'ah scholars. But in Islamic banking in Bahrain, interest rates remained, while profit-sharing contracts did make some difference, although not through improved productivity or in the efficient allocation of funds. What emerged was not a form of ethical capitalism but a growth in traditional Islamic finance, yielding to aggressive state intervention yet rarely developing a professional dynamism. Ironically, the limit to change was bolstered by the IMF and its complacent attitude when appraising the efficiency of Shari'ah-compliant finance (although it did not accept Shari'ah-compliant finance within IMF aid programmes because of the absence of rigorous financial instruments and its inadequate accounting discipline). This indulgence towards religious-rooted networks embedded within resource-rich hierarchies propels a financial system from Malaysia to the Middle East, and to Africa, Europe, and even in the USA, although fear of funding terrorism persisted in the latter.[49] In Bahrain an important institution for strict financial governance was the Central Bank of Bahrain.

The Central Bank of Bahrain produced 15 principles of risk management under six categories, and Islamic banks were registered under this regulatory framework. The six categories are credit risk, equity investment risk, market risk, liquidity risk, rate of return risk, and operational risk. State intervention in Bahrain, which hitherto had been light and somewhat random, now increasingly became highly bureaucratic. The Islamic Financial Services Board, which in turn guided the Basel Committee on Banking Supervision (Basel 1, 2, 3) made concerted efforts to create market transparency in Islamic finance. In 2013, the CBB regulated takaful business with respect to solvency, corporate governance, and actuarial reporting within the insurance sector. AAOIFI, IIFM, and the International Islamic Finance Rating Agency acquired authority in governing Islamic finance in Bahrain. There emerged 26 accounting standards, five auditing standards, seven governance standards, two ethics standards, and 45 Shari'ah rules and perceived standards. However, despite such dense financial regulation, there is a lack of rigour,

---

[49] Haider Ala Hamoudi, 'Muhammad's Social Justice or Muslim Cant? Langdellianism and the Failures of Islamic Finance', *Cornell International Law Journal*, vol. 40 (2007).

and this inevitably disrupted international expansion, except through Islamic windows within conventional banks.[50]

The Shari'ah boards are funded by the very banks they monitor. There is a marked lack of legal control, and insider dealing can occur. The multiple boards add to the confusion because there is a shortage of fully trained Shari'ah scholars and financial experts. Issues of compliance are not clear. This limits the evolution and reform of banking and the banks' ability to achieve high standards. Often the IMF is too obsequious when praising the efficiency of Shari'ah-compliant finance. The IMF praises the Shari'ah scholars who sit on the boards in the Gulf states for providing consistency, when, in reality, they comprise a club of relatives, and governance is often undermined by serious misdemeanours.

In September 2017, the Central Bank of Bahrain introduced a code of practice involving the establishment of an external, independent audit for all Islamic banks. This would replace the earlier decentralized approach where Islamic banks had relied on in-house scholars, for the efficacy of internal control was now seriously disputed. Beyond the boardroom, unethical behaviour could be criminalized. The Central Bank would issue training and competence requirements for members of Shari'ah boards and Shari'ah auditors. Hitherto board members had possessed inadequate Shari'ah qualifications, had been fed inadequate financial information, had risked privileged contacts similar to insider dealings, and had relied on subordinates, while huge oil wealth had swirled around, demanding far tighter accounting. Bahrain's ambitions for global prominence in Islamic finance drove the creation of improved corporate governance.

The legal system in Bahrain has facilitated the regulation of Islamic finance, although local jurisdictions have produced variants of Islamic financial law which, in turn, have fed into a diverse global law. Backed by oil revenues and facilitated by transnational firms with advanced technological, managerial, and entrepreneurial resources, Islamic Finance Law (IFL) has thrived in global financial markets, notwithstanding its lack of systemic coordination. Business environments characterized by resource dependency, reckless private credit, and weak bankruptcy laws and liquidation procedures have enabled IFL to extend into over 70 jurisdictions worldwide, even though Islamic financial instruments do not necessarily meet consumers' demands

[50] AAOIFI, *Accounting, Auditing, and Governance Standards for Islamic Financial Institutions: Financial Accounting Standards* (2010). See also ICD-Thomson Reuters, *Islamic Finance Development Report*, 2015, 'Global Transformation'; Central Bank of Bahrain, press release, 17 March 2017; Central Bank of Bahrain, 'Shariah Compliant Wakalah Liquidity Management', press release, 2015; AAOIFI website, 'Announcement on Sharia Standards on Murabahah, March 2017'; AAOIFI on Sukuk, February 2017; Bankscope, *Islamic Finance Reports*; Islamic Financial Services Board, *Annual Stability Report*, June 2016.

for Shari'ah compliance. English law has been called upon to resolve IFL disputes in English courts. IFL is thus a market-generated amalgamation, a creature of a global financial system in which cross-pollination of legal ideas is driven by market forces.[51]

Securing an Accommodation between Islamic Finance and Shari'ah

Legal pluralism involves an awkward inclusion of Shari'ah within secular constitutions. In Bahrain there is limited commercial legislation, although a new Civil and Commercial Code based on Egyptian civil principles is proposed. The Commercial Code of 1987 did provide for interest income in banking and commercial transactions.[52] This was followed by the Civil Code of 2001 which adjusted commercial attitudes and legal principles to the financial infrastructure of Bahrain. This new Civil Code relegated Shari'ah to third place as a founding authority, below customary law. In other words, there was flexibility in the application of Shari'ah. In Bahrain, the key role for Shari'ah is in matters of personal status, as is the case too in Malaysia and Thailand. This approach was given further substance in the 2002 Judicial Authority Law, with the creation of Sunni and Ja'fari courts.[53] Yet it is crucial to emphasize that Shari'ah still validates Islamic financial institutions and operations in Bahrain.

As noted earlier, Bahrain operates a dual regulatory framework for Islamic finance, with the establishment of the Central Bank of Bahrain in 2006 to replace the Bahrain Monetary Agency. The CBB has created institutional safeguards for Shari'ah compliance, a compliance that is also rigorous in improving corporate governance. Limiting Shari'ah in its legal system and yet engaging actively in Islamic finance, Bahrain has created a modern, sophisticated Islamic financial infrastructure while reassuring its wealthy conservative neighbours. Its centralized system of Shari'ah governance provides clarity, despite a prominent legal pluralism and the arbitration of financial disputes across regional, local, and international jurisdictions. When a dispute over a financing arrangement between an international investor, KCSC

---

[51] Chibli Mallat, 'Commercial Law in the Middle East: Between Classical Transactions and Modern Business', *American Journal of Comparative Law*, vol. 48, no. 1 (2000); A. E. Mayer, 'The Shariah: A Methodology or a Body of Substantive Rules?', in *Islamic Law and Jurisprudence*, edited by N. Heer (Seattle, WA: University of Washington Press, 1990); Ercanbrack, *The Transformation of Islamic Law*, pp. 237–62.

[52] Ercanbrack, *The Transformation of Islamic Law*, p. 245.

[53] Ercanbrack, *The Transformation of Islamic Law*, p. 246.

Kuwait, and Sanghi Polyester involving istisna (contract of hire, manufacture) came to arbitration in London, a Shari'ah specialist confirmed that the dispute could be settled under English law despite inevitable conflict with Shari'ah.[54] Financial transactions and contracts need certainty and here English courts and English law provided that assurance.[55] In a second case, between Shamil Bank of Bahrain and Beximco Pharmaceuticals in 2003, a murabahah financing arrangement was found to be inadequate. The court accepted that the contract should be governed by English law and this was later upheld by the English Court of Appeal. Here it can be argued that English courts can provide flexibility and accuracy to Shari'ah decisions.[56]

To resort to English law and English courts for dispute resolution involves a reconciliation between secular and religious laws, and one can question whether this 'manipulation' in fact strengthens the commercial tenets in Islamic finance. Arbitration is not an alternative to Shari'ah and domestic courts but reflects a decision to settle 'disputes within a forum which is free from the constraints of "social engineering" objectives or values with which national courts are concerned'. Grigera Naon calls this cultural openness and neutrality in the arbitration of disputes.[57]

The legal and regulatory gaps and ambiguities that exist between Islamic financial law and municipal legal systems and the resulting operational difficulties were demonstrated in the Dana Gas claim, in 2017, that sukuk is not Shari'ah compliant. The UAE legal system, although based on the 1971 constitution, constitutes a series of syntheses modelled on Egyptian, Sudanese, and other Arabic derivations. The resulting hybrid legal system within this municipal jurisdiction lacks legal rigour because of its failure to conform to

---

[54] *Sanghi Polyesters (India) Ltd v International Investor KCSC (Kuwait)*, WL 389643 (2000). ALL ER (D) 93 (2000), 1 Lloyd's Law Report 480 (2001) CLC748. Thompson-Reuters, Practical Law, 'Islamic Finance in International Arbitration', 25 September 2001.

[55] Ercanbrack, *The Transformation of Islamic Law*, pp. 223–36; Nigel Blackaby, Constantine Partasides, Alan Redfern, and Martin Hunter, *Redfern and Hunter on International Arbitration* (Oxford: Oxford University Press, 2015); Aida Maita, 'Arbitration of Islamic Financial Disputes', *Annual Survey of International and Comparative Law*, vol. 20, no. 1, article 7 (2014).

[56] *Shamil Bank of Bahrain EC v Beximco Pharmaceuticals Ltd*, 2003, EWHC2118 [Comm]: 20032 ALL E.R. [Comm] 849; *Shamil Bank of Bahrain EC v Beximco Pharmaceuticals Ltd*, 2004 EWCA Civ19 [1]: 2004 1WLR1784 at 1801. See also Denton Wilde Sapte, 'Recent Decisions on Islamic Finance Transactions in Bank Briefings', Denton Wilde Sapte Law Office, April 2004.

[57] Grigera Naon, 'The Role of International Commercial Arbitration', *Arbitration*, vol. 65 (1999), pp. 266–77; Aisha Nadar, 'Islamic Finance: Potential Implications for Dispute Resolution', *Arbitration*, vol. 75, no. 3 (2009), pp. 296–308. See also F. E. Vogel and S. L. Hayes, *Islamic Law and Finance: Religion, Risk and Return* (The Hague: Kluwer International Law Publishers, 1998), chapter 5; Mallat, 'Commercial Law in the Middle East', pp. 81–142. For an overview of the relationship between arbitration and Islamic jurisdiction, see C. N. Browser and J. K. Sharpe, 'International Arbitration and the Islamic World: The Third Phase', *American Journal of International Law*, vol. 97 (2003); Hassan Ali Radhi, *Judiciary and Arbitration in Bahrain* (Leiden: Kluwer Law International, 2003), pp. 168–212; Aseel Al-Ramahi, 'Competing Rationalities: The Evolution of Arbitration in Commercial Disputes in Modern Jordan', PhD thesis, University of London, 2008.

the rules of the AAOIFI (Accounting and Auditing Organization for Islamic Financial Institutions) and the Islamic Financial Services Board (IFSB). Even in the Shamil Bank of Bahrain and the Beximco Pharmaceutical arbitration cases of 2003, it was confirmed that English law could not engage in the interpretation of the Shari'ah as the governing law of a financial transaction. Rather, *Shamil Bank v Beximco Pharmaceuticals Ltd* illustrated that Islamic finance was attempting to provide choice in mediation through international commercial arbitration, while accepting the chasm that could exist between Islamic finance and international settlements. The UAE case of Dana Gas also shows legal hybridity at the municipal level. The use of English courts ensured sustainable, commercially viable arrangements. But were the arrangements strictly Shari'ah compliant? International commercial arbitration is serving as a nexus to, rather than a divorce from, Shari'ah law. Although the power of Shari'ah provides a foundation for ethical capitalism, it would be misleading to assume that the coexistence of Shari'ah within legal pluralism was without problems.

Paradoxes in Islamic Banking

When Shari'ah conflicts with English common law in commercial disputes, English law is paramount. In *Shamil Bank v Beximco Pharmaceuticals Ltd*, the secular court was decisive. In Saudi Arabia this would not be possible, as Shari'ah is the sole source of legitimacy. Another glaring tension arises from the Shari'ah prohibition on speculation, for hedging is a crucial instrument in modern finance and without hedging Islamic finance would be trapped at an immature stage of global finance. Bahrain sought a plausible escape by discrete, sophisticated manipulation. In the Gulf states, high oil prices help to sustain these sophisticated financial manipulations. Finally, Bahrain was eager to diversify and modernize its financial infrastructure but again faced serious constraints. It sought to break those constraints by creating a banking sector offshore, securing funds from wealthy neighbours and Western banks and in this way integrating international and regional finance. This also protected the domestic economy from aggressive foreign banks. Offshore banking is also exempt from taxation. As early as 1976, National Westminster, Banque Nationale de Paris, Societé Generale, Citibank, and Bank of America were involved in Bahrain's offshore banking. By 1980, the total Offshore Banking Unit (OBU) assets were US$37.5 billion.[58]

---

[58] Bean, 'The Contemporary Financial Development of Kuwait and Bahrain', p. 89.

The involvement of the state in Islamic finance facilitates a measure of deception. For example, a heavy concentration of investment in low-risk short-term murabahah financing artificially creates profits. Islamic finance cannot face genuine competition in such short-term financing and leaves high-risk long-term financing to state infrastructural projects. Islamic finance has a high preponderance in short-term financing, trade, or currency-secured loans. Islamic banks have a dualism through such investments, and this illustrates their Shari'ah compromises.[59]

The Central Bank, as well as the capital market authorities and other regulators, control banks, insurance companies, mutual funds, hedge funds, and issuers of Islamic bonds. International regulatory institutions such as AAOIFI, established in Bahrain, prepares, promulgates, and interprets accounting, auditing, and governance standards for Islamic finance. The Islamic International Financial Market, established in Bahrain in 2009, encourages the self-regulation of money and capital markets. The institutions in Bahrain, together with the international standards being advanced by Basel, AAOIFI, and IFSB, secure Bahrain's position as the second largest centre for Islamic finance, after Malaysia. These institutions provided the necessary legal, corporate governance, technology, and certainly the standard for Bahrain to achieve global ambitions. Critically, this explains why Bahrain achieved better corporate governance than her Gulf neighbours. The World Bank Global Financial Development Database demonstrated that Bahrain outstrips Saudi Arabia, Kuwait, and the UAE in financial success and corporate governance and therefore was able to compete in international markets.[60] Finally in this chapter, it would be useful to sketch in the structure of Islamic finance in Malaysia.

Islamic Finance in Malaysia: The Contrasting Dynamics of Financial Instruments and Shari'ah Compliance

In Malaysia, Islamic finance had its origins in the Pilgrim Fund (Lembaga Tabung Haji), protected within the 'Inculcation of Islamic Values' policy of Prime Minister Mahathir in 1981. The first Islamic Bank, Bank Islam Malaysia Berhad, was established in 1983 and the following year saw the establishment of Takaful Malaysia Berhad (Islamic Insurance). But the

---

[59] Turen, 'Performance and Risk Analysis of Islamic Banks'.
[60] Data from World Bank World Development Indicators for 2015; ICD-Thomson Reuters, *Islamic Finance Development Report 2016*, pp. 30–1; COMCEC, *Diversification of Islamic Financial Instruments*, pp. 8–9, 68–182; Bean, 'The Contemporary Financial Development of Kuwait and Bahrain', p. 76.

critical move in creating an Islamic capital market came in 1995 with the establishment of the Securities Commission, followed by the Shari'ah Advisory Committee in 1996, charged with Shari'ah interpretation and ensuring compliance. An attempt to validate Islamic windows in conventional banks posed a serious challenge to Shari'ah compliance. The determination to consolidate Malaysia's commitment to Islamic finance had led to the introduction of the world's first Islamic inter-bank money market in January 1994. Malaysia's position in Islamic finance is reinforced through financial instruments such as sukuk (Islamic bonds). Sukuk issuers receive tax deductions and exemptions. Many of the issuers were foreign companies such as Shell MDS, a subsidiary of the Anglo-Dutch oil company. There was also an innovative application of sukuk Ijarah and sukuk Musharakah. As in Bahrain, sukuk was used to finance state-led projects. Between 2001 and 2015, while Malaysia's sukuk issues accounted for 67 per cent of global issues, Bahrain accounted for a mere 3 per cent.[61]

A compelling explanation for the growing power of Malaysia in global Islamic finance is, paradoxically, its flexibility in achieving the standardization of IFL. Bank Negara's understanding of the constraints imposed by IFL has led to the establishment of a regulatory system that is standardized and yet innovative in response to market needs.[62] Bahrain, it should be noted, accommodates AAOIFI standards but ignores certain aspects which are viewed as imposing constraints on market competition. A common dispute is over the recognition of bay' al-'inah, a legal strategy in which a person sells an asset to another for a deferred payment, the seller buying back the asset for a cash payment before having to make the full payment at the deferred price. This arrangement involves gharar, uncertainty as to whether the obligations could be fulfilled, and also conceals riba. Bahrain accepted the use of riba, an acceptance that has underpinned its market impetus.

Tawarruq (a sale and resale transaction exploited to create liquidity) has been accepted in both Bahrain and Malaysia, despite objections by the jurist Ibn Tamiyyah of AAOIFI. The Malaysian Shari'ah Advisory Council of the Malaysian Securities Commission considers a debt as a financial right that is capable of being bought and sold.[63] Both Malaysia and Bahrain pushed for the standardization of Islamic finance in order to reflect market needs. Malaysia sought institutional connections with Arab states to achieve compromises.

---

[61] IIFM (International Islamic Financial Market) Sukuk Database; Securities Commission Malaysia, RAM (Rating Agency Malaysia).
[62] Jonathan Ercanbrack, 'The Standardization of Islamic Financial Law: Lawmaking in Modern Financial Markets', *American Journal of Comparative Law*, vol. 67, no. 4 (2019).
[63] Ercanbrack, 'The Standardization of Islamic Financial Law'.

Malaysia's Central Bank and the Bahrain and Dubai regulatory authorities sought standardization of IFL. They were aware of the risks involved in legal transplants but also aware of the impact of AAOIFI Shari'ah standards on market needs.[64] Bahrain and Malaysia both recognize that traditionally interpreted Shari'ah may obstruct Islamic finance in developing adaptable commercial practices. Thus, standardization through knowledge of the existing legal system and the imposition of Shari'ah need to be complementary. Both countries have a base in common law, although in the last two decades Bahrain has adopted civil law in its regulatory infrastructure to enforce Islamic financial transactions. Bahrain has grappled with the role of Shari'ah in its municipal system and has also used English courts in complex disputes, as in the Beximco case. That case exposed two important principles. First, that an English court will use only English law, and second, that Islamic principles can be incorporated into a contract governed by English law. This reduces the pressure to secure Shari'ah validation. 'Islamic standards such as AAOIFI standards when mandated by law have shown to achieve the highest degree of standardization.'[65]

The most reasoned articulation of IFL in Malaysia was in the development of a specialized legal and regulatory system that gave a minimal role to traditional jurists. As a multi-ethnic nation, Article 121 of the Malaysian constitution makes a clear distinction between federal jurisdiction and the jurisdiction of the Shari'ah courts.[66] Article 74 gives federal courts jurisdiction over civil law and criminal law, including a wide range of civil law matters as well as finance and contract law. It also gives state courts jurisdiction over Islamic law, including Islamic personal and family law. Islamic financial disputes are often dealt with in secular civil law courts. Although the jurisdiction of Shari'ah courts is constrained, the clarity of its constitutional and legal framework assists market manipulation, as in sukuk. This has assisted in the creation of a state-mandated version of IFL that van Santen criticizes as a conventional clone.[67] This flexibility has promoted IFL

---

[64] Gunther Teubner, 'Legal Irritants: Good Faith in British Law or How Unifying Law Ends Up in New Divergences', *Modern Law Review*, vol. 61, no. 1 (1998). See also Brown, review of Ercanbrack, *The Transformation of Islamic Law*.

[65] Ercanbrack, 'The Standardization of Islamic Financial Law'.

[66] Emma van Santen, 'Islamic Banking and Finance Regulation in Malaysia: Between State Sharia, the Courts and the Islamic Moral Economy', *Company Lawyer*, 2018.

[67] van Santen, 'Islamic Banking and Finance Regulation', p. 27.

in Malaysia. Bahrain too has pursued similar compromises to secure its position as a major centre for Islamic finance.

Conclusion: Continuities and Contrasts

The key focus in this chapter has been on the accommodation of Shari'ah principles and the manner in which ethical dilemmas have been reconciled. In fact, this mixed effect of Islamic banking in Bahrain has sustained a stronger economic performance. In this, the taming of Shari'ah resembles the approach of behavioural economics, in which different contexts call for tailored interpretive strategies. Scholars such as Mahmoud El-Gamal have called the bluff of the Islamic finance industry's claim that its products and services align with traditional Islamic ethical aspirations.[68] But I have argued that hybrid legal structures are legal composites reflecting state law, religious law, and international financial standards in particular historical contexts. Much of the existing scholarly work on Islamic finance remains wedded to the notion that we are dealing with classical Islamic law and some of it is too uncritical or insufficiently theorized. My empirical dissection of Islamic finance in Bahrain, including its application in municipal legal systems, including English courts, has exposed the intricacies and dynamics that allows it to thrive in Bahrain, Malaysia, and even in Britain and Ireland. It is the interdisciplinary pluralistic legal ordering which is responsible for the creation of two financial hubs, one in Bahrain and the other in Malaysia. The financial hub in Bahrain resembles that in other cities such as Singapore and Hong Kong, where domestic and foreign transactions have developed institutions and a legal framework within a larger international context.[69] Bahrain also operates a unique offshore financial centre to shape laws and institutions to meet the needs of clients outside Bahrain and to a degree outside the GCC jurisdiction. In some respects, the Bahrain hub resembles London. But clearly there are differences as Bahrain has an embedded dependence on the oil wealth of its neighbours and a religious and social structure that synthesizes a unique blend of rights-based and relationship-based culture in finance, both in conventional banking and in Islamic banking.

Tables 3.1 to 3.8 below capture Bahrain's globalization in Islamic finance.

---

[68] Mahmoud El Gamal, *Islamic Finance, Law, Economics and Practice* (Cambridge: Cambridge University Press, 2006).

[69] David C. Donald, with contributions by Jiangyu Wang and Jefferson P. Vanderwolk, *A Financial Centre for Two Empires: Hong Kong's Corporate, Securities and Tax Laws in its Transition from Britain to China* (Cambridge: Cambridge University Press, 2014).

Table 3.1 Subsidiaries of the Al Baraka Banking Group: held directly by the bank

	Ownership in 2018 (per cent)	Ownership in 2017 (per cent)	Year of incorporation	Country of incorporation	No. of branches, 31 December 2018
Banque Al Baraka D'Algerie	55.90	55.90	1991	Algeria	31
Al Baraka Islamic Bank—Bahrain (AIB)	91.12	91.12	1984	Bahrain	200
Al Baraka Bank Tunis	78.40	78.40	1983	Tunisia	37
Al Baraka Bank Egypt	73.68	73.68	1980	Egypt	32
Al Baraka Bank Lebanon	98.98	98.94	1991	Lebanon	6
Jordan Islamic Bank (JIB)	66.01	66.01	1978	Jordan	105
Al Baraka Turk Participation Bank	56.64	56.64	1985	Turkey	230
Al Baraka Bank Limited (ABL)	64.51	64.51	1989	South Africa	11
Al Baraka Bank Sudan	75.73	75.73	1984	Sudan	28
Al Baraka Bank Syria	23.00	23.00	2009	Syria	13
BTI Bank	49.00	49.00	2017	Morocco	4

Table 3.2 Subsidiaries of the Al Baraka Banking Group: held indirectly by the bank

	Subsidiary held through	Effective ownership in 2018 (per cent)	Effective ownership in 2017 (per cent)	Year of incorporation	Country of incorporation
Al Baraka Bank (Pakistan)	AIB	53.88	53.88	2010	Pakistan
Itqan Capital	AIB	75.69	75.69	2007	Saudi Arabia
Al-Omariya School Company	JIB	62.31	65.61	1987	Jordan
Al-Samaha Real Estate Company	JIB	62.97	66.01	1998	Jordan
Future Applied Computer Technology Company	JIB	66.01	66.01	1998	Jordan
Sanable Alkhair for Financial Investment	JIB	66.01	66.01	2006	Jordan
Al Baraka Properties (Pty) Limited	ABL	64.51	64.51	1991	South Africa

Table 3.3 Al Baraka Bank: distribution of assets, liabilities, and equity of investment account holders by economic sector, 2017 and 2018

	2018			2017		
	Assets US$ 000	Liabilities US$ 000	IAH US$ 000	Assets US$ 000	Liabilities US$ 000	IAH US$ 000
Manufacturing	3,670,844	100,106	277,065	4,272,944	219,771	202,767
Mining and quarrying	122,771	4,647	21,572	182,855	6,902	27,252
Agriculture	179,627	21,003	4,999	127,190	7,246	7,294
Construction and real estate	2,796,364	21,853	25,271	3,259,085	21,663	36,223
Financial	4,493,331	2,081,910	1,690,425	3,646,634	2,703,293	1,759,254
Trade	1,608,667	254,441	175,776	1,622,738	222,384	161,548
Personal and consumer finance	2,834,613	3,933,665	8,954,660	2,926,192	4,025,988	9,716,539
Government	5,648,272	55,087	70,743	6,177,308	78,584	164,559
Other services	2,476,749	1,980,171	1,901,857	3,238,265	1,774,610	1,806,673
	23,831,238	8,452,883	13,122,368	25,453,211	9,060,441	13,882,109

Table 3.4 Al Baraka Banking Group: consolidated statement of financial position, as of 31 December 2018

	2018 US$ 000	2017 US$ 000
Assets		
Cash and balances with banks	5,008,009	5,430,085
Receivables	10,303,868	12,001,050
Mudarabah and Musharakah financing	2,718,906	2,377,654
Investments	3,067,008	2,888,334
Ijarah Muntahia Bittamleek	1,770,833	1,856,018
Property and equipment	406,564	430,192
Other assets	556,050	469,878
Total Assets	*23,831,238*	*25,453,211*
Liabilities, Equity of Investment Account Holders and Owners' Equity		
Liabilities		
Customer current and other accounts	5,325,924	5,465,433
Due to banks	1,178,758	1,322,470
Long-term financing	976,891	1,236,555
Other liabilities	971,310	1,035,983
Total Liabilities	*8,452,883*	*9,060,441*
Equity of Investment Account Holders	13,122,368	13,882,109
Owners' Equity		
Share capital	1,242,879	1,206,679
Treasury shares	(9,203)	(9,550)
Share premium	18,829	18,644
Perpetual tier 1 capital	400,000	400,000
Reserves	165,551	199,282
Cumulative changes in fair values	31,929	40,443
Foreign currency translations	(861,313)	(706,242)
Retained earnings	519,587	530,615
Proposed appropriations	37,286	60,334
Equity attributable to parent's shareholders and Sukuk holders	1,545,545	1,740,205
Non-controlling interest	710,442	770,456
Total Owners' Equity	*2,255,987*	*2,510,661*
TOTAL LIABILITIES, EQUITY OF INVESTMENT ACCOUNT HOLDERS AND OWNERS' EQUITY	*23,831,238*	*25,453,211*

Sources: Unified Sharia Supervisory Board Report; Report of the Board of Directors; Independent Auditors Report; Consolidated Financial Statements, 31 December 2018.
Note: The figures in brackets indicate ownership by special institutions, such as the Treasury and foreign currency.

Table 3.5 Al Baraka Banking Group: structure of ownership—directors' and executive management's direct and indirect interests in bank's shares, 2017 and 2018

Name of director	Position	Nationality	Number of shares, 2017	Number of shares, 2018
Saleh Abdulla Kamel	Chairman	Saudi	660,613,269	680,431,667
Abdulla Ammar Saudi	Vice Chairman	Bahraini	646,942	666,350
Abdulla Saleh Kamel	Vice Chairman	Saudi	328,736	338,598
Mohydin Saleh Kamel	Board Member	Saudi	687,356	707,976
Abdul Elah Sabbahi	Board Member	Saudi	219,320	225,899
Adnan Ahmed Yousif	Board Member (President & Chief Executive)	Bahraini	352	362
Abdulrahman Shehab	Executive Vice President, Head of Operations and Administration	Bahraini	232,274	339,231

Table 3.6a Global performance of Al Baraka Banking Group, I

	2018			2017		
	Assets US$ 000	Liabilities US$ 000	IAH US$ 000	Assets US$ 000	Liabilities US$ 000	IAH US$ 000
Middle East	11,594,671	2,907,485	7,338,507	11,154,872	2,976,028	6,827,712
North Africa	2,743,750	1,429,458	1,042,643	2,691,890	1,355,042	1,042,965
Europe	7,919,036	3,662,996	3,768,663	9,538,495	4,034,513	4,847,691
Others	1,573,781	452,944	972,555	2,067,954	694,858	1,163,741
	23,831,238	8,452,883	13,122,368	25,453,211	9,060,441	13,882,109

Table 3.6b Global performance of Al Baraka Banking Group, II

	2018			2017		
	Total operating income US$ 000	Net operating income US$ 000	Net income US$ 000	Total operating income US$ 000	Net operating income US$ 000	Net income US$ 000
Middle East	414,924	198,191	114,643	370,546	175,270	101,964
North Africa	132,279	68,822	37,792	103,291	41,437	22,265
Europe	347,782	155,280	48,415	407,474	185,536	60,534
Others	92,834	25,069	15,878	117,379	28,130	22,156
Total	987,819	447,362	216,728	998,690	430,373	206,919

Table 3.7 Al Baraka Banking Group: distribution of specific financial instruments (in US$ 000)

	Cash	Sales receivables	Mudarabah financing	Investment in real estate	Ijarah Muntahia Bittamleek	Investments	Others	Total
Balance at 1 January 2018	33,196	177,793	292,657	48,411	112,345	190,788	48,190	903,380
Deposits	165,784	335,471	256,093	529	59,876	13,421	-	831,174
Withdrawals	(168,533)	(216,196)	(219,844)	(937)	(21,762)	(54,930)	(48,190)	(729,852)
Income net of expenses	-	34,160	7,787	465	8,782	2,883	20	54,097
Mudarib's share	-	(6,657)	(1,405)	-	(107)	(177)	(20)	(8,366)
Foreign exchange translations	-	(29,570)	-	-	-	(26,825)	-	(56,395)
Balance at 31 December 2018	*30,447*	*295,001*	*335,288*	*48,468*	*159,134*	*125,700*	-	*994,038*
Balance at 1 January 2017	73,558	223,323	286,201	38,150	82,962	157,672	10,177	872,043
Deposits	209,723	235,941	193,416	10,624	48,757	78,964	63,233	840,658
Withdrawals	(250,085)	(299,601)	(193,622)	(450)	(22,081)	(39,760)	(26,495)	(832,094)
Income net of expenses	-	30,793	6,662	366	3,321	1,558	(233)	42,467
Mudarib's share	-	(6,790)	-	(279)	(614)	(370)	(104)	(8,157)
Foreign exchange translations	-	(5,873)	-	-	-	(7,276)	1,612	(11,537)
Balance at 31 December 2017	*33,196*	*177,793*	*292,657*	*48,411*	*112,345*	*190,788*	*48,190*	*903,380*

Note: Bracketed figures identify special Arabic commercial involvement.

Table 3.8 Al Baraka Banking Group: alignment with specific banks in the various states

Country	Name	Former Name	Branches
Saudi Arabia	Itqan Capital		1
Jordan	Jordan Islamic Bank		97
Indonesia	Al Baraka Bank Representation		1 Representative Office
Pakistan	Al Baraka Bank		138
Bahrain	Al Baraka Islamic Bank (AIB)	Al Baraka Islamic Investment Bank B.S.C. (E.C.)	19
Turkey	Al Baraka Tűrk Participation Bank	Albaraka Tűrk Őzel Finas Kurumu A.Ş.	213
Syria	Al Baraka Bank Syria		12
Lebanon	Al Baraka Bank Lebanon		23
Tunisia	Al Baraka Bank Tunisia		22
Algeria	Banque Al Baraka D'Algerie		30
South Africa	Al Baraka Bank Limited		17
Sudan	Al Baraka Bank Sudan		27
Egypt	Al Baraka Bank Egypt	Al Ahram Bank (also formerly known as Egyptian Saudi Finance Bank)	31
Libya	Al Baraka Bank Representation		37
Iraq	Al Baraka Tűrk Participation Bank		42

4

The Bahrain Stock Market

Law, Growth, and Performance

This chapter on the Bahrain stock market examines the legal advances that shaped the regulatory protection of investors while examining the juxtaposition of significant institutional change and governance. Important here is the synchronicity of the shared influence of colonial legal traditions in crafting an indigenous jurisdiction with Shari'ah interpretations. Securities laws involve the imposition of disclosure duties and the banning of insider dealing and on stock price manipulation. With Bahrain as the financial hub of the Gulf states and with increasing globalization, cultural and legal mediation is important.

The dynamics of Bahrain's stock market and capital market follow from two aspects of Islamic banking as a distinct institution linked to its oil-wealthy Gulf neighbours. Bahrain's emergence as a financial hub is derived from numerous factors ranging from oil wealth, speculative behaviour in stocks, the scandal of Souk al-Manakh in Kuwait in 1982, and a standardization of Islamic financial law through compromises on Shari'ah. Financial integration, offshore banking, and commercial arbitration through both local municipal courts and English courts further strengthened the regulatory regime for the often state-dominated enterprises of Bahrain and the Gulf states.

This chapter addresses contests over law and operational issues, and the use of sukuk and corporate bonds. Important here were problems of asset pricing and of commercial arbitration. A further, almost political and legal, contest exists within the framework of bankruptcy and liquidation. In effect, financial support came, in many cases, from commercial banks and state-owned corporations. The power of the state waned to a degree when alternative legal autonomy was exercised through local municipal courts and through the arbitration of commercial disputes in London courts. Contested plural legalism and jurisdictional fluidity demonstrates the scale and scope of Bahrain and its moderate legal colonial heritage, providing a framework for its relations with conservative, oil-wealthy Gulf neighbours. The stock market

Islam and Capitalism in the Making of Modern Bahrain. Rajeswary Ampalavanar Brown, Oxford University Press.
© Rajeswary Ampalavanar Brown (2023). DOI: 10.1093/oso/9780192874672.003.0004

in Bahrain provides for an understanding of the Bahrain model of modernity and globalization in finance, in contrast to the fragmenting Islamic parochialism and limiting stance of Saudi Arabia and even the UAE.

The Bahrain stock market was established in 1989 when trading was conducted manually. An automated trading system was introduced in 1999 when all transactions were carried out electronically. In the same year, 1999, the Bahrain Government relaxed ownership restrictions to allow GCC nationals to list and own 100 per cent equity in listed corporations on the Bahrain stock exchange, while foreign investors were permitted to control up to 49 per cent of local company shares. This change was accompanied in 2002 by the transfer of regulatory supervision of the Bahrain stock exchange from the Ministry of Commerce to the Central Bank of Bahrain. In 2010, the BSE, the Bahrain Stock Exchange, was replaced by a shareholding company, the Bahrain Bourse (BHB), which has since joined international organizations such as the Union of Arab Stock Exchanges, the Federation of Euro-Asian Stock Exchanges, the World Federation of Exchanges, Africa and Middle East Depositories, and the Association of National Numbering Agencies. This was to enhance its grasp of legislative, technical, and administrative developments in the global capital markets sector. In 2012, there were 43 companies listed on the Bahrain Bourse. As stated earlier, Bahrain's listed companies faced restrictions on foreign ownership, which was limited to 49 per cent. However, some listed companies are fully open, while others are fully closed to foreign investment, as occurs in Bahrain's Gulf neighbours. Total market capitalization on the Bourse increased by nearly 67 per cent, from US$9.7 billion in 2003 to US$16.1 billion in 2012, an impressive growth in light of the 2008 financial crisis. The total volume of shares traded in 2012 rose by 13 per cent, to reach US$0.31 billion as compared to US$0.27 billion in 2003.[1] Some words of caution. It is hard to explore a correlation between the ability to survive global economic pressures and the power of state listings on the stock market. A number of Bahraini listed corporations are closed. These closed joint stock companies may be privately held or closely held and managed by a small group of shareholders, perhaps by the state, or by connected businessmen. As a result, they are less exposed to periodic disclosure, and face less compliance to securities regulation and effective governance requirements. Morck, Schleifer, and Vishny see capital markets as 'not solely driven by fundamentals but by investor sentiment'.[2]

---

[1] Central Bank of Bahrain, Annual Reports, 2002–14.
[2] Randall Morck, Andrei Schleifer, and Robert W. Vishny, 'Do Managerial Objectives Drive Bad Acquisitions?', *Journal of Finance*, vol. 45, no. 1 (1990), pp. 31–48; Randall Morck, Andrei Schleifer, and Robert

Intimate Markers of History and Modernity

How do we reconcile the disparities between Bahraini modernity and state control of the Bourse? A sharper understanding of jurisdictional uncertainties would help. In pre-colonial times, limited commercial activity led to simple legal institutions, first with rulers' courts settling social disputes, then tribal arbitration involving both intra-tribal processes and a broader conciliation process. There were also specialized tribunals that solved disputes between merchants. Finally, there were Shari'ah courts which specialized in family law and dispute settlement procedures.[3] In comparison with the desultory nature of legal institutions in Saudi Arabia, Bahrain, from 1930, possessed legal independence, despite its strong inter-regional culture and commercial links with its Gulf neighbours.

E. P. Thompson famously saw the rule of law as 'a cultural achievement of universal significance'.[4] My study of Bahrain illustrates this and agrees with Thompson: the colonial state modernized Bahrain through legal changes. The British in Bahrain introduced administrative reforms to secure political control, civil society, and popular participation. Ironically these reforms may have also contributed to a rise in political conflicts. But overall, local tribal hegemony in Bahrain permitted negotiation between Shiite leaders and tribal chiefs, a process that secured more moderate Shiite leaders and powerful Shiite businessmen, collaborating with forms of associated state capitalism.

By 1820, under the rule of the Khalifahs, Bahrain had signed an abstention from piracy treaty with the East India Company. The creation of extra-territorial British jurisdiction was in force in 1913 and this led to vibrant commercial relationships, which had an impact on the legal system. Unique again for Bahrain, as compared to other Trucial States, was the emergence of a form of legal pluralism with, first, the jurisdiction of the British Crown and second, the jurisdiction of local rulers' courts.[5] Hence, British legal influence was strong in Bahrain.[6]

W. Vishny, 'The Stock Market and Investment: Is the Market a Sideshow?', *Brookings Papers on Economic Activity*, vol. 21, no. 2 (1990), pp. 157–216.

[3] Nathan Brown, *The Rule of Law in the Arab World: Courts in Egypt and the Gulf* (Cambridge: Cambridge University Press, 1997), p. 130.

[4] E. P. Thompson, *Whigs and Hunters: The Origins of the Black Act* (New York: Pantheon Books, 1975), p. 67. He then stepped back: 'I do not lay any claim as to the abstract, extraterritorial impartiality of these rules' (p. 266). See also Ranajit Guha, *Dominance Without Hegemony: History and Power in Colonial India* (Cambridge, MA: Harvard University Press, 1997), pp. 85, 66–7.

[5] George N. S. Feir, *Modernization of the Law in Arab States: An Investigation into Current Civil, Criminal and Constitutional Law in the Arab World* (San Francisco, CA: Austin and Winfield Publications, 1998), p. 47.

[6] William Ballantyne, *Legal Development in Arabia* (London: Graham and Trotman, 1980), p. 8.

The British Advisor, Charles Belgrave, was involved in the development of the Bahraini legal system and also acted as a judge. Bahrain agreed with the Trucial States to introduce mixed courts that employed English and local judges to investigate cases involving both locals and foreigners. By 1955–57, with the introduction of special laws for English courts in regions of Bahrain, William Ballantyne urged the British Government to further encourage the modernization of the region's legal system to secure London's commercial involvement even after the withdrawal of Britain. Bahrain thus undertook the translation of some English codes into Arabic to maintain the British legal heritage. In contrast, the other Gulf states reverted to Shari'ah.[7] However, undermining Ballantyne's position, there existed the supremacy of tribal power insisted on by Belgrave, and that imposed limits on each type of community and emphasized tribal hegemony.[8]

Rulers historically also functioned as judges. However, regional rulers were hostile to the principle of an independent judiciary, and this hostility delayed the emergence of an efficient, structured legal system. Rulers regarded legal, and particularly judicial development to be a threat to their inherited authority. Hence, the British withdrawal left a major legal gap, and the discovery of oil and soaring commercial activity undermined the immature legal system. Following the failure of the British to impose an Anglo-Saxon legal model in the Gulf, the regional rulers, except Saudi Arabia, opted for the Egyptian-French model.[9]

After 2002, Bahrain underwent further dramatic change when it became a kingdom and adopted a new constitution. The constitution was formed through a referendum that took place in February 2001. The constitution states that there are other sources of law in addition to Shari'ah. The influence of Islamic law is manifested in the civil codes but overall, in Bahrain, Islamic law is less influential than in Kuwait and the UAE.[10] The new Civil Code organizes the sources of law as follows: first is the civil code, then custom, then Islamic law, and finally natural and equity law.[11] This hierarchy can be linked to British influence, as seen in Article 12, section 3 in the Bahrain Order.

Commercial law in Bahrain is less observant of Shari'ah than the civil codes. Indeed, commercial codes may contradict Islamic principles, such as

---

[7] Ballantyne, *Legal Development in Arabia*, p. 10.
[8] Mansoor Al-Jamri, 'Conclusion: Birth of a New Legal System—Anglo-Muhammadan Law', Middle East Studies Association, 32nd Annual Meeting, Chicago, 6 December 1998.
[9] Fahad Al-Zumai, 'Protection of Investors in Gulf Cooperation Council Stock Markets: A Case Study of Kuwait, Bahrain and United Arab Emirates', PhD thesis, University of London, 2006, p. 54.
[10] Al-Zumai, 'Protection of Investors', p. 56.
[11] Article 1, Civil Code No. 19/2001.

in permitting riba.[12] The legal gaps in customary commercial law had to be filled by Western law. Unlike jurisdictional politics in other former British colonies, Bahrain rarely judged commercial disputes but instead sought resolution through the London courts.[13]

I have argued so far that multicentric legal codes promoted a pattern of legal pluralism and jurisdictional complexity that was exploited in commerce and on the stock market. This is clearly demonstrated in the growth and diversification of the Bahrain Bourse from 1989 to 2019. As the main investors are the state and its associated merchants, and as a major portion of investment is in state infrastructural projects, the principal mandatory commercial rules may be replaced by contract rather than governed by the rule of law. Such contractual characteristics carry risks and rewards. Here the role of human perception and innate cognitive bias towards familiarity may play a role in minimizing legal threats. This study will interrogate this protean emotion.[14]

Negotiating the Tangled Inheritance of Shari'ah

The first law regulating the Bahrain stock market was passed in 1987, the Amiri Decree No. 4/1987 securing its establishment. In 1988, the internal regulation of the exchange was instituted under Decision No. 13, which set out the regulations for stockbroker conduct, the listing rules, the arbitration process, and the trading mechanism. The Bahrain Monetary Agency acted as the supervisory and regulatory body for the Bahrain Stock Exchange. In 2004, the Capital Market Division issued a consultation paper for substantial reform of the exchange's legal framework. Bahrain underwent rapid reform after the appointment of King Hamad Al-Khalifah. The Commercial Companies Act No. 21/2001 provides the framework for companies in Bahrain. Civil Code No. 19/2001 governs all civil transactions, Commercial Law No. 7/1987 deals with commercial transactions, and Bankruptcy Law No. 11/1987 deals with insolvency among companies and individual traders. In 2001, the free trade agreement negotiated with the US attracted FDI and created the Bahrain Financial Centre.

Bahrain acknowledges that Shari'ah has not evolved since the tenth century and thus argues that the modernization of commercial law is essential, through transplants and the use of foreign courts, as in the Beximco case

---

[12] Article 1, Bahraini Commercial Law No. 7/1987.

[13] Jonathan Ercanbrack, *The Transformation of Islamic Law in Global Financial Markets* (Cambridge: Cambridge University Press, 2015), pp. 236, 326.

[14] Daniel Kahneman, *Thinking Fast and Slow* (New York: Penguin Random House, 2011).

heard in London.[15] The Beximco case reaffirmed that English law would not decide the case on the basis of Shari'ah, since a contract governed by a non-state law is not permitted under English law. This is in line with the UK's then membership of the European Union. Moreover, AAOIFI Shari'ah standards can be incorporated into a contract governed by English law, thereby resulting in a high degree of standardization.[16] Bahrain recognizes also that the way in which the civil legal system was adopted restricts the ability of judges to participate in legal development, unlike common law jurisdictions where the judiciary is in contact with local interests and is aware of the practical legal problems that arise. Consequently, Bahrain relies on several tactics to standardize and conform, and this is discussed later in detail.

Dark Pools Alternative Trading Systems Where Oil Wealth Dictates Liquid Markets

Commercial activities accelerated dramatically after the discovery of oil. Bahrain's first oil concession was signed in 1925, with the Eastern Company. But the firm faced difficulties, and in 1928, the ruler signed an agreement with Standard Oil California, although the British authorities at first refused approval. In 1930, the US Government finally persuaded the British to approve. This led to the entry of foreign corporations into Bahrain's financial markets. Bahrain had had a bank in Abushahr since 1901 but it failed because of the opposition of Indian traders who had their own informal financial institutions. In 1957, the National Bank of Bahrain was created, and this drew attention to the absence of effective commercial codes and company law. In 1975, Bahrain introduced the Commercial Companies Law, with provision for limited liability. Limited liability applies only to those companies with limited partnerships, closed joint stock corporations, and public joint stock companies.[17]

Within the Gulf states (Bahrain, Kuwait, and the UAE) from the 1950s to the 1960s, the total number of public companies incorporated was 45. Twenty-five were incorporated in Kuwait, 14 in Bahrain, and only six in the UAE. After introducing Decree No. 28/1975, which regulated local public companies, Bahrain had restricted Gulf companies incorporated in Bahrain from engaging in commercial activities for fear of instability. But Bahrain soon liberalized, as part of its determination to develop an offshore banking

---

[15] *Shamil Bank v Beximco Pharmaceuticals Ltd* (2004) EWCA Civ 19 (1).
[16] Ercanbrack, *The Transformation of Islamic Law*, pp. 227–32.
[17] Article 42, Bahrain Commercial Companies Law, 1975.

hub. In 1981, 78 Gulf companies were registered in Bahrain. In the same year, permission was granted for Bahrainis to become co-owners of these public companies, and this accelerated the growth in stock market trading. The Souk al Jawharah (Jewel Market) was not regulated but its operations were monitored by Bahraini officials, although they traded with the Souk al-Manakh in Kuwait, an unregulated market for trading in securities.[18] The Souk al-Manakh traded in a huge unregulated expansion of credit. The crash came in 1982, with total outstanding trading amounting to US$94 billion from 6,000 investors. Individual families were severely affected and only one bank remained solvent, supported by the National Bank of Kuwait. The government rescue was still incomplete when Iraq invaded Kuwait in 1990.[19] For Bahrain, trading on the Souk al-Manakh was encouraged by the lack of regulatory insight and government controls. Bahrain's liquidity rose between 1979 and 1983, from BD411 million to BD843 million, and credit facilities rose from BD41 million to BD128 million, largely through trading on the Souk al-Manakh.[20]

This collapse led Bahrain to establish an official stock exchange in 1987 and trading started in 1989. In 1983, the International Finance Corporation had already advised the creation of an information centre in Bahrain, to regulate the secondary market and carry out studies on existing corporations.[21] However, Bahrain's relations with Kuwait had a serious spillover impact. Fully aware of Kuwait's fractured stock market and the proliferation of fraud encouraged Bahrain's legal rigour and its expansion into Western markets with improved governance and ethics.

Kuwait's World of Speculation with No Moral Turning Point

In the 1970s, Kuwait had experienced a recession because of speculative activities. In 1974, the Minister of Trade and Industry had banned the sale of futures. But this ban was quickly lifted by the Securities Commission in order to stimulate trade.[22] In addition, a provisional suspension was imposed on

---

[18] Al-Zumai, 'Protection of Investors', pp. 69–70.

[19] Al-Zumai, 'Protection of Investors', p. 69.

[20] Fida Darwiche, *The Gulf Stock Exchange Crash: The Rise and Fall of Souq al-Manakh* (London: Croom Helm, 1986), pp. 69–70.

[21] 'The Keynesian natural laws of development of capitalist economies leads to the emergence of conditions conducive to financial instability.' Masami Hayashi, 'Financial Crisis Prevention: A Psychological Approach from Behavioral Science', MPhil dissertation, Institute of Development Studies, University of Sussex, 2001, pp. 69–72.

[22] Ministerial Order No. 31/1977.

the creation of new public companies, while increases in capital for existing listed companies was restricted until 1979. Banks also agreed to lower interest rates to ease the burden. The government meanwhile began to increase capital input by purchasing private sector shares at low prices. The total value of shares thus purchased is estimated at US$450 million.[23] This encouraged speculators, leading to insecure investment by speculators confident of state support. The creation of new companies and capital increased hugely and these companies traded on an unofficial stock market. This attracted Gulf corporations and by 1982 there were 49 Gulf companies set up by Kuwaiti investors in Bahrain and the UAE, with shares traded in Kuwait. The legal exemption by the Bahrain Government was also speculative. The Kuwaiti law forbidding the sale of shares in public companies in the first three years after founding was ignored and trading volume escalated. Total trading volume ranked third behind the US and Japanese stock markets.[24]

The Kuwaiti government, by requesting annual accounts in 1981, was only encouraging more speculation. Future deals escalated with deferred payments and post-dated cheques, thus creating irreconcilable transactions. In addition, 'movable banks' were created, and an estimated US$89 billion flowed into the Souk al-Manakh.[25] Commercial bank loans totalled US$12 billion. This speculation had involved ministers, MPs, and royal family members.[26] The total value of post-dated cheques was three times that of loans from the IMF in 1981. In 1982, the government suspended all future transactions, introduced laws on forward dealings, and established arbitration boards to resolve disputes. In 1983, bankruptcy processes were improved, through a special body to fast-track decisions on bank assets and payments.[27] However there was corruption, as the law benefited MPs, major traders with connections to the state, and members of the royal family. 'Eight knights' of the Souk debacle owed US$63 billion. These developments affected the Bahraini al-Juhra market and it dropped 50 per cent of its links with the Souk al-Manakh.[28] The Bahrain government refused to intervene.

Kuwait's banks incurred huge bad debts as these loans were not asset-based. Legal prudence was absent. Insider information was widely employed. It has been suggested that this debacle was part of a government conspiracy to

[23] Fawzi Al Sultan, 'Averting Financial Crisis—Kuwait', World Bank Working Paper No. 243 (1989), p. 5.
[24] Al-Zumai, 'Protection of Investors', p. 80. Frank Veneroso, 'Memories of the Souk Al Manakh', see http://www.dfm.co.ac/dfm/main/main.htm.
[25] Al-Zumai, 'Protection of Investors', p. 82.
[26] Darwiche, The Gulf Stock Exchange Crash, p. 92.
[27] Al-Zumai, 'Protection of Investors', pp. 86–7.
[28] Al-Zumai, 'Protection of Investors', p. 88.

paralyse democracy in Kuwait, a diversion from the dissolving of parliament in 1976.[29] The government bought shares in the Souk and when the crisis struck, it bought all the banks' debts. In May 1993, the state raised the salaries of public sector workers, just three months before an election.[30]

Bahrain: From Maturity to Renaissance through Oil

In Bahrain the discovery of oil marginalized the private sector, while the state and its cronies benefited. Before oil, the state often relied on the private sector for finance but after the rise of oil, the state absorbed major industries, and this is reflected on stock markets. Islamic banking insurance, Takaful, and investment corporations ensured that society's institutions evolved and thrived within this authoritarian state. In Bahrain, the social-religious element is crucial for Shi'ites.[31] Bahrain also modernized its financial regulations as a result of the Souk crisis, and, as seen above, a stock market was established. Law and vigilant supervision were seen as essential.

The Bahrain Stock Market requires a minimum capital for listing. For public companies, the minimum was BD500,000 (£695,000) while for closed joint stock companies not open to public trading it was BD200,000.[32] Capitalization is a serious issue, as both Bahraini and Kuwaiti markets insisted that a listed company had 50 per cent of shareholder equity as fully paid-up capital. This requirement is designed to offer protection for both shareholders and creditors of the company. Bahrain has been less rigorous over minimum equity in order to attract more companies. When the stock exchange was established it had only 45 listed companies. Bahrain also has less stringent rules on the profitability of these companies. Total turnover should be not less than BD500,000 (£695,000) and the listed company should have generated profits in the two years prior to listing.[33] However the additional requirement of 'financial stability' is rather ambiguous and this led to the listing of 'paper companies' during the Souk al-Manakh. Another confusing feature is the existence of parallel markets: one, Souk al-Jat, has hardly any regulations. In addition, Bahrain applies separate listing rules for foreign companies, which must have a representative office in Bahrain.

---

[29] Al-Zumai, 'Protection of Investors', p. 91.
[30] Al-Zumai, 'Protection of Investors', p. 91.
[31] Al-Zumai, 'Protection of Investors', p. 93.
[32] Article 1 in Decision Number 1/1993 for listing of Closed Joint Stock Companies in Bahrain.
[33] Resolution No. 13/1988, Article 39/10, Bahrain.

Corporate Governance in GCC States

In Bahrain, as in the Gulf states, board structures reveal associated clans rather than a separation of ownership from management. The new Bahrain commercial companies law laid down the responsibilities of directors and made clear where conflicts of interest could occur. The pursuit of directors' self-interest is prohibited except with shareholder approval.[34] Listing on the stock market is regarded as one method of securing scrutiny but with associational links between owners and managers, this is undermined. The agency problem, which exposes inherent conflicts of interest, is difficult to overcome in family and state-dominated firms.[35]

In the US, all publicly traded companies have strict guidelines on appropriate practices and experience. In Bahrain this is lacking as nepotism governs recruitment.[36] Cross-listing, even on overseas stock markets, can improve corporate governance. In the Middle East, the Union of Arab Stock Exchanges and Securities Commissions created a network through cross listing.[37] There were also bilateral agreements between Bahrain and Kuwait.

Moreover, in Bahrain, Articles 41, 42, and 43 of Resolution No. 13/1/1988, 'on the issuance of internal regulations', governs the suspension of listed corporations or delisting. The Commercial Companies Act imposes penalties if a public company issues debt securities that violate the law and damage investors and the market. Investors are thus protected.[38] Bahrain has restricted the rights of individual shareholders to sue the directors of the company.[39] Injured parties cannot seek redress easily.[40] Bahrain, the financial hub in the Gulf and without oil wealth, must attract listed companies. With electronic book-keeping slow to develop, Bahrain created the Central Depository System, which is part of Clearance and Settlement, managed by the Stock Exchange. But registrars of companies used their power and influence to resist the establishment of a compulsory Central Depository System. Hence there are risks associated with clearance and settlement.

---

[34] Saleh H. Hussain and Chris Mallin, 'The Dynamics of Corporate Governance in Bahrain: Structure, Responsibilities and Operations of Corporate Boards', *Corporate Governance Journal*, vol. 11, no. 3 (2003).

[35] See similarities with China: Rajeswary Ampalavanar Brown, *The Chinese and Indian Corporate Economies: A Comparative History of Their Search for Economic Renaissance and Globalization* (Abingdon: Routledge, 2017), pp. 115–52, 302–49.

[36] NYSE Corporate Accountability and Listing Standards Committee Report, June 2002, p. 2.

[37] Al-Zumai, 'Protection of Investors', p. 125. See United Nations, *Responding to Globalization: Stock Market Networking for Regional Integration in the ESCWA Region*, 2003, pp. 6, 8.

[38] Al-Zumai, 'Protection of Investors', p. 127.

[39] Al-Zumai, 'Protection of Investors', p. 132.

[40] See Article 187, Commercial Companies Law No. 21 /2001.

In Bahrain, as in the majority of Gulf states, only a few shares are traded. The rest are either not active or remain as liquid shares. On 13 April 2005, only 16 of the 47 listed companies traded.[41] With this limited market participation, none of the GCC stock markets experienced volatility, despite the absence of efficient clearance and settlement systems. The Souk al-Manakh had occurred because of uninhibited speculation.

The Bahrain Monetary Authority's *Guidelines on Insiders* of 2004 divides primary insiders into (1) 'statutory insiders', directors or auditors of listed companies; and (2) 'insiders by definition', accidental insiders receiving inside information. Bahrain and the UAE have strict rules against the use of inside information. Bahrain's guidelines are borrowed from the Helsinki laws on insider information.[42] There are sanctions for offences committed by primary insiders, imprisonment for five years and a fine of from BD5,000 to 10,000.[43]

These sanctions are targeted at listed companies, brokers, and market makers. But their weakness lies in the institutions that dominate the stock market. A significant number of banks and infrastructure firms are owned by the state, and this undoubtedly influences the behaviour of the market. Nevertheless, Bahrain's stock market is the only one in the Gulf that provides protection for investors, including the right to cancel trades based on inside information.[44] Another protection is provided by arbitration committees, which act when a dispute involves a criminal offence and is referred to the public prosecutor.

Market Manipulation

In Bahrain, the regulator did not define market manipulation but adopted a broad approach by prohibiting only 'irregular and suspicious' trading.[45] The manipulator can buy large blocks and influence the price.[46] Important here is the presence of rumours that sway prices and profits. Also trading activities are lower in Bahrain than in other GCC markets.[47] Trading volume on

---

[41] Al-Zumai, 'Protection of Investors', p. 149. See Article 15 of Resolution No. 4/2000: with Respect to the Establishment of a Guarantee Contribution Fund at the Bahrain Stock Exchange.

[42] Al-Zumai, 'Protection of Investors', p. 191.

[43] Article 361 of Commercial Companies Law No. 21/2001. Bahrain's Commercial Companies Act No. 2/2000 also requires those who commit insider trading to compensate the victims. These sanctions already existed in Article 14 of Decree No. 4 /1987: With Respect to the Establishment and Organization of the Bahrain Stock Exchange.

[44] Al-Zumai, 'Protection of Investors', pp. 219–21, 225.

[45] Article 7 of the Bahrain Stock Exchange Law Decree No. 4/1987.

[46] Steve Thel, '$850,000 in Six Minutes: The Mechanics of Securities Manipulation', *Cornell Law Review*, vol. 79 (1994), p. 239.

[47] Al-Zumai, 'Protection of Investors', p. 243.

23 May 2006 was BD324,671 (US$861,492) while on the Saudi market on the same day it was SR13,564,302,532 (US$3,616,954,437).[48]

Since the establishment of its stock market, Bahrain has adopted many administrative sanctions to prohibit market manipulation. In addition, several measures were taken to combat suspicious and irregular trades. Article 7 of the BSE Law (Decree Law No. 4/1987) targeted suspicious transactions and Article 5.7 of the BSE internal regulations also condemned transactions that were irregular. But there were difficulties in imposing specific penalties. Consequently, the potential for irregular transactions that affect the transparency, efficiency, and stability of the market persist and increase the risks for investors.[49] There was considerable fear of price manipulation.

Price manipulation, in particular last-minute suspicious trading, causes speculative bubbles.[50] But the lack of a direct prohibition on market manipulation makes this difficult to avert. The absence of effective sanctions, as well as the obvious difficulties in securing proof, makes action near-impossible. 'Buy back' schemes are used to manipulate the market in some GCC markets. As regulations are weak in deterring 'buy back', this hinders good governance. Moreover, brokerage firms can be a single trader or simply unsophisticated.[51] The level of education and professionalism is low and accentuated by the absence of effective sanctions against market manipulation. According to Fahad Al-Zumai, market manipulation was widespread, almost 59 per cent in Bahrain and in Kuwait, 70 per cent.

Another serious issue concerns the lack of regulatory rigour on the disclosure of interests by companies. In Bahrain in 2003, disclosure guidelines were issued to govern direct and indirect interests of more than 5 per cent.[52] The existence of proxies to undertake purchases adds to the confusion and affects investment decision-making. Coverage of disclosure in Bahrain is poor. The disciplinary board of the Bahrain Stock Market can suspend violators for a maximum of four months, but such measures are ineffective.

Another weakness concerns accounting standards. The IMF argues that there are no adequate regulations and procedures to monitor compliance by the operators and supervisors of the GCC stock exchanges.[53] Al-Zumai argues that the IMF had in its possession flawed accountancy records on

---

[48] See http://Bahrain Stock Exchange.com/bdsx/index.htm. Cited in Al-Zumai, 'Protection of Investors', p. 243.
[49] Al-Zumai, 'Protection of Investors', p. 247.
[50] Al-Zumai, 'Protection of Investors', p. 253.
[51] Al-Zumai, 'Protection of Investors', p. 278.
[52] Al-Zumai, 'Protection of Investors', pp. 291–2.
[53] International Monetary Fund, *Kingdom of Bahrain: Financial Stability Assessment, Including Reports on the Observance of Standards and Codes on the Following Topics: Banking Supervision, Insurance Supervision, Securities Regulation, and Anti Money Laundering and Combatting the Financing of Terrorism.* IMF Country Report No. 06/91, March 2006, p. 65.

Bahrain but had not included them in its report.[54] This failure is compounded by the absence of clear anti-fraud rules and precise punishments, which are in any case difficult to enforce.[55]

In Bahrain, the Bahrain Monetary Authority issued guidelines to regulate directors' rights. The register of trades by insiders (board members, senior management) is linked to the Bahrain Stock Exchange Central Depository System.[56] Article 8.3.1 of the *Guidelines on Insiders* of 2004 required those who issued stock to disclose information and reduce information asymmetry in the market. Bahrain has an obligation to confirm or deny rumours. Kuwait had introduced this obligation because of the Souk al-Manakh crisis. The international standards of the IOSCO are relevant here. In Bahrain, the adoption of foreign laws is common but investor protection is still inadequate.[57] Insider dealing and market manipulation are still prevalent. The structure of shareholding reinforced these inadequacies. The law is crucial but rigorous practice is also required.

Institutional Flaws

Gatekeepers, especially lawyers and accountants, can detect flaws but an immature regulatory framework undermines safeguards. GCC stock markets failed to develop security analysts, professional lawyers, a vigilant press, and efficient accountants. Another significant feature is political reform, although oil creates an authoritarian hold over business and the economy.[58]

Al-Zumai points to emotion and chaos in the rise of GCC stock market prices between 2000 and 2005, driven by manipulation and the creation of non-operational profits that impact on the non-institutional investor.[59] Governments in the GCC learnt from the moral hazard of speculation under the Souk al-Manakh. Companies in a frenzy for quick profits turned traders, both institutional and individual, into speculators. The absence of robust tax regimes exacerbates this greed. Institutional fragility, a cultural vacuum, and weak educational backgrounds pose serious challenges to law and reform. Modernizing the judiciary and the emergence of a shrewd investment culture could have created an effective stock market with substantial oil wealth. Bahrain's reliance on expatriates is not very effective as locals have better

---

[54] Al-Zumai, 'Protection of Investors', pp. 303–4.
[55] Al-Zumai, 'Protection of Investors', p. 322.
[56] Bahrain Monetary Authority, *Insider Guidelines*, 2004, Article 6.2.
[57] Al-Zumai, 'Protection of Investors', pp. 341–2.
[58] Ian Ayres and Jonathan R. Macey, 'Institutional and Evolutionary Failure and Economic Development in the Middle East', *Yale Journal of International Law*, vol. 30 (2005), p. 428.
[59] Al-Zumai, 'Protection of Investors', pp. 354–5.

connections and better knowledge if they receive professional training. The failure to develop a long-term strategy to advance financial expertise among locals was damaging. Local training could have led to the exploitation of Bahrain's huge oil wealth to create a sophisticated stock market not subject to volatility.[60] Historical evidence suggests that legal developments have tended to follow rather than precede economic change.[61]

The failure of Middle East stock markets to develop into vibrant institutions is striking. The Saudi market is the largest in the Middle East yet shows little sophistication. Would the integration of GCC stock exchanges help? Legal differences would pose a serious barrier. The emergence of financial centres in Dubai, Qatar, and Bahrain have achieved limited global accreditation. Bahrain is the financial hub of the Gulf. But why is Malaysia *the* global Islamic financial market? This point was discussed in Chapter 3 on Islamic finance.

The shift to state hegemony in the structure of listed corporations, in ownership concentration, in pursuit of an emphasis on state projects, in infrastructural, industrial, and urban modernization, sharpened the legal reforms and eliminated to a degree the speculative stock market seen in 1982. The special legal and cultural role of state intermediaries in the stock exchange protected the powerful banks and other institutional investors. The ability to develop market power and to incorporate the price-setting ability of stocks created economies of scope and scale. There is, in concentrated ownership, both a value-creating and price-setting power. This is not necessarily innovative and competitive, but it does achieve scale and scope, largely through the maximization of economic power by the state. Pitelis sees the firm not as a black box structure delineated by ownership criteria but as a fluid coordinating organization, sharpened by a nexus of contracts. He further sees concentrated ownership as being able to create competitive advantage and avoid speculative tactics and volatility.[62]

Listings with concentrated ownership on the Bahrain Bourse did expose contradictions that questioned the legitimacy and corporate governance of the Bourse. The dominance of the state and the state's role in legal matters is reflected in the weaknesses of default rules. These rules are burdened by mandatory requirements that undermine growth and diversification. State paternalism dictates and shapes corporate rules and this affects the freedom

---

[60] Stephen J. Choi, 'Law, Finance and Path Dependence: Developing Strong Securities Markets', *Texas Law Review*, vol. 80 (2002), p. 1698.

[61] John Coffee Jr., 'The Rise of Dispersed Ownership: The Roles of Law and the State in the Separation of Ownership and Control', *Yale Law Journal*, vol. 111 (2001), p. 7.

[62] C. N. Pitelis, *Market and Non-Market Hierarchies: Theory of Institutional Failure* (Oxford: Blackwell, 1993); Alfred D. Chandler, *Scale and Scope: Dynamics of Industrial Capitalism* (Cambridge, MA: Harvard University Press, 1990).

of contract and corporate governance in Bahrain and the GCC countries. Competition laws and capital market regulations are in the grip of the state and the business elite, mainly Shiites, although powerful Sunnis linked to the Royal family too were pervasive.[63] However, the interventionist nature of the paternalistic state did move later towards a contract-influenced market. There is a requirement that no public company can be incorporated without the consent of Bahrain's Ministry of Commerce and Industry. The Ministry can also dissolve a board of directors for taking 'pernicious' economic decisions.[64]

The large, often state-dominated oligopolists were canny operators who drew in investment from wealthy Gulf neighbours. Clusters concentrated in listed public sector institutions, the holding companies, financial institutions, banks, and elite families, dominate the stock market. This undoubtedly has important implications for debt and insolvency measures and corporate governance. Nevertheless, as illustrated in Tables 4.1, 4.2, and 4.3, there was impressive stock market growth despite misjudgements in overvaluing some stocks.

Table 4.1 Bahrain Bourse: market capitalizations as of 17 February 2019

ABC	521,749,150	BNH	42,903,000	SEEF	103,960,000
ALBH	568,000,000	CINECO	76,426,691	SICO-C	66,415,600
APMTB	77,400,000	CPARK	9,492,826	SOLID	26,400,000
ARIG	34,420,100	DUTYF	108,126,673	TAIB	116,068,211
AUB	2,433,848,466	ESTERAD	15,400,000	TAKAFUL	7,650,000
BANADER	11,704,577	FAMILY	3,240,000	TRAFCO	25,493,316
BARKA	147,598,185	GFH	353,935,465	UGH	512,088,567
BASREC	27,720,000	GHG	101,697,688	UGIC	20,000,000
BATELCO	502,286,400	INOVEST	28,083,830	UPI	5,889,675
BBK	497,558,058	INVCORP	292,552,000	ZAINBH	33,856,000
BCFC	130,680,000	ITHMR	97,120,545	Total	11,311,575,573
BFM	8,691,375	KHCB	72,450,000		
BISB	144,711,968	NASS	22,220,000		
BKIC	45,760,000	NBB	954,035,415		
BMB	17,200,000	NHOTEL	30,870,000		
BMMI	112,017,840	POLTRY	7,864,738		
BMUSC	2,696,882,653	SALAM	199,106,560		

[63] Fahad Al-Zumai, 'The Evolution of Corporate Law in the Arab World: the Everlasting Grip of the State', unpublished paper, Kuwait University, no date.
[64] Article 72 of the Bahrain Commercial Companies Law No. 21 of 2001 states this requirement. This reflects the principle that public companies are established under the political authority of the state. David L. Ratner, 'Corporations and the Constitutions', *University of San Francisco Law Review*, vo. 15 (1981); Otto Kahn-Freund, 'On Uses and Misuses of Comparative Law', *Modern Law Review*, vol. 37 (1974), pp. 1–27; Fahad Al-Zumai and Mohammed Al-Wasami, '2008 Financial Crisis and Islamic Finance: An Unrealised Opportunity', *International Journal for the Semiotics of Law*, vol. 29 (2016), pp. 455–72; Andre Oliveira Santos, 'Integrated Ownership and Control in GCC Corporate Sector', IMF Working Paper, 2015, pp. 1–24.

Table 4.2 Bahrain Bourse: financial details, 1 January 2001 to 17 February 2019

Symbol	Company	Share Turnover (per cent)	Symbol	Company	Share Turnover (per cent)
AUB	Ahli United Bank BSC	31.13	DUTYF	Bahrain Duty Free Complex	37.72
SALAM	Al Salam Bank, Bahrain BSC	143.47	BASREC	Bahrain Shipping Repairing and Engineering	5.77
AUB.N	AUB New Issuance Share	N/AP	BATELCO	Bahrain Telecommunications Company	68.27
AUB.P.T.	AUB Ordinary Converted Shares	N/AP	BMMI	BMMI BSC	48.30
AUB.R	AUB Pre-emptive Right Shares	N/AP	NASS	Nass Corporation BSC	219.41
BISB	Bahrain Islamic Bank	117.43	SEEF	Seef Properties	48.19
BBK	BBK	122.07	TRAFCO	TRAFCO Group BSC	60.17
ITHMR	Ithmaar Holding BSC	224.02	ZAINBH	Zain Bahrain BSC	8.94
KHCB	Khaleeji Commercial Bank BSC	130.39	**Services**		**56.47**
NBB	National Bank of Bahrain	13.84	ALBH	Aluminium Bahrain BSC	16.42
BSB	The Bahraini Saudi Bank	NA	BFM	Bahrain Flour Mills Company	4.42
Commercial Bank		**51.98**	BLICO	Bahrain Light Industries Company	NA
BARKA	Al Baraka Banking Group BSC	43.8	POLTRY	Delmon Poultry Company	23.75
ABC	Arab Banking Corporation	13.34	**Industrial**		**16.34**
BCFC	Bahrain Commercial Facilities Company	42.1	FAMILY	Bahrain Family Leisure	95.98
BIB	Bahrain International Bank	NA	BTC	Bahrain Tourism Company	NA
BMB	Bahrain Middle East Bank	35.50	BANADER	Banader Hotels Company BSC	27.80
SHAMEL	Bahrain Shamel Bank	NA	GHG	Gulf Hotel Group BSC	6.35

ESTERAD	Esterad Investment Company BSC	402.63	NHOTEL	National Hotels Company	4.10
GFH	GFH Financial Group BSC	92.61	**Hotels and Tourism**		**16.63**
GMG	Gulf Monetary Agency	NA	**Market (Local Public Companies only)**		**48.62**
INOVEST	Inovest BSC	227.20	TAMEER	Al Khaleej Development Company	NA
INVCORP	Investcorp Bank	19.54	SICO-C	SICO BSC (c)	44.03
TAIB	Taib Bank	49.92	UPI	United Paper Industries BSC (c)	25.58
UGB	United Gulf Bank	NA	**Closed Companies**		**42.77**
UGH	United Gulf Holding Company BSC	8.00	BMUSC	Bank Muscat	0.02
UGIC	United Gulf Investment Corporation BSC	114.17	GLOBAL	Global Investment House (Kuwait)	NA
Investment		**48.93**	IIG	International Investment Group	NA
AHLIA	Al-Ahlia Insurance Company	NA	QTEL	Qatar Telecom	NA
ARIG	Arab Insurance Group	68.44	SDTL	Sudan Telecommunications Company	NA
AIIC	Arab International Insurance Company	NA	TII	The International Investor	N/AP
BKIC	Bahrain and Kuwait Insurance Company	22.25	UFC	United Finance Company SAOG	NA
BNH	Bahrain National Holding Company	32.73	**Non-Bahraini Companies**		**0.91**
SOLID	Solidarity Bahrain BSC	0.01	AUB.PREF.A	AUB Class A Preference Share	NA
TAKAFUL	Takaful International Company	130.01	INV.PREF	Investcorp Bank EC	NA
Insurance		**49.75**	**Preferred Share**		**0.00**
CPARK	Bahrain CarPark Company	12.80	NM: Not Meaningful		
CINEMA	Bahrain Cinema Company	NA	NA: Not Available		
CINECO	Bahrain Cinema Company	0.80	N/AP: Not Applicable		

Table 4.3 Value of shares exchanged on Bahrain Stock Exchange

	1995	1996	1997	1998	1999	2000
January	5107	2939	476	11,024	8429	11,363
February	1869	3281	5065	7106	11,395	10,944
March	2015	5602	8940	13,692	8018	15,434
April	3025	4318	9293	9586	18,523	6558
May	4537	3561	9232	21837	25176	5053
June	3365	3357	11227	29218	13503	5471
July	4386	3125	12076	30628	32924	2393
August	3378	3823	17042	27517	7032	2857
September	2243	2532	22872	26128	14861	2824
October	4291	15440	33839	15204	9872	5380
November	2847	9598	13371	13012	9755	4453
December	2932	9995	28333	12346	8467	19803

Source: Bahrain Government web, Statistical Abstracts for the years 1996, 1999, and 2000, and Bahrain Stock Exchange

The tables above provide insights for understanding elite networks, alliances, and syndicates in Bahrain and challenge the Santos argument that debt concentration is maximized under state influence. My research on the Bahrain stock exchange suggests that Bahrain, as a financial hub, significantly raised monopoly profits and was not inhibited by ownership and control links on the Bourse. Even the Mumtalakat Holding Company, Bahrain's sovereign wealth fund controlled by the Central Bank of Bahrain (CBB), successfully tapped sukuk markets in Bahrain, Malaysia (dual listing sukuk for US$1 billion), and the UK. An unprecedented 30-year bond issued at US$1.25 billion later reached US$5.75 billion and was priced to produce a yield of 6 per cent.[65] Santos's thought-provoking interpretation emphasizes the problems of concentrated ownership and control in public corporations, holding companies, financial institutions, and family-owned corporations. But this is not always supported by the statistical evidence of growth and performance in Bahrain. Despite concentration, in Bahrain there are multi-divisional hierarchies within the holding companies, with powerful institutional investors to make the market more, not less, efficient and coordinate even global interaction through sukuk.[66] Concentration of ownership and control cannot

[65] CBB, *Financial Stability Report*, 2011–17; Hatim El-Tahir, 'Bahrain's Islamic Capital Markets—a Case Study', in *Islamic Capital Markets and Products: Managing Capital and Liquidity Requirements under Basel III*, edited by Simon Archer and Rifaat Ahmed Abdel Karim (Chichester: Wiley, 2018), p. 274.
[66] Annual reports and full consolidated financial statements of Mumtalakat for the years ended 31 December 2011–17, and associated notes for half-yearly financial statements for 2018.

be equated with or implicated in either incompetence or random profits and growth.

Having highlighted these issues, it is important to examine the different forms of distribution of consolidated debt and examine how the Bahrain Bourse and the GCC nations vary in their responsibility for settling debts. Large industrial and commercial groups have stakes in banks and the state and recorded the highest annual increases in market capitalization between 2002 and 2017. Market capitalization leapt by 12.9 per cent between 2014 and 2015.[67] Some financial institutions were exposed by the global crisis of 2008 and the Arab Spring of 2011 but this is analysed later in this chapter. Corporate structure and concentration can be explored in the work of David Landes and Joseph Schumpeter.[68] Hatim El-Tahir's empirically rigorous work on Bahrain's Islamic capital markets showed that concentration of ownership and control, particularly in industrial companies and the hotel and tourism sector, were no less competitive.[69]

Bahrain's financial renaissance in the period from 1970 to 2008 was impressive in commercial terms and innovation. But it was the legal structure that secured stability, notably during the 2008 Global Financial Crisis. In April 2014, the Basel Committee on Banking Supervision published a supervisory framework for measuring and controlling large exposures. In Bahrain, public sector institutions are at the centre of concentrated corporate power through holding companies, banks, and family groups, and although cross-holdings are not widespread, hierarchical structures with multiple lines of authority and control emerge.[70] Integrated ownership leads to failure in one sector affecting other sectors and in particular banks. In addition, ownership information does not always show the ultimate shareholder. In holding companies, it is difficult to determine responsibility for ownership as the records are not always available: moreover, there are often interconnected shareholdings. Foreign majority ownership is not encouraged and is subject to government approval.[71] The GCC has highly concentrated ownership, with Kuwait and Saudi Arabia having the highest concentrations. It is of course arguable that the Santos position is plausible and that there were inadequate governance procedures to regulate the divorce of ownership from control. But

---

[67] Bahrain All-Share Index, February 2011 to 2015.

[68] David Landes, *Prometheus Unbound* (New York: Cambridge University Press, 1969); Thomas K. McCraw, *Prophet of Innovation: Joseph Schumpeter and Creative Destruction* (Cambridge, MA: Harvard University Press, 2007), 251–78 and 471–4. See also Leslie Hannah, 'Strategic Games, Scale, and Efficiency, or Chandler goes to Hollywood', in *Business in Britain in the Twentieth Century: Decline and Renaissance*, edited by Richard Coopey and Peter Lyth (Oxford: Oxford University Press, 2009), p. 20.

[69] El-Tahir, 'Bahrain's Islamic Capital Markets', pp. 267–70.

[70] Santos, 'Integrated Ownership and Control in GCC Corporate Sector', p. 5.

[71] Santos, 'Integrated Ownership and Control in GCC Corporate Sector', p. 10.

Bahrain had a substantial presence of institutional investors and waves of regulatory reform to improve corporate governance and attract European and American funds. In August 2006, the CBB introduced a financial trust law to govern financial trusts. In June 2007, the Collective Investment Undertakings (CIU) Law was passed, and this further improved regulatory governance. This investment module widened the range of investment services and products available to include hedge funds and derivatives. In addition, the CBB introduced rules to govern real estate investment trusts and Private Investment Undertakings (PIU), improving the flexibility of Shari'ah-compliant investment instruments and widening the portfolios of investors. These reforms increased the pressure to invest in state infrastructural programmes, thus improving state–private sector alliances.[72]

In 2015, a corporate governance code was introduced which encouraged institutional investors to become active shareholders. In addition, a higher proportion of independent executive members was recruited to corporation boards. Public sector institutions in Bahrain, such as the Social Insurance Organization, are highly concentrated. Holding companies, such as Mumtalakat Holding in Bahrain and the National Bank of Bahrain and Kuwait Finance House, each possess concentrated hierarchical ownership and multiple lines of influence and control.[73] But Bahrain has better governance through both legal regulation and fiduciary legal discipline. At times, large shareholding concentrations inhibit the appointment of independent directors, and therefore minority shareholders are not protected. In addition, a few members have positions on different boards, making it difficult to monitor agreements or enforce compliance. This raises issues of risk tolerance and compensation systems. More serious is the lack of qualified corporate figures in Bahraini society, which weakens governance and undermines the Basel core principles for effective supervision. Public sector institutions have the highest number of ownership links, family networks, and holding companies. In Bahrain the banks, as a group, rule the Bahrain Bourse. This triggers fear of irrational exposures as losses have to be borne by the very same banks, although Bahrain has legal conventions to avert such crises.[74]

---

[72] El-Tahir, 'Bahrain's Islamic Capital Markets', p. 271.

[73] Bloomberg, Bahrain Bourse, All Share Index, March 2016. See F. Brioschi, L. Buzzacchi, and M. Colombo, 'Risk Capital Financing and the Separation of Ownership and Control in Business Groups', *Journal of Banking and Finance*, vol. 13 (1989), pp. 747–72.

[74] G. Rotundo and A. M. D'Arcangelis, 'Ownership and Control in Shareholding Networks', *Journal of Economic Interaction and Coordination*, vol. 5 (2010), pp. 191–219; Paulo F. Alves, 'The Puzzle of Corporate Control', *International Research Journal of Finance and Economics*, no. 99 (2012).

Asset Pricing: Continuities and Consequences of State Power in the Bahrain Bourse

It is important, in assessing the stock market in Bahrain, to understand how its efficiency is affected by the close relationship with Gulf neighbours and the grip of the Bahrain state on state-owned listed companies. One of the reasons for the great sustainability of listed firms is that they are state-owned and assisted by the Shiite and Sunni business elites. While there are conventional factors behind the stability of the Bourse, it is the consolidated industrial power of the state that is crucial, as with the Mumtalakat corporation. Schumpeterian creative destruction of market leaders by more dynamic new firms rarely occurred. Most of the firms were created through state and historical business lineages. The Al-Khalifah regime reserved for itself one-third of the funds derived from oil exports in the 1980s.[75] In the mid-1990's, efforts to promote private enterprise, senior Al-Khalifah sheikhs acted as silent partners in firms in diverse sectors: hotels, tourism, Gulf Air, and in the development of the harbour and related infrastructural projects. Economic liberalization through privatization further enhanced the power of the state and ruling families. However, as part of its economic liberalization programme, the Ministry of Commerce also adopted international accounting standards and all listed companies had to publish quarterly financial statements reviewed by external auditors.[76] The aim here was to attract foreign investment, which involved a move towards a more cosmopolitan, competitive business culture of listed companies, for example those involved in projects in the new industrial zone created on reclaimed land along the coast at Al-Hidd in 2005.[77]

However, the integration of the Bahrain Bourse, with the economies of the Gulf states and the international linkages that arose through listing on stock markets in Europe and the US, exposed Bahrain to the impact of the financial crisis of 2008. This is covered in detail later in this chapter. While the conventional and radical theories of Fama and Shiller are of considerable value in understanding stock markets in general, the central strategy of corporate diversification in Bahrain and abroad was facilitated by state control and the holding company Mumtalakat. The use of historical research and

---

[75] The evolution of royal family power as an invisible entrepreneur is evident throughout Bahrain's modern history. Fuad I. Khuri, *Tribe and State in Bahrain: The Transformation of Social and Political Authority in an Arab State* (Chicago, IL: Chicago University Press, 1980), p. 104.
[76] *Middle East Economic Review*, July 1997, p. 15: see also Abdulhadi Khalaf, Unfinished Business: Contentious Politics and State-Building in Bahrain, Research Report in Sociology 1, Lund University, 2000, pp. 37–9.
[77] *Gulf Daily News*, 14 November 2005; *Daily Star* (Beirut), 28 December 2005.

evidence produces a more selective, disciplined narrative of the role of quantitative indicators such as market capitalization, trading patterns, and share turnover, besides macro and micro data on ownership, managers and bureaucrats, the role of banks, and industrial firms (see Tables 4.1–4.3). It is still important to outline the theories on successful stock markets to point out the contrast with inadequately structured and managed Bahraini firms that achieved success owing to state monopolies. Perhaps their greater sustainability is achieved through the oil wealth flowing into the Bourse from the 1990s, and this continued even after the financial crisis.

Stock Market Efficiency

A stock market can be in one of three states: a fundamental state in which share prices are determined, as in the efficient markets hypothesis (EMH); a bubble or bull market state in which share prices are above their fundamental levels but rise because asset holders expect still higher prices in future; and a bear state where shares are held by irrational agents and rational agents cannot exploit the over-valuation because of short-selling constraints. This is captured in the Souk al-Manakh in Kuwait in 2008. There are also heterogeneous rational expectations that explain stock market behaviour. The fundamental state may change into a bubble or the bubble may collapse, and the market enters a bear state. The bulk of the empirical work on stock exchanges is carried out on exchanges in the West. The only exception for the Middle East is the article by Iqbal Thonase Hawaldar, Babitha Rohit, and Prakash Pinto.[78]

This study of Bahrain has sought to test the weak form of EMH for individual stocks, the randomness of individual stock prices, and the individual independence of stock price changes within a sample of 43 companies listed on the Bahrain Bourse for the period 2011–15. It is important to be cautious in appraising stock exchange securities and their floatation and price earnings ratio, as the institutional underpinnings and prospects of high capital gains for the insider group that owns the most stock is difficult to assess accurately. The majority of the companies tested were banks and these are largely state owned. The conclusions do not exhibit any rigour in identifying dramatic changes in prices, profits, or overall performance. I have, with Alaa Alabed's

[78] Iqbal Thonase Hawaldar, Babitha Rohit, and Prakash Pinto, 'Testing of Weak Form of Efficient Market Hypothesis: Evidence from the Bahrain Bourse', *Investment Management and Financial Innovations*, vol. 14, 2 (2017), pp. 376–85.

assistance, produced a set of tables on market capitalization, trading patterns, and performance for important years from the 1990s to the present.[79] One of the main reasons for the sustainability of the Bahrain Bourse may be the role of the institutional investor. Personal ownership is perhaps more fickle and more prone to financing problems. Therefore, the influence of the state through institutional investors may secure greater stability.

However, analysis of the Bahrain stock market from empirical sources, and emphasizing its position as an Islamic financial hub, concludes with a rejection of the weak market hypothesis. Rather, it is crucial to emphasize the role of the institutional investor and to focus on the impact of oil wealth on the finances of the stock exchange, stock options, exchange securities, and restructuring in global financial markets, as well as the impact of the 2008 financial crisis. It is also important to explore the impact of the Arab Spring, and to understand how selective qualitative and quantitative features disciplined the grip of the Al-Khalifah family and the business elites. The corporate governance techniques responsible for the stock exchange's sustainability were further developed by the state's growing global ambitions. From the analysis presented in this book we may conclude that much of Bahrain's success is explained by the social and legal structure. Its economy and much of its regulation was outward-looking. It is an international Islamic financial centre and yet the dominant shareholder in the stock exchange is the state, along with its long-rooted capitalist networks who brought power and hierarchy into its governance. It is also a stock exchange with companies from the wealthy Gulf states and Western firms seeking a share in oil wealth. Therefore, the concentrated shareholding and successful performance has to be examined beyond company and securities law and fair commercial activity. What is crucial is the employment of particular financial instruments and their individual efficacy.

Stock Market Financial Instruments and Governance of Dominant Corporate Groups

The aim in this section is to examine the institutional investors, including their levels of concentration, their control, and their institutions: investment

---

[79] Tables 4.1–4.3, the source is Bahrain Bourse data 2001–18; researched and collected by Alaa Alabed in Bahrain: tables on market capitalization, share turnovers and on trading patterns (the last from the late 1980s).

funds, pension funds, mutual funds, state and sovereign wealth bonds such as Mumtalakat, and the private investors.[80]

The diverse stock options and the generous proportions permitted within their clustering are shown in the statistics for 2015. In that year there were 44 listed companies, with a market capitalization of US$17,152 million. Bahrain attracted a high ratio of intra-regional flows of investment, 12 per cent compared to Kuwait's 10 per cent, the UAE 27 per cent, and Saudi Arabia 7 per cent.[81] Sovereign investors in Bahrain accounted for 49 per cent of total investors, while for Saudi Arabia the figure was 45 per cent and for the UAE, a remarkable 75 per cent. Banks retained a dominant position. Non-financial institutions accounted for an insignificant amount of total investment. In general, investment accruing from insurance companies in Bahrain was higher than in the stock markets of Kuwait, Saudi Arabia, and the UAE throughout the 1990s through to 2017.[82]

Bahrain has a low level of investment originating from mutual funds, despite its impressive range of domestic mutual funds. Perhaps new entrants were locked out by regulations relating to the listing of mutuals on the Bourse.[83] Although the Bahrain Bourse took an impressive share of investment from the Gulf states, the volume from the West was low. The Bahrain Bourse attracted a mere 1 per cent while Saudi Arabia attracted 14 per cent, Kuwait 1 per cent, and the UAE 4 per cent.[84] The low figure for Bahrain was possibly related to its size, a small island economy with declining oil reserves. Other factors such as weak corporate governance, a lack of sufficient liquidity, and above all limited diversity in financial instruments also explains the low inward investment. A large proportion of shares on the Bahrain exchange are rarely traded and this encourages speculative trading by retail investors and therefore trading instability.[85] Regional investments flowing into Bahrain remained significant, amounting to 12 per cent of funding on the Bourse, compared to Saudi Arabia attracting 20 per cent, the UAE 5 per cent, and

[80] 'What Role for Institutional Investors in Corporate Governance in the Middle East and North Africa?', report issued by GOVERN, the Economic and Corporate Governance Centre, in joint collaboration with Bogazici University, Centre for Research in Corporate Governance and Financial Regulation, coordinated by Alissa Amico, Vedat Akgiray, and Zeynep Ozcelik, October 2016. The sources are Thomson Reuters, Datastream and stock exchange and company websites.

[81] Central Bank of Bahrain Rulebook, vol. 2, Islamic Banks, Thomson Reuters, 2015.

[82] Central Bank of Bahrain, Bahrain All-Share Index, February 2011–June 2015; Central Bank of Bahrain, Financial Stability Report, August 2017. Important data sources are the Bahrain Financial Exchange and Deloitte Research and Analysis, 2017.

[83] GOVERN, 'What Role for Institutional Investors?', p. 26.

[84] GOVERN, 'What Role for Institutional Investors?'.

[85] Bahrain's government owned Mumtalakat sovereign fund, established in 2006, signed a memorandum of understanding with the Russian Direct Investment Fund in 2011. Central Bank of Bahrain Rulebook, vol. 2, Islamic Banks, Thomson Reuters, 2015; Zawya, MENA Mutual Funds Quarterly Bulletin, 2012; Central Bank of Bahrain, BR-CBB, Rulebook on Islamic Banks, July 2021.

Kuwait 10 per cent. Bahrain was playing a major role in processing and exporting oil for Saudi Arabia and Kuwait. This relationship proved innovative and led to the successful listing of Bahrain firms in Ireland, the UK, and the US.[86]

The Bourse's performance and sustainability were secured by many features of the institutional investors within large state enterprises.[87] The institutional investors held substantial stakes and proved more resilient, despite occasional below par performances, as with Gulf Air. Institutional ownership and the choice of income growth strategy in non-financial companies was relatively impressive.[88]

Institutional ownership has an important influence on stock value, performance, incentives, strategic decisions, social responsibility, and governance mechanisms.[89] Bahrain's market is characterized by a high ownership concentration. On average, 45 per cent of shares in non-financial listed companies are in the hands of institutional investors. In addition, 45 per cent of non-financial listed companies are controlled by large block holders. These powerful elite entrepreneurs dominate as institutional investors. In its early stages, such entrepreneurial concentration delivered significant economies of scale and attracted foreign businesses. Foreign business was keen to negotiate through modern corporate structures in Bahrain, and in this way creative initiatives were sustained. Bahrain's non-financial listed companies, by employing international linkages, and through officially adopted International Financial Reporting Standards (IFRS) retained sustainability. Thus, while political pressure on the non-financial companies was intense, creating a degree of fragility, they also benefited from the inclusion of public and private corporations within their clusters. Aggregate growth and the sustainability of the non-financial listed companies in the face of the 2008 financial crisis, as well as the inevitable volatility arising from the Arab Spring, are captured in the tables on market capitalization, trade frequency, and share turnover (Tables 4.1–4.3). Their strength came from the commitment of the state to provide financing and professional management, as revealed in Mumtalakat. Institutional investors could rely on government intervention.

---

[86] Central Bank of Bahrain Rulebook, vol. 2, Islamic Banks, Thomson Reuters, 2015.

[87] See Listed Companies on Bahrain Bourse 2018.

[88] Yarob Kullab and Chen Yan Dongbei, 'The Impact of Institutional Ownership on Income Accounting Strategy: Evidence from Bahrain', *Academy of Accounting and Financial Studies Journal*, vol. 22, no. 1 (2018), pp. 1–17.

[89] Won Yong Oh, Young Kyun Chang, and Aleksey Martynov, 'The Effect of Ownership Structure on Corporate Social Responsibility: Empirical Evidence from Korea', *Journal of Business Ethics*, 104 (2011), pp. 283–97; M. Jensen and W. Meckling, 'Theory of the Firm: Managerial Behavior, Agency Costs and Ownership Structure', *Journal of Financial Economics*, vol. 4, no. 3 (1976), pp. 305–60.

The list below shows the corporations with institutional investors, of both industrial and non-financial listed companies, and their presence in major industries.

Zain Bahrain Bahrain Share-Holding Company (BSC)
Bahrain Tourism Company
BMMI BSC
Gulf Hotel Group BSC
Al-Matahin Company BSC
Bahrain Cinema Co. BSC
Bahrain Car Parks Company BSC
Bahrain Duty Free Shop Complex BSC
Bahrain Ship Repairing and Engineering Company BSC
Delmont Poultry Company BSC
Trafco Group BSC
National Hotels Company BSC
Aluminium Bahrain BSC
NASS Corporation
SEEF Properties BSC
Bahrain Telecommunications Company BSC
Bahrain Family Leisure Company BSC

While concentrated ownership does allow management to adopt accounting methods that protect their own interests, membership of IFRS would restrain such manipulation.[90] Bahrain has capitalist elites that attract institutional investors. It also has strong growth and seeks global competitiveness. However, non-financial listed companies do not disclose information regarding debt contracts, and therefore accountants use leverage as a proxy and concentrate on an income-increasing strategy. The benefit from tax exemptions is not an issue in Bahrain as local companies are not subject to tax.[91] In addition to this advantage, non-financial companies listed on the BSE operate in a monopolistic market along with state-owned listed banks. However, the listed banks produce substantial accounting information within a three-pronged strategy: disclosure of the financing in each initiative, performance, and management. This is financing that is pro-business, with the emphasis on the state's infrastructural drive and ambition. Therefore, state-dominated stock exchange and securities trading in Bahrain and successful growth pose

---

[90] Omar Juhmani, 'Corporate Governance and the Level of Bahraini Corporate Compliance with IFRS Disclosure', *Journal of Applied Accounting Research*, vol. 18, no. 1 (2017), pp. 22–41.
[91] Bahrain Economic Development Board, *Islamic Finance Report*, 2015, p. 73.

serious challenges to Michael Porter's model of the competitive advantage of nations.[92]

Institutional investors influence business organizations. They process information and can efficiently manage owners and directors as necessary. In Bahrain, institutional investors reduce agency costs compared to dispersed ownership, as in the USA.[93] Of course, managerial greed does exist in Bahrain, with ambitions for profit growth and corporate expansion, despite the concentrated institutional ownership. Fifty per cent of Bahrain's non-financial listed companies are owned by institutional investors. Consequently, minority investors are muted on the Bahrain Bourse. Small investors are not particularly active and often simply follow the state's predicted path. The Bahrain Government adopts expansionary economic policies, reducing the pressures on management. Concentrated ownership is closely connected to politicians, more so than with dispersed ownership.[94]

Stock Market Investment Patterns, Risks, Mispricing of Assets, and Volatility

The writings of Eugene Fama, Lars Peter Hansen, and Robert Shiller have helped us to understand asset prices. Shiller places behaviour biases, market frictions, and mispricing centre stage in the appraisal of asset pricing.[95] Understanding asset prices is important as risks, returns, and prices are indicative of investment decisions and may predict potential bubbles and crashes. The relationship between risk and asset prices has led to distinctive approaches to pricing, ranging from rational investor assumptions to behavioural finance, which emphasizes behavioural biases, market instability, and direct mispricing. There are also institutional complications with diverse investors and psychological distortions. Notable in Bahrain is state dominance and its intersection with business elites, involving an inordinate degree of secrecy. Even after the Commercial Companies Law of 2001

[92] Michael Porter, 'Capital Disadvantage: America's Failing Capital Investment System', *Harvard Business Review*, vol. 70, no. 5 (1992), pp. 65–82.

[93] Andrei Shleifer and Robert W. Vishny, 'A Survey of Corporate Governance', *Journal of Finance*, vol. 52, no. 2 (1997), pp. 737–83.

[94] Randall Morck, 'On the Economics of Concentrated Ownership', *Canadian Business Law Journal*, vol. 26 (1996), pp. 63–75. For the Bahrain Bourse market, see http://www.bahrain bourse.com and OSIRIS database on financial information; company annual reports. Non-financial listed companies were dominant in industry, hotels, tourism, services, and telecommunications in 2013–18, as there had been substantial growth and diversification of non-financial companies between 2000 and 2013.

[95] Eugene F. Farma, 'Efficient Capital Markets: A Review of Theory and Empirical Work', *Journal of Finance*, vol. 25, no. 2 (1970), pp. 383–417; Eugene Farma, Lars Peter Hansen, and Robert Shiller, 'Empirical Asset Pricing', *Scandinavian Journal of Economics*, vol. 116, no. 3 (2014).

(and subsequent amendments of 2014, 2015, and 2018) required publication of corporate details, listing was still cloaked in secrecy. Bahrain's state dominance did push rational investors to take advantage of arbitrage opportunities, and behavioural elements with arbitrage may result in stochastic features. In addition, strong information may lead irrational investors to put their trust in state protection, as when, for example, action by Mumtalakat Corporation may lead to imitative betting on asset prices. There is also short-term predictability because of changes in oil prices. Unpredicted liquidity may lead to large-sector trading and therefore short-term price pressure. But overall, as the majority of shares were held by the state, investors lacked the power to influence the market.

In a 1979 paper, Shiller found evidence of excess volatility in government bonds in the US. In contrast in Bahrain, government bonds were stable except if they were in listed firms in overseas markets, for example in Ireland or London. In 1981, Shiller argued that excess volatility may be a product of fads and fashions. Such psychological behaviour leads to asset pricing anomalies, overreaction to information, overconfidence, or to bounded rationality, each creating excess volatility, momentum, and psychological evidence, as in Prospect Theory.[96]

A related issue is the Capital Asset Pricing Model (CAPM) of William Sharpe. This asserts that assets correlate more strongly with the market and this involves risk that requires a higher return in compensation. Fama showed that adding a stock market value and its ratio of book value to market value greatly improves the understanding of the CAPM. Individuals are subject to biases, and notably so on the Bahrain stock market with its various cultural and nepotistic biases. Psychological biases are reinforced by social movements because investors are subject to group psychology and peer pressure. Fads and fashions contributed to market booms and busts.[97] The Kahneman and Tversky 1979 Prospect Theory and the Thaler 1985 Mental Accounting are psychology-based responses. Overconfidence or bounded rationality leads to excess volatility and therefore reversion in asset prices.[98] In Bahrain

[96] Daniel Kahneman and Richard H. Thaler, 'Anomalies, Utility Maximization and Experienced Utility', *Journal of Economic Perspectives*, vol. 20, no. 1 (2006), pp. 221–34; Daniel Kahneman and Amos Tversky (ed.), *Choices, Values, and Frames* (Cambridge: Cambridge University Press, 2000).

[97] Robert J. Shiller, 'Investor Behavior in the 1987 Stock Market Crash: Survey Evidence', NBER Working Paper No. 2446; Robert J. Shiller and J. Pound, 'Survey Evidence on Diffusion of Interest and Information among Investors', *Journal of Economic Behavior and Organization*, vol. 12 (1989), pp. 47–66.

[98] Daniel Kahneman and Amos Tversky, 'Prospect Theory: An Analysis of Decision under Risk', *Econometrica*, vol. 47 (1979), pp. 263–92. R. H. Thaler, 'Mental Accounting and Consumer choice', *Marketing Science*, vol. 4 (1985), pp. 199–214; Nicholas Barberis, Ming Huang, and Tano Santos, 'Prospect Theory and Asset Prices', *Quarterly Journal of Economics*, vol. 116 (2001), pp. 1–53; M. M. Carhart, 'On Persistence of Mutual Fund Performance', *Journal of Finance*, vol. 52 no. 1 (1997), pp. 57–82; J. H. Cochrane, 'The Dog That Did Not Bark: A Defense of Return Predictability', *Review of Financial Studies*, vol. 21 (2007),

there are different forms of saving and investing as distinct institutions and psychological biases occur within Islamic finance and conventional finance, as a result of changing oil prices, from the impact of global financial crises (as in 2008), and from unpredictable inward flows of foreign direct investment.

Shiller's argument was that stock prices are particularly vulnerable to psychological biases, because of uncertainty in the true valuation of a stock. Opinions flow through people, and stock markets react to fads and fashions. Another point made by Shiller concerns ordinary investors who respond to expected returns and smart money investors who respond to rationally expected returns but are limited by wealth. Consequently, the former will create temporary deviations of stock prices from their fundamental value, leading to overreactions to dividend news and excess volatility. Shiller emphasized the importance of social psychology using evidence from investor surveys.[99] Case and Shiller elaborated further on fads and bubbles to housing markets. Black and Scholes, and Xiong and Yu document a bubble in the pricing of Chinese warrants in the late 2000s, which revealed trading far above their fundamental value. They argued that short sales constraints prevented the mispricing from being arbitraged away.[100]

A number of studies have focused on liquidity and its impact on asset pricing. In these models, investors demand an additional risk premium for holding illiquid assets that cannot be easily sold when investors need liquidity. Models based on financial frictions and liquidity had been shown to have explanatory power during the 2008 financial crisis.[101] Jensen's analysis of the performance of mutual funds suggests similarities with mutual funds in Bahrain.[102] Jensen evaluated mutual fund performance and found that the majority of funds did not generate any excess risk-adjusted returns. Subsequent studies of mutual fund performance have failed to find positive excess performance but, rather, negative excess performance. Fama and French have shown that only the extreme tails of active mutual funds generate significant

pp. 1533–75; E. F. Fama and K. R. French, 'Luck Versus Skill in the Cross Section of Mutual Fund Returns', *Journal of Finance*, vol. 65, no. 5 (2010), pp. 1915–19.

[99] Robert J. Shiller, 'The Use of Volatility Measures in Assessing Market Efficiency', *Journal of Finance*, vol. 36, no. 2 (1981), pp. 291–304; Robert J. Shiller, 'Stock Prices and Social Dynamics', Carnegie Rochester Conference Series on Public Policy, 1984, pp. 457–510; Shiller, 'Investor Behavior in the 1987 Stock Market Crash'; Shiller and Pound, 'Survey Evidence on Diffusion of Interest and Information among Investors'.

[100] F. Black and M. Scholes, 'The Pricing of Options and Corporate Liabilities', *Journal of Political Economy*, vol. 81 (1973), pp. 637–54; Wei Xiong and Jialin Yu, 'The Chinese Warrants Bubble', *American Economic Review*, 101 (2011), pp. 272-3-53.

[101] Markus Brunnermeier, 'Deciphering the Liquidity and Credit Crunch of 2007–2008', *Journal of Economic Perspectives*, vol. 23, no. 1 (2009), pp. 77–100; Markus Brunnermeier and L. H. Pedersen, 'Market Liquidity and Funding Liquidity', *Review of Financial Studies*, vol. 22, no. 6 (2009), pp. 2201–38.

[102] M. C. Jensen, 'The Performance of Mutual Funds in the Period 1945–64', *Journal of Finance*, vol. 23, no. 2 (1968), pp. 389–416.

negative and positive returns respectively, and that in fact the aggregate port-folio of active mutual funds is close to the market portfolio.[103] This means that the sector as a whole gives negative excess returns to investors.[104] Another important stock in the stock market infrastructure is the Real Estate Invest-ment Trust (REIT). In Bahrain this investment trust is popular, including Shari'ah REITs.

Real Estate Investment Trusts: A Shari'ah-led Collective Investment

REITs are listed stocks in real estate properties, that is, shares in prop-erty companies. Investopedia lists five kinds of REITs: retail, residential, healthcare, office, and mortgage REITs. The investment may be of a mixed character or specialized in a particular asset market. Islamic REITs filter for Shari'ah compliancy through their appraisal of tenants and rentals, and cer-tainly avoid restaurants serving alcohol. Property insurance has to be takaful, although conventional insurance is permitted in the absence of a takaful cover. Another approach used by the REIT is sale and leaseback under an Ijarah contract. This provides a REIT with a stable income and reduces risk arising from the acquisition of different tenancies. Shari'ah conformity is also achieved by using sukuk al-ijarah (Islamic securitization based on a lease) or sukuk al-murabahah (a sale with a mark-up profit). The rate of return would depend on earnings and operating expenses.[105]

In 2015, new listing rules were introduced for REITs listed on the Bahrain Bourse. The requirement was a minimum of two properties, with a combined value of at least US$20 million. Also, the CBB authorizes and regulates REITs before they are listed. Another regulation was that the dividend payout of a REIT had to be at least 90 per cent of its net realized income. Eskan Bank appointed SICO as lead manager for its first REIT listed on the Bourse: it was Shari'ah compliant with a total value of BD20 million and was offered to the public through an IPO.[106] Eskan Bank's properties included Segaya Plaza in Segaya and Danaat Al Madina in Isa Town. REITs provide investment in real

---

[103] Fama and French, 'Luck versus Skill', pp. 1915–47.

[104] Carhart, 'On Persistence of Mutual Fund Performance', pp. 57–82.

[105] Simon Archer and Brandon Davies, 'Islamic Collective Investment Schemes', in *Islamic Capital Markets and Products: Managing Capital and Liquidity Requirements under Basel III*, edited by Simon Archer and Rifaat Ahmed Abdel Karim (Chichester: Wiley, 2018), pp. 75–6.

[106] SICO is a leading regional asset manager, broker, and investment bank and is controlled by the CBB. It also has international operations.

estate, regular income, and diversification, while increasing liquidity in their portfolios.[107]

An interesting comparison is with Malaysia, where REIT investments are in properties related to healthcare, in plantations, and in a shopping complex at Petronas Twin Towers.[108] Malaysia has a total of 16 listed REITs, three of which are Shari'ah compliant because of constraints on rental income and on investment in pubs and restaurants selling alcohol. In 2017, Islamic REITS accounted for 42 per cent of total listed REITs by market capitalization. The next section examines the central role of banks and financial institutions on the Bahrain Bourse.

The Role of Banks in the Stock Market

Large-scale commercial banks and investment banks assumed a dominant position on the Bahrain stock exchange, assisted by their involvement in the large state infrastructural, industrial, and services sectors since the 1990s. The ambition of the banks to be powerful investors on Bahrain's stock exchange was driven by their exploitation of oil revenues. Between 1997 and 2012, Bahrain's oil revenues averaged 22 per cent of GDP, much of it imported from other Gulf states to be processed.[109] A further feature in the acceleration in the banks' growth was that it was intra-regional. In the 1970s, Bahrain had invited international banks to establish offshore banking units to attract oil revenues from oil-wealthy Gulf neighbours, thereby establishing Bahrain's reputation as the financial hub of the Gulf. These offshore units rose to 77 within 10 years.[110] The Chandlerian concept of personal capitalism with individualistic traits does not permeate these dense business networks. The Middle East, with tribal loyalties and strongly embedded regional loyalties, has also evolved powerful and cohesive traits in individual sectors within their own state, and hence they were not 'espousing virtues of district wide governance derived from deep implantation of actors in robust regional socio-cultural structures'.[111]

---

[107] El-Tahir, 'Bahrain's Islamic Capital Markets', p. 273.

[108] Obiyathulla Ismath Bacha and Daud Vicary Abdullah, 'Malaysia's Islamic Capital Markets—a Case Study', in *Islamic Capital Markets and Products: Managing Capital and Liquidity Requirements under Basel III*, edited by Simon Archer and Rifaat Ahmed Abdel Karim (Chichester: Wiley, 2018), p. 250.

[109] Hoda Selim and Chahir Zaki, 'Business Cycle Synchronization in the Arab Region: Recycling Petrodollars through Trade Finance and Remittances', August 2015, http://fesp-eg.org, pp. 334–49.

[110] William Bean, 'The Contemporary Financial Development of Kuwait and Bahrain: A Study of Contrasts', PhD thesis, Princeton University, 1988, pp. 84–140; A. S. Gerakis and O. Roncesvalles, 'Bahrain's Offshore Banking Center', *Economic Development and Cultural Change*, vol. 31, no. 2 (1983).

[111] Bean, 'The Contemporary Financial Development', pp. 84–140. This is reminiscent of Kahneman, *Thinking Fast and Slow*.

As Febvre argued, 'reconstituting the emotional life [la vie affective] of a given era is a task that is both extremely seductive and terribly difficult but one that a historian has no right to desert'.[112] Bahrain had learnt a severe lesson with the Souk crisis in Kuwait in 1982, and increased legal constraints to reduce speculative behaviour. This was accompanied by the growth of sophisticated financial instruments, involving diverse aspects of Islamic finance that included sukuk. While establishing the Liquidity Management Centre in 2002 to check excess liquidity and inflation, Bahrain was using the stock exchange and listed banks to promote high-growth industries, involving multinational cooperation. These listed banks were involved in funding technology-intensive projects such as the Hidd power project, requiring US$55 million within a funding tranche of US$300 million. Aluminium Bahrain held an investment of US$250 million as part of a US$1.55 billion expansion funding facility. First Islamic Investment Bank completed a UK direct equity deal with the acquisition of a 33 per cent stake in Beaufort Wind, in cooperation with the BSEC Investment Bank of Lebanon, and launched its first auto-backed sukuk.[113]

These measures were also to avert speculative behaviour in stocks. Since the Kuwait Souk crisis of 1982, Bahrain has been vigilant against speculative frenzy. After the failure of its US$100 billion real estate venture, IPO was converted into Gulf Medical. Speculators floated US$55 billion in post-dated cheques and this led to the collapse, with severe repercussions for Bahrain, which now became far more cautious. The presence of banks and funding on the Bahrain Bourse rose.[114] The increased inflow of FDI, from US$0.2 billion in 2003 to US$1.1 billion in 2006, was evidence of the increased stimulus from the CBB, encouraging Bahrain banks to engage in collaborative projects with multinationals.[115]

A Felix Rioja and Neven Valev study of stock markets and banks as sources of capital accumulation illustrates how banks not only secure capital but also overcome transaction costs and informational asymmetries to reduce liquidity constraints and improve the allocation of capital, thereby achieving greater

---

[112] Lucian Febvre, 'La sensibilite et l'histoire: comment reconstituer la vie affective d'autrefois?', *Annales d'histoire sociale*, vol. 3 (1941), p. 21.
[113] Bahrain Centre for Islamic Banking Report, 2005.
[114] Ross M. K. Kaiser and N. Mazaheri, 'The Resource Curse in MENA: Political Transitions, Resource Wealth, Economic Shocks and Conflict Risk', World Bank Policy Research Working Paper No. 5742, Washington, DC, 2011.
[115] Central Bank of Bahrain, Annual Reports, 2002–08.

productivity growth.[116] Beck and Levine also illustrate the role of banks in securing economic growth.[117]

On the Bahrain stock market, it is possible to measure changes in market capitalization. But perhaps more importantly, turnover measures the value of shares traded and thus illustrates how active or liquid the stock market is in relation to its size. Values traded are also measured as a percentage of Bahrain's GDP. Stock market capitalization was 54.4 per cent of GDP in 2012. Another useful measure is that of loans to government and state enterprises as a percentage of GDP, which was 20.7 per cent in 2012. International debt issue was 32.7 per cent of GDP, and private credit by financial institutions and intermediaries was 97.6 per cent of GDP, both in 2012.[118] The international debt issues include long-term bonds and notes as well as money market instruments placed on international markets. Private credit to financial institutions also includes private credit to banks.

Bahrain's stock market is the largest in the GCC by capitalization, where Saudi Arabia is 48.4 per cent and the UAE is 18.4 per cent. Bahrain is also the largest within the GCC in terms of the value of international debt issues relative to GDP, with the UAE at 28.1 per cent. Saudi Arabia does not publish this data, perhaps because of its transfers to groups in Sudan, Iraq, and Syria, and to Malaysia under Najib. Another interesting feature is that private credit by financial institutions in Saudi Arabia is dramatically less than in Bahrain at 46.5 per cent.

Bahrain's market capitalization can be disaggregated into industrial stocks, which experienced an increase in 2014–15 of 12.9 per cent, followed by hotels and tourism, 7.7 per cent, and services, 5.2 per cent.[119] The role of the banks on the stock market is clear, as well as Bahrain's adaptation to globalization. From 1990 to 2014, GDP growth against stock market indicators, such as size, liquidity, the All Share Index, turnover, and market capitalization, is impressive. Bahrain, lacking oil, had made efforts to diversify the economy. It focused on the financial sector and securities markets. As the financial hub of the Gulf, it increased investment, stabilized and mobilized savings, allocated resources, diversified risk, and increased the savings ratio. That financial mobilization enabled stock markets to borrow at lower cost.

---

[116] Felix Rioja and Neven Valev, 'Stock Markets, Banks and the Sources of Economic Growth in Low and High Income Countries', *Journal of Economic Finance*, vol. 38 (2014), pp. 302–20.

[117] Thorsten Beck and Ross Levine, 'Stock Markets, Banks, and Growth: Panel Evidence', *National Bureau of Economic Research*, 2004; also *Journal of Banking and Finance*, vol. 28, no. 3 (2004).

[118] World Bank, Global Financial Development Database.

[119] Central Bank of Bahrain, *Financial Stability Report*, August 2015; Batool K. Asiri and Mohamed A. Abdalla, 'Economic Growth and Stock Market Development in Bahrain', *Journal of Applied Finance and Banking*, vol. 5, no. 2 (2015), pp. 67–80.

By 2014, Bahrain had 400 licensed financial institutions.[120] Currently finance contributes 16.7 per cent of GDP and the sector's employees are 60 per cent Bahrainis. The number of listed companies rose from 29 in 1989 to 47 in 2014. The total assets of the Bourse increased to BD (Bahrain Dinar) 9,397,052 in 2013, from BD8,961,272 in 2012: liabilities were BD969,517, compared to BD1,205,617 in 2012. In addition, shareholder equity rose from BD7,755,655 in 2012 to BD8,427,535 in 2013. The Bahrain All Share Index increased by 17.2 per cent in 2013. The value of shares traded increased by 104.88 per cent in 2013, as against the value in 2012. The volume of shares traded rose by 197.55 per cent and the number of transactions increased by 39.62 per cent.[121]

Particularly important to the stable growth is the increase in the banks' trading value on the stock exchange. In 2012–13, the commercial banks captured 68.01 per cent of total trading value, followed by the investment sector with 14.13 per cent. The services sector accounted for 8.7 per cent, the industrial sector only 2.47 per cent, the insurance sector 0.34 per cent, and finally the hotels and tourism sector just 0.14 per cent.[122] Crucial in this impressive growth was the state and oil wealth inflows. The market capitalization of Bahrain's public holding companies increased from BD5.86 billion at the beginning of the year to BD6.96 billion at the end, an increase of 18.91 per cent. By June 2015, a different picture had emerged. The industrial sector recorded an increase in market capitalization to 12.9 per cent, followed by hotels and tourism, 7.7 per cent, and services at 5.2 per cent.[123]

There are three indices in the Bahrain Stock Exchange: the Bahrain All Share Index, the Dow Jones Bahrain Index, and the Estirad Index. Foreign investors enjoy the same rights as domestic investors, and even have the right to vote on important decisions for their company. They are also permitted not to be taxed on dividends. They can buy and sell their own properties and bonds, units of mutual funds, and warrants of domestic joint stock companies on the Bahrain Stock Exchange. Trading is carried out through 14 securities brokers active in daily trading. The Central Bank's Capital Market Supervision Directorate supervises and regulates primary and secondary markets. In 2006, the Central Bank of Bahrain and Financial Institutions Law was

---

[120] Central Bank of Bahrain, *Financial Stability Report*, 2014.
[121] Central Bank of Bahrain, *Financial Stability Report*, 2012; Bahrain Bourse website; Bahrain Bourse Profile and Bahrain Bourse Publications; Bahrain Economic Development Board, *Islamic Finance Report*, 2015.
[122] Central Bank of Bahrain *Financial Stability Report*, 2011–15.
[123] El-Tahir, 'Bahrain's Islamic Capital Markets', pp. 267–9. See Asiri and Abdalla, 'Economic Growth and Stock Market Development in Bahrain', pp. 67–80; Hisham Handal Abdelbaki, 'Causality Relationship between Macroeconomic Variables and Stock Market Development: Evidence from Bahrain', *International Journal of Business and Finance Research*, vol. 7, no. 1 (2013), pp. 69–78.

introduced. The Capital Markets rule book has market-disclosure regulations and provides transparency in capital market transactions. Activity on the BSE is measured by total value traded relative to GDP. This reflects the value of stock transactions relative to economic activity. The value-traded ratio of the BSE declined from 9.33 in 1998 to 2.18 in 2001, then increased, reaching 8.77 in 2006 but then declined again in 2007 to 5.8. The global crisis in 2008 affected FDI and Sovereign Wealth Funds.[124] Market capitalization decreased from BD10,185 million in 2007 to BD7,520 million in 2008, and then to BD6,131 million in 2009. The number of listed companies declined from 51 in 2008 to 48 in 2009. The value of shares traded declined from BD787.3 million in 2008 to BD178.4 million in 2009. The turnover ratio declined from 10 per cent in 2008 to 2.9 per cent in 2009.[125]

As argued earlier, one of the long-term characteristics of the corporations listed on the stock market is the concentration in ownership and control. Here I add statistics to reinforce the nature and level of concentration. Although the Bahrain Bourse ruled that the largest shareholder should not hold more than 20 per cent of the shares in a firm, just 58 per cent of firms adhered to this regulation. Thus 42 per cent of listed firms were dominated by a single owner. Moreover, the Board of Directors was restricted to between 7 and 13 members. However, the independence of the directors was often compromised by an inability to recruit sufficient professional managers and members of boards of high quality. Their connections rather than their talent dictated their appointment. This was further complicated by the creation of two posts, of Chairman and Chief Executive. Nevertheless, at least 50 per cent of firms had independent directors.[126]

It appears that dependent board members had knowledge and commitment, while independent directors had less, and this weakens performance.[127] Mubarak and Hamdan found poorer governance in large corporations, compared to small companies. But the difference is marginal. In terms of financial leverage and corporate governance, there is an absence of firm control by creditors over companies in Bahrain, as lending appears

[124] Abdelbaki, 'Causality Relationship between Macroeconomic Variables and Stock Market Development'.

[125] Central Bank of Bahrain, *Annual Trading Bulletin*, various issues. GDP, the investment rate, savings rate, credit to private investors, per capita income, M2, and GDP inflators are each from *Annual Trading Bulletin*, numbers 1, 18, 25. Data on Bahrain Stock Exchange are from *Annual Trading Bulletin* and CBB economic indicators. FDI data from *World Investment Report*, 2006, 2007, 2008, 2009, and from United Nations, *Foreign Direct Investment Report*, 2008. *Source: Annual Trading Bulletin*, stock market, various years, 1998–2008. Muneer Mohamed Saeed Al-Mubarak and Allam Mohammed Mousa Hamdan, 'The Impact of Corporate Governance on Market Capitalization: Evidence from Bahrain Bourse', *Corporate Ownership and Control Journal*, vol. 13, no. 3 (2016), pp. 121–30.

[126] Al-Mubarak and Hamdan, 'The Impact of Corporate Governance', p. 125.

[127] Al-Mubarak and Hamdan, 'The Impact of Corporate Governance', p. 126.

to be free of restraint. Perhaps this is because lenders are not familiar with governance issues, or perhaps because the state and the banks are the main lenders. Also, in Bahrain more than 50 per cent of shares are in the hands of three shareholders who thus dominate the market. Does that concentration secure strong commercial performance? This study indicates a positive relationship between ownership and the market performance of a firm, although the quantitative data is often thin and the time span for analysis is short. In addition, voluntary mergers were used as a less stressful form of growth and even survival. There were few competitors. The next significant issue concerns sukuk bonds, their multiple Shari'ah structures, and their global economic diversification.

Sukuk: Seeking Aggressive Market Growth through Shari'ah Standardization and Overseas Listings: Comparative Modelling in Bahrain and Malaysia

There are several aspects of sukuk that differentiate them from conventional bonds. The most important is that sukuk should not provide guaranteed returns. Investors must not expect the return of principal plus dividends/profit without incurring risk of loss. In essence, sukuk are asset based, and therefore structured to resemble the risk and payment profile of a conventional bond. The most common way of making this possible is to include a purchase undertaking requiring the originator to buy back the sukuk assets upon default or maturity of the notes. Investors are compensated in full. A so-called true sale has not taken place, for that would be contrary to Islamic commercial principles. There is no such thing as a beneficial sale in Islamic law, unlike in English law where a sale is outright, immediate, and allows the buyer unfettered disposition of the asset. This is not the case in almost all sukuk issues.

Close analysis of sukuk and its application in Bahrain and Malaysia shows that Islamic financial law is a modern hybrid, reflecting market needs and practices: it grapples with realities. This refashioning of appropriate elements of Shari'ah to adapt to market needs shows the transformative moments of Shari'ah with greater precision. Unger, for example, describes customary law as patterns of interactions to which moral obligations adhere.[128] But within

---

[128] Roberto Mangabeira Unger, *Knowledge and Politics* (New York: The Free Press, 1975); Roberto Mangabeira Unger, 'The Critical Legal Studies Movement', *Harvard Law Review*, vol. 96, no. 3 (1983).

this there nestle legal orders relevant for efficient operations in modern markets. This is more than legal pluralism in a Hobbesian world. Sukuk involves standardization of Shari'ah, revealing jurisdictional rationality and arbitration to adapt to market needs, besides the role of human perception and our innate cognitive bias for familiarity in minimizing legal differences.[129] Multinational banks, such as Barclays Capital and Deutsche Bank, are among the world's major issuers of sovereign sukuk. The inducement for sovereign sukuk in international markets was replicated in retail finance. This led to the establishment of secondary markets, as in the UK.[130] Islamic financing through sukuk assisted the acquisition of the Chelsea Barracks site, played a role in the construction of the Shard, and enabled the purchase of properties in London by Arabs. Here the commodity murabahah emerged as the preferred instrument for interbank lending across diverse jurisdictions.[131]

AAOIFI provides 16 different standards for sukuk issuances. But the market is not easily standardized. Sukuk issuances are structured around the assets, risks, and credit structure of specific transactions, and pursue a close adherence to the documentation used in international bonds issuances. Adhering to the legal similarities and seeking Shari'ah authenticity proves vexatious. In 2008, the Chairman of AAOIFI's Shari'ah Committee, Sheikh Mohammed Taqi Usmani, questioned the Shari'ah compliance of Mudarabah- and Musharakah- based sukuk.[132]

Both Bahraini and Malaysian jurisprudence are permissive here because of an innovative culture ordered by the central bank in both countries. Hence, with the sovereign sukuk, both Malaysian and Arab scholars approved the structure. Bahrain consistently worked with Bank Negara Malaysia in interpreting Shari'ah compliance, creating a framework that is culturally distinctive and yet could manoeuvre across markets. These cross-regional ties, already strong with Bahrain's Gulf neighbours, were reinforced by sukuk's local and transnational Islamic financial cosmology. This success is captured in Mumtalakat, a closed joint-stock company incorporated under Bahrain's Commercial Companies Law of 2001 and fully established in 2006. By 2014,

---

[129] Kahneman, *Thinking Fast and Slow*, pp. 60–1; Jonathan Ercanbrack, 'The Standardization of Islamic Financial Law: Lawmaking in Modern Financial Markets', *American Journal of Comparative Law*, vol. 67, no. 4 (2019).

[130] HMRC, *Impact Assessment of Sukuk [Islamic Bonds] Legislation* (London: HM Revenue & Customs, 2008), p. 5.

[131] Maxwell J. Fry, *Emancipating the Banking System and Developing Markets for Government Debt* (New York: Routledge, 1997); Paul Furneaux, Samer Hijazi, John Lee, and Jamal Fakhro, 'Cross-border Development in Islamic Banking', *Islamic Finance Review, Euromoney Yearbooks*, 2008–09, p. 45.

[132] Farmida Bi, 'AAOIFI Statement on Sukuk and Its Implications', Norton Rose Fulbright, September 2008; AAOIFI, 'Shari'ah Standard No. 17, Investment Sukuk 5/1/8/7', in AAOIFI, *Sharia Standards for Islamic Financial Institutions*, 2015.

it held minority or majority stakes in 35 commercial enterprises. Its diversified industrial portfolio is sustained in the following companies: ALBA, representing 40 years of Bahrain's industrial heritage, becoming the leading producer in aluminium; Gulf Air, connecting Bahrain with regional and global markets; Batelco, the national telecommunications corporation in a deregulated market; Bahrain Livestock Company and Bahrain Flour Mills Company, responsible for livestock and wheat; NBB, Bahrain's first local bank and involved in retail and commercial banking; and finally the Formula 1 race track operated by Bahrain International Circuit Company. With Mumtalakat it is important to show how the structure, the underlying assets, the profits created, the agreed price, the role of government, and the process and security of investment utilize all the variants of sukuk. Bahrain, a small island economy, created legal certainty with commercial aspirations, as evident in Mumtalakat.[133] This acceptance of transplants, derived law, legal structures, institutions, and the power of the ruling elite make possible the application of legal transplants.[134]

Although owned by the government, Mumtalakat is a commercial entity, regulated by the Ministry of Industry and Commerce as a private commercial company. The interdependence and separateness of Mumtalakat is illustrated in its complex use of sukuk. Bahrain also made subtle but important shifts in the legal definition, and used the two variants of sukuk, asset-backed or asset-based. Asset-backed involves securitization of tangible assets with recourse in case of default: and asset-based is where responsibility lies with the issuing entity, if transferred by true sale to a Special Purpose Vehicle, which holds and can issue shares. The most popular sukuk is sukuk al ijarah, which can be compared to a fixed rate coupon bond with Shari'ah compliance. Its international pre-eminence is seen in the sukuk issuances between 2001 and 2014, within the different Muslim-dominated states. In Bahrain, sukuk accounted for 3 per cent of investment, Malaysia 67 per cent, while in Saudi Arabia it was 8 per cent.[135] Most of the sukuk issued in Malaysia is in state-led investments in infrastructure and critical industries but a substantial proportion is issued in global markets. Each sukuk issue had either tax advantages or posed as a variant of a convertible bond, with the aim of conversion into listed shares. Powerful oil corporations, both indigenous as well as in partnership with Western companies, used sukuk. In 1990, sukuk financing for the Malaysian

---

[133] Emma van Santen, 'Islamic Banking and Finance Regulation in Malaysia: Between State, Shari'a, the Courts and Islamic Moral Economy', *Company Lawyer*, vol. 38, no. 1 (2018), pp. 21, 26; Ibrahim Warde, *Islamic Finance in the Global Economy* (Edinburgh: Edinburgh University Press, 2010), p. 12.

[134] Kahn-Freund, 'On Uses and Misuses of Comparative Law', p. 37.

[135] IIFM, Sukuk Database, sukuk issuance by country, 2001–14.

subsidiary of Shell, the Anglo-Dutch oil company, was succeeded in 1993 by sukuk investment in Petronas. These high-profile sukuk investments were replicated further by Kentucky Fried Chicken (KFC) with a global sukuk in 1997, and in 2001 by the powerful plantation firm Guthrie (a mortgage company), Cagamas, and Khazanah Nasional (an investment group). In each of these, the use of sukuk as a financial instrument was accompanied by a series of inducements such as tax exemptions or guaranteed musharakah certificates with redeemable papers, where sukuk was a variant of the convertible bond and permitted conversion into listed shares. Guthrie Plantations used a US$-denominated ijarah sukuk wedded to seminal payments, referenced on LIBOR. With Khazanah the innovation was in sustainable and responsible investments. Highly innovative manipulation of sukuk continued in 2013 when the world's first perpetual sukuk was issued by MAS (Malaysian Airlines System). In 2014, Malaysian regulators even approved the potential use of intellectual property as an underlying asset for sukuk. The brilliantly theatrical search for Shari'ah compliance has to be examined against existing commercial and investment legal rules. These developments raise the obvious question: why are ethical standards in Shari'ah allowed to weaken? The markets, business organization, and business technology are experiencing dramatic change, change which becomes urgent in sukuk markets. It is state intervention that makes possible high-risk financial behaviour, as in the perpetual sukuk in MAS and the ijarah sukuk referenced on LIBOR by Guthrie Plantations.

Bahrain, while releasing a series of sovereign issues of sukuk and long-term Islamic securities, took legal precautions through the Central Bank. In 2001, it issued short-term as well as long-term tradeable asset-backed sukuk but protected them by establishing the Liquidity Management Centre to facilitate the creation of an inter-bank money market. Later it issued short-term sukuk that accommodated Basel 111 through the Liquidity Coverage Ratio (LCR), supplemented by level 1 High Quality Liquid Assets (HQLA). Besides these legal defences, state possession of institutional investment was invoked. The majority of government sukuk are either not listed or not actively traded.[136] The sharpest critic of such economic behaviour would have been Adam Smith, proclaiming the sovereignty of the market and the separation of economics and business from religion and ethics. Another compliance tactic used in Bahrain was arbitration through local municipal courts or resolution in English courts.

---

[136] Standard & Poor, *Islamic Finance Outlook*, 2015.

Bahrain, like the UAE in the Dana Gas sukuk case, sought to overcome the restrictions of Shari'ah through local municipal courts or through the English courts. In the *Shamil Bank v Beximco Pharmaceuticals Ltd* case, the courts in London decided an Islamic finance contract dispute. In appealing to multiple legal authorities, AAOIFI Shari'ah standards can be incorporated into contracts governed by English law. Malaysia employed a distinct state-centred standardization model with top-down legal administration and a diminished role for traditional jurists. Bahrain refashioned legal tools to identify and achieve transformative moments with greater precision. This contrast between Bahrain and Malaysia points to the use of jurisdictional politics in achieving sukuk and Shari'ah compliance.

Malaysia, more than Bahrain, created its own special inducements. In Malaysia, the hybrid character of Shari'ah, challenging authenticity in Islamic finance by employing pluralistic manipulations and innovative economic interpretations, identifying alternatives in the choice of sukuk finance for large state projects, saw the country emerge as the global hub of Islamic finance. In an influential paper, Killian Balz has argued that Shari'ah scholars no longer play the central role in determining Islamic financial law. Instead, traditional legal concepts have been transformed by global financial markets to conform to international commercial practices, thus rendering Shari'ah a code of ethics rather than a fully fledged legal system. He minimizes the role of the state but emphasizes the trend towards a harmonization of Shari'ah through transnational legal operations.[137] In Bahrain, Shari'ah is a source of jurisprudence for Islamic finance law. But the conduct of commerce and finance involves a secular mixture of Western-derived civil law and modern jurisprudence. Only in Saudi Arabia has Shari'ah not been modified from its traditional form.

Bahrain maintained an emphasis on liquidity and the investment needs of Islamic financial institutions through its regular issue of short-term sukuk and through mergers of banks in 2017. The long-term capital needs of industry were satisfied by the state and innovative sovereign sukuk, while small businesses required frequent short-term sukuk. Important here was the increasing involvement of the International Islamic Liquidity Management Corporation (IILM) in the short-term international sukuk market. A fortuitous by-product of the intervention by the IILM was that Islamic financial institutions were active in the short-term sukuk market, seeking low-risk securities.[138]

---

[137] Killian Balz, 'Shari'a Risk? How Islamic Finance Has Transformed Islamic Contract Law'. Islamic Legal Studies Program, Harvard Law School, Occasional Publications 9, September 2008.
[138] International Islamic Financial Market, *IIFM Sukuk Report*, 2018, pp. 194–7.

Potential Development and Problems in the Sukuk Market

Bahrain issued the first sovereign sukuk in 2001 through the Bahrain Monetary Authority. This first international sukuk programme established Bahrain's reputation as a hub of Islamic finance, conducive to economic integration within the Gulf. In 2002, Malaysia followed with its first global sovereign sukuk. Between 2001 and 2017, Malaysia issued the highest number of domestic and international sukuk with a total value of US$612 billion, followed by Saudi Arabia at US$95 billion. Bahrain concentrated on the domestic issue of sukuk. These domestic sukuk were promoted largely by the Central Bank of Bahrain and were principally sovereign al-ijarah sukuk in 2011, 2012, and 2015. In 2014, the CBB had issued a Sukuk-al Wakalah. In 2016, the CBB issued four sovereign sukuk, structured on sukuk al salam. On the corporate sukuk side, progress has been limited, with only nine issues from 2004 to 2011. In 2012, Celcom Transmission issued a sovereign al-ijarah sukuk. Corporate sukuk were less popular in Bahrain, perhaps because of the fragmented legal order and the conflicts it generated, in contrast to the position of sovereign funds where a government-owned company possessing more capital created less risk. In this financial landscape, corporate issuers face a scarcity of professional talent, of trained personnel with the ability to expand into international markets. Their performance consists of jurisdictional jockeying, unleashing disputes that create problems for corporate sukuk. The leading feature in sovereign sukuk, particularly in issues of impending default and restructuring, was a discourse on the state, law, political affiliations, and tribal loyalties that surfaced within sovereign sukuk. Islamic and conventional banks and clusters of state-driven financial intermediaries have been crucial agents in the sukuk market. The CBB issued medium- to long-term sukuk and also retained a regular programme of short-term sukuk. A curious but revealing transaction was a 30-year bond issued by the CBB which raised US$1.25 billion, rising to US$5.75 billion within a short space of time. The bond was priced to yield 6 per cent.[139]

It is, of course, arguable that in Malaysia, in contrast to Bahrain, the corporate sukuk market exercised influence partly because of the role of the National Investment Corporation, Permodalan Nasional Berhad (PNB). It was established on 17 March 1978 to secure Malay privileges in commerce within the associational economics monopolized by Malaysian-Chinese

---

[139] El-Tahir, 'Bahrain's Islamic Capital Markets', p. 274.

capitalists. This powerful investment group, PNB, brought about the transformation of Malaysia from a jaded presence in Islamic finance to the major corporate issuer of sukuk, followed by Saudi Arabia, the UAE, Qatar, Turkey, and then Bahrain. In contrast, Bahrain's state-consolidated business leadership, entrenched by financial institutions, was followed by industrial and infrastructural corporate issuers. This offers an interesting theoretical comparison. Karl Polanyi argued that economic acts occur in socially constructed frameworks, with interactions of capital, political power, and social organization determining capitalist evolution[140]. Malaysian state economic hegemony prospered through alliances with local Chinese capitalists. But the creation of a powerful state investment company, PNB, produced rising Malay economic power exploiting Western and Arab Islamic networks. And here sukuk was a core instrument. Bahrain, a pioneer in establishing trading and financial hubs in the Persian Gulf from the mid-fifteenth century, and now embedded in financial networks with the oil-wealthy Gulf states, employed sukuk finance to advance solar power and sustainable development while creating investment opportunities in social welfare, the ma'tam and waqf infrastructure, through Green Sukuk and Social Sukuk.[141]

Bahrain's financial and industrial competitive advantage since 2006 involved specialization and the clustering of technology within the holding company Mumtalakat, and its portfolio of specialized interests in aluminium (ALBA), aviation (Gulf Air), Edamah (land), Batelco (telecommunications), NBB (a local bank), real estate and tourism, food, telecommunications, financial services, the automotive industry, and dispersed ownership in Gulf states corporations. Mumtalakat, Bahrain's Sovereign Wealth Fund, a holding company established in June 2006, pursued an aggressive policy of industrial financial integration while promoting inward investment from wealthy Gulf neighbours. The two most powerful forces affecting sukuk was the continuing shift to listing on Western stock exchanges and the fact that these major quoted companies absorbed a large proportion of the oil wealth flowing into Bahrain. In November 2014, Mumtalakat raised US$600 million from the sale of sukuk in an attempt to refinance its debt. To achieve this, it created a hybrid structure comprising a commodity murabahah and a wakala based on Mumtalakat's stake in a diverse portfolio of commercial interests and tapped the pool of liquidity within Islamic finance. The listing of this transaction was on the Irish stock exchange. The transaction was advised by BNP

---

[140] Karl Polanyi, *The Great Transformation: The Political and Economic Origins of our Time*. Boston: Beacon Press, 1957.

[141] Deloitte Research and Analysis, 'Sustainable Finance: Can Sukuk Become a Driver of Solar and Green Energy Growth?', 2018; *IIFM Sukuk Report*, 2018.

Paribas, Deutsche Bank, MUFJG, and Standard Chartered Bank, while the Arab Banking Corporation and National Bank of Bahrain were involved as managers.[142]

The preference for a Keynesian policy of macro-management exploited global talent and foreign stock markets while preserving traditional Shari'ah identity through Islamic banks and the articulation of dual sukuk instruments, thereby strengthening innovation and market success. The virtues of Islamic finance were exploited, aiming at growth sectors like aluminium, oil processing, telecommunications, real estate, and land and harbour development. From the perspective of intra-regional cohesion, the principal innovation was diverse sukuk investment, largely in sovereign equity funds and less through corporate issuers of sukuk. In the use of domestic and foreign markets to legitimize market-driven Islamic products, Mumtalakat has a long history. In October 2012, Mumtalakat had marked a milestone in its dual listing with CIMB Investment Bank Berhad Malaysia, with a ringgit-denominated murabahah sukuk, valued at close to US$1 billion. This had secured a high rating from RAM, the Ratings Agency of Malaysia.[143]

Shari'ah and the Securitization of Gold Assets on the Bahrain Stock Market

The principal impetus for gold investment assets has been the diversified gold investor base in the US, China, and India. The US launched gold asset investment in 2003 and it has emerged as a safe, lucrative investment, performing well in both rising and falling markets.[144]

Gold is seen as a complement to stocks and bonds on American stock markets, for it generates long-term returns but is also an effective diversifier and therefore restricts losses in periods of market stress. It provides liquidity and hence reduces credit risk, while improving overall performance. Part of gold's success is that the investor is able to track performance on the stock market while also tracking changing gold prices in retail markets. The Central Bank of Bahrain holds large gold reserves as a monetary asset and to hedge against market risk. Gold is also a store of value against inflation. Moreover, investors

---

[142] Mumtalakat Holding Company, cited in El-Tahir, 'Bahrain's Islamic Capital Markets', pp. 262–79.

[143] El-Tahir, 'Bahrain's Islamic Capital Markets', p. 274; A. Roger Wedderburn-Day, 'Sovereign Sukuk: Adaptation and Innovation', *Law and Contemporary Problems*, vol. 73, 4 (2010), pp. 325–33; Deloitte Research and Analysis cited in El-Tahir, 'Bahrain's Islamic Capital Markets', pp. 274–5. RAM ratings from Malaysia for sukuk programmes are frequently laxer than Fitch Ratings.

[144] World Gold Council, 'The Relevance of Gold as a Strategic Asset, Individual Investors', World Gold Council: https://www.gold.org/goldhub/research/relevance-ofgold-as-a-strategic-asset-2020-individual.

can invest in gold-mining companies, for example in South Africa and Sudan, where the return will be in the company's future earnings and not just in the price of gold. However, investments in Sudan and South Africa, countries with marked political volatility, may experience poor returns. Therefore, Bahrain focuses on Western markets, notably those of the US, where an average annual return of 10 per cent has been recorded over the past four decades. Part of gold's stability derives from the fact that production rises are limited to 1.6 per cent per annum.[145] It is also arguable that gold's strategic role is broad based: it is a store of wealth to hedge against systemic risk, currency depreciation, and inflation, and it also provides returns. World currencies remained pegged to gold until 1971 and the disintegration of the Bretton Woods structure. But in a world of great economic volatility, gold is on its way back.

In the 2008 financial crisis, while stocks fell and real estate shares tumbled, gold rose by 14 per cent.[146] Gold provides protection in periods of economic uncertainty: it significantly improves risk-adjusted returns across various levels of risk.[147] Gold can enhance the performance of investment portfolios.[148]

Sustaining and Integrating Shari'ah in the Growth of Gold Assets Investment

FinTech has made possible efficient Shari'ah-compliant gold asset operations on the stock market, with the International Islamic Financial Market (IIFM) and the World Gold Council (WGC) developing standards for gold-based Islamic contracts. In 2018, the WGC and the Bahrain-based International Islamic Financial Market attempted to introduce Shari'ah-compliant gold contracts for use in Islamic finance. Gold contracts are for calculating credit risk and include periods of maturity. In addition, all assets and liabilities must be included at closing mid-market spot exchange rates. The Central Bank of Bahrain also ensured that Wakalah investment products can be traded on foreign exchange markets.[149] The Commodity Murabahah Transaction (CMT), a sale with a mark-up profit was used in this complex transaction. The CBB

---

[145] World Gold Council, 'The Relevance of Gold as Strategic Asset, Individual Investors', report, 27 May 2020, p. 5.

[146] Bloomberg Commodity Index, a 20-year Commodity Index, 1999–2019; World Gold Council, 'The Relevance of Gold', p. 11.

[147] World Gold Council, 'The Relevance of Gold', p. 9.

[148] Oxford Economics, 'The Impact of Inflation and Deflation on the Case for Gold', July 2011.

[149] Wakalah is a form of special agency that has the authority to invest funds in Shari'ah-compliant institutions or in specific financial instruments.

also regarded Wakalah investments in gold as being the same as investments in foreign currencies. This is crucial as the CBB is attempting to promote gold investments, gold savings, gold certificates, and gold Exchange Traded Funds (ETF) while promoting gold transactions.[150] However, for Islamic banks the credit risk was zero as their transactions were backed by gold bullion held in their own vaults. Overall, the AAOIFI's Shari'ah standards were maintained in gold trading. The Accounting and Auditing Organization for Islamic Financial Institutions had introduced the Shari'ah Standard No. 57 on gold and its trading partners in 2016, with technical support from the World Gold Council. This standard covers Shari'ah rules for gold both in trade and in the creation of gold-based financial products, and this was critical for Islamic banks and other financial institutions that sought to retain gold as an investment asset in a Shari'ah-compliant account. The regulatory authorities remained the Central Bank of Bahrain, AAOIFI, and the National Bureau for Revenue (NBR). An important element in the regulatory structure was strict coordination between the financial regulators and commercial and government agencies. This required collaboration with the industry to maintain the sustainability of investment and trade as Exchange Traded Funds (ETFs). Al Bahrain Jewellers LLC became an associate member of the London Bullion Market Association (LBMA), an international group representing the gold and silver bullion market since 2011.[151]

Significant environmental issues became important here, particularly for European investors. Mining (largely in Third World countries) involved water-intensive and chemical-laden operations, posing risks to local communities and to the environment.[152] This led the World Bank to create the Climate-Smart Mining Initiative. This was a joint action with the UN Sustainable Development Goals (SDGs) to ensure the decarbonization of the mining and energy sectors, including the mining of gold in Africa. In 2019, the WGC launched the Responsible Gold Mining Principles, which complemented the London Bullion Market Association's Responsible Sourcing Programme, an ambitious initiative to eliminate money laundering, terrorist-financing, and human rights abuses within the gold-producing sector. These responses imply an exacting culture of ethics and governance often missing in

---

[150] *IIFM Sukuk Report*, 2018.
[151] Deloitte & Touche, Middle East, 'The Global Gold Investment Market: Traits for Shari'ah-based Investment Solutions', 2021, pp. 40–3; F. A. O'Connor, B. M. Lucey, J. A. Batten, and D. G. Baur, 'The Financial Economics of Gold—a Survey', *International Review of Financial Analysis*, vol. 41 (2015), pp. 186–205.
[152] OECD, 'Investment Governance and the Integration of Environmental, Social, and Governance Factors', 2017.

capitalist operations. The OECD and WGC reforms made possible a Shari'ah-compliant market in gold and in gold assets on the Bahrain Stock Market, which attracted Islamic investors to what they saw as risk-free diversification in investments.[153]

In pursuit of these financial innovations, Bahrain adopted appropriate technologies. In 2016, the CBB introduced electronic systems and regulations in the financial services sector, including electronic transfer systems and private networks for interbank transfers. It also introduced the Regulatory Sandbox deal with FinTech and blockchain products and services, as well as open banking rules and rules pertaining to Crypto-Asset platform operations (CPO), a Crypto-Asset Module.[154]

Gold and Shari'ah-compliant Investment on the Bahrain Stock Market: From a Safe Haven to a Problem?

Gold assets investment includes derivatives based on the price of the refined metal (for which there is evidence of a considerable trade) and shares or Exchange Traded Funds (ETFs) that track both gold prices and also corporations involved in gold mining and the use of gold in jewellery production.[155] One should not exaggerate the importance of gold to Bahrain's financial structure: in August 2020, Bahrain's gold reserves amounted to only 4.7 tons or 6.1 per cent of total reserves. However, the AAOIFI's Shariah Standard on Gold, which permitted various Islamic capital market instruments backed by gold, did open up investment opportunities. Another significant opportunity for gold investment came through the Al Bahrain Jewellers LLC. Further encouragement came when the Central Bank of Bahrain treated gold contracts like foreign exchange contracts.[156] The CBB also introduced measures to protect gold trading in foreign markets, as shares or commodities, and also the gold held in a bank's own vaults.

The New Scepticism towards Gold Assets

In 2019, Bahrain exported US$316m in gold, US$315m to the United Arab Emirates and US$1.18m to Hong Kong. In the same year, Bahrain imported

[153] World Gold Council, report 2019; OECD, 'Investment Governance'; OECD, 'Due Diligence for Responsibility Supply Chains of Minerals from Conflict and High Risk Areas', 2019.
[154] Deloitte & Touche, Middle East, 'The Global Gold Investment Market', p. 18.
[155] See https://en.asinko.com/trading/gold-bahrain.
[156] Deloitte & Touche, Middle East, 'The Global Gold Investment Market', pp. 40–1.

US$445m in gold from the UAE, US$260,000 from Italy, US$92,500 from Turkey, US$16,100 from Germany, and US$8,970 from France.[157] In 2019, Bahrain exported US$13.2 billion in refined petroleum (down from US$23.9 billion in 2014), mainly to the UAE, Saudi Arabia, the US, and to South Korea. Other exports included raw aluminium and iron ore.

It has been argued that gold is a conservative diversifier that dampens down volatility to provide safe returns on investment.[158] Gold is certainly a safe haven in the investment strategies of the Gulf states. Moreover, in recent global financial crises there has been a clear advantage for Shari'ah-compliant securities because of their religious ethics and the state's ability to inject emergency funds. Gold in Bahrain is both a stable investment and a precious asset because of the CBB's strict legal governance. Gold is attractive because of its Shari'ah and Islamic sectorial advantages.[159] Gold and Islamic stocks provide a safe haven during times of market turbulence.

Legal Regimes and Challenges

The fluidity of the legal order, the jurisdictional complexity involved in utilizing Shari'ah and Western civil and common law, and listing overseas is captured in two interesting cases: one in the UAE, a bold attempt to evade debt; and the Beximco case in Bahrain.

The Dana Gas Sukuk of the UAE was unprecedented, but it may produce new legal and policy rules for corporate financiers. In 2017, Dana Gas told investors that it could not make payments on its US$700 million sukuk issue because the underlying structure was no longer Shari'ah compliant. The company filed a motion in the UAE court declaring the Mudarabah sukuk unlawful under UAE law. It also obtained injunctions in the UAE court and English court prohibiting investors from suing under the Mudarabah agreement or the purchase undertaking until a final decision was reached in those proceedings.[160] Dana Gas wanted to restructure the US$700 million issue so that profit distributions were halved, on the grounds that the structure had

---

[157] Gold in Bahrain/OEC—The Observatory of Economic Complexity 2021: https://oec.world/en/profile/bilateral-product/gold/reporter/bhr,p.3.

[158] Eugene J. Sherman, 'Gold: A Conservative Prudent Diversifier: Gold has Lowered Volatility and Improves Returns in almost all Environments', *Journal of Portfolio Management*, vol. 8, no. 3 (1982).

[159] Muhammad Abubakr Naeem, Fiza Qureshi, Muhammad Arif, and Faruk Balli, 'Asymmetric Relationship between Gold and Islamic Stocks in Bearish, Normal, and Bullish Market Conditions', *Resources Policy*, vol. 72 (2021), pp. 3–4.

[160] *Dana Gas PJSC v Dana Gas Sukuk Ltd*, 2017; EWHC2340 (Comm); Ercanbrack, 'The Standardization of Islamic Financial Law'.

become unlawful 'due to the evolution and continual development of Islamic financial instruments and their interpretation.[161]

This was an attempt to avoid responsibility for debt by claiming a lack of Shari'ah compliance within the Mudarabah sukuk. This highlights the hybridity of Islamic financial law and the consequent gaps between it and the municipal legal systems. It also exposes serious deficiencies in Islamic financial law in industry-specific legal jurisdictional boundaries. Subsequently, AAOIFI issued a statement that, with respect to sukuk modelled on Mudarabah and Musharakah contracts, the purchase undertaking should be based on the net asset value, market value, cash equivalent, or any price agreed upon at the time of purchase. The full value of capital can be repaid to sukuk investors only in the event of negligence or malfeasance. The principle here is that the sukuk bears the risk of the underlying assets. However, the hybridity of Islamic financial law leads to conflicts, with parties seeking to invalidate contracts in multiple jurisdictions in an attempt to escape the debt payment on the grounds of a lack of Shari'ah compliance.[162]

In the controversial case of *Shamil Bank v Beximco Pharmaceuticals Ltd*, resolution was sought in an English court, an attempt to govern a contract according to both Shari'ah and English law. The case focused on the Beximco Group's efforts to seek working capital from the respondent, Shamil Bank. Two murabahah financing agreements with Shamil Bank in 1995 and 1996 secured first US$15 million and then another US$15 million but by 1999 the Beximco Group had defaulted. Frustrated by failures in subsequent negotiations, Shamil Bank initiated proceedings in an English court.[163] But the English Court of Appeal ruling was that only the law of the country concerned could govern a contract.

The Court of Appeal has thus indirectly defined the limits of Shari'ah commercial and contract law in foreign courts. In Bahrain, the Commercial Code of 1987 resolved some of the clashes between Shari'ah and secular law. There is an agreement that there must not be conflict between Shari'ah and mandatory legislative provisions. Legislators have adopted in the Commercial Code the Western notion of freedom of contract. In commercial custom, the civil code is consulted first, followed by Shari'ah, and then the principles of natural justice. Thus, the Commercial Code, in Articles 76 and 275, allows for commercial loans or deposits with interest, despite the conflict with Shari'ah. The

[161] Dana Gas, 'Dana Gas outlines broad terms for Sukuk discussions', UAE Government, 13 June 2017.
[162] Ercanbrack, 'The Standardization of Islamic Financial Law', pp. 825–60.
[163] *Shamil Bank v Beximco Pharmaceuticals Ltd* (2004), EWCA Civ 19[1]; Lawrence Collins, *Dicey, Morris and Collins on the Conflict of Laws, Vol. 11* (London: Sweet and Maxwell, 2006), pp. 1568, 1571.

Civil Code of 2001 confirmed this.[164] This new Code, which replaced the contract law and law of civil wrongs, accepts this interpretation of Bahraini law, in effect relegating Shari'ah below customary law. Disputes involving commercial interests are resolved in secular civil law but Shari'ah has an influence in Islamic financial law through the Bahrain Financial Centre.[165]

Keeping in focus these structural adaptations, Sheikh Taqi Usmani, Chairman of the AAOIFI Shariah Board, declared that 85 per cent of the Sukuk market was not Shari'ah compliant.[166] There was a subsequent decline in sukuk issuances. This downturn ironically corresponded with the 2008 financial crisis, thereby confusing the impact of his statement.[167]

Global Financial Crisis of 2008 and Its Impact on Sovereign Sukuk

The scepticism of prominent Islamic scholars as to the authenticity of sukuk in Islamic finance, and fears of an adverse impact on sukuk from the 2008 Global Financial Crisis, are not supported by the data in Moody's Investors Report of 2009. The precise dimensions of the rise and decline in sukuk issues are related to a wider context: growth in sukuk after 2009 was through sovereign and government-related issuers. The increase of issues was through the Ijara sukuk (sale and lease back) structure. The sukuk revival in domestic markets was not reproduced in the UK or the US, which were affected seriously by the 2008 crisis and were fearful of new challenges posed by sukuk. The dominant narrative is of an expansion in sukuk issues between 2004 and 2007, growing from US$7.2 billion in 2004 to US$12.0 billion in 2005, to US$27.4 billion in 2006, and to US$38.6 billion in 2007. Towards the end of 2007, sukuk issues had exceeded US$90 billion. Standard and Poor's Report in 2009 revealed a dramatic decline in 2008 to US$15 billion. This provided ammunition for sceptics of the standardization of Islamic finance in market-led economies. In appraising the impact of the financial crisis, the precautionary actions of the CBB against any rigging of the Bahraini

[164] Legislative Decree no. 7 of 1987, Promulgating the Commercial Code; Legislative Decree no. 19 of 2001, Promulgating the Civil Code, Art. 1, s[b].

[165] Ercanbrack, *The Transformation of Islamic Law*, pp. 246–7.

[166] Bi, 'AAOIFI Statement on Sukuk and its Implications'.

[167] Simon Archer and Rifaat Ahmed Abdel Karim, ed., *Islamic Capital Markets and Products: Managing Capital and Liquidity Requirements under Basel III* (Chichester: Wiley, 2018), pp. 37, 43, 78, 81, 221; Wedderburn-Day, 'Sovereign Sukuk', pp. 331–43; AAOIFI, 'Accounting and Auditing Organization for Islamic Financial Institutions', Shari'ah Board Resolutions on Sukuk 2–3, 2008; International Islamic Financial Market (IIFM), 'Sukuk Report', April 2018: 'A Comprehensive Study of the Global Sukuk Market'.

dinar meant speculative behaviour was absent in Bahrain's financial markets, although it did experience a deficit caused by a dramatic fall in oil prices, estimated at BD450 million, but domestic and foreign loans were used to overcome the deficit. The losses in sovereign funds were severe. The foreign portfolio of Gulf countries decreased from US$1.3 trillion in 2007 to US$1.2 trillion in 2008.[168]

Constructing and Diagnosing the Multiple Corporations within Mumtalakat's State Ownership

The corporate industrial success within Mumtalakat contradicts Schumpeter's paradigm of corporate success through small-state ownership, weak cartels, and market competition. Mumtalakat's major quoted companies were quasi-monopolized by the state, and this secured their success in securities markets in Bahrain as well as in listings in other Gulf states. In view of the inadequate governance procedures and an immature capital market, in Bahrain it limited the agency problems arising from the divorce of ownership from control. It is also arguable that in Arab states, the institutional underpinnings of close interaction between state and business, particularly strong in Bahrain, assisted Mumtalakat's impressive growth between 2006 and 2018. This holding company assembled interests in aluminium; in a state owned airline, Gulf Air, supported by state funding; Edamah, an investment property company; Batelco, a leading integrated telecommunications provider in Bahrain; NBB, the National Bank of Bahrain in retail and commercial banking; and GIC, a Gulf investment company incorporated in Kuwait in 1983, owned equally by Bahrain, Kuwait, Oman, Qatar, Saudi Arabia, and the UAE, with a paid-up capital of US$2.1 billion. GIC's aim was to nurture diverse economic growth and the creation of efficient capital markets in the Gulf region. Mumtalakat possessed a 16.67 per cent stake in GIC.

---

[168] B. Setser and R. Ziemba, 'GCC Sovereign Funds: Reversal of Fortune', Council of Foreign Relations, January 2009; Andreas Jobst et al., 'Islamic Bond Issuance—What Sovereign Debt Managers Need to Know', International Monetary Fund, July 2008; Standard & Poor, 'Sukuk Market Has Continued to Progress to 2009, Despite Some Roadblocks', press release, September 2009, on file with Law and Contemporary Problems; Moody's Investors Service, 'Sukuk Issuance Surges, Dominated by Government Related Issuers', press release, 10 November 2009, on file with Law and Contemporary Problems; Wedderburn-Day, 'Sovereign Sukuk', pp. 324–33. Mumtalakat is a prime user of sukuk al ijarah, sukuk murabahah, wakalah, mudarabah, and sukuk al salam. A study of its operations is useful in showing the growth and diversification of the Bahrain economy through the sukuk financial instrument. It also illustrates a model of state and oligopolistic entrenchment in the portfolio of the companies within Mumtalakat, which is a holding company.

ALBA, the Bahrain aluminium company, was established in 1971 and was the first smelter in the Middle East. In November 2010, Mumtalakat's ordinary shares in ALBA were listed on the Bahrain Bourse and on the London Stock Exchange. Mumtalakat retained a 69.38 per cent equity shareholding in ALBA. On ALBA's nine-member board, six are from Mumtalakat. By June 2014, ALBA's market capitalization was BD630.5 million (US$1,676.9 million). Total assets for 2011, 2012, 2013, and 2014 were BD1,304.8 million, BD1,211.9 million, BD1,178.3 million, and BD1,169.1 million respectively. Total liabilities were BD496.0 million, BD382.3 million, BD309.8 million, and BD 298.7 million for 2011, 2012, 2013, and 2014 respectively. Net profit was BD211.9 million, BD96.5 million, and BD79.8 million, for 2011, 2012, and 2013 respectively. It is the largest employer in Bahrain and 87 per cent of employees are Bahraini nationals.[169]

Gulf Air was established in 1950. Until 2002, it was jointly owned by Bahrain, Qatar, Abu Dhabi, and Oman. In November 2007, Mumtalakat assumed sole ownership, as the other partners established their own carriers and withdrew from the joint shareholding company. Total assets were BD600.0 million, BD749.3 million, and BD660.3 million for 2011, 2012, and 2013 respectively. Total liabilities were BD486.1 million, BD716.8 million, and BD640.5 million in 2011, 2012, and 2013 respectively. It achieved a net profit of BD1.5 million in 2014 after a loss of BD18.6 million. Gulf Air recorded losses of BD210.7 million, BD81.5million, and BD12.0 million in 2011, 2012, and 2013 respectively. In 2014, it recorded a net profit of BD1.5 million. Its losses are clearly as a result of competition from Emirates, Etihad, Qatar Airways, and Air Arabia. The regional unrest after 2011 was another contributory factor. It has received aid from Mumtalakat to offset losses as well as to purchase new aircraft. The funding in loans rose from BD168.9 million in 2008 to BD196.7 million in 2009. In October 2010, Mumtalakat gave Gulf Air a further BD400.0 million. In 2012–13, restructuring costs were BD185.0 million and BD95.0 million and there was a shareholder loan of BD30.0 million in 2012. From January 2012 to June 2014, Gulf Air received a total of BD317.5 million from the government.[170]

The Edamah property investment company is wholly owned by Mumtalakat. The state transferred substantial land and properties to Edamah, to a total value of BD132.8 million by June 2014. The state restricts sales and mortgages of properties by Edamah. Revenues were BD2.7 million, BD2.2 million, and BD3.1 million for 2011, 2012, and 2013 respectively. The net

---

[169] Annual Report of Mumtalakat, 2010 to December 2014, pp. 108–9.
[170] Report of Mumtalakat, 2007–14, pp. 109–11.

loss for 2011 was BD209.3 million because of market volatility. Net profit in 2012 was BD0.4 million followed by BD1.6 million in 2013.

The most prominent high-volume, mass-marketing, and quintessentially modern company within Mumtalakat is Batelco Telecommunications, established in 1981 and offering mobile services, international roaming, high-speed Internet connections, WIFI, VPN network management, data communications, and information and telecommunications services, integrated within an innovative structure. Its quest for a global presence is clear in its acquisition of Cable & Wireless Communications in the Maldives, Sure Channel Islands and the Isle of Man, and Sure Falkland Islands, St Helena, Ascension and Diego Garcia, as well as a 25 per cent stake in Compagnie Monegasque de Communications has a 55 per cent stake in Monaco Telecom. Batelco also sought shareholdings in Cable and Wireless Seychelles but failed to secure regulatory approval. Batelco also has subsidiaries and joint ventures in Kuwait, Yemen, Saudi Arabia, Jordan, and Egypt, which contributed 54 per cent of gross revenues for 2013. By 2014, Batelco's overseas interests contributed 57 per cent of its gross revenues.[171]

Batelco owns 96 per cent of shares in Umniah Mobile Company PSC Jordan. By 2014, Umniah had over 3 million mobile customers and a market share of 31.5 per cent. Umniah also provides 80 per cent of the Internet services in Jordan.[172] In February 2014, Batelco acquired a 46 per cent shareholding in Qualitynet, a data and Internet provider in Kuwait, later increasing its stake to 90 per cent. Batelco also held a 27 per cent stake in Yemen's Sabafona mobile operator. Batelco also acquired shares in Etihad Atheeb Telecom in Saudi Arabia but faced serious problems. However, most impressive was its creation of a subsidiary, Batelco Millennium India Company, with a stake of 42.7 per cent in S Tel, an Indian mobile company. But Batelco was dragged into legal suits which dented its global aspirations.

Until 2002, it had a monopoly in Bahrain but it then faced competition from a Saudi telecommunications company. This eroded what was already a small market in Bahrain. Revenues were BD327.0 million, BD304.7 million, and BD370.6 million for the years 2011, 2012, and 2013 respectively. Net profit was BD80.0 million, BD60.3 million, and BD43.6 million for 2011, 2012, and 2013 respectively. Batelco, with its international investment in a high-technology industry, was central to Bahrain's economic diversification, particularly after the fall in oil prices after the 2008 financial crisis. Industrial policy was used to determine the structure of existing industries like

---

[171] Mumtalakat Annual Reports for 2011–14, pp. 112–13. See also *IIFM Sukuk Report*, 2017.
[172] Mumtalakat Annual Reports for 2011–14, p. 113.

aluminium but also to drive innovative competitive sectors offering prospects for global expansion. In a small island economy, selective policies were crucial, financed by a global sukuk market. Particularly impressive was the fact that 90 per cent of the labour force in Batelco were Bahraini nationals.

One reason for the sustainability of the divergent industrial and service corporations held within the holding company is that finance is secured from an extensive pool of liquidity, with the National Bank of Bahrain acting as joint lead manager with foreign banks, BNP Paribas, and Deutsche Bank, along with the Arab Bank Corporation in seeking listings in overseas stock markets. The NBB was established in 1957 as Bahrain's first locally owned bank and it grew to become a leading provider of retail and commercial finance and of treasury and investment services. It is the biggest bank in Bahrain. Its activities focus on the inter-bank market, purchase of treasury bills, property deals, investment in securities, derivatives, managed funds, equities, international markets, and private deals with clients. A growing focus on corporate banking led to expansion in Abu Dhabi and Riyadh. It was listed on the Bahrain Bourse in 2014 and the public held 43.9 per cent of shares, with 11.1 per cent held by SIO, and 45.0 per cent by Mumtalakat. The combined shares of the SIO and Mumtalakat gave the government a controlling stake. Mumtalakat is also represented by four directors on the NBB board.

NBB's market capitalization was BD715.1 million. The total shareholder equity increased by 4.1 per cent between 2013 and 2014, from BD274.7 million to BD378.0 million. The total shareholder equity was BD274.7 million in 2011 and BD318.9 million in 2012. The figures for net income show an impressive increase of 7.1 per cent in 2014, to BD28.7 million, up from BD26.8 million in 2013. The net income was BD45.6 million, BD47.5 million, and BD51.4 million for the years 2011, 2012, and 2013 respectively. The treasury and investment sector was the largest segment in operating income and increased by 28.9 per cent between 2013 and 2014 while business banking decreased by 79.5 per cent in those years. The personal banking sector increased by just 5.9 per cent.[173] Non-performing loans increased by 15.9 per cent in 2014, up from BD66.7 million in 2013 to BD77.3 million in 2014. Non-performing loans were BD18.0 million in 2011 but rose to BD69.8 million in 2012. NBB's total assets were BD2,857.7 million in 2014, an increase of 3.9 per cent, from BD2,749.2 million in 2013, while in 2012 total assets had been BD2654.6 million. NBB's capital adequacy ratio was 31.2 per cent in 2013 and 30.8 per cent in 2014. The capital adequacy ratio, including credit, operational, and market risk is well above the Basel requirement of 8 per cent

[173] Mumtalakat Annual Reports for 2010–16.

and indeed above the 12 per cent set by CBB. The main factors that con-tribute to NBB's strong capital adequacy ratio are a relatively high capital base and the relatively low-risk profile of NBB's on-balance sheet and off-balance sheet exposures, which include lower-risk weighted assets, namely loans to governments, public sector undertakings, banks, and financial institutions.

The next investment institution in Mumtalakat is GIC, incorporated in Kuwait in 1983 as a Gulf shareholding company owned by six member states: Bahrain, Kuwait, Oman, Qatar, Saudi Arabia, and the UAE, with a paid-up capital of US$2.1 billion. Mumtalakat holds Bahrain's 16.67 per cent stake in GIC. GIC invests in finance, telecommunications, petrochemicals, metal and electricity, and global markets, including equities, bonds, hybrid securi-ties, and property. Its investors range from governments, quasi-governments, the corporate sector, and other investors in the Gulf. Its innovations are in stock and bond mutual funds. Its revenues were US$344.0 million, US$273.0 million, and US$359.0 million for 2011, 2012, and 2013 respectively. Its prof-its were US$182.0 million, US$131.0 million, and US$165.0 million for 2011, 2012, and 2013 respectively. Net operating income was US$292.0 million, US$222.0 million, and US$302.0 million for 2011, 2012, and 2013 respec-tively. The total share equity was US$2,405.0 million, US$2,303.0 million, and US$2,578.0 million for 2011, 2012, and 2013 respectively.

Market Capitalization and Corporate Governance

The main driver for the survival of large national firms such as Mumtalakat in Bahrain was consolidated state ownership, assisted by a penchant for legal security. A Corporate Governance Code developed in consultation with the Ministry of Industry and Commerce was introduced in January 2011. The Code applies to all companies incorporated under Legislative Decree No. 2001 with respect to the Bahrain Commercial Companies Law relating to companies listed on the Bahrain Bourse. The Code could also apply to non-listed firms and foreign companies based in Bahrain. The Code is based on nine core principles of corporate governance, relating to board evaluation, internal control, remuneration of officers and directors, shareholder par-ticipation, and publicly available written governance guidelines. The Code goes beyond the Companies Law and includes the recommendations that the chair of the board and the CEO should not be the same person and that 50 per cent of members of the Board of Directors should be non-executive directors. Boardroom issues were undoubtedly subject to political influence. The main influence, however, was the rise of Bahrain as an Islamic finance hub with economic ties with its Gulf neighbours. Rigorous industrial and commercial competition and transparency were sought through institutions: boards of directors, board compensation and governance committees, boards of risks and audit committees, boards of investment, management executive committees, and management investment committees. There is a subtle hierarchy in this structure. Mumtalakat is at the core of this governance. It submitted annual and half-yearly reports on its activities, asset allocation, and investment details. The audit and risk committee approved the internal audit, accountability, and internal policies. Its members were all independent non-executive directors. The investment committee investigated both investment and divestment strategies and credit risk. It had at least one independent director. The management committee supervised all investment operations while the investment committee reported weekly on investment plans. Bahrain's economic stability, even following the 2008 financial crisis, is testament to these institutional strengths and corporate social responsibility, achieved through adherence to Shari'ah and Islamic finance in a compliant alignment with market economics.

Sukuk and Its Engagement with Environmental Issues and Projects

Policy debates on environmental problems were complex in Bahrain. As a small-scale producer of crude oil and as an important producer of refined oil and natural gas, processing much of the oil from wealthy Gulf neighbours, Bahrain's energy sector was dependent on fossil fuels. Saudi Arabia, Kuwait, and the UAE hold approximately a third of the world's proven reserves, while Bahrain was a tiny oil producer, accounting for less than 0.4 per cent.[174]

Oil and gas accounts for a major part of Bahrain's current energy consumption and exports but several environmental initiatives have been introduced, mainly solar power plants. In 2014, BAPCO, the National Oil and Gas Authority (NOGA), and the US-based Petra Solar built Bahrain's first solar power plant, which uses Petra Solar's smart grid technology to provide energy to BAPCO's Awali township and the University of Bahrain. The investment was US$25 million. Bahrain PV Park with US$360 million and then a further US$720 million was also developed by the Bahrain Petroleum Company. Two other initiatives were the Al Dur PV plant and the Al Dur Wind Farm,

---

[174] US Energy Information Administration, *Oil and Gas Journal*, 2013.

at a cost of US$17.18 million but the project developers have not been disclosed. Tatweer Petroleum built a solar plant in 2015 which was generating 1.5 per cent of the company's power consumption by 2017.[175] In January 2017, the Bahrain cabinet approved another solar plant project. This was followed by investment by a consortium comprising Saudi-based ACWA, Japanese contractor Mitsui, and Bahrain industrial conglomerate Al Moayyed for the construction and operation of a further solar power plant.

These projects need sustainable long-term funding, usually through a Special Purpose Vehicle to act as a trustee for sukuk holders and investors. Gulf Solar Sukuk SPV signed an istisna contract with project founder (GM) to construct Gulf Solar Farm. A technology firm (First Gulf Solar) was then engaged to deliver the project. Upon completion in two years, by 2020, the title and asset would pass to Gulf Solar Sukuk SPV. This financing strategy ensured that all stakeholder interests were protected, particularly crucial as the project carries risk. Sale-based, lease-based, and equity-based Shari'ah-compliant financing structures, murabaha, ijarah, and Mudarabah respectively, are designed to reflect solar project risks and timeline requirements in the different phases of the project. The solar asset sukuk form of financing brings benefits and skills along the entire value chain. Its transactional structure is divided into different phases to reflect each stage of project implementation and capital expenditure, and this suits both developers and investors. The issuers include the asset originator, which is Gulf Municipality, the project asset is Gulf Solar Farm, the developer is First Gulf Solar, and the electricity distributor is GEWA. The financiers are Sukuk Holders, a Special Purpose Vehicle and credit enhancement institution, and the service manager is Gulf Solar. There are social ethics both in securing green energy principles and in using sustainable finance. In achieving sustainable industry partnerships, both domestic and foreign sukuk are the core. The tapping of Islamic finance makes these projects global while securing socially responsible energy programmes. This maturing of Islamic finance within a globally integrated green energy programme establishes ethical environmental disclosure and accountability.[176]

The performance of sukuk in capital markets in the Middle East and across the globe rests on contract enforceability. The business culture, the firm and industry responses and governance, and above all the role of the state in securing sukuk acceptance have been examined here. Throughout the period from 2001 to 2015, sovereign sukuk by the state holding company

[175] Oxford Business Group, 'New Solar Power Projects in Bahrain add to the Country's Energy Mix', 2017.
[176] Deloitte Research and Analysis, 'Sustainable Finance'; *IIFM Sukuk Report*, 2018.

has dominated. By 2014, global sukuk entered a period of consolidation, with the Government of Bahrain registering global sukuk of US$600 million, rising to US$660 million in 2015, while there was a doubling of domestic issuance to US$3 billion. The expansion of domestic sukuk was in state projects through the oligopolist Mumtalakat and its individual corporate interests. The international sukuk was largely Sukuk al Ijarah.[177] The second most popular was Sukuk al Musharakah from 2001 to 2008 but it declined after the 2008 financial crisis by 23 per cent.[178] The decline in the use of diverse sukuk instruments in international markets while clinging to ijarah can be explained by the fact that Musharakah structures are adapted to property markets and were affected by international property cycles. In addition, sukuk al wakala replaced sukuk al musharakah in popularity in 2009–12, a consequence again of the 2008 Global Financial Crisis. Wakala rose from 1 per cent in international sukuk issuances in 2001 to 29 per cent in 2008 and to 38 per cent in 2013–14, while ijarah held a 42 per cent stake in the international sukuk market overall. In domestic markets in all countries the preference was also for sukuk al murabahah.

In 2007, Sheikh Taqi Usmani, chairman of the Shari'ah Board of AAOIFI, criticized the sukuk instruments used in these markets, in particular mudarabah, wakala, and musharakah, as not being Shari'ah compliant. In 2008, the AAOIFI issued strict rules on ownership of assets, clarity on debt, liquidity, purchases at market value, and purchase of assets at a price agreed by an independent agent. This has led to the evolution of a hybrid sukuk structure, with flexibility in the types of assets used. Consequently, sukuk issuance is on a more efficient basis than with a single instrument like ijarah. In addition, the Shari'ah-compliant index stipulates that issuance be made by reputable organizations with strict AAOIF standards. And the underlying assets in sukuk must be screened for compliance by the Shari'ah Supervisory Board. Also, S & P Dow Jones has a trio of sukuk indices aimed at MENA and Islamic investors. These are the S & P MENA Bond and Sukuk Index, and two sub-indices, S & P MENA Bond Index and S & P MENA Sukuk Index. In addition, for Islamic finance to operate in the US there was the option of issuing securities through Rule 144A and flexibility through Regulation S of the US Securities Act of 1933. This was to avoid the constraints

---

[177] IIFM Sukuk Database.

[178] Simon Archer, Brandon Davies, and Rifaat Ahmed Abdel Karim, 'Overview of the Islamic Capital Market', in *Islamic Capital Markets and Products: Managing Capital and Liquidity Requirements under Basel III*, edited by Simon Archer and Rifaat Ahmed Abdel Karim (Chichester: Wiley, 2018), pp. 12–13.

of the Sarbanes–Oxley Act of 2002 and the higher costs if registered with US underwriters.[179]

With different standards within the AAOIFI, variation is inevitable. Appraising assets, risk, and credit structure varies according to the transaction and to the region in which it is carried out, whether domestic or international. But sukuk achieves a high degree of legal similarity while attempting to preserve Shari'ah compliance. In addition, when operating in wholesale markets, investor preference and industry and commercial practices help to minimize legal differences. Furthermore, the Beximco arbitration in London showed that, ultimately, classical law is no longer relevant in modern markets. Sukuk is a shrewd operator in international markets and the new challenges have enabled it to invert the classic paradigm and pursue the quest for animating Islamic finance in both domestic and international markets, and utilize both corporate and sovereign sukuk structures.[180]

Predicting, Providing, Sustaining, and Achieving Success with Diverse Financial Portfolios: Mutual Funds and Foreign Investors

Mutual funds represent an active part of the Bahrain Bourse. The first overseas mutual fund was initiated in the 1980s and the first indigenous mutual fund was launched in 1984. Growth has been strong since regulations governing mutual funds were introduced in 1992. The first Collective Investment Schemes Rules were issued by the CBB in the same year and further reforms were introduced in June 2007. These provided comprehensive rules and regulations governing the registration and supervision of mutual funds based in Bahrain. Despite the financial crisis of 2008, the mutual funds domiciled in Bahrain grew at an average of 15 per cent.[181] By the end of June 2019 there were 2,136 mutual funds, of which 74 were based in Bahrain. There were 80 Shari'ah-compliant funds in June 2019. The net asset value of these mutual funds was US$7.534 billion at the end of March 2019, compared to US$7.877 billion in 2018. Of the total net asset value, US$3.340 billion was invested locally and US$1.325 billion in Shari'ah-compliant funds.[182] This apparent

---

[179] Archer, Davies, and Karim, 'Overview of the Islamic Capital Market', pp. 18–35. See also the IIFM Sukuk Database, January 2001 to December 2015.

[180] Sovereign sukuk by contract, 2001–16: sukuk Wakalah 23.00 per cent; sukuk Salam 4.27 per cent; Sukuk Murabaha 0.21 per cent; Sukuk Ijarah 71.00 per cent; Hybrid 2.18 per cent. Corporate sukuk and sovereign sukuk by contract: Ijarah 32 per cent; Musharakah 16 per cent; Murabaha 8 per cent; Mudarabah 11 per cent; Wakalah 23 per cent; Hybrid 3 per cent; Exchangeable 7 per cent. *IIFM Sukuk Report*, 2018.

[181] Deloitte Research and Analysis, *Global Impact Report*, 2012.

[182] Central Bank of Bahrain, 'Collective Investment Undertakings', April 2019.

decline could be the result of 'spin-offs' into diverse investments, as well as the impact of overseas entrants into Bahrain.

With strong government intervention in Bahrain's stock market, the foreign benefits are clear. There is a consensus that, in addition to the spillover effects from the wealthy Gulf states, there is optimism surrounding the encouragement of foreign companies into Manama. There is an exchange of technical ideas, financial market intelligence, and skills. The Capital Market Law 95 of June 1992 and the Banking Law of June 2003 granted foreigners full access to Bahrain's capital markets. In 2012, the Global GCC Islamic Fund and the IIAS Islamic Mena Fund were both listed on Bloomberg. Bahrain is the third largest mutual fund area in the GCC. The three largest mutual fund managers are Lebanon's Blominvest Bank, which has assets of US$372 million (under Assets Under Management (AUM)), Kuwait's Global Investment House (US$235 million), and GIC Funds Company (US$234 million).[183] All transactions within the mutual funds are through the Mutual Funds Exchange's automated trading system.

Bahrain's mutual fund managers operate internationally but local markets are prominent, as almost half of AUM is directed at fixed income funds compared to the regional average of 6 per cent. By 2016, the Bahrain Bourse had a total of 19 mutual funds, all of them open-ended. Global Investment House is the largest investor with five funds traded on the market, followed by the Securities & Investment Company, a prominent financier in Bahrain associated with innovative initiatives. Other mutual fund institutions investing on the Bahrain Bourse included the National Bank of Kuwait and the Makaseb Fund Company.

Despite the financial crisis, mutual funds in Bahrain have grown at 15 per cent in recent years. In 2015, there were a total of 88 Islamic mutual funds with assets of US$1.4 billion. The same year the number of open-ended mutual funds with various providers rose to 2,743, with a net asset value of US$9.74 billion. The providers included retail banks, wholesale banks and institutions, and individual investors.[184]

The pattern of fund distribution and the specific institutions involved (financial intermediaries, wholesale banks, and retail banks) have been identified in 2015 by the Central Bank of Bahrain. This pushed investors to a position of dominance and showed that financial institutions were important

---

[183] Oxford Business Group, 'Several Innovations in the Pipeline to Deepen Bahrain's Capital Markets', *Bahrain Report 2017*, p. 3.
[184] See Figure 13.5 in El-Tahir, 'Bahrain's Islamic Capital Markets'. See also Central Bank of Bahrain: http://www.cbb.gov.bh/page-p-11th-annualworld-islamic%96funds%96and%96financial-markets-conferences-2015.htm

in developing the Bahrain Bourse, while encouraging the formation of rival clusters for investment in the insurance and bond market, such as Mumtalakat. The highest volume of funds is derived from financial intermediaries to institutions, ranging from US$2,698,352,000 to US$3,172,184,000. The flow from financial intermediaries to individuals was US$859,724,000 to US$1,048,040. The next category of fund provision was from retail banks to individuals, ranging from US$994,015,000 to US$1048,557,000. The provision from retail banks to institutions was US$759,037,000 to US$822,087,000. The third category was wholesale banks to individuals, US$69,208,000 to US$67,876,000; and from wholesale banks to institutions, from US$1,083,938,000 to US$1,064,088,000.[185]

The popularity of mutual funds in Bahrain can be contrasted with Malaysia where Islamic mutual funds invest in sukuk and IIFM instruments. In Malaysia, the allocation strategies of both Islamic mutuals and conventional mutuals are established by the Permodalan Nasional Berhad, the state investment agency, directing funds into infrastructural and industrial projects. This was ensured by conventional mutual funds investing stocks, bonds, and cash. Islamic mutual investment remained small, 17 per cent in December 2014, while conventional finance, less Shari'ah-observant, exploited sukuk as the major investment tool. In Bahrain, too, legal hybridity existed, where regulatory rigour was achieved through a 1992 law governing mutual operations. Bahrain retained a more diverse but strong growth through mutuals investing on the Bourse.[186]

We need now to analyse briefly the pattern of mutual fund and investment strategies in international comparison, to understand the lock-in by the Bahraini state and how that was the keystone for growth on the Bourse. When Hoepner, Rammal, and Rezec investigated investment patterns and the size of investments in 20 countries, it was evident that Islamic mutual funds gravitate towards growth and small capital stocks but also may invest in a diverse way when investing abroad.[187] This is clearly rooted in Bahrain's access to oil wealth from her Gulf neighbours. Mutual funds are invested in energy, petrochemical and related processing industries, property throughout the Gulf states, and in financial intermediaries. The result was that these institutional investments enabled the mutual funds to be highly competitive because of superior information and knowledge spillover from the Gulf neighbours,

---

[185] Central Bank of Bahrain, 2015, cited in El-Tahir, 'Bahrain's Islamic Capital Markets', p. 272.

[186] Central Bank of Bahrain, April 2019, Appendix 1, Mutual Funds–Asset Classes, Bahrain Bourse.

[187] Andreas G. F. Hoepner, Hussain G. Rammal, and Michael Rezec, 'Islamic Mutual Funds' Financial Performance and International Investment Style: Evidence from 20 Countries', *European Journal of Finance*, vol. 17, no. 9–10 (2011).

with such competitiveness enabling Bahrain to expand its stock market operations despite its exchange being smaller than the stock exchanges in Saudi Arabia and the UAE. Furthermore, the investment mode of Islamic mutual funds is more standardized than that of their conventional counterparts because Shari'ah has a narrow range of permissible activities. Islamic funds are invested in smaller stocks for fear of investing in Shari'ah forbidden stocks. In fact, their returns may turn negative when funds are invested in unfamiliar areas, which may not be Shari'ah compliant. In addition, Islamic mutuals may invest less in overseas foreign companies due to the risk of investing in prohibited activities. Despite these restrictions, mutual funds in Bahrain outperform mutual funds in international equity markets because of Bahrain's prominence as the Islamic financial hub for the Gulf states.[188]

A vital attraction, inspiration, and influence for the Bahrain Bourse was the New York Stock Exchange. Therefore, an assessment of the NYSE may be useful in identifying trends in the Bahrain Bourse. Here Falkenstein's work may help understand why Bahrain, in contrast to Saudi Arabia and Kuwait, encouraged foreign investment into its stock exchange. Bahrain was simultaneously building a common law and civil law structure to improve accountability and governance, while seeking to create networks with Islamic countries in the MENA region to centralize and decentralize their operations.[189]

As the Mutual Fund Portfolio on the NYSE has illustrated, mutual fund preferences for stocks are not driven only by conventional proxies for risk. They show significant preferences for various investment characteristics relevant for understanding the behaviour of these institutions. First, they display a non-linear preference towards stocks with high-value volatility. Mutual funds show an aversion to low-price stocks, while demand is consistently increasing in liquidity, as measured by trading volume divided by shares outstanding. Other than the small capital sector, which specializes in small firms, mutuals show an aversion to small firms. They avoid stocks with little information. Mutual fund owners are sharp on risks, transaction costs, and information on the firm. In Bahrain, it was state involvement that created interest in mutual funds. The interest was accentuated by the Financial Trust Law enacted in August 2006, governing financial trusts, while the Collective Investment Undertakings (CIUs) Law and the CBB rules governing real estate investment trusts and private investment undertakings both increased the flexibility of Shari'ah-compliant investment institutions, thus attracting

---

[188] Hoepner, Rammal, and Rezec, 'Islamic Mutual Funds' Financial Performance', p. 27.
[189] Eric G. Falkenstein, 'Preferences for Stock Market Characteristics as Revealed by Mutual Fund Portfolio Holdings', *Journal of Finance*, vol. 51, no. 1 (1996), pp. 111–35.

a large portfolio of investors, as seen in the list of mutual funds and REITS listed on the Bourse.

Clearly, some investors have comparative advantages in buying certain assets, and therefore their preferences are clear. The appendix on mutual funds in Bahrain shows considerable diversity. Furthermore, mutual funds in Bahrain often direct investment towards small firms where there is evidence of good performance and an acceptable cost of equity. This appears to be the key component of the CAPM, which often does not incorporate firm and sustainable information. Precision and credibility are secured through contacts and knowledge of the Bahrain state and its investment ambitions and successes. In Bahrain, despite investment in small firms, mutual funds face lower information asymmetry because of their contacts with the state, the main financier.

The major questions are: Who owns the mutual funds? What percentage are open-ended mutual funds? And is the total equity owned by mutual funds really small?[190] The small company funds represent a sizeable proportion of investor demand, and this is part of small firm preferences. Are there institutional constraints on funds? In his research in 1991–92, Falkenstein discovered that mutual funds have a preference for stocks with high visibility and low transaction costs. There is an emphasis on investor recognition, a potential agency problem in mutual funds, and herd behaviour by mutuals and their links to corporate finance.[191] In Bahrain's case, the state is the resource provider. Its cliques are, to a degree, broken by foreign direct investment. The 'associational economy' has a different framework for resource distribution and resource dependency. This shows how unique Bahrain is compared to her conservative neighbours.

Mutual funds' aversion to risky stocks often leads them to prefer stocks with a long period of listing.[192] This helps institutions to justify their portfolios to investors. Falkenstein has shown that share price, volatility, liquidity, age of listing, and size are all relevant for the mutual funds' approach to investment. There is a preference for small capital stocks, and most are concentrated in stocks with relatively low liquidity. Mutual funds are sensitive to proxies for transaction costs (price, liquidity) and to information flows. Mutual funds behave less like 'insiders' and more like the general public. Mutuals are influenced by media information. Sirri and Tufano argue that mutual fund

---

[190] See the capitalization figures above on mutual funds and the institutional and individual funds. Central Bank of Bahrain: http://www.cbb.gov.bh/page-p-11th_annual-world-islamic-funds-and-financial-markets-conferences-2015.htm.

[191] Falkenstein, 'Preferences for Stock Market Characteristics', p. 111.

[192] Falkenstein, 'Preferences for Stock Market Characteristics', p. 128.

performance affects net capital for the highest-ranking funds.[193] The low-risk funds receive large inflows of money. This is true of Bahrain's SICO and Mumtalakat investments.

Mutual funds seem more poised to take advantage of relative rather than absolute performance, as funds are not simply buying high-priced stocks. Moreover, mutual funds do not prefer the most highly volatile stocks but, rather, avoid the lowest volatility stocks. The statistics for the Bahrain Bourse show low volatility. In addition, there is little evidence of avoidance of newly listed stocks by Bahrain's mutual funds or of herd behaviour in support of certain stocks. This improved sense of balance may be attributed, in part, to a lack of tension between the state, the resource provider, and the Islamic constraints on Islamic mutual funds. However, the closure of certain bank-funded mutuals and private mutuals suggests that there exists market-driven performance but not unfettered capitalism.

On the Bahrain Bourse, market efficiency and state support attract mutual funds, while low-skilled managers are dealing in stocks that are largely risk free. Shari'ah is implicated in the choice of stocks, while in overseas markets, Bahrain's mutual funds avoid poor performance stocks and seek predictability in returns. Bahrain, like Kuwait and Qatar, demonstrate low reporting (the infrequency of NAV reporting) with investment funds, representing 40 per cent or more of sector-wide AUM, providing only monthly updates. This may also reflect a higher proportion of closed-end investment funds.[194] Bahrain's position as the powerful Islamic finance hub of the Middle East has been accelerating since the 1990s. The Makaseb, Markaz Arabian, and Lebanese funds use Bahrain for cross-border portfolio investments, especially in equities.[195]

[193] Erik R. Sirri and Peter Tufano, 'Costly Search and Mutual Fund Flows', Journal of Finance, vol. 53, no. 5 (1998), pp. 1589–622; Alexander Kempf and Stefan Ruenzi, 'Status Quo Bias and the Number of Alternatives: An Empirical Illustration from the Mutual Fund Industry', Journal of Behavioral Finance, vol. 7, no. 4 (2006), pp. 204–13.
[194] Zawya and CBB calculations. In addition to the retail and wholesale banks, the following also provide mutual funds. SICO Selected Securities; Global Distressed Fund (GLBL.DSF); Global Energy, Petrochemical and Downstream Industries Fund (GLBL.EPDIF); Global GCC Islamic Fund (GLBL.GIF); Global GCC Large Cap Fund (GLBL.LCF); Global GCC REAL Estate Fund (GLBL.GREF); Global Islamic Fund of Funds (GLBL.IF); Global Opportunistic Fund (GLBL.OF; Khaleej Equity Fund (KLJ.EQ.fund); Makaseb Arab Tigers Fund (MAKASEB.AT); Makaseb Income Fund (MAKASEB.IF); Markaz Arabian Fund (MGF); NBK Gulf Equity Fund (NBK.GEF); NBK Qatar Equity Fund (NBK.QEF); SICO Fixed Income Fund (SICO.FIF); SICO Gulf Equity Fund (SICO.GEF); SICO Kingdom Equity Fund (SICO.KEF); The Zenith Fund (GLBL.TZF); Unit Investment Bank (UNITINVEST): Source: Bahrain Bourse Investor and Challenges, 1 August 2019.
[195] William Macko and Diego Sourrouille, Investment Funds in MENA (World Bank, 2010), pp. 15–16, 21–3.

Liquidity and Concentrated Shareholding

Having examined in detail the fundamental strengths and weaknesses of the major financial instruments exploited on Bahrain's stock market, it is clear that the dogmatic adherence to concentrated shareholding was an enervating position. The Bahrain stock market also provided a central mantra in rejuvenating the market forces in both Islamic finance and conventional finance.

The role of liquidity in assisting allocational efficiency within the stock market is important but complex. Liquidity assists investors to trade with less price anxiety. However, market imperfections exist within the Bahrain Bourse because of concentrated corporate ownership, with a few families, aristocratic Sunnis and Shiite merchant elites, holding a disproportionate share of stocks, both openly and concealed. This ownership concentration affects market liquidity.

The role of banks on the stock market, often as intermediaries, exposes the banks and the stock market to unnecessary risk. The 2008 crisis exposed the ambiguous nature of funding by the inter-bank and money markets. In periods of liquidity stress, these markets faced problems of capital adequacy and credit availability. Islamic banks face even more difficulties, as using inter-bank and money markets involves interest-based instruments: but Bahrain is in a stabler position because it has permitted the charging of interest.[196] The argument here is that the different corporate structures and stock market instruments affect governance, with the threat of insider trading and stock manipulation. It is generally accepted that dispersed ownership creates market liquidity.[197]

Jacques Hamon and Edith Ginglinger assert that trading or free float creates liquidity, increasing the market capitalization of a firm.[198] When a firm has concentrated ownership, free float is limited, and with less trade, liquidity is decreased. Ownership concentration may also affect liquidity through information access. Concentration of ownership produces less need for information, less need to invest, and less stock engagement in free float.

A further explanation for disruption of liquidity is the adverse selection hypothesis. Concentrated ownership, with block holders with private information about a firm's value, are held in a comfort zone with less complex and

---

[196] Archer and Karim, *Islamic Capital Markets and Products*, pp. 237–42.

[197] P. Bolton and E. L. Von Thadden, 'Blocks, Liquidity, and Corporate Control', *Journal of Finance*, vol. 53, no. 1 (1998), pp. 1–25.

[198] Jacques Hamon and Edith Ginglinger, 'Ownership, Control and Market Liquidity', *Finance*, vol. 33, no. 2 (2012), pp. 61–99.

locally shared knowledge. It is a model of mutually limited active interaction with the market. Liquidity providers may respond to informed trading with wider spreads. It is necessary here to be cautious in accepting the conventional view as to the role, origins, and impact of liquidity. With the MENA countries, oil capital flows often seek stock listing to launder wealth accrued through high prices, and the Bahrain Bourse is a secure hub for investment. Institutional investors on the Bahrain Bourse possess a high level of information.

Rubin sees a high negative correlation between insiders' block holdings and institutional holdings, confirming that institutions are more willing to invest in firms with less concentrated insider ownership.[199] But US stock markets have independent institutions free of connections. In Bahrain, institutional investors may have close ties to the state and to merchant elites, and raiding certain stocks as high earners is inevitable.

However, there are reasons to suggest that ownership concentration improves control of management. A larger deviation from control of ownership may be associated with problems between the major group and minority shareholders. Given Bahrain's access to oil wealth from her neighbours, does its concentration of ownership and control produce less information asymmetry? Bahraini investors, although familiar with the financial benefits from investing in particular stocks, may also be influenced by emotion. Human perceptions and the cognitive bias for familiarity may dictate investment strategies.[200] One fruitful approach here is to trace the diverging investment strategies on the Hong Kong Stock market as compared with China. Investors in China do not always exhibit profound insight in investing in particular stocks: historical persecution and emotion hold greater sway over stock selection.[201] The divergence between Hong Kong and China reflects not just the efficient legal structures in the Hong Kong Stock Exchange that provide investor protection. Good governance will undoubtedly affect investment strategies in Hong Kong. But it is important to add that in China, with its highly speculative culture, stock listing is often driven by emotion and group instinct.

My later analysis of corporate structure and ownership in Bahrain may also shed light on investment strategies on the stock exchange. When a firm's ownership is concentrated, the availability of shares is limited, for there are fewer shareholders to engage in trading and frequency in trading is low. And

---

[199] Hamon and Ginglinger, 'Ownership, Control and Market Liquidity'.
[200] Kahneman, *Thinking Fast and Slow*, pp. 60–1.
[201] See P. Brockman and D. Y. Chung, 'Investor Protection and Firm Liquidity', *Journal of Finance*, vol. 58, no. 2 (2003), pp. 921–38.

liquidity is decreased. However, in Bahrain, liquidity is also determined by intra-regional capital flows of oil from Saudi Arabia, Kuwait, and the UAE. It is also possible that there is a positive association between spreads and block ownership, including insider and institutional blocks. We thus find that the spread is positively related to institutional ownership.[202] La Porta et al. demonstrate the importance of an economy's legal system for the degree of investor protection and the development of liquidity in financial markets.[203] Bahrain is a clear example of legal rigour in finance and stock market operations, as explained in the section on the impact of the Souk al-Manakh in 1982 and the Global Financial Crisis of 2008. It should be emphasized that control by concentrated owners of corporations when listing can generate private benefits for those owners, and outside investors may be dissuaded and therefore liquidity falls. But often, associational or cronyistic investors follow the dominant players on the Bahrain Bourse.[204]

Islamic banks face serious challenges in securing both funding and market liquidity, as operations in the interbank and money markets involve riba. Liquid assets such as cash, bank reserves, government bonds, and highly rated corporate bonds involve challenges in liquidity risk management. They also face difficulties in ensuring that contractual liquidity facilities are Shari'ah compliant. Consequently, there is evidence for the manipulation of Shari'ah-compliant products such as sukuk.[205]

It is also important to assess the impact of a large volume of capital held by institutions and wealthy individuals on liquidity in the Bahrain Bourse. The McKinsey Global Wealth Management Survey estimated that personal wealth finance in the four GCC countries (Saudi Arabia, Kuwait, the UAE, and Bahrain) amounted to US$2.7 trillion in 2015, having seen a dramatic rise from US$1.6 trillion in 2011. Rising investment in sovereign wealth funds and GCC pension funds in Bahrain, and increasing fears of a volatile market, prompted Bahrain to introduce institutional and legislative reforms. In 2015,

---

[202] A. Sarin, K. A. Shastri, and K. Shastri, 'Ownership Structure and Stock Market Liquidity', Working Paper, Santa Clara University, 2000.

[203] Rafael La Porta, Florencio Lopez-de-Silanes, Andrei Schleifer, and Robert Vishny, 'Investor Protection and Corporate Valuation', *Journal of Finance*, vol. 57, no. 3 (2002), pp. 1147–70; Rafael La Porta, Florencio Lopez-de-Silanes, Andrei Schleifer, and Robert Vishny, 'Investor Protection and Corporate Governance', *Journal of Financial Economics*, vol. 58 (2000), pp. 3–27. See also Morck, Shleifer, and Vishny, 'Do Managerial Objectives Drive Bad Acquisitions?', pp. 31–48; Morck, Shleifer and Vishny, 'The Stock Market and Investment'.

[204] A. Bhide, 'The Hidden Costs of Stock Market Liquidity', *Journal of Financial Economics*, vol. 34 (1993), pp. 31–51. Bhide argues that because of information asymmetry, the spreads of closely held firms are higher, which hinders a float and therefore impacts on liquidity. N. L. Beny, 'A Comparative Empirical Investigation of Agency and Market Theories of Insider Trading', University of Michigan Legal Working Paper Series, 2004, reports that weaker insider trading regimes have less liquid equity markets.

[205] Archer and Karim, *Islamic Capital Markets and Products*, pp. 240–1.

a clearing, settlement, and depository electronic registry was established, and simultaneously a secondary market was activated to include exchanges, bulletin boards, and trading systems, together with an increasing number of off-market systems administered by the stock exchange. Secondary market activity in the electronic age is created as a global institution with regulatory frameworks. Hence Bahrain, with US$100 million in liquidity funds in 2016 and with a 63 per cent trading value in the market, now attracted foreigner investors representing the remaining 37 per cent. Initially struggling to attract foreign investment from outside the Gulf, Bahrain was now in a favourable position with Basel 111: the liquidity coverage ratio and liquidity risk monitoring tools that featured prominently in the BCBS document in January 2013.[206]

It is also the case that the domination of Bahrain's capital markets by large institutions, a relatively small group of investors, exacerbated by oil flows from Saudi Arabia and Kuwait, led to misjudgements in the valuing of assets. While liquidity has an important role in asset pricing in small firms, for the large listed firms, Bahrain relies on state investment, foreign oil capital flows, and FDI. Consequently, the role of liquidity is impossible to determine accurately. In addition, access to insiders and private information is near impossible to appraise.[207] Bahrain's commitment to the power of the state now needs to be analysed through the efficient markets hypothesis, to assess whether deficient governance practices are hidden under liquidity. In addition, a comparative international examination would throw light on any puzzling behavioural anomalies in the Bahrain Bourse.

A useful comparison here would be the US stock exchanges, where tighter regulation aimed at greater responsibility followed the 2008 crisis. The American Securities and Exchange Commission has protected investors and maintained an orderly market.[208] Reform in the US has led Europe to establish disclosure rules and impose sanctions against insider trading. But Bhide cautions that these rules and sanctions have promoted market liquidity at the expense of the efficient governance of firms[209]. The US model discourages what Jensen called 'active investors' who provide valuable internal

---

[206] Simon Archer and Rifaat Ahmed Abdel Karim, 'Liquidity Risk Management and High Liquid Assets', in *Islamic Capital Markets and Products: Managing Capital and Liquidity Requirements under Basel III*, edited by Simon Archer and Rifaat Ahmed Abdel Karim (Chichester: Wiley, 2018), p. 238. See Bahrain Bourse Report, December 2016; Oxford Business Group, *A Developing Market in Equities in Bahrain*, 2017, p. 2; Yakov Amihud, Haim Mendelson, and Lasse Heje Pedersen, 'Liquidity and Asset Prices', *Foundation and Trends in Finance*, vol. 1, no. 4 (2005), pp. 269–364.
[207] Bhide, 'The Hidden Costs of Stock Market Liquidity', pp. 31–51.
[208] Bhide, 'The Hidden Costs of Stock Market Liquidity', pp. 31, 32.
[209] Amar Bhide, 'The Hidden Costs of Stock Market Liquidity', *Journal of Financial Economics*, vol. 34, no. 1 (1993), pp. 31–51.

monitoring and control of managers. Now shareholders are passive and play no part in internal governance. Thus, attempts to protect small investors and liquidity in US equity markets has led to passivity and fragmentation in stockholding.[210]

Disclosure rules and sanctions against insider trading reduce the costs of breaking up concentrated holdings and diversifying portfolios by sustaining market liquidity. Conversely, policies that promote the fragmentation of portfolios increase market liquidity. The liquidity of a securities market refers to the extent to which it is continuous without large price changes. Liquidity increases with the number of stockholders. Stocks may be held by few active investors, and this impairs the continuity and depth of markets. Essential thus for Bahrain is the large number and widely dispersed class of individual and small institutional investors.[211] Bahrain, unlike the early London Stock Exchange and the Souk Al-Manakh in Kuwait, was not populated by rogue promoters.

Dealing with such new challenges did not, of course, eradicate corporate misdemeanours. With Bahrain's large stockholders, such as the state, entrenched as oligopolists, it was difficult to evolve a serious commitment to transparency. Disclosure by banks of management perks lacked certification as the headquarters of many corporations are based in the Cayman Islands. The incentive to fragment portfolios in Bahrain's stock market to secure market liquidity was absent. The presence of gentlemanly, elitist, passive stockholders on Bahrain's Bourse had serious consequences for liquidity as they neglect potential growth firms to achieve more diversified portfolios. Bahrain needed economic diversification to survive. Financial reporting is less frequent in Bahrain, and funds moving in and out are difficult to trace. Consolidated annual statements and disclosures are not regular. Japan, too, is implicated in such habits and practices.[212]

In Bahrain, a drive to achieve economic diversification internationally, as well as to attract inward investment, led to a three-pronged emphasis on banks, investment trusts, and financial institutions that would create sustainable growth in the capital markets of the Gulf. There was a further emphasis on mutual funds and insurance firms, which often hold more than 10 per cent of a listed firm's stock. As well as increasing the involvement of institutional investors in listed stocks, individuals shifted from direct investment in equities to holding mutual fund shares and public pension funds and nonprofit endowments. Institutional investors face lower transaction costs than

---

[210] Michael C. Jensen, 'Eclipse of the Public Corporation', *Harvard Business Review*, 1989, pp. 61–74.
[211] Bhide, 'The Hidden Costs of Stock Market Liquidity', p. 34.
[212] Bhide, 'The Hidden Costs of Stock Market Liquidity', p. 40.

individual investors and do not face high commission rates. New methods in exploiting sukuk finance to absorb liquidity from the traditional aristocratic families of Saudi Arabia and Kuwait led to the transformation of sukuk into a Shari'ah-compliant instrument. The state, funding infrastructure projects through sukuk finance, stabilized the stock market.

This reluctance to diffuse shareholdings is reminiscent of Warren Buffet's reluctance to sell stocks to both highly and less-efficient firms. The turnover in his business is also constrained by holdings of privately placed convertible preferred stocks. In Japan, 48 per cent of stocks are held on a near permanent basis by a network of banks, insurance companies, suppliers, and customers. Corporate cross ownership is also present in Germany, Austria, Spain, and Italy.[213] Liquid markets can utilize cash assets quickly and diversify cheaply and with speed, but they can be exposed and weaken governance.[214] Buffet's structure of active shareholders with full access to information has considerable advantages in making correct evaluations, as was shown by his response to the 2008 Global Financial Crisis. He emerged unscathed.

It is perfectly plausible that increased liquidity on the Bahrain Bourse can overcome the problem of fragmented stockholding by using intermediaries to maintain sales. Warren Buffet, as a major investor in Saloman, had the confidence to identify rising risk in the firm and he replaced the CEO. Managers need substantial information, both confidential and contextual.[215] The US experience shows that exceptional liquidity on the part of American firms does not necessarily provide traded firms with advantages in issuing equity.[216] Established firms rarely raise significant funds. Earnings retained by American firms with liquid stocks are more highly valued by investors. However, the regulation of increased securitization of pension benefits and mutual funds is difficult to measure.

Firms usually start with fully concentrated stockholding, with all investors active in governance. It is important to recognize social norms and psychology, as, for example, on the Tokyo Stock Exchange, which is an insider's paradise. The firms there are complacent about self-dealing by stockholders who provide goods and services to firms they control. The chains in the Keiretsu (the Japanese business network) can result in a decline in corporate principles. Japanese firms can place a high proportion of stocks with active investors, thus providing few safeguards to diffuse stockholdings but

---

[213] Bhide, 'The Hidden Costs of Stock Market Liquidity', p. 43.
[214] Shleifer and Vishny, 'A Survey of Corporate Governance'.
[215] Bhide, 'The Hidden Costs of Stock Market Liquidity', p. 44.
[216] Jonathan Barron Baskin, 'The Development of Corporate Financial Markets in Britain and the US 1600–1914: Overcoming Asymmetric Information', *Business History Review*, vol. 62, no. 2 (1988), p. 213.

without significant loss of liquidity. Japan has consistently viewed the macro-economy through venture capital firms, family trust Japanese keiretsu firms with strategies in R&D, marketing, production, and management.[217] Porter suggests that firms reveal strategies as well as financial data by fostering better governance, more protection for small stockholders, and liquid markets.[218]

An analysis of the investors on the Bahrain Bourse shows that, because of state dominance, pension funds and endowments do not need high liquidity. In addition, the wealthy treat stocks as long-term holdings. The stock markets in the Gulf are premature frontier stock exchanges. Yet, even under the crippling weight of weak organizational capabilities, amateurish professionals still had listings in London and New York. Nonetheless, they have been slow to grasp the power of venture capital liquidity.[219]

There have been three major innovations to boost liquidity. First, 2010 saw the creation of the Bahrain Financial Exchange, trading international derivatives, structured products, and Shari'ah-compliant and cash instruments. Second, 2015 saw the establishment of an Islamic Finance Index of all Shari'ah-compliant companies. Then, in January 2015, the CBB introduced access to government debt, which permitted both institutions and individual investors to purchase government bonds from the primary market through licensed brokers.

In 2016, nine of the top stocks had a free float of lower than 25 per cent, and outside of the blue chips the proportion of company shares publicly traded on the market was smaller.[220] Important here was the clustering of shares within family-owned businesses, which inevitably maintain a high degree of ownership. The state, through its control of major state programmes undertaken by state-owned corporations, also abstained from active trading. Consequently, the dynamics of the spread dictates the trade volume. While it is accepted that frequency of trading increases liquidity, it also has market impact but retains control of major corporations. A small proportion of shares is available for investors. Short-term traders seek opportunities with low free floats where volatility is low, although this is not very attractive.

[217] N. Kawabe, 'The Development of Distribution Systems in Japan before World War II', *Business and Economic History*, vol. 18 (1989), pp. 33–44; J. Muranaga and T. Shimizu, 'Market Microstructure and Market Liquidity', mimeo, 1999; J. Muranaga and M. Ohsawa, 'Measurement of Liquidity Risk in the Context of Market Risk Calculation', in *The Measurement of Aggregate Market Risk*. Bank for International Settlements, 1997; Bruce N. Lehman and David M. Modest, 'Trading and Liquidity on the Tokyo Stock Exchange: A Bird's Eye View', *Journal of Finance*, vol. 49, no. 3 (1994).
[218] Michael E. Porter, 'Capital Disadvantage: America's Failing Capital Investment System', *Harvard Business Review*, vol. 70, no. 5 (1992), pp. 65–82.
[219] William A. Sahlman, 'The Structure and Governance of Venture Capital Organizations', *Journal of Financial Economics*, vol. 27 (1990), pp. 473–521.
[220] Oxford Business Group, 'Several Innovations in the Pipeline'.

In 2014, the CBB tackled the free float issue through an amendment to its securities-offering module, proposing a free float of 20 per cent of total issued shares. The CBB retains the right to control the market, as in the floatation of ALBA in 2010, in which 10 per cent of shares were offered, with the minimum float reduced to 10 per cent, consistent with BHB listing rules. This was to encourage more listing of family-owned companies. In tackling liquidity through the free float, the CBB and BHB sided with the market resolution of 2015, which obliged all listed companies to have a minimum free float of 10 per cent of issued and fully paid-up shares. The profits the market makers derive are relatively small in size but big in volume. They will create a balance between supply and demand and bridge the gap between buying and selling prices. In May 2016, Manama-based Securities and Investment Company, SICO, signed an agreement with BHB as first market maker on the Bourse. The liquidity fund's investors were Osoolasset Management, an arm of the Social Insurance Organization and the Military Pension Fund. Since 2011, it has invested in private equity programmes such as Bahrain Pharma and the Bank of Bahrain and Kuwait, which has operated in Bahrain for 45 years and dominates the retail market and the Financial Mall. Finally, another significant strategy was the ambitious expansion and power through mergers of prominent banks. Entrepreneurship, management, and state power are increasingly concentrated within banks through mergers, and it remains a major factor in the economic renaissance of the stock market in Bahrain.

The Banks' Mergers and Acquisitions in Seeking Scale, Scope and Survival

The close relationship of the banks to the state discouraged competition across a wide range of financial sectors and products. The banks concentrated on mergers and acquisitions, dominated by state and metropolitan interests. They did this with support from the CBB, not least in providing legal protection. This did pose risks to foreign investors.

Al Salaam Bank acquired 100 per cent equity in Bahraini Saudi Bank and swiftly recorded a 95 per cent increase in net profits in 2012. First Leasing Bank merged with Ithmaar Bank to increase its paid-up capital to US$758 million. Capivest, ElfBank, and Capital Management House also merged, raising shareholder equity to US$350 million and assets to over US$400 million. These mergers increased the total assets of seven banks in this group to US$6.3 billion. Only clusters of influence within the oil-rich Gulf could sustain Bahrain, as it was restricted by its limited population of 1.2 million.[221] Consolidation of ownership was achieved between the Islamic Retail Bank and Al Salam Bank Bahrain and conventional retail bank BMI Bank in February 2014; and between Elaf Bank, Capivest, and Capital Management House with Ibdar Bank in December 2013.[222] Bahrain's banks are characterized by high asset concentration. They financed commercial real estate institutions, where exposure stood at 29.4 percentage in September 2016.[223] However, it was the funding of state programmes that often rendered these banks vulnerable.[224] With phenomenal growth, reliance on external resources such as oil, and the inherent instability of transient foreign banks, there were huge risks.

The rise of investment banks added to these risks, but they were alleviated by the state's presence. Invest Corp, the dominant investment bank in Bahrain, had pursued retail banking with outstanding success, despite fluctuating profits in the mid-1980s. In 2010, Invest Corp's acquisition of Coral Palm Plaza, a shopping centre in Coral Springs Florida, as part of a joint venture with Lincoln Equities, for US$120 million signalled its global ambitions. But Arcapita's purchasing of a stake in J. Jill, a retailing giant in America, in 2011 was a serious misjudgement. Arcapita filed for bankruptcy in March 2012. It had had a fascinating history, being incorporated in Bahrain in November 1996 as a joint stock company (closed) and operating as an Islamic wholesale bank licensed in Bahrain. It was privately owned by 360 shareholders, although 70 per cent of shares were held by a small number of prominent individuals and institutions in the Gulf, the remaining 30 per cent by Arcapita's management. Its subsidiary AIHL was incorporated in 1998 as a holding company in the Cayman Islands. Prior to filing for bankruptcy, it was a powerful investment company listed on the Bahrain Bourse and owned by Gulf elites and by sovereign wealth funds. The investors came from Saudi Arabia, Kuwait, the UAE, Qatar, Oman, and Malaysia. Its investments were principally in real estate and state infrastructure. In 2004, it had invested in Bahrain's infrastructure programme and had expanded into Europe and Asia between 2002 and 2008, in wind turbine technology, rail network projects, and gas companies, with equity holding companies and special purpose vehicles providing the finance.[225] The opportunities offered by oil wealth,

---

[221] Hatim El-Tahir, 'Bahrain: Threads of Growth Markets in Islamic Finance', in *The Islamic Finance Handbook: A Practitioner's Guide to the Global Markets*, edited by Sasikala Thiagaraja, Andrew Morgan, Andrew Tebbutt, and Geraldine Chan (Singapore: Wiley, 2014), pp. 31–2.

[222] Bahrain Economic Development Board, *Islamic Finance Report*, 2015; websites of banks; Central Bank of Bahrain, *Financial Stability Report*, February 2015, 2017.

[223] Central Bank of Bahrain, *Financial Stability Report*, February 2017, p. 49.

[224] Central Bank of Bahrain, *Financial Stability Report*, February 2017, p. 53.

[225] Michael J. T. McMillen, 'The Arcapita Group Bankruptcy: A Restructuring Case Study', International Shari'ah Research Academy for Islamic Finance and the Thomson Reuters Report, 8 November 2015.

intra-regional links, and the combination of conventional and Islamic banking, drove attempts to become global but with little rationality. Arcapita had global ambitions but without the required financial, manufacturing, and technology skills. It was merely exploiting a lucrative oil market but had no thought-through plan for investment. It ended up bankrupt because of the American legal rigour demanded by the Sarbanes–Oxley Act of 2002. In Bahrain it would not have faced bankruptcy or even have been forced to repay its debts.

Paradoxically, it was the CBB that assumed corporate social responsibility, by its commitment to a comprehensive reporting framework that, in 2013, issued 15 risk management rules, under six categories. Islamic banks were also registered under this regulatory framework. The six categories are credit risk, equity investment risk, market risk, liquidity risk, rate of return risk, and operational risk. State intervention in Bahrain, which hitherto had been light, now increasingly became bureaucratized. The Islamic Financial Services Board, which in turn guided the Basel Committee on Banking Supervision (Basel 1, 2, 3) introduced concerted efforts to shape market transparency in Islamic finance. In 2013, the CBB regulated takaful business on issues of solvency, corporate governance, and actuarial reporting within the insurance sector. In 2012–13, Bahrain came under AAOIFI Islamic Standards, consisting of 26 accounting standards, five auditing standards, seven governance rules, two ethical standards, and 45 Shari'ah regulations.[226]

The AAOIFI, IIFM, and the International Islamic Finance Rating Agency acquired authority in governing Islamic finance in Bahrain. However, despite those financial frameworks, there was a lack of legal rigour, and this inevitably disrupted international expansion, both through Islamic windows within conventional banks and in Islamic financial institutions.

There are serious impediments to any form of convergence between Islamic banks and conventional banks, as illustrated in the market shares of Islamic banks. In Bahrain, Islamic banks held 14 per cent of the market, while in Kuwait they took 22 per cent. In Indonesia, Islamic banks held 1 per cent of total banking assets and in Malaysia, despite state dominance, just 11 per cent of the financial market. There were increasing doubts over the long-term ability of Islamic finance to compete in international markets. In the oil-rich GCC countries, cocooned by high liquidity, it was possible to forge a protected financial sector sheltered from global shocks. What were the features that provided that protection?

---

[226] El-Tahir, 'Bahrain: Threads of Growth Markets in Islamic Finance', p. 39.

External shocks on the assets side can be passed to investment depositors. Conversely, Islamic banks are reluctant to engage in risky initiatives, because of their need to provide stable and competitive returns to investors. Investors, in turn, retained a commitment to tight discipline, since all shared the risks. Islamic banks hold a larger share of assets in reserve accounts with central banks, a commitment to the indigenous characteristics of society within an authoritarian state fuelled by oil revenues.

Western economists Adam Smith, F. A. Hayek, and John Maynard Keynes were concerned at the inherent problems with interest rates. Even Joseph Stiglitz argued that interest rates were responsible for economic and financial fluctuations and hit the poor most severely. The advantage of Islamic banking is that a profit-sharing contract makes the return to capital depend on productivity, the allocation of funds, growth potential, and the viability of enterprise. The reality was that the Bahrain government was interventionist rather than cautious.

With government prompting, the volume of projects and investments will increase because of the underlying risk-averse accountability. Islamic finance reduces speculation in financial markets, and the secondary markets for stocks and certificates are based on profit-sharing principles. Islamic finance can be less inflationary because the supply of money is not allowed to exceed the supply of goods. Islamic banking is less risky in terms of external shocks, liquidity risks, and insolvency risks than are conventional banks. But this is difficult to substantiate because often the two systems coexist. At the same time the need for frameworks of support for Islamic finance and for diversification into new financial products is clear.

In tackling problems in regional expansion, it becomes apparent that Islamic finance was a double-edged sword. For example, the use of Special Purpose Vehicles in offshore accounts and the off-the-balance-sheet nature of many transactions may disguise links to terrorism as well as raise fears of money laundering by the oil-rich Middle East states. This weakness is assisted by the confused structure of the regulation of Islamic banking, both within Bahrain and across the MENA countries, through AAOFI, IIRA, IIFM, LMC, GCIBFI, and BIBF.[227]

---

[227] AAOIFI: Accounting and Auditing Organization for Islamic Financial Institutions, established in 1990 in Bahrain as an international standard regulator for finance, providing governance and transparency. IIR: International Islamic Rating Agency, to provide rating services for Islamic financial instruments. IIFM: International Islamic Financial Market started in 2002 in Bahrain to provide a cooperative framework for Shari'ah interpretations and to encourage the creation of a secondary market. LMC: Liquidity Management Centre, established in 2002 to facilitate the creation of Shari'ah-compliant financial products. Its main aim is the creation of an interbank money market, provide investment opportunities, short-term liquidity, and tradeable instruments, and to expand the market. GCIBFI: General Council for Islamic Banks and Financial Institutions, organizes seminars, training opportunities for financial sector employees. BIBF: Bahrain Institute of Banking and Finance, provides courses focused on Islamic finance.

Table 4.4 Average annual OPEC crude oil price, 1960–2018
(US$ per barrel)

1960	1.63	1980	35.52	2000	27.60
1961	1.57	1981	34.00	2001	23.12
1962	1.52	1982	32.38	2002	24.36
1963	1.50	1983	29.04	2003	28.10
1964	1.45	1984	28.20	2004	36.05
1965	1.42	1985	27.01	2005	50.59
1966	1.36	1986	13.53	2006	61.00
1967	1.33	1987	17.73	2007	69.04
1968	1.32	1988	14.24	2008	94.10
1969	1.27	1989	17.31	2009	60.86
1970	1.21	1990	22.26	2010	77.38
1971	1.70	1991	18.62	2011	107.40
1972	1.82	1992	18.44	2012	109.00
1973	2.70	1993	16.33	2013	105.87
1974	11.00	1994	15.53	2014	96.29
1975	10.43	1995	16.86	2015	49.49
1976	11.60	1996	20.29	2016	40.76
1977	12.50	1997	18.86	2017	52.51
1978	12.79	1998	12.28	2018	69.78
1979	29.19	1999	17.44	2019	64.62

Source: See https://www.statista.com/statistics/262858/change-in-opec-crude-oil-prices-since-1960/

5

The Stock Market

Dynamics of Socially Responsible Oil and Gold

Oil provides a major explanation for the emergence of Bahrain as the hub of Islamic finance in the GCC states from the 1970s. One of the reasons for the sustainability of the Bahrain stock exchange had been the oil wealth which provided it with funding. Personal ownership in listed companies is limited, as the state is the major investor on the stock exchange. The power dynamics of oil and the Sunni-dominated Gulf allowed Bahrain to undertake the refining of oil from Saudi Arabia and Kuwait. Bahrain had exhausted her own oil reserves by the early 1970s. However, despite the decline in her own oil reserves, discovered in 1931, by the 1970s Bahrain had consolidated its financial leadership through oil capital flows within the GCC countries. Bahrain was in the vanguard of GCC financial vitality and economic resurgence. In 2018, oil and gas reserves were discovered in the Khaliji-al Bahrain basin, located off the western shore. It has been estimated that 14 trillion cubic feet of gas will be produced in five years. The existing oil fields in the Bahrain field pump 45,000 barrels a day while the Abu Sada offshore field, with 160,000 barrels a day, is shared with Saudi Arabia.

With British technological input, Bahrain had developed a sophisticated oil infrastructure and after 1971 concentrated on exports of refined oil. This refining compensated for the decline in her own oil reserves. BAPCO, founded in 1929 by Standard Oil, had opened its first refinery in 1936. By the 1970s the Bahrain Natural Gas Company had BP and Caltex as shareholders, although the state was the major shareholder.[1] Despite this local development, revenues from oil were remarkably low in Bahrain compared even to Kuwait. The average contribution of oil revenues to Bahrain's state budget was 53 per cent between 1934 and 1971.[2] In 1985, oil revenues accounted

---

[1] S. H. Longrigg, *Oil in the Middle East* (London: Oxford University Press, 1968).
[2] M. G. Rumaihi, *Bahrain: Social and Political Change Since the First World War* (London: Bowker, 1976), p. 75.

Islam and Capitalism in the Making of Modern Bahrain. Rajeswary Ampalavanar Brown, Oxford University Press.
© Rajeswary Ampalavanar Brown (2023). DOI: 10.1093/oso/9780192874672.003.0005

for US$1 billion when Kuwait had US$7.8 billion. By 2013 Bahrain earned US$16.5 billion in oil revenues.[3]

Table 5.1 below demonstrates Bahrain's diversification away from its dependence on oil. Oil refining grew and aluminium production increased more than sixfold between 1979 and 2013. In addition, petrochemical production, of ammonia and methanol, increased after the creation of the Gulf Petrochemical Industries Company (GPIC), a joint venture involving the Government of Bahrain and two petrochemical companies from Kuwait and Saudi Arabia, which began operation in 1985.[4] Shipbuilding increased, in response to the oil transport needs of Bahrain. The Arab Shipbuilding and Repair Yard, a Bahraini shipyard jointly owned by the Government

Table 5.1 Bahrain: indicators of economic activity

	1979	1990	2000	2013
Oil and natural gas production				
Crude oil (million metric tons/year	9.5	9.4	9.3	9.9
Natural gas (billion cubic metres/year	2.9	4.3	6.1	14.2
Manufacturing production				
Aluminium (thousand metric tons/year)	139	213	509	913
Refined oil (1,000 barrels/day)	254	254	262	265
Ammonia (1,000 metric tons/year)	0	325	350	378
Electricity production				
Gross Domestic Production (TWh)	1.5	3.5	6.3	25.9
Wholesale Trade Seaports				
Containers handled (1,000 TEU/year)	43	69	122	356
Air Transport				
Airport arrivals (1,000 passengers/year)	450	995	1,682	3,627
Financial Sector				
Total assets financial sector (per cent of GDP)	1,019	1,321	1,174	584
Of which: Offshore banks	951	1,219	1,027	355

Sources: Yesenn El-Radhi, *Economic Diversification in the Gulf States: Public Expenditure and Non-oil Economic Growth in Bahrain, Oman and Qatar* (Berlin: Gerlach Press, 2018), p. 140. International Energy Agency (IEA), *Oil Information*, various issues; IEA, *Natural Gas Information*, various issues; IEA, *Energy Statistics of Non-OECD Countries*, various issues; IEA, *Electricity Information*, various issues; US Geological Survey, *Minerals Yearbook*, various issues; Containerisation International, *Containerisation International Yearbook*, various issues; BH/CSO (1991); BH/CIO (2001, 2014); BH/MFNE (1991); BH/CBB (2001, 2005, 2006, 2014); UN Data, *National Accounts Main Aggregates Database*.

[3] Hoda Selim and Chahir Zaki, 'The Institutional Curse of Natural Resources in the Arab World', in *Understanding and Avoiding the Oil Curse in Resource-rich Arab Economies*, edited by Ibrahim Elbadawi and Hoda Selim (Cambridge: Cambridge University Press, 2016), pp. 326–7, 328, 341.

[4] R. E. Looney, 'An Economic Assessment of Bahrain's Attempts at Industrial Diversification', Industrial Bank of Kuwait Papers, 1989, pp. 17–18; R. E. Looney, *Manpower Policies and Development in the Persian Gulf Region* (Westport, CT: Praeger, 1994).

of Bahrain and six petroleum exporting companies, began operating in November 1977.[5]

The emergence of Islamic finance in the 1970s is related to the rise in oil revenues. Prices fell briefly in the late 1980s, affecting Bahrain. Kuwait suffered a 22 per cent fall in revenues in the 1980s. The bulk of Bahrain's oil revenues was directed into infrastructural development and economic diversification projects. While Kuwait directed its oil revenues into investment funds, in Bahrain, petro-dollars served to advance political, economic, and social reforms. In the mid-1970s Bahrain invited major international banks to establish offshore banking units. Its close connections to Kuwait, however, produced adverse effects, notably following the speculative frenzy surrounding the Souk al Manakh. Oil wealth was threatened in 1973 by Kuwait and its aggressive, unregulated strategy, that led to the collapse of Souk al Manakh with a loss of US$94 billion in 1982. However, by 1973 Bahrain had already created a sophisticated financial infrastructure. The impact of oil on the indirect as well as direct financing of Bahrain's private sector occurred through her capital markets. The interplay of oil revenues and the emergence of Bahrain as a financial hub for the oil-rich countries of the GCC involved increasing industrial investment of oil revenues as well as greater funding of development projects within the waqf and ma'tam in Shiite and Sunni areas. By 2007, oil and gas accounted for 25 per cent of GDP, and diversification into aluminium and steel, ship building, metallurgy, and textiles was notable in providing Bahrainis with medium- and low-skilled employment, particularly for the Shias. The growth was largely through foreign multinationals. Transactions in Islamic finance often involved technology-intensive projects in cooperation with Arab neighbours and Western multinationals. The Hidd Power Project involved US$55 million within a funding tranche of US$300 million. Aluminium Bahrain held an investment of US$250 million in Islamic finance as part of a US$1.55 billion expansion funding facility. First Islamic Investment Bank completed its first UK direct equity deal with the acquisition of a 33 per cent stake in Beaufort Wind, an owner of a portfolio of energy farms in the UK. Finally Shamil Bank of Bahrain, in cooperation with BSEC Investment Bank of Lebanon, launched the first auto-backed sukuk.[6]

One of the important long-term characteristics of Bahrain has been the role of foreign direct investment and in this period large investment banks and oil wealth flowed in from Saudi Arabia and Kuwait. Foreign direct investment

---

[5] A. Al-Yousef, 'An Evaluation of Bahrain's Major Industries and Their Future Prospects', in *Bahrain and the Gulf*, edited by J. B. Nugent and T. H. Thomas (London: Croom Helm, 1985), pp. 123–31.

[6] Zawya Sukuk Database, *Bahrain as a Centre for Islamic Banking*, 2005.

in Bahrain expanded from US$0.2 billion in 2003 to US$1.1 billion in 2006. This was the stimulus for further growth in inward investment through subsidiaries of overseas British and European corporations. The impact of these overseas entrants was extremely positive, diffusing better living standards as well as technology and managerial and entrepreneurial skills appropriate for Bahrain.[7] This economic vibrancy, with corporate governance rated the best in the GCC area, subdued the repercussions of the 2008 financial crisis.

Despite a sound institutional framework regarding contracts, financial deepening was weak because of spillovers from the GCC crises, as well as the Kuwait crisis in 1982. Instability through the high ratio of private credit (almost 50 per cent in Bahrain and 60 per cent in Kuwait) created concern and yet Bahrain remained rather sanguine.[8] Bahrain's lead in syndicated lending and in cross-border banking and its expansion into sovereign wealth funds did include generous social welfare programmes. But because Bahrain's population in 2011 was only 1.22 million (including national foreigners), its reduced dependence on oil revenues (85.5 per cent in 1970 but 25.1 per cent in 2011) had consequences for the economy. Ironically, Kuwait's revenues from oil rose from 43.25 per cent in 1970 to 51.3 per cent in 2011.[9] Although Bahrain achieved a more diversified development into non-oil industrialization, which now accounted for 75 per cent of GDP, exports are still principally of oil, not all its own but flowing from GCC countries. Bahrain's hydrocarbon revenues constituted three-quarters of total revenues, resulting in a rise in tax revenues. Bahrain's restructuring of its economy towards higher-growth sectors was exposing its rural areas, occupied by Shias, to economic decline. These features intensified the state's repressive rule, accompanied by an increase in violence and civil unrest.[10]

Between 1997 and 2012, Bahrain's oil revenues were high, averaging 22.0 per cent of GDP. The GCC countries, with the exception of Bahrain, remained tax free. Bahrain introduced taxes although they remained low. Bahrain focused on diversification through manufacturing, which accounted for 15 per cent of GDP and 24 per cent of total merchandise exports in 1980–2011.[11] This produced flexible labour recruitment, with an emphasis on the service sector rather than rapid industrialization. Bahrain expanded across

[7] Annika Kropf, *Oil Export Economies: New Comparative Perspectives on the Arab Gulf States* (Berlin: Gerlach Press, 2016), p. 25.
[8] Hoda Selim and Chahir Zaki, 'The Institutional Curse of Natural Resources in the Arab World', in *Understanding and Avoiding the Oil Curse in Resource-rich Arab Economies*, edited by Ibrahim Elbadawi and Hoda Selim (Cambridge: Cambridge University Press, 2016), pp. 352–3.
[9] Selim and Zaki, 'The Institutional Curse of Natural Resources in the Arab World', p. 329.
[10] Selim and Zaki, 'The Institutional Curse of Natural Resources in the Arab World', p. 334.
[11] Selim and Zaki, 'The Institutional Curse of Natural Resources in the Arab World', p. 346.

the GCC countries through joint ventures with foreign and GCC partners.[12] This coincided with high rates of investment in Bahrain, amounting to 25 per cent of GDP. Financial intermediation increased in the private credit sector, accounting for 50 per cent of GDP, while private credit in Kuwait is 60 per cent of GDP.

Bahrain's reliance on Saudi Arabia is an element in Bahrain's intra-regional growth. In the 1970s, Bahrain invited international banks to establish off-shore banking units to attract oil revenues from oil-rich neighbours. These offshore units rose to 77 within 10 years. Saudi development programmes stimulated financial growth in banking investment, with Islamic finance emerging dominant. Bahrain's offshore banking handled trade and con-struction programmes with private companies throughout the Gulf. This was accompanied by the growth of sophisticated financial tools and a revival of Islamic finance, strong enough to challenge Malaysia and Pak-istan. This introduced a range of Islamic finance instruments, although the pre-eminence of sukuk showed that Bahrain's share was high in funding infrastructural growth. Bahrain's story of revival is a compelling one within Islamic finance, greased as it was by abundant oil flows with Saudi Arabia and Kuwait, the main partners of Bahrain. A flexible specialization frame-work emerged with syndicated loans, club deals arranged for forward markets in diverse currencies, dollars, riyals, and regional currencies, developed to a sophisticated international standard. In this way Bahrain grew as a vibrant international financial centre. By the 1970s and 1980s, offshore banking units had 60 to 70 per cent of their business in Saudi riyals.[13] Saudi authorities, secretive and conservative, used Bahrain to bear the burden of the inter-nationalization of their financial infrastructure. Equally, the debacle of the 1981 financial crisis and the 1990s suspicions of funding terrorism were concealed. Saudis remain opposed to the internationalization of the riyal. This constrained Bahrain because the Saudis were determined to protect the riyal. Bahrain's offshore banks, two-thirds of whose business derived from Saudi Arabia, were affected. Free transfer of riyals was restricted. Bahrain's difficulties persisted, a consequence of the Saudi Government's forward mar-ket contracts being in dollars and not riyals. These constraints were related to the wider political context, where all Saudi transactions required the approval of the Saudi Arabian Monetary Agency (SAMA). Local Saudi banks were prohibited from conducting foreign transactions without approval from

---

[12] Selim and Zaki, 'The Institutional Curse of Natural Resources in the Arab World', p. 349.

[13] A. S. Gerakis and O. Roncesvalles, 'Bahrain's Offshore Banking Center', *Economic Development and Cultural Change*, vol. 31, no. 2 (1983), pp. 271–93.

SAMA. The free flow of capital was a casualty.[14] The recession in 1983 led to regional expansion into Asia, particularly after the collapse of Kuwait's Souk al-Manakh in 1982.

The Souk collapse of 1982 had both positive and negative influences on Bahrain's financial sector. The Bank of Bahrain and Kuwait (BBK), which had concentrated shareholding in powerful individuals who had abused the bank's lending policies, was now, with declining oil prices, faced by a dramatic fall in earnings, from 18 per cent in 1983 to 7 per cent in 1984. This resulted in a 35 per cent fall in dividends.[15] BBK bad loans originating from the Souk collapse were estimated at 85 per cent, and this led to the creation in 1984 of a special loan loss reserve account, into which a third of BBK earnings were deposited. Yet BBK struggled: new capital was raised while no dividends were paid.

Oil capital flows from the Gulf states to Bahrain are closely connected to the stock market. Two features dominate the shareholding structure. One is the use of liquidity by the authoritarian state acting as an institutional investor and second, the use of sovereign bonds and sukuk to finance state infrastructural projects. Of particular interest is Bahrain's ambition to diversify from oil into industry. Oil has led to Bahrain's rise as a financial hub, involving the sophisticated use of sukuk in state projects and the creation of Islamic financial instruments, notably wakalah, mudarabah, and mushrakah.[16]

Oil and Impact

This section examines the effects of oil price shocks on stock markets in the GCC countries. Rising oil prices increase stock returns only when stock markets are bullish or normal, and falling oil prices lower stock returns only when stock markets are bearish or normal. This suggests that stock markets are more likely to boom together or crash together.

An analysis by Diaz and Perez de Gracia of the impact of oil price shocks on stock returns for four oil and gas corporations listed on the NYSE between January 1974 and December 2015 suggests a significant positive short-term

---

[14] Rodney Wilson with Abdullah Al-Salamah, Monica Malik, and Ahmed Al-Rajhi, *Economic Development in Saudi Arabia* (London: Routledge Curzon, 2004), pp. 56–74.

[15] William Bean, 'The Contemporary Financial Development of Kuwait and Bahrain: a Study of Contrasts', PhD thesis, Princeton University, Princeton, NJ, 1988, p. 76.

[16] Salah A. Nusair and Jamal A. Al-Khasawneh, 'Oil Price Shocks and Stock Market Returns of the GCC Countries: Empirical Evidence from Quantile Regression Analysis', *Economic Change and Restructuring*, vol. 51, no. 4 (2018).

impact.[17] Oil is regarded as the main driver of economic activity in a GCC dependent on oil revenues. In 2013, oil revenues in the GCC accounted for 83 per cent of government revenues, 73 per cent of total exports, and 44 per cent of GDP.[18] In turn, this impacts on the stock market.[19] Falling oil prices obviously influence corporate earnings and thus determine share prices.[20] A further major impact on the stock market came with the financial crisis of 2008 and then the Arab Spring in 2011.

Rising oil prices lead to increased income flows from oil importing countries to oil exporting countries, and result in increased economic activity in the latter. Oil exporters increase their earnings, and Bahrain handles this capital through its position as a financial hub. The value of stock is equal to the sum of expected future cash flows, calculated using a discount rate that makes allowances for inflation and the real interest rate. Thus movement in the oil price affects inflation and expected real interest rates and in that way influences stock prices.[21] The response of the stock market to oil price changes also reflects the stability or volatility of the economic environment. Volatility is evident in the series for oil and stock prices.[22] The sharp increase in oil prices in 2005–06 led to a rise in stock prices, but these fell during the 2008 financial crisis, followed by another fall during the Arab Spring from December 2010. With political unrest, the stock market declined but oil prices rose. Though a volatile situation—oil prices swung between US$22 and US$139— the Bahrain Bourse was less affected because Bahrain is not an oil producer but a processor and exporter.

Oil prices have a greater impact on stock prices in bullish times because of investor sentiment and but also because the state and banks have the largest presence on the Bahrain Bourse. Oil price shocks are related to the wider economy. Thus, oil and stock markets boom together and crash together.[23]

[17] Elena Maria Diaz and Fernando Perez de Gracia, 'Oil Price Shocks and Stock Returns of Oil and Gas Corporations', *Finance Research Letters*, vol. 20 (2017), pp. 75–80.

[18] Salah A. Nusair, 'The Effects of Oil Price Shocks on the Economies of Gulf Cooperation Council Countries: Nonlinear Analysis', *Energy Policy*, vol. 91 (2016), pp. 256–67.

[19] Nusair, 'The Effects of Oil Price Shocks on the Economies of Gulf Cooperation Council Countries', pp. 256–67.

[20] Shawkat Hammoudeh and Elsa Aleisa, 'Dynamic Relationships among GCC Stock Markets and NYMEX Oil Futures', *Contemporary Economic Policy*, vol. 22, no. 2 (2004), pp. 250–69.

[21] Nader Naifar and Mohammed Salah Al Dohaiman, 'Nonlinear Analysis among Crude Oil Prices, Stock Markets' Return and Macro-Economic Variables', *International Review of Economics and Finance*, vol. 27 (2013), pp. 416–31.

[22] Nusair and Al-Khasawneh, 'Oil Price Shocks and Stock Market Returns of the GCC Countries', p. 345.

[23] Nusair and Al-Khasawneh, 'Oil Price Shocks and Stock Market Returns of the GCC Countries', p. 370.

Impact of Oil Prices on Stock Markets: Evidence from GCC Financial Markets

In 1981, the GCC completed an agreement between Saudi Arabia, Kuwait, Qatar, the United Arab Emirates, Bahrain, and Oman to secure free trade in agricultural and industrial products but excluding petroleum.[24] In addition there was free movement in factors of production. In 2002, proponents of more intensive integration pushed for a single market and the prospect of monetary union. In 2010, approval for monetary union was sought through the Statute of the Monetary Council of the Cooperation Council for the Arab States of the Gulf. This was ambitious. It sought the progressive liberalization of financial controls and the coordination of monetary and exchange rate policies for national currencies, until the establishment of a GCC central bank that would be responsible for the issue of currency and the pricing of financial assets, each of which would improve transparency and reduce transaction costs. But financial integration was difficult to achieve. As the GCC financial system was dominated by commercial banks with varying strategies to limit cross-border equity flows, compliance would face serious obstacles. Only Bahrain, with the least oil resources, would benefit. Another difficulty obstructing integration is the different size of the individual stock markets, ranging from the highly capitalized stock market in Saudi Arabia down to those with weak operational experience and transparency. Morgan Stanley Capital International stigmatized GCC stock markets as frontier markets because of their often-inadequate liquidity levels, poor payment systems, weak regulation of disputes caused by the presence of powerful Saudi families who often failed to settle debts, and an uncompromising adherence to Shari'ah. There were also limits on foreign investment, although Bahrain was most liberal towards foreign ownership through its offshore banking units.

GCC Integration and a Culture of Financial Extravagance Aided by Oil

Bahrain, as the beneficiary of spillovers from Kuwait and Saudi Arabia, became a focus for integration in the Gulf. Bahrain's capital surpluses from oil, its cosmopolitan legal framework, and its relatively sophisticated organizational capabilities were crucial here. The Supreme Council of the GCC

---

[24] Abdullah R. Alotaibi, 'Financial Integration in the Gulf Region', PhD thesis School of Business, University of Western Sydney, 2014.

appointed the Secretary General. The Ministerial Council, composed of foreign ministers from the GCC nations, facilitated cooperation between the ministries of finance and industrial units.[25] Crucial here was the implementation of technical standards in industries, the undertaking of commercial arbitration, and the registration of patents. Underpinning this were appropriate institutions: the Standardization and Metrology Organization; the Technical Telecommunications Bureau; the Regional Committee for Electrical Energy Systems; and the Patent Office. In 2003, a customs union agreement was signed with a single common external tariff of 5 per cent. By 2007, an agreement on GCC monetary and fiscal convergence was being sought. By 2008, the GCC had a common market.

Adam Hanieh has demonstrated that the international circulation of oil, capital, and commodities such as aluminium, has reintegrated regional clusters into threads of globalization. Here the question is: has the stock market integration achieved through the GCC diminished global and local market risk or has it strengthened the existing religious and cultural features that secure Bahrain's economic position?[26]

Oil Price Shocks and Stock Markets

The US stock market reacts to oil shocks rationally.[27] There is little evidence of market overreaction. But does the Bahrain stock market overreact to oil price shocks? Does the price of crude oil respond to the same forces that drive stock prices? In effect, it is the demand and supply for crude oil that determines the oil price. Through oil capital transfers during the oil boom, the GCC experienced some growth. With this capital-driven growth, Bahrain improved its physical infrastructure and pursued diversification in order to prepare the economy for a decline in oil income. Bahrain also recycled oil revenues through its offshore banks to invest in foreign assets. These spillovers from oil have benefited specific industries. They have encouraged clustering of investment in specific sectors, and in this way improved market intelligence for the Bahrain stock exchange, as well as for the stock exchanges of Kuwait

---

[25] Alotaibi, 'Financial Integration in the Gulf Region', p. 25.

[26] GCC economic indicators for 2012 show strong GDP growth. In 2012, GDP per capita ranged from US$23,554 in Bahrain to US$104,756 in Qatar. GDP per capita in Kuwait and the UAE was US$48,761 and US$43,733 respectively, in Oman US$25,536, and Saudi Arabia US$24,523. Average GDP per capita was US$45,120. Bahrain is the smallest GCC country, with a population of 1.2 million, just 3 per cent of the total GCC population. In 2010, Bahrain's non-citizen population and non-citizen labour force was 54 per cent and 76 per cent respectively. Alotaibi, 'Financial Integration in the Gulf Region', p. 81.

[27] Charles M. Jones and Gautam Kaul, 'Oil and the Stock Markets', *Journal of Finance*, vol. 11, no. 2 (1996).

and Saudi Arabia. The expertise available to local firms has increased, commercial networks have been established, and links to stock exchanges in the West have been created.

In 2001, the Bahrain stock exchange index (BSEI) covered 42 listed companies with a market capitalization of US$6 billion. The stock market is led by financial institutions: 5 banks, 10 investment firms, and 7 insurance companies. There are also 8 service companies, 3 industrial corporations, and 4 companies in the hotel and tourism sector. Bahrain's financial position was led by her offshore banks, 8 banks that accounted for 19 per cent of market capitalization. Companies from both GCC and non-GCC countries were listed on the Bahrain stock exchange, and this confirmed the close links between GCC oil and the Bahrain economy. The close financial links through the GCC have encouraged flexible collaborative structures such as FinTech in global finance. Ownership of these listed companies was mainly in the hands of the state. The Bahrain Stock Exchange Index, with its inclusion of offshore companies, showed relatively little volatility during the 2008 financial crisis, for the state used its huge oil wealth to provide liquidity. Kuwait was the most volatile.[28] The companies in Bahrain that absorbed the largest share of national capital were also less prone to speculation, in contrast to Kuwait which was seriously vulnerable. The Kuwait capital market was sclerotic, with cartels that maintained the earlier inadequate governance, as demonstrated in the Souq al-Manakh in 1982.

To assess the impact of movements in oil prices on the Bahrain stock market requires an understanding of the factors determining oil prices over time.[29] For Bahrain, fluctuations in oil production and price are exogenous to the economy. High oil prices are often driven by global activity. GCC markets regularly experience low levels of trade, which is in the hands of the state and a small number of private traders. In Bahrain, such foreign involvement in the economy is limited, although oil market fundamentals are important for liquidity on the bourse. Saudi Arabia accounted for 21 per cent of OPEC reserves and 18 per cent of global reserves in 2014. Bahrain has a high concentration of financial and banking services, but these markets are prone to only limited volatility as the state acts to pump in liquidity at the first sign of trouble. The relationship between oil prices and stock market returns permeates

---

[28] Hammoudeh and Aleisa, 'Dynamic Relationships among GCC Stock Markets and NYMEX Oil Futures', p. 256.

[29] L. Kilian, 'Not All Oil Price Shocks Are Alike: Disentangling Demand and Supply Shocks in the Crude Oil Market', *American Economic Review*, vol. 19 (2009), pp. 1053–69.

all the GCC countries except Bahrain.[30] Despite diminished oil resources in Bahrain, oil price changes did have an impact there because of cross-listing on GCC stock markets and increased integration within the GCC.[31]

Oil Business: Responses, Renaissance, and Reverberations in the Regions and across International Clusters

It is important in exploring the influence of oil price shocks on stock markets to analyse regional and international economic forces and their impact on oil production, revenues, and prices. Bahrain's oil economy accounts for only 2 per cent of GCC GDP. Saudi Arabia accounts for 47 per cent, the UAE 26 per cent, Qatar 12 per cent, Kuwait 8 per cent, and Oman 5 per cent.[32] In 2013, oil revenues in the GCC accounted for 83 per cent of government revenue, 73 per cent of total exports, and 44 per cent of GDP, and this in turn has a major impact on the stock market.[33]

Sharp oil price increases in 2002 to 2008, resulting in vastly increasing oil revenues, created high economic growth. GCC oil earnings had averaged US$146 billion per year over the period 1997–2002 but US$327 billion per year between 2002 and 2006; real GDP growth averaged 3.2 per cent per year in 1999–2002 but 7.1 per cent per year in 2003–07.[34] As oil prices then fell, oil revenues averaged US$211 billion per year in 2012–13 while real GDP growth averaged 4.5 per cent.[35] That put a brake on corporate earnings and thus share prices.[36]

---

[30] See Table 5.3 in the appendix on stock market trades in Bahrain; Syed Abul Basher and Perry Sadorsky, 'Hedging Emerging Market Stock Prices with Oil, Gold, VIX and Bonds: A Comparison between DCC, ADCC, and Go-Garch', *Energy Economics*, vol. 54 (2016), pp. 235–47.

[31] Elie Bouri, 'Oil Volatility Shocks and the Stock Markets of Oil Importing MENA Economies: A Tale from the Financial Crisis', *Energy Economics*, vol. 51 (2015), pp. 590–8; Shawkat Hammoudeh, Huimin Li, and Bang Jeon, 'Causality and Volatility Spillovers among Petroleum Prices of WTI, Gasoline and Heating Oil in Different Locations, *North American Journal of Economics and Finance*, vol. 14, no. 1 (2003), pp. 89–114; Shawkat Hammoudeh and Elsa Alesia, 'Relationship between Spot/Futures Prices of Crude Oil and Equity Indices for Oil Producing Economies and Oil Related Industries', *Arab Economic Journal*, vol. 11 (2002), pp. 37–62.

[32] Hani El-Chaarani, 'The Impact of Oil Prices on Stock Markets: New Evidence during and after the Arab Spring in Gulf Cooperation Council Economies', *International Journal of Energy Economics and Policy*, 2019, p. 21.

[33] Nusair, 'The Effects of Oil Price Shocks on the Economies of the Gulf Cooperation Council Countries', pp. 256–67.

[34] B. Momani, 'Gulf Cooperation Council Oil Exporters and the Future of the Dollar', *New Political Economy*, vol. 13, no. 3 (2008), pp. 293–314.

[35] Nusair, 'The Effects of Oil Price Shocks on the Economies of the Gulf Cooperation Council Countries'.

[36] Hammoudeh and Aleisa, 'Dynamic Relationships among GCC Stock Markets and NYMEX Oil Futures', pp. 250–69.

Oil wealth flows affected stock markets in the GCC, creating a link between oil prices and stock market returns. The GCC accounted for 30 per cent of world oil reserves, quasi-monopolized by the oil-rich Gulf states. But the Gulf stock markets could still be hit by a world economic recession, as happened in 2008, and from the Arab Spring of 2011. For Bahrain, the impact of these external shocks on the stock exchange was brief but it strengthened the ambition to diversify the economy away from its dependence on oil.

Rising oil prices, creating substantial flows of oil wealth, result in increased economic activity. This is clear in the case of Bahrain, as the financial hub of the Gulf. Rising oil prices influence stock prices, although the influence may be minimal because the bourse is small and is controlled by state investors.[37] The response of stock markets to oil price changes also reflects the broader economic environment. This is clear from the series on oil prices and stock prices.[38]

Thus the sharp increases in oil prices in 2005–06 led to a rise in stock prices. But these fell back with the 2008 global crisis and again with the Arab Spring from December 2010. However, the Bahrain Bourse was less affected because Bahrain is not an oil producer as such. More important for the stability of the Bahrain stock market during these periods of turmoil was that the state and banks are the largest shareholders and speculation is limited. The Bahrain stock market is marked by a mature competitiveness that includes seeking out investment opportunities in Western markets.

Table 5.2 Financial valuations of the six GCC stock markets, end of 2000

Market	Market capitalization (US$ billion)	P/E	P/BV	Dividend Yield (per cent)	As percentage of GDP
Bahrain	6.643	15.88	1.04	5.34	83.0
Kuwait	25.615	17.64	1.91	2.58	67.8
Oman	3.386	12.85	0.99	7.12	17.1
Qatar	6.324	12.84	2.66	3.62	43.7
Saudi Arabia	68.000	17.63	2.25	3.50	39.9
UAE	22.364	11.77	1.31	3.49	38.2
Total GCC	132.332	14.50	1.87	4.34	47.6
S&P 500	11,713.754	26.40	6.20	1.21	117.0
Dow Jones	3,472.541	22.20	8.20	1.60	35.0

Source: Sawkat Hammoudeh and Elsa Aleisa, 'Dynamic Relationship among GCC Stock Markets and NYMEX Oil Futures', *Contemporary Economic Policy*, vol. 22, no. 2 (2004), p. 253.

[37] Naifar and Al Dohaiman, 'Nonlinear Analysis among Crude Oil Prices, Stock Markets' Return and Macro-Economic Variables', pp. 416–31.
[38] Nusair and Al-Khasawneh, 'Oil Price Shocks and Stock Market Returns of the GCC Countries', pp. 339–72. See also tables on Bahrain stock markets.

Table 5.3 GCC: stock market valuations by economic sector, end of 2001

Sector	Market Capitalization (US$ billion)	P/E Ratio	P/BV	Dividend Yield (per cent)
Bahrain				
Banks	1.850	11.54	1.24	6.85
Investment	2.595	20.82	0.70	4.15
Insurance	0.236	−2.89	0.90	2.65
Service	1.891	10.73	2.03	6.86
Industry	0.033	−46.90	0.60	6.21
Hotel and Tourism	0.124	9.89	0.68	6.96
Kuwait				
Banks	12.375	13.0	2.1	5.8
Investment	3.224	15.6	1.2	5.3
Insurance	0.575	10.5	1.2	7.7
Real Estate	1.591	25.2	1.1	5.5
Industry	2.652	9.5	1.5	16.0
Service	4.500	12.5	2.8	7.1
Food	0.696	7.3	1.4	0.0
Oman				
Banks	NA	16.5	NA	NA
Insurance	NA	NA	NA	NA
Service	NA	NA	NA	NA
Saudi Arabia				
Banks	35.123	17.47	3.72	5.24
Industry	17.398	12.70	1.63	2.83
Cement	7.641	22.51	3.45	4.04
Service	3.008	25.44	1.30	2.71
Electricity	9.810	NA	1.55	NA
Agriculture	0.302	37.06	0.44	0.9
UAE				
Banks	13.256	12.52	1.66	4.06
Insurance	1.301	14.24	1.39	5.18
Service	13.246	14.25	1.36	4.24

Source: Sawkat Hammoudeh and Elsa Aleisa, 'Dynamic Relationship among GCC Stock Markets and NYMEX Oil Futures', *Contemporary Economic Policy*, vol. 22, no. 2 (2004), p. 254.

Table 5.4 GCC: average annual real GDP growth, 1991–2008 (per cent change)

	Oil Real GDP			Non-oil Real GDP			Overall Real GDP		
	1991–2002	1997–2002	2003–08	1991–2002	1997–2002	2003–08	1991–2002	1997–2002	2003–08
Bahrain	5.7	6.7	−3.1	4.5	4.0	9.3	4.8	4.7	6.9
Kuwait	12.3	9.1	7.3	7.5	6.8	9.8	8.1	7.2	8.7
Oman	9.7	15.0	1.0	6.3	6.5	9.2	7.3	9.3	5.8
Qatar	9.8	16.1	10.8	4.1	5.5	15.6	6.8	10.6	13.0
Saudi Arabia	1.2	−1.7	5.8	3.0	3.5	4.6	2.4	1.7	4.9
UAE	−1.6	−0.1	3.9	8.6	7.3	9.9	4.1	4.7	8.3
GCC	5.1	1.7	5.6	4.7	4.8	7.3	4.0	3.7	6.6

Sources: International Energy Agency (IEA), *Oil Information*, various issues; International Energy Agency, *Energy Statistics of Non-OECD Countries*, various issues, 1991–2009; BH/CIO 2001, 2013; BH/Ministry of Finance and National Economy (MFNE), 1991–2009; BH/CBB, 2001–2010; UN Data, National Accounts Main Aggregates Database. For Kuwait and others, collated from Yesenn El-Radhi, *Economic Diversification in the Gulf States: Public Expenditure and Non-oil Economic Growth in Bahrain, Oman and Qatar* (Berlin: Gerlach Press, 2018); Rodney Wilson with Abdullah Al-Salamah, Monica Malik, and Ahmed Al-Rajhi, *Economic Development in Saudi Arabia* (London: Routledge Curzon, 2004); Annika Kropf, *Oil Export Economies: New Comparative Perspectives on the Arab Gulf States* (Berlin: Gerlach Press, 2016); World Bank Reports on the individual Gulf States Economic Transformation, 1991, 1994, 1997, 2004, 2008, 2013; IMF selected country reports; IMF World Economic Outlook Database April 2014; IMF, *Regional Economic Outlook: Middle East and Central Asia*, October 2015.

Table 5.5 GCC: selected economic indicators for 2008

	Bahrain	Kuwait	Oman	Qatar	Saudi Arabia	UAE	GCC total
Population (millions)	0.8	3.4	2.8	1.1	24.9	4.8	37.8
Nominal GDP (US$ billions)	21.2	148.2	59.9	100.4	469.4	261.4	1,060.6
GDP per capita (US$ thousands)	27.2	43.0	21.6	91.5	18.9	54.8	28.4
PPP GDP per capita (US$ thousands)	34.7	39.9	24.7	86.0	23.8	38.9	35.9
Oil reserves (per cent of global reserves)	0.0	8.7	0.4	2.2	21.0	7.8	40.1
Gas reserves (per cent of global reserves)	0.1	2.0	1.3	33.5	10.0	8.5	55.3
Spare capacity (per cent of OPEC capacity)	0.0	8.0	0.3	1.7	56.5	7.6	74.1
Growth (average 2004-08)	6.9	5.1	6.9	14.3	4.3	7.6	6.0
Fiscal balance (per cent of GDP)	8.0	34.0	13.9	11.5	33.0	20.5	26.5
Current account balance (per cent of GDP)	10.6	43.7	9.1	33.0	28.6	8.5	24.7
Oil revenue (per cent of total revenue)	85.3	76.8	87.4	56.8	89.3	80.4	82.1
Oil exports (per cent of total exports)	79.6	95.0	76.0	91.4	89.6	42.8	78.1
Inflation (year average)	3.5	10.6	12.6	15.0	9.9	11.5	10.7
Share of GCC nominal GDP (per cent)	2.0	14.0	5.7	9.5	44.3	24.6	100.0

Source: As shown in Table 5.4.

Table 5.6 Average annual OPEC crude oil price, 1960–2018 (US$ per barrel)

1960	1.63	1980	35.52	2000	27.60
1961	1.57	1981	34.00	2001	23.12
1962	1.52	1982	32.38	2002	24.36
1963	1.50	1983	29.04	2003	28.10
1964	1.45	1984	28.20	2004	36.05
1965	1.42	1985	27.01	2005	50.59
1966	1.36	1986	13.53	2006	61.00
1967	1.33	1987	17.73	2007	69.04
1968	1.32	1988	14.24	2008	94.10
1969	1.27	1989	17.31	2009	60.86
1970	1.21	1990	22.26	2010	77.38
1971	1.70	1991	18.62	2011	107.40
1972	1.82	1992	18.44	2012	109.00
1973	2.70	1993	16.33	2013	105.87
1974	11.00	1994	15.53	2014	96.29
1975	10.43	1995	16.86	2015	49.49
1976	11.60	1996	20.29	2016	40.76
1977	12.50	1997	18.86	2017	52.51
1978	12.79	1998	12.28	2018	69.78
1979	29.19	1999	17.44	2019	64.62

Source: See https://www.statista.com/statistics/262858/change-in-opec-crude-oil-prices-since-1960/.

6

The Impact of the Global Financial Crisis of 2008 on the Bahrain Economy

Bahrain did not escape the impact of the 2008 Global Financial Crisis. How-ever, the oil price boom of her GCC neighbours and a major capital inflow had, from the 1990s, fuelled credit growth, inflation, and a rise in real estate and harbour construction. The corporate sector, too, had ridden the boom in credit although with increased vulnerabilities. However, in Kuwait the global crisis did impact the unofficial stock market, Souq Al-Manakh, and it col-lapsed. Bahrain's banks retained profits and were a major source of liquidity for the Bourse during the crisis.[1]

The oil price boom from 2003 to 2008 intensified infrastructural invest-ment, the development of the harbour areas and housing, and the expansion of industries such as aluminium. Gross value added by economic activity and capital expenditure averaged 9.3 per cent of non-oil GDP from 1976 to 2013, while mining and the production of oil and gas and the manufacture and refining of petrochemicals and aluminium accounted for 27.8 per cent of total gross value in the same period. Construction was around 8 per cent in 1976 but declined to 5.9 per cent in 2013. Wholesale and retail trade maintained 14.5 per cent growth in 1976 but declined to 4.2 per cent by 2013. Transport and telecommunications recorded a steady 7 per cent growth throughout. Real estate and social services registered around 6.0 per cent growth through-out the three decades. The financial sector recorded growth at 6.6 per cent in 1976, rising to 11.7 per cent in 2000, 19.2 per cent in 2006, and 15.3 per cent in 2013. Offshore banking rose throughout 1976–2013, averaging around 8 per cent.[2] Thus, while the oil boom in Saudi Arabia, Kuwait, and Qatar cre-ated large fiscal and external surpluses, these could not counteract the asset and credit misfortunes unleashed by the financial crisis in November 2007.

---

[1] International Monetary Fund, Middle East and Central Asia Department, Washington, DC, 'Impact of the Global Financial Crisis on the Gulf Cooperation Council Countries and Challenges Ahead', 2010, prepared by May Khamis, Abdelhak Senhadji, Maher Hasan, Francis Kumah, Ananthakrishnan Prasad, and Gabriel Sensenbrenner.

[2] UN Data, National Accounts, Official Country Data; World Bank (1993), p. 178: BH/CSO (1985, 1991, and 1996): BH/CIO 2005, 2014.

Islam and Capitalism in the Making of Modern Bahrain. Rajeswary Ampalavanar Brown, Oxford University Press.
© Rajeswary Ampalavanar Brown (2023). DOI: 10.1093/oso/9780192874672.003.0006

Bahrain, as their financial hub and oil processing centre, experienced a credit squeeze in 2008. Swift intervention by the Central Bank of Bahrain in providing capital for the banks, produced a slight increase in liquidity, which fuelled credit growth, inflation, and rise in asset prices. Bahrain experienced some distress from 2007 because of its increased dependence on foreign financing and, in particular, its exposure to real estate and construction lending, which had a cumulative impact on the equity market. Both the housing boom and intense and diversified corporate growth ran into difficulties. Bahrain also experienced a fall in profits from oil processing for her Gulf neighbours. The peaks and falls in oil prices and production volumes added to the problems in Bahrain's mining, oil refining, and manufacturing industries. These were the causes of Bahrain's difficulties, not the financial crisis in the West. Thus, in Bahrain, in contrast to the US and UK, banks remained profitable, both Islamic and conventional banks. In December 2009, Bahrain's financial sector, accounting for 25.1 per cent of GDP, remained stable, while the total assets of the retail banks stood at BD22.5 billion. Moreover, total outstanding credit increased as a result of the drive to diversify from the existing oil dependency. At the end of 2009, this credit facility was BD5,884.9 million, compared to BD5,887.6 million at the end of 2008. A stimulus package in Saudi Arabia of US$400 billion also had a positive impact in Bahrain.[3]

A selection of economic indicators contrasting Bahrain and Kuwait would capture the differences in the impact of the 2008 financial crisis between the two economies. The nominal GDP in US$ billions was 21.2 for Bahrain, 148.2 for Kuwait. GDP per capita in thousands of US$ was 27.2 for Bahrain and 43.0 for Kuwait. Oil reserves as a percentage of global reserves was nil for Bahrain, while for Kuwait it was 8.7 per cent. Gas reserves are 0.1 per cent for Bahrain and 2.0 per cent for Kuwait. Kuwait had 8.0 per cent of OPEC capacity while Bahrain had nil. Yet Bahrain's growth between 2004 and 2008 was 6.9 per cent average while Kuwait recorded 5.1 per cent. The fiscal balance as a percentage of GDP was 8.0 per cent for Bahrain but 34.0 per cent for Kuwait: oil revenue as a percentage of total revenue was 85.3 per cent for Bahrain and for Kuwait 76.8 per cent. Oil exports as a percentage of total exports was 79.6 per cent for Bahrain and 95.0 per cent for Kuwait. The average annual inflation was 3.5 per cent for Bahrain but 10.6 per cent for Kuwait. Finally, the share of GCC nominal GDP was 2.0 per cent for Bahrain and 14.0 per cent for Kuwait.[4]

---

[3] International Monetary Fund, 'Impact of the Global Financial Crisis on the Gulf Cooperation Council Countries', p. 1.

[4] Country authorities and IMF staff estimates as cited in International Monetary Fund, 'Impact of the Global Financial Crisis on the Gulf Cooperation Council Countries', p. 5.

The contrasting circumstances of Bahrain and her Gulf neighbours is captured in the holdings of sovereign wealth funds. Sovereign wealth funds ranged from US$600 billion to US$1 trillion in 2008. Saudi Arabia dominated. Bahrain's Mumtalakat had diverse holdings but often benefited from investment by wealthy neighbours in the Bahrain Bourse. Sovereign wealth funds were affected by the decline in international asset prices in 2008, with losses of 20–30 per cent. For Bahrain, real estate prices fell: but Dubai suffered severely with the collapse in 2009 of the holding company Dubai World, owned by the Dubai Government. This collapse had a serious impact on sovereign wealth funds throughout the region, including Bahrain. However, Bahrain's position as the financial hub for the Gulf and its financial institutions experienced only limited stress, partly because Bahrain's banks had been supported with credit from September 2008. Bahrain also maintained state fInancing of non-bank corporate institutions from December 2003 through to September 2009.[5] Dubai's economy accounts for less than 10 per cent of GCC GDP and intra-GCC trade is less than 10 per cent of total GCC trade.[6]

Tight credit withheld or postponed the implementation of projects. At the end of 2009, Bahrain held back only 2 per cent of projects valued at US$13 billion. In contrast, Kuwait withheld 8 per cent of projects valued at US$44 billion. But the UAE withheld 79 per cent, valued at US$451 billion.[7] Bahrain's Central Bank had been quick in responding through liquidity support, retaining long-term government deposits in the banks and financial institutions, and reducing interest rates and modifying reserve requirements. Despite these measures, two Bahrain-based wholesale banks, the International Banking Corporation and Awal Bank owned by Saudi conglomerates, were put into administration by the Bahrain authorities after defaulting in May–June 2009. The two banks were part of the Algosaibi and Al-Saad Saudi business groups.

Another two Bahrain-based wholesale banks, Gulf International Bank (GIB) and Arab Banking Corporation (ABC) incurred large debts, US$1.3 billion in the case of GIB, US$1.2 billion in the case of ABC, between 2008 and 2009, but they maintained stable capitalization.[8] The problems of the

[5] Central Bank of Bahrain, *Financial Sector Review*, December 2010; BIS Consolidated Banking Statistics.

[6] International Monetary Fund, 'Impact of the Global Financial Crisis on the Gulf Cooperation Council Countries', p. 23.

[7] *Middle East Economic Digest*, 26 June 2009; Kristian Coates Ulrichsen, 'The GCC States and the Shifting Balance of Global Power', Center for International and Regional Studies, Georgetown University, Occasional Paper 6, 2010.

[8] International Monetary Fund, 'Impact of the Global Financial Crisis on the Gulf Cooperation Council Countries', p. 32.

wholesale banks arose from their global links. Retail banks, less exposed to regional and international links, were secure. They did endure some losses as the wholesale banks made reduced contributions to the economy. (See Tables 6.1 and 6.2 on bank performance, 2003–09, and Appendix below on major banks' performance 2008–15.)

Weaknesses occurred in construction and real estate development. This boom, rising from 15 per cent in 2002 to 30.5 per cent in 2008, often resulted in increased lending for the purchase of securities. This growth, funded by domestic deposits, also increased the banks' foreign liabilities.[9] In 2007–08, banks used short-term speculative foreign deposits to finance their lending, exacerbating funding mismatches and often creating a refinancing risk. Capital adequacy ratios, although well above regulatory requirements, could still expose vulnerability, as high credit growth in the year before the crisis had now given way to a credit crisis. However, Bahrain did not experience a drastic credit decline and the financial hub held firm. The capital adequacy ratio for Bahrain was almost 25 per cent in 2003, declining to 17 per cent in 2008. All the other Gulf nations, including Kuwait, Qatar, and Saudi Arabia, recorded figures lower than 17 per cent in 2008.[10]

Non-performing loans, NPLs, are low in Bahrain but the banks' exposure in asset markets, their increasing dependence on foreign financing, and the presence of low liquidity are troubling. Often liquidity problems arise because short-term speculative capital inflows cause credit crises, even in Bahrain which is closely regulated. The banks' violation of the loan-to-deposit ratio is low in Bahrain because they are largely state-owned and the law is rigorous. The banks that did violate loan-to-deposit ratios are usually foreign-owned banks based in Bahrain, as in the case of the two Saudi-owned banks that faced liquidation. Bahrain's offshore banking is more exposed, while the retail banks can be affected by interbank exposures.[11] The non-bank financial sector was more affected as its regulatory frameworks were weak.

Although Bahrain held limited oil reserves, she was closely involved in oil refining for her neighbours. Consequently, the decline in oil prices and cuts in oil production affected Bahrain's links with global equity and credit markets. Economic activity contracted from late 2008, accompanying a decline in credit and investments and a fall in speculative capital flows, with the inevitable impact on banking and corporate liquidity. Now with the

---

[9] International Monetary Fund, 'Impact of the Global Financial Crisis on the Gulf Cooperation Council Countries', p. 10.

[10] GCC bank data, 2003–08; Central Bank of Bahrain, financial stability data, 2003 to 2008.

[11] International Monetary Fund, 'Impact of the Global Financial Crisis on the Gulf Cooperation Council Countries', p. 38.

Global Financial Crisis, liquidity shortages triggered falls in asset prices and increased government intervention.

The measures taken in October 2008 to improve market liquidity included interest rate changes and the introduction of a new FXSwap facility to assist banks in foreign exchange operations. The CBB also expanded the range of collateral and new Islamic liquidity instruments. But the CBB, in particular, concentrated on controlling the level of real estate risk, in view of the Dubai crisis. Dubai had borrowed extensively between 2004 and 2008 to fund expansion in commercial and residential properties, creating a property bubble, and the UAE incurred a US$100 billion credit excess as a result of government compliance with the risk. The immediate market reaction was disastrous, with equity falls on the stock markets in Dubai and Abu Dhabi transmitted throughout the GCC, including Bahrain. Bank stocks were most affected, but Bahrain's CBB contained this through liquidity monitoring and management, identifying the banks' deficiencies, and strengthening deposit protection. In October 2008, the monitoring of foreign bank branches was enhanced. In particular, the CBB monitored the use of Special Purpose Vehicles by locally incorporated banks. The CBB identified this as the major culprit in the crisis, calling it a 'shadow banking sector'. It called for strict regulation and supervision of SPVs and other off-balance sheet funding arrangements. It also monitored to see whether Bahrain's own banks were exploiting this vehicle. These measures greatly increased the flow of information to the public.

As part of these improvements, the CBB established a global communications network, SWIFT, strengthening its communications with the retail banks. It also upgraded the cheque-clearing technology and issued new licences to local banks, foreign banks, asset management companies, insurance institutions, and investment companies. This was to attract foreign investment and enhance competition. The UAE and Saudi Arabia, unlike Bahrain, did little to enhance disclosure, reduce defaults, break market concentrations, or seek economic diversification. Bahrain was never cosseted by oil revenues and this explains its constant vigilance of international shocks. Kuwait issued a Financial Stability Law to secure the rapid restructuring of failing banks, while the UAE sought to enhance its central bank's regulatory powers.

One crucial response to the crisis was to enhance liquidity support. The CBB provided deposits of US$150 million in three retail banks and reduced the repo and discount rates. The state used oil exports to increase government deposits in banks experiencing liquidity shortages. But the main measure was to lower the reserves requirements for banks as an emergency initiative. From

October 2008, acceptable collateral for overnight funds was now to include government Islamic securities (Ijara Sukuk). Anxiety over liquidity was so strong that it was suggested that the loan-to-deposit ratio should be 60–65 per cent for most banks and 70–75 per cent for those with no large investments other than loans. Liquid assets as a percentage of total assets were to be 25 per cent, close to Saudi Arabia's ratio of 20 per cent. With regard to liquidity management, Bahrain stipulatd that reserve requirements would ensure that 5 per cent of total deposits (based on end of previous month data) be maintained on a daily basis.

The real estate sector suffered in the 2008 crisis. In October 2009, the CBB imposed a 30 per cent cap on bank lending for real estate as a share of total bank lending. Also, the banks' own investments in real estate were capped at 40 per cent of their capital base. This was suspended in November 2009 as development projects were being hampered and there was need for caution. A capital adequacy ratio of 125 was insisted for all Bahraini banks. There was also an insistence that NPLs should be recognized within 90 days, thereby restricting exposure to bad-performing loans.

The majority of Bahrain's wholesale banks do not serve the local economy.[12] Bahrain's financial centre has been the base for regional operations, including Saudi Arabia's project finance market directing investment from private wealth into the MENA region, South Asia, and the West. Thus, between 2006 and 2008, Bahrain's private sector credit rose from 15 per cent to 40 per cent. This involved concentration on real estate and infrastructural construction projects, resulting in lower bank liquidity and a dependence on foreign borrowing. Bahrain's problems were in this sector and it escaped difficulties in domestic lending. Foreign ownership of banks was highest in Bahrain at 57 per cent, even higher than in the UAE, at 21 per cent. Bahrain had limited public sector ownership of banks until 2008, and after that, major shareholding was vested in the state and associated business elites. It is relevant here to note the structure of bank ownership in 2006–07. Private ownership was greater than public ownership until 2007. State ownership accounted for 20.4 per cent, of which government held 9 per cent, quasi-government institutions 11.4 per cent, and the royal family nothing. In contrast, private domestic financial institutions held 41.8 per cent of total domestic banking. The private foreign share of total assets was 37.8 per cent, GCC ownership was 34.7 per cent, and non-GCC was 3.1 per cent. The domination of Bahrain's banks by domestic private owners and foreign owners

---

[12] International Monetary Fund, 'Impact of the Global Financial Crisis on the Gulf Cooperation Council Countries', p. 62.

was a consequence of Bahrain's dependence on domestic business lineages, both Sunni and Shiite, and on oil-wealthy neighbours and their connections to core industrial and financial groups in Bahrain. The apparent absence of the royal family is explained by their shadowy financial connections with domestic business elites and foreign financial and insurance institutions. Quasi-government investors include public pension funds and social security investment institutions.[13]

State power in finance remains considerable. The CBB is responsible for regulating and supervising the whole of Bahrain's financial sector. This includes the retail banks, wholesale banks, the insurance sector, investment firms, brokers, investment advisers, the Bahrain Stock Exchange, finance companies, and mutual funds. Even personal credit is within the Benefit Company launched in 2005, owned by 17 commercial banks and providing credit information.

The weaknesses in the non-bank financial sector revolved largely around risk and difficulties over capital requirements. To avoid a high-risk culture within these institutions, the state adopted tighter conditions for granting licences. The need for better management was apparent, particularly after the start of the crisis. There was an urgent need for a stronger disclosure culture, to avert constant pressure for recapitalization of financial institutions facing liquidation. The CBB's authority over all financial institutions helped to insulate them from the recurring oil cycle, by ensuring that fluctuations there were not transmitted to the non-oil sector and then to the stock market. The CBB also undertook cross-border surveillance, frequently off-loading vulnerable financial interests onto off-shore banks, because Bahrain's off-shore banking was more secure, being capitalized mainly through Saudi Arabia, Oman, and Kuwait. The CBB focused on the stability of the financial system as a whole.

Bahrain also pursued a strict policy on bank capitalization, creating a buffer against the bubbles that emerged from indiscriminate speculation during the boom years. It included avoiding high leverage in the corporate sector, which had increased vulnerabilities in 2008. Also, the CBB sought to strengthen cross-border cooperation and strengthen regulation and off-shore banking. The crisis in regional banks had an impact on domestic banks. Here improvements through the credit bureau were sought. Within this, the CBB sought awareness of cross-border structures, hard-to-value instruments, and off-balance-sheet vehicles, all of which complicated the CBB's analysis and tracking of risk in financial institutions.[14]

---

[13] Abdullah Al-Hasan, May Khamis, and Nada Oulidi, 'A Topography and Analysis of the GCC Banking Systems', IMF Working Paper, WP/10/87, 2010.

[14] Moody's Global Corporate Finance, 'Gulf Corporates: The Flip Side of Globalization', June 2009.

The Contrasting Experience of Islamic Banks in Bahrain

Islamic banks initially experienced less exposure to the 2008 financial crisis. The new wave of Islamic finance generated by Bahrain's position as the Islamic financial hub of the Gulf states, emphasized innovation in the creation of Islamic instruments and was driven by the flow of funds from oil-wealthy Saudi Arabia and Kuwait rather than by exposures in the US. Their broadly ethical character prohibited the financial anarchy exhibited in Kuwait with its Suq Al-Manakh episode in 2008. Bahrain's Islamic banks increased their assets between 2000 and 2008. The share of Islamic bank assets in total bank assets in 2008 was 29.9 per cent. Between 2000 and 2008, the assets of Islamic banks increased by 37.6 per cent, while assets in the total banking system (including Islamic banks) grew by 9.6 per cent. This last figure indicates a major decline in conventional banking assets.[15]

If Islamic banks were initially less affected by the crisis, in 2009 they still experienced a decline in profits, the result of difficulties in the macro-economy and in particular losses in the real estate and construction industry. Although Islamic banks in Bahrain have less exposure in the real estate sector, they were affected by problems in Dubai and Qatar. Islamic banks are, however, better placed to ride challenges in the wider economy, partly because of their risk-averse culture, with an emphasis on capital adequacy, liquidity protection, and risk-sharing Shari'ah-compliant contracts. Pre-crisis capital provisions provided the necessary protection. Islamic banks have much higher equity-to-asset ratios than conventional banks. This means they have lower returns on equity than the conventional bank but they endure less risk. Also, Islamic banks are not permitted to engage in financial derivatives, and it was this sector that suffered the major decline in asset prices in 2008.

A further set of figures is useful in explaining the sustainability of Islamic finance in the crisis. In 2008, the capital adequacy ratio of Islamic banks in Bahrain was 24.5 per cent, while for banks it was 18.1 per cent. Islamic banks increased profitability by 14.7 per cent while the entire banking system suffered losses, of 4.8 per cent in 2007–08. The increase in profitability in 2008–09 for Islamic banks was 57.6 per cent while for the total banking sector

---

[15] Central Bank of Bahrain, *Financial Stability Report*, 2012. For a critical understanding of the complex regime of Islamic instruments, see Brandon Davies, 'Eligible Capital and Capital Instruments', in *Islamic Capital Markets and Products: Managing Capital and Liquidity Requirements under Basel III*, edited by Simon Archer and Rifaat Ahmed Abdel Karim (Chichester: Wiley, 2018), pp. 208–20; Central Bank of Bahrain, *Financial Stability Report*, March 2017; Naser J. Najjar, 'Can Financial Ratios Reliably Measure the Performance of Banks in Bahrain?', *International Journal of Economics and Finance*, vol. 5, no. 3 (2013), p. 161.

it was 36.8 per cent. The exposure of Islamic banks to real estate and construction as a percentage of total loans was 11.3 per cent, compared to 26.2 per cent for the whole banking sector. Weak attitudes and practices towards liquidity affect Islamic banks during a crisis, as in 2008. The International Islamic Liquidity Management Corporation (IILM), established in 2008 as a direct response to the crisis, adopted strict measures for liquidity risk management. Regulations relate to the disclosure of risky assets, crucial in an active market seeking to avoid severe volatility.[16]

A Saviour or a Problem? The Gulf States and 2008 Volatility

Between 1980 and 2011, cross-border portfolio equity assets in the GCC countries increased from US$4,528 million to US$501,487 million; FDI assets increased from US$1,186 million to US$191,026 million; and total external assets increased from US$238,349 million to US$2,561,286 million.[17] The GCC, established in 1981, had free trade agreements in agricultural and industrial products and the free movement of labour. In 2008, the GCC established a single market. The financial system, dominated by commercial banks, imposed greater discipline on cross-border equity flows. Bahrain, in contrast to her neighbours, was more liberal towards corporate ownership by foreigners. Bahrain and Oman have the most open banking sectors, where foreign investors hold between 30 and 40 per cent of domestic banking assets. In Bahrain, foreign investment ceilings for listed stocks are 49 per cent in general and 10 per cent for a single equity. Some banks and insurance companies are 100 per cent open to foreign ownership and 100 per cent open to GCC nationals.[18]

Bahrain is the most integrated in the GCC. Saudi Arabia is the most segmented, although it offers portfolio diversification to regional GCC and international investors mainly through mutual funds, and this provided some protection from the impact of the 2008 financial crisis for Bahrain and Kuwait. Bahrain experienced a smaller stock market decline while the GCC's stock market capitalization fell by 40 per cent after the collapse of Lehman Brothers in 2007. Volatility was considerable: the standard deviation of daily

[16] Central Bank of Bahrain, *Islamic Finance*, 2007.
[17] Philip R. Lane and Gian Maria Milesi-Ferretti, 'Oil Shocks and External Balances', IMF Annual Research Conference, 3–4 November 2016, pp. 1–2; Abdullah R. Alotaibi, 'Financial Integration in the Gulf Region', PhD, School of Business, University of Western Sydney, 2014, p. 67.
[18] *Standard & Poor's Global Stock Markets Factbook*, 2012.

average returns doubled between August 2008 and February 2009, compared with January 2007 to August 2008.[19] Bahrain, where Islamic banks are the dominant providers of Shari'ah-compliant finance, immediately used its IILM membership to improve liquidity. In a further response to the crisis, the government placed deposits of US$150 million in the banks. In addition, providing banks with a penalty free credit facility for short-term dollar swaps indicated official concern that banks might fail. Two banks that ran into financial difficulties were taken over by the Central Bank to protect the other banks. The CBB also raised the commercial banks' deposit guarantee from 15,000 to 20,000 Bahraini Dinars.[20] Bahrain also reduced the reserve requirement rate from 7 per cent to 5 per cent. This followed a reduction in the one-week deposit rate by 25 bps and the overnight repurchase rate by 125 bps. Bahrain was also helped indirectly by Saudi Arabia's large stimulus of a US$400 billion investment plan over five years. These recovery measures meant that Bahrain experienced only a modest decline. Saudi Arabia had a distinct relationship with Bahrain. In 2012, Saudi Arabia's exports to Bahrain, at US$5294.87 million, exceeded its exports to all other GCC countries. Saudi Arabia's imports from Bahrain, at US$1292.9 million, were greater than its imports from Oman, Kuwait, and Qatar.[21]

The Bahrain Bourse experienced only a modest decline as a result of the 2008 financial crisis. Market capitalization was US$10 billion in 2003, US$14 billion in 2004, and US$17 billion in 2005. It then rose to US$21 billion in 2006 and to US$28 billion in 2007, falling to US$21 billion in 2008 and then to US$17 billion in 2009. It recovered in 2010 to US$20 billion but dipped in 2011 to US$17 billion and in 2012 to US$16 billion.[22] However, the benefits of large inflows of capital can be disrupted by sudden outflows that can weaken the financial system. In Bahrain, efficient supervision of capital markets and reduced dependence on oil and gradual economic diversification averted dramatic capital outflows in 2008–09.[23]

The integration of Bahrain within the GCC, stimulating trade, was complemented by the sustainable growth in credit. Financial integration also increased the efficiency of financial intermediaries and the stock market

---

[19] International Monetary Fund, 'Impact of the Global Financial Crisis on the Gulf Cooperation Council Countries'.

[20] D. Lidstone, 'Sector Regaining Its Confidence after the Shock of Crisis', Economic and Social Commission for Western Asia, 2009; Financial Times, 10 November 2009.

[21] Alotaibi, 'Financial Integration in the Gulf Region', p. 179; A. Mishra, International Investment Patterns: Evidence Using a New Dataset', Research in International Business and Finance, vol. 21, no. 2 (2007), pp. 342–60.

[22] Bahrain Bourse website 2013; ICD-Thomson Reuters, Islamic Finance Development Report, 2015.

[23] Yesenn El-Radhi, Economic Diversification in the Gulf States: Public Expenditure and Non-oil Economic Growth in Bahrain, Oman and Qatar (Berlin: Gerlach Press, 2018).

through increased competition.[24] Trade, turnover, inflation, domestic credit, oil production, and institutional vigour each had an impact on Bahrain, together with regional spillovers from Saudi Arabia and Kuwait. The next section will analyse the impact of oil, the long-term link between oil prices and the Bahrain Bourse.[25]

Thus, despite the uncertainty and vulnerability that gripped Bahrain's banking sector between 2007 and 2009, it quickly regained its usual vitality. No bank collapsed and the two that faced serious problems were Saudi banks in Bahrain. Bank profitability has been moderate as a result of assistance from government long-term deposits, the Central Bank's infusion of liquidity, and the introduction of monetary measures to ease the financial crunch. In addition, the CBB also limited Bahrain's exposure to external sources of credit and credit default swap spreads, which were particularly serious between March 2008 and November 2009. The CBB's monetary easing policies have been impressive. The decline in oil prices and the accompanying plunge in asset prices did affect Bahrain through its trading in oil and refining, but the impact was moderate. Bahrain's involvement in real estate and construction programmes was low in comparison to Dubai and Qatar. Bahrain also addressed the risk from multiple exposures created by family conglomerates by tightening external credit to banks.[26]

Aggregate data on Non-performing Loans (NPLs), Capital Adequacy Ration (CAR), Return on Asset (ROA), and Return on Equity (ROE) demonstrate both the mildness of the impact of the 2008 financial crisis on Bahrain and the effectiveness of the recovery measures initiated by the Government and CBB. Non-performing loans in 2007 were 2.3 per cent, and rose to 3.9 per cent; the capital adequacy ratio declined from 21.0 per cent in 2007 to 19.6 per cent in 2009; the banking sector return on assets remained at 1.2 per cent in 2007–09; and the return on equity declined from 18.4 per cent to 10.6 per cent.[27]

It can also be argued that the Islamic bank model of financing helped to contain the financial crisis. In Bahrain, leasing or hire purchase (ijarah) is the second most common method of financing, while murabahah and mudarabah account for 50 per cent of total financing.[28] This is assisted

[24] Alotaibi, 'Financial Integration in the Gulf Region', p. 100.

[25] F. S. A. Balli and R. Louis, 'Sectoral Equity Returns and Portfolio Diversification Opportunities across the GCC Region', *Journal of International Financial Markets, Institutions and Money*, vol. 25 (2013), pp. 33–48.

[26] BIS Consolidated Banking Assets; Central Bank of Bahrain, *Financial Stability Report*, 2003 to 2017.

[27] Central Bank of Bahrain, *The Review*, 2007 and 2009; International Monetary Fund, 'Impact of the Global Financial Crisis on the Gulf Cooperation Council Countries'.

[28] Salman Syed Ali, *Islamic Banking in the MENA Region* (World Bank and Islamic Development Bank, Islamic Research and Training Institute, February 2011), p. 18.

further by three types of customer account: demand deposits that do not pay any return; unrestricted investment accounts; and restricted investment accounts that share in profits. Mudarabah-based deposit accounts are required to keep the funds invested in real activities in order to accrue profits for themselves and their depositors. Invariably, such utilization provides stability. In Bahrain, the asset utilization ratio (total investment against total assets) increased by 73 per cent between 2006 and 2009. This increase in asset utilization, accompanied by an increase in the proportion of liquid assets, was a result of an increase in demand for Islamic finance in Bahrain. Islamic banking in Bahrain, unlike in Iran, was devoid of Qard al-Hasan loans (interest-free loans) which also contributed to stability.[29] One small flaw was that in Bahrain in 2008, the financing component of total assets increased faster than their portfolio investment, which was affected by constraints in financial markets. This inevitably strained liquidity but was swiftly counteracted by the CBB's capital injection.[30]

The fact that the bulk of financing was through murabahah and ijarah explains to a degree Bahrain's sustainability, as both instruments operate with high transparency: credit is tracked throughout its tenure. They are also protected by assets. Despite globalization, Bahrain's Islamic banking is not exposed to derivatives, unlike the conventional banks which faced severe international economic downturns. There is the argument that the Black-Scholes equation, upon which a prominent hedge fund was based, contributed to the 1997 crash in Asia and Russia. The hedge fund lost US$4.6 billion within four months.[31]

Law, Culture, and Institutional Structure

The financial crash of 2008 has encouraged considerable modelling and quantification of the Bahrain stock market. But the focus here is on the legal order and how it shaped institutional reform to secure a stable global Bahrain Bourse. Bahrain had a vital role historically as a trading diaspora with international interactions. From the 1970s, Bahrain became a powerful

---

[29] Farhad Nili, 'Iran: Islamic Banking and Finance', in *The Islamic Finance Handbook: A Practitioner's Guide to the Global Markets*, edited by Sasikala Thiagaraja, Andrew Morgan, Andrew Tebbutt, and Geraldine Chan (Singapore: Wiley, 2014), pp. 176–212.
[30] Najjar, 'Can Financial Ratios Reliably Measure the Performance of Banks in Bahrain?', p. 161.
[31] Geoffrey M. Hodgson, 'The Great Crash of 2008 and the Reform of Economics', *Cambridge Journal of Economics*, vol. 33, no. 6 (2009), p. 1212; Uskali Maki (ed), *Fact and Fiction in Economics: Models, Realism, and Social Construction* (Cambridge: Cambridge University Press, 2002); Thorsten Beck, Asli Demirgüç-Kunt, and Ouarda Merrouche, 'Islamic Banking vs. Conventional Banking: Business Model, Efficiency and Stability', World Bank Policy Research Working Paper No. WPS5446, 2010.

unifying economic force within the GCC. Bahrain is the Islamic finance hub of the GCC. Its institutional cross-regional ties expanded to include the stock exchange, as part of the process of developing sophisticated financial instruments. With these developments there emerged prescient legal and economic responses to the financial crisis of 2008. Bahrain had had a rigorous legal regime since 1971 and faced little danger from expanding derivative markets or excessive debt. It faced very few bank failures and those few were banks owned by the GCC neighbours. Credit spreads with potentially high default rates and a negligent appraisal of financial risk against assets were constrained, partly by the fact that the banks were owned by the state, partly by the power of institutional investors in the grip of the state, but ultimately by legal constraints on speculative behaviour. Real estate valuations did pose risks on the bourse. But business equity is held by the state and by wealthy business elites who are close associates of the state. In addition, there is investment through mutual funds: in 2009 there were 2,747 with assets of US$5,580 million, accounting for 8.3 per cent of assets under management and contributing 25.5 per cent of GDP. Of these Bahrain-domiciled funds, 53 are Islamic funds.[32]

Only a third of mutual funds are open, using proceeds to make individual investments. A large share of these open funds are money market funds used by corporations for short-term liquidity management. The share of mutuals investing directly in mutual funds (pension funds, insurance companies) is small, only 10 per cent. These mutuals are diversified and add liquidity to the stock holdings. Investment ranges from real estate securities, local bond markets, and shareholdings in government enterprises. All these strategies encourage the growth of non-bank securities firms and an increase in foreign fund managers, thereby enhancing talent and encouraging the acquisition of sub-par funds to stabilize the bourse. They contribute to market turnover, effective price discovery, and lower costs of capital, and they have a positive impact on corporate governance. The result is an improvement in investor safeguards to the level of IOSCO (International Organization of Securities Commission) standards, while contributing to the formation of a global interstate order. This explains why the crisis was muted in Bahrain.[33]

[32] NCB Capital (2010) on institutional investors in the GCC: Zawya database of listed local mutual funds. These investments are in petroleum-related industries, telecommunications, and finance. Bahrain Bourse report 2010; Central Bank of Bahrain, *Financial Stability Report*, 2010: mutual funds focus on equity but rarely on IPO funds.

[33] International Organization of Securities Commission, *IOSCO Principles for Collective Investment Schemes*, 1995. This provides legal form and structure, custodian rules and supervision, and addresses conflicts of interest and asset valuation and pricing. J. Carmichael and M. Pomerleano, *The Development and Regulation of Non-Bank Financial Institutions* (Washington, DC: World Bank, 2002); X. Chen, J. Harford, and L. Kai, 'Monitoring: Which Institutions Matter?', *Journal of Financial Economics*, vol. 86 (2007),

Mutual funds also encourage the holding of Shari'ah-compliant assets including sukuk, and in Bahrain this accounts for US$193 million out of total assets amounting to US$1,208 million. This is 16 per cent of total Shari'ah-compliant assets, while conventional assets account for 84 per cent of mutual funds.[34] The juxtaposition of a state-centred capital market alongside traditional mutual funds has, to a degree, driven Bahrain's emergence as a powerhouse of both Islamic and conventional finance and secured the stability of the Bahrain Bourse, in contrast to Kuwait.

Twenty-one mutual funds were located locally while 706 were located within the GCC and 276 in the MENA countries. The mutual funds that were focused on external investment account for 98 per cent of the total investment of Bahrain's mutual funds. This confirms the extraterritoriality developed since the 1990s.[35] Ultimately, a significant part of the economy is built on business assets and equity markets but the organizational capabilities of the state and its institutions protected it from the impact of the 2008 crisis. Only the real estate sector suffered, but then only modestly and briefly.[36]

Why did Bahrain and the GCC countries not struggle with the effects of the 2008 financial crisis? Tables 6.1 and 6.2 illustrate a swift recovery after 2009 and a remarkable return to stability. Bahrain felt the tremors in a series of runs on financial institutions but the economy never fell to pieces, as it did in the US.[37] (See the tables of major banks 2008–15 in the Appendix.)

Despite being the hub of Islamic finance in the Gulf, Bahrain had not pursued financial liberalization through de-regulation to create new and profitable financial sectors. The growth of the financial sector was not fuelled by increasing debt or by an asset price boom, as in the Suq al-Manakh in Kuwait. The banks in Bahrain, both Islamic and conventional, are mainly owned by the state and were not over-leveraged or burdened by sovereign debt. There were small tremors from the distressed Kuwait Finance House based in Bahrain, because of the fall in stock market prices and decline in real estate values. Bahrain's resilience was maintained through stable oil prices.

pp. 279–305; Paul A. Gompers and Andrew Metrick, 'Institutional Investors and Equity Prices', *Quarterly Journal of Economics*, vol. 116, no. 1 (2001), pp. 229–59. Large MENA investment funds in 2009 included: NCB Capital, EFG Hermes, Riyadh Capital, Beltone Asset Management, HSBC Saudi Arabia Limited, Al-Rajhi Capital, EL-Ahly Fund Management, CI Asset Management, Samba Capital, Caam Saudi Fransi. These, the largest of the MENA investment funds, account for 27 per cent of total investment: Zawya Database; NCB Capital, 'The Rise of Institutional Investors', 2010.

[34] Zawya data of listed local funds in Bahrain.

[35] International Monetary Fund, 'Impact of the Global Financial Crisis on the Gulf Cooperation Council Countries', pp. 5–12.

[36] William Macko and Diego Sourrouille, *Investment Funds in MENA* (Washington, DC: World Bank, 2010). Zawya Thomson Reuters is part of Thomson Reuters Middle East and is a major source of financial and business news.

[37] Robert E. Hall, 'Why Does the Economy Fall to Pieces after a Financial Crisis?', *Journal of Economic Perspectives*, vol. 24, no. 4 (2010), pp. 3–20.

Table 6.1 Kuwait Finance House

	Return on equity ratio	Financial leverage margin	Cost income ratio	Risk provision ratio
2003	22.18	10.71	34.95	5.97
2004	23.93	10.61	29.77	15.22
2005	22.00	7.80	35.00	21.89
2006	28.21	8.99	44.03	12.00
2007	27.68	7.27	36.56	10.19
2008	14.52	8.50	41.38	53.92
2009	4.90	7.21	51.10	72.76

Table 6.2 Al Baraka Bank

	Return on equity ratio	Financial leverage margin	Cost income ratio	Risk provision ratio
2003	8.38	8.39	32.45	56.32
2004	10.62	8.94	39.39	25.89
2005	14.25	8.22	34.46	22.76
2006	11.53	6.30	34.60	19.12
2007	15.64	6.44	31.90	8.94
2008	17.10	7.04	33.11	15.44
2009	12.70	7.58	35.63	32.07

Source: Banks' annual reports and calculations in Rania Abdelfattah Salem and Ahmed Mohamed Badreldin, 'Assessing Resilience of Islamic Banks: An Empirical Analysis', in *Islamic Banking and Financial Crisis: Reputation, Stability, and Risks*, edited by Habib Ahmed, Mehmet Asutay, and Rodney Wilson (Edinburgh University Press, 2014), pp. 50–1.

The performance of leading Islamic banks will be appraised by an analysis of liquidity, stability, and risk. At the outset it is important to appreciate that the 2008 crisis revealed a failure of risk management in the private sector, a failure of public sector governance of the financial system, and that globalization of trade, finance, and labour had created a risky interdependence. Despite the externalization of financial resources within the GCC, Bahrain was less exposed as government intervention overlay the financial and trading framework. A trigger of the 2008 crisis was excessive liquidity and weak liquidity management. In 2002, the Bahrain Monetary Agency had established the Liquidity Management Centre which controlled the sale of Shari'ah-compliant securities, including sukuk al-salam and ijarah sukuk, thereby averting predatory pricing. Islamic banks in Bahrain assessed the level of liquidity in investment, savings, and current accounts. That rigorous supervision led to speedy intervention in periods of crisis, as in 2007.[38] The prudent culture of banks in Bahrain, compared to those in Kuwait, is captured in the contrast between the Al Baraka Bank of Bahrain and Kuwait Finance House. The Kuwait Finance House followed a strategy of maintaining a higher financing margin as compared to its deposits, while for the Al Baraka Bank, the deposit margin is greater than its financing margin. The cost–income ratio provides an indicator of a bank's profitability before deduction of impairment provisions, and clearly confirms the positive performance of the Islamic banks. However, the important ratio is the RPR—the risk provision ratio. This shows the level of gross profit that has been allocated for the impairment or the rescue of bad debts. The banks showed an increase in RPR in 2007, 2008, and 2009 for both KFH and Al Baraka Bank. This increase is explained by rescue strategies during the financial crisis, while between 2003 and 2006, the risk provision ratio indicates the quality of the banks' financing policy and capitalization, with an equity ratio varying from 9 per cent to 20 per cent. Before the financial crisis, the Islamic banks were lax in providing capital assigned for risky assets. But after 2008, they were aware that the RPR ratio is crucial if they were to operate successfully in global markets. From 2006, the Central Bank of Bahrain, aware of impending problems, had injected state deposits in listed banks to avert risk. However, although the CBB sought greater transparency, from 2002 the Islamic banks were slow to improve disclosure, as profit equalization reserves and investment risk reserves were still not shown in their financial statements. The quantification of risk is important as Bahrain's financial institutions have impressive global ambitions.[39]

Kuwait Finance House had a financing leverage margin above 70 per cent between 2003 and 2008 but it fell to 50 per cent in 2009. Al Baraka maintained a stable deposit margin higher than its financing leverage margin.

Conclusions and Contrasts

It is important, as a conclusion, to review the factors responsible for the 2008 crisis and the major reasons why its impact was mild in Bahrain. With

---

[38] Noraini Mohd Ariffin and Salina Hj. Kassim, 'Liquidity Risk Management and Financial Performance of Islamic Banks: Empirical Evidence', in *Islamic Banking and Financial Crisis: Reputation, Stability, and Risks*, edited by Habib Ahmed, Mehmet Asutay, and Rodney Wilson (Edinburgh: Edinburgh University Press, 2014), p. 127.

[39] Rania Abdelfattah Salem and Ahmed Mohamed Badreldin, 'Assessing Resilience of Islamic Banks: An Empirical Analysis', in *Islamic Banking and Financial Crisis: Reputation, Stability, and Risks*, edited by Habib Ahmed, Mehmet Asutay, and Rodney Wilson (Edinburgh: Edinburgh University Press, 2014), pp. 40–57.

respect to the causes, Mirakhor and Kirchener identify high liquidity, the creation of innovative financial instruments not suitable for existing markets, information asymmetry, lax structure of credit instruments, high risk-taking, associational links of financial institutions with real estate developers and insurance companies, and faults in the pricing of assets. But serious empirical case studies with qualitative and quantitative evidence are lacking.[40] My focus here has been on the regulation of debt and investment financing by Central Bank of Bahrain directives.[41] Conventional banks in Bahrain were cautious when restructuring debts, and the CBB gave clear direction on the tools to be adopted when rescheduling non-performing loans. Although Tawarruq (a sale and resale transaction used to generate liquidity) was frowned upon as creating more debt, it still prevailed. But in the 2008 Global Financial Crisis, the state intervened to provide increased liquidity for the banks through deposits. Shaykh Muhammad Taqi Usmani had proposed that the current debt-based financial system be replaced by an equity-based system linked to the market economy.[42]

The main factor mitigating the impact of the crisis in Bahrain was its emergence from 2003 as a hub of Islamic finance, thereby creating inflows of capital from oil-rich GCC countries and channelling surplus funds into Bahrain's economic diversification. Dramatic increases in oil prices, from US$30 per barrel in 2003 to US$100 at the end of 2007, producing real GDP growth of 6 to 7 per cent per annum, softened the impact of the 2008 crash. The figures below clearly show the dramatic recovery of banks in Bahrain by 2012. Even Kuwait Finance House, which earlier had faced serious financing problems, recovered.

In assessing the impact of the 2008 crisis, it is important to recognize that there was no systemic breakdown and that bank profitability declined only marginally. Non-performing loans rose from 2.3 per cent in 2007 to 3.9 per cent in 2009; the capital adequacy ratio fell from 21.0 per cent in 2007 to 19.6 per cent in 2009; and return on assets remained the same, 1.2 per cent in 2007 and 1.2 per cent in 2009. The return on equity was 18.4 per cent in 2007 and in 2009, 10.6 per cent. The only weakness was in domestic and regional

---

[40] Abbas Mirakhor and Noureddine Krichenne, 'The Recent Crisis: Lessons for Islamic Finance', IFSB Public Lecture on Financial Policy and Stability, Kuala Lumpur, Islamic Finance Services Board, 2009. See also Hyman Minsky, *Stabilizing an Unstable Economy* (New York: McGraw-Hill Professional, 2008); Y. Mersch, 'About the Role of Central Bank in Financial Stability and Prudential Liquidity Supervision and the Attractiveness of Islamic Finance', IFSB Public Lecture on Financial Policy and Stability, Kuala Lumpur, Islamic Financial Services Lecture, 2009.

[41] Central Bank of Bahrain, *Financial Stability Report*, April 2012, March 2017.

[42] Shaykh Muhammad Taqi Usmani, 'Post-crisis Reforms: Some Points to Ponder', in World Economic Forum, *Faith and the Global Agenda: Values for the Post Crisis Economy* (Geneva: World Economic Forum, 2010), pp. 51–4.

credit flows for banks and non-bank financial institutions. Important here were the commercial ambitions of the state, the ruling family, tribal kinship ties, and associational business links with Shiite business elites. Those crony connections were further encouraged by the poor performance of the regional banks in oil-wealthy Saudi Arabia and Kuwait. The crisis prompted change in this 'noble gentlemanly capitalism nirvana of ownership' towards the diverse, modern, pro-manufacturing, professional dynamism on which modern capitalism thrives. The diversification of commercial power in the state and private sectors is the route to improving corporate governance and long-term financing strategies. Here the risks facing financial and corporate institutions will be rigorously evaluated and liquidity standards improved in order to cope better with shifts created by economic and business cycles.

Appendix: The Performance of Major Banks in Bahrain, 2008–15

The following figures demonstrate the banks' recovery after the financial crisis. The sources for all the figures are the Central Bank of Bahrain, the reports of each of bank, the annual reports of the Economic Development Board Bahrain and the Bahrain Financial Services Focus 2013; Deloitte Research and Analysis, 2012, 2013; and Zawya Sovereign Database 2005–13. These were kindly given to me by Omid Torabi, and Alaa Alabed, and Hatim El-Tahir, Director of the Islamic Finance Group and Leader of the Deloitte and Touche-Bahrain. A further source was Salman Syed Ali, *Islamic Banking in the MENA Region* (World Bank and Islamic Development Bank, Islamic Research and Training Institute, February 2011).

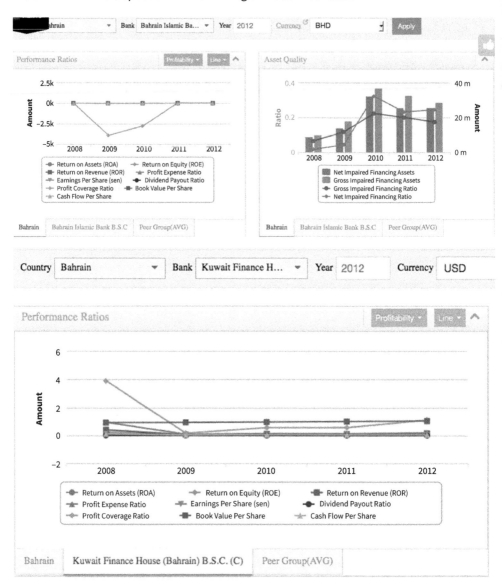

No.	Country	Bank	Total Assets						
			2009	2010	2011	2012	2013	2014	2015
1	Bahrain	ABC	-9.78%	-5.86%	-16.62%	3.09%	-6.09%	28.32%	1.20%
2		Albaraka	-7.15%	44.81%	18.66%	-11.23%	15.00%	12.49%	1.07%
3		Alsalam	41.74%	8.99%	7.86%	1.98%	15.50%	79.67%	-15.27%
4		Islamic	4.35%	2.60%	-10.32%	-0.76%	9.30%	-3.85%	11.56%
5		First Energy	20.83%	-2.76%	2.57%	13.79%	1.20%	-4.07%	-22.75%
6		Gulf Finance House	-52.87%	-38.00%	-18.89%	7.82%	1.95%	43.76%	102.88%
7		International Investment	-17.94%	-10.76%	-7.29%	11.29%	5.74%	55.32%	-15.54%
8		Khaleeji Commercial	1.85%	-11.48%	6.75%	5.73%	14.60%	9.16%	10.48%
9		Kuwait Finance House	6.90%	5.34%	6.27%	-4.15%	6.22%	-5.31%	-2.14%
10		Seera	-18.57%	36.16%	26.11%	-31.61%	-13.78%	-34.98%	-16.29%

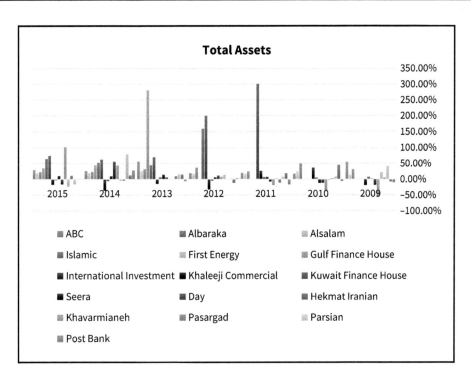

No.	Country	Bank	Financing Assets						
			2009	2010	2011	2012	2013	2014	2015
1	Bahrain	ABC	−16.05%	−10.72%	−9.43%	15.54%	3.66%	26.34%	−7.60%
2		Albaraka	−13.66%	38.38%	12.64%	−12.65%	18.34%	14.41%	8.14%
3		Alsalam	20.95%	44.82%	35.82%	20.88%	18.48%	56.31%	9.53%
4		Islamic	2.67%	−28.07%	−5.00%	1.27%	5.38%	19.95%	13.22%
5		First Energy	-	92.85%	18.65%	−100.00%	-	-	124.25%
6		Gulf Finance House	−57.84%	−50.64%	−100.00%		-	-	-
7		International Investment	-	-	-	-	-	-	286.80%
8		Khaleeji Commercial	37.06%	5.79%	−0.81%	21.92%	4.66%	34.88%	11.41%
9		Kuwait Finance House	13.88%	−2.79%	−6.12%	−8.23%	8.85%	−6.77%	−4.37%
10		Seera	−7.89%	-	179.04%	−6.14%	−87.64%	−87.07%	−100.00%

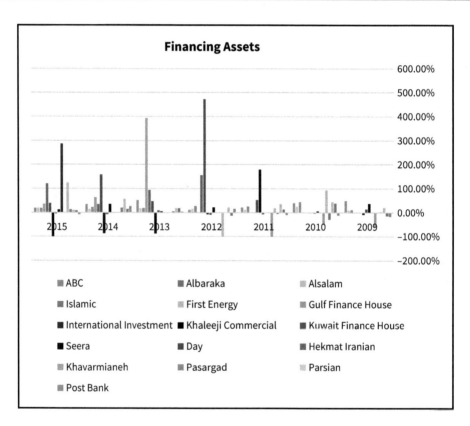

No.	Country	Bank	Total Liabilities						
			2009	2010	2011	2012	2013	2014	2015
1	Bahrain	ABC	−12.72%	−10.55%	−20.98%	2.94%	−9.32%	31.88%	−0.33%
2		Albaraka	−5.21%	50.34%	22.05%	−11.93%	17.15%	13.74%	0.93%
3		Alsalam	52.92%	12.08%	10.47%	1.50%	14.71%	93.13%	−17.82%
4		Islamic	9.04%	8.32%	−11.70%	3.42%	9.06%	−4.33%	8.88%
5		First Energy	747.52%	−10.31%	16.94%	28.13%	−8.27%	9.06%	15.07%
6		Gulf Finance House	−51.99%	−25.40%	−34.31%	−14.06%	−24.78%	14.72%	299.28%
7		International Investment	−81.01%	−36.41%	−10.77%	99.82%	−9.51%	3199.02%	−3.02%
8		Khaleeji Commercial	6.12%	−13.25%	9.15%	7.64%	25.03%	10.55%	10.92%
9		Kuwait Finance House	9.23%	6.28%	7.18%	−6.25%	9.68%	−6.36%	−3.59%
10		Seera	−52.45%	279.48%	57.33%	−15.15%	−32.59%	−45.97%	−62.23%

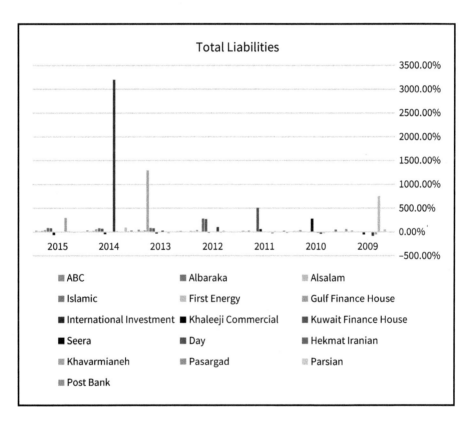

			Deposits from Customers						
No.	Country	Bank	2009	2010	2011	2012	2013	2014	2015
1	Bahrain	ABC	-	-	-	-	-	-	11.28%
2		Albaraka	24.83%	56.65%	6.95%	−7.53%	−84.69%	794.29%	−1.81%
3		Alsalam	−14.68%	80.07%	9.25%	23.37%	−5.69%	164.38%	12.53%
4		Islamic	20.98%	13.13%	−9.80%	7.53%	9.49%	−2.68%	7.48%
5		First Energy	-	-	-	-	−100.00%	-	-
6		Gulf Finance House	-	−34.61%	0.96%	23.97%	−8.41%	−22.83%	67210.70%
7		International Investment	-	-	-	-	-	-	-
8		Khaleeji Commercial	−16.31%	−12.37%	10.35%	−1.29%	36.50%	30.97%	14.83%
9		Kuwait Finance House	51.62%	−7.74%	2.03%	−3.02%	5.24%	15.95%	−6.68%
10		Seera	-	-	-	-	-	-	-

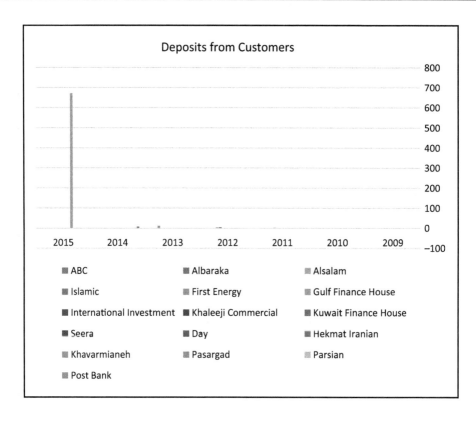

No.	Country	Bank	Total Shareholders' Equity						
			2009	2010	2011	2012	2013	2014	2015
1	Bahrain	ABC	15.35%	24.49%	3.63%	3.62%	5.27%	15.73%	7.47%
2		Albaraka	−15.66%	3.26%	−2.89%	−4.09%	0.00%	0.78%	2.56%
3		Alsalam	14.90%	−0.16%	−0.71%	5.90%	13.08%	35.40%	0.11%
4		Islamic	−15.59%	−28.78%	1.27%	−31.15%	10.19%	2.87%	38.48%
5		First Energy	1.70%	−1.53%	0.36%	2.95%	1.83%	−6.06%	−26.65%
6		Gulf Finance House	−55.18%	−73.16%	100.71%	63.38%	37.64%	29.28%	2.52%
7		International Investment	−13.04%	−10.32%	−8.22%	6.72%	6.06%	−2.66%	−21.27%
8		Khaleeji Commercial	−8.27%	−6.65%	0.65%	0.44%	−16.27%	3.05%	4.70%
9		Kuwait Finance House	1.44%	3.31%	4.38%	2.79%	−3.78%	1.06%	3.16%
10		Seera	−12.16%	2.89%	21.88%	−42.73%	0.94%	−28.41%	1.79%

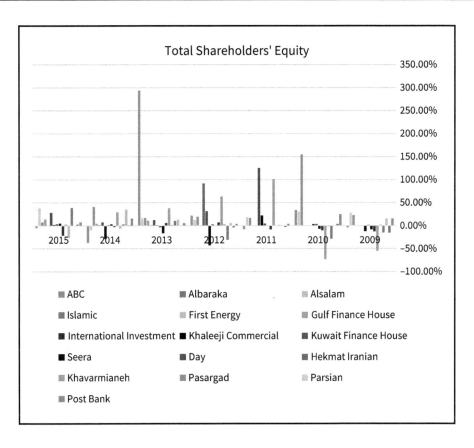

			Total Income						
No.	Country	Bank	2009	2010	2011	2012	2013	2014	2015
1	Bahrain	ABC	−39.77%	−22.03%	−4.89%	6.04%	12.79%	46.78%	23.26%
2		Albaraka	−15.14%	58.57%	12.28%	−8.98%	11.08%	14.19%	15.23%
3		Alsalam	−16.82%	−11.91%	−20.74%	49.60%	−39.60%	75.72%	25.51%
4		Islamic	−57.06%	−102.75%	3695.43%	−13.64%	74.55%	20.33%	−2.64%
5		First Energy	218.59%	−10.86%	−38.29%	210.85%	−12.58%	105.64%	−92.72%
6		Gulf Finance House	−99.46%	120.73%	898.73%	−10.93%	−35.53%	281.44%	−41.69%
7		International Investment	−79.82%	−46.64%	−114.29%	3930.59%	−30.41%	−70.68%	41.78%
8		Khaleeji Commercial	−49.92%	−42.26%	18.12%	−17.06%	−48.16%	107.95%	46.17%
9		Kuwait Finance House	−49.66%	40.91%	4.03%	−5.89%	−44.15%	149.16%	16.93%
10		Seera	−61.71%	137.87%	427.15%	−85.65%	203.28%	−135.56%	171.65%

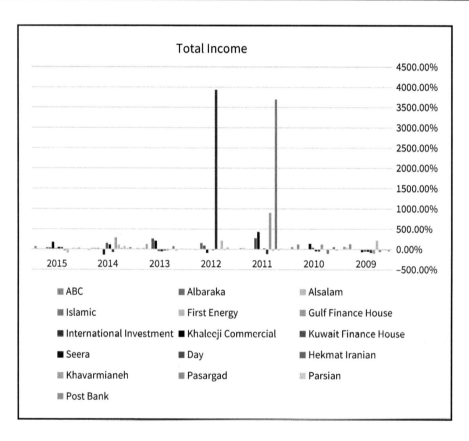

No.	Country	Bank	Total Expenses and Provisions						
			2009	2010	2011	2012	2013	2014	2015
1		ABC	−25.11%	−35.47%	50.73%	−11.60%	25.58%	−1.62%	−7.52%
2		Albaraka	−97.93%	36.34%	−20.75%	−32.66%	18.82%	−9.66%	−5.83%
3		Alsalam	−11.33%	−5.39%	3.27%	−17.03%	57.48%	−116.24%	−54.98%
4		Islamic	−29.90%	9.78%	−4.91%	−38.13%	47.87%	−13.73%	9.06%
5	Bahrain	First Energy	−117.88%	−63.99%	57.91%	−87.06%	32.23%	−354.14%	−218.56%
6		Gulf Finance House	−154.24%	54.32%	80.09%	24.58%	35.16%	−301.24%	43.19%
7		International Investment	−97.31%	29.46%	62.87%	−11.63%	33.62%	−78.67%	−166.37%
8		Khaleeji Commercial	−1.85%	2.25%	22.38%	19.09%	−105.33%	56.03%	−15.21%
9		Kuwait Finance House	16.96%	−33.70%	−5.67%	11.47%	44.84%	−181.59%	−10.97%
10		Seera	−31.58%	77.88%	−177.86%	77.09%	472.19%	−34.03%	84.86%

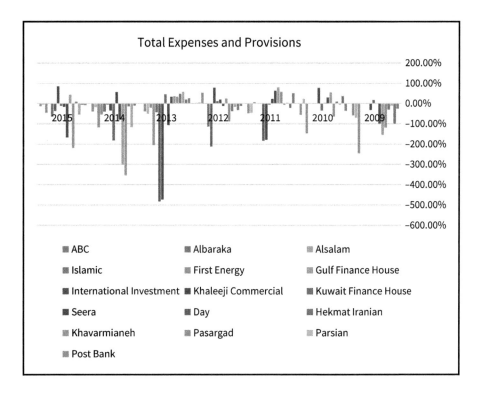

No.	Country	Bank	Profit for the Year						
			2009	2010	2011	2012	2013	2014	2015
1		ABC	−60.46%	−79.49%	292.91%	1.57%	47.60%	84.94%	30.75%
2		Albaraka	−1153.89%	117.58%	−44.21%	−509.29%	108.62%	126.09%	191.00%
3		Alsalam	−45.34%	−47.60%	−93.21%	1974.04%	20.02%	27.88%	−33.33%
4		Islamic	−186.93%	−104.73%	56.31%	−108.59%	116.87%	52.24%	20.52%
5	Bahrain	First Energy	33709.52%	−171.30%	135.01%	944.70%	8.28%	−59.43%	−2407.43%
6		Gulf Finance House	−366.32%	55.05%	100.11%	2531.76%	−37.50%	171.80%	−29.41%
7		International Investment	−306.41%	25.64%	54.66%	186.97%	−26.51%	−235.10%	−223.18%
8		Khaleeji Commercial	−88.65%	−310.74%	107.93%	44.98%	−2657.79%	115.86%	163.33%
9		Kuwait Finance House	−82.82%	52.07%	2.80%	4.77%	−26.40%	−30.78%	109.85%
10		Seera	−152.80%	124.77%	597.74%	−87.67%	−46.75%	−1536.39%	104.75%

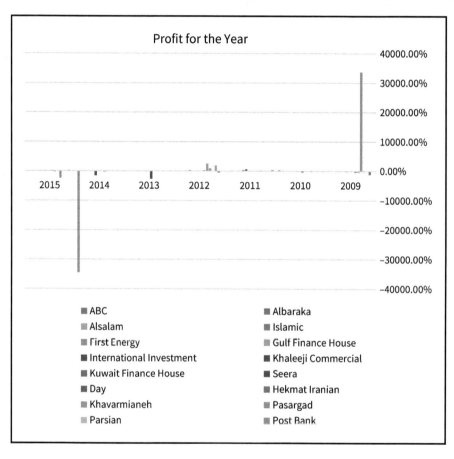

7
Bahrain's Arab Spring

Economic inequality and unemployment trigger riots. Eric Hobsbawm sees riots as a form of collective bargaining, while Charles Tilly argues that when the people believe that they are being unjustly deprived of food, they have a moral and political right to riot. In Bahrain, the poor, and in particular the Shi'a, endured state repression and economic discrimination, set against rising state and elite privilege and increasing oil wealth. Economic deprivation became the trigger for protest, as the Shi'a majority saw the growing disparities of wealth and power, particularly after the surge in oil capital from Saudi Arabia and Kuwait in the 1980s and 1990s. Resistance and protest, as well as the government response, took on a distinctly sectarian character. The accession of Shaikh, later King, Hamad bin Isa initially eased tensions as he made concessions, for example abolishing some intrusive and repressive security laws, releasing political prisoners, and inviting exiles to return and set up political parties and newspapers. He also promised the establishment of a constitutional monarchy under a new constitution, with parliamentary elections in which women would be allowed to vote. The National Action Charter to approve the new constitution received 98 per cent of votes in a 2001 referendum. Although the constitution of 2002 did not meet all promises, many were implemented. However, the major opposition parties, Shi'i Islamist, socialist, and Arab nationalist, boycotted the parliamentary elections of 2002. The sectarian groups in Bahrain, until then engaged in episodic protest, became a major movement seeking change in existing structures of power.[1]

With rising violence by the police and security services against these protests, the action now moved to villages and certain towns, where resistance was orchestrated by a core community. Films and broadcasts of the protests showed how the state was abusing civic rights. In 2007, fishermen in Malakiyya village protested against a cousin of the king who had appropriated

---

[1] Michel Foucault, *Power/Knowledge: Selected Interviews and Other Writings 1972–1977*, translated and edited by Colin Gordon and Leo Marshall (New York: Pantheon Books, 1980), pp. 78–107; Charles Tripp, *The Power and the People: Paths of Resistance in the Middle East* (Cambridge: Cambridge University Press, 2013), pp. 106–17.

Islam and Capitalism in the Making of Modern Bahrain. Rajeswary Ampalavanar Brown, Oxford University Press.
© Rajeswary Ampalavanar Brown (2023). DOI: 10.1093/oso/9780192874672.003.0007

the land on the seafront and thereby denied the fishermen their livelihood. This protest led to police brutality: particularly serious were the battles between the youth of the village and the riot police. The King intervened and forced the cousin to abandon the land he had seized.[2] In Sitra, a coastal town, a land reclamation had been ordered by the Ministry of Defence: but the local residents resisted, although the authorities ultimately pushed through the reclamation. In this way the state provoked long-simmering resentment but resistance was held back by fear. The Arab Spring involved not the overcoming of fear but the creation of hope. Frank Furedi has argued that although 'fear often serves as the foundation for public discourse, historians should not mistake moods or episodes for timeless and essential historical truths or conditions': and further, that the 'politics of fear [is] a sensibility towards life in general'.[3]

The protests and demonstrations were also a response to the state's repression through the police and the Special Security Force. Repression by the authoritarian state was taken under the State Security Measures Law of 1974 and the Penal Code of 1976 and its subsequent amendments.[4] Moreover the Lower House had limited powers and its legislation could be vetoed by the unelected Upper House. And then the authorities arrested 300 people in 2010 on charges of threatening state security. They included members of the parties that were boycotting the elections, as well as bloggers and human rights activists. The authorities also expelled foreign human rights activists.[5] In the parliamentary elections, the Shi'i dominated Al-Wifaq Party won almost half of the seats in the 40-seat chamber, while the rest fell to independent candidates.[6] Government attempts to smear the Al-Wifaq Party, by alleging electoral irregularities, could not be sustained. In fact the party had demonstrated the strength of the electoral process in resisting the authoritarian state. However, the absence of real political change was shown by the fact that the King's uncle, Shaikh Khalifa bin Salman al-Khalifa, remained as Prime Minister, a post he had held for 40 years. He was a hated figure, long associated

---

[2] Land reclamation and seizures by the royal family and their associated merchant cliques are discussed in Fuad Al-Ansari, 'Public Open Space on the Transforming Urban Waterfront of Bahrain: The Case of Manama City', PhD thesis, Newcastle University, 2009, chapters 7–9.

[3] Frank Furedi, *Politics of Fear* (New York: Continuum, 2005), pp. 130, 140. See also Max Weiss, 'Fear and its Opposites in the History of Emotions', in *Facing Fear: The History of an Emotion in Global Perspective*, edited by Michael Laffan and Max Weiss (Princeton, NJ: Princeton University Press, 2012), pp. 1–9; Tripp, The Power and the People, p. 5.

[4] Joe Stork, *Routine Abuse, Routine Denial: Civil Rights and the Political Crisis in Bahrain* (New York: Human Rights Watch, 1997).

[5] Human Rights Watch, 'Bahrain: Elections to Take Place Amid Crackdown', 20 October 2010: http://www.hrw.org/en/news/2010/10/20/bahrain-elections-take-place-amid-crackdown.

[6] Tripp, The Power and the People, p. 109.

with the regime's brutal acts. As a final rebuke, in the purported constitutional monarchy, the king retained supreme executive power.[7]

With growing resentment over the unfulfilled promises of the National Action Charter of 2001, and inspired by the events in Egypt, in February 2011 there was a call for a 'Day of Rage'.[8] Mobilization was achieved through networks of parties, activists, and human rights organizations, using electronic communication. A Facebook page described the state crushing any move towards democracy and economic empowerment. The protesters demanded the dissolution of parliament, the redrafting of the 2002 constitution, and the creation of an elected prime minister heading a representative government sensitive to popular wishes. They demanded that the Al-Khalifah family should not possess executive powers. They also demanded a halt to the policy of tajnis (naturalization of foreign immigrants) that was altering the balance between Sunni and Shi'a. This manifesto attracted thousands of supporters.[9]

By 14 February 2011, the protests had spread from Manama and Muharraq to numerous Shi'i villages, from Nuwaidrat in the east of the island to Karzakan to the west, and to Daih, Sanabis, and Barhama on the outskirts of Manama. The riot police responded with violence. Many were injured and one demonstrator, Ali Abd al-Hadi Mushaima, was killed. His funeral procession, with mourners waving Bahraini flags and Shi'i banners, drew the security force into further violence and another protester, Fadhil Matrouk, was killed. Demonstrators descended on Pearl Roundabout, demanding citizen rights and political change. The Al-Wifaq Party announced that it was withdrawing its members from parliament in protest against the killings. This was a turning point in the resistance movement.[10] The royal household expressed concern but made no concessions.

King Hamad appeared on television to offer condolences to the bereaved but the next day the security forces moved against the Pearl Roundabout protesters, a repression recorded by foreign journalists and television crews. When the security forces attacked the funeral processions of those killed on the Pearl Roundabout, Crown Prince Salman bin Hamad ordered the security forces back to their barracks. But such apparently conciliatory

[7] Ian Black, 'Bahrain Election Puts Shia Opposition as Largest Single Group', The Guardian, 24 October 2010: http://www.guardian.co.uk/world/2010/oct/24/bahrain-poll-shia-opposition.
[8] For an analysis of resistance through non-violence in Tahrir Square in Egypt, see Tripp, The Power and the People, pp. 71–5, 88–106. The evasion of state control is considered in James C. Scott, Domination and the Arts of Resistance: Hidden Transcripts (New Haven, CT: Yale University Press, 1990), and in his The Art of Not Being Governed: An Anarchist History of Upland Southeast Asia (New Haven, CT: Yale University Press, 2009).
[9] Tripp, The Power and the People, pp. 110–11.
[10] Martin Chulov, 'Bahrain's Quiet Anger Turns to Rage after Brutal Attack', The Guardian, 18 February 2011.

interventions by the royal family merely added to the protesters' anger. They called for the release of all political prisoners and the resignation of the prime minister and of the appointed members of the government, principally relatives of the Al-Khalifah family. On 22 February 2011, a procession stretched from Bahrain Mall to the Pearl Roundabout (Martyrs' Square), led by youth activists, trade unionists, teachers, lawyers and other professionals, and members of the opposition political parties. The Al-Wifaq, Wa'ad, and the Haq movement supported the procession. Support for political change was markedly egalitarian. During the protest, committees were formed to organize communal cooking, medical provision, and childcare. In addition, there was political debate, focused on the needs of the villages. There was little division within the clerics between political aims and social identity through the waqf and ma'tam, reminiscent of Max Weber's 'the management of the goods of salvation'.[11] Secret negotiations with the Crown Prince yielded little. The state television ignored the protests but focused on a smaller counter demonstration supporting the King, taking place in front of the main Sunni mosque in Manama.[12]

The protestors sought to challenge the government's naturalization of immigrant Sunni Arabs and non-Arabs, intended to alter the sectarian balance in Bahrain. On 8 March 2011, they targeted the Immigration Office in Manama, shouting 'the naturalized must get out'. They then attempted to march on Rifaa, the home of the royal household, but they were blocked by supporters of Al-Khalifah. Subsequently, pro-regime forces rapidly moved onto the campus of the university, provoked by rumours in the government media that the anti-government protests had been instigated by foreign powers such as Iran. As argued earlier, Shi'ites in Bahrain had never been dependent on Iran, as was Hezbollah in Lebanon. In Bahrain the Shi'ites used charities, Ashura, to attract public and state support. Hezbollah preferred resistance, a war of national liberation, and in that Iran was an inspiration. In contrast, Bahrain Shi'ites used religious symbols and charities to reach what is essentially a secular goal, control over a given territory.[13] In Iraq, the political religious divisions were more complex. The Da'wah Party was established to combat the declining influence of the Shi'ite ulama and Shi'ite regions. In opposing the Sunni dominated Iraqi state, the Shi'ites, who formed the

---

[11] Max Weber, *Economy and Society: An Outline of Interpretive Sociology* (Berkeley, CA: University of California Press, 1978).

[12] Omar al Shehbai, 'The Community at Pearl Roundabout Is at the Centre', The National, 1 March 2011.

[13] Brian P. Maynard, 'The Role of the Ulama in Shi'ite Social Movements: Bahrain, Lebanon and Iraq', MA thesis, Main National Security Affairs, Naval Postgraduate School, 2005, p. 64: Michael Cook, *Commanding Right and Forbidding Wrong in Islamic Thought* (Cambridge: Cambridge University Press, 2000), pp. 252–301.

majority, were drawn towards the communist party because of its philosophy of equality and social justice. The communist aim to overthrow an oppressive state resonated with Shi'ite ambitions. But Muhammad Baqir al Sadr sought to reform Iraq's religious hierarchy and here the Iranian Revolution inspired support: he was called the Khomeini of Iraq. Eventually he was executed. Iraq was failed by the hierarchic structure of religious leadership and by internal rivalries. Sadam Hussein used his security forces to suppress internal opposition. If Da'wah had adopted a cellular structure it may have escaped annihilation.[14]

The royal family was caught between violent suppression of the demonstrations and dialogue. The demonstrations on 13 March 2011 in the financial district of Manama led the Crown Prince to assert on television that 'any legitimate claims must not be made at the expense of security and stability'. There were rumours that the Saudi National Guard was preparing to intervene. And indeed, a thousand-strong contingent of Saudi troops, accompanied by 500 police from the UAE, crossed the causeway into Bahrain.[15] This was described by Al-Wifaq as an outright 'declaration of war'.[16] The number of Saudi troops may have been substantially more than acknowledged.[17] The military intervention by the Gulf Cooperation Council (GCC), supported subtly by the USA, gave the Bahrain authorities the confidence to seek a violent suppression of this month-long mass demonstration. Martial Law was declared: and this encouraged the security forces to use violence against all forms of protest. The authorities killed those they recognized as organizers of the protests. With Saudi assistance the security forces cleared the Pearl Roundabout and demolished the monument in the Square that had become a focus of popular resistance. Around 20 were killed, hundreds wounded, and many arrested, detained, and tortured, while prominent individuals associated with human rights organizations, as well as journalists and bloggers, disappeared.[18] Students and academics were dismissed for participating in the demonstrations or voicing dissent. Thousands of Shi'ites lost their jobs in a purge infused with sectarian prejudice and revenge. The government sought

---

[14] Talib Aziz, 'The Role of Muhammad Baqir al-Sadr in Shii Political Activism in Iraq from 1958 to 1980', *International Journal of Middle East Studies*, vol. 25, no. 2 (1993), p. 209; Keiko Sakai, 'Modernity and Tradition and the Islamic Movements in Iraq: Continuity and Discontinuity in the Role of the Ulama', *Arab Studies Quarterly*, vol. 23, no. 1 (2001), p. 38.

[15] The Guardian, 14 March 2011.

[16] Tripp, The Power and the People, p. 114.

[17] Martin Chulov, 'Saudi Arabian Troops Enter Bahrain to Help Regime Quell Uprising', The Guardian, 15 March 2011.

[18] The Bahrain Center for Human Rights listed the people killed and wounded in Bahrain from 14 February 2011.

to prevent more protests by mounting raids on centres of dissent such as San-abis, Budaiya, Janussan, and Malkiyya.[19] As late as 2019, news emerged that tortured activists were to be executed. Britain was asked to intervene because of its multi-million-pound support for rule of law programmes in Bahrain. Britain had allocated £5 million to Bahrain out of £80 million for security ini-tiatives in the Gulf states. Mohammed Ramadhan, 37, and Husein Moussa, 33, leading figures in the 2011 uprising, were convicted in 2014 of the murder of a police officer.[20]

This increasing violence led the king to set up an independent commis-sion of inquiry in June 2011 under the chairmanship of Cherif Bassiouni, an Egyptian jurist. Its task was to examine the circumstances of the 2011 Spring Uprising, the actions of the security forces, and the behaviour of the protestors. But there were also demands for a United Nations inquiry. In June 2011, the United States called on the UN to investigate the human rights record of the Bahrain government. The Commission, reporting in November 2011, established that human rights abuses had been committed earlier that year and that Iran did not pose a threat to Bahrain. However, victims were exasperated by the failure to identify systematic abuse by the security services. Moreover, no individuals were identified as committing human rights abuses. This report was vacuous. And the opposition was fur-ther angered by the death of Abdulnabi Kadhem at the hands of the police in the village of A'ali just before the report was published.[21]

There was a gulf between the Bahrain state and Bahrain's population, and as a result popular protest was determined to force the state to concede economic and political reform. Much of the protest involved poor Shi'ites, claimed by the authorities to be stooges of Iran. But Bahrain's Shi'ites are culturally and psychologically different from the Shi'ites of Iran: not least, they do not seek the creation of an Islamic state. To identify sites as a focus for resistance was an important factor in organizing the protest, win-ning national and international recognition, and in securing concessions. Disgruntled unemployed Bahraini youth presented a vivid example of the resistance and political drive created by resentment and grievance towards the state. But it is important to emphasize that Bahrain did not see the extreme barbarity that marked conflict in Syria and Iraq in this period. The protests in Bahrain certainly unleashed violence but the social order held.

---

[19] Tripp, The Power and the People, pp. 114–15.
[20] Interview with Akbar Busheri of Manama; reported in the UK press.
[21] Toby Jones, 'We Know What Happened in Bahrain: Now What?', Carnegie Endowment for Interna-tional Peace, 1 December 2011.

Economics of Inequality and the Arab Spring

It would be misleading to see Bahrain's Arab Spring of 2011 purely or even largely from a political perspective, to focus solely on the political organization and alliances, the protests, and their suppression, or indeed to see 2011 as simply the most recent stage in a century or more of political disaffection. For underpinning Bahrain's Arab Spring were serious long-standing economic fractures: the dispossession of certain important sections of Bahrain's population, and the denial of educational and economic opportunity to others, both the consequences of Bahrain's economic transformation in the previous decades.

Bahrain's annual GDP growth exceeded 10 per cent, which allowed the provision for education, health, and infrastructure also to expand considerably. Growth is driven by high levels of public expenditure, largely financed by Bahrain's offshore financial sector, itself driven by the flow of oil wealth into Bahrain from its Gulf neighbours. However, these growth rates mask increasing socio-economic inequalities, deprivation, and a growing alienation against the Al-Khalifah family and its associated mercantile elites, many of whom are Shi'ites. Inequality is a consequence of state control over oil and property resources, a Weberian form of monopoly that Charles Tilly categorizes as 'opportunity hoarding', and it is economic inequality among the young and the deprived farmers and the fishermen that drove support for the Arab Spring.[22]

Rapid economic growth, economic diversification, and urbanization increased socio-economic inequalities within the Sunni-dominated state.[23] Despite high economic growth and a relatively high rating of 0.794 on the Human Development Index (Egypt stood at 0.661 and Tunisia at 0.71), resentment was pervasive, particularly among middle-class youth in the first decade of the twenty-first century. The uprising in Bahrain was, to a degree, non-ideological but dominated by the issues of youth unemployment, lack of housing, income inequality created by poor education, and even food insecurity. The prices of the major staples of rice, corn, and wheat rose by 15 per cent between October 2010 and January 2011, while local food production had been disrupted by land reclamation projects.[24]

---

[22] Charles Tilly, *Durable Inequality* (Berkeley, CA: University of California Press, 1998).

[23] Asya El-Meehy, 'Relative Deprivation and Politics in the Arab Uprisings', research report, 'Social Justice and Development Policy in the Arab World' programme, Issam Fares Institute for Public Policy and International Affairs, American University of Beirut, 2014.

[24] World Bank, 2011, Food Price Watch: http//www.world bankorg/foodcrisis/foodpricewatch report-feb2011.ml.

The national economic fortune and performance indelibly associated with oil and an authoritarian state were evident in new centres of economic power in Muharraq. Thus, the ambition of protesting youth was to seek a share of this wealth, increasingly associated with the formation of the GCC in 1981 and the spillovers of oil riches. It is commonly acknowledged that the Arab Spring also reflected the region's unique demographic pyramid with, on average, 30 per cent of the population aged 14–25. The median age is the second lowest in the world, with only Sub-Saharan Africa being lower.[25]

Poverty estimates are scarce in Bahrain. Indeed, the authorities often deny the poverty that clearly exists in rural areas and among fishing communities. A report by the Centre for Human Rights in 2004 argued that 25 per cent of the population in Bahrain were in poverty, and even official reports stated that almost 22 per cent of Bahrain nationals were relatively poor.[26] The concentration of oil wealth in the hands of a small section of the population may explain the dramatic effect of fuel and food crises. In Egypt and Tunisia, growth in per capita GDP declined to 6.2 per cent in 2008 and to 3.9 per cent in 2010 compared to 10.4 per cent and then 9.0 per cent during 2005–07.[27] In the crisis years, Bahrain expanded both Islamic and conventional finance as well as pursuing economic diversification. Unwittingly, this created a degree of fragility. Real per capita GDP fell by 10 per cent during the recession years of 2008–10 and by 14 per cent during 2005–07. This reversal in earlier gains in real per capita GDP was serious.[28] The decline in oil prices in the summer of 2008 and early 2009 had serious consequences for Bahrain. Although Bahrain had limited oil reserves, it depended on budget support from the GCC to provide subsidies for essential food products. Food subsidies were allowed to rise from BD88.9 million, or 1.1 per cent of GDP in 2009–10, to almost BD133 million, 1.6 per cent of GDP, in 2011 and 2012.[29] These subsidies assisted mainly the middle classes. Further examples of inequalities in treatment were seen in pensions reform implemented with ILO consultation in 2000. This introduced a two-tier unemployment insurance scheme, a departure from fixed benefit social security for workers in the public and

---

[25] World Bank, *Middle East and North Africa Economic Developments and Prospects: Navigating through the Global Recession* (Washington, DC: 2009); Robert Springborg 'The Precarious Economics of Arab Springs', *Survival: Geopolitics and Strategy*, vol. 53, no. 6 (2011); El-Meehy, 'Relative Deprivation and Politics in the Arab Uprisings', p. 5.

[26] Bahrain Centre for Human Rights, 2004; Bahrain Economic Development Board, 2011.

[27] World Bank Data from Global Economy.com.

[28] World Bank Data from Global Economy.com; IMF World Economic Outlook Database, April 2011; F. Iqbal, *Sustaining Gains in Poverty Reduction and Human Development in the Middle East and North Africa* (Washington, DC: World Bank, 2006).

[29] IMF World Economic Outlook, 2010; Habib Toumi, 'Bahrain Announces Measures to Help Needy Families', *Gulf News*, 3 February 2011.

private sector, including foreigners. Enterprises with less than five employees were not covered in the new scheme, thus depriving the largely Shi'a working poor of unemployment benefits. The second tier of this insurance system aided first-time job seekers, who had to accept training and career guidance. By 2009, 87 per cent of those receiving unemployment benefits under this scheme were middle class, with half holding university degrees. State philanthropy towards the middle classes further fuelled resentment by the poor. During the financial crisis of 2008, when food and fuel prices rose, the government had increased subsidies to benefit the middle classes. Yet it was these same privileged citizens who led the Arab Spring. A sense of entitlement on the part of the educated middle classes provided fierce resistance to the state. Resistance did not come from the rural poor or fishermen deprived of their livelihoods by land reclamation and state infrastructure projects. This suggests that it is misleading to assume that the economic pressures alone were the trigger for the revolt in 2011.[30] Despite significant poverty among the rural and urban poor of Bahrain, they did not lead the uprising. Authoritarian regimes in Bahrain, Tunisia, and Egypt had pursued new social benefit initiatives in the previous two decades to protect the interests of the middle classes and, to a lesser extent, the health and welfare of the poor. Thus, by 2010 Bahrain had a debt-to-GDP ratio of 32.0 per cent, Egypt 85.7 per cent, and Tunisia 45.7 per cent.[31]

Although Bahrain's economy has been vibrant, it has suffered with sharp setbacks. In recent decades its strength had derived from its position as a financial hub and from its integration with its oil-wealthy GCC neighbours. The benefits have been concentrated in the oligarchs of the state and their merchant elite allies. This created resentment that led the middle classes to participate in the Arab Spring. Middle-class participation was seen, too, in both Egypt and Tunisia.[32] The protests were driven by increasing deprivation and unemployment among middle-class youth. Yet this alone cannot explain the rioting. There was also an economic context. This was Bahrain's oligarchic rule in the 1990s, King Hamad's ascent in 1999, and the attempts by Crown Prince Sheikh Salman to usurp power through the Economic Development

---

[30] Aysa El-Meehy, 'Welfare Restructuring in Rentier Arab States: The Case of Bahrain', Paper presented at Gulf Research meeting, Cambridge, July 2011.

[31] Calculations from El-Meehy, 'Relative Deprivation and Politics in the Arab Uprisings'. See also El-Meehy, 'Welfare Restructuring in Rentier Arab States', p. 10; Aysa El-Meehy, 'Rewriting the Social Contract: The Social Fund and Egypt's Politics of Hidden Retrenchment', University of Toronto dissertation, 2009.

[32] Hazem Kandil, 'Why Did the Egyptian Middle-Class March to Tahrir Square?', *Mediterranean Politics*, vol. 17, no. 2 (2012); 'What lies beneath the so called "Jasmine Revolution" is increasing intolerance towards inequality between regions, social classes and generations': Hela Hermassi, 'Tunisian Revolution and Regional Imbalance', *Global Advanced Research Journal of Management and Business Studies*, vol. 2, no. 2 (2013), p. 80.

Board and Chamber of Commerce, which threatened to destabilize powerful vested interests like the Kanoo oligarchs. The attempts by King Hamad to protect those interests produced divisions within the royal family. This drove the demand for political change, a demand by the middle classes for democracy and economic reform.

During this period, inflation in Bahrain and Tunisia stood at 4 per cent, while in Egypt it was 13 per cent. In Bahrain, the consumer price index rose from 109 to 115 between 2008 and 2010. In Egypt it rose from 139 to 173, and in Tunisia from 113 to 123. Can rising prices in 2010, adding to middle-class anxieties, explain the protests? The historical context is important here. In the 1950s, the middle classes were increasingly bound to the state, beneficiaries of land reform, free education, and guaranteed public employment for graduates. From independence in 1971, the inflow of oil wealth from Bahrain's neighbours led to market-oriented reforms by the Bahraini state and these threatened parts of the middle class and their links to the rulers. The 1950s nurtured links between middle-class merchants and the state but with independence the links were between multinationals, foreign and local capitalists, and sections of the royal family. This new phase created a super-rich class, unseating the highly educated middle class. Concurrently, there emerged a resource dependency embedded in oil, tourism, and the leisure industries. Increasing dependence on the GCC and international markets further disadvantaged the educated middle classes who suffered high levels of unemployment, with little ameliorative action by the state.[33]

The middle classes were still taking state benefits but were being deprived. The self-immolation of a Tunisian fruit vendor in December 2010 inspired middle-class youth in Bahrain to challenge the autocratic state and to seek democracy. They were driven by more than their well-being. In 2010, per capita income in Bahrain stood at US$20,000, compared to US$2,070 in Egypt and US$3,720 in Tunisia. And yet Bahraini youth was not appeased. Their comparator was not Egypt or Tunisia but the super-rich in Bahrain. They sought to evict the oligarchs and reform the Al-Khalifah family. They demanded democracy, press freedom, education, and jobs.[34]

In 2003, the poorest 20 per cent of the population of Bahrain received 9.3 per cent of income, the richest 20 per cent received 41.6 per cent.[35] Data

[33] Filipe R. Campante and Davin Chor, 'Why Was the Arab World Poised for Revolution? Schooling, Economic Opportunities, and the Arab Spring', *Journal of Economic Perspectives*, vol. 26, no. 2 (2012), pp. 167–88.

[34] World Bank Databank: http//databank.worldbank.org/data/databases.aspx; El-Meehy, 'Relative Deprivation and Politics in the Arab Uprisings', p. 12.

[35] UNDP International Human Development Indicators: http/hdrstats, undp.org/en/tables, 2003, 4; UNDP, *The Arab Human Development Report*, New York, 2003–10, 2014.

from 2002 to 2014 appears to show little distress. But Bahrain's middle-class youth were comparing themselves to Bahrain's rich and the global rich.[36] There was in Bahrain an alarmingly high level of dissatisfaction even when the income figures did not show a sharp fall.[37] The Bahrain state had become more interventionist in social and political matters after independence in 1971. The majority of Sunnis in Bahrain were employed in government, while the majority of the population were concentrated in SMEs, with low skills and low incomes. The large private companies, in particular those with highly skilled foreign expatriates, paid high wages, to the anger of middle-class youth perched just above the poverty line.[38] A large-scale campaign for minimum wage legislation was orchestrated by the new social movements, the political opposition, and the trade unions. The rise of new industries in information technology, finance (the rise of Bahrain as the financial hub of the Gulf states), and tourism, with high wages and lavish lifestyles, created a wealthy, segmented society within gated accommodation. Bahraini youth felt lost. The glamour of shopping malls in urban and coastline Bahrain added to this growing sense of deprivation. Rises in house and food prices, and the increasing volume of personal loans for housing and cars, fuelled growing anger with the ruling family and its alliances with local and expatriate business elites.[39] The growing anxiety over unemployment was particularly acute within the 15–29-year-old cohort: a quarter were unemployed just prior to the Arab Spring. University graduates were most vocal in expressing their resentment of the rich. And Bahrain's unskilled poor faced serious competition from migrant workers, who were largely from India.[40]

Inequality in income, lifestyle, and education created not just unemployment but also psychological misery. However, dramatic changes in the Bahrain state also increased the polarization of the working class and unemployed middle-class youth. As already noted, land reclamation in Bahrain had created luxurious housing and leisure haunts, not just for rich Bahrainis but also for Saudis and Kuwaitis, escaping the social repression of their own societies. There was a shift in Bahrain, dominated by a ruling family boosted by oil wealth, towards extreme material ostentation. Inevitably there were social and political consequences.

[36] El-Meehy, 'Relative Deprivation and Politics in the Arab Uprisings', p. 12.
[37] See tables on economic performance in Bahrain; Clemens Breisinger, Olivier Ecker, Perrihan Al-Riffai, and Yu Bingxin, *Beyond the Arab Awakening: Policies and Investments for Poverty Reduction and Food Security* (Washington, DC: IFPRI, 2012).
[38] Springborg, 'The Precarious Economics of Arab Springs', pp. 87–8.
[39] H. Kotb, 'Protest Movements in Bahrain: Developments in Bahrain's Political Society', in *Protest Movements in the Arab Nation*, edited by Amr Al Shobky (Beirut: Center for Arab Unity Studies, 2011).
[40] IMF World Economic Outlook Database, April 2011; World Bank Database, 2011 and 2014; UNDP, *The Arab Human Development Report*, 2003–10 and 2014.

Educational Inequality and Income Inequality

The pessimism of youth was built on frustration over access to good education and to well-paid jobs. Education expenditure is heavily weighted in favour of the interests of the ruling and business elites. There are fine private schools, of course, but they are not open to the ordinary poor. In turn, lack of educational opportunity reinforces income inequality and limits increases in labour productivity. Increasing labour productivity reduces income inequality, although that can also be reduced by labour organization.

The literacy rate for adults in Bahrain rose from 84 per cent in the period 1985–94 to 88.8 per cent in the period 1995–2007. In 2007, enrolment in public and higher education accounted for 90.4 per cent of the relevant age cohorts, and this rate exceeded the global average and placed Bahrain first in the Gulf states. Female enrolment in education reached 95.3 per cent, and that of males, 85.8 per cent in the same period. The United Nations reported enrolment in education at 89.3 per cent in Bahrain, in the Arab states 72.6 per cent, and in the Gulf states 83.4 per cent. The global average was 75.3 per cent. In Bahrain in 2010, primary school enrolment was over 98 per cent.[41] In 2012, the Ministry of Education in Bahrain indicated that primary school enrolment had reached 100 per cent. This was in response to the Education Act of 2005, which made education compulsory (attendance was closely monitored) and reduced the drop-out rate in primary education. In addition, the number of students and teachers in primary schools had risen since 1990, and spending on education had increased. In brief, Bahrain's performance in education had been impressive. Enrolment for males and females was high, literacy rates for adults extremely good, while gender equality and reduced drop-out rates had been achieved in both primary and secondary education.[42] Yet despite these achievements, income inequality remained severe. In Bahrain in 2018, 70 per cent of income was held by 10 per cent of the population.

The state provides high-quality education to wealthy families in Manama, Muharraq, and the central, southern, and northern districts.[43] Spending on education is strongly focused on the wealthy. Private schools, both foreign and local, pursue rigorous curricula and teaching. The fees for foreign private

---

[41] UNESCO, *Global Monitoring Report on Education for 2010*, 'General Regional Overview: Arab Countries Path to Equality'.

[42] Hisham H. Abdelbaki, 'An Analysis of Income Inequality and Education Inequality in Bahrain', *Modern Economy*, vol. 3, no. 5 (2012), pp. 675–85; Hisham H. Abdelbaki, 'The Impact of Macroeconomic Policies on Income Distribution: an Empirical Study of Egypt', PhD, Development and Project Planning Centre, Bradford University, 2001.

[43] Bahrain Central Informatics Organization, *Household Expenditure and Income Survey*, 2005–06.

schools are exorbitant, which clearly promotes access for the wealthy. Children of middle-class families have access only to national private schools and children of low-income families go to state schools where education is free. This disparity in educational opportunity, and the corresponding impact on employment opportunities, enraged the middle-class protestors in 2011.[44]

The Links to Political Protest

Thus, the prime cause of Bahrain's Arab Spring protests was the instability of the state, with Sheikh Isa Al-Khalifah and then son Hamad, facing challenges, responding with reforms that were either then withdrawn or were too weak. The challenges came from a youth population experiencing increasing prices and rising unemployment. The protesters demanded democracy, an end to corruption, and the introduction of press freedom. Middle-class youth, with good educational and skills attainments, were prominent in demanding democracy and economic opportunities. As Samuel Huntington has argued, 'The higher the level of education of the unemployed ... the more extreme the destabilizing behavior which results.'[45] Between 1980 and 2010, Bahrain achieved a doubling in average years of schooling from 4.92 to 9.59, greater than in Tunisia, Saudi Arabia, the UAE, Iran, Jordan, Libya, and Egypt.[46] And yet it was the youth in Bahrain who drove the protest movements throughout the 1990s through to 2011. It is important to note that Bahrain's education system had not responded to major changes in the labour market by providing training in technology and in information systems, and consequently, despite increasing years at school, there was no improvement in job prospects. An increasingly educated youth faced greater unemployment because of radical change in Bahrain's economy. There was high demand for technological skills which local youth could not meet but expatriates could. Equally important, Bahrain's youth had a passion for change in politics.[47] Modernization can be destabilizing when Bahrain lacked a tested institutional infrastructure, such as an efficient bureaucracy,

[44] Bahrain Central Informatics Organization, *Household Expenditure and Income Survey*, 1983–84, 1995–96, and 2005–06; Bahrain Central Informatics Organization, *Report for Establishment Survey of Wages Structure and Distribution Survey*, 2006; Vinod Thomas, Yan Wang, and Xibo Fan, 'Measuring Education Inequality: Gini Coefficient of Education', World Bank Research Paper no. 2525, Washington, DC, World Bank, 2001.

[45] Samuel P. Huntington, *Political Order in Changing Societies* (New Haven, CT: Yale University Press, 1968), p. 48.

[46] Robert Barro and Jong-Wha Lee, 'A New Dataset of Educational Attainment in the World, 1950–2010', NBER Working Paper No. 15902, 2010.

[47] Willa Friedman, Michael Kremer, Edward Miguel, and Rebecca Thornton, 'Education as Liberation?', NBER Working Paper No. 16939, 2011.

law, and governance.[48] Education increases awareness of political issues, fosters socialization, increases civic skills, and drives a passion to ameliorate injustice.[49]

Did a Food Crisis Incubate the Arab Spring?

With the encroachment of land reclamation from the late 1990s on agriculture and fishing, together with the drive towards non-oil economic diversification, food security emerged as a significant issue in Bahrain. The increase in global food prices, which occurred in the financial crisis of 2008, together with high unemployment in 2010–11, triggered by major labour movements, contributed to the political unrest that swept through the Middle East, including Bahrain, Tunisia, Morocco, Libya, and Egypt in 2011. Rising food prices added considerably to the cost of living. Many Bahraini nationals faced an erosion of living standards, while elites were living in oil-infused luxury. Bahrain's government, which had earlier maintained subsidies for food, housing, and fuel and had guaranteed employment in exchange for political loyalty, was now cutting these subsidies as unrest broke out in parts of Manama and the seaboard.

GDP per capita in Bahrain had been US$8,896 in 1985 but by 2010 had risen to US$11,236.[50] But during that same period, Bahrain, as part of the Gulf states, had come in the top fifth of per capita cereal importers in the world.[51] Between 1990 and 2010, Bahrain's agricultural value added per capita fell on average by 1.6 per cent per year. For Saudi Arabia, the decline was 5.3 per cent.[52] In Bahrain, food prices rose substantially from 2007. The rise was related to economic diversification which reduced food production and increased food imports. Following Amartya Sen's concept of entitlement, an individual's income and assets, as well as prices, determine access to food.[53] Food security is less for the poor. Bahrain sought to lease land in Turkey,

[48] Campante and Chor, 'Why Was the Arab World Poised for Revolution?'; Edward Glaeser, Giacomo Ponzetto, and Andrei Shleifer, 'Why Does Democracy Need Education?', Journal of Economic Growth, vol. 12, no. 2 (2007), pp. 77–99.
[49] Marcus Noland and Howard Pack, The Arab Economies in a Changing World (Washington, DC: Peterson Institute, 2007); Henrik Urdal, 'A Clash of Generations? Youth Bulges and Political Violence', International Studies Quarterly, vol. 5, no. 3 (2006), pp. 607–29.
[50] World Bank, World Databank: http://databank.worldbank.org/data/home.aspx.
[51] FAO STAT online database: http//faostat.fao.org: FAO Committee on Food Security, Price Volatility and Food Security: High Level Panel of Experts on Food Security (Rome: Food and Agriculture Organization, 2011); FAO, FAOSTAT, The State of Agricultural Commodity Markets: High Food Prices and the Food Crisis: Experiences and Lessons Learned (Rome: Food and Agriculture Organization, 2009).
[52] Calculated from Breisinger et al., Beyond the Arab Awakening, table 2.
[53] Amartya Sen, Poverty and Famines: An Essay on Entitlement and Deprivation (Oxford: Clarendon Press, 1981).

Africa, and the Philippines for food production.[54] The US, Australia, Canada, the EU, and Argentina accounted for 73 per cent of world cereal exports. The Gulf states have a high import dependency but because of their oil wealth that dependency does not translate into vulnerability.

The sharp increase in food prices in the Gulf from 2007 was due principally to population increase and to economic growth, which brought changing patterns of food consumption, notably increased meat consumption.[55] Increased demand for land also pushed up food prices. The Arab world faced an increased dependence on food imports.

Inflation in the MENA countries was more than twice the global rate in 2007–08, the result of increases in food prices, public sector wages, and welfare payments.[56] It is estimated that in these parts of the world, almost 40 per cent of income is spent on food, and therefore rising food prices can cause considerable distress and political protest.[57] In 2007–08, there were demonstrations against rising food prices in Jordan, Lebanon, Morocco, Saudi Arabia, and Yemen, as well as in Bahrain. In Bahrain, autocratic rule had been accepted because the government had provided subsidies for food, housing, and fuel as well as jobs. There were also welfare provisions within the waqf and ma'tam. These now came under strain.

The Arab Spring in Bahrain reflected the failure of government to appease the demands of middle-class youth for economic improvement and political reform. Rising food prices were the main trigger for protest. When Egypt removed food subsidies at the instigation of the IMF in the mid-1970s, there were riots and the policy was immediately reversed. Arezki and Bruckner have investigated the relationship between food prices and democracy and state conflict, using data from 120 countries over the period 1979–2007. They found that in low-income countries, increasing food prices threatened democratic institutions and provoked anti-government riots. But this did not occur in high-income countries.[58] In Bahrain, the protest movements can

[54] United Nations Economic and Social Commission for Western Asia, *Food Security and Conflict in the ESCWA Region*, New York, 2010; Jane Harrigan, *The Political Economy of Arab Food Sovereignty* (Basingstoke: Palgrave Macmillan, 2014), pp. 132–4.

[55] FAO, *Near and Middle East and North Africa: Agriculture Towards 2050: Prospects and Challenges* (Rome, 2008); Credit Suisse Research Institute, *Emerging Consumer Survey*, 2011; World Bank, *Improving Food Security in Arab Countries* (Washington, DC: World Bank, 2009).

[56] Jane Harrigan, 'Did Food Prices Plant the Seeds of the Arab Spring?', Inaugural Lecture, School of Oriental and African Studies, 28 April 2011, p. 12; Harrigan, *The Political Economy of Arab Food Sovereignty*, pp. 54–70; IMF, World Economic and Financial Survey, 2008: www.imf.org/externalpub/ft/weo/2008/02/weodata/index.aspx.

[57] 'Percentage of Income Spent on Food', US Department of Agriculture website; Harrigan, 'Did Food Prices Plant the Seeds of the Arab Spring?', p. 13.

[58] R. Arezki and M. Bruckner, 'Food Prices, Conflict, and Democratic Change', University of Adelaide, Department of Economics, Research Paper no. 2011–04, 2011.

be explained more accurately by the Acemoglu and Robinson argument that political institutions are vulnerable to transitory economic shocks.[59]

From Home to Global Food Production

As part of its ambitious programme of economic diversification, Bahrain sought to lease agricultural land in Asia, Turkey, and Africa. This strategy aimed to improve food security but also to save scarce water resources. Renewable water per capita in MENA is only 17 per cent of the world average. Agriculture requires huge volumes of water. With its substantial financial resources, Bahrain could easily contemplate the outsourcing of food production overseas and indeed the World Bank and FAO had advocated a move towards trade-based food security in the region. This strategy was also sensible in the light of the ecological problems confronting the Middle East.[60] Bahrain's search for food sovereignty rested on the belief that the state can maintain political control only by securing access to food, and that that necessitated out-sourcing food production to distant parts of the world, such as the Philippines, through leasing arrangements. In the late 2000s, this became a major strategy for the MENA countries.[61] Since 2000, China has followed the same path in parts of Africa. These ventures were undertaken either by the state or by companies that are state-owned or owned by business elites with close links to the state. In Bahrain, the Crown Prince and the Prime Minister, a relative, were closely involved. There is potential here for labour abuse and ecological damage, as well as the transmission of religious radicalism. The Saudi charity IIROSA was accepted in Thailand because of its restrained commercial behaviour.[62] Indonesia discontinued a Saudi bin Laden US$4.3 billion rice project after violent protests in the country. There was serious controversy. Saudi Arabia imported rice, wheat, and barley on land leased in Ethiopia, at the same time as the World Food Programme spent US$116 million providing 230,000 tonnes of food aid to 4.6 million Ethiopians threatened by famine.[63] Sudan, too, shipped food to the Middle East while its

---

[59] D. Acemoglu and J. Robinson, 'A Theory of Political Transitions', *American Economic Review*, vol. 91 (2001), pp. 938–63; D. Acemoglu and J. Robinson, *Economic Origins of Dictatorship and Democracy* (New York: Cambridge University Press, 2006).
[60] A. Richards and J. Waterbury, *A Political Economy of the Middle East* (Oxford: Westview, 2006), chapter 6; H. Lofgren and A. Richards, *Food Security, Poverty and Economic Policy in the Middle East and North Africa* (Washington, DC: IFPRI, 2003).
[61] World Bank, *Improving Food Security in Arab Countries*.
[62] Rajeswary Ampalavanar Brown, *Islam in Modern Thailand: Faith, Philanthropy, and Politics* (London: Routledge, 2014), chapter 9.
[63] South Asia Partnership, SAP-Pakistan Blog, 'Poor Farmers', 22 May 2011, cited in Harrigan, 'Did Food Prices Plant the Seeds of the Arab Spring?', p. 22.

people were starving. FAO chief Jacques Diouf described these projects as neo-colonialist.

Constructing Al-Khalifah Power: Winner Takes All

For a deeper understanding of the nature of the inequalities that character-ized Bahraini capitalism we need to introduce some mainstream debates on the state and capitalism. Thomas Piketty argues that market economies have an underlying dynamic that ushers in the concentration of capital indepen-dent of political institutions.[64] But politics can disturb this dynamic through wars, revolutions, and democratic transitions or through a radicalized labour movement. He also explores the paradox that as capital grows relative to the economy, the holders of capital acquire even greater political power and influence and thus can protect their assets. In Bahrain, the state, the Al-Khalifah ruling family, acquires greater power through economic change, and the old clique of merchants is replaced by a new, subservient class of entrepreneurs. Karl Polanyi argued that capital agglomeration is a politi-cal project driven by clusters of merchant elites using all political resources, including violent coercion.[65] Polanyi saw the formalization of property rights as key to blocking the market. In Bahrain, land, once the preserve of the rural communities, became the private property of the Al-Khalifah family. This usurpation is associated with rising inequalities. Again, the rapid expansion of private housing impacts on social housing. Bahrain is a perfect example of what Jacob Hacker has referred to as 'pre-distribution', to change the way mar-kets are regulated to achieve greater equality through taxation.[66] In Bahrain there is no redistribution of wealth through taxation (except through state beneficence). The unfair distribution of housing is a political phenomenon. The Global Financial Crisis of 2008 led Bahrain to rescue banks as well as increase subsidies for poor farmers and fishermen. But as Picketty would point out, the holders of capital sought to protect their assets, although they were soon after faced by the young protesters of the Arab Spring.

It is useful here to pause and trace how the authoritarian state evolved in Bahrain. The relationship between state politics and economic power was secured through the merchant elite. The relationship between the Kanoos,

---

[64] Thomas Piketty, *Capital in the Twenty-First Century* (Cambridge, MA: Belknap Press of Harvard University Press, 2014).
[65] Karl Polanyi, *The Great Transformation: The Political and Economic Origins of Our Time* (Boston, MA: Beacon Books, 1957).
[66] Jacob Hacker, 'How to Reinvigorate the Centre-Left: Pre-Distribution', The Guardian, 12 June 2013.

heading powerful multinational corporations, and state institutions continued into the twenty-first century. But other merchant elites became far less
secure. The Bahraini state, which had emerged in part out of family politics
and the rule of law under the British, evolved from the 1970s into a powerful authoritarianism, and that in turn created tension within the Al-Khalifah
family. In the final decades of the twentieth century, economic diversification
driven by the state and business elites was accompanied by increasing divi
sions within the royal family. The accession of King Hamad in 1999 restored
order, although the ambitions of Crown Prince Salman and his technocrat
friends ignored rising inequalities in education and increasing food prices.
The King attempted to reduce Prince Salman's authority and the power of
the technocrats but with little effect. The internal politics of the ruling family drove it to grab reclaimed land to build hotels and commercial properties
and to secure government contracts. As part of this aggrandizement, in 2005
Prince Sheikh Salman replaced Khalid Kanoo as head of the Chamber of
Commerce. The merchant elite had dominated the Chamber of Commerce
since 1939 but were now replaced by members of the royal family, increasing
the dependence of private business on the royal family for commercial opportunities. Salman replaced EDB members with Western-educated expatriates
and Sunni national technocrats, mainly in their 30s and 40s. Following the
death of Sheikh Isa Al Khalifah in 1999 and the accession of his son Hamad,
a more formidable state apparatus drove on with luxury real estate projects,
but these initiatives deprived middle-class youth of housing and job opportunities. Some 30 per cent of the population were unemployed, 55 per cent
in the 17–25 age group.

Moreover, crony capitalism deprived the middle classes of opportunities
for wealth creation. Gulf Finance House, an important Islamic bank headed
by Isam Jinahi, was now powerful in real estate and infrastructural developments, including the construction of the Bahrain Financial Harbour. Another
elite capitalist close to the royal household was Khalid Abd al-Rahim, responsible for Bahrain's Formula 1 racing circuit. Those capitalists not affiliated
to the Al-Khalifah family were highly resentful. In effect, the royal family
controlled all wealth creation. Lacking institutional constraints, it focused on
acquiring resources and fought over even the smallest prerogative.

In summary, the Arab Spring drew support from a wide range of interests, the Shi'ites, the young, the political opposition, farmers, fishermen, and
sections of the business elite. It was not a narrow response. The Shi'ites did
not protest on sectarian lines but focused on the abuses of class and privilege. They also sought the restoration of villages for food security and public
housing. But the business elite tied to the royal family remained loyal, and the

state in turn dismissed the protests as interference by Tehran. The allegation of an Iranian conspiracy was levelled at the Pearl Roundabout protesters on 15 February.[67]

Conclusion

A major part of the Arab Spring in Bahrain involved disputes over constitutional and legal structures. Jurisdictional politics calmed sectarian and cultural differences, despite the Sunni links to Saudi Arabia. State-centred legal pluralism and the legitimacy of moderate Shi'ism, endowed with autonomy through the waqf and ma'tam, were central to religious and cultural self-definition, the display of diverse 'emotion' without threatening the rule of law. It led to what Cortni Kerr and Toby Jones call 'a revolution paused'.[68] In contrast, Bashar al-Assad's response to protest was savage repression, and a descent into civil war and the displacement of millions of Syrians.[69]

Central to Bahrain's future will be the satisfaction of the economic and political demands of educated youth. It need only be noted that the shadowy 'February 14th' movement that emerged at the time of the 2011 uprising, 'a confederation of loosely organised networks ... faceless, secretive and anonymous', simply despaired at the loss of leadership within the political opposition.[70]

But splits within the ruling family, with the Crown Prince Salman bin Hamad Al-Khalifah being marginalized and power shifting to hardliners around the bin Ahmed brothers, made political recovery near impossible. The erosion of reforming institutions such as the Economic Development Board added to the crisis. To attract foreign investment, particularly from the US and Europe, required new leadership of the EDB. Khalid Al-Rumaihi was succeeded as CEO by Khalid Humaidan, who had been on the EDB board since 2014 and previously had been head of Global Markets MEA at BNP Paribas. The EDB then revived because of its close links with Mumtalakat, Bahrain's sovereign wealth fund. Bahrain's close ties with Saudi Arabia

---

[67] Ned Parker, 'Bahrain Protestors Celebrate as Police, Soldiers Withdraw from Pearl Square', Los Angeles Times, 19 February 2011; Omar AlShehabi, 'The Community at Pearl Roundabout is at the Centre', The National, 1 March 2011.

[68] Cortni Kerr and Toby Jones, 'A Revolution Paused in Bahrain', in The Arab Revolts: Dispatches on Militant Democracy in the Middle East, edited by David McMurray and Amanda Ufheil-Somers (Bloomington, IN: Indiana University Press, 2013), pp. 208–14.

[69] Thomas Pierret, Religion and State in Syria: Sunni Ulama from Coup to Revolution (Cambridge University Press, 2013); Thomas Pierret, 'Merchant Background, Bourgeois Ethics: The Syrian Ulama and Economic Liberalization', in Syria from Reform to Revolt: Culture, Society and Religion, edited by Christa Salamandra and Leif Stenberg (Syracuse, NY: Syracuse University Press, 2015), pp. 130–46.

[70] T. C. Jones and Omar AlShehabi, 'Bahrain's Revolutionaries', Foreign Policy, 2 January 2012.

(demonstrated by its brief incursion into Bahrain in 2011) secured economic support.[71] But to secure an accommodation between the protestors and the ruling Al-Khalifah family was near impossible. Hard repression briefly crushed the protesters. But a divided ruling family was still required to resolve its divisions, appease Saudi Arabia, and maintain the confidence of the Western powers. Bahrain has few resources and is highly dependent on intra-regional and global trade.

In final summary: prominent in the Arab Spring protests in Bahrain in 2011 were protests over constitutional, political, and legal structures. But underpinning the rising were long-festering economic grievances. The Arab Spring drew support from a wide range of interests, Shi'ites, the young, the political opposition, of course, farmers, fishermen, and indeed sections of the business elite, although ultimately the latter remained loyal to the regime. It was not a narrow-based rising. Much of the protest involved poor Shi'ites, dismissed by the authorities as stooges of Iran. The Shi'ites did not protest on sectarian lines but focused on the economic and political abuses arising from class and privilege. They also sought the restoration of villages for food security and public housing. Bahraini youth, long denied educational and employment opportunities, further drove the protests. The Arab Spring of 2011 exposed the gulf between the Bahrain state and Bahrain's population, determined to force the regime to concede economic and political reform. Identifying sites as a focus for resistance was important in organizing the protest, winning national and international recognition, and in securing concessions from the state. The protests in Bahrain certainly unleashed violence. But the social order held, for Bahrain did not see the descent towards barbarity that marked conflict in Syria and Iraq in this same period.

---

[71] R. Mills, 'Pioneering Bahrain Finds Itself Reliant on Saudi Largesse', The National, 1 May 2012.

8
A Place for the State

In Bahrain's pre-colonial and colonial history, legal concepts and practices shaped the transformation of the economy and the state. The grip of the state was tempered by law. And in recent decades, there has been an urgent need to liberate the economy and business through the evolution of a legislative framework.[1]

The power of the Bahrain state in the economy grew with the power of oil, principally after 1971. High oil prices, particularly after 2004–09, have coincided with further changes in the role of the state, involving economic diversification and the reform of labour markets from a high dependence on foreign labour to an emphasis on local labour and its acquisition of essential skills. Of particular concern were reforms in education to facilitate advances in local employment and the creation of multicentric legal orders, in other words legal pluralism.[2] These legal orders are patterned on Bahrain's colonial inheritance, religious sectarianism, and institutional changes.

A study of the state in Bahrain reveals contentious politics, driven by regime manipulation and, most recently, youth radicalization. Political and economic resentment on the part of the young has been exacerbated by divisions within the ruling family. A close analysis of politics and the state, during and after the Arab Spring, reveals important shifts in Islamist politics and state authoritarianism. Finally, the Bahraini state is riven with disputes both within the ruling family and within business. To understand the complex interactions between the ruling family and business demands insights from several disciplines. Marc Valeri's writings on the Bahrain state has drawn attention to the rise of diverse factions, including youth movements and numerous strands of Islamists. The golden age of oil in the Gulf since 1971 has paradoxically driven economic diversification in Bahrain and encouraged Bahrain's globalization. Bahrain is unique in that religious

---

[1] Fahad Al-Zumai, 'The Evolution of Corporate Law in the Arab World: The Everlasting Grip of the State', unpublished paper, Kuwait University, no date; Fahad Al-Zumai, 'Rentier States and Economic Regulation Infrastructure: Kuwait as a Case Study', *Journal of Law*, vol. 31, no. 3 (2007).
[2] Marc Valeri, 'Oligarchy vs. Oligarchy: Business and Politics of Reform in Bahrain and Oman', in *Business Politics in the Middle East*, edited by Stephen Hertog, Giacomo Luciani, and Marc Valeri (London: Hurst, 2013), pp. 17–41 and notes 292–6.

Islam and Capitalism in the Making of Modern Bahrain. Rajeswary Ampalavanar Brown, Oxford University Press.
© Rajeswary Ampalavanar Brown (2023). DOI: 10.1093/oso/9780192874672.003.0008

and cultural oppositions, as well as youth movements pressing for good education, employment, and wealth, have each challenged the state. But government repression, though strong, has not led to state collapse, as it has in Syria, Lebanon, or Egypt. In Bahrain, the law and religious authority, including charitable institutions such as the waqf and ma'tam and the Ashura festivals, have restrained disorder and helped moderate religious, political, and legal demands. The legitimacy of the state creates legal pluralism without threatening the rule of law. Tolerance and imagination have enabled the Sunni state to survive in a Shia majority nation and to counter religious threats from Iran and Iraq. It is often said that Bahrain's authoritarian state survives through oil wealth and the co-option of business elites. But I argue that Bahrain is unique in the Middle East, in that the state there is responsive to secular institutions and political pressures through the law. There is juridical space for the state.

Discernible Patterns of Influence: Law, Business, and the State

The dominance of the state in Bahrain is clear. How then does business thrive? The right to incorporate a public company is shaped by political decision.[3] The establishment of a public company requires the approval of the political authorities. In Bahrain, the Minister of Trade and Commerce also has the power to dissolve the board of directors of a public company if its decisions were seen as having negative effects.[4] Such interventions by the state are legitimized on the grounds of protecting society. The Minister of Trade and Commerce also has the power to extend the term of a board of directors for up to six months.[5]

Contract law is central to Bahrain's corporate economy. The 2001 Act defines corporations as 'a contract under which two or more persons are committed to participate in an economic enterprise with the objective of profit realization by contributing a share in capital or work and dividing between themselves the profit or loss resulting from the enterprise'.[6]

[3] Al-Zumai, 'The Evolution of Corporate Law in the Arab World', p. 6. Article 72 of the Bahrain Commercial Companies Law, No. 21 of 2001, states: 'The founders shall submit an application for incorporating a company to the Ministry of Commerce and Industry.'
[4] Article 197 of the Bahrain Commercial Companies Law, No. 21 of 2001.
[5] Article 172 of the Bahrain Commercial Companies Law, No. 21 of 2001.
[6] Article 1 of the Bahrain Commercial Companies Law, No. 21 of 2001. See also W. Bratton, Jr., 'The Nexus of Contracts Corporation: A Critical Appraisal', *Cornell Law Review*, vol. 74, pp. 407–65; Nicholas H. D. Foster, 'Company Law Theory in Comparative Perspective: England and France', *American Journal of Comparative Law*, vol. 48, no. 4 (2000), pp. 573–621.

In Bahrain, the government attempts to protect private investors through extensive regulation. Consequently, in corporate law, 78 per cent of rules are mandatory, just 14 per cent are enabling. The mandatory rules provide protection for minority shareholders.[7]

There is a serious failure to provide distinct rules governing public and private companies.[8] Bahrain's corporate law has rules governing the establishment of statutory legal reserves to protect creditors.[9] The governing framework on directors' liabilities is modelled on the French Commercial Code, which provides strict regulations and articles of association to guard against fraud. In addition, in exceptional circumstances courts have the power to dissolve companies, although this power is rarely used.[10] The capitalization of corporations is, of course, in the hands of the investors and here the state and large private investors are powerful, as they have access to funds through the Central Bank of Bahrain and the Bahrain Development Board. However, there is protection here as majority consent is needed for companies raising capital, while for listed companies stock exchange approval is essential. In brief, through corporate law and governance, the state is both visible and a shadow in working through the jurisdictional complexity of the political and corporate economy of Bahrain.[11] The state's pre-eminence is encouraged by the lack of active intervention by courts, lawyers, and academics. Many of the laws are transplanted from common law and civil law but with detailed reassessment through the evolution of legal structures that are missing.[12]

State-making in the Middle East always involved contests over the configuration of religion, ethnicity, and legal systems. But in Bahrain, Sunni–Shi'a relations held a less prominent place in cultural and political discourse than is often assumed. The political and legal manoeuvring around Sunni–Shi'a relations came to the fore only when Iran's influence on the Shi'ites arose. Quietist Shi'ism in Bahrain remained cautious of Iran and Iraq.

---

[7] Al-Zumai, 'The Evolution of Corporate Law in the Arab World', p. 15.
[8] Article 227 of the Bahrain Commercial Companies Law, No. 21 of 2001.
[9] Article 224 of the Bahrain Commercial Companies Act, No. 21 of 2001.
[10] Al-Zumai, 'The Evolution of Corporate Law in the Arab World', p. 29; Lefevre Pelletier & Associates, 'Doing Business in France 2005', World Bank Publications, June 2006; article 321 of the Bahrain Commercial Companies Law, No. 21 of 2001.
[11] Article 210 of the Bahrain Commercial Companies Law, No. 21 of 2001.
[12] Al-Zumai, 'The Evolution of Corporate Law in the Arab World', p. 31; Otto Kahn-Freund, 'On Uses and Misuses of Comparative Law', *Modern Law Review*, vol. 37 (1974), pp. 1–27; Maren Hanson, 'The Influence of French Law on the Legal Development of Saudi Arabia', *Arab Law Quarterly*, vol. 2, no. 3 (1987), pp. 274–91; D. Berkowitz, K. Pistor, and J. F. Richard, 'Economic Development, Legality and the Transplant Effect', *European Economic Review*, vol. 47 (2003), pp. 165–95.

Islamist Political Parties and the State: Continuity and Change

Shia movements achieved political importance in conflict with the state particularly after the Arab Spring of 2011. But the tension had long been present in the economic deprivation of Shi'ites from the end of pearling in the 1950s, through the rise of oil and the increasing power of the ruling family. Indeed, increasing economic deprivation, arising particularly from economic development programmes from the 1970s, had a crushing impact on Shi'ites, with land grabs by the state resulting in the loss of fishing and agricultural employment. A fortuitous by-product of the Arab Spring was that Islamist groups were constrained, as they cooperated with Sunni protestors. This restrained 'cosmopolitanism', in contrast to Syria, was a product of legal reform in the 1990s, along with action by civic- and religious-based associations to revive non-state and diverse forms of authority within the waqf and ma'tam. The power of the ulama within Bahrain Shi'ism secured loyalty to a legal–religious order that tipped it towards a less violent Arab Spring. The institutional modernity of the ulama has been analysed in detail earlier. The Shia Islamist force al-Wifaq, which had been transformed by the regime into an institutional safety valve in 2006, after 2011 faced difficulties in overcoming its sectarian identity. Its desire to be an intermediary between the throne and the revolutionary Shi'a movements became a fading hope. This disappointment for Shi'ites coincided with the Sunni Islamist groups loyal to the regime, now falling victim to manipulation by members of the fragmented ruling family. On 17 July 2016, the High Civil Court of Manama sought the dissolution of the pre-eminent political society, the Shi'a Islamist, Jam'iyyat al-Wifaq al Watani al-Islamiyya (the Entente-National Accord Islamic Society, abbreviated to al-Wifaq). Al-Wifaq's Secretary General, Ali Salman, was sentenced to nine years in prison on charges of 'promoting forceful change of the regime'. This was followed by the stripping of citizenship from Bahrain's most prominent cleric, al-Wifaq's spiritual leader, Isa Qasim. This further destabilized the fragile relations of the state with secular and Islamist political opposition groups in an already turbulent atmosphere following the 2011 uprising. This aggressive mood on the part of the regime is attributed to intervention by Saudi Arabia and the calm response to the intervention by the US, which maintained a security base in Bahrain. These two shadowy influences appear to have shaped Al-Khalifah assertiveness. It is clear, however, that divisions within the ruling family increased the tension with Shi'ites.[13]

---

[13] 'High Court Dissolves Al-Wifaq', *Bahrain News Agency*, 17 July 2016; Marc Valeri, 'Islamist Political Societies in Bahrain: Collateral Victims of the 2011 Popular Uprising', in *Islamists and the Politics of*

The first decade of King Hamad's reign, 1999–2011, was marked by selective legal reform to restore stability following the economic unrest resulting from the fall in oil prices in the 1980s and the absence of political institutions after the dissolution of the first parliament in 1975.[14] Keeping in focus the need to strengthen the legitimacy of the ruling family, a National Action Charter, outlining the future structure and principles of government, was presented to a popular referendum on 14 February 2001. This was approved by 98.4 per cent of voters.[15] A few days earlier, Hamad had smoothed the political scene by abolishing the 1974 decree on state security measures, announcing the release of all political prisoners and detainees, and allowing the return of Bahraini opposition activists who had been in exile for years.[16] Without claiming that the politics of legal pluralism determined these changes in the politics of the kingdom, the crucial advance had come in 1989 with the granting of permission to register political societies under a general law governing civil, social, and cultural societies (No. 21 of 1989), making Bahrain the first Gulf monarchy to legalize political organizations. In August 2005, the law on political societies (No. 26 of 2005) was passed. It required the registration of political societies with the Ministry of Justice and stipulated that they should not have organizational or financial affiliations to non-Bahraini organizations. In addition, they were not allowed to build on narrow ethnic, linguistic, geographic, gender, class, or sectarian identities. This introduced a rise in political parties, both pro-regime and in opposition.

Sunni and Shi'a Islamist societies functioned like political parties until the Arab Spring of 2011. The most powerful society was Shi'a Islamist al-Wifaq, created with the aim of gathering all Shi'a Islamic groups under one banner headed by Ali Salman, a cleric who had been one of the leaders of the 1990s Bahraini Intifada. It sought the establishment of a constitutional monarchy with a cabinet accountable to an elected unicameral legislature committed to end sectarian discrimination. The traditional form of politics, cognitive and functional, was now accompanied by a structural transformation. Many of the activists of the Islamic Enlightenment Society, the legal face in Bahrain of Hizb al-Da'wa (Da'wa Party), were either members from the beginning or

the Arab Uprisings, edited by Hendrik Kraetzchmar and Paolo Rivetti (Edinburgh: Edinburgh University Press, 2018).

[14] Munira Fakhro, 'The Uprising in Bahrain: An Assessment', in The Persian Gulf at the Millennium: Essays in Politics, Economy, Security, and Religion, edited by Gary Sick and Lawrence G. Potter (New York: St Martin's Press, 1997), pp. 167–88.

[15] Valeri, 'Islamist Political Societies in Bahrain', p. 167.

[16] Katja Niethammer, 'Voices in Parliament, Debates in Majilis, and Banners on Streets: Avenues of Political Participation in Bahrain', EUI Working Paper No. 27, Robert Schuman Centre for Advanced Studies, Florence, 2006, p. 4.

were closely affiliated. Isa Qasim, although not a formal member, was revered as al-Wifaq's spiritual leader.

Another Shi'a Islamist society, founded in 2002, was Jam'iyyat al-Amal al-Islami (Islamic Action Society), which, like al-Wifaq, was committed to constitutional reform.[17] IAS also appealed to the followers of Ayatollah Shiraz in Bahrain. It is an offshoot of the former al-Jabha al-Islamiyya li Tahrir al Bahrayn (the Islamic Front for the Liberation of Bahrain, IFLB), founded in exile in 1975. In December 1981, 60 IFLB members were accused of plotting against the ruling family.

The establishment of cosmopolitan, outward-looking political dynamics can also be seen in the emergence of secular opposition societies. The former clandestine Arab nationalist Jabhat al-Sha'biyya li Tahrir al-Bahrayn (Popular Front for the Liberation of Bahrain) created Wa'd (Promise) in 2005, and participated in the 2006 Council of Representatives election. One Wa'd candidate was successful. A second new society, Jam'iyyat al-Minbar al-Dimuqrati al-Taqaddumi (Progressive Democratic Tribune Society, PDTS) was established in 2002 by returning exiles from the Marxist-Leninist National Front of Bahrain. Its candidates stood in the parliamentary election in 2002 and won three seats. There were also pro-regime societies, the most prominent being the liberal Jam'iyyat Mithaq al-'Amal al-Watani (National Action Charter Society), composed of businessmen. The NACS won three seats in the Council of Representatives in 2002.[18]

Among the pro-regime institutions established in the early 2000s was the Islamist Jam'iyyat al-Minbar al-Watani al-Islam (National Islamic Tribune) which was recognized as the political affiliate of the Bahraini al-Ikhwan al-Muslimun (Muslim Brotherhood). The Muslim Brotherhood focused on educational charities and was opposed to the political sympathies of Arab nationalists and Shi'a Islamists during the Intifada of the 1990s. Its membership was drawn mainly from the urban middle class and civil servants and thus it had considerable influence within government departments, including the education department. The party included members of the ruling family and the former Labour Minister, Isa bin Mohamed Al-Khalifah, who chaired it for five decades, from 1963 to 2013.[19] According to leaked US diplomatic cables, it appears that the royal court and Islamic banking sector funded this

[17] International Crisis Group, 'Bahrain's Sectarian Challenge', Middle East Report, no. 40 (2005), p. 15.
[18] Valeri, 'Islamist Political Societies in Bahrain', pp. 178–9.
[19] Ghassan al-Shihabi, 'Al-Ikhwan al-Muslimun fi-l-Bahrain: Tahulat al-"Aqud al-Sab'a"' [The Muslim Brotherhood in Bahrain: the Seven Decades' Transformations], in Al-Ikhwan al-Muslimun fi-L-Khalij, The Muslim Brotherhood in the Gulf (Dubai: Al-Mesbar Studies and Research Centre, 2014), p. 163.

society.[20] Another strong supporter of the state was al-Asala al-Islamiyya (the Islamic Authenticity Society), a political wing of the main Salafi organization in Bahrain, the Islamic Education Society. Members of this society formed influential clusters in the Ministries of Justice and of Islamic Affairs and Endowments. It registered as a society in 1990 and attracted support from among poor tribal Sunnis from Muharraq and al-Rifa' as well as from among naturalized Sunnis who had been granted citizenship, perhaps to enhance the Sunni position within a Shi'ite majority state. Political rapprochement was sought with the Muslim Brotherhood, Salafis, and other Sunni groups led by Abd al-Latif al-Mahmood, the founder of a small independent charity, the al-Jam'iyya al-Islamiyya (Islamic Society). Abd al-Latif al-Mahmood was educated at al-Azhar University, was Professor of Arabic at the University of Bahrain, and had been one of the leaders of the 1992 petition presented to Emir Isa demanding the restoration of the 1973 National Assembly. This petition, the inspiration of a coalition supported by leftists and Sunni and Shi'a Islamist societies, failed.

This failure by political religious societies to secure restoration of the National Assembly drew together disparate opposition groups into a coalition to boycott the first parliamentary elections of October 2002. It published a pamphlet seeking a revision of the 2002 constitution to secure full legislative powers in an elected chamber as well as a redrawing of electoral constituencies in order to readdress the imbalance between Sunni and Shi'ite electorates. Al-Wifaq favoured participation but was disturbed by the prospect that the redrawing of constituencies would be to its electoral disadvantage. In contrast, the pro-regime Sunni societies participated in the 2002 elections with the political wing of the Muslim Brotherhood winning seven seats and the Salafi al-Asala six, out of a total of 40.

Al-Wifaq regretted non-participation in 2002 and therefore registered under the new law on political societies in 2005. This led to the departure of some of its members, including its deputy leader Hasan Mushaima' and the cleric Abd al-Wahab, who, together with a number of secular political societies, founded the Right Movement for Freedom and Democracy (the Haqq). This coalition had dual Shi'a and Sunni leadership, campaigned for a new constitution, and even considered civil disobedience. In 2006, the Muslim Brotherhood resorted to street activism, calling for constitutional reform, in part a recognition of its growing popularity among the people. Haqq attracted underprivileged youth and decided to participate in the 2006 elections with

---

[20] 'A Field Guide to Bahraini Political Parties', Wikileaks, Cable from US Embassy in Bahrain, 4 September 2008, cited in Valeri, 'Islamist Political Societies in Bahrain', p. 168.

IAS. It formed a cross-ideological pact with the Arab nationalists, Jam'iyyat al-'Amal al-Watani al-Dimuqrati-Wad (National Democratic Action Society-Promise). In the 2006, elections the Islamist parties triumphed, within both opposition and pro-regime groups. The Islamists took 32 seats out of the 40 seat Council of Representatives. This victory was in part due to the Muslim Brotherhood and Salafi al-Asala not putting up candidates in certain seats in order to maximize the Sunni Islamist vote, a tactic that clearly succeeded. This tactical voting also benefited the Muslim Brotherhood, which won seven seats, and Salafi al-Asala, which won eight seats. All al-Wifaq candidates, 17 in total, were successful despite the party conforming to the rules of the regime in these elections. In the 2010 elections, al-Wifaq secured 18 seats while the Muslim Brotherhood won only two seats: the Salafis gained three seats while losing five.

The 2006 elections marked a triumph for Islamist political parties, both pro-regime and opposition. Their success indicated a subtle capitulation to the state, a state that held power through oil wealth. However, the arrangement with the Muslim Brotherhood and the Salafi was fragile, and in the 2010 elections only two of the former's candidates and just three of the latter's won seats. The opposition group led by al-Wifaq retained its position, winning 18 seats. These electoral accomplishments revealed that politics was not seriously sectarian. The demands were not religious but for a constitutional monarchy, with government made accountable to a parliament. The opposition saw the Prime Minister, Khalifa bin Salaman, as a major obstacle, and they sought his dismissal. But the pre-eminence enjoyed by the ruling classes was accepted as 'the dominant fraction of the dominant class', in Bourdieu's analysis[21]. The opposition was not attempting to unseat the ruling family. Political groups were, to a degree, moderate, following the historical legacy of the rule of law, an inheritance of British colonialism. Al-Wifaq's political stance of participating in institutional change, in adopting a conciliatory attitude towards the regime, weakened its reputation, particularly after the 2011 demonstrations at the Pearl Roundabout. The 18 Al-Wifaq MPs resigned from the Council of Representatives on 27 February 2011 following the violence of the security forces against the protestors. Moreover, the military intervention by the Gulf Cooperation Council joint force on 14 March 2011 destroyed al-Wifaq's daily communication with the Crown Prince, which sought to restrain the rising violence.[22]

[21] Pierre Bourdieu, *Language and Symbolic Power*. London: Polity Press, 1992.
[22] Valeri, 'Islamist Political Societies in Bahrain', pp. 170–1.

The Arab Spring and Tangled Politics

The Arab Spring of 2011 reversed the significant achievements of conciliatory politics sought through electoral changes since 2000. Hamad's regime now presented Shi'ites as a radical threat while encouraging loyal Sunni political organizations to work with the regime. On 19 February 2011, Sunni political parties, including the Muslim Brotherhood, Salafi al-Asala, the Sunni nationalist Harakat al-ʿAdala al-Wataniya (National Justice Movement Society), and the Nasserist-cum-Islamist al-Wasat al-ʿArabi al-Islami (Arab Islamic Centre Society), agreed to create a new movement, the Tajammu al-Wahda al-Wataniya (National Unity Gathering, NUG), to be a dominant Sunni voice, supporting political reform and rejecting revolution.[23] They elected Abd al-Latif al-Mahmood as NUG spokesperson. Their rallies at Al-Fatih Mosque on 21 February and 2 March affirmed their loyalty to the ruling family and expressed solidarity.[24] Praise from the Prime Minister and the King for the NUG led it to proclaim that the Sunnis were an abandoned community and should be reconstituted, thus creating three powerful camps, the regime, the Shi'ites, and the Sunnis. Abd al Latif al-Mahmood urged that these three forces had to be consulted on political and constitutional reform and that the consent of all three was mandatory for any decision by the regime.[25] The NUG lashed out at the sectarianism of Al-Wifaq and accused it of seeking the introduction of Wilayat al-Faqih in Bahrain (rule and guardianship by a jurist), the exclusive right of clerics to the interpretation of Islamic law. That would put ultimate power in the hands of clerics, as in Iran since 1979.

Rising pressure on the NUG to affirm the legitimacy of the ruling Al-Khalifah family and to reject calls for the resignation of the cabinet and an end to the demonstrations, as well as veiled allegations that Al-Wifaq was close to Iran, played into the hands of the regime. However, the NUG was shifting its stance. It had established a reformist process by collaborating with Al-Wifaq.[26] The NUG also insisted on substantial social and political reform, involving more power being transferred to the people. It also sought a balanced revision of the constitution 'to ensure people are the sources of authority under the kind custodianship of the King.'[27] The NUG pressed for

[23] Valeri, 'Islamist Political Societies in Bahrain', p. 172.
[24] Bahrain Independent Commission for Inquiry Report, 10 December 2011, p. 87; Nancy A. Youssef, 'Huge Bahraini Counter Protest Reflects Rising Sectarian Strife', *McClatchy Newspapers*, 21 February 2011; Habib Toumi, 'Bahrain's National Unity Rally Turns into a Political Society', *Gulf Daily News*, 11 June 2011.
[25] Andrew Hammond, 'Bahraini Sunni says Opposition Must Change Leader', *Reuters*, 28 May 2011: www.reuters.com/article/us-bahrain-cleric-interview-idUSTRE74R18Q20110528.
[26] Bahrain Independent Commission for Inquiry Report, p. 135.
[27] Bahrain Independent Commission for Inquiry Report, p. 87.

the release of political prisoners arrested during the Arab uprising and for the prosecution of those responsible for the killing of protestors. It also sought wage increases for both public- and private-sector employees, increased provision for housing, greater independence of the judiciary, and an end to corruption. This led the NUG to engage with the seven opposition parties, including al-Wifaq, in March 2011. It worked to condemn inter-communal clashes and warned of the dangers of sectarianism. But any progress towards conciliation was interrupted by the GCC's military intervention to clear the Pearl Roundabout on 14 March. The intervention was triggered by allegations that the protesters had Iranian connections. A state of emergency was imposed between 15 March and 1 June. Shadowy allegations of external threats created problems for Bahrain's moderate opposition and for the pro-regime parties such as the NUG.

The so-called authoritarian state in Bahrain needs to be seen in the context of largely decentralized governance with external allies subtly intruding in Bahraini politics. The NUG persevered with its mission for reform. It sought a coalition of independent political parties, and this was also the aim of the Muslim Brotherhood. A second option was to evolve the NUG into a charity involved in social and economic issues confronting the poor and youth. That would provide a possible solution for the sectarian and class-infused politics of resentment. This was supported by the Salafi al-Asala party. A third option was to transform the NUG into a registered political party. This was supported by Abd al-Latif al-Mahmood but opposed by al-Minbar and al-Asala, as the law did not permit simultaneous membership of two political parties. Both al-Minbar and al-Asala were anxious not to lose members to the NUG. And indeed, registration of the NUG as a political party on 28 June led to a break with al-Minbar and al-Asala and growing tensions within the pro-regime parties. A further crisis had been caused by the resignation of all 18 Al-Wifaq MPs from the Council of Representatives in February 2011. A by-election organized in September 2011 following the resignations was boycotted by the NUG in order to preserve 'national unity'. The Muslim Brotherhood and Salafi parties refrained from contesting this election, on the rather flimsy grounds that they had not been prepared to participate in what were strong Shi'a constituencies. They supported candidates with 'acceptable' political programmes.[28]

The boycott by these major parties led to the election of pro-government deputies, labelling themselves as 'independent candidates'. This marked a serious decline in the ability of Sunni political parties to overcome political

---

[28] Valeri, 'Islamist Political Societies in Bahrain', p. 174.

lock-in. The pro-regime Sunni parties, the Muslim Brotherhood, its affiliate al-Minbar, and other Salafis dependent on support from the Al-Khalifah
family, declined when the ruling family concluded that they were now super-
fluous to the regime, as shown by the failure to suppress the Pearl Roundabout
protests.[29] The ruling family concluded that as the Arab Spring was a Shi'a
performance, a Sunni coalition challenging the Shi'ites was beneficial. But
following the Arab Spring, a more dynamic Sunni Islamist political presence
came to threaten the ruling oligarchy. As soon as the end of 2011, the NUG
had lost much of its value to the regime.

By January 2012, a second wave of young NUG sympathizers created the
Sahwat al-Fatih (al-Fatih Awakening) and organized a rally to commemo-
rate the anniversary of the first NUG gathering at al-Fatih Mosque in 2011.
The occasion involved none of the original NUG leaders.[30] This society was
thought to be a creation of the ruling family and the Muslim Brotherhood,
both seeking to weaken the NUG. Al-Fatih also sought to weaken the link
between the NUG and Al-Wifaq, describing the latter as a terrorist group.
It also whipped up anti-American sentiment, accusing the US of exploiting
Bahrain for its own geopolitical interest. By 2012, al-Fatih had faded but it
had helped the state to portray the NUG and the break-up of its coalition
with al-Minbar and al-Asala as responsible for the failure to negotiate an
agreement between the regime and the legal opposition. This strengthened
the state's ability to resist sectarian demands as well as absolve it from responsibility for the failure of the 'National Dialogue'. Beginning in early 2013, this
initiative, chaired by the Justice Minister, was termed a 'national dialogue'
and not a crude political gathering. Government officials moderated the
discussions between representatives of the opposition and nationalist societies while refraining from direct intervention. This approach failed, as the
opposition insisted on high-level government participation. This refocused
concern that Sunnis had no representative in the government and alluded
to the view that the royals were more tribal than Sunni. Sunnis had always
feared being let down by the Al-Khalifah family, not from malice but from
political expediency. Thus the 2011 uprising had created more Sunni political
frustration.[31] However the regime's attempt to place Sunni–Shia divisions at
the centre of politics backfired and instead there emerged anti-Shi'ite propaganda from within the regime's own security apparatus, professing sympathy

[29] Hasan T. Al-Hasan, 'Sectarianism Meets the Arab Spring: TGONU a Broad-Based Sunni Movement
Emerges in Bahrain', *Arabian Humanities*, vol. 4 (2015): https://cy.revues.org/2807
[30] Al-Hasan, 'Sectarianism Meets the Arab Spring'.
[31] Justin Gengler, *Group Conflict and Political Mobilization in Bahrain and the Arab Gulf: Rethinking the
Rentier State* (Bloomington, IN: Indiana University Press, 2015), pp. 136–8.

for the Islamic State and attracting Bahrain's youth.[32] As Justin Gengler has argued, 'Bahrain's capacity for sectarian manipulation is a political tool at least as powerful as its capacity to enrich.'[33] This 'protection racket politics', as Daniel Brumberg describes many post-Arab Spring societies, is a common feature of Arab autocracies, which display 'an uncanny knack for manipulating a wide array of ethnic, religious and sociocultural groups by playing upon their fears of political exclusion (or worse) under majority rule and offering them Godfather-style protection in return for political support.[34] Thus facing a confluence of political and legal slyboots, the state's strategy remained to favour pragmatic businessmen and tribal leaders, both susceptible to manipulation to support the regime's policies.

The problems facing Sunni Islamist political parties increased in the November 2014 elections for the Council of Representatives for, in September, the government had announced a plan to redraw constituency boundaries with the explicit intention of reducing the chances of victory for Sunni Islamists. The gerrymandering acted to favour independent tribal candidates. The re-drawn boundaries neither helped nor hindered Al-Wifaq's electoral prospects but they led to an opposition boycott of the 2014 elections on the grounds that government had failed to support Sunni Islamist and populist candidates in favour of independent tribal candidates. This was evident in the Sunni-dominated south where the creation of new neighbourhoods affected local bases of support in and around Rifa. Several Islamist MPs displaced existing Sunni legislators. In Muharraq, the Salafi and the Muslim Brotherhood did not gain seats as a result of the constituency changes.[35]

In retrospect, it is apparent from the 2010 election results that land development extending from the north of the island, converted into commercial and industrial sites, followed by development on the island of Muharraq, with the construction of an airport, dry docks, and warehouses, produced a substantial demographic transformation. The man-made Amwaj islands off the north-east coast of Muharraq became an expensive expatriate area. Manama, too, experienced a transformation with the establishment of the Bahrain

---

[32] Valeri, 'Islamist Political Societies in Bahrain', pp. 175–6; Noor Mattar, 'Bahrain's Shia Muslims Tense as Politicians and Preachers Pledge Allegiance to ISIS', *Global Voices*, 24 July 2014: https://globalvoices.org/2014/07/24/bahrains-shia-muslims-tense-as-politicians-andpreachers-pledge-allegiance-to-isis/; Andrew Hammond, 'Bahrain Sunnis Warn Government over Dialogue at Rally', *Reuters*, 22 February 2012: http://uk.reuters.com/article/uk-bahrain-protest-talks-idUKTRE81LOXK20120222; Laurence Louer, 'Sectarianism and Coup-Proofing Strategies in Bahrain', *Journal of Strategic Studies*, vol. 36, no. 2 (2013), p. 246.
[33] Gengler, *Group Conflict and Political Mobilization in Bahrain and the Arab Gulf*, p. 141.
[34] Daniel Brumberg, 'Transforming the Arab World's Protection-Racket Politics', *Journal of Democracy*, vol. 24, no. 3 (2013), pp. 88–103.
[35] Gengler, *Group Conflict and Political Mobilization in Bahrain and the Arab Gulf*, pp. 155–6.

Financial Harbour. The Shi'a-dominated Northern Governate included mansions, resorts, and a causeway to Saudi Arabia. The dramatic transformation of coastal areas and the construction of Hamad Town involved the appropriation of the destitute Shi'a villages of Dumestan, Karzakan, al-Malkiya, Sadad, Shahrakan, and Dar Khalib. This naturally led to violent confrontation with the government. Sunnis were also affected by industrial development on the eastern coast. New sites for the Bahrain Petroleum Company, other petrochemical firms, and for Aluminium Bahrain attracted expatriate workers. But Sunni and Shi'a displacement was growing, and the regime feared more dissent after the Arab Spring of 2011. It therefore engineered boundary changes to prevent domination by Islamists, both Sunni and Shi'a.[36]

The Intimate Markers of a Tribal Royal Counter-Revolution

This determination to prevent parliament being controlled by Islamists arose from a growing fear of transnational Sunni Islamist movements, the Islamic State, and Shi'a activism inspired by Iran. The radical imam Turki al-Binali's support for IS leader Abu Bakr al-Baghdadi's assumption as the righteous caliph was highly disturbing. His urging of fellow Sunnis to join the resistance against Shi'a in Syria and Iraq posed a serious threat to the Al-Khalifah regime. Pressure from Saudi Arabia and the UAE to limit Sunni Islamist influence led Bahrain to loosen its ties with the Salafis and with the Muslim Brotherhood in March 2014. With tensions rising, it was inevitable that in the November 2014 election the NUG failed, all seven of its candidates losing, while al-Minbar, an affiliate of the Muslim Brotherhood, secured only one seat out of the seven it contested. Salafi al-Asala won three out of the six seats it contested.[37]

Al-Wifaq struggled to contain pressure from its members while maintaining its privileged access to the crown prince and the royal family. It also had to mediate between the society's moderate wing and the radical demands of the February 14 Youth Coalition. Five opposition groups, including Al-Wifaq and IAS, decided to boycott the elections. They gave as their reasons the unjust imprisonment of 4,000 political prisoners, including the leaders of Al-Wifaq and Haqq, since the uprising in 2011. The earlier conciliatory

---

[36] Gengler, *Group Conflict and Political Mobilization in Bahrain and the Arab Gulf*, pp. 96–101.

[37] Justin Gengler, 'Electoral Rules and Threats Cure Bahrain's Sectarian Parliament', The Monkey Cage, 1 December 2014: www.washingtonpost.com/blogs/monkey-cage/wp/2014/12/01/electoral-rules-and-threats-cure-bahrains-sectarian-parliament/.

effort of Al-Wifaq to appease the regime by participating in electoral politics in 2006 had been ignored by the state, which rejected appeals to release
political prisoners and then redrew constituency boundaries to preserve its
hegemony not through Islamists but through state-supported 'tribal independent' candidates. Al-Wifaq's failure to secure concessions from the regime led
to the fiasco of the election boycott in November 2014. Al-Wifaq's dissolution in 2016 and the continued imprisonment of its Secretary General, Ali
Salman, from December 2014 meant that an opportunity was lost to create
a hegemony of a different kind, one based on allegiance to the Al-Khalifah.
Equally dispiriting was the regime's abandonment of the Sunnis, as it had
been Sunni support in 2011 and 2012 that had enabled the ruling family to
deal with the Shi'a. The Al-Khalifah regime had then denounced the Shi'ites
as terrorists. But the final blow was the defeat of Sunnis in the Muslim Brotherhood, Salafis, and the NUG in the 2014 elections by state manipulation and
electoral engineering to advantage state cronies. The regime's fear of sectarian politics, Sunni and Shi'ite, has been driven by the rise of Islamic State
and the violence of Jihadism. Institutional insecurity and fear of global terror
determined the actions of the state.[38]

The 2018 elections, held in November and December to elect 40 members
of the Council of Representatives, also met with resistance. Both Al-Wifaq
and the secular Waad were barred from fielding candidates. Independent candidates monopolized the 40 constituencies. But a record number of Bahraini
women were elected.[39] This subtle repression of both Sunnis and Shi'ites in
Bahrain stands in sharp contrast to the brutal repression in Syria.

The Rise of Youth and Left-wing Politics

The challenges to the state from youth protest movements arose principally
from problems in education and employment.[40] The construction of an
authoritarian state, contested by political and cultural challenges, has been
the foremost theme in the literature on the Bahrain state. However, a
closer analysis and comparison with other Gulf states suggests a revision

---

[38] Farishta Saeed, 'Bahrain Asks Court to Suspend Main Opposition Bloc's Activities', *Reuters*, 20 July
2014: www.reuters.com/article/us-bahrain-politics-alwifaq-idUSKBNOF-PONZ20140720.
[39] 'Record Number of Bahraini Women elected to Parliament': https://www.aljazeera.com/news/2018/
12/2/record-number-of-bahraini-women-elected-to-parliament; 'Bahrain Opposition: Voter Turnout
Did Not Exceed 30%': https://www.middleeastmonitor.com/2018 1126-bahrain-opposition-voter-
turnout-did-not-exceed-30/, 26 November 2018.
[40] Marc Valeri, 'Contentious Politics in Bahrain: Opposition Cooperation between Regime Manipulation and Youth Radicalization', in *Opposition Cooperation in the Arab World: Contentious Politics in the
Time of Change*, edited by Hendrik Kraetzschmar (London: Routledge, 2012), pp. 129–49.

to the oft-quoted paradigm of authoritarianism. One revision is that youth political protest involved cross-ideological and cross-sectarian cooperation, particularly in the 1970s, 1980s, and most dramatically during and after the Arab Spring of 2011. King Hamad's canny efforts to break cooperation between these opposition groups fashioned a route for an increase in state power despite the divisions within the ruling family. William Zartman has argued that in Tunisia, Egypt, and Morocco, dictatorial rule in the 1980s owed much to the moderate opposition, successful in securing its demands without provoking the ruling power.[41] For Bahrain to achieve a similar outcome involved manipulation of elections and the incitement of boycotts by political parties, who thus chose abstention rather than a direct challenge. Gause sees this as a pressure valve releasing political tensions in order to maintain authoritarian rule.[42]

The Transition from Sunni–Shia and Cross-Ideological Cooperation

There are three points of entry when analysing the fragmentation of Bahrain's political opposition. The first requires an appreciation of the alliance of cross-sectarian opposition that existed in the 1950s, again at the height of Arab nationalism in the 1990s, and again in 2000. This cross-sectarian opposition posed a serious threat to the survival of the authoritarian regime, fully under-stood by Hamad who had been Commander-in-Chief of the Bahrain Defence Force since 1969 and who came to power in 1999 following the death of his father Shaykh Isa bin Salman Al-Khalifa (1961–99). This cross-sectarian coalition had sought reform before independence in 1971 but now circled peacefully around well-structured labour movements. However, after independence, these political coalitions also moved into left-wing political parties and challenged the legitimacy of the Al-Khalifah dynasty.[43] The repressive acts of the regime, including the dissolution of the first parliament in 1975, resulted in considerable political protest between 1975 and 1999. Hamad's

---

[41] I. W. Zartman, 'Opposition as Support of the State', in *Beyond Coercion: The Durability of the Arab State*, edited by A. Dawisha and I. W. Zartman (London: Croom Helm, 1988), pp. 61–87.

[42] F. Gregory Gause III, 'The Middle East Academic Community and the "Winter of Arab Discontent": Why Did We Miss It?', Report for the Stimson Center: www.Stimson.org/images/uploads/research-pdfs/Academic_Community.pdf. 2011, p. 15; Daniel Brumberg, 'The Trap of Liberalized Autocracy', *Journal of Democracy*, vol. 13, no. 4 (2002), pp. 56–67; Lisa Blaydes, *Elections and Distributive Politics in Mubarak's Egypt* (Cambridge: Cambridge University Press, 2011); H. Kraetzschmar, 'Mapping Opposition Cooperation in the Arab World: From Single-Issue Coalitions to Transnational Networks', *British Journal of Middle Eastern Studies*, vol. 38, no. 3 (2011), pp. 287–302.

[43] Valeri, 'Contentious Politics in Bahrain', p. 131.

accession to the throne in 1999 was also accompanied by serious civil unrest, fuelled by falling oil prices and declining living standards but also nurtured by a sense of loss of political participation since the closing of parliament in 1975. The repression then pushed the opposition underground. Cooperation among the opposition factions was maintained largely in the exiled Shi'i Islamists and leftist groups.

To emphasize the emergence of a new liberal monarchy, Hamad changed his title from Emir to King. With his accession in 1999, political societies were legalized, marking a shift towards cross-ideological and cross-sectarian political structures. This was a clear basis for electoral democracy, but the ruling family was astute in reinforcing recognition of the regime as a powerful entity, able to regulate electoral politics to maintain control. Religious and class factions were restrained by the regime, justified, it said, by the need to achieve secular modernity. There was a strong contrast to the pre-independence period, when Sunni Shi'a politics was marked by militant labour demands, general strikes, and demands for the release of political prisoners. In summary, it was the loss of institutional protection for the religious and secular opposition in the National Assembly that resurrected the fragmentation of the opposition and weakened political stability by 1999. Now opposition unity rested on petitions on single issues and electoral boycotts.[44] The reforms initiated during the early reign of King Hamad proved deceptive and discontent persisted. In February 2002, he introduced a new constitution, under which he held absolute executive power, with the ability to dissolve the new bicameral National Assembly composed of a Council of Representatives elected every four years. There was also provision for a Consultative Council appointed by the King. Legislation could be proposed by members of the National Assembly. However, jurisdictional boundaries remained, as only the King could amend the constitution by formal decree. The concentration of power in the monarch disrupted the dynamics of opposition and the ability to liberalize politics and seek change. To interpret Hamad's breach of the processes of reform, it is necessary to trace the roots of opposition politics in Bahrain.

The Dynamics of Youth Radicalism

The early signs of opposition activism and youth radicalism are found in the indigenous Baharina, the Arab Shi'a, in 1921, when they demanded

---

[44] M. Al-Jamri, 'Shia and the State in Bahrain: Integration and Tension', *Alternative Politics*, special issue no. 1 (2010), p. 18.

protection from the royal family and sought fair taxation under the British Protectorate. This was a challenge to Sunni merchants and resulted in sectarian tension. British intervention resulted in the abdication of Shaykh 'Isa bin Ali (1869–1923). The reign of his son Shaykh Hamad from 1923 to 1942 was marked by labour unrest because of the collapse of the pearling industry. There was now a wider labour movement. In 1938, Bahraini workers of the Bahrain Petroleum Company (BAPCO) organized strikes for better wages and working conditions. This was supported by the Sunni merchants. Fearing a Sunni–Shi'a labour coalition, the authorities arrested the strike leaders and deported them to India. With the emergence of Arab nationalist movements in Bahrain in the mid-1950s, sectarian riots erupted. In September 1953, the Ashura festival ignited fierce clashes, and there was real concern about violent sectarianism. Arab nationalists, including 'Abd al-'Aziz al-Shaman and 'Abd al-Rahman al-Bakr who had created cultural clubs and political publications, now sought to establish a cross-sectarian reformist movement. In October 1956, the National Union Committee (NUC), with representatives from villages and urban communities, recruited four Sunnis and four Shi'a. The main demands were for the establishment of an elected Legislative Council, the legalization of trade unions, and the removal of the ruler's British advisor Charles Belgrave. The NUC succeeded in establishing a labour union with more than 14,000 workers, and the ruler agreed to the creation of a tripartite committee, representing the authorities, employers, and workers, to prepare a Labour Code. But in October 1956, student demonstrations against the Israeli invasion of Sinai turned into an anti-British protest and the NUC called for a general strike. There followed arrests and a state of emergency was declared. From the late 1950s, there was harsh political repression. In 1965, a major strike in the BAPCO developed into a brief uprising but the leaders were forced into an underground organization of Arab Nationalists, Ba'thists, and communists. The Emergency Law of 1956 was revived and this caused further fragmentation of opposition politics, posing a threat to Sunni–Shi'a unity. Within this fragmented politics, labour activism gathered strength, particularly after independence in 1971. Labour activists cooperated with underground left-wing political groups and organized a mass rally in March 1972.[45] The arrest of the leaders and other repressive measures was always accompanied by constitutional changes.

The period after 1975 saw a reconfiguration of ideologies within the opposition. The religious activists were forced underground. Many of those forced into exile faced difficulties in coordinating the remaining activists at home. Only the followers of the Iraq–Iranian Ayatollah Muhammad Shirazi openly

---

[45] Valeri, 'Contentious Politics in Bahrain', pp. 132–5.

defied the authorities but even they were forced to retreat. It was the left-wing opposition that was most affected by state repression. The Popular Front for the Liberation of Bahrain (PFLB) leaders forced into exile attempted to maintain links with al-Da'wa activists. Mansur al-Jamri created the Islamic Bahrain Freedom Movement (IBFM) in London in 1982. But it lost credibility in Bahrain itself. The decline of the Arab nationalists and the communists accelerated after the late 1970s. The end of the oil boom and the 1991 Gulf War hit workers, with unemployment rising to 30 per cent. The deteriorating economy and political paralysis in the 1990s unleashed violence, an Intifada during which 40 people died.[46] Many of these clashes were in Shi'a villages. Sunni leftist activists, too, called for an end to the discrimination against Shi'i and for the restoration of parliament. The harsh repression did lead to a movement seeking collaboration between Sunni and Shi'a. The regime targeted activists such as the leaders of the Shi'i protest movements, including 'Abd al-Amir al-Jamri and 'Abd al-Wahhab Husayn. The young Shi'i cleric Ali Salman was arrested and expelled.[47] However, state repression also united Shi'i Islamists and many Bahraini citizens to demand a representative parliament that would include the opposition, a cross-sectarian opposition that would drive political mobilization. This was the main driver from the 1950s for political and social reform. Such ideological and religious contests can simultaneously produce institutional patterns and expectations. As Clifford Geertz has argued, the global institutional order has its origins in the stories people tell themselves about others.[48]

Prospects for Change under Hamad: Order Out of Trouble?

After the violent era of his father, Shaykh 'Isa bin Salman Al-Khalifa (1961–99), a violence accentuated by falling oil prices and political paralysis, strikingly, the succession of King Hamad was marked by political reforms. The perception of liberalism was evident in his abolition of the 1974 Decree on State Security, the release of all political prisoners and detainees, and an amnesty towards all opponents forced into exile. Political pluralism was evidently encouraged. Numerous political societies were allowed to register under the 1979 law governing civil and cultural societies.[49] But behind

---

[46] Fakhro, 'The Uprising in Bahrain', pp. 167–88.
[47] Valeri, 'Contentious Politics in Bahrain', pp. 136–8.
[48] Clifford Geertz, 'Religion as a Cultural System', in *Anthropological Approaches to the Study of Religion*, edited by Michael Banton (London: Tavistock Publications, 1966), pp. 1–46.
[49] Niethammer, 'Voices in Parliament, Debates in Majilis, and Banners on Streets', p. 5.

this apparent tolerance lay the fear of Shi'ism and the influence of Iran, and of Marxist activism. The power of centralized political authority had been demonstrated in August 2005 when a new law decreed that political societies could not be affiliated to any non-Bahrain organization, and could not be based on ethnic, sectarian, or class identity. Formerly banned political societies, arguing for a constitutional monarchy, re-emerged. Even 'involvement in the Intifada was really the main yardstick of political legitimacy among the Shia population'. Here the Shia relationship to the marja'iyya and Iran was not relevant in politics but was often in 'competition for social power'.[50]

By 2002, Hamad had cannily ensured that while there was freedom of speech and political association, he had reinforced his grip on power by limiting the ability of the opposition to control the elected chamber. Sunni areas were given additional constituencies and Sunni expatriates, the majority working in the security services, were offered naturalization and thereby granted political rights. These measures led to the regrouping of leftists and Arab nationalists, and the Al-Wifaq and Islamic Action Society boycotted elections, seeking to overturn the 2002 Constitution and force a return to the 1973 Constitution. A more dramatic conflict was the Arab Spring of February 2011, with youth demanding fundamental reform of the political system and major improvements in employment and training. A majority of the protestors were Shi'ites but the demands were not sectarian or religious.[51] The increasing violence of the police and the 14th of March military intervention by the GCC provoked deep resentment. The National Security Agency and the Ministry of the Interior mounted a crackdown on the opposition leaders. This led to calls for a republican state by radical youth. Al-Wifaq, Wa'ad, and six legal societies with close contacts with Crown Prince Salman lost leadership to radicalized youth, the February 14 Youth Coalition. This youth populism was fed by resentment of a regime which was constantly attributing the uprising to sectarianism. Tension also rose as Sunni cadres of the ex-Communist (PDTS) movement were critical of the growing youth protests. The cohesion of the opposition was further weakened by the imposition of a five-year jail sentence on Ibrahim Sharif, the Secretary General of the Sunni Wa'ad Society. This brutal sentence created fear of a conspiracy by the regime to split Sunni–Shi'a unity. Although the Pearl Roundabout pro-democracy protests had not resulted in political change, its impact on youth had been enormous. The young protesters have been deeply affected by the

[50] Laurence Louer, *Transnational Shia Politics: Religious and Political Networks in the Gulf* (London: Hurst, 2011), pp. 238–9.

[51] International Crisis Group, 'Popular Protests in North Africa and the Middle East [111]: the Bahrain Revolt', *Middle East /North Africa Report* 105, 6 April 2011, p. 6.

arrests of their leaders and by a heightened awareness of economic divisions and the failures of the state.[52]

Populism and Youth Protests in the Arab Spring and After

The youth protests in 2011 coincided with low economic growth, a decline in oil prices, increasing youth unemployment, and loss of land and housing. There was a speculative boom in land development affecting Shi'ite villagers, fishermen, and industrial workers. The failure of the state to win over factions within the opposition parties drove youth towards protest. Richard Hofstadter has examined the relative legacies of populist movements led by farmers in the late nineteenth-century United States and of progressive liberals. He re-presented the populists as losers, infused by irrational resentments and drawn to politics by an agrarian myth.[53]

In Bahrain, youth populism was driven not by narrow sectarianism but by a demand for reform of the economy, politics, and society. It has leftists, but even as it failed in 2011 it left behind the memory of a repressive state and the torture of young activists.[54] Moreover, present-day Bahraini young populists are not simply resentful losers. They are forward-looking radicals seeking a democratized industrial society and the transformation of social values to protect youth employment and skills. This has been described by Goodwyn as 'a self-generated culture of collective dignity and individual longing'. As a movement 'it was expansive, passionate, flawed, creative— above all, enhancing in its assertion of human striving'. As a mass movement it resists corporate financial interests and privileges.[55] Also relevant here for a deeper understanding of Bahraini youth populism is Michael Kazin's analysis of the diversity of parties, social movements, and labour unions within populism. He stresses the pragmatism prevailing in populism and its flexibility in shifting from left to right.[56] Charles Postel was highly critical of Hofstadter's account of populism as resentful and backward-looking, of populists as losers in the process of modernization. He asserted that the agricultural

---

[52] Valeri, 'Contentious Politics in Bahrain', pp. 146–7.
[53] Richard Hofstadter, *The Age of Reform: From Bryan to FDR* (New York: Vintage, 1955), pp. 47, 50–9.
[54] Bahrain Independent Commission for Inquiry Report, 10 December 2011, chapter 5; Toby Jones, 'Bahrain's Revolutionaries Speak: An Exclusive Interview with Bahrain's Coalition of February 14th Youth', *Jadaliyya*, 22 March 2012.
[55] Lawrence Goodwyn, *Democratic Promise: The Populist Moment in America* (New York: Oxford University Press, 1976), pp. 11–14, 17–18, 26–31, and 276–306; Hofstadter, *The Age of Reform*, pp. 47, 50–9, 73, 95–6, and 101.
[56] Michael Kazin, The *Populist Persuasion: An American History* (Ithaca, NY and London: Cornell University Press, 1998), pp. 28, 30, 38.

populists of late nineteenth-century America were not ignorant farmers but were well connected commercially and intellectually to the wider world. They were seeking to ensure that the world, although changing, would still provide a place for their localism and solidarity. These debates on American populism resonate with Bahrain's youth populism of the 1950s, 1970s, 1980s and into the twenty-first century.[57]

But in Bahrain the ruling family was powerful. In the earlier decades of populism, there was flickering protest against big business, financial capitalism, and business oligarchs. In contrast, the populism of the Arab Spring was more pragmatic. The shift from left to right too was shaped by pragmatism. Bahrain's youth sought to persuade the state to give them greater access to education, employment, and housing. They were never critical of the monarchy until the state unleashed violence against them in 2011 and they faced arrest and exile. They then sought a move from a monarchy to a republic. That was a response to state repression. Youth populism was opposed to sectarianism and to the West. Its core membership in the cities protested against elitism in business and oligarchic elitism, although many were from an oligarchic business background. Hence Bahrain's populism differed from that of Hofstadter's American liberalism which, while accepting insights from Darwin, Marx, and Freud, was explicitly tied to a 'paranoid style of politics rooted in status anxiety'.[58] Bahrain's youth populism emphasized none of these anxieties. And it exhibited no trace of anarchy. It was never a status-seeking revolution. Its only resentment was fear of foreign labour as a threat to their jobs.[59]

The Art of Government: An Internal Form of Colonialism

Joseph Kostiner, Lisa Anderson, Michael Herb, and Gregory Gause III have argued that institutional flexibility, cohesion within the ruling elite, and vast

---

[57] Charles Postel, *The Populist Vision* (Oxford and New York: Oxford University Press, 2007), pp. 173–203, 205–42; E. Bellin, 'The Robustness of Authoritarianism in the Middle East: Exceptionalism in Comparative Perspective', *Comparative Politics*, vol. 36, no. 2 (2004), pp. 139–57.

[58] Hofstadter, *Age of Reform*, pp. 73, 101.

[59] Abdulhadi Khalaf, 'Labour Movements in Bahrain', MERIP reports, 132, 1985, p. 25; Paul Dyer and Samer Kherfi, 'Gulf Youth and the Labour Market', in *Young Generation Awakening: Economics, Society, and Policy On the Eve of the Arab Spring*, edited by Edward A. Sayre and Tarik M. Yousef (Oxford: Oxford University Press, 2016), pp. 88–109; Jeffrey B. Nugent, 'Does Labor Law Reform Offer an Opportunity for Reducing Arab Youth Unemployment?', in *Young Generation Awakening: Economics, Society, and Policy on the Eve of the Arab Spring*, edited by Edward A. Sayre and Tarik M. Yousef (Oxford: Oxford University Press, 2016), pp. 188–203. There is an impressive study on populism by Christian Lekon, 'United States Populism from Reform to Reaction 1880s–1920: Myths in the Writing of Ignatiss Donnelly, Thomas E. Watson and William Jennings Bryan' (forthcoming monograph). For my understanding of Bahraini youth, I am indebted to Ali Akbar Bushehri and our frequent discussions since 2015, as well as to Alaa Alabed. National Archives, London, BW144, British Council: Registered Files, Persian Gulf, 1947–80.

patronage networks greased by oil revenues explains the resilience of dynastic monarchies in the Gulf. I would argue that the state in Bahrain from the 1870s through to the present has produced various responses to the threats to its survival. The responses might be understood in terms of E. P. Thompson's *Whigs and Hunters*, the paradox of plebeian loyalty to a legal order greatly nuanced in favour of the ruling class. The core of capitalist relations in Bahrain, from the days of pearling in the nineteenth century through to the era of oil, was protected by the rule of law and belief in democratic institutions. In Thompson, an oppressed population remains willing to appeal to authoritarian institutions. So, too, in Bahrain, despite the Al-Khalifah regime constantly altering the constitution to their advantage, the people showed patience, although they had their own customs and autonomous power through religion, rituals, and ethnic and sectarian structures. Seymour Martin Lipset argues that there is a linear path to the attainment of democracy, through education, urbanization, industrialization, and political mobilization.[60] But in contrast, in Bahrain after independence, economic development has consolidated authoritarianism. Neither has the wealthiest state in the region, Saudi Arabia, been characterized by cosmopolitanism, freedom, the rule of law, or a transition to democracy. But the authoritarian states here are vastly different. Cultural and religious factions in Bahrain have constrained the state's authoritarianism while Saudi Arabia has chosen a fragmenting conservatism.

Authoritarianism is far less rigid in Bahrain. It is the product of tribalism and the patriarchy of Islam, reinforced by the insecurity of a Sunni ruling family in a Shi'ite- dominated state. The political importance of these identities is further driven by the historical conflicts between Shia Iran and Sunni Saudi Arabia. Alongside tribalism and religion, the state had an economic dependence, on pearling in the nineteenth century and oil in the twentieth century. These economic and political linkages create a fragility that prompts the ruling oligarchy to resort to protective authoritarianism.[61]

The Kamrava, Lipset, and Sharabi argument that the Middle East as a region does not possess the social or cultural pre-requisites necessary for

---

[60] Seymour Martin Lipset, 'Some Social Requisites of Democracy: Economic Development and Political Legitimacy', *American Political Science Review*, vol. 53, no. 1 (1959), p. 84. Michael Hudson draws attention to economic development as 'the engine of social mobilization' and the path to democracy: Michael Hudson, *Arab Politics: The Search for Legitimacy* (New Haven, CT: Yale University Press, 1977), p. 126.

[61] Mehran Kamrava, *Politics and Society in the Third World* (London: Routledge, 1993), pp. 121, 136; Hisham Sharabi, *Neopatriarchy* (Oxford: Oxford University Press, 1988), pp. 7, 31; Roy R. Andersen, Robert F. Seibert, and Jon G. Wagner, *Politics and Change in the Middle East: Sources of Conflict and Accommodation* (Hoboken, NJ: Prentice Hall, 6th ed., 2001), p. 151.

democratization is provocative.[62] It fails to recognize the individuality of states such as Bahrain and Kuwait, which are radically different from Saudi Arabia and the UAE.[63] In Bahrain, the monopoly of the Al-Khalifah family in the cabinet, bureaucracy, and in the military, and above all the oil wealth held within the family and their associates, provides a cohesive loyalty that renders any opposition weak. There were divisions within the royal family, but they did not seriously undermine the institution of a monarchic state. Michael Herb rightly attributes the fear of Islamists and the difficulties in understanding terror and jihadism to the reinforcement of the authoritarian state. He also argues that, in the long term, these monarchies could negotiate a solution through elected assemblies. However, Bahrain has shown that elections can be manipulated by the state. Even when sectarian, secular, and class-motivated parties formed coalitions to contest elections in 2000, 2006, and 2014, they were manipulated by the state. Al-Khalifah can exploit split identities to undermine the opposition in elections. The Islamists and secular parties did not concede defeat. Rather, they resorted to a dignified exit through a boycott. Consequently, it is not inter-elite and inter-class conflicts that hinder democratization but fears of Iran and of radical, violent Islamism. The Islamists in Bahrain are not an obstacle to democracy. The obstacle is fear of collapse, as in Egypt, Syria, Yemen, and Algeria after 2011. Lisa Anderson has argued that there is a 'historical precedent that is indicative of the monarchy's flexible nature—which allows a top down democratization model of political pacts while preserving the ruling elites.'[64] In Bahrain it is the legal codes that underpin progress. In its ambition to advance as the financial hub of the Middle East, Bahrain used the transnational common and civil law to expand its offshore banking into the UK, Ireland, and the US. Cosmopolitan ideals and pluralism created tolerance and respect between opposing groups

[62] Martin Seymour, 'The Social Requisites pf Democracy Revisited', American Sociological Review, 59, 1 (1994), pp. 1-22; Mehran Kamrava, The Political Economy of the Persian Gulf. New York: Columbia University Press, 2012; Hisham Sharabi, The Next Arab Decade: Alternative Futures. Abingdon: Routledge, 2019.

[63] Edward Said, Orientalism (New York: Vintage, 1979), pp. 3, 12; Martin Kramer, Ivory Towers on Sand: The Failure of Middle Eastern Studies in America (Washington, DC: Washington Institute for Near East Policy, 2001), p. 29; Mathieu Kissin, 'Explaining the Failure of Political Liberalization in the Persian Gulf and Assessing the Prospects for Democratization: The Case of Bahrain', 11 December 2007: https://ssrn.com/abstract=2338947, 26, posted 11 October 2013.

[64] Lisa Anderson, 'Absolutism and the Resilience of Monarchy in the Middle East', Political Science Quarterly, vol. 106, no. 1 (1991), pp. 1, 2. (See earlier sections in this chapter on elections in Bahrain under King Hamad from 2000 to 2014.) Michael Herb, 'Islamist Movements and the Problem of Democracy in the Arab World', Paper delivered to the MESA Annual Conference, November 2005; Suzanne Karstedt, 'Democracy, Values, and Violence: Paradoxes, Tensions and Comparative Advantages of Liberal Inclusion', The Annals of the American Academy of Political and Social Science, vol. 605, no. 1 (May 2006), p. 58; Joseph Kostiner (ed.), Middle East Monarchies: The Challenge of Modernity (Boulder, CO: Lynne Rienner, 2000), p. 56.

in politics and society. This in turn created a more humane form of authoritarianism in Bahrain, although repressive action by the police and security
services does persist. Instrumental in this harsh repression was Sheikh Khalifa bin Salman, the world's longest serving prime minister, from 1971 to
2020. Though pro-Western and an Anglophile, he resisted political liberalization, while seeking economic diversification and economic modernization,
notably through the construction of the King Fahd Causeway and Bahrain
Financial Harbour. Oil revenues flowing into Bahrain from Saudi Arabia and
Kuwait financed the creation of a modernized bureaucracy and a modern
economy, popularizing the monarchy further with non-tax incentives.[65] King
Hamad was able to retain his authority in the face of divisions with Prince
Salman and with the Prime Minister. The ability of Hamad to build and maintain complex patronage networks without seriously alienating any group was
particularly impressive. That success is captured by Joseph Kostiner, when he
draws attention to the 'ability of a leading family—a dynasty—to form a coalition among various social segments, drawing on earlier monarchical legacies,
by using bargaining methods'.[66]

Gregory Gause attributes the success of monarchies in the Gulf to oil revenues. This is certainly true of Bahrain, for oil has sustained institutions
and economic development. The monarchy has large revenues and generous welfare systems.[67] And as oil revenues have receded, Bahrain has sought
economic diversification. The emphasis on Bahrain's authoritarian state has
tended to obscure the fluidity of state power and the legal order. Power was
not one-sided and many interests, both Islamic and secular, challenged the
Al-Khalifah dynasty. This complexity contrasts with Syria where the inter-
connecting religious challenges had poor institutional, bureaucratic, and
legal bases.

Bahrain's Cosmopolitanism and Liberalism

Having outlined in detail the institutional differences within the authoritarianism of monarchies in the Middle East, it is clear that what distinguishes
Bahrain is its heritage of law and bureaucracy arising from the informal

---

[65] Interview with Ali Akbar Bushehri and access to Bushehri Archives; Michael Herb, 'Princes and
Parliaments in the Arab World', *Middle East Journal*, vol. 58, no. 3 (2004), p. 2.

[66] Kostiner (ed.), *Middle East Monarchies*, p. 5; Anderson, 'Absolutism and the Resilience of Monarchy
in the Middle East', pp. 1, 2.

[67] F. Gregory Gause III, *Oil Monarchies: Domestic and Security Challenges in the Arab Gulf States* (New
York: Council on Foreign Relations Press, 1994), pp. 42–118.

empire and the grace of oil capital flows and rapid commercialization, including the creation of a global Islamic finance. Also, the regime is sustained to a degree by the GCC, as in the 2011 military intervention. The American military presence, too, provides support. But above all it is the moderate character of the Muslim Brotherhood that is crucial in preserving stable party politics in Bahrain.

I will next outline another significant feature of the resilience of the Sunni monarchy in Bahrain. First is political ethnicity, a Sunni–Shi'ite trait in the Gulf that provides a concept of community and religious network. Second, Sunni hegemony in the Gulf provides a strong incentive to avoid conflict. This stable community has been sustained by long-distance trade and economic expansion that strengthens the state, for commercial integration and business alliances with powerful Shi'ite merchants, the Kanoos and Safar families, reinforce that stability. Thus, legal traditions and rapid economic growth promote confidence in the state, particularly when neighbours are in chaos, especially after the Arab Spring of 2011. The economic roots in religion are captured in peaceful Sunni–Shi'ite relations. Hence, economic shifts promote political integration far more rapidly. The poor Shi'ites protest but cultural integration held firm through regional autonomy and the power of the ulama and Ja'fari jurisprudence. Sunni youth collaborated with Shi'ite farmers and fishermen. The flow of capital resources favoured identification with the state, which retained a monopoly over commerce. Thus, one can chart the process of integration of sovereign authority and social hierarchies that shaped a distinct form of authoritarianism. The monarchy under Hamad was created as a hereditary institution dedicated to social order, while Hamad made political gestures of parliamentary politics and promised a return to the 1973 constitution, which provided for a unicameral legislature. But the 2002 constitution put greater power in the hands of the monarch, with a bicameral legislature in which the elected and the royal appointees were given equal authority. As it was, economic growth absorbed the upheavals of the Arab Spring without the political revolution or social breakdown that occurred in much of the Middle East. While Bahrain was clearly not a functioning democracy, the diverse political parties were able to pressure the state to create and sustain the legislature. The populists were promised political reform, increased employment, and greater access to education and skills training. These commitments resolved some of the tensions between the state, on the one hand, and the youth and vulnerable Shi'ites, on the other. Legal entitlements and religious identity calmed the activists. But sovereignty lay with the monarch.

Bahrain also pursued a secular culture. In parts of Bahrain such as Manama, liberal cosmopolitanism was sustained, as indicated by greater economic diversification and increased tourism and leisure services. Economic diversification strengthened cohesion despite increasing economic inequalities. And increasing economic and commercial integration strengthened the monarchy while sustaining liberalism. The powerful influence of the consumer culture encouraged social fluidity and this assisted monarchic stability. A unique sovereignty and the primacy of secular over religious institutions mark modern Bahrain.

A Radical Comparison: The Ba'athist Authoritarian Republic in Syria from 1963 to the Present—Contentious Salafis, Ulama, Charities, and Transnationalism

The main drivers in modern Syrian politics and society have been the power politics of Salafism, the role of the ulama and opposition movements in the aftermath of the Gulf War 1990–91, and the increasing violence following the Arab Spring of 2011. An authoritarian republican government in Syria had been challenged by Salafism with intra-regional links since 1963. The Syrian Muslim Brotherhood, established in 1946, had put religion to the fore, through educational institutions and Islamic charities built on tribal and merchant networks. They threatened Ba'athist power and were exiled after the insurrection of 1982. The power of two cities, Damascus and Allepo, further threatened the state.

The vast difference between Syria and Bahrain derives from the dominance of religion in Syria. The religious shaykhs, although often experiencing dramatic change, retained power as the 'old houses of knowledge', until the cultural transformations brought by Western-based educational institutions just before the First World War.[68] These retreating religious dynasties were followed by an incursion of merchants and ulamas, overlapping to form influential regional clusters. The period after the First World War therefore saw the evolution of a religious hierarchy and jurisdictional complexity. For centuries, Damascus had received refugees and migrants from Palestine (during the Crusades), then Kurds, followed by Caucasians from the eighteenth century and Albanians in the twentieth century. The most dramatic change within the religious hierarchy came with the French invasion of Algeria in

[68] Thomas Pierret, *Religion and State in Syria: Sunni Ulama from Coup to Revolution* (Cambridge: Cambridge University Press, 2013), pp. 26–7.

the 1830s. This led to North Africans exerting religious influence in Damascus. In brief, Syria was marked by the co-existence of religious groups with separate legal authorities, unlike Bahrain with its identifiable Sunni–Shi'a identities. Two Algerians, Emir 'Abd al-Qadir (1807–82) and Tahir al-Jaza'iri (1852–1920) introduced local reforms, while new forms of Sufism became prominent. This period also saw the emergence of a more powerful politicized group of Moroccans, in which Makki al-Kittani (1890–1973), whose father was head of the League of Ulama and who represented the World Islamic League, was prominent.[69]

These new religious elites had to reconcile themselves to increasing secularization on the part of some of the clergy. One member of the Atasi family, who monopolized the position of mufti in Homs from 1553 to 1984, was the last Sunni President, the Ba'thist physician Nur al-Din (1929–92). Arguably more important was the loss of the awqaf (charitable endowments) which were a crucial source of local hegemony and status. The ulama in the pre-2011 period typically exhibited an amalgam of religious and bourgeois ethical ideology. They valued self-employment and were disciplined for hard work and success in the professions. They saw that their prosperity sustained generosity towards the underprivileged members of society. Muslim clerics were adjusted to capitalism through the development of ethical institutions and Islamic finance. In the Sunni tradition, wealth was ethically secured and morally neutral. Even the Sufi-oriented ulama defined asceticism as the route to spending money 'in the path of God'.[70] The partial nationalization of awqaf had also led to ulamas being excluded from the judiciary, including the religious courts. Under the French Mandate, a degree in secular law was compulsory for judges. The new hybrid order struggled with the challenges posed by religion and its charitable institutions.

The religious endowments derived their economic power from alliances with local merchants. This enabled them to finance mosques, Islamic schools, and welfare societies. The dependence of the clergy on merchants, principally local entrepreneurs with small and medium-sized enterprises, increased their independence from the state. In strategic terms, this led to an increase in charities, particularly in the twenty-first century. In Damascus many of these merchant-ulama clusters were members of the Zayd movement. For

[69] Pierret, *Religion and State in Syria*, p. 27; David Dean Commins, 'Wahhabis, Sufis and Salafis in Early Twentieth Century Damascus', in *Guardians of Faith in Modern Times: 'Ulama' in the Middle East*, edited by Meir Hatina (Leiden: Brill, 2009), pp. 231–46.
[70] Thomas Pierret, 'Merchant Background, Bourgeois Ethics: The Syrian Ulama and Economic Liberalization', in *Syria from Reform to Revolt: Culture, Society and Religion*, edited by Christa Salamandra and Leif Stenberg (Syracuse, NY: Syracuse University Press, 2015), pp. 131–2, 136.

the Syrians, 'ulama' piety and wealth were aligned to provide religious free-dom. However, between 1946 and 1963, Islamic socialism was popularized by the Muslim Brotherhood. This was not nurtured through class identity but was a response to the growing strength of the communists, Ba'thists, and Nasserites. The close ties between clergy and the merchant community are also part of a long-entrenched Sunni hostility to the state, stigmatized as a rapacious power in the economy. This distrust of the Ba'thists after 1970 was further driven by the latter's embezzlement of public funds. The clerics also accepted the nationalization of banks and large corporations but resented any incursion by the state into private SMEs. Ironically, the ulama had earlier, in the 1960s, also opposed the socialist measures of the Ba'thist regime and promoted the laissez-faire policies of the private sector. This was bred out of fear that an absolutist regime would use the economy for social control.[71] In addition, after 1963 the Muslim Brotherhood followed the clerics by aban-doning their particular form of Islamic socialism. This continued into 2004. The Muslim Brotherhood thus sought private capitalism to thwart totalitari-anism. Their seeking of an alliance with private capitalism to resolve tensions inside the Islamic groups provoked the Ba'th party in 2005 to announce the introduction of a 'social market economy', a programme that included the state creating three Islamic banks, the International Bank of Syria, al-Sham Bank, and al-Baraka Bank.

The Syrian Ulama's support for more humane capitalism thus allowed for a more harmonious co-existence with the ruling classes. The outcome was also a link with global ethical Islamic capitalism, its perceived superiority being vindicated during the Global Financial Crisis of 2008. The growing influence of neoliberal ideology in the wider Arab world is seen in preachers such as the Egyptian 'Amr Khalid, Kuwaiti Tariq Suwaydan, the Saudi 'Aid al-Qarni, and the Syrian 'Abd al-Karim Bakkar, identifying the formation of a new global order. The attempt to create a non-state moral and religious authority was joined by secular specialists in neuro-linguistic programming (NLP) in per-sonal development. This would have been alarming to the Syrian regime, and perhaps led it to create its own secular repression to counter the rising pop-ulism. The assassination of the popular Syrian cleric from Aleppo, Mahmud Ghul Aghasi, alias Abu al-Qa'qa', in September 2007 was a mystery as he had close ties to Bashar al-Assad. However, he had been highly critical of police treatment of poor agriculturalists.[72] Viewed broadly, in seeking an auton-omy sustained by their connections with private entrepreneurs and less with

---

[71] Pierret, 'Merchant Background, Bourgeois Ethics', p. 139.
[72] Pierret, 'Merchant Background, Bourgeois Ethics', pp. 142–3.

the state, the clerics sought both protection from Bashar al-Assad and growing transnational links. The Syrian ulama saw socialism as a form of social
control by the state. Consequently, from the 1950s through to 2011, they
pursued an ethical form of capitalism, through charities, the awqaf, religious
institutions, and Islamic finance, and endorsed non-violent protest against a
repressive, corrupt state and crony capitalism. In this split from the regime,
private merchants were their financiers. But the clergy was not wholly united.
Some clerics supported the regime and its policy of economic liberalization
as it was of substantial economic benefit to them.

This ulama–merchant nexus, although tolerated by the state, remained a
thorn in its side. From the 1990s, the state in Syria was strained by rapid population growth and weak economic structures. It thus struggled to maintain
its legitimacy and power. It feared the increasing closeness of local religious
influences and political power, shown most clearly by the Zayd movement
and its control of powerful charities in Damascus. The 'charitable empire'
run by Zayd was a threat to the state. Zayd had concentrated for decades
on mosque building while proselytizing at the grassroots level, providing
education and building ties with merchants. In contrast, the Ba'th regime
lacked the religious and material resources needed to secure control of the
people.[73] From October 2008, the government tightened control, although
there were rifts between Bashar al-Assad and his brother. The drought from
2006 to 2010 and the 2008 Global Financial Crisis had further undermined
the authoritarian state. Bashar al-Assad concentrated on the creation of a
social market economy while retaining his existing patronage networks. The
reforms included a coalition of military–commercial interests between 2004
and 2005. The creation of private banks from December 2000 was financed by
Lebanese banks. Islamic finance and trade and investment with the Greater
Arab Free Trade Area increased. The privatization of state resources in fact
supported the state. The plunder of the economy, first through nationalization then by privatization, enabled powerful capitalists to create corporations
from the state sector, blurring the distinction between public and private corporations. Rami Makhlouf, a cousin of the President, rose to become the main
private investor in the state-initiated social market economy. His skilled and
ruthless acquisitions in industries ranging from oil, tobacco, banking, high-
tech, media, airways, and tourism met with little resistance. Rami Makhlouf

[73] Thomas Pierret and Kjetil Selvik, 'Limits of Authoritarian Upgrading in Syria: Private Welfare, Islamic Charities, and the Rise of the Zayd Movement', *International Journal of Middle East Studies*, vol. 41, no. 4 (2009).

and his 70 entrepreneurs held control through two holding companies with a capitalization of US$350 million.[74]

The President, Bashar al-Assad, used IT and telecommunication companies to expand his networks and to draw scientists into his military and technological interests. These provided vital intelligence for the military, controlled by the state. They were efficient forms of political and technological control, essential for Bashar al-Assad to maintain his authoritarian rule. Between 2005 and 2010 he also exploited the charities' networks through NGOs that were part of the state apparatus called GONGOs. These were funded by the state to concentrate on rural development and the empowerment of women. The Syrian Trust for Development (STFD) was under the first lady, Asma al-Assad. These institutions provided education, training, and loans to create a social market economy.[75] The Syrian Young Entrepreneur Foundation (SYE) had access to funds to develop business and to strengthen contacts with private banks. These measures were targeted to where the state was vulnerable, in an attempt to regain control through the creation of a civil society. This was a challenge to the powerful private charities in Damascus and Aleppo, the cities with advanced mercantile sectors with transnational links. Upgrading the state through civic measures, through technology and intelligence networks, as well as through the co-option of the military, was driven by rivalry with the private charities in the two cities. But Rami Makhlouf's commercial power now emerged as a threat to Bashar al-Assad and the Ba'th Party. The Syrian case demonstrated the limits of privatization, which had led to monopolies in the hands of Rami Makhlouf and not Bashar al-Assad. The relationship between commercial patronage and the regime weakened. The state also faced the power of the Salafis and Islamic institutions, the Awqaf, and Islamic finance. This was prominently seen in the Arab Spring protests of 2011. The irony is that Bashar al-Assad introduced technological advance and empowered private corporations to secure his authority: and yet each of these reforms posed a serious challenge to the Ba'th Party and to himself. The result was a return to the Syrian tradition of repression.

Has Syria been a troubled country throughout its modern history? First the Great Syrian Revolt of 1925 under the French Mandate, then the 1948

---

[74] Caroline Donati, 'The Economics of Authoritarian Upgrading in Syria: Liberalization and the Reconfiguration of Economic Networks', in *Middle East Authoritarianisms: Governance, Contestation, and Regime Resilience in Syria and Iran*, edited by Steven Heydemann and Renoud Leenders (Stanford, CA: Stanford University Press, 2013), pp. 35–60.

[75] Beatrice Hibou, *Privatising the State* (London: Hurst, 2004); Donati, 'The Economics of Authoritarian Upgrading in Syria', pp. 44–6.

Syrian involvement in the Arab–Israeli War, the Suez Crisis of 1956, the military coup of September 1961, followed by the October 1973 involvement of Syria and Egypt in the Yom Kippur War against Israel, the preceding January 1973 Muslim Brotherhood uprising, the Hama Massacre of 1982, then Syria's participation in the Gulf War of 1990 in the US-led coalition against Saddam Hussein, and finally the Syrian Civil War following the Arab Spring in 2011.[76] Bahrain, in contrast, saw two centuries of Al-Khalifah rule and a peaceful independence from British control. How is Syria's fearful captivity to violence to be explained?

Bahrain was distinguished first by a specialized pearling industry and then by oil from the 1930s. When oil declined, it diversified economically, notably becoming the financial hub for the oil-wealthy Gulf states. These transitions were contingent upon Bahrain's regional and international links, both commercial and political, for example membership of the Gulf Cooperation Council. Thus, Bahrain and Syria inhabit very different spaces, exposure to contrasting forces, and national economic fortunes. Bahrain appears to be in the vanguard of Middle East economic vitality with diminished political conflict.

Revival and Decline in Syria

The reorganization of patronage networks under the impact of privatization eroded the loyalist connections of Bashar al-Assad. It resulted in the creation of predatory networks, including those centred on his cousin and other relatives and their cronies, who extracted vital resources and challenged the Ba'th Party's political control. The Ba'th Party was corrupt and increasingly fragile. Moreover, Islamic institutions such as Islamic banks were attracting diasporic funds as well as local investment. Aleppo's SMEs and small urban industrialists, seeking to avoid the corrupt private banks, traded in cash, and the regime was increasingly fearful of this autonomous Islamic sector. Moreover, the wealthy entrepreneurs nurtured by the state, as powerful landlords, created tension among local tribal elites from the north of Raqqa and to the south. The 2007 parliamentary elections demonstrated the regime's loss of control over rural areas. The welfare state had been in decline for some time, weakening the social pact that had guaranteed stability. It was now confronted by social and political anger. By fostering a diverse range of entrepreneurs

---

[76] Rifaat Ali al-Assad, a younger brother of Hafiz al-Assad, is said to have been the commanding officer responsible for the Hama Massacre in 1982. But this is disputed and other members of the Assad family are incriminated.

to control production, trade, and finance, the regime had simply allowed those entrepreneurs to create personal wealth and status. The Islamic charities had followed the same path, for the Ulama–merchant clusters, including the Jama'at Zayd, created a wealthy economic base within the Sunni majority.[77] The state's reform towards socio-economic liberalization had failed to develop a path towards democracy but instead was confronted by challenges from Makhlouf and his cronies, and above all from the Salafis and other Islamic groups. Bashar al-Assad then resorted to authoritarianism, following in the footsteps of his father. Bashar al-Assad's return to authoritarianism was further driven by the shrinking communal base of the military, as recruits, who were largely Alawite, became disaffected. The rural Sunnis who had earlier dominated the military were now subordinate to the regime's Alawite elites. Sectarian divisions widened, and many of the disaffected defected to the Free Syrian Army to defend civilians from the repressive regime.[78] Syrian ethnic and religious division now gave vent to Kurdish riots and Salafis participation in the Arab Spring protests in Homs in 2011 and 2012. The Republican Guard, mainly composed of Alawites, was sent to quell these protests.

Increasing the power of authoritarianism through private merchants and charities, the latter both state-owned and private, created new challenges. Syrian authoritarian corporatism was also frustrated by wealth-seeking relatives and cronies. The structure was unstable from the outset. Economic interests blended with political interests to create instability. Hence Bashar al-Assad achieved a weakening of his control rather than an upgrading of power. In Syria, new networks competed with the old, retarding the growth of a global market. 'Thus the 2011 Uprising … is the ultimate expression of resistance by Syrians to the economic and social costs of reconfiguring authoritarian governance in Syria: it has involved populations that have been excluded from economic success, faced new patterns of predatory redistribution of wealth. What we are also seeing is an attempt to redefine or to overthrow, from below, a ruling coalition that has become a minority.'[79]

The Authoritarian State, Salafism, the Economy, and the Aftermath of the Arab Spring

A spectacular rise of Salafism followed the Arab Spring of 2011. By October 2013, Sunni–Alawite polarization was pronounced, and Salafi networks

[77] Pierret and Selvik, 'Limits of Authoritarian Upgrading in Syria'.
[78] Donati, 'The Economics of Authoritarian Upgrading in Syria', pp. 56–8.
[79] Donati, 'The Economics of Authoritarian Upgrading in Syria', p. 60.

dominated villages, provincial towns, and rural suburbs of Damascus and Aleppo. This coincided with the growing influence of Salafi networks in Iraq and the Arabian Peninsula. Within the Salafi networks, the conflicting political orientations of jihadism, political Haraki, and quietist Salafism shaped the insurgency and increasingly challenged the authoritarian state of Bashar al-Assad. Salafis embraced a military agenda that involved the creation of military forces and projected power across borders.[80] The rebel groups included the Jihadi al-Nusra, the 'Salafi lite' Haraki Syrian Islamic Front, the Haraki Syria Islamic Liberation Front, and the 'quietist' Front for Authenticity and Development. They spent 2013 alternately merging or splitting within themselves. Al-Nusra was ultra-Islamist, sectarian, and anti-Western, an organization made up predominantly of foreign guerrillas engaged in suicide bombings against government offices in densely populated areas. The Syrian Islamic Front, established in 2012, was a coalition of groups from different provinces in Syria. It also had Kuwaiti supporters. The Syrian Islamic Liberation Front (SILF) was different from the Syrian Islamic Front (SIF) in a number of respects. First it had different forms of authority and leadership in each city, Idlib, Damascus, Homs, and Aleppo. The SILF was more moderate than the SIF. It was more conciliatory towards the Alawites. It adopted a similar position to that of the Muslim Brotherhood on the implementation of Shari'ah and on support for a strong electoral system. SILF also promoted the Syrian National Coalition. Its pragmatism was inspired by the Qatar–Turkey cooperation. SILF secured most of its funds from the Gulf-based Haraki Salafis. Its supporters were not the Kuwaitis but the Syrian cleric Muhammad Surur Zayn al-'Ab'in of Haraki Salafism. He had been in exile in Saudi Arabia in 1965 but had then moved to Kuwait, Britain, Jordan, and in 2013 to Qatar. He constructed an integrated Salafi doctrine while preserving the Muslim Brotherhood's political interests.[81] Zayn al-'Abdidin exploited his regional networks to raise funds for the Syrian opposition. The SILF also maintained close links with the Sham Islamic Committee, a missionary society with leaders in Saudi Arabia and Bahrain. In Syria, it was funded partly by the Qatari 'id Charitable Foundation, a major patron of global Haraki Salafism. It maintained a moderate ideology, unlike the Kuwaiti Harakis. It remained quietist in opposing the 2011 uprising but then changed and joined the Syrian rebels. The constant shifting of loyalties and the support

---

[80] Thomas Pierret, 'Salafis at War in Syria: Logics of Fragmentation and Realignment 2017'. HAL Id:hal 01753795: https:/hal.archives-ouvertes.fr/hal-01753795. submitted 29 March 2018.
[81] Stephane Lacroix, *Awakening Islam: The Politics of Religious Dissent in Contemporary Saudi Arabia* (Cambridge, MA: Harvard University Press, 2011); SILF Facebook Page, 9 March 2013.

for extremism created still greater instability.[82] One opposition group, led by Khalid al-Hammad, a Syrian cleric, was based in the Emirates. It had to rely on a heterogeneous alliance of former jihadis who had repented and now sought alternative methods of revival. It attracted defectors from Assad's army and tribesmen from the eastern province of Deir ez-Zor. FAD had an identity crisis, supporting the flying of the Syrian flag while its closeness to Riyadh Salai factions raised suspicions that its 'Awakening Councils' were similar to those established by the United States in Iraq to fight ISIS a decade earlier.[83]

The SIF and SILF merged into the Islamic Front in 2013, a response to growing radicalism and marking increasing sectarian division. The Alawite militia, the National Defence Army, and the involvement of Lebanese Hezbollah to recapture al-Qusayr near Homs marked the extreme militarization of the conflict and the deepest social upheaval in Syria since the Ba'ath's 'revolution from above' in the 1960s.[84] The Sunni bourgeoisie of Damascus and Aleppo felt threatened by the Bashar al-Assad regime from late 2012. Many clerics opted to go into exile, driven out by chaos, terror, dislocation, and the constant fear of international intervention. Throughout this violence, the wealthy maintained a neutral stance.[85]

Political and religious polarization, as well as constantly shifting alliances, posed an unending struggle for the al-Assad regime. The inter-sectarian conflict added to Bashar al-Assad's paranoia. Even Assad's brother and cousins turned disloyal. The First Lady's corruption and greed for glamour only added to the alienation of the masses from Bashar al-Assad. There were also American pressures. In contrast, Bahrain has American military bases but there was no threat of American meddling. Syrian instability was exacerbated by the absence of defined institutions, a bureaucracy, and a secular institutional framework to meet the diverse threats. Syria had abandoned the ulama, who remained outside the state: in other words, religious leadership could not be coordinated through a religious bureaucracy. The radical religious, social, and cultural movements from the 1960s had converted the ulama in Syria into a more influential force. The blossoming of the charitable sector and mass media added to their power. The civil war in Syria was

[82] Pierret, 'Salafis at War in Syria', p. 27.

[83] Pierret, 'Salafis at War in Syria', pp. 24–8.

[84] Thomas Pierret, 'The Syrian Baath Party and Sunni Islam: Conflicts and Connivance', *Middle East Brief*, no. 77 (2014), pp. 1–7; International Crisis Group, 'Tentative Jihad: Syria's Fundamentalist Opposition', *Middle East Report*, no. 131, 12 October 2012.

[85] Thomas Pierret, 'Les oulémas: une hégémonie religieuse ébranlée par la revolution', in *Pas de printémps pour la Syrie*, edited by Francois Burgat and Bruno Paoli (Paris: La Découverte, 2013); Aron Lund, 'Syria's Salafi Insurgents: The Rise of the Syrian Islamic Front', Swedish Institute for International Affairs, UI Brief 17, 17 March 2013.

principally a conflict of economic interests and religious power. In contrast Bahrain had religious autonomy in its regions, with independent Ja'fari courts and leaders. The Ashura festival was a powerful symbol of Shi'ite autonomy, particularly in rural Bahrain. Bahrain had less religious anxiety, resistance, and protest. In Syria, the ruling oligarchy were Alawites who felt socially distanced even from Iranian Shi'ism and maintained a secular identity. But secularization did not lead to a liberal democratic public sphere, for religious division inexorably pushed Bashar al-Assad 'not to a religiously informed cultural identity but to politics of cultural nationalism'.[86] In Bahrain, the ascent of King Hamad in March 1999 restored stability that enabled the country to cope with the turmoil during the Arab Spring. Economic diversification ensured economic growth and viability within a global economy. Throughout, Bahrain's cosmopolitanism and liberalism had to be sustained in the global push.

This account of contemporary Syria suggests why a republican state is more vulnerable to breakdown for it pushes for control of all sectors of the state. The challenges to the authority of the ulama, the loss of regional autonomy in Damascus and Aleppo, and the brutality of the regime led to devastation. In contrast, Bahrain's political stability arose from the dynamics of oil and of global Islamic finance.

---

[86] See Ayesha Jalal, 'Exploding Communalism: The Politics of Muslim Identity in South Asia', in *Nationalism, Democracy and Development: State and Politics in India*, edited by Sugata Bose and Ayesha Jalal (Delhi: Oxford University Press, 1997), p. 79.

9
Transnational Trading Networks

The Role of the Pearling Industry in Mercantile Power and in the Growth of Port Cities

To understand the importance of oil as a tool of statecraft and in the rise of mercantile power in Bahrain it is necessary to explore the migration of Utub and their allies from Najd, from the late seventeenth century, and their presence in the pearling industry. They founded Muharraq, the largest pearling town in the Gulf by the 1820s, and Hidd, also on Muharraq Island, the second prominent pearling city.[1] The pearling boom from the late nineteenth century to the early twentieth century was secured by the maritime treaties imposed by the British, beginning with the General Treaty of Peace in 1820, to suppress plunder, piracy, and slavery.[2] A further series of treaties in the 1880s and 1890 imposed British protectorate status upon Bahrain, as well as on Oman, the Trucial Coast, and Kuwait. Bahrain had the largest pearling fleet in the Gulf and accounted for more than half of total pearl exports from the region. Between 1900 and 1912 the value of Bahrain's pearl exports rose sixfold, principally through rising sales to France. Bahrain's wealth was evident in Manama's expansion and in the rise of Persian merchant elites and trading networks. Leading members of the Al-Khalifa family were pearl merchants. Pearling sustained a mobile population, shifting alliances, and a constantly changing political and commercial environment. Bahrain retained stability through the loyalty of its pearl merchants and divers, secured by a decision not to impose taxes or customs duties.[3] The relatively low proportion of men engaged in pearling encouraged diversification into agriculture in order to provide food security. One-third of the inhabitants of Sitra, Nabih Salih, and Muharraq were pearl divers.

---

[1] Robert A. Carter, *Sea of Pearls: Seven Thousand Years of the Industry that Shaped the Gulf* (London: Arabian Publishing, 2012), p. 111.
[2] Carter, *Sea of Pearls*, p. 141.
[3] Carter, *Sea of Pearls*, pp. 157–63.

Islam and Capitalism in the Making of Modern Bahrain. Rajeswary Ampalavanar Brown, Oxford University Press.
© Rajeswary Ampalavanar Brown (2023). DOI: 10.1093/oso/9780192874672.003.0009

Western merchants crowded into Bahrain. French firms but also business elites in Bombay rose to finance the pearl divers, the latter supplying the Indian princely market, such as the realm of the Maharaja of Baroda. Bombay also entered the global pearl trade, with Leonard Rosenthal as the 'Napoleon of Pearls'. In addition, wealthy Arab merchants from the Gulf engaged in pearl trading. A fifth of pearls traded internationally were from Bahrain.[4] Personal capitalism was the main driving force behind the successful family firms of al-Haj Yusuf bin Ahmad Kanoo, Ali bin Ibrahim Al-Zayani, the Saudi merchant Muqbil Abdal-Rahman al-Dhukair, and Al-Haj Abdal-Rahman bin Aydan, who operated from Muharraq in the 1910s.[5] The most significant rivals to Bahrain were Ceylon and India, specifically the Gulf of Manar, but their output was unpredictable. Leonard Rosenthal estimated that at the beginning of the twentieth century, 80 per cent of the world's fine pearls came from the Gulf but by 1905–08 that figure had dropped to 65 per cent.[6] By that time Bahrain accounted for 40 per cent of the world's pearl trade.[7]

The prominent family merchants were also financiers of the pearl trade. Moreover, they often owned the boats. In addition, the European merchant firms provided working capital for the major pearl dealers. Lending was regulated by customary law but also obeyed Shari'ah law. A shares system involved a promise that debt would be repaid. In detail, 20 per cent was subtracted from the gross profits of the owner of the boat: then the costs for food, water, and maintenance of the boat were subtracted, leaving the earnings to be divided among the crew. The owner of the boat finally took 10 per cent of the profits. Those involved were close family and co-religionists, though working in a strictly hierarchical structure, frequently tied into the Al-Khalifa ruling family. That structure and those alliances would, in time, be duplicated in Bahrain's Islamic finance sector.

The pearling industry declined inexorably over the first half of the twentieth century, the victim of changes in fashion and the rise of the cultured pearl, which employed new labour-saving technologies. Loans helped to sustain operations in the short term but provided no long-term security. The decline of the Bahrain pearling industry was dramatic, as noted by Adam Villiers: 'The pearlers lie almost as thick as the discarded shells of empty oysters on a pearling beach—big ships and little ships, jailboots, sambuks, belems, skewes. The shapely timbers of the little craft throw long shadows under the

---

[4] Carter, *Sea of Pearls*, p. 170.
[5] Carter, *Sea of Pearls*, p. 171.
[6] Leonard Rosenthal, *The Kingdom of the Pearl* (London: Nisbet & Co, 1920, reprinted 1984), cited in Carter, *Sea of Pearls*, p. 179.
[7] Carter, *Sea of Pearls*, p. 180.

moon and beautify the beach but they are warped and rotted now and they can sail the seas no more.'[8]

Business in Bahrain: An Historical Audit of Oligarchs and Merchants

Nelida Fuccaro's path-breaking studies have drawn out the links between tribal and regional associations within Bahrain from the fifteenth century onwards, as well as an increasingly important diasporic capitalism.[9] Tribalism enmeshed with increasing urbanism was central to the development of modern economic and sociopolitical ties. In the fifteenth century, the islands of Bahrain were ruled by the al-Jabr family from Najd, with powerful links to Hormuz under Portuguese rule. By the eighteenth century, the al-Madkhur family from Oman governed Bahrain as a dependency of Iran. In 1783, Utub tribes from the Arabian peninsula occupied these islands and this ended Iranian power. Subsequently, within the Utub confederation, the Al-Khalifa family became identified with an increasingly important British presence. There soon evolved a modern state under the British. These political changes took place alongside a vibrant commercial culture, a booming trade in Gulf pearls and then, in the nineteenth century, the exploitation of oil. Until the last decades of the nineteenth century, British interests in Bahrain were mainly economic and Manama was the commercial centre. By agreements in 1880 and in 1892, Bahrain became an informal British colony. British interference in the affairs of Bahrain intensified, creating a power struggle between the Al-Khalifa rulers and the British. An important legacy of this contest was the creation of Manama as a powerful mercantile city under British control.

This commercial development was further driven by the rise of oil-rich Gulf neighbours, Saudi Arabia, Kuwait, Qatar, Oman, and the UAE by 1930. In recent decades, Bahrain's own oil reserves have greatly declined, and it has responded by creating an innovative, competitive financial sector to serve Bahrain's oil-rich neighbours. Bahrain now flourishes as a financial centre, a powerful hub of Islamic finance. In this it has been assisted by the huge flow of oil wealth from the Gulf producers. Gulf oil revenues drove the urbanization and financial development of Bahrain. In the 1980s, Bahrain, using its

---

[8] Alan Villiers, *Sons of Sinbad: An Account of Sailing with the Arabs in their Dhows*. Introduction by W. Facey, Y. Al-Hijji and G. Pundyk (London: Arabian Publishing, 2006), p. 325.
[9] Nelida Fuccaro, 'Understanding the Urban History of Bahrain', *Critique: Critical Middle Eastern Studies*, vol. 17 (2000), pp. 49–81.

offshore banking sector, transferred Gulf financial surpluses into US treasury and North American securities. Important here were the Al-Baraka Banking Group, an investment bank that is both an Islamic bank and a conventional bank, Gulf Finance House, and Ahli United Bank. The ruling families are pervasive in business, while private sector conglomerates are frequently represented in the state apparatus.

Bahrain's aluminium conglomerate ALBA (Aluminium Bahrain) is owned by the Bahrain Mumtalakat Holding Company and Saudi SABIC. In telecommunications, Viva Bahrain is a subsidiary of Saudi telecom but Batelco is fully owned by Bahrain. By 2015, four Gulf telecommunications firms, including Batelco, Zain Ooredoo, and Etisalat, earned 60 per cent of their revenues outside their domestic markets.[10] Many of their international markets were in Arab countries, although Asia and Africa are also targeted. Bahrain's BMMI Group, in food and agriculture, operates supermarkets in Saudi Arabia.

Among the financial institutions, a pan-GCC ownership structure marks Bahrain's offshore banking sector. Gulf capital is mostly drawn from Saudi Arabia and Kuwait. Oil wealth flows into the GCC banks, as they are mainly state-owned and are therefore secure. Banks are closely interlocked through shared directorships. In addition, they often own non-banking subsidiaries, for example in construction, retail, and telecommunications. The Kuwait Government owns 18.1 per cent of Bahrain's Ahli United Bank, 10.1 per cent being held by the Bahrain Government. Interlocking directorships are significant, for example tying together the Bahrain Petroleum Company, the Bahrain Stock Exchange, Ahli United Bank, the Tamdeen Real Estate Company, and Global Omani Development and Investment. The Al-Baraka Banking Group had a stake in the Dallah al Barakh Group.[11] The ABC Islamic Bank and the Ahli United Bank have interlocking directors. Investment banks such as the Al-Baraka Banking Group operate in both Islamic and conventional finance.

Management was often through Gulf private equity firms. In 2015, these firms raised US$1 billion and most were based in the GCC, with owners and board directors drawn from across the Gulf.[12] These private equity firms also had ownership outside the GCC. The rapid growth of private equity firms from the 1990s is related to oil wealth and spillovers from Saudi Arabia, Kuwait, and the UAE. The most powerful firm is UAE-based Abraaj Capital,

[10] Adam Hanieh, *Money, Markets, and Monarchies: The Gulf Cooperation Council and the Political Economy of the Contemporary Middle East* (Cambridge: Cambridge University Press, 2018), p. 89.
[11] Hanieh, Money, Markets, and Monarchies, p. 107.
[12] Adam Hanieh, *Capitalism and Class in the Gulf Arab States* (New York: Palgrave Macmillan, 2011), pp. 140–5; Hanieh, Money, Markets, and Monarchies, p. 109.

worth an estimated US$9 billion. In 2007, it raised US$6 billion but in 2009 it experienced some distress.[13]

How does the GCC link all these regional and global interactions? First, the Arab–Persian hybrid merchant families, the Safars and Kanoos, with their transnationalism through the nineteenth and twentieth centuries, were joined in the 1990s by powerful groups from Saudi Arabia and the UAE, al-Kharafi, Olayan, Al Rajhi, Ghurair, Al Futtaim, and Al Shaya, to create close networks within the authoritarian states of the GCC. Saudi Arabia and the UAE form the apex. Kuwait and Qatar were autonomous zones of capital accumulation, while Oman and Bahrain were dependent on their wealthy neighbours. However, Bahrain outranked these states with its outstanding success in emerging as a financial hub with a liberal interpretation of Islamic finance law. The benefits brought by oil capital flows transformed the economy and in particular banking, creating a globalized economy through international partnerships. The state, employing sovereign wealth funds and its commercial agencies, formed cartels with a compliant merchant class. This is evident in the petrochemical corporations producing and refining oil, real estate developers, telecommunications corporations, and the banks. However, despite a commitment to joint management by state and family and to existing business networks, Bahrain employed professionally intermediated finance both at home and abroad. Overall, the separation between private and public control is vague, as ruling families are major shareholders. But cross-border mergers and listing on stock markets in the US and Ireland provided forms of internationalization in GCC capital markets. FDI brought crucial forms of liberal economic behaviour and thus the GCC possessed dynamic concentrations of industrial clusters in aluminium, cement, and oil refining but also reshaped food production, water, electric power, telecommunications, and transport, particularly air transport.

The roots of this business culture and industry structure can be sought through detailed historical case studies of the pre-eminent merchant families, the Safar family and the Kanoo family.

Transnational Trading Networks

'The coastline of Bahrain, a permeable border, nurtured the coexistence of diverse religious and ethnic communities under local tribal rulers who

---

[13] *MENA Private Equity and Venture Capital Report*, 2015, p. 5; E. McBride, 'The Story behind Abraaj Group's Stunning Rise in Global Private Equity', Forbes, 4 November 2015, https://www.forbes.com/sites/elizabethmacbride/2015/11/04/the-story-behind-abraajs-stunning-rise/?sh=c20be1c20ac7

enjoyed the protection of foreign powers: the Portuguese, the Persians and Omanis, and since the early 19th century the Government of India. The Al-Khalifa family who conquered the islands in 1783 brought in different material cultures, political loyalties and legal traditions which through a long process of strategic negotiation established the pre-eminence of their particularistic Sunni/Bedouin tradition of family rule.'[14] This Sunni-dominated state survives today. Although Britain's informal empire established a framework of politics and of legal pluralism, it was the merchant–ruler relations and the subtle legitimization of Sunni-Shi'a cooperation that drove a dynamic economic evolution in Bahrain, most clearly seen in the growth of Manama, the capital city.

The history of Manama emphasizes its external links, principally with Iran and most of Arabia. External links underpinned its economic vitality in each historical era, as far back as the Portuguese between 1515 and 1521 and the Persians, following the Safavid conquest of Hormuz in 1621. By 1736, Nadir Shah had built a new fort on the southern outskirts of Manama. This was a natural harbour for commercial and naval shipping, and thus attracted immigrants. By the early nineteenth century, the economic evolution of the fort and port in Manama drew it apart from the seat of the tribal power of the Al-Khalifa dynasty in Muharraq. Spatial proximity was a boon to corporate magnates, the Safar and Sharif families and the Kanoo group, providing resources to the ruling Al-Khalifa family.

Customs payments collected in the port remained an important resource for the rulers, and profits from maritime trade, together with the revenues accruing from the agricultural hinterlands of Manama, accounted for virtually the entire income of the Shaykh of Bahrain in the early 1870s. By the beginning of the twentieth century, that income secured the finances of the rulers and stabilized their power.[15] One of the factors most critical in determining the power of the monarchy between 1869 and 1923 was its acquisition of land on the island. This imposed a coercive structure of taxes and corvée on the agricultural population. It also became a principal source of political control by the extended family of the ruler. The Governor of Manama city was a member of Al-Khalifa Shaykh's family. This created rigidity in resource

---

[14] Nelida Fuccaro, 'Mapping the Transnational Community: Persians and the Space of the City in Bahrain, c.1869–1937', in *Transnational Connections in the Arab Gulf*, edited by Madawi al-Rasheed (London: Routledge, 2005), p. 41.

[15] John George Lorimer, *The Gazetteer of the Persian Gulf, Oman and Central Arabia* (Calcutta: Office of the Superintendent Government Printing, 1908; republished Farnborough: Gregg International, 1970), vol. 2, p. 251; 'Administration Report on the Persian Gulf Political Residency and Maskat Political Agency for 1873–74', in *The Persian Gulf Administration Reports 1873–1949* (Gerrards Cross: Archive Editions, 1986), vol. 1, p. 66.

ownership and power, a rigidity that later increased after Bahrain became independent. While the actual collection of these revenues was farmed out to Indian merchants from the late nineteenth century, ultimate control of the revenues was vested in the royal family. The ruler also controlled markets, shops, and warehouses. But the traders with transnational connections were the merchant families, notably the Kanoos. They dominated trade, the money economy, and the construction industry. Between 1894 and 1899, the British Native Agent, Rahim Safar, a member of the prominent Safar family, was distributing cash loans to Shaykh Isa. This economy remained in the hands of powerful merchants. Fuccaro also identifies the support provided by merchant elites as a subtle form of accepting the authority of the Shaykh.[16] In the context of relatively weak institutional safeguards, the merchants and their co-religionists, the Shi'ites, created long-distance networks rooted in the pearl trade. Between 1873 and 1900, the value of pearl exports increased sevenfold.[17] This extensive externalization of the economy sustained the royal family and its ties with powerful merchants. This was not Chandler's personal capitalism but associational economics. It reflects to a degree Granovetter's 'strong embeddedness' perspective on regional business networks.[18]

Manama's prosperity was dependent on its regional links, its economic and commercial expertise, and on immigrant labour. The population was diverse. In 1904, half of its residents, some 25,000, were from Basrah, al-Ahsa, Qatif, Kuwait, Najd, and Iran, with small communities of Indians, Jews, and Europeans.[19] The freedom and power of the merchants were enhanced by the imposition of British extraterritorial jurisdiction over the immigrant communities in 1861, which released them from the power of the Shaykh. The courts established in 1919 applied British Indian law and operated in parallel with Sunni and Shi'i religious courts and with the tribal councils controlled by the ruler.[20] These new institutions for arbitration and mediation in commercial and in civil and criminal disputes through British extraterritorial jurisdiction empowered the merchants.[21]

---

[16] Fuccaro, 'Mapping the Transnational Community'.

[17] Lorimer, The Gazetteer of the Persian Gulf, Oman and Central Arabia, vol. 1, p. 2252.

[18] M. Granovetter, 'Problems of Explanation in Economic Sociology', in Networks and Organizations: Structure, Form and Action, edited by N. Nohria and R. Eccles (Cambridge, MA: Harvard University Press, 1992), p. 5; U. Staber, N. Schaefer, and B. Sharma (ed.), Business Networks: Prospects for Regional Development (Berlin: de Gruyter, 1996).

[19] Lorimer, The Gazetteer of the Persian Gulf, Oman and Central Arabia, vol. 2, p. 1160.

[20] James Onley, The Arabian Frontier of the British Raj: Merchants, Rulers, and the British in the Nineteenth-century Gulf (Oxford: Oxford University Press, 2007), pp. 104–213, 281.

[21] On the history, administration, and records of the court of the Political Agent in Bahrain, see IOR series R/15/3, 'Political Agency, Bahrain: Political Agent's Court, 1913–1948', and its introduction, pp. 107–22.

The reconfiguration of land ownership in favour of merchants created further decline in the rulers' control over Manama. Sale of land and the appropriation of land owned by rulers in return for cash loans provided by wealthy merchants increased the power of the merchants. The Land Registration Act, enforced in 1925, enabled merchants to acquire permanent property rights. The creation of a property market regulated by law and modern institutions weakened the monopoly exercised by the Al-Khalifa Shaykhs. Particularly significant in commercial specialism was the merchants' ownership of land and property located in the suq. To some extent the allegiance to the suq was emotional and psychological, with its roots in local craft, a key identification for local and foreign Persian and Indian merchants. The influx of Persians unseated the existing Indian merchants from 1902.[22] The Persians identified with their places of origin in Iran, and here the Busheris, Shirazis, Farsis, Ahwazis, and Bastekis were pre-eminent too, through their ma'tams and through their marriage links with other rich and powerful merchants. This created a web of capitalist hegemony through religious connections reinforced by privileged access to the British Agency and to the rulers.[23]

The Safar and Sharif families, the rich and influential Ajam Shi'i cluster that emerged in the pre-oil era, enjoyed British support in their international trade. These political connections were first established by Muhammad Ali Safar, who had settled in Bahrain in 1833 as Native Agent for the British Resident in Bushehr, a position then held by the family without interruption until 1900 with the formal establishment of a British Political Agency. The Safar family also maintained a close relationship with Shaikh Isa. Such powerful connections helped the family to consolidate its position in the trade in arms, coffee, rice, dates, and tea. The family also controlled the pearling fleets. It had vast landholdings in southern Iraq and urban properties in Bombay and the Gulf. Its power was contested only by other families like the Kanoos. The powerful family-managed firms were successful because of their multiple industrial and commercial interests and their cosmopolitan ties with Persian traders, Western businesses, and governing elites. They enjoyed strong competitive advantage in, for example, pearls and food products. Their high social status and marriage connections were also a route to business success. Their multiple commercial and industrial enterprises were strengthened by their links to British political agents and to the ruling Shaykh Isa family. Their

[22] Administration Report for the years 1902–03 in *Persian Gulf Administration Reports 1873–1949*, vol. V, pp. 35, 180.
[23] Fuccaro, 'Mapping the Transnational Community', pp. 46–7.

ambition was to use local advantage and later GCC wealth to achieve international trade links. Britain's informal empire brought a legal and institutional framework that enabled family firms to establish long-run strategies and structures. Aspects of modernity can be traced back to Bahrain's past powerful commercial and trading interests. Nelida Fuccaro emphasizes the ability of the Safar and Sharif families, despite intermarriage, to maintain strict ethnic and linguistic identity, separate from the Arabs. They resisted claiming Arab or tribal descent to demonstrate loyalty to the ruling family. But nationality and property laws introduced in 1937 forced these merchants to disown their historical links with Iran, although it was Bahrain's independence in 1970 that finally clinched this separation.[24]

However, it was religion, and in particular the Shi'ite ma'tams, that provided a power base visible and eternal. This base was later reinforced through the creation of autonomous Shi'i courts. Here the Kazruni and Bushehri families not only maintained religious institutions but also provided economic support for the community, essential with the demise of the pearling industry in the early 1930s. Their loans to the ruling families and assistance in the collection of customs duties further engendered public trust and respect.[25]

The Ma'tam al-Ajam al-Kabir, established in 1892 as the centre for the celebration of Ashura and for the organization of the Tamthiliyyah, the procession, ceremonial flagellation, and passion commemorating the martyrdom of Imam Husayn, was supported by merchants. The Bushehri and Safar families contributed two-thirds of the initial capital for this celebration. The Safars later distanced themselves from the ma'tam while the Bushehri family controlled it from 1927 to 1967. Several ma'tams acquired luxurious houses owned by one of the wealthiest merchants. In 1952, one ma'tam was funded by the rent income from three houses, six shops, and one hawtah in the city of Manama. These properties also provided refuge for homeless unemployed workers, particularly vital following the collapse of the pearling industry in the early 1930s. These ma'tams were funded by Ali Kazim Bushehri, a labourer who became an international trader in food and commodities and had made his fortune speculating on food prices in Iran. His business expanded into Lingah, Bandar Abbas, and Bombay. From the wealth created through the food trade, the Bushehri family moved into building construction, booming since the 1920s, where they exploited family and ethnic networks and employed skilled labourers from Iran. The patronage of charities assisted their rise, as they undertook the construction of notable

[24] Fuccaro, 'Mapping the Transnational Community', pp. 48–52.
[25] A. A. Bushehri, 'Struggle of [sic] National Identity', unpublished typescript, 1995; A. A. Bushehri, 'The Master Builder of Bahrain', *The Gulf Mirror*, no. 8, February 1987.

buildings. Abd al-Nabi Bushehri built the British Political Agency building in 1900 and renovated both the Khamis Mosque and the British base in 1927.[26]

The control of the construction industry and real estate, as well as food importing and distribution, secured a golden age for mercantile capitalism in the pre-oil era. It required a clustering of charities and the negotiation of long-term alliances with the Sunni state. The merchants' Persian ethnic patronage networks were also bolstered by links with dock workers, construction workers, and urban labour. The Persian ma'tams fostered close links with Iran, as mullahs and theologians were recruited from Bushehr, Shiraz, and Qum. This recruitment had the potential to become politically charged, particularly during the celebration of the martyrdom of Husayn. And between 1913 and the 1950s, Persia's education system emphasized international linkages through Shi'ism. But Bahrain's external links were curbed by nationality and property laws in 1937, which brought in tighter definitions of citizenship and restricted the ownership of immovable property to Bahraini citizens.[27] The extent of the property owned by the Ajam community became clear with the registration of citizenship. The power of the Ajam elite on the municipal council of Manama, in the police force, and in commercial courts (majlis al-urf) heightened fears of Iranian interference in Bahrain. Fear of Iran was instigated by the loyalty towards it shown by students in the Persian school in the 1920s and 1930s.[28] The 1937 legislation provided social, religious, and political dynamism to Bahrain's Shi'ites. Their impact in Bahrain entered a mature phase when Shi'ite notables with substantial interests in the economy and in property made the decision to remain. Those with close links to Iran left. Iran did not recognize Bahrain as a sovereign state until independence in 1970. Thus 'the adoption of Bahraini nationality in the late 1930s represents ... the single most important event which started to alienate those strong historical links between the Ajam of Bahrain and Iran.'[29] Bahrain's Shi'ites, their economic future underpinned by increasing involvement in property and trade, while maintaining close ties to Islamic charities, had created new centres of economic power in Manama and the regions. That power was effected through participation in local municipal councils and arbitration

---

[26] Bushehri Archieve (BA), 'Daftar ma'tam al-ajam al-kabir (1929–1951)'. Information on Waqf properties in BA, 'Daftar buzur (1 muharram 1932–1933); 'Ilan amin al-sunduq (Ali Kazim Bushehri), 19 Dhu al-Hijjahseptember 1952'; A Seyf, al-Matam fil bahrayn (Manamah: Matba'ah al-Sharqiyyah, 1995), pp. 108–11: kindly provided from the archives of Akbar Busheri. Hawtah is a sacred enclave, an enclosure where certain actions are prohibited. It can also mean a protective place for women.

[27] Bahrain Nationality Law, 17 February 1937, King's Regulation no. 1 of 1937, under Article 70 (b) of the Bahrein Order in Council, 8 May 1937, in *King's Regulations Order in Council and Bahrain Regulations, 1913–1958* (London: HMSO, 1958).

[28] Fuccaro, 'Mapping the Transnational Community', p. 53.

[29] Fuccaro, 'Mapping the Transnational Community', p. 53.

through Shi'ite courts. In securing a balance between cooperation with the ruling Al-Khalifa family and competition with indigenous and foreign merchants, the Shi'ites maintained a moderate religious adherence. The passion exhibited during the Arab Spring was largely a consequence of the poor education and employment prospects facing youth, while farmers and fishermen were protesting against the seizure of land by the state for housing and leisure facilities.

It would be useful here to pause to analyse the evolution of the Kanoo business group. The Kanoos were Persian Arabs (Hawalah) from Najd. The founder of the family business was Hajjii Yusuf bin Ahmed Kanoo (1868–1945), who was involved in the import trade with India. Later he emerged as a banker, with branches in Bombay, and as the Bahrain agent for major companies, Anglo-Persian Oil (later British Petroleum), the Bombay and Persia Steam Navigation Company, the Kerr Steamship Company, Studebaker, and Ford. From here Kanoo interests evolved into a large conglomerate in the Gulf, Y. B. A. Kanoo in Bahrain, in Saudi Arabia, and the UAE/Oman with headquarters in Dubai. Competitive advantage was secured through quasi-monopoly control of shipping and imports. After the Second World War, Kanoo diversified into travel, lighterage, aviation, insurance, construction, labour recruitment, oil supplies, aircraft services, ship repairs, the processing of chemicals, and retailing. All these subsidiaries were owned by the family with authority and decision-making devolved within family hierarchies. This facilitated multinational operations in key industries in the Gulf.[30]

Kanoo is a transnational with its main headquarters in Bahrain from 1890. It then expanded into Saudi Arabia, to Ras Tannurah and Ras Mishab in 1950, Dammam in 1953, Riyadh in 1963, and Jeddah in 1968. In the 1960s, Kanoo moved into Dubai, Abu Dhabi, and Sharjah, followed by Oman and the US in 1975 and London in 1978.[31] All these firms were family owned and managed by family members. Although many of the heads of these companies held MBAs from the United States, their training in business was essentially through family hierarchies. The Kanoos were an established business elite. Their integration into the elite classes, including the royal families in the Gulf states, served their business purposes. Their high performance in quasi-monopolistic corporations was secured more by access to the Gulf elite than through business excellence. Glamour connections have been prominent in Gulf business since the eighteenth century, displaying an ability to operate in

---

[30] James Onley, 'Transnational Merchant Families in the Nineteenth and Twentieth Century Gulf', in *The Gulf Family: Kinship Policies and Modernity*, edited by Alanoud Alsharekh (SAQI in association with London Middle East Institute SOAS, 2007), pp. 46–55.

[31] Onley, 'Transnational Merchant Families in the Nineteenth and Twentieth Century Gulf', p. 52.

weak institutional and legal frameworks. Their entrepreneurial achievement was to maintain a tightly knit conglomerate through each generation. But the challenges of the twenty-first century are enormous, not least the challenge of diversifying from oil. Their expansion in the 1960s and 1970s involved little structural change and was facilitated by oil and substantial labour immigration. But it secured the position of transnational merchants like the Kanoos and the Safars.

The Safar family lost leadership after the death of Agha Muhammad Khalid Safar in 1900. His successors struggled to improve management either through recruitment from outside or by training family members. An important factor in the earlier success of the Safars had been a close alliance with the ruling families in Bahrain and Kuwait, who depended on the merchants to collect revenues and provide loans. The Safars' close ties as agents of the British obviously lost their effectiveness with the British withdrawal on independence.[32] Also, the oil wealth of the 1950s and 1960s had loosened the ties between the political elite and merchants, including the Safars.

Economic Diversification and the Rise of Small and Medium Enterprises

The dominant narrative in the corporate history of Bahrain focused on the powerful trans-national merchants and the state until the 1950s, and then the rise of state-owned corporations, bolstered by oil capital flows both from within Bahrain and from its oil-wealthy neighbours. Missing was the growth of the small and medium enterprise (SME), securing positions in niche sectors in trade, manufacturing, finance, transport, construction, and in food and agriculture. The SME was little seen throughout the oil era until 2000 but came into its own with economic diversification. In the challenge to achieve economic diversification, SME entrepreneurial drive was crucial. SMEs were particularly prominent in trade and in construction.[33]

The retail market and the import–export sector proved to be particularly attractive for the SMEs. In mining, financial services, manufacturing, construction, transport and communications, the wholesale and retail trades, and in hotels, restaurants, and tourism, the SMEs were involved only in

[32] IOR R/15/1/330, British Representation at Bahrain: Appointment of a Political Agent to Bahrain, 1898–1908 (Gulf Residency Bushehr).

[33] Bahrain Ministry of Industry, Commerce and Tourism, number of SMEs by sector 2017; *Bahrain Human Development Report 2018*; UNDP, *Pathways to Sustainable Economic Growth in Bahrain*, 2018; Bahrain Centre for Strategic International and Energy Studies, 'Economic Diversification, Competitiveness and the Role of SMEs: Challenges and Opportunities', pp. 50–101.

outsourcing. In 2017, there were 30,478 SME firms in retailing, trading, and repair; 13,107 in construction; and 8,462 in manufacturing. Agriculture, transport and storage, food, communications, and professional services involved far fewer SMEs, as these sectors were dependent on advanced technology and foreign connections.

The contribution of the oil and gas industries to GDP declined from 28 per cent in 2005 to 18 per cent in 2017. In contrast, electricity, water, business services, and real estate flourished. However, the extraction of oil in the Abu Sa'fa oil field, shared with Saudi Arabia, and in Bahrain's major onshore oil field in Jabal Al Dukhan, was maintained.[34] Downstream of extraction was the manufacturing or refining of oil to produce basic chemicals, fertilizers, man-made fibres, and plastic products, and SMEs were significantly involved here, driving forward Bahrain's economic diversification.[35] SMEs continued to grow in the first two decades of the twenty-first century. In 2017, they accounted for 56 per cent of total employment.[36]

The SMEs frequently involved co-ownership with large, often state corporations. The ambition of the state to achieve economic diversification and reduce dependence on oil was undoubtedly secured in part by the growth of SMEs. Often the SMEs had to grapple with technological complexity in industries where large firms had to combine with SMEs to remain competitive. The growth in SMEs reduced the presence of public sector state-owned monopolies. The increasing contribution of the private sector was particularly important in fisheries, water, electricity, aquaculture, food processing, and tourism.[37]

Earlier, Bahrain's dependence on oil had created a powerful state with a large public sector, sustained by huge oil revenues. SMEs had been marginalized.[38] SMEs were hindered by the strict regulations of the Central Bank of Bahrain, while the banking sector was dominated by the state. The abundance of cheap immigrant labour undermined the pressure on SMEs to increase productivity: in fact, local workers accounted for only 11 per cent of employment in the SME sector. In Bahrain, as in the other Gulf states, the economic power of the state and its associated capitalists determined the development

---

[34] Bahrain Information and Government Authority, 'Cumulative Growth Percentage by Sector of GDP, 2005–2017'.

[35] Bahrain Economic Development Board, 'Report by HE Mr. Khalid Al-Rumaihi', CEO, 2018.

[36] Bahrain Ministry of Industry, Commerce and Tourism, 'SME Contributions in Percentage in Bahrain, 2017': The World Bank and OECD confirm this figure.

[37] Bahrain Ministry of Industry, Commerce, and Tourism, 'SME Contributions in Percentage in Bahrain'.

[38] J. Kotilaine, 'Turning Entrepreneurship into a Growth Driver', Bahrain National Human Development Report Background Paper, 2018; 'Laying the Foundations for Sustainable Growth', Bahrain National Human Development Report background paper, 2018.

of the firm and its organizational structure. Marx and classical economists who recognized the labour theory of value, including Thompson, Braverman, and Marglin, have focused on the control of labour. The exploitation of labour is acute in Bahrain, because access to immigrant labour drives down labour costs.[39] Monopolistic firms not only possess concentrated ownership but also draw on close alliances with elite families, bureaucrats, and merchants.[40]

An Ancient Heresy of Corporate Opportunism: Aluminium and Petrochemical Companies and SMEs

Aluminium Bahrain was innovative in three respects. It produced a non-oil export, it facilitated metal production downstream through a number of smaller companies, and it raised productivity. Aluminium Bahrain had the largest smelter in the Middle East, located in Bahrain. It was established in 1971 and is jointly owned by the Bahrain Government (77 per cent), SABIC (20 per cent), and a German investment firm, Bretton Investments (3 per cent). A large proportion of the aluminium produced was for the domestic market but there were also exports to international markets. Production rose from 120,000 metric tonnes in 1971 to 971,000 metric tonnes in 2017. It produced high-grade aluminium products, including standard and T-ingots, extrusion billets, rolling slab, properzi ingots, and molten aluminium.[41] There was a commitment to expand production through the 'Alba line 6 Expansion Project', seeking to increase productivity and drive innovation and create new business formations in January 2019. This will be ALBA's largest single site aluminium smelter in the world.[42] The raw aluminium produced by ALBA is used by smaller companies involving major Bahraini capital groups. One of these companies is Midal Cables, established in 1977, which uses aluminium to produce cables and rods. It grew to become the world's largest producer of aluminium conductors, exporting to 60 countries. Midal is jointly owned by the Bahraini conglomerate, Al Zayani investments (AZI), and the Saudi conglomerate, Ali Reza (Xenel Group). This is an example of the strong connections between GCC capitalists. The Zayani conglomerate is involved

---

[39] Karl Marx, *Capital: A Critique of Political Economy*, vol. 1 (London: Lawrence & Wishart, 1972); E. P. Thompson, *The Making of the English Working Class* (Harmondsworth: Penguin, 1991); H. Braverman, *Labour and Monopoly Capital: The Degradation of Work in the Twentieth Century* (New York: Monthly Review Press, 1974); S. A. Marglin, 'What Do Bosses Do? The Origins and Functions of Hierarchy in Capitalist Production', *Radical Review of Political Economics*, vol. 6, no. 2 (1974).
[40] C. N. Pitelis, *Market and Non-Market Hierarchies: Theory of Institutional Failure* (Oxford: Blackwell, 1993).
[41] ALBAsmelter.com 2017.
[42] ALBAsmelter.com 2018.

in automobiles as agents for BMW, Rolls Royce, Mitsubishi, Ferrari, and Hyundai. Its capital is secured through Investcorp, the Bahraini Islamic Bank, and Bahrain Kuwait Insurance Company. The Zayani conglomerate also held interests in manufacturing. Xenel is active in petrochemical production, with the first private company in the Middle East at Yanbu. It also has interests in construction, real estate, and information technology.[43] While the upstream component of aluminium production was dominated by state capital with a significant involvement of foreign capital, there were 20 smaller firms from the GCC processing aluminium, especially for building construction in Bahrain, and these often involved ownership, control, and funding within families from Bahrain and the GCC. It is estimated that 90 per cent of the aluminium used in the Middle East was in the real estate sector.[44] Three-quarters of downstream aluminium firms were private companies, established in earlier phases of industrialization. These manufacturing companies contribute 10–12 per cent of Bahrain's GDP. These downstream companies utilize about 40 per cent of ALBA's aluminium production.[45] These companies commonly involved joint GCC ownership and capital: Balexo, held by Gulf Finance House, which is controlled by the Al Shaya group, Kuwait; Midal Cables is controlled by Al Zayani Corporation Bahrain and Ali Reza group from Saudi Arabia.

Bahrain's major contribution in the petrochemical sector was not in oil and gas directly but in its derivatives. It was engaged in the refining of crude oil to produce chemicals, polymers, fertilizers, and metals. These downstream operations were principally through the Gulf Petrochemical Industries Company (GPIC), a joint venture between the Government of Bahrain and two petrochemical companies from Kuwait and Saudi Arabia. It commenced operations in 1985.[46] There were some smaller firms linked to GPIC in some of these sectors but were more often state owned. The petrochemical sectors were important in manufacturing. Crude oil and natural gas production remained at around 9 per cent of economic activity between 1979 and 2013 but refining and downstream manufacturing was more substantial.[47] GPIC uses natural gas to produce fertilizer and petrochemicals, including ammonia, urea, and methanol, totalling 1.4 million tonnes each year. In 2018, GPIC

---

[43] Hanieh, Capitalism and Class in the Gulf Arab States, pp. 72–3, 116–17, 216.

[44] Global Investment House (GIH), 2007, p. 23.

[45] Hanieh, Capitalism and Class in the Gulf Arab States, p. 117.

[46] R. E. Looney, 'An Economic Assessment of Bahrain's Attempts at Industrial Diversification', Industrial Bank of Kuwait Papers, 1989, pp. 17–18; R. E. Looney, *Manpower Policies and Development in the Persian Gulf Region* (Westport, CT: Praeger, 1994).

[47] International Energy Agency, *Oil Information*, 1979–2013, various issues; Yesenn El-Radhi, *Economic Diversification in the Gulf States: Public Expenditure and Non-oil Economic Growth in Bahrain, Oman and Qatar* (Berlin: Gerlach Press, 2018), pp. 140–1.

contributed over US$271 million to the Bahrain economy.[48] It sought to employ and train local labour. In 2018, 90 per cent of the company's 444 employees were Bahrainis. The company funds professional training for its labour force. It also employs women through an equal opportunities committee. GPIC seeks sustainable industrial expansion. In 2010, seeking to reduce its carbon emissions, it established the region's first carbon dioxide recovery plant. It has won awards for its contributions to environmental sustainability and corporate rigour. The ALBA smelter has also invested in a local workforce. Of 2,700 employees in 2017, 84 per cent were Bahrainis, and a significant proportion were female.[49]

SME Growth and Competition: An Uneven Playing Field?

For a number of reasons, the growth of SMEs was limited. First, the state's huge oil revenues were mainly distributed to government projects and public sector firms where SMEs were little involved except as sub-contractors in the construction sector. But then this emerged as a powerful sector after the decline of oil from the 1990s. Between 2005 and 2017, individual SME registrations rose from 5,000 to 25,000. Large company registrations rose from 2,000 to 5,000 in the same period. The SME growth was heavily in fisheries, aquaculture, food processing, and tourism.[50] In 2017, SME registrations were 4,388 in agriculture; 8,462 in manufacturing; 13,107 in construction; 30,478 in trading; 1,191 in transport; 5,131 in food processing; and 5,542 in professional services.[51] Though the increase in SME registrations was substantial, their contribution to GDP was low and they accounted for only 56 per cent of total employment.

The centralization of financial institutions imposed by the Central Bank of Bahrain created problems for mergers, acquisitions, and the expansion of small firms. In addition, the internationalization of Bahrain's economy because of oil wealth encouraged the proliferation of firms and increased the need for technological specialization. In other words, the SMEs were forced into niche production. That said, access to low-wage immigrant labour

---

[48] GPIC *Annual Report*, 2018.
[49] Albasmelter.com 2017; corporate profile online at http://www.albasmelter.com/ 2018.
[50] Bahrain Ministry of Industry, Commerce, and Tourism, 'New Commercial Registrations and SME Growth 2005–17 in Bahrain'.
[51] Bahrain Ministry of Industry, Commerce, and Tourism, 'Number of SMEs by Sector, 2017'; *Bahrain Human Development Report 2018*, 'Economic Diversification, Competitiveness and the Role of SMEs: Challenges and Opportunities', pp. 57, 58, 60.

enabled the SMEs to concentrate on cheap production rather than to aim for high productivity.

This would be an appropriate point to examine Bahrain's attempts to diversify the economy. Although diversification had been sought since the 1960s, the main drive came with the launch of Economic Vision 2030 in 2008. FDI accounted for 80 per cent of GDP in 2009–17, rising from 5,000 million Bahrain dinars to 9,000 million over that period.[52] FDI from GCC territories accounted for 66 per cent of the total, with Kuwait and Saudi Arabia the two largest contributors, followed by the UAE, Oman, and Qatar.[53] Finance remained the main sector of growth, although investment in real estate remained a major attraction.

Bahrain's diversification strategy strengthened its integration within the GCC. This involved the establishment of the GCC Customs Union in 2003, followed by the creation of a single market in 2008.[54] The most promising sector in diversification was telecommunications, although the sector did not involve substantial SME participation. The state never involved itself in start-ups in technology, as skills were limited in the local workforce. In 2002, Bahrain established the Telecommunications Regulatory Authority (TRA). It permitted two foreign providers to operate in the market: Zain, a Kuwaiti company in 2003; and Viva, a Saudi company in 2008. There were opportunities for SMEs in mobile phones and Internet operations. The social media platform became the preferred platform for many home-based family-run businesses, from clothes, accessories, to food and translation services. To regulate this sector, the Ministry of Industry and Commerce and Tourism initiated the Sijilat, a commercial registration system in December 2016. This permits any citizen to operate a business in 39 specified commercial activities without registration. It has resulted in greater economic inclusion and reduced business costs.[55] The transition to a knowledge and digital economy involved diverse participants, and if education standards improved, SMEs would play a major role in the economy.

The Economic Vision of 2030 initiated in 2008 assisted the growth of SMEs, through creating a relatively liberal legal and economic system. Alfred

---

[52] Information and eGovernment Authority Bahrain, 'FDI Stocks in Bahrain from GCC Countries, 2009–2017'; *Bahrain Human Development Report 2018*, pp. 62–3.

[53] O. Al-Ubaydli and A. Jones, 'GCC Economic Integration: Opportunities and Challenges', *Bahrain National Human Development Report*, Background Paper, 2018, p. 61.

[54] M. Abdulghaffar, O. Al-Ubaydli, and O. Mahmood, 'The Malfunctioning of the Gulf Cooperation Council Single Market: Features, Causes, and Remedies', *Middle Eastern Finance and Economics*, 2013, pp. 54–67.

[55] Bahrainedb.com 2016.

Chandler saw personal capitalism as the main cause of failure in new industries, noting its inability to evolve the organizational capabilities needed
for modern industrial enterprise. But in the corporate history of Bahrain,
innovative SMEs and family firms loosened the grip of the state. Crucial here was the introduction of laws to facilitate fair funding, improved
governance structures, and the creation of strategies to secure niche markets. The number of start-ups increased by 46 per cent between 2004 and
2017.[56] Chandler's theories of strategy, structure, scale, scope and managerial capitalism were criticized by Leslie Hannah in 2009.[57] Government and
semi-governmental agencies, for example the Bahrain Development Bank,
are providing funding and advisory services for start-ups and SMEs. Tamkeen, the semi-governmental agency established in 2006 as a labour fund
to secure growth of the private sector, offered a successful model for the
reconfiguration of large and small firms. The start-up incubators included
the Ebdaa Bank for micro-financing, Bahrain Fashion, the Bahrain Business
Incubator (BBIC), and the Riyadat programme for women entrepreneurs. In
addition, there were technology agencies such as Fin Tech Bay, C5Accelerate,
Ch9, LevelZ, Rukn, the Hive, and Brinc. Another vital influence came
through community-wide corporations, investors, and educational institutions appealing to the young. Accounting firm Ernst & Young estimated that
70 per cent of Bahrain's youth were keen to start their own business, the highest percentage in the Gulf.[58] While diversifying the economy by investing
in non-oil sectors such as finance, real estate, tourism, logistics, information, and communication technologies, they were simultaneously assisting
SME growth. Tamkeen also recognized the benefits percolating down to
SMEs, which lacked the resources to invest in innovation. It fostered 300
programmes to improve skills through training and therefore raise productivity.[59] Tamkeen was assisted in these SME programmes by the Bahrain
Development Bank, established in 1992. Sijilat, introduced by the Ministry
of Industry, Commerce and Tourism in December 2016, is a commercial
registration initiative encouraging small projects put forward by individual commercial enterprises. The commercial interests that were supported
included professional, scientific, and technical services, information and
communications, education, leisure, personal services, basic manufacturing,

---

[56] *International Finance*, 3 April 2018, 'How Bahrain is Providing a Fillip to SMEs and Entrepreneurs',
available at: http:www.internationalfinance.com/sme/Bahrain-smes-entrepreneurs-startups.
[57] Leslie Hannah, 'Strategic Games, Scale, and Efficiency, or Chandler goes to Hollywood', in *Business
in Britain in the Twentieth Century: Decline and Renaissance*, edited by Richard Coopey and Peter Lyth
(Oxford: Oxford University Press, 2009), pp. 15–47.
[58] Ernst & Young, 'How Will the GCC Close the Skills Gap?', 2015, p. 25.
[59] *Bahrain Human Development Report 2018*, p. 66.

and trading activities. It prohibited employment of foreign labour as the aim was to involve local men and women in these ventures. There were further changes introduced to assist SMEs, for example reducing the minimum capital required for business registration. Furthermore, an amendment to the commercial companies law enabled foreign investors to acquire 100 per cent ownership across diverse industries, for example real estate and food. GCC capital is already dominant in Bahrain's real estate sector. In financial services, the most important innovation came with the arrival of FinTech.

The Commercial Companies Law and the Success of SMEs

Central to securing SME growth was the creation in 2017 of the SME Development Board (SDB) headed by the Minister of Industry and Commerce and Tourism. Its aims were to ensure that SMEs contributed 40 per cent of GDP and 20 per cent of exports, and to increase the number of Bahrainis working in SMEs to 43,000.[60] This initiative involved creating access to finance, developing skills, and accelerating innovation through the UN Enterprise Development and Investment Promotion (EDIP) programme. It led to the creation of the Arab International Centre for Entrepreneurship and Investment, its activities being coordinated by the UNIDO Investment and Technology Promotion Office in Bahrain in collaboration with the Ministry of Industry, Commerce, and Tourism and the Bahrain Development Bank. In the state-facilitated transition to the digital economy, Tamkeen provided cloud computing credits to SMEs after the decision by Amazon WebService to use Bahrain as its regional hub.

Amendments to Bahrain's Commercial Companies Law of 2001, introduced in 2014, 2015, and 2018, sought to improve international competitiveness. It was now permitted for a shareholder in one company to be a shareholder in a competing company. There was greater transparency in personal interests and increased protection for investors. The SMEs benefited from this greater openness as improved compliance with regulations on the part of large companies was often to the advantage of SMEs in aligned industries. The amendments to the Commercial Companies Law in effect provided greater opportunities for major concerns to negotiate with competing companies and with SMEs. They reinforced Bahrain's 2030 Economic Vision to

---

[60] *Bahrain Human Development Report 2018*, 'Pathways to Sustainable Economic Growth in Bahrain', pp. 80, 82; Bahrain Centre for Strategic International and Energy Studies, 'Economic Diversification, Competitiveness and the Role of SMEs'.

encourage more diverse participation in the corporate economy.[61] Bahrain is unique in the Gulf states for achieving greater commercial visibility through legal, political, and financial measures.

Women and Business

The following section will explore the increasing role of women in business and in the wider labour market, notably in the service sector. Their increased participation in the service sector provided more opportunities for their involvement in entrepreneurship and management. Bahrain has been a leader in the Gulf states in the empowerment of women since the turn of the twentieth century.[62] This improved their socio-economic position (the constitution of Bahrain emphasizes women's rights and gender equality) built on the provision of educational opportunities for girls from as early as the 1920s. The first girls school opened in 1920, just a few years after the establishment of the boys school. Latifa Al-Zayani and Maryam Alzayani were the first female teachers in Bahrain and in the GCC. Women were also offered education and training abroad. Bahraini women were granted equal rights in political participation by the 1930s. These changes provided women with the intellectual skills to create independent enterprises and invest in commercial ventures, as well as to participate in family business. By the 1940s, much of this interest involved the service sectors, including nursing and teaching.[63] The 1950s saw increased participation by women in the media, including the prominent female journalists Shahla Al-Khalifan and Moza Abdulla Al-Zayed.[64] By 2005, 50 per cent of newspaper editors working in the Ministry of Information were female. In the 1960s, increasing numbers of women were appointed as executives in the service sector, and in the establishment of Bahrain's financial hub from the 1970s, women played key roles as employees and directors. In 1998, Ms. Sabah Khalil Al Moayyed was appointed Director General of Eskan Bank.[65] By the 1970s, women had

[61] Al Tamimi and Company's Corporate Structuring Team, Eman Al Isa, Report, March 2018; see also Zu'Bi and Partners, 'Recent Amendments to the Commercial Companies Law', published in Oxford Business Group, *The Report: Bahrain 2019*.

[62] K. Young and T. Al-Hashmi, 'Women's Economic Inclusion in Bahrain', *Bahrain National Human Development Report*, Background Paper, 2018, pp. 202–12; World Economic Forum, *Global Gender Gap Report* (Geneva: World Economic Forum, 2015), available at http://www3.weforum.org/docs/GGGGR 2015/cover.pdf.

[63] Supreme Council for Women (SCW), 'Bahraini Women in the Financial Sector', 2015, available at: file:///C:/Users/dcrsgaa//Downloads/Bahraini%20women%20%financial.pdf; Supreme Council for Women, 2016, statistics at: http://www.scw.bh/en/About Council /Pages/record2016.aspx.

[64] Supreme Council for Women, 'The Reality of Bahraini Women in Media', 2013, available at http://www.scw.bh/ar/MediaCenter/Publications/Miscellaneous/mediastudy.pdf.

[65] Supreme Council for Women, 'Bahraini Women in the Financial Sector'.

also advanced in law enforcement and in the military. In 1999, Shaikha Haya bint Rashed Al Khalifa was appointed Bahrain's first female ambassador to France and in 2006 she became President of the 61st UN General Assembly. Also in 2006, Lateefa Al-Gaood was elected to the Bahrain Council of Representatives. In 2004, Nada Haffdah had been appointed Minister for Health. During this period women also became more prominent in the labour market and in small business. In this, women were assisted by greater legal protection, advanced by the Supreme Council for Women (SCW), which had been established in 2001. The Enterprise Development and Investment Promotion (EDIP) and the Investment and Technology Promotion Office (ITPO) provide training in enterprise creation and self-employment. The EDIP programme increased the percentage of female entrepreneurs from 28 in 2003 to 51 in 2014. Bahrain also registered the highest percentage of companies in the Gulf that had women board members and heads of corporations.[66] Significant expansion was achieved through the availability of start-up funding, especially in technology. The Women Entrepreneurship Program was launched by SCW with Tamkeen in 2010. This programme included training, direct grants, and loans at subsidized interest rates, all targeted at female entrepreneurs. More than 80 training programmes were run for 15,000 women, with a US$2.56 million micro-financing portfolio for participants.[67] Women's participation was also encouraged through Riyadat, a business programme for female entrepreneurs set up in 2013 by SCW, Tamkeen, and the Bahrain Development Bank.

The increase in female labour force participation generated new possibilities for women beyond the workforce. Women acquired experience and opportunities for self-employment. The Bahrain Labour Law for the Private Sector No. 36 of 2012 prohibited discrimination on the grounds of gender, ethnicity, language, or religion. In the public sector, wages were set by the Civil Service Bureau and were equal between men and women. The Supreme Council for Women amended considerable legislation and promoted new laws to preserve equality. The Global Gender Gap Report of 2015 from the World Economic Forum showed that Bahrain had the closest wage equality and highest female educational attainment in the region.[68]

---

[66] International Labour Organization, 'Women in Business and Management', 2016, available at http://www.ilo.org/wcmsp5/groups/public/arabstates/-ro-beirut/documents/publications/wcms-446104.pdf.
[67] Young and Al-Hashmi, 'Women's Economic Inclusion in Bahrain', p. 209.
[68] Central Bank of Bahrain, *Statistical Bulletin*, 2018.

The renaissance of family firms, often involving cooperation with the state, frequently required technology transfer from foreign firms in the Gulf. Resource redistribution and knowledge acquisition through supply chain relationships has been central to the success of family firms in Bahrain from the 1970s. At the heart of this is trust, access to state contracts and state funding, and access to sources of innovation and technology that has received criticism from various quarters, particularly in Europe. Fahad Al-Zumai, in his unpublished paper, accused Bahrain firms of 'being in the grip of the state', but European firms have always exploited their links to government.[69] Western corporate evolution has been driven by industrial innovation, competitiveness, and productivity agendas, while the loosening of state control in Britain under Thatcher saw the transfer of automobile production to Ford, General Motors, and numerous other foreign companies, ICI chemical plants to foreign business, and British Steel to Tata Steel. Sir John Rose, Chairman of Rolls-Royce, declared that the UK was becoming an 'aircraft carrier for foreign companies and warned that those [new] owners might take decisions in their own national interest rather than Britain's'.[70] Yet British MP Michael Heseltine, Secretary of State for Trade and Industry in 1992, recognized the importance of the state to the British corporate economy: 'If I have to intervene to help British companies I'll intervene before breakfast, before lunch, before tea and before dinner. And I'll get up the next morning and I'll start all over again.'[71] Business historians have recognized the importance of the state, regional industrial clusters, and foreign multinational collaborators.[72]

Family Entrepreneurship: Continuity and Change

This section provides an analysis of family firms in Bahrain. It will consider whether elitism is the crucial factor in the firms' success, and whether family firms are listed in order to secure more funds or in order to seek a stronger identity in the market in the GCC and abroad. It must be acknowledged that the survival rate among family firms is high. Why is that so? Some family firms survive through the building of trust but in the Middle East this is not

[69] Fahad Al-Zumai, 'The Evolution of Corporate Law in the Arab World: The Everlasting Grip of the State' (unpublished paper, Kuwait University, no date) captures the differences between the Kuwaiti, Bahraini, Omani, Qatari, Jordanian, and Egyptian legal systems and their inheritance from French, British, and Ottoman legal systems but perhaps overstates the 'grip of the state' argument.

[70] Financial Times, 10 February 2007.

[71] Heseltine speech at Conservative Party Conference 1992.

[72] A. M. Pettigrew and E. Fenton (ed.), The Innovating Organization (London: Sage, 2000), pp. 295–6; Kevin Morgan and Philip Cooke, The Associational Economy: Firms, Regions and Innovation (Oxford: Oxford University Press, 1998); Christopher Bartlett and Sumantra Ghoshal, Managing Across Borders: The Transnational Solution (Cambridge, MA: Harvard University Press, 1989).

always necessary. Another important issue concerns the protection of capital gains for the insider core. David Landes accused third generation business-men of amateurism, where the young who inherit lack the combative and innovative drive of the founder.[73] For many family firms, success derives from social status and access to finance. In the case of Bahrain, it is connections to the state.[74]

Before 1940, family firms accounted for 10 per cent of business in Bahrain. This declined in the 1960s to 7 per cent but then rose to 14 per cent in the 1970s following independence. In the 1980s and 1990s it was 19 per cent and by 2000 it had risen to 21 per cent.[75]Almost 54 per cent of these family firms were located in Manama, a concentration reflecting their historical trading and international connections. In contrast, 27 per cent of family firms were in Sitra, Nuwaidrat, Ma'meer, and Salmabad in the Central Governate, where the principal industries were located. The remaining 15 per cent were in the Southern Governate. An interesting point concerned the number of employ-ees in family firms. The earlier Bahrain Centre for Studies and Research (BCSR) report had calculated the average number of employees in family firms at less than 50. But the 2009–10 survey calculated an average of between 51 and 100. Thirteen per cent of family firms had 500 or more employees. Approximately 72 per cent of family firms recorded an annual revenue of below US$20 million while 5 per cent recorded an annual revenue of US$100 million. Two per cent of family firms recorded an annual revenue of between US$200 and 500 million. As these revenues were not taxed, it can be assumed that these figures are transparent and accurate.[76]

Both David Landes and Alfred Chandler have argued that family firms and 'personal capitalism' rarely survived into the third generation.[77] Landes accused Western Europe of losing innovative zeal because of the prominence of family firms. Bahrain presents a more variegated and fairly successful form of personal capitalism. In Bahrain, just 28 per cent of family firms survived into the second generation and this proportion declined still further in the third generation. The PwC Global Report of 2010 indicated that in 36 per cent of family firms, leadership had been retained into the second generation.

[73] David Landes, *The Unbound Prometheus: Technological Change and Industrial Development in Western Europe from 1750 to the Present* (New York: Cambridge University Press, 1969).
[74] Bahrain Family Business Association, *Assessment of Family Business Enterprises in the Kingdom of Bahrain*, 2010. A survey of 100 family business enterprises in the Kingdom of Bahrain was carried out by Ernst & Young in 2009–10. An earlier report in 2003 by the Bahrain Centre for Studies and Research had conducted research on 102 family firms, while the Pricewaterhouse Coopers 'Family Business Survey' of 2010–11 surveyed 1,600 family businesses across 35 countries.
[75] Ernst & Young, 'Survey on Family Business in the Kingdom of Bahrain, 2009–10', p. 21.
[76] Ernst & Young, 'Survey on Family Business', p. 23.
[77] Landes, *The Unbound Prometheus*; Alfred D. Chandler, *Scale and Scope: Dynamics of Industrial Capitalism* (Cambridge, MA: Harvard University Press, 1990).

However, crucially, ownership can remain within the family while leadership can be broadened by bringing in outsiders. Moreover, 59 per cent of family firms reported 10 family members working in the firm, while 23 per cent had between 11 and 20 members as employees. Those with more than 60 family members were often established before 1960. But at the same time, family businesses were recruiting professionals from outside. This may have been motivated by the need for Bahrain to diversify from its dependence on oil from her Gulf neighbours. The importance of innovation and organizational ability in modern industrial enterprises was recognized.[78] The proportion of family members working in family firms was significantly lower in the Bahrain Center for Studies and Research study of 2003. It recorded that 97 per cent of family businesses had less than 10 family members, and none had more than 20 family members in the company.[79] This is an interesting change in the composition of family members working in family firms.

In Bahrain, family firms acquired more diversified leadership as they acquired diverse industries. Outside of family, executives were often appointed on the basis of an existing position within the firm but also from outside.[80] There was also an element of arbitrariness in the selection of elites but this was restrained as family businesses had operations across multiple sectors as a consequence of the diversification of the economy from the 1970s. According to Ernst & Young data, in 2010, 47 per cent of family firms operated in a number of economic sectors.[81]

Family firms constituted only 10 per cent of firms in technology, 9 per cent in medical and health services, and a mere 2 per cent in financial services, because family firms lack the capital resources required to compete with state-owned banks and large private banks. In tourism and hospitality, family firms accounted for 9 per cent, 13 per cent in professional services, and in real estate and construction, an impressive 52 per cent. The state was commissioning huge building programmes from the 1990s and often subcontracting to family firms. In manufacturing, family firms accounted for 32 per cent, and in retail and consumer products, 35 per cent. From the late 1990s, family firms came to prominence in those sectors vital for economic diversification.

[78] Ernst & Young, 'Survey on Family Business', pp. 24–5.
[79] Bahrain Centre for Studies and Research, 2003.
[80] Israel M. Kirzner, *Competition and Entrepreneurship* (Chicago, IL: University of Chicago Press, 1973).
[81] Ernst & Young, 'Flexible, Focussed and Forward Looking: How a Distinctive Business Approach is Sustaining Family Firms through the Downturn', 2010, online at http//www.ey.com/Publication/wxLUAssets/Flwxible-focused and forward-looking /SFile /Family%20business%20report%200410k. pdfv. See also Bahrain Family Business Association, *Assessment of Family Business Enterprises in the Kingdom of Bahrain*, p. 25.

At first, Bahrain's family firms expanded into the GCC, seeking shares in the oil wealth of neighbours. But the expansion stagnated after the 2008 financial crisis. The general trend was for Bahrain's family firms to restrict their operations to Bahrain: 64 per cent did so, while 24 per cent operated in the GCC market and 16 per cent ventured into other parts of the Middle East. Six per cent operated in Europe and 5 per cent in the USA.[82] These firms are family owned and led by family members: 44 per cent are controlled by the first generation and around 38 per cent are in the hands of the second generation.

Clearly, a huge contribution was made by SMEs to the evolution of the corporate economy and to economic growth in Bahrain from the 1970s. A detailed consideration of two companies, the Nass Group and the Al Zayani Investment Group, would throw light on the reasons for their success, drawing on such theories of entrepreneurial performance as Schumpeter's creative destruction, Kirzner's arbitrage, Casson's judgemental decision-making, or Chandler's preoccupation with strategy, scale, and scope.[83] Is Bahrain's corporate history really a demonstration of obedience to the state, as is repeatedly stated? The classical school, from Adam Smith to Stigler, would assert that long-run markets are sustained by information, in the form of capabilities, become transformed into codified information in the form of routines, and are transferable between organizations.[84] In family firms, control is critical even when outsiders are appointed to the board. The family-managed institution also works within a value chain mechanism. Markets and hierarchies may be regarded as interchangeable, but the firm remains dominated by the family and historical linkages. Family ownership is secure but operates within a fluid coordinating organization characterized by alliances with the state, with large private corporations, and with international firms in the Gulf. This is the transaction cost approach of Pitelis.[85]

The Search for Success

The corporate history of family firms is complex and multifaceted, embracing vibrant growth but often disintegration and decline. The Al Zayani Investments Group, established in 1977 by Khalid Rashid Al Zayani and

[82] Ernst & Young, 'Flexible, Focussed and Forward Looking', pp. 27, 41.

[83] J. Schumpeter, *The Theory of Economic Development* (Cambridge, MA: Harvard University Press, 1911); Kirzner, Competition and Entrepreneurship; Mark Casson, *The Entrepreneur: An Economic Theory* (Oxford: Oxford University Press, 1991); Mark Casson, *Enterprise and Competitiveness: A Systems View of International Business* (Oxford: Oxford University Press, 1990); Chandler, Scale and Scope.

[84] Adam Smith, *The Wealth of Nations* (London: Penguin, 1986); George Stigler, *The Organization of Industry* (Homewood, IL: R. D. Irwin, 1968).

[85] Pitelis, Market and Non-Market Hierarchies.

his brothers, grew through the creation of subsidiaries and joint stock ventures. Manufacturing formed a significant part of its activities. The Group created Midal Cables in 1978. The first smelter was established by ALBA. It began operations in 1971. It established Aluwheel in 1992 as a joint venture for the manufacture of closures for beverage companies, creating Gulf Closures in the same year. The Group then expanded into automobiles with Zayani Motors in 1994 and Euro Motors in 1998, distributing such premium brands as BMW, Rolls Royce, Ferrari, Maserati, Land Rover, and MG. A further major development came with Zayani Properties in 2001, which was concerned with real estate development and the leasing of commercial and residential properties in Bahrain and in the Gulf region. But problems arose as family members took up leadership positions in the Group, for often they lacked expertise and experience for such responsibilities. Family feuds in 1984 led to management of the business being handed over to a custodian. Khalid and his brothers created a new company, recognizing that governance had to improve.

The Al Zayani Investments Group was a strictly regulated institution with a separation between ownership and management, a separation that secured growth in the aluminium industry, automobiles, and real estate. Family dominance and the family's lack of entrepreneurial efficiency may well have dampened its enthusiasm for business. A failure to establish close relations with financial institutions may well have been a further disadvantage. But with the rise of Bahrain as the financial hub of the Gulf from 1981, that problem was solved for elite families like the Al Zayani family.

Khalid Rashid Al Zayani pursued a strict separation between ownership and management of the family business. Family members sought out high-value industrial opportunities but operational matters were left to professionals. 'The companies are operated entirely as profit centres. If the CEO achieves his targets he and his staff will earn bonuses to keep them highly motivated.'[86] Fifty per cent of the dividends were retained within the company to maintain capital adequacy. To avoid situations in which senior family leaders refused to step down, there was a clear succession plan to transfer both ownership and management to a succeeding generation. Khalid established a 'graduation date', one that required the Chairman of the Board to retire at 65. One essential principle for the group was to seek out new industries, to be constantly innovating. Khalid emphasized innovation, risk taking, and forward thinking. He believed that the advantage of family business as against public companies lay in the willingness to take risks. He therefore opposed

[86] Ernst & Young, 'Survey on Family Business', p. 54.

conversion of the group into a public company. For Khalid, culture, tradition, and heritage played a pivotal role in the development of the group. Even so, he sought out expatriate expertise to secure the group's expansion into engineering, automobiles, aluminium, transport, construction, and information systems.

The Nass Group: First Mover Advantage, Finance, and Market Success

The Nass Group had success partly because of its first mover advantages in specific industries with complex chains of small firms. It was also the first family firm to convert itself into a public company, although it remained substantially family owned. Abdulla Ahmed Nass founded the group in 1963 with his father and younger brother. It became a public company in 2005, with 24 per cent of the company sold to investors and 25 per cent listed on the Bahrain Stock Exchange through an initial public offering. The family retained 51 per cent. This public conversion was a strategic decision to raise capital and strengthen management while sustaining business continuity through the generations. Nass is an industrial conglomerate and a construction powerhouse, encompassing 34 companies and 6 associated firms with operations throughout the Gulf. It moved into manufacturing, trade, marine services, transport, ship repairs, offshore engineering, and dredging and land reclamation to emerge as a pioneer giant. It rode the construction boom of the 1980s, creating a small empire of companies to serve Bahrain's construction sector. In the mid-1960s, Nass had established the first cement plant in the GCC, meeting its own construction needs. In the 1980s it improved the quality of cement produced and became the major provider of cement for the construction sector. Nass was also prominent in marine dredging, sand processing, and landscaping for housing projects. It was a compelling example of the rise of a major conglomerate, not on the back of the state but through entrepreneurial drive and imagination. The founder's experience in the construction industry in Saudi Arabia between 1953 and 1963 provided him with knowledge and skills. The Nass Group has survived into the second generation, when only 30 per cent of family firms in Bahrain survive and only 10 per cent of the third generation retain leadership roles.[87] Nass has promoted family members on merit but has also recruited management professionals from outside, even expatriates. The success of Nass derives from its engagement in

---

[87] Ernst & Young, 'Flexible, Focussed and Forward Looking'.

industries that are essential for Bahrain's diversification away from oil dependence. The decentralization of management in Nass has provided each family member with the opportunity to build his reputation by operating in a flexible manner: it involved a 'very democratic and effective selection of brains', that Schumpeter recognized as resulting from market competition among owners and tycoons.[88]

When Nass became a public company in 2005, the family shares were divided according to Islamic law. The daughters were given shares with the opportunity to sell them, while the sons received equal shares. Abdulla Nass himself retained a 20 per cent stake. Abdulla had identified construction as the group's core interest, with an extension into electrical services, plumbing, joinery, and the manufacture of cement. These were provided by his companies that were established in the 1970s', followed in the 1980s by specialist firms to provide services and materials for shipping and offshore industries. He then entered the food import and wholesale business. In the 1990s, the group expanded into scaffolding and prefabricated pipe assembly in a large shipyard and into the production of organic fertilizers.

Explaining Inertia in Labour

Bahrain's business environment has been constrained by inefficiencies in local labour and the consequent dependence on foreign labour. The power of the state in the corporate economy is acknowledged in many analyses of large companies, both state-owned and private-owned, in Bahrain from the 1930s to the present. The power of the state was driven in large part by its huge oil and gas resources. But there was a sustained effort to achieve corporate pluralism, seen not least in the persistence of powerful family firms. But the lack of employment opportunities for Bahraini youth in the large state and private companies provoked resentment. Private sector jobs at high wages were filled by expatriates who had the required education, skills, and experience. With the need for economic diversification, in 2006 Tamkeen expanded skills training and education in accounting and marketing, each geared towards small and medium firms. Direct financial assistance through the Bahrain Development Bank (BDB) from 2012 provided funds for technical training for Bahrainis. The Bahrain Institute for Entrepreneurship and Innovation, another subsidiary of the BDB, also provides technical training.

---

[88] Thomas. K. McCraw, *Prophet of Innovation: Joseph Schumpeter and Creative Destruction* (Cambridge, MA: Harvard University Press, 2007), pp. 159, 251–78, 471–4.

The Ministry of Industry and Commerce Small and Medium Enterprises unit carried out research on sectoral distribution and marketing strategies in order to accelerate the recruitment of Bahraini employees in preference to expatriates. In 2012, the Bahrain Chamber of Commerce and Industry established the SME Development and Support Centre to organize workshops in business skills and to improve access to funding and service providers such as Zain Bahrain, Ebtikar Society, and the Arab Investment and Export Guarantee Corporation. From 2008, there was increased government intervention to reduce the recruitment of expatriates and to give preference to locals. This was achieved slowly through the Labour Market Regulatory Authority and Tamkeen. The persistent complaints directed towards the 'rentier state' and a weak and bloated bureaucracy led to institutional and legal reform after the 2008 financial crisis. Most notable here was an attempt to improve labour productivity. This was particularly important for the private sector.[89] Bahraini nationals still prefer to work in public companies or in large private companies because of higher wages. This created a challenge for SMEs. Raising finance for start-ups remained within the embrace of 'family, friends and fools'.[90]

To assuage youth resentment over poor job opportunities, Bahrain limited work visas for foreign nationals. But flexibility in recruitment was essential for high-skill, technology-intensive enterprises. Only 12 per cent of CEOs in Bahrain felt that there were sufficient numbers of skilled Bahrainis. Consequently, highly skilled expatriates were essential. Moreover, foreign low-cost workers filled private companies. It followed that Bahrainis with inadequate skills were attracted to state and public companies. Labour inertia was the core problem. However, the 2008 financial crisis and the Arab Spring of 2011 forced Bahraini youth to question its prejudices against foreign labour and to focus on improving local skills. In the attempt to improve education and skills, Bahrain's Vision 2030, launched in 2008, focused on high-value-added industries in the private sector, especially in the financial sector.[91] But there was poor coordination between training programmes and, in addition, duplication between the Tamkeen and Ministry of Labour programmes to encourage the hiring of unemployed Bahraini youth.

The inefficiency of these programmes could be attributed to state factionalism. The divisions within the ruling family had been apparent since 2011.

[89] Bahrain Economic Development Board, 2013, pp. 65–7.
[90] Jessie Moritz, 'Rents, Start-ups, and Obstacles to SME Entrepreneurialism in Oman, Bahrain and Qatar', in *Employment and Career Motivation in the Arab Gulf States: The Rentier Mentality Revisited*, edited by Annika Kropf and Mohamed A Ramady (Berlin: Gerlach Press, 2015), pp. 211, 218.
[91] Bahrain Economic Development Board, 2014.

The BDB reforms unleashed a power struggle between the reformist Crown Prince Salman bin Hamad bin Isa Al-Khalifa and the conservative Prime Minister, Khalia bin Salman Al-Khalifa. There was a suspected plan by the Prime Minister to force suspension of LMRA (Labour Market Regulatory Authority) fees in 2011, simply in order to disrupt the economic reforms and thereby diminish the influence of the Crown Prince. The feud within the ruling family created confusion, raising the wages of workers but suspending the LMRA levy on expatriates and thereby reducing the proportion of Bahrainis employed in the private sector, which had risen to 67 per cent in 2009, but fell to 63 per cent in 2014.[92] To the extent that the Bahrain state was powerful in the economy, it was often as a result of personal ambition within the ruling family. Thus, in violation of the aims of Bahrain's 2030 Vision, not least to raise the prospects for local labour, short-term security was accorded priority over long-term economic sustainability, simply to meet the threats to the political order created by the 2011 uprising. The core strategy for the state had to be to work closely with SMEs, to provide funding, and to raise the educational and training standards of the local population. That was a long-term task.

---

[92] Labour Market Regulatory Authority (LMRA), based on data from the Bahrain Labour Market Indicators website http://www.lmra.bh/blmi.

10

Labour Regimes, Mobility, Productivity, and Migrant National Workers

The dominant narrative of labour history in Bahrain has been the overwhelming presence of foreign labour, particularly in the private sector, while locals were attracted to the public sector, as the state provided subsidies to enhance earnings. This segmentation of labour created long-term consequences for acquiring essential skills and improving labour productivity. Some industries, such as telecommunications, defense, electronics, and engineering, depended on highly skilled Indian and Egyptian technocrats. Improved productivity in the labour market required advances in education and in skills-training, rather than securing cheap Indian labour in labour-intensive industries such as construction, oil, aluminium, in retail and the wholesale sectors, and in infrastructural projects including transport.

This chapter attempts to examine changes in labour structure and in recruitment resulting from the economic initiatives of the state. These initiatives included shifting from oil into diversified industries from the late 1990s. Recognizing the importance of clusters in oil processing through BAPCO and aluminium production through ALBA, government sought to regulate the employment of expatriates while educating locals for telecommunications, electronics, and technology. There was hoarding of cheap foreign workers within the private sector. This suggests that the cause of poor labour productivity in the 1990s was the hoarding of unskilled foreign labour. The public sector performed even more poorly than the private sector. Subsidies in the public sector to maintain wages led to locals hanging on to inefficient posts and resisting opportunities to acquire skills and move into more competitive sectors.

Bahrain's population of 1,501,116 in 2017 included 823,610 foreign nationals, or 55 per cent, of whom 85 per cent were from Asia. In 2018, 70 per cent of expatriates were employed in unskilled and highly skilled jobs.[1] Most of the expatriates were in the private sector. Although Bahrain had had Arab and

---

[1] Bahrain Central Informatics Organization, *Population Statistics*, 2018.

Islam and Capitalism in the Making of Modern Bahrain. Rajeswary Ampalavanar Brown, Oxford University Press.
© Rajeswary Ampalavanar Brown (2023). DOI: 10.1093/oso/9780192874672.003.0010

Persian workers before 1970, the government now feared interference from Iran and other countries in the Middle East and opted to recruit Asian workers. From the mid-1970s through to 2008, the oil boom led to an influx of foreign workers, many on menial wages. Bahrain's indigenous labour dominated the public sector with higher wages. They were also employed in industrial state joint ventures, such as BAPCO and ALBA, the aluminium company. The oil slump of the 1980s and 1990s produced a decline in the public sector leaving many Bahrainis unemployed.[2] The economic diversification from the 1990s led to an influx of foreign workers. This persisted despite the introduction of labour reforms aimed at reducing the dependence on foreign labour. Unemployment among Bahrain nationals, in particular Bahraini youth, posed a threat. The law aimed at liberalizing the labour market by reducing the divide between nationals and expatriates through structural change in the economy, notably expansion of the service sector and economic diversification within the small business sector. There was an attempt to reduce the cost of employing locals who were highly paid and also received welfare subsidies. The Labour Market Regulation Authority (LMRA), established in May 2006, sought to control the issue of work permits for expatriates and the self-employed in an attempt to increase competition between expatriates and locals. In August 2009, it abolished the 'No Objection Certificate', thereby reducing the professional mobility of expatriate workers. Prior to 2009, the certificate prevented foreign workers switching from kafala sponsorship.[3] Kafala was a form of recruitment in which the worker was linked to a specific job, but it often involved violence and abuse. Kafala had emerged as an organized labour system in the pearling industry. In 2011, a new law, responding to employers' protests against the abolition of Kafala, contained a clause that allowed switching only with the consent of the employer and only after a full year of employment with that employer. Bahrain had no minimum wage for foreign workers in the private sector: wages had been negotiated with the sponsor in the country of their origin, although those agreements were rarely respected. However, the 2012 Labour Law provided access to Ministry of Labour mediation services for domestic workers, with complaints over contracts, as well as annual vacation and severance pay. But it did not cover hours of work and overtime pay. Further legislation in October 2017 provided for a wage protection system and free healthcare for domestic workers.[4]

---

[2] Francoise De Bel-Air in Gulf Labour Markets and Migration, GLMM-EN-No6/2016, Gulf Research Center, p. 4.

[3] Labour Market Regulation Authority (LMRA), *Bahrain Labour Market Indicators*, no. 27, 2014: http://lmra.bh/portal/files/cms/shared/file/Newsletter/NewsletterQ3[En].pdf.

[4] Human Rights Watch, 'For a Better Life: Migrant Worker Abuse in Bahrain and the Government Reform Agenda', HRW, 30 September 2012, https://www.hrw.org/report/2012/09/30/better-life/

One of the long-term characteristics of the Bahrain labour market was the peculiarly important role played by foreign workers. They came to dominate both the low-paid sector and the skilled professional group in a number of key industries. Large numbers of low-paid foreign workers were kept in labour camps, a practice accelerated by economic diversification and the globalization of the economy. The influx of foreign workers also created rising unemployment among Bahrainis, in particular Bahraini youth. Sunni Muslims, Jordanians, Syrians, Yemenis, and Pakistanis were naturalized and recruited into the security services. This was an issue in the Arab Spring of 2011. Labour from Asia accounted for 79 per cent of the private sector workforce in 2018, a slight decline from 2010. In 2018, only 15 per cent of expatriates, largely Asians, held highly skilled jobs in the scientific and technical sectors.[5]

Expatriates were concentrated in certain sectors. The bulk of foreign workers in 2010 were in the construction sector (27.9 per cent), in the wholesale and retail trades (16.3 per cent), in private domestic work (16.0 per cent), and in manufacturing (12.4 per cent). In contrast, Bahrainis were employed in public administration and in security services (31 per cent). Bahrainis in the wholesale and retail trades were just 13.2 per cent, and in manufacturing 10.8 per cent. These figures confirm Bahrain's high dependence on foreign workers. Expatriates from Asia constituted 84.4 per cent of the total in 2010, while Arabs accounted for 4.5 per cent.[6] This inflow of foreign workers had continued through the 2008 financial crisis and the Arab uprising of 2011, through the tactic of labour hoarding. In a period of trauma, foreign recruitment was deeply engrained in the mindset of Bahrain's employers. This interpretation fits with the data from the LMRA and the Ministry of Labour for the years 2009–14.[7]

---

migrant-worker-abuse-bahrain-and-government-reform-agenda;   http://blog.lmra.bh/en/2017/09/19/new-contracts-for-domestic-workers-to-be-enforced-from-from-October-1/;   Francoise De Bel-Air, 'Demography, Migration and the Labour Market in Bahrain', explanatory note No. 1/2019, Gulf Labour Markets, Migration and Population, GLMM programme of the Migration Policy Centre (MPC) and the Gulf Research Center (GRC): http://gulfmigration.org; Oxford Business Group, Bahrain: Year in Review 2018, 2 January 2019: https://oxford businessgroup.com/news/bahrain-year-review-2018.

[5] LMRA, *Bahrain Labour Market Indicators*, no. 42, Q2, 2018: http://blmi.lmra.bh/2018/06/newsletter_en.pdf Andrew Gardner, 'Strategic Transnationalism: The Indian Diasporic Elite in Contemporary Bahrain', *City & Society*, vol. 20, no. 1 (2008), pp. 54–78.

[6] Bahrain Census data: http://gulfmigration.eu/population-by nationality-group-and sex-2010/.

[7] See also Omar AlShehabi, 'Rootless Hubs: Migration, Urban Commodification and the "Right to the City" in the GCC', in *Transit States: Labour, Migration and Citizenship in the Gulf*, edited by Abdulhadi Khalaf, Omar AlShehabi, and Adam Hanieh (London: Pluto Press, 2015); Laurence Louer, 'The Political Impact of Labour Migration in Bahrain', *City & Society*, vol. 20, no. 1 (2008), pp. 32–53; Ian Secombe and Richard Lawless, 'Foreign Worker Dependence in the Gulf and the International Oil Companies 1910–50', *International Migration Review*, vol. 20, no. 3 (1986), pp. 548–74.

Youth Labour

The youth labour market illustrates that Bahrain's reliance on cheap foreign labour contributed to high youth unemployment. In 2001, the unemployment rate in the 15–64 age group was 6 per cent; the adult unemployment rate was 3 per cent; the rate for the 15–24 age group was 20 per cent; the youth/adult unemployment rate was 6.8 per cent. Unemployment among the young remained high, in 2003 accounting for 25 per cent of total unemployment.[8] The rise in female labour participation, with women often possessing better educational qualifications, made it more difficult for youth to secure jobs. Labour market rigidities, between public and private enterprises, also reduced opportunities in youth employment. A significant part of the productivity problem in many manufacturing and industrial sectors in the 1950s through to the 1990s arose from the employment of low-skilled local workers in the public sector, where wages were high and where incomes were bolstered by state subsidies.

Often the young struggled to find work because of their inferior educational qualifications and lack of experience. Bahrain and Saudi Arabia registered relatively higher youth unemployment, 28 per cent and 20 per cent respectively, than the UAE and Kuwait. Bahrain and Saudi Arabia experienced substantial cheap foreign labour immigration. In Bahrain, first-time jobseekers accounted for more than two-thirds of the unemployed.[9] A sluggish economy in the 1990s produced persistently high levels of youth unemployment. By 2002, the unemployment rate among local Bahrainis was 13 per cent: among adults it was 7 per cent, among the young, 31 per cent. In contrast, expatriate youth unemployment was 0.5 per cent, and for adult expatriates, 0.2 per cent. In Saudi Arabia, unemployment among the local population ran at 10 per cent, within which adult unemployment stood at 5 per cent, youth unemployment, 37 per cent. For expatriates in Saudi Arabia, unemployment ran at 0.8 per cent, within which adult unemployment was 0.5 per cent and youth unemployment was 6 per cent.[10] Labour reforms sought to assist youth employment through improved education and reduce recruitment from overseas.

---

[8] ILO LABORSTA 2004; Gustavo Crespi Trantino, 'Computation, Estimation and Prediction Using the Key Indicators of the Labour Market (KILM) data set', Employment Strategy Paper, 2004/16, International Labour Organization, Employment Strategy Department, Geneva.

[9] ILO LABORSTA 2004, International Labour Organization of the United Nations, Geneva, Global Employment Trends for Youth, data set, 2004.

[10] Bahrain Central Informatics Organization (CIO), 2002: Basic Results: Population, Housing, Buildings and Establishments Census.

Gender and Employment

Labour force participation trends between the 1970s and 1990s indicate that the labour market first restricted women's access to paid work but that opportunities then opened up. The labour force participation of females aged 15–19 rose from 3.1 per cent in 1971 to 8.4 per cent in 1981 and to 8.3 per cent in 1991. For the age group 20–24, the rate in 1971 was 11.6 per cent; in 1981, 31.5 per cent; and in 1991, 37 per cent. For the age group 25–29 it was 10.02 per cent in 1971; 31.1 per cent in 1981; and by 1991, 42 per cent. Finally, for females aged 30–54, participation rate was 5.8 per cent in 1971; 15.7 per cent in 1981; and 33.6 per cent in 1991.

In Bahrain, the share of young female workers in the labour force rose from 18 per cent in 1980 to 31 per cent in 2000, the highest in the MENA countries. The largest cohort increase was in the 15–24 age group.[11] However, female labour participation rates increased among all age groups in Bahrain between the 1970s and 1990s. The increases are attributed to declining fertility rates, higher educational attainment, and a trend towards female emancipation. Women in Bahrain secured the highest educational attainment in the region, along with Kuwait and Jordan. The average length of schooling in Bahrain is estimated at almost seven years.[12] The large increase in female participation rates during the 1990s also produced high rates of unemployment among young females. In 2001, male youth unemployment was at 17 per cent while for women it was 27 per cent.[13] In Bahrain in 2000, unemployment among young females was 50 per cent higher than for young males. The causes of the higher rates of unemployment among women are diverse. Women work in particular occupations and face different challenges on entry. They also face different family requirements: marriage and children cause a quarter of the gender difference. Cultural traditions may also explain gender differences in labour participation rates.

As is evident in Table 10.1 for males, labour participation rates among the 30–54 age group was fairly constant at over 90 per cent. The problem for youth is that labour markets are not sufficiently flexible to absorb new young entrants. Rising population growth also has an impact on youth employment.

---

[11] World Development Indicators (WDI) 2004, World Bank, Washington, DC.

[12] Robert Barro and Jong-Wha Lee, 'International Data on Educational Attainment: Updates and Implications', Centre for International Development, Working Paper No. 42, Harvard University, 2000; World Bank 'Reducing Vulnerability and Increasing Opportunity: Social Protection in the Middle East and North Africa', Washington, DC, 2002; World Bank, MENA Development Report, *Gender and Development in the Middle East and North Africa* (Washington, DC: World Bank, 2004).

[13] ILO LABORSTA, *2004 Global Employment Trends for Youth.*

Table 10.1 The male labour force participation rate by age group, 1971, 1981, 1991, by percentage

	15–19	20–24	25–29	30–54
1971	42.8	88.4	97.7	97.0
1981	30.0	89.2	98.1	98.4
1991	24.7	87.9	98.0	99.0

Note: The aggregate male participation rates during 1971–91 were: –42 per cent in first age group 15–19; –1 per cent for 20–24 age group; 0 per cent for 25–29 age group; and 2 per cent for the age group 30–54. ILO LABORSTA, *2003 Global Employment Trends*, Geneva. All data are accumulated from population census, household survey, and from labour force survey: Nader Kabbani and Ekta Kothari, 'Youth Employment in the MENA Region: a Situational Assessment', Special Protection Paper No 0534, September 2005, p. 10.
Sources: BH/MFNE, 1972; BH/MCA, 1982; BH/CIO, 2001, 2004, 2011.

The labour market segmentation between males and females is also shaped by the transition from rural to urban employment as well as by the increasing opportunities for women in self-employment. David Blanchflower notes that 'self-employment is the simplest kind of entrepreneurship'.[14] A notable feature of women's involvement in work was the extensive reliance on technology. Technology allows for outsourcing, downscaling, de-concentration, and the subcontracting of labour-intensive service jobs, each stimulating self-employment.[15] Ironically, Geert Hofstede's index on individualism, masculinity, power-distance, and risk-taking reflect the position of women in employment in the Middle East.[16]

Migration and Employment

The data on labour confirms that migration across the MENA countries increased opportunities for youth employment, alongside the migration to urban areas within Bahrain. Bahrain, together with the UAE and Kuwait, exhibited higher net migration across the MENA countries (per thousand)

---

[14] David G. Blanchflower, 'Self-employment in OECD Countries', NBER Working Paper No. 7486, Cambridge, MA, 2000, p. 3.
[15] Ferry de Goey, 'Economic Structure and Self-employment during the Twentieth Century', Paper for 8th EBHA conference, 16–18 September 2004, Barcelona.
[16] Geert Hofstede, *Culture's Consequences: International Differences in Work-Related Values* (London: Sage Publications, 1980); Geert Hofstede, *Cultures and Organizations: Intercultural Cooperation and its Importance for Survival* (New York: McGraw Hill, 2010).

between 1995 and 2000 than between 2000 and 2005.[17] The high net migration between 1995 and 2000 is related to the labour demands of the oil industry, which then declined after 2000, although industrial diversification created new labour demands. Overall, expatriate workers within Bahrain remained highly important, which further restricted employment opportunities for the young, although the majority of migrant workers were in low-paid service jobs or in technical posts where local workers lacked the necessary skills. In other words, youth unemployment is only partly linked to poor education and low skills and to state-subsidized employment in the public sector.

The labour theory of value, derived from Marx and the classical economists, has been revived by a number of modern economists including Thompson, Braverman, and Marglin, who have concentrated on the importance of capital and the division of labour.[18] The state in Bahrain did not maximize the power of markets and hierarchies, nor did it employ efficient transaction systems, but instead directed its own nationals into public sector jobs and subservience, while increasing dependence on foreign labour.[19] Moreover, significant sections of Bahraini youth and older workers were also disadvantaged through their poor educational levels. The instabilities of Bahrain in the period after the 2008 crisis were heightened by employment insecurities, particularly among the young, rather than by the often-exaggerated religious divisions between the Sunni state and Shi'a majority, although much of the present literature sees the Middle East uprisings as the culmination of disputes between Sunnis and Shi'ites.

The next section will focus on Bahrain's educational reforms and their impact on labour. Expatriates remained at around 60 per cent of Bahrain's labour force between 1975 and 2001.[20] In Qatar, the figure increased to 88 per cent.[21] The proportion of expatriate workers in Saudi Arabia fell to 50 per cent in 2002, principally by an increasing employment of Saudi nationals, particularly in the public sector.[22]

---

[17] United Nations Population Division, *World Population Prospects: The 2002 Revision* (New York: United Nations, 2003).

[18] Karl Marx, *Capital: A Critique of Political Economy, Vol. 1* (London: Lawrence & Wishart, 1972); E. P. Thompson, *The Making of the English Working Class* (Harmondsworth: Penguin, 1991); H. Braverman, *Labour and Monopoly Capital: The Degradation of Work in the Twentieth Century* (New York: Monthly Review Press, 1974); S. A. Marglin, 'What Do Bosses Do? The Origins and Functions of Hierarchy in Capitalist Production', *Radical Review of Political Economics*, vol. 6, no. 2 (1974).

[19] C. N. Pitelis, *Market and Non-Market Hierarchies: Theory of Institutional Failure* (Oxford: Blackwell, 1993).

[20] Bahrain Central Informatics Organization (CIO), *Basic Results: Population, Housing, Buildings and Establishments Census*, 2002.

[21] Qatari Planning Council, March 2004 Population Census, 2005.

[22] Saudi Arabia Central Department of Statistics, *Social Statistics Labour Force Survey 2002*, Ministry of Economy and Planning, Riyadh, 2003. See also Ugo Fasano and Rishi Goyal, 'Emerging Strains in GCC

Youth unemployment has been explained by poor education and training, as well as by the competition from foreign workers. However, MENA governments were committed to education, and the average number of years of schooling for those 15 years and older increased by more than four times between 1960 and 2000. For Bahrain, there were two years of schooling in 1960, five in 1980, and six years in 2000.[23] The ratio of female to male years of schooling increased from 0.51 in 1960 to 0.8 in 1980 and finally to equality in 2000. Kuwait had similar figures. Relatively large gender differences in literacy persisted among the less-educated segments of the Bahrain and Kuwait populations. Illiteracy among young females in Bahrain fell from 22 per cent in 1970 to 2 per cent in 2000.[24] Gross enrolment rates in Bahrain for primary education rose to almost 100 per cent in 2000, but for secondary education the rise was to 85 per cent, and in tertiary education to 20 per cent. Increases in school enrolment coincided with a decline in standards, the result of shortages in teaching specialists, a failure to establish a progressive curriculum, and budget constraints. In particular, there was limited focus on teaching the skills essential for employment in the private sector. Kuwait had lower enrolment rates in primary and secondary education than was the case in Bahrain.[25]

Labour Productivity: An Alternative Narrative on Public–Private Sector Scale and Efficiency

The dominant position of public-sector employment often concealed low productivity as many state employees were secondary school graduates with low educational achievement.

As is evident in Table 10.2, the adult literacy rate as a percentage of adults aged over 15 was 25.3 in 1960, 50.9 in 1970, 71.2 in 1980, 82.1 in 1990, 87.5 in 2000, and 94.6 in 2010. There were 21 public schools in 1950, 55 in 1960, 111 in 1970, 125 in 1980, 158 in 1990, 193 in 2000, and 206 in 2013. Gross enrolment figures divide the total number of students enrolled (regardless of age)

Labour Markets', Topics in Middle Eastern and North African Economics: Proceedings of the Middle East Economic Association, vol. 6, September 2004.

[23] Robert Barro and Jong-Wha Lee, 'International Data on Educational Attainment: Updates and Implications', Centre for International Development, Working Paper No. 42, Harvard University, 2000.

[24] World Development Indicators (WDI) 2003.

[25] WDI 2004; World Bank, 'Reducing Vulnerability and Increasing Opportunity: Social Protection in the Middle East and North Africa', Washington, DC, 2002; Sebastien Dessus, 'Human Capital and Growth', World Bank, Middle East and North Africa, Working Paper No. 22, April 2001.

Table 10.2 Enrolment in primary, secondary, and tertiary education as percentage of age cohort, 1950–2012

	Primary	Secondary	Tertiary
1950	24.0		
1960	72.0		
1970	98.4	51.3	1.4
1980	104.2	59.0	5.1
1990	110.0	87.0	16.7
2000	103.4	100.1	21.0
2012		95.5	33.5

Source: World Bank, World Development Indicators.

by the population in the age cohort of the respective educational level.[26] Weak labour productivity is partly the result of inadequate education, clearly evident throughout secondary and tertiary education. This led to the creation of low value-added sectors, even in periods of increased employment. Periods of falling labour productivity (1979–86, 2005–09) coincided with high rates of growth in Bahrain's labour force, as a substantial part of the increased employment was in the low value-added sectors of the non-oil economy.[27]

The state's generosity in subsidizing high wages as well as providing benefits resulted in low productivity and a weak work ethic.[28] There was also a relationship between productivity and vocational education and training. In Bahrain, 20 per cent of secondary students are enrolled in vocational programmes: 16 per cent of female students are enrolled in vocational programmes and 25 per cent of male students.[29] The weaknesses in Bahrain's vocational technical education were its lack of coordination with market demands and poor links with the private sector. Important reform came through school enterprises and internships that encouraged employment in the private sector.[30]

[26] Bahrain Central Informatics Organization, 2001–2014; World Bank, 'The Road Not Travelled: Education Reform in the Middle East and North Africa', World Development Indicators, Washington, DC, 2008; Yesenn El-Radhi, *Economic Diversification in the Gulf States: Public Expenditure and Non-oil Economic Growth in Bahrain, Oman and Qatar* (Berlin: Gerlach Press, 2018), p. 132.

[27] Bahrain Central Informatics Organization, various issues, 2001, 2004, 2011, 2014; BH/CIO 2011, *Results of Census 2010*; Bahrain, Ministry of Finance and National Economy, *Statistics of the Population Census*, 1971, 1981, 1991, 2001, 2010.

[28] Lant Pritchett, 'Has Education Had a Growth Payoff in the MENA Region?', World Bank, Middle East and North Africa Working Paper No. 18, December 1999; Ryan Paul, 'The School-to-Work Transition: A Cross-National Perspective', *Journal of Economic Literature*, vol. 39 (2001), pp. 34–92.

[29] United Nations Educational, Scientific & Cultural Organization, 2004.

[30] David Neumark and Donna Rothstein, 'School-to-Career Programs and Transitions to Employment and Higher Education', NBER Working Paper No. 10060, Cambridge, MA, 2003.

There is little evidence that government intervention assisted youth employment. Public-sector employment has been a welfare provision for workers who could not find jobs in the private sector at comparable wages, what the World Bank suggests is a form of social contract with youth for securing stable living standards.[31] Few opportunities were created for the young in the high-grade technological industries: the workforce was in government administration, health, and education. The public sector accounted for 13 per cent of total employment, while its wage bill was high. This impeded the development of a vibrant private sector, creating substantial numbers of high-paid jobs.[32] Dependence on the state also meant that minimum wage requirements in Bahrain, as in Oman, were not enforced. Eligibility for social benefits was pervasive. Collective bargaining was not allowed by law in Bahrain, in contrast to Kuwait where it was permitted with restrictions.[33] Consequently, minimum wage regulations have little impact for males but do affect females as they are frequently in lower-paid jobs. In Bahrain, as in most Arab countries, the public voice is weak. But the Bahrain government is efficient in seeking economic growth, and it recognizes the rule of law and seeks to limit corruption. There is political stability and modest regulatory authority but this is rarely discussed in public.[34] Nevertheless, youth unemployment in Bahrain is high, contributing to popular protest during the Arab Spring of 2011.

Higher wages and social and welfare benefits for the public sector limited access to high-productivity, high-paying jobs in the private sector. This was evident in the recruitment of skilled foreign workers for the high-productivity industries, leaving Bahrainis either trapped in the public sector or in unemployment. Public sector employment grew by 16 per cent between 2001 and 2013, while private sector employment grew by 3 per cent. Job creation between 2009 and 2011 was 0.3 per cent and between 2012 and 2013 it was 3.3 per cent.[35] Oil price increases sustained the employment of local and foreign workers until after the financial crisis of 2008. In 2013, the high-skilled, including those with tertiary education, accounted for 15 per cent

[31] World Bank MENA Development Report, *Unlocking the Employment Potential in the Middle East and North Africa* (Washington, DC: World Bank, 2004).

[32] Alan Abrahart, Iqbal Kaur, and Zafiris Tzannatos, 'Government Employment and Active Labour Market Policies in MENA in a Comparative International Context', in *Employment Creation and Social Protection in the Middle East and North Africa*, edited by Heba Handoussa and Zafiris Tzannatos (Cairo: AUC Press, 2002).

[33] ILO, 2004; United States Department of State, Bureau of Democracy, Human Rights and Labor, *Country Reports on Human Rights Practices* (Washington, DC: US Department of State, 2002).

[34] Daniel Kaufmann, Aart Kraay, and Massimo Mastruzzi, 'Governance Matters 111: Governance Indicators for 1996–2002', World Bank Policy Research Working Paper No. 3106, Washington, DC, 2003.

[35] Bahrain Economic Development Board, 2004–13; Bahrain Ministry of Finance and National Economy, 2000–13.

of the labour force, and were largely foreign. The low-skilled accounted for 80 per cent of the labour force in 2013. Only the UAE had a higher percentage of skilled workers, almost 40 per cent.[36] As foreign labour took 75 per cent of private sector jobs, a significant proportion were low skilled. The public sector wage bill in Bahrain was 12 per cent of GDP in 2000, 8 per cent in 2008, and 10 per cent in 2013, among the highest in the developing world. Bahrain was able to support this high ratio through its oil exports, which accounted for 78.4 per cent of total exports. Whatever the inefficiencies in its labour structure, Bahrain was able to create successful industries through economic diversification from the late 1990s.[37] It should be added that Bahrain has a relatively flexible labour market, and has done much to encourage female employment, unlike its Gulf neighbours. As a result of massive investment in infrastructural projects, Bahrain has recruited large numbers of foreign workers, many on temporary contracts in construction. The Bahrain Government has realized that employment quotas are necessary in targeting high-skilled foreign workers, and to restrict the recruitment of unskilled foreign workers, as it depresses both employment opportunities and wages for local unskilled labour. Thus, job creation and elasticity of employment are important in increasing labour productivity. In recent decades, Bahrain's great economic successes have been in finance and in aluminium, both of which require highly skilled and experienced employees.

Labour Reforms: From Stagnation to Renaissance through Vocational Education

Labour reforms undertaken by the Bahrain state have included the expansion of school-based vocational education, support for entrepreneurs, expanded employment in public construction projects, high wage allocations subsidized by the state, and welfare provisions. However, state investment projects did not always greatly expand skills-intensive employment but rather employment opportunities for the low-skilled. Moreover, capital-intensive manufacturing industries, petrochemicals and aluminium for example, often partly state-owned, were dominated by skilled foreign workers. Bahrainis were in construction and trade, low-productivity sectors. The size of the labour force in Bahrain rose more substantially than labour productivity,

---

[36] Bahrain Central Informatics Organization, 2014; Gulf Cooperation Council, 'Labour Market Reforms to Boost Employment and Productivity in the GCC: an Update', 25 October 2014, prepared by IMF staff, pp. 10–13.
[37] Gulf Cooperation Council, 'Labour Market Reforms', p. 14.

Table 10.3 Bahraini employment by sector: per cent

	1971	1981	1991	2001	2010
Public administration	9.8	19.2	34.7	29.9	31.1
Wholesale and retail trades	11.9	9.6	7.9	9.4	13.3
Manufacturing	4.6	6.7	8.3	12.2	10.8
Education and health	14.1	15.0	13.7	14.5	10.7

Sources: Yesenn El-Radhi, *Economic Diversification in the Gulf States: Public Expenditure and Non-oil Economic Growth in Bahrain, Oman and Qatar* (Berlin: Gerlach Press, 2018), pp. 284–5; BH/MFNE, 1972; BH/MCA, 1982; BH/CIO2001, 2004, 2011.

despite accelerated economic diversification after the 1990s. Annual average productivity per worker rose by 0.2 per cent in 1980–2013, while the labour force increase was 5.5 per cent.[38]

As is evident from Table 10.3 public education and health expenditures rose to 4.3 per cent of non-oil gross value but the stock of skills and employment in the private sector was low. Bahrain favoured employment over productivity, notably in a public sector supported by subsidies. More relevant was the segmentation of the labour market between the public sector and private sector. Kuznets has shown that strongly rising output levels per worker are associated with large structural shifts in employment and production from agriculture to industry and subsequently to services.[39] Bahrain would have been well advised to follow greater privatization and liberalization of product and factor markets. Instead, it retained heavy state involvement even in listed corporations. In 2010, the combined employment of public sector activities in public administration, public education, and health services was 41 per cent of total employment. This, and subsidized public sector wages, discouraged the employment of Bahrainis in the private sector: and when they were employed in the private sector, they were in low-productivity industries, construction, trade, and household services. The sectorial structure of employment of Bahrainis is illustrated in the following table.

As is evident from Table 10.4 the increase in construction during the 2000s involved real estate and prestige projects such as Bahrain Bay and Bahrain Investment Wharf, the building of ports and logistics facilities, and

[38] United Nations Statistics Division, National Accounts Main Aggregates Database; and ILO LABORSTA Database.

[39] Simon Kuznets, 'Quantitative Aspects of the Economic Growth of Nations: Industrial Distribution of National Product and Labor Force', *Economic Development and Cultural Change*, vol. 5, no. 4, Supplement, 1957, pp. 1–119.

Table 10.4 Non-Bahraini employment by sector: per cent

	1971	1981	1991	2001	2010
Construction industries	21.3	31.4	18.2	12.2	27.9
Wholesale and retail trades	9.6	11.4	12.6	13.3	16.4
Household services	11.2	14.9	13.1	16.3	16.0
Manufacturing	10.4	9.3	15.0	20.2	12.4

Sources: Yesenn El-Radhi, *Economic Diversification in the Gulf States: Public Expenditure and Non-oil Economic Growth in Bahrain, Oman and Qatar* (Berlin: Gerlach Press, 2018), pp. 284–5; BH/MFNE, 1972; BH/MCA, 1982; BH/CIO2001, 2004, 2011.

electricity projects. In all these, Bahraini nationals were involved in high-skilled positions, but more were in low-skilled employment. Bahrain sought higher-skilled positions for its nationals through joint ventures with international companies such as the petrochemical and IT corporations, for example Microsoft. Bahraini nationals working in the public sector in 2014 earned on average US$2,176 while in the private sector US$1,774, a clear disincentive for nationals to move into the private sector. Also, the private sector was attracting cheap immigrant labour.[40] The government's policy of protecting nationals within public companies resulted in low productivity. Hence, reform was sought through the law.

Labour Productivity and Structural Change

El-Radhi suggests that the experience of Bahrain's labour structures and institutions challenges the view that education exerts a direct impact on labour productivity. High oil and gas export revenues between 1974 and 2013 enabled Bahrain to invest in infrastructural change. But although public education improved, with increased secondary school enrolment and advances in adult literacy, this did not result in increased labour productivity.[41] The structure of Bahrain's labour markets is the more crucial factor in raising labour productivity. Skills should match labour market needs, in particular

[40] BH/SIO (Bahrain Social Insurance Organization), 2015; Information Technology; Bahrain MFNE Ministry of Finance and National Economy, 1972; Bahrain/MCA (Bahrain Ministry of Cabinet Affairs), 1982; Bahrain CIO (Bahrain Central Informatics Organization), 2001, 2004, 2011; Steffen Hertog, 'Defying the Resource Curse: Explaining Successful State Owned Enterprises in Rentier States', *World Politics*, vol. 62, no. 2 (2010), pp. 261–301; Steffen Hertog, 'A Comparative Assessment of Labour Market Nationalization Policies in the GCC', in *National Employment, Migration and Education in the GCC: The Gulf Region: Economic Development and Diversification*, edited by Steffen Hertog (Berlin: Gerlach Press, 2013), pp. 65–106.
[41] El-Radhi, *Economic Diversification in the Gulf States*, pp. 270–1.

the demands for skilled labour in advanced manufacturing.[42] Employment quotas have been introduced to increase the proportion of Bahrain nationals in the private sector labour force. But implementation was difficult as Bahrainis were paid higher wages in the public sector and also lacked the skills sought by the private sector.[43] Employment quotas were often used to recruit highly skilled foreign workers. Increasing the internal mobility of foreign workers could make the labour market more competitive and efficient. Moreover, employers need incentives to invest in training. The 2012 labour law, amending the 1976 act, sought to stimulate the private sector labour market by enhancing employee rights, for example imposing leave entitlements, end of service protection, and maternity leave and childcare provisions. Bahrain then introduced a self-sponsorship scheme for expatriate workers, although 54 per cent of employees in Bahrain were already foreign.[44] A retirement residence permit was introduced, which enabled expatriates to apply for residence after at least 15 years of employment in Bahrain. A property ownership permit gave ownership rights to expatriates, dependent on income and a deposit. The 2012 law also defined unfair termination of employment, set the components of entitlement, and established the procedures for the settlement of labour disputes, including access to the High Court. Employers faced tough penalties if they failed to comply with the new legislation. Bahrain sought international standards and best practices.[45]

Further legislation in 2020 covered such issues as representation in industrial disputes, discrimination, maternity and family leave, termination of employment, and data protection. But it failed to introduce measures to improve labour productivity, essential as Bahrain pursued industrial diversification and a huge expansion in financial services, both of which involved major advances in technologies. Outsourcing and the creation of supply chains with external economies have a substantial direct impact on Bahraini labour. Firms are building hierarchies and networks, and these require advanced training for employees and the establishment of performance measures and accountability. These are far from Bahrain's earlier culture of state-subsidized labour and a high dependence on oil revenues and foreign labour.

[42] J. W. Rojewski (ed.), *International Perspectives on Workforce Education and Development* (Greenwich, CT: Information Age Publishing, 2004); E. Hanushek, L. Woessmann, and L. Zhang, 'General Education, Vocational Education and Labour Market Outcomes over the Life Cycle', NBER Working Paper No. 17504, National Bureau of Economic Research, 2011.

[43] IMF, 'Labour Market Reforms to Boost Employment and Productivity in the GCC: An Update', 25 October 2014, p. 29.

[44] Bahrain Central Informatics Organization, Census 2010.

[45] Oxford Business Group, *Report Bahrain*, 2013, 2020.

Migrant Labour and Cognitive Lock-in and Dependence

It is important to trace the extent to which the dependence on foreign migrant labour, in particular on 'docile' Indian labour, in a range of industries created a labour congestion that disadvantaged local labour. Certainly, youth was resentful of the dominant presence of foreign labour. Sponsorship systems in labour recruitment gave employers an increasingly flexible labour market, reduced labour power, and held down wages. Low-skilled foreign labour dominated the private sector as labour legislation limited minimum wage requirements there to local employees. Private sector business had no incentive to advance into high-skilled production.[46]

In 2014, Bahraini nationals in the public sector earned an average monthly wage of US$2,176, while in the private sector they earned an average of US$1,774. In contrast, non-Bahraini employees earned US$566 in the private sector.[47] That wage discrepancy was a result of the availability and docility of Indian labour, as foreign Arab labour would not accept such low wages. There is no data available for non-Bahraini employees in the public sector.[48]

Indian labour was attractive to employers in Bahrain because of its low cost and docility. Bahrain, engaged in rapid industrial change, needed a flexible employment structure, an ability to offload workers when projects were completed, and a non-unionized workforce. In addition, Indian workers were politically acquiescent. In 1972, Robert Teash alluded to the government's reluctance to recruit Palestinians, Iraqis, Syrians, and Egyptians because of a fear of political extremism.[49] However, some Egyptians were selected for higher-level positions.[50] Heightened sensitivity to the presence of religious sects following the Iranian Revolution and the Iran–Iraq war further reduced and then ended the recruitment of Syrians, Iraqis, and Yemenis, who had earlier been prominent in the security services. The most powerful factor determining labour recruitment has been the investment in infrastructure and manufacturing, and here cheap Indian labour, 30,000 by 1974, was crucial.[51]

[46] Francoise De Bel-Air, 'Demography, Migration and the Labour Market in Bahrain', Gulf Research Center and Migration Policy Centre, European University Institute, GLMM-EN-No. 6, 2015, p. 5.

[47] BH/Social Insurance Organization (SIO), 2015.

[48] El-Radhi, *Economic Diversification in the Gulf States*, p. 288.

[49] R. M. Teash, 'Bahrain: Annual Review for 1972', National Archives, FCO 8/1974.

[50] Miriam Joyce, *Ruling Shaikhs and Her Majesty's Government, 1960–1969* (London and Portland, OR: Frank Cass, 2003), p. 63.

[51] R. M. Teash, 'Internal Political 1974', 17 December 1974, National Archives, FCO 8/2180; Marc Owen Jones, *Political Repression in Bahrain* (Cambridge: Cambridge University Press, 2020), pp. 83–5.

In 2001, there had been 181,220 non-Bahrainis in the workforce. By 2015, the figure had leapt to 551,859.[52]

Mapping the Kafala System of Organized Migrant Labour and Potential Abuse

The kafala system of sponsoring labour migration into Bahrain drew a substantial number of Indians from Kerala and Gujarat, seeking to support their families in India. Indian farming had undergone substantial decline as a result of rapid industrialization and environmental degradation. But sponsorship often involved exploitation of the migrant. First, Indian labourers had to pay a substantial sum for the right to work in the Gulf. In 2002–03, US$2,000 was required to work in Bahrain. The risk for the foreign worker was that he was bound to the recruiter, who could seize his assets if any problem arose. There was the threat of deportation. The fear of returning home stripped of earnings and burdened with debt led many to work illegally in Bahrain, their passports being retained by the sponsor, although this was forbidden by legislation.[53] Living in labour camps far from the city centre where they worked, they were vulnerable to violent attacks from local youth, angered that the recruitment of foreign labour had left them unemployed. The control of these poor foreign workers has been called 'contract slavery'.[54]

In 2009, legislation was introduced to allow free labour movement without the consent of the initial employer. However, as a result of inertia and confusion in the legal system, this was not implemented. The Bahrain state often fails to monitor employer compliance in maintaining the rights of sponsored migrants.[55] As the employer had paid for all migrant expenses, including education and training, it was difficult to challenge him. Bahrain, like its GCC neighbours, has ratified the ILO international conventions concerning migrant labour since December 1978, and in particular the protection

---

[52] Bahrain Central Informatics Organization, Labour Force by Nationality and Sex in Census Years 1959, 1965, 1971, 1981, 1991, 2001; Bahrain Labour Market Indicators, Labour Market Regulatory Authority, Q2, 2015 Rob Franklin, 'Migrant Labor and the Politics of Development in Bahrain', *Middle East Report*, 132 (1985).

[53] Andrew M. Gardner, *City of Strangers: Gulf Migration and the Indian Community in Bahrain* (Ithaca, NY: Cornell University Press, 2010), p. 60.

[54] Kevin Bales, *Disposable People: New Slavery in the Global Economy* (Berkeley, CA: University of California Press, 2004); Kevin Bales, *Understanding Global Slavery: A Reader* (Berkeley, CA: University of California Press, 2005).

[55] Hanan N. Malaeb, 'The "Kafala System" and Human Rights: Time for a Decision', *Arab Law Quarterly*, vol. 29 (2015), p. 322.

of domestic workers regulation of June 2011.[56] In April 2012, the Bahrain National Assembly passed a private sector labour law which increased sick leave and annual leave entitlements, provided for compensation for unfair dismissal, and increased the fines and jail terms for employers who violated these labour laws. The legal reforms also protected workers from abuse, important when they faced the pressures of long hours and unhealthy, congested dwellings, far from their workplace. The threat of deportation increased the docility of Indian labour. These legal interventions were crucial, as for much of this time the Kafala system was only partly codified in law. Particularly significant was the intervention of the Labour Market Regulatory Authority after 2009 to hear petitions from workers. But Bahrain, a small island economy with reduced oil reserves, was highly dependent on cheap, exploited labour if it was to maintain its position in the regional and global economy. Lacking oil wealth, it can no longer employ its citizens in the public sector on high wages. Hence, the state struggled to modify the Kafala system.[57]

Law: Is It a Classic Hallucination or a Search for a Solution and Global Acceptance?

Bahrain consistently sought to reform its labour laws but was inconsistent in their implementation. Facing a flood of foreign workers, in April 2016 it introduced a resolution to the effect that if an employer did not meet Bahraini employment quotas, he or she had to pay BHD300, in addition to the established fees for renewing a visa or issuing a new visa. This was an attempt to encourage employers to recruit local Bahraini workers and not use cheap labour strategies. Another pressure came through work permits. The Labour Market Authority would collect fees in proportion to the required number of work permits. More advanced technology was used in approving visas, and this, to a degree, reduced visa abuse. However, the visa requirement was separate from the requirement to have a work permit, and therefore the employment of cheap foreign labour continued. The most important new measure to be introduced was the Flexi-Work Permit for expatriates in 2017. This allows eligible expatriates to work and live without sponsorship or a

---

[56] ILO, 'International Labour Migration: A Rights-based Approach', Geneva, 2010; Malaeb, 'The "Kafala System" and Human Rights', p. 328.

[57] Anh Longva, 'Keeping Migrant Workers in Check: The Kafala System in the Gulf', *Middle East Report*, no. 211 (1999), pp. 20–2; Anh Longva, *Walls Built on Sand: Migration, Exclusion and Society in Kuwait* (Boulder, CO: Westview Press, 1997).

work permit. It must be renewed every two years. But these attempts to control the influx of foreign workers did not impact on the majority, that is, those in poorly paid jobs and living in labour camps. For that group, the most significant legislation came in December 2018, an amendment to the Bahrain Labour Law, making it unlawful for an employer to abuse or harass workers.[58] Indeed, a central theme in the modernization of Bahrain's labour law has been the attempt made to define the responsibilities of Bahraini employers towards foreign workers, although the law still struggles to protect foreign workers. But the United Nations has been impressed. In 2018, it declared that Bahrain's Flexi-Work Permit model offered the best international practice, although the cost to the expatriate employee, BHD1169 to be paid every two years, was high.

The attempts to reform the Kafala system failed to offer protection through collective bargaining or the establishment of a minimum wage. The legislation also lacked protective measures for foreign domestic workers, who were principally women. In 2006, the LMRA had been mandated to regulate work permits for migrant workers. As part of this process, in 2008 it introduced the Anti-Trafficking Law that forbade the withholding of workers' passports or their wages. It also investigated violations involving forced labour recruitment or sex trafficking. But trafficking offences continued, despite the introduction in 2017 of a National Referral System, a hotline, to track offenders and protect victims. In May 2009, the LMRA had formally abolished the Kafala system and now the LMRA itself directly controlled the sponsorship of migrant workers, providing more liberal protection. But Human Rights Watch reported that the Kafala labour system remained in place. To acquire the right to work in Bahrain still required a sponsor. In 2011, the government introduced the requirement that a migrant worker must stay with his or her initial employer for a minimum of a year. This reflected the inefficiency of the LMRA, together with allegations of corruption in the organization. Even when, in 2012, legislation was introduced to provide rights on pay and sick leave in the private sector, with increased fines for employers who breach those rights, implementation is poor, the result of employer greed and the docility and easy availability of foreign workers. Among the 1.6 million residents of Bahrain, more than 0.6 million are migrant workers, accounting for 54.7 per cent of the workforce and concentrated in low-skilled, low-paid jobs. Just under 100,000 are domestic workers, including 75,305 women.[59] Thus, the Government claimed in April 2017 that it would abolish the Kafala

---

[58] Bahrain Report 2020 on Labour Law.
[59] European Centre for Democracy and Human Rights, 'Advocating for Human Rights in the Gulf Region; Bahrain Migrant Workers Rights', Brussels, June 2019, p. 1.

system. But it has not accepted the International Convention on the Protection of the Rights of All Migrant Workers. Bahrain's National Institution for Human Rights (NIHR) 2017 Report declined to explain its refusal to comply with the International Convention. However, Bahrain, together with Oman, were the only countries in the GCC that sought to reduce inequalities in pay and residence for foreign workers. In 2017, the LMRA announced that all recruitment agencies in Bahrain must, from the 1st of October, adopt a new mandatory contract for domestic workers, which laid down the nature of the job, work hours, leave provisions, wages, employee's residence, and welfare provisions. But responsibility for determining those rights remained with the employer, and therefore enforcement remained arbitrary. Labour inspectors have no authority to inspect private homes and the contract does not fall within the provisions of Bahrain legislation on labour inspection. Such inspection provisions are essential as domestic workers are largely immigrants. They face difficulties in reporting to the authorities, not least because of language difficulties, and fear abuse and retaliation if they do submit complaints. Karim Radhi of the General Federation of Bahrain Trade Unions (GBTU) has called for stronger protection of domestic workers.[60]

Women and Greater Visibility

Female participation in public sector employment rose from 5 per cent in 1971 to 46 per cent in 2011.[61] The greatest increase was between 1980 and 1997, 10.3 per cent to 20.6 per cent.[62] This coincided with an increase in migrant labour during the oil boom and an expansion in the non-oil economic sectors since 1990. The increase in foreign direct investment accounted for the expansion in Bahraini female employment but ironically was followed by an increase in Bahraini youth unemployment. Public sector expansion also increased the female labour participation rate. Bahraini women comprised 65 per cent of the female workforce at the end of 2010.[63] This was part of the government initiative to nationalize the labour force. The labour and economic reforms of 2006 further stimulated job creation, including in the private sector, through the provision of technical training

[60] 'Assessing Bahrain's New Standard Contract for Domestic Workers', Migrant-Rights.Org, 2018: https://www.migrant-rights.org/2018/03/assessing-bahrains-new-standard-contract-for-domestic-workers.
[61] Bahrain Central Informatics Organization, Statistical Abstract, Kingdom of Bahrain: www.cio.gov.bh 2011.
[62] International Labour Organization, World Employment Report, Geneva, 1998, pp. 217–20, table 7.
[63] Bahrain Central Informatics Organization, Statistical Abstract, Kingdom of Bahrain.

for Bahrainis and reductions in the salary differentials between nationals and foreigners. The 2009 revision of the Kafala system, giving foreign employees freedom to change employer, increased opportunities for Bahrainis in the private sector.[64]

Bahraini women were largely employed in education, healthcare, and childcare. Oil revenues increased from the 1980s, drawing in foreign female workers from poorer Arab countries and from Asia. They concentrated in domestic employment.[65] Gulf Air recruited Bahraini and European women as flight attendants, and there was an influx of foreign women into the leisure and sex industries.[66] In domestic jobs there was recruitment from Indonesia, the Philippines, and South Asia. The expansion in regional tourism and increased consumerism drove the construction of shopping centres, amusement parks, hotels, and restaurants, each of which recruited foreign workers.[67] The retail sector employed Bahrainis in sales and clerical positions working alongside foreign colleagues. But the entertainment and personal service sectors remain, together with domestic employment, dominated by foreign women and men. Foreign labour remained in the unskilled, low-paid, private sector, while Bahraini women were manoeuvring themselves into the teaching sector and into public schools. Teaching in Bahrain's public schools, which had opened for girls in 1928, was popular for foreign women. Many also worked in foreign firms as clerks and secretaries. Healthcare shifted away from its reliance on foreign labour but at a slower pace than education.[68] Paying greater attention to gender and ethnicity is important in increasing female entry into diverse jobs and in acquiring education and skills. Domestic work to healthcare remain dominant spaces for South Asian and South East Asian females, while Bahraini women are increasingly in clerical work, healthcare, as well as working for the Bahraini airline Gulf Air, besides being self-employed in SMEs.[69] The rise of private entrepreneurship and self-employment among Bahraini women is not difficult to understand,

---

[64] Sharon Nagy, 'Bahraini and Non-Bahraini Women in Bahrain's Workforce: Gender, Work and Nationality', *Arabian Humanities: International Journal of Archaeology and Social Sciences in the Arabian Peninsula*, 2013: https://journals.openedition.org/cy/2144, 4.

[65] Michele Ruth Gamburd, *The Kitchen Spoon's Handle: Transnationalism and Sri Lanka's Migrant Housemaids* (Ithaca, NY: Cornell University Press, 2000): Caitrin Lynch, 'The Good Girls of Sri Lankan Modernity: Moral Orders of Nationalism and Capitalism', *Identities*, vol. 6, no. 1 (1999), pp. 55–89.

[66] Gulf Air, 'Gulf Air Celebrates First All-Bahraini Female Cabin Crew Graduation with Tamkeen Support, 2 August 2010: http://www.gulfair.com/English/aboutgulfair/Pages/News.aspx? newsno=180.

[67] Staci Strobl, 'Policing Housemaids: The Criminalization of Domestic Workers in Bahrain', *British Journal of Criminology*, vol. 49, no. 2 (2009), pp. 165–83.

[68] Nagy, 'Bahraini and Non-Bahraini Women in Bahrain's Workforce', pp. 11–12.

[69] S. Al-Najjar, 'Women Migrant Domestic Workers in Bahrain', International Migration Papers, 47, International Migration Programme, International Labour Office, Geneva, 2002.

as they are often better educated than Bahraini men. Structural change in the economy through outsourcing increased opportunities for women in private business and in self-employment. A woman would face less public exposure by being self-employed and working from home.

New Economy and New Opportunities for Women

Reducing the gender employment gap has been made possible by the expansion in digital financial services, which offers significant opportunities for women. Moreover, FinTech has built trust and attracted savings from domestic workers. Digitalized services provide flexibility, security, and transparency. Financial networks attract female agents responsible for e-payment, for example through Fawry in Egypt and Dinarak in Jordan, to reach female customers. Migrant workers, both men and women, have access to universal digital provision. More than 50 per cent of workers in Bahrain are of foreign origin but digital access provides them with stability in their financial transactions. It is important to emphasize that, for example, the Hawiyati platform developed by Making Cents International has provided migrant women with an entry point to build their credit rating and history, and so acquire personal or business loans. These financial institutions are of immense value in a society that still discriminates against women, although Bahrain and Oman are more progressive than their Gulf neighbours. The inclusive financial structure is even more critical for lower-income workers, both local and foreign.[70] In March 2016, Bahrain launched a US$100 million fund for female entrepreneurs, supported by the Bahrain Women Development Fund, the Supreme Council of Women, Tamkeen (with an emphasis on education), and the Bahrain Development Bank. This was solely for Bahrainis and had no impact on migrant workers. In contrast, the Arab Women's Enterprise Fund (AWEF), a five-year project funded by the British DFID and established in 2015, had an immense impact in the MENA countries, including in Bahrain. AWEF's Practitioner Learning Brief offered courses to women through DFS (Digital Finance Services) on innovative digital finance. AWEF also encouraged e-payments to assist foreign female workers. But it is perhaps ironic that while advances in technology and education empowered women, Bahrain's youth experienced high unemployment.

---

[70] Chloe Gueguen, Sabal Al Majali, and Julia Hakspiel, 'Making Digital Finance Work for Women in the MENA Region: 8 Lessons from the Field', Information and Communications Technology.

Explaining Inertia of Youth and Employment in Bahrain

In the midst of economic growth and job creation between 2000 and 2011, there was persistent youth unemployment, and in part this explains the prominent role of the young in the Arab Spring. Young Bahrainis, in particular the privileged, had enjoyed educational and employment opportunities but often waited for high-paid jobs in the public and semi-public sectors. This preference for public employment partially explains the high level of unemployment among the youth. It is also explained by the high population growth between 1970 and 2010, an increase from 8 million to 45 million across the GCC.[71]

Table 10.5 indicates that in 2010–11, those in the 15–29 age group accounted for 52 per cent of the total population. This bulge did not coincide with youth employment rates.[72] The labour force participation rates for Bahrain nationals of working age 15–64 was 51 per cent. This low participation rate partly reflects the high proportion of jobs being created in the private sector, where Asians with skills fill low-paid jobs. The female labour participation rate was close to 30 per cent in 2010.[73] The participation rate

Table 10.5 Annual percentage growth in Bahrain population, 1950–55 to 2010–11

1950–55	2.91
1955–60	3.10
1960–65	4.04
1965–70	2.79
1970–75	4.28
1975–80	4.86
1980–85	3.51
1985–90	3.39
1990–95	3.12
1995–2000	2.21
2000–05	1.68
2005–10	1.33
2010–11	1.29

Sources: 'Labour Migration to the GCC Countries', Baqer Al-Najjar, 2006; Bahrain Central Informatics Organization, 2011.

[71] United Nations, Economic and Social Affairs, Population Division, '2013 World Population Prospects: The 2012 Revision', DVD ed.
[72] Bahrain Central Informatics Organization, 2011.
[73] ILO, October 2011, 'Economically Active Population, Estimates and Projections', 6th ed.: http://laborsta.ilo.org/applv8/data/EAPEP/eapep_E.html.

for males in Bahrain approached 71 per cent. But for young men it was low. The Male Labour Force Participation Rate (LFPR) rose within the 15–29 age cohort but fell in the 30–64 cohort.[74] Despite staying longer in school than young women, young men are in low-paid jobs, because of their inferior educational achievements and consequent low skills. They are often in self-employment or in the army, police, or the security sector.

A major factor in the high-unemployment rate among Bahraini youth is that the new jobs created by the oil boom and economic diversification in the first decade of the twentieth century were taken mainly by foreign workers.[75] In 2010, 34 per cent of working Bahrainis were in the public sector, down from 49 per cent in 2004.[76] Wages in the public sector are generally higher than in the private sector, and those in the public sector also enjoy welfare subsidies, in particular substantial pensions.

The Legal Arc of National Labour Protection from Migrant Threat

To discourage private sector employment being dominated by expatriates, in 1995 Bahrain imposed a broad quota for all private sector recruitment. This required firms to ensure that 20 per cent of their workforce were Bahraini, adding that firms had to increase the proportion of Bahraini employees by 5 per cent each year. This had serious implications for labour productivity. First, Bahrainis were often low-skilled and could move jobs easily. Second, there was the option for Bahraini youth to be self-employed: in 2010 it was estimated that 9 per cent of Bahrainis were in their own or family firms.[77] This led to a black market in the private sector, where employers used expatriates under the guise of being locals. These expatriates also worked in several places illegally.[78]

---

[74] Bahrain Ministry of Labour and Bahrain Centre for Studies and Research, Report, 2004.
[75] International Monetary Fund, 'Gulf Cooperation Council Countries: Enhancing Economic Outcomes in an Uncertain Global Economy', Washington, DC, 2011.
[76] Bahrain Central Informatics Organization, 2011, results of census, 2010: http://www.cio.gov.bh/cio_eng/SubDetailed.aspx? subcatid=256; Bahrain Ministry of Labour and Bahrain Centre for Studies and Research, *Labour Force Survey*, November 2004.
[77] Bahrain Central Informatics Organization, 2011.
[78] Paul Dyer and Samer Kherfi, 'Gulf Youth and the Labour Market', in *Young Generation Awakening: Economics, Society, and Policy on the Eve of the Arab Spring*, edited by Edward A. Sayre and Tarik M. Yousef (New York: Oxford University Press, 2016), pp. 98–9.

Thus, despite reform, there was rising youth unemployment at the same time as a boom in job creation.[79] In 2010, Bahrain's unemployment rate was 4.7 per cent: but the youth unemployment rate was 10.7 per cent, although the labour force survey of 2004 had recorded an unemployment rate for Bahraini youth of 29.2 per cent.[80] Young females, in the age cohort 25–29, recorded an unemployment rate of 43 per cent, despite possessing superior educational levels. Employers' reluctance to employ women could be related to their family and childcare positions, or to the possibility that they would soon leave to marry.[81] Bahrain increased its investment in secondary and tertiary education and in training but the young still sought employment in the public sector, instead of acquiring technology skills and science training perhaps more suited to the private sector.

The Bahrain government persevered to force youth into certain occupations. It sought first to eliminate wage differentials between the public and private sectors. The employment quotas were abolished, as they were being manipulated by employers and were creating a black economy. The Kafala system of hiring and firing workers was discouraged and the state now regulated working conditions and allowed trade unions to operate. The authorities also introduced unemployment insurance schemes and training programmes, and increased wages. Fees for the recruitment of foreign workers were increased. In 2007, all labour issues became the responsibility of the newly established Labour Market Regulatory Authority. But vested interests resisted the removal of the Kafala system and the increased fees for foreign worker visas. Bahraini workers also raised objections to the levy on wages, regarding it as a tax on wages instead of seeing it as an insurance provision. All these measures have had a significant impact.[82]

[79] D. Salahi-Isfahani and N. Dhillon, 'Stalled Youth Transitions in the Middle East: A Framework for Policy Reform', Middle East Youth Initiative, Working Paper No. 8, Washington, DC: Wolfensohn Center for Development, Brookings Institution, 2008.

[80] Bahrain Central Informatics Organization, Census 2011.

[81] N. Ridge, Education and the Reverse Gender Divide in the Gulf States: Embracing the Global, Ignoring the Local (New York: Teachers College Press, 2014); Dyer and Kherfi, 'Gulf Youth and the Labour Market', p. 102.

[82] Steffen Hertog, 'Arab Gulf States: An Assessment of Nationalization Policies', Gulf Labour Markets and Migration Programme, Research Paper no. 1, 2014: http://cadmus.eui.eu/bitstream/handle/1814/32156/GLMM%20Research Paper_01-2014.pdf?sequence=1; Paul Dyer, 'Human Capital and the Labour Market in Bahrain', in Bahrain Country Profile: The Road Ahead for Bahrain (Cairo: Economic Research Forum, 2008); I. Forstenlechner and E. Rutledge, 'Unemployment in the Gulf: Time to Update the "Social Contract"', Middle East Policy, vol. 17, no. 2 (2010), pp. 38–48.

Youth at Risk: Political Impact from Migrant Labour Hoarding, 1950s–1990s

The youth and labour struggles in Bahrain can perhaps be examined through the perspective of E. P. Thompson's construction of English labour struggles and political activity from the late eighteenth century.[83] Thompson sees English working-class movements as serious political movements. In Bahrain, class did exist but the class structure was loose because industrial work was limited: industrial discipline and labour collective consciousness was shaped by tradition, family, and culture. Moreover, capitalism in Bahrain, from pearl diving to the oil industry and later manufacturing, drew on both foreign and local labour, often in conflict with each other. The merchants were of diverse backgrounds, with complex ties to the state. The high proportion of docile immigrant labour undermined class solidarity. An obedient workforce allowed for the imposition of restrictive practices on migrant workers, while Bahrainis were cushioned within public sector companies. There were, of course, worker protests from the 1950s but it was the Arab Spring of 2011 that created a class solidarity among the Bahraini workforce. The Bahrain Labour Federation, a trade union, was established in October 1955 by BAPCO workers but membership was limited to Bahraini citizens, and it was less concerned with labour grievances than with calling for the establishment of democratic institutions, independence, and with wealth redistribution. This approach was too political and hazy to have an impact.[84] Labour rights were only seriously established in the Workers Trade Union Law passed by King Hamad bin Isa Al-Khalifah on 24 September 2002. This recognized the right of workers to organize collectively. The law had provisions for strikes but restricted union activities in essential industries. In October 2006, the King introduced a law banning the sacking of employees engaged in union activities. Batelco was one significant company that had union protection.[85] There have been few high-profile strikes and disputes appear to have been commonly settled within the corporation.

[83] Thompson, *The Making of the English Working Class*. See also Frederick Cooper, 'Work, Class and Empire: an African Historian's Retrospective on E. P. Thompson', *Social History*, vol. 20, no 2 (1995), pp. 235–41.
[84] Emile A. Nakhleh, *Bahrain: Political Development in a Modernizing Society* (Lexington, MA: Lexington Books, 1976), p. 78.
[85] Bahrain Central Informatics Organization, 2010: see also https://www.paulhastings.com/area/international-employment-law/Bahrain.

Thompson's emphasis on the fluidity of inequality in models of class domination was perhaps evident in Bahrain when workers flocked into the urban areas from the 1950s as a result of the oil boom. This tied economic grievances to the increasing authoritarianism of the monarchy, bolstered by merchant elites, from both the traditional merchant classes and the new merchant elite, emerging from within the Royal Family from the 1970s. The uneven development of capitalism led Bahrainis to seek well-paid public sector jobs. Labour disturbance is usually met by soothing responses from the Al-Kahalifah family, often with legislation for dealing with worker complaints. Only the Arab Spring of 2011 showed serious divisions.

Labour's tensions with the state in Bahrain is sporadic populism and not Thompson's class war against capitalism. There are diverse ways of analysing Thompson's English working-class ideology, where conflict with capitalism arises from real labour power. Thompson remains an inspiration in understanding the relationship between capitalism and the authoritarian monarchy in Bahrain. Bahrain was part of Britain's informal empire until 1971, a time when the state was not aggressively interventionist. Only after independence did state power grow, and it was not until the late 1990s that Bahrain's transnational corporations exerted substantial pressure. The working class is not an opponent of the state, although protests are frequent. In reality, capitalists are subservient to the monarchy. Perhaps Bahrainis are trapped in an ethnic sectarian culture, although it must be said that sectarianism more readily expresses the economic grievance of poor Shi'ites in deprived urban areas. Tensions in Bahrain are often driven by external forces, such as by Iran and its need to exert Shi'ite power. William Sewell provides an apt analysis of labour power that is relevant for Bahrain. Current social theory, instead of dividing economics from the political or social, now claims that these are cultural or discursive.[86]

Wages are at the core of dissent among urban Bahraini workers, alongside race, as migrant workers dominate the private sector. Chakrabarty disputes Thompson's articulation of English equality before the law as being a crucial heritage of the English working class.[87] I would argue that class identity is missing in Bahrain, from the time of the pearl industry, as the divers were

[86] William Sewell, 'Toward a Post-Materialist Rhetoric for Labor History', in *Rethinking Labor History: Essays on Discourse and Class Analysis*, edited by Lenard R. Berlanstein (Champaign, IL: University of Illinois Press, 1993), p. 18; Dipesh Chakrabarty, *Rethinking Working-Class History: Bengal 1890–1940* (Princeton, NJ: Princeton University Press, 1989); David Featherstone and Paul Griffin, 'Spatial Relations, Histories from Below and the Makings of Agency: Reflections on The Making of the English Working Class at 50', *Progress in Human Geography*, vol. 40, no. 3 (2016), pp. 375–93.
[87] Dipesh Chakrabarty, *Rethinking Working-Class History: Bengal 1890–1940* (Princeton, NJ: Princeton University Press, 1989)

poor in contrast to the affluent pearl merchants and boat owners. However, there was a form of equality among the divers, often linked to tribal families within a salafiyya system (mutual collectives) of loans and support. The salafiyya were not monopolies. Monopolies emerged in pearl trading only with the rise of the wealthy merchant families. They evolved from salafiyya, from sharing the cost of dives through a network of loans and mutual obligations that proved useful in providing support to divers in dire times.[88] This form of labour could not be sustained by the oil industry, dependent as it was on machinery and technical expertise. The salafiyya identity vanished with the end of pearling. The oil industry brought new structures and relationships with labour that would be difficult to term as class relations. Thompson's emphasis on notions of the freeborn Englishman, of equality before the law, of articulations of liberty and responsibility, each a heritage of the English working class, could survive only in a particular economic and cultural environment. In Bahrain, the emergence of the oil industry fractured traditional internationalism in trading and pearl diving. This challenge to Thompson, that English class experience was not necessarily unique, is captured by Chakrabarty.[89]

Thompson's emphasis on the particular geographical contexts for class and spatial politics, and his stress on the barriers between places and on international exchange, are debated by Third World scholars. His work had a very significant impact on Indian subaltern studies with criticisms of his focus on English distinctiveness in class and internationalism.[90] Paul Gilroy argues that 'the laudable, radical varieties of English cultural sensibility' celebrated by Thompson 'were not produced spontaneously from their own internal and intrinsic dynamics'.[91] Catherine Hall calls for a focus on the intersection of race, class, nation, and gender divisions both at home and across the empire to understand the imagined homogeneity with home.[92] Bahraini youth competed with skilled Bahrainis and skilled foreign workers, but rarely with unskilled immigrants.

---

[88] Robert A. Carter, *Sea of Pearls: Seven Thousand Years of the Industry that Shaped the Gulf* (London: Arabian Publishing, 2012), pp. 109–282.

[89] Dipesh Chakrabarty, 'Fifty Years of E. P. Thompson's The Making of the English Working Class', *Economic and Political Weekly*, 21 December 2013, pp. 24–6; Chakrabarty, *Rethinking Working Class History*.

[90] Ranajit Guha, *Elementary Aspects of Peasant Insurgency in Colonial India* (Durham, NC and London: Duke University Press, 1999); Raj Chandavarkar, 'The Making of the Working Class: E. P. Thompson and Indian History', in *Mapping Subaltern Studies and the Postcolonial*, edited by Vinayak Chaturvedi (London: Verso, 2000), pp. 50–72.

[91] Paul Gilroy, *The Black Atlantic: Modernity and Double Consciousness* (London: Verso, 1993).

[92] Catherine Hall, 'The Rule of Difference: Gender, Class and Empire in the Making of the 1832 Reform Act', in *Gendered Nations: Nationalisms and Gender in the Long Nineteenth Century*, edited by Ida Blom, Karen Hagemann, and Catherine Hall (Oxford: Berg, 2000), pp. 107–36.

The labour market in Bahrain is not competitive but segmented between migrant labour and local youth. Foreign workers were seen as adjuncts of the Western workforce and the absence of trade union activity within immigrant labour further estranged the two segments. The presence of migrant workers was resented, even though they occupied miserable, low-paid jobs and had little freedom to leave. Despite the desperate conditions of migrant workers, Bahrainis were angry, and occasionally erupted in political mobilization, as occurred in the 1950s when BAPCO employees demanded Bahrainization of the entire workforce. The share of migrant workers in the workforce increased from 37.6 per cent in 1971 to 58.8 per cent in 1981. In 1981, Bahrainis accounted for 33 per cent of workers in the private sector and 67 per cent in the public sector.[93] Most of the resentment was directed at low-paid Asian workers, not at the Arabs and Persians.[94]

In the period after 1991, economic diversification led to a decline in public sector employment and increased resentment on the part of Bahraini workers against the state. This, and earlier changes in power relations within the Al-Khalifah family, fuelled anti-government protests. The ruling family held positions on the boards of BAPCO, ALBA, and other corporations, and was further strengthened by Sunni recruits from Najd into the army and security services. Sunnis close to the royal family were prominent in the Ministry of Information and the Ministry of Foreign Affairs. This grip on the bureaucracy, corporations, and social networks was engineered by the Al-Khalifah family. This added to the anger and volatility of unemployed youth.[95] Rising anger had followed the elimination of Parliament in 1975, a harbinger of increasing authoritarianism and political unrest until Hamad's reign. The rise of Islamic activism attracted both Shi'a and deprived Sunnis, already antagonistic towards foreign workers, and now seeking accountability from the state. The Intifada of 1994–99, punctuated by demonstrations and petitions, targeted violence towards foreign workers, seen as the primary cause of the protesters' economic woes. 'Unskilled immigrants … occupy the bottom of the income distribution and thus contribute to measured inequality.'[96]

---

[93] Franklin, 'Migrant Labor and the Politics of Development in Bahrain', p. 9.

[94] Franklin, 'Migrant Labor and the Politics of Development in Bahrain', p. 132; Nelida Fuccaro, 'Mapping the Transnational Community: Persians and the Space of the City in Bahrain, c.1869–1937', in *Transnational Connections in the Arab Gulf*, edited by Madawi al-Rasheed (London: Routledge, 2005); Ian Secombe and Richard Lawless, 'Foreign Worker Dependence in the Gulf and the International Oil Companies 1910–50', *International Migration Review*, vol. 20, no. 3 (1986).

[95] Fuad I. Khuri, *Tribe and State in Bahrain: The Transformation of Social and Political Authority in an Arab State* (Chicago, IL: Chicago University Press, 1980), p. 123.

[96] Raghuram G. Rajan, *Fault Lines: How Hidden Fractures Still Threaten the World Economy* (Princeton, NJ: Princeton University Press, 2010), p. 28. See also Nolan McCarthy, Keith Poole, and Howard Rosenthal, *Polarized America: The Dance of Ideology and Unequal Riches* (Cambridge, MA: MIT Press, 2008).

Shi'a Employment and Sectorial Distribution

The government was mindful, too, of Shi'a employment in strategically important industrial and technological sectors. In 1984, of the BATELCO (Bahrain Telecommunications) total workforce of 1,800, Shi'a accounted for 87 per cent. In BANOCO (Bahrain National Oil Company), of a total workforce of 4,500, Shi'a accounted for 80 per cent. In ALBA (Aluminium Bahrain), of a total of 2,000 workers, Shi'a accounted for 79 per cent. In BSED (Bahrain Electricity), the figures were 1,900 and 78 per cent.[97] By 1997, Shi'a dominance was restricted to non-sensitive industries and did not include security services. As Shi'a employment diminished, there were protests. In the Arab Spring of 2011, youth protests over unemployment fused with protests by displaced and disenfranchised Shi'a.[98] The state exploited its increasing control over labour selection based on ethnic, religious, and tribal identity, while clamping down on union activity. This discrimination against Shi'a in employment aroused the ire of the ITUC. 'These violations are continuous and recurrent and the labour legislation fails to protect workers.'[99]

It is important to recognize that modern Bahrain is largely urban, and that agrarian labour is much diminished. There is now a substantial economic, political, and social distance between the metropolitan Manama and Muharraq and the agricultural hinterland.[100]

The Paradoxes of Agriculture and Fisheries: Labour Decline

Why is agricultural labour insignificant in modern Bahrain? The challenges to the farmer and the fisherman first came from the pearling industry but it was the rise of tribal mercantilism and urbanization along the coasts of Bahrain from the 1840s that transformed the agricultural hinterland.

[97] S. P. Collis, 'The Shi'a in Bahrain', Bahrain Internal Political, 1984, TNA FCO8/5422.
[98] Luayy Bahri, 'The Opposition in Bahrain: A Bellwether for the Gulf', *Middle East Policy*, vol. 5, no. 2 (1997), pp. 42–57.
[99] International Trade Union Confederation, 'Countries at Risk: Violations of Trade Union Rights', 2013, p. 36; Omar AlShehabi, 'Contested Modernity: Divided Rule and the Birth of Sectarianism, Nationalism and Absolutism in Bahrain', *British Journal of Middle Eastern Studies*, vol. 44, no. 3 (2017), pp. 335–55; Austin T. Turk, *Political Criminality: The Defiance and Defence of Authority* (Beverly Hills, CA: Sage Publications, 1982); Fred H. Lawson, 'Repertoires of Contention in Contemporary Bahrain', in *Islamic Activism: A Social Movement Theory Approach*, edited by Quintan Wiktorowicz (Bloomington, IN: Indiana University Press, 2004).
[100] Nelida Fuccaro, *Histories of City and State in the Persian Gulf: Manama since 1800* (Cambridge: Cambridge University Press, 2009), p. 219.

Al-Khalifah and his tribal entrepreneurs created a new economy with shrinking agricultural hamlets occupied by Shi'ites. By 1836, the villages of al-Diraz and al-Shakurah lay in ruin. Shaykh Isa's agricultural revenue halved between 1873 and 1904. In 1906, Bahrain's date production collapsed, and the increased import of dates reflected the decline of the farmer and growing resentment between Shi'i notables of rural origins and the largely Shi'i agrarian population.[101] The rapid growth of Manama and Muharraq, and the state's approach to land reclamation, had major consequences for agriculture and the farming and fishing communities. The loss of land to oil caused rioting by farmers in the 1950s. Land loss was increasingly equated with sectarianism and the immigration of Sunnis and foreign workers taking Shi'is' jobs. 'Petro-urbanism' and increasing globalization marginalized agricultural workers by the 1980s.[102] Old villages such as Jidd Hafs and Bilad al-Qadim were transformed into satellites of Manama, termed by Fuad Khuri as 'dormitory communities', marginalizing rural communities and agrarian labour.[103] These new suburban Shi'i dormitory communities were still identified as backward, 'villager, farmer or labourer, illiterate, emotional and revolutionary', in contrast to Sunnis, 'peace-loving, urban, wealthy and educated'.[104]

Law remained a useful deterrent to land grabs and in protecting the agricultural economy, and therefore preserving employment in the agrarian and fisheries sectors. Islamic endowments also helped to sustain an efficient and mature institutional framework for land registration and transfers, securing opportunities for fishermen and farmers to prevent fragmentation and to use land as collateral for obtaining formal credit. In a rural agricultural context, the waqf can sustain employment, although often awqaf failed to register land and therefore failed to secure ownership. Ma'tams did preserve special rights of ownership and preserved special rights in the face of a variety of legal reforms. The cash waqf also sustained local farmers and fishermen, despite the fact that cash does not have an enduring quality like real estate. Bahrain witnessed a considerable expansion between 1980 and 2000 in the number of mortgaged parcels of land and in the percentage of properties purchased through an Islamic Bank.[105] As argued by Singer, awqaf were thus integral to the neighbourhood economy and society, being 'affected by a whole range

---

[101] Fuccaro, *Histories of City and State in the Persian Gulf*, pp. 27–9.
[102] Fuccaro, *Histories of City and State in the Persian Gulf*, pp. 222–3.
[103] Khuri, *Tribe and State in Bahrain*, pp. 253–4.
[104] Ilsa Amelia Schumacher, 'Ritual Devotion among Shi'i in Bahrain', PhD dissertation, University of London, 1987, p. 53.
[105] Manaf Yousuf Hamza, 'Land Registration in Bahrain: its Past, Present and Future within an Integrated GIS Environment', PhD dissertation, University of East London, 2003.

of local factors from weather to urban development'.[106] While the Kuwait Awqaf Public Foundation (KAPF) used modern computerized information to sustain local financial and investment support, Bahrain had a backlog of problems through weak management. It also had poor coordination with ministries and local institutions in the provision of land and housing, both essential for agriculture and fishing.[107] The Islamic moral economy provides instruments for survival in the modern economy, challenging Timur Kuran's assertion that Islamic financial institutions have not revolutionized the economic lives of Muslims but merely created sub-economies that offer cultural and interpersonal bonding.[108] It is valuable now to examine the maintenance in Bahrain of agrarian performance and productivity through an agribusiness culture after 1980, the 'creation of an agro-commodity circuit and capital accumulation'.[109]

The expansion in innovative agribusiness is impressive given the pressures of securing food within a global food chain. In many of the Gulf states, large agribusiness firms emerged which outsource food production through the acquisition of land and resources in Africa and Asia. Bahrain, the least wealthy of the Gulf states, exploited foreign sources far less than did Kuwait, the UAE, and Saudi Arabia. But at the end of 2009, following protests against rising food prices in the previous year, Bahrain invested in agriculture and fisheries through Nader, Ebrahim, and Hassan (NEH), to secure rice, bananas, and fish from the Philippines, and US$500 million in an agricultural project in Turkey.[110] Bahrain uses the Philippines to grow rice, wheat, and sugar, employing cheap labour within a secure political environment that protects investors. But outsourcing food production overseas makes the position of farming communities in Bahrain more difficult, and may provoke rising food prices and food riots. Transnational agri-business has hit the agricultural chain in Bahrain. Bahrain continues to farm less water-intensive crops such as fruits (although date production has declined) and vegetable and food-processing industries have expanded.[111] Bahrain's inadequate food production and rising unemployment is strangely related to a heavy reliance

---

[106] Amy Singer, 'A Note on Land and Identity: From Zeamet to Waqf', in *New Perspectives on Property and Land in the Middle East*, edited by Roger Owen (Cambridge, MA: Harvard University Press, 2001).

[107] S. A. Salih, *The Challenges of Poverty Alleviation in IDB Member Countries* (Jeddah: Islamic Development Bank, 1999).

[108] Timur Kuran, 'Islamic Economics and the Islamic Sub-economy', *Journal of Economic Perspectives*, vol. 9, no. 4 (1995), pp. 155–73.

[109] Adam Hanieh, *Money, Markets, and Monarchies: The Gulf Cooperation Council and the Political Economy of the Contemporary Middle East* (Cambridge: Cambridge University Press, 2018).

[110] Eckart Woertz, *Oil for Food: The Global Food Crisis and the Middle East* (Oxford: Oxford University Press, 2013), figure 7.1 for details of agro-projects established between 2008 and 2011.

[111] Alpen Capital GCC food industry: www.alpencapital.com/.2016May.

on food subsidies, price controls, cash transfers to farmers and fishermen, and school feeding programmes. It should be added that Bahrain's youth are keen on high wages and secure jobs in the public sector, and are little attracted by poorly paid work in agriculture.

As a consequence of the low level of agricultural production in the Gulf states, reliance on food imports is high and that reliance can create distress for the poor in the host countries. In Bahrain, private agri-business and state-owned corporations are aligned in seeking agricultural land abroad. Saudi Arabia's land grabs in Ethiopia have threatened food security there, forcing the World Food Programme to spend US$116 million in providing 230,000 tons of food aid to Ethiopia between 2007 and 2011, feeding 4.6 million Ethiopians threatened with hunger. Yet, the Ethiopian Government boasts about its lease of 3 million hectares of its most fertile land to rich-country investors by the end of 2015.[112] Bahrain, in contrast, had chosen the Philippines and Turkey, focusing locally on areas not prone to hunger and malnutrition. 'These internationalization tendencies are evident—evident also in integrated circuits that extend across the production, circulation and realization of agro-commodity value.'[113] However, this global food production chain, dependent on state support, denies employment for Bahrainis in food processing, production, and marketing. It also increases the monopoly position of Bahrain's food corporations. Seeking food security through conglomerates operating globally has disturbed local farming and diminished local employment opportunities. The internationalization of agribusiness is embedded in state control and is connected to local capitalists in the host economy, although to a lesser degree for Bahrain and Oman compared to Saudi Arabia, Kuwait, and the UAE. Saudi Arabia has ruthlessly intervened in Yemen in order to curtail Iran's growing power in the Middle East, unleashing war and hunger. Bahrain has avoided foreign interventions. It has not sought political influence overseas, only food security. In Bahrain, food riots in response to rising food prices, as occurred in 2018, encouraged the outsourcing of food production overseas. Bahrain's food and retail corporations, ranging from BMMI, food retailers and wholesalers in Sitra since 1883, and Al-Muntazah in Muharraq, established in 1984 as a supermarket chain, do provide work for the young.[114] But agrarian employment has been lost in a frenzy of construction and urbanization. NASS Corporation BSC, a powerhouse in Bahraini industry and heavy construction, and established in Manama in 1963, is responsible to a degree for diminishing the lands long

[112] Jane Harrigan, *The Political Economy of Arab Food Sovereignty* (Basingstoke: Palgrave Macmillan, 2014), p. 150; World Food Programme 2009 Operations, 'Targeted Food Support to Vulnerable Groups Affected by High Food Prices'.
[113] Hanieh, *Money, Markets, and Monarchies*, p. 119.
[114] *Economic Development Board Annual Report*, 2010–19.

cultivated by farmers. The Fakhro Group, established in Manama in 1888, has food interests as well as shipping. Bahrain remains the most food secure nation in the region and in seeking to establish food production overseas, it wishes to maintain that security and to keep food prices low. But, inevitably, the poor in the host country suffer, even to the extent of facing famine.[115]

Land Reclamation on Bahrain's Seafront and Loss of Employment for Fishermen

Land reclamation presented serious problems for many in Bahrain, concentrated in villages and cities along the coast. The most affected were those engaged in pearl diving, agriculture, and fishing. Pearl diving had declined but fishing and agriculture remained essential sources of employment and food security. The newly created islands had a devastating impact on both occupations. Annual fish catches declined from 16,000 tons to 6,000 between 2006 and 2010. It was estimated that 90 per cent of fishing grounds had been partially or completely destroyed. This brought serious deprivation to Sunnis, although Shi'ites were the most affected group.[116] The collapse of fish stocks led growing numbers to abandon fishing. Bahrain's Fishermen Protection Society had campaigned for a GCC law to facilitate fishing outside Bahrain's borders. Further pressure was exerted by the UN Food and Agriculture Organization, which called for a halt to reclamation, dredging, and the destruction of the reef in order to protect the livelihood of fishermen.[117] A further pernicious development involved illegal reclamation by unlicensed individuals. In September 2012, the Manama Municipal Council reported that nine separate reclamation projects had been carried out in Manama and Karbabad, in violation of environment laws.[118]

Reclamation Projects Focus on Luxury Real Estate and Tourism Development

Reclaimed lands include Diyar al-Muharraq, a residential and tourism development of 12 square kilometres; Dilmunia Health Island, 1.25 square

---

[115] Amartya Sen, *Poverty and Famines: An Essay on Entitlement and Deprivation* (Oxford: Clarendon Press, 1981).

[116] S. Al-Halwachi, 'Land Reclamation Shrinks Fish Production in Bahrain', *Al-Wasat*, 20 November 2010; A. al-Maskati, *Al-Wasat*, 14 June 2010; Omar AlShehabi, 'Radical Transformations and Radical Contestations: Bahrain's Spatial Demographic Revolution', *Middle East Critique*, vol. 23, no. 1 (2014), p. 32.

[117] 'New GCC Bid to Tackle Territorial Waters Row', *Gulf Daily News*, 24 May 2010.

[118] Al-Aali, 'Reclamation Halted?', *Gulf Daily News*, 27 September 2012.

kilometres; and Amwaj Island, a mixed residential and tourism project, 2.8 square kilometres. The Northern City, allocated for government-funded housing, occupied 7.4 square kilometres. More prestigious projects include Bahrain Bay, Reef Island, and Bahrain Financial Harbour.[119] On Bahrain's southern tip, the Durrat Al Bahrain reclamation includes six atolls and five pearl-shaped islands spread over 21 square kilometres. Another major development was in Muharraq, the traditional home of the royal family, which had quadrupled in land area since 1950 through the constant reclamation of land.[120] A further ambitious state project involved the creation of a 40-kilometre-long bridge between Bahrain and Qatar, which involved the construction of a road on reclaimed land. Qatar's commitment was driven by the glamour project of hosting the FIFA World Cup in 2022.[121] But at the same time, Qatar was arresting Bahraini fishermen. In 2010, Qatar seized 260 men while one fisherman was killed by a Qatari coast guard patrol. Arrests continued into 2011. There had long been tension between Bahrain and Qatar, for example over coral reefs and islands, but now Qatar was seeking to challenge Bahrain's increasing power and its alignment with Saudi Arabia.[122]

The reclamation of land also involved the transfer of land to private interests associated with the Al-Khalifah family. In 2010, the Investigative Committee of State Public and Private Properties in the Bahrain Chamber of Deputies provided evidence of the transfer of public lands to private entrepreneurs. It estimated that 90 per cent of reclaimed land was now privately owned, with plans for prestigious real estate and infrastructure projects.[123]

Natives, Expatriates, and Naturalized Citizens

Land reclamation had particularly significant consequences for farmers and fishermen. Since the mid-1990s, more than 70 square kilometres of seafront

---

[119] Elham Fakhro, 'Land Reclamation in the Arabian Gulf: Security, Environment, and Legal Issues', *Journal of Arabian Studies*, vol. 3, no. 1 (2013), pp. 36–52.

[120] Mohammed Basma, 'Reclamation Costs Bahrain Millions', *Gulf Daily News*, 7 March 2009; Mohammed Basma, 'Muharraq Grows by Four Fold', *Gulf Daily News*, 22 June 2010.

[121] Lidstone Digby, 'Qatar-Bahrain Causeway: A Bridge between Two Cultures', *Financial Times*, 18 November 2009; Benjamin Millington, 'KBR Awarded Qatar-Bahrain Construction Contract', *Construction Week Online*, 16 November 2008.

[122] Robert Meyer and Henry Tuttle, 'Bahrain Shuts Al-Jazeera Television Channel as Tensions Flare with Oil Rich Qatar', *Bloomberg*, 19 May 2010.

[123] M. Mahdi, 'Bahrain Public Lands Sold to Private Investors', *The National*, 25 March 2010; H. Al-Madhoob, 'National Properties Committee: The Struggle Will Continue Until Retrieval of Citizen's Lands', *Al-Wasat*, 12 May 2010.

have been reclaimed, 50 square kilometres between 2001 and 2011.[124] In 2008, 13 square kilometres of sea were reclaimed. The reclamations were concentrated around the northern coast of Bahrain, increasing the land area by 10 per cent. The city area of Muharraq expanded four times between 1951 and 2008, principally through reclamation from the sea.[125] Much of the reclaimed land was for commercial projects and for housing. Real estate and construction accounted for 9.8 per cent of GDP in 2007, with an annual growth rate of 7.1 per cent. It ultimately accounted for 33 per cent of domestic bank loans.[126] In addition, Bahrain was the location for prestigious building projects undertaken by UAE real estate corporations.[127] The commercial and real estate development was intended for wealthy entrepreneurs, both local and from the GCC. It was not intended for the inhabitants who had been displaced, the poor farmers and fishermen. By 2008 more than 20 large gated-housing projects had been built, providing 60,000 new residential units with commercial and office facilities.[128] The development was driven by the oil boom and the rise in oil prices.

The emergence of Bahrain as the financial hub of the Gulf also attracted funds from GCC investors for real estate development. From 2006, liberal property laws allowed GCC nationals to base their construction corporations in Bahrain. In 2007, the largest contractor in Bahrain was from the UAE.[129] The huge inflow of oil wealth accelerated the pace of land reclamation on the northern coast of the island and in parts of Muharraq and Manama, involving the construction of roads and real estate. By 2010, 65 square kilometres of reclaimed land were valued at US$40 billion, and the combined value of the projects under construction there were valued at US$28.6 billion.[130] The projects included the construction of a Formula 1 track at US$300 million, the Financial Harbour at US$1.3 billion, and the Bahrain airport expansion,

---

[124] Data compiled from Central Informatics Organization cited in Omar AlShehabi, 'Radical Transformations and Radical Contestations: Bahrain's Spatial Demographic Revolution', *Middle East Critique*, vol. 23, no. 1 (2014), p. 29.

[125] Mohammed Basma, 'Muharraq Grows by Four-Fold', *Gulf Daily News*, 22 June 2010.

[126] P. Devaux, 'Oil Bonanza and Banking Activity in the GCC Countries', *Conjuncture* (Economic Research-BNP Paribas), December 2006; Global Investment House, 'GCC Real Estate Sector-Changing Times!', February 2009.

[127] Adam Hanieh, *Capitalism and Class in the Gulf Arab States* (New York: Palgrave Macmillan, 2011), pp. 104–6, 114–16.

[128] DTZ Middle East Market Update Series, Bahrain, September 2008.

[129] B. Redfern, 'Private Developers Drive Boom', *Middle East Economic Digest*, 1 February 2008; Global Investment House, 'GCC Real Estate Sector-Changing Times!', February 2009; Shereef Ellaboudy, 'The Global Financial Crisis: Economic Impact on GCC Countries and Policy Implications', *International Research Journal of Finance and Economics*, no. 41 (2010), pp. 180–94. See also Hanieh, *Capitalism and Class in the Gulf Arab States*, p. 105.

[130] 'A Steady Approach Benefits Bahraini Property and Tourism Sector', *Middle East Economic Digest*, 29 October 2009.

costing US$200 million.[131] Bahrain also became involved in projects in the UAE. In 2007, a Cebarco subsidary was heavily committed in building the infrastructure for the Abu Dhabi Grand Prix. In 2009, there were six large building construction projects in the GCC being carried out by Bahraini companies, compared to seven by companies from Saudi Arabia, three from Kuwait, two from Oman, 13 from the UAE, and nine from Qatar. That interdependence was a major dynamic in the regional economy.[132] Bahrain's interests were held by long-established business tycoons such as Yusef Kanoo and other members of the Kanoo family. The reclamation projects also greatly strengthened private entrepreneurs with links to the royal family. The reclamation divided the population into expatriates and locals and divided, too, religious sect and class. Division inevitably increased the power of entrenched royal absolutism.

Demographic Employment Transformation through Sectarianism, Nationalism, and Royal Absolutism

From the 1980s and 1990s, land reclamation strengthened the position of the rich with powerful ties to the state. An increase in private ownership of land accelerated that trend. The division of the population on sectarian and ethnic grounds and by class and region was long pursued by local rulers to counter political opposition.[133] The rulers also sought to condemn any protest as a Shi'te attempt to undermine the country and threaten the regime. The oil boom brought in two classes of expatriate: managers and professionals, living in luxurious homes built on reclaimed land; and migrant labour, largely Indians, living in labour camps. In 1941, there were 16,000 expatriates out of a population of 90,000, and they worked mainly in the oil industry. By 1957, there were 24,401 expatriates out of a population of 143,145.[134] By 1975, the number of expatriates had tripled to 60,000, accounting for 22.9 per cent of the population and 37 per cent of the workforce. By 2000, this number had almost quadrupled to 261,000, accounting for 40 per cent of the population and 63 per cent of the workforce. In 2008, expatriates became the majority, 570,000, accounting for 51 per cent of the population and 78

---

[131] AME info, 'Bahrain Boosts Infrastructure Expenditure', 7 March 2009, cited in AlShehabi, 'Radical Transformations and Radical Contestations', pp. 32–3.
[132] Hanieh, *Capitalism and Class in the Gulf Arab States*, pp. 114–15, 122–3.
[133] AlShehabi, 'Radical Transformations and Radical Contestations', p. 34.
[134] FO 371/149151, Population Census of Bahrain, 31 December 1955.

per cent of the workforce.[135] The 2010 census recorded that, out of a total of 666,000 non-citizens, 54 per cent of the population, 562,000 were Asians, of whom an estimated 300,000 were Indians. Arabs, including GCC nationals, accounted for less than 67,000. North Americans and Europeans numbered 16,000. The majority of the expatriate labour force, 307,000 in 2009, were unskilled workers. The construction industry accounted for 32.8 per cent of total employment, and within this, foreign workers accounted for close to 89.8 per cent of workers in the sector. Wholesale and retail accounted for 17.9 per cent of total employment, with foreign workers accounting for 81.6 per cent of employment in that sector. Foreign workers accounted for 75.1 per cent in manufacturing and 87.9 per cent in domestic service.[136] Illegal workers were estimated to account for 10 per cent of the total workforce.[137]

There was clearly a vast gulf between the North American and European expatriates, on the one hand, and labourer expatriates, mainly Indians, although there were also middle-class expatriates from Asia. The Western expatriates lived in private villas and flats while the foreign workers lived in labour camps. The low-pay labourers from South Asia experienced considerable brutality. Underpinning this flow of cheap labour was the kafala system of indentured labour, present since the pearling era.[138] In the oil era it brought about a pernicious binary divide, leading to violence against foreign labour. The steady decline in the number of Arab workers since the 1970s, as Bahrain sought to prevent the entry of Pan-Arab revolutionary sentiments, may have strengthened local Shi'ite labour. Arabs from poorer nations in the Middle East, largely Shi'ites, were feared, as the Bahrain state was engineering a Sunni dominance by offering foreign Sunnis lucrative jobs and residence with local citizenship. These Sunni were largely Bedouin Arabs from Jordan, Saudi Arabia, Syria, and Yemen, and included Baluchis from Baluchistan in Pakistan. Between 2001 and 2007, some 61,000 were selected to become naturalized citizens, increasing the local citizen population by 15 per cent. They were employed in security and defence services. This strategy of using 'safe' persons from 'safe' states for defence, depriving locals of employment on sectarian lines, is reminiscent of the British policy in the nineteenth century to recruit soldiers from Baluchistan and parts of India with a martial tradition. In independent Bahrain, it became an effective strategy to strengthen the minority Sunni authoritarian state. Exploiting Indian labour while creating

---

[135] M. Baldwin-Edwards, 'Immigration and Labour Markets in the GCC Countries: National Patterns and Trends, Kuwait', Programme on Development, Governance and Globalization in the Gulf States, London School of Economics, Working Paper No. 15, 2011.
[136] Baldwin-Edwards, 'Immigration and Labour Markets in the GCC Countries'.
[137] AlShehabi, 'Radical Transformations and Radical Contestations', p. 35.
[138] Gardner, *City of Strangers*, chapter 2.

citizens from neighbouring Sunni enclaves strengthened Sunni loyalty and confidence. The Al-Khalifahs therefore faced the Arab Spring confident that the protests could be suppressed. Immigrant labour was extremely marginalized through the labour camps, while Western expatriates were rewarded with lucrative jobs and posh homes. Overarching this was solidarity within the GCC. While Syria declined into chaos, tightly controlled Bahrain rose as a major hub of Islamic and international finance.

Urban Zones of Concentrated Labour Participation

In summary, a modern Bahrain was created that secured the power and wealth of the state and its ruler. The oil boom from 1973 brought in huge numbers of foreigners requiring vastly different housing and employment facilities. As Charles Tilly has noted, in European cities like Berlin and Madrid, rulers fed these cities at great effort and at great cost to their hinterlands.[139] Housing for citizens and expatriates grew at a phenomenal rate. Those on the outskirts of the two major cities accounted for 54,983 out of the total of 93,653 households in Bahrain.[140] The inhabitants in this semi-urban sprawl received benefits from the government that included free healthcare, education, and subsidized housing. Between 1975 and 2002, 61,509 families received housing loans.[141] Such subsidies secured political allegiance. The building of Isa Town in the late 1990s exemplified such state 'imaginings', now replacing a history of semi-statelessness with a powerful ruler.

But for the local population, the cruel reality was that they were being pushed out of both jobs and housing, as old districts were rebuilt with shopping malls and hotels, catering for tourists. Saudis and other GCC nationals flooded in at weekends, seeking sex, gambling, and alcohol. Major features of this transformation included a new architecture and changing employment patterns. Overlooking the old city centres of Muharraq and Manama were the twin towers of the World Trade Centre and the twin towers of Bahrain's Financial Harbour, both built on reclaimed land. The old architecture, the palm grove, and the coastline were obscured or simply disappeared. Centuries-old dilapidated buildings confronted new skyscrapers. The government, greased with oil money, grabbed public lands, in particular

---

[139] Charles Tilly, 'War Making and State Making as Organized Crime', in *Bringing the State Back In*, edited by Peter Evans, Dietrich Rueschmeyer, and Theda Skocpol (Cambridge University Press, 1985), p. 178.
[140] O. Al Hassan, 'Khalifa bin Salman: He Chose Achievements, so the Prize Chose Him', *Bahrain News Agency*, 28 April 2007.
[141] M. Saeed, 'Al-Dhahrani Refuses to Ratify MPs' Letter Demanding the Lands' Master Plan from the Political Leadership', *Al-Wasat*, 18 June 2008.

on the coast, and pushed aside the poor. The rising politics of exclusion translated into resistance. The Arab nationalism and leftist opposition which had been present in the 1950s and in the 1970s gave way to a politics based on religion and sect. Haq, which attracted both Shi'ites and secular members, opposed the 2002 constitution which allowed only limited political participation. The secular leftist organizations, Wa'ad and Al-Menbar, declined after the 1970s. Sunni religious organizations, the Muslim Brotherhood, the Al-Menbar Islamic Society, and the Salafist Al Asala were largely supportive of the state.[142]

But it was the issues of public land and the naturalization of foreigners to secure the political hegemony of the al-Khalifah that created the most serious resistance. The limited availability of land, coupled with rapid population growth, created a dramatic need for housing and also squeezed out opportunities for the existing local workers. The waiting list for government-assisted housing exceeded 45,000 households, and was increasing by 7,000 each year. It was estimated that BD2.25 billion of government expenditure would be required to meet that housing need.[143] There was anger that new, luxurious developments were being built on stolen lands. Two parliamentary enquiries were launched, one to investigate the theft of public lands and the other, land reclamation. A loose coalition of environmentalists, fishermen, politicians, and local councillors organized meetings and demonstrations against land reclamations. A major focus concerned the Lulu project, built on reclaimed land and overlooking the reclaimed shoreline. On one side was Al Lulu Towers, a real estate project on reclaimed land. On the other side were the Shia villages of Burhama, Sanabis, Jedhafs, and Daih, close to the shoreline. Eventually Lulu was abandoned because protestors had camped there. Al Fateh, the National Unity Gathering, accused the protesters of treason. But it was the issue of political naturalization that, in 2009, drew the biggest demonstration, leading to clashes between local youths and the recently naturalised immigrants.[144] The foundations were laid for the Arab Spring protests of 2011.[145]

---

[142] Chibli Mallat and J. Gelbort, 'Constitutional Options for Bahrain', *Virginia Journal of International Law*, vol. 2, no. 1 (2011), pp. 1–16; K. Katzman, 'Bahrain: Reform, Security and US Policy', Congressional Research Service, 2 March 2011.

[143] N. Zain, '2.25 Billion Dinars Needed to Meet the Demand for Housing', *Al-Waqt*, 17 April 2010.

[144] M. Abdulla, 'A Huge March Demands the Cessation of Political Naturalization', *Al-Wasat*, 31 January 2009.

[145] Reuters, 'Sectarian Clashes Erupt in Bahrain', 3 March 2011; Omar AlShehabi, 'The Community at Pearl Roundabout is at the Centre', *The National*, 1 March 2011; Amal Khalaf, 'Squaring the Circle: Bahrain's Pearl Roundabout', *Middle East Critique*, vol. 22, no. 3 (2013); James C. Scott, *The Moral Economy of the Peasant: Rebellion and Subsistence in Southeast Asia* (New Haven, CT: Yale University Press, 1976); James C. Scott, *Weapons of the Weak: Everyday Forms of Peasant Resistance* (New Haven, CT: Yale University Press, 1985); Ian Brown, *A Colonial Economy in Crisis: Burma's Rice Cultivators and the World Depression of the 1930s* (Abingdon: Routledge, 2005); Ian Brown, *Burma's Economy in the Twentieth Century* (Cambridge University Press, 2013).

11
Economic Diversification

Bahrain's access to oil wealth through both domestic sources and external flows of oil capital provided scope for low taxation, political patronage, and strong economic growth. But the depletion of Bahrain's oil reserves from the 1950s drove economic diversification into non-oil sectors, notably in aluminium, with the establishment of Aluminium Bahrain (ALBA) in 1968, a joint venture between the Bahrain state and four international companies. It was the first aluminium producing company in the GCC. Oil refining had been established in 1937 by BAPCO (Bahrain Petroleum Refinery Company).[1] It grew slowly but aluminium production increased more than sixfold between 1979 and 2013.[2] This period also saw the production of the petrochemical products ammonia and methanol, with the creation of the Gulf Petrochemical Industries Company (GPIC) in 1985. This was a joint venture between the government of Bahrain and two petrochemical companies from Kuwait and Saudi Arabia. Earlier, in November 1977, the Arab Shipbuilding and Repair Yard (ASRY) was established as a partnership between the Bahrain state and six other petroleum-exporting countries. These joint ventures with other GCC countries and with multinationals drove international competition in trade and attracted investment from elsewhere in the Gulf. These energy-intensive manufacturers also had an impact on electricity production. The expansion of these industries has been sustained by the increasing production of natural gas, allocated to domestic power companies or energy-intensive manufacturing sectors such as aluminium or petrochemicals.[3]

In explaining the success of these manufacturing initiatives, it is important to note that a modern service sector was already in place. The international operations of Gulf Air expanded when, in 1973, Bahrain joined Oman, Qatar,

---

[1] S. H. Longrigg, *Oil in the Middle East: Its Discovery and Development* (London: Oxford University Press, 1968), p. 103.
[2] Yesenn El-Radhi, *Economic Diversification in the Gulf States: Public Expenditure and Non-oil Economic Growth in Bahrain, Oman and Qatar* (Berlin: Gerlach Press, 2018), p. 140.
[3] Bahrain Central Informatics Organization, Results of Census 2010, table 13.08, 2011.

Islam and Capitalism in the Making of Modern Bahrain. Rajeswary Ampalavanar Brown, Oxford University Press.
© Rajeswary Ampalavanar Brown (2023). DOI: 10.1093/oso/9780192874672.003.0011

and Emirate Abu Dhabi as major shareholders.[4] The Bahrain Telecommunications Company (Batelco) was a joint venture between Bahrain and the British company Cable and Wireless, involving the transfer of Western technology while preserving a state monopoly in an essential service. The Bahrain Government provided the capital investment, foreign corporations provided the technology. Oil revenues contributed 53 per cent to the state budget between 1934 and 1971, funding that infrastructure investment.[5] A lower ratio of public spending is indicated for Bahrain's non-oil economy, and this is a result of declining oil reserves. Total public expenditure in Bahrain amounted to only 33.2 per cent of non-oil GDP between 1976 and 2013. This is a relatively small proportion compared to Oman, where the share of total public expenditure in non-oil GDP was 86.1 per cent, and to Qatar, where it was 81.5 per cent. Despite this restricted financial outlay, Bahrain developed the non-oil economy through diverse initiatives.[6]

Important in promoting economic diversification was the construction of economic zones: the Bahrain Logistics Zone, the Bahrain Investment Wharf, and the new Khalifa bin Salman Port. Collaboration with foreign multinationals assisted in the creation of industrial areas in Manama, working closely with intermediaries, suppliers, and subcontractors. The encouragement of non-oil production involved lifting restrictions on foreign investment and encouraging local private investment, thereby eroding government monopolies in real estate and telecommunications. In addition, Bahrain's vibrant financial sector became the main force in innovative technology, such as FinTech banking and the introduction of Sukuk Islamic Green Bonds to assist in climate change projects.[7]

Economic diversification involved the increased use of natural gas. Bahrain's electricity-generating capacity depended heavily on natural gas, and gas consumption rose by 85 per cent between 1999 and 2009.[8] Bahrain's ALBA, the largest aluminium smelter in the world, was a heavy consumer of energy.[9] Bahrain recognized its urgent need for alternative sources of energy. In May 2006, Bahrain ratified the Kyoto Protocol and signed the statute for the International Renewable Energy Agency (IRENA). It established

[4] Gulf Air, *History of Gulf Air*, 2013.
[5] BH/MFNE: 1991, p. 146; World Bank, *Bahrain Current Economic Position and Prospects*, Report no. 2058, Washington, DC, 1978; World Bank, *Bahrain: The Requirements for Economic Diversification and Sustainability*, Report no. 11281-BH, Washington, DC, 1993, p. 178.
[6] El-Radhi, *Economic Diversification in the Gulf States*, pp. 125–6.
[7] K. Thomas, 'Kingdom Takes on Gulf Shipping Giants', *Middle East Economic Digest*, vol. 53, no. 16 (2009), pp. 40–1; Bahrain Ministry of Works, *Annual Report 2008*, p. 19; Gulf Research Center, 'Renewable Energy in the GCC Countries', 2012; Imen Jeridi Bachellerie, *Renewable Energy in the GCC Countries: Resources, Potential and Prospects* (Jeddah: Gulf Research Center, 2012), pp. 21–46.
[8] US Energy Information Administration, Statistics for 1999–2010: Bahrain's Energy Profile: at http://www.eia.gov/countries/cab.cfm?fips==BA.
[9] ALBA website: http://www.aluminiumbahrain.com/en/default.asp?action=article and id ==224.

a Designated National Authority for the consideration of energy projects within the Clean Development Mechanism. IRENA is based in Abu Dhabi. Bahrain's National Oil and Gas Authority (NOGA) calculated the rising danger of carbon emissions, and its chairman, Abdul Hussain bin Ali Mirza, Minister for Oil and Gas Affairs, sought international collaboration. BAPCO, GPIC (the Gulf Petrochemicals Industries Company), and Banagas (Bahrain National Gas Company) were each involved in this 'green policy'. NOGA's enthusiasm for tackling environmental problems led, in 2009, to the creation of sustainable projects with Abu Dhabi, based at Masdar. From 2009, the University of Bahrain undertook work on renewable energies. The Engineering Faculty was involved in the design and construction of a mobile solar water desalination unit and collaborated with Long International in creating a hybrid solar/wind power generation system.[10]

Buildings in Bahrain were not energy efficient, and this encouraged the installation of solar thermal devices and photovoltaic (PV) panels on roofs. It is estimated that up to 30 per cent of electricity consumed in buildings could be produced through Building Integrating Photovoltaics (BIPV). But the high initial cost of this technology and the lack of local expertise to maintain the sophisticated equipment was a serious obstacle.[11] A joint project by the University of Reading and the University of Bahrain analysed the application of these technologies in two large buildings, the Almoayad Tower and the Bahrain International Circuit, and estimated that the installation of PV panels would reduce the consumption of electricity considerably and of annual CO_2 emissions by 3,000 tons.[12] The commitment to energy saving was illustrated in the construction of the Bahrain World Trade Center Building in 2008: three parallel wind turbines were installed by 2009. However, these measures were not regarded as impressive in comparison to European and international standards.

These experimental energy projects suggested that the costs associated with solar and wind technologies inhibited change. Electricity production from fossil fuels was heavily subsidized by the state, and hence renewable energy faced severe cost competition. Equally important in the adoption of alternative technology was the structure of decision-making. In Bahrain, the committee responsible for renewable energy projects included representatives from the Ministry of Industry and Commerce, the National Oil and Gas Authority, the Bahrain Petroleum Company, ALBA, the University of Bahrain, and the Public Commission for the Protection of Marine Resources,

[10] Bachellerie, *Renewable Energy in the GCC Countries*, pp. 34–5.
[11] N. W. Alnaser, R. Flanagan, and W. E. Alnaser, 'Potential of Making-over to Sustainable Buildings in the Kingdom of Bahrain', *Energy and Buildings*, vol. 40 (2008), pp. 1304–23, in particular p. 1312.
[12] Bachellerie, *Renewable Energy in the GCC Countries*, p. 38.

Environment and Wildlife. Between 2008 and 2013, two projects were set up to develop solar and wind power, but little progress was made despite a collaboration with Fichtner Consulting Engineers of Germany. Bahrain announced that it aimed to produce 5 per cent of its energy from renewable sources by 2030. These proposals involved large capital expenditure and aroused great enthusiasm, but change was limited. One characteristic of these initiatives was the important role of foreign companies. In December 2010, the Minister for Electricity and Water Affairs declared that Bahrain had plans for the installation of nuclear power by 2017. But this prospect was not thought through, as Bahrain struggled to find alternatives to combat its shrinking oil resources. However, Bahrain remained determined to diversify, and the aim was to attract GCC wealth as well as international expertise. Bahrain had the ability to achieve economic diversification, frequently with Western collaboration. BAPCO's joint venture with German Heliocentris, a Berlin specialist in clean energy, led to the installation of clean energy systems, while NOGA persisted with its association with American Petrosolar for transforming the city of Awali into a solar energy city.[13] At the same time the UN Development Programme (UNDP) and NOGA sought to establish a think tank on energy conservation, clean technologies, and training in these fields.[14] In contrast to Saudi Arabia, Bahrain and Qatar sought improved economic performance with a lower dependence on oil.

These clean energy projects were also undermined by weaknesses in the law, in particular an absence of rigorous legislation. Moreover, there was a severe shortage of local technical expertise, which diminished the confidence of foreign experts. The absence of legislation to regulate energy use, contradictory policy statements and strategies related to clean energy, and a failure to engage with the public in sustainable technologies were severe obstacles to change. Between 2013 and 2018, Bahrain reassessed its policy on subsidizing electricity and fuel. The government increased the price of car fuel and the price of electricity for expatriate residences.[15]

Historical Continuities and Problems of Change

As an island, Bahrain faced serious environmental challenges with its marine life and wildlife. Bahrain had engaged in trade for 5,000 years. It was

---

[13] *Reuters*, 'Bahrain Plans to Use Nuclear Power by 2017', 23 December 2010.
[14] UNDP website: http://www.undp.org.bh/energyandenv.html.
[15] *Bahrain Human Development Report 2018*, 'Pathways to Sustainable Economic Growth in Bahrain'; Bahrain Center for Strategic International and Energy Studies, 'Economic Diversification, Competitiveness, and the Role of SMEs: Challenges and Opportunities', pp. 50, 101, 181, 242–76.

identified as ancient Dilmun, as recorded in the Bible, and as the Garden of Eden and the landing place of Noah after the flood. It was also the centre of a flourishing pearling trade from ancient times to the 1930s, when artificial pearls undermined this bedrock of Bahrain's prosperity. Diversification into an oil-dominated economy occurred as pearling diminished. Now the challenge was to revive the fisheries sector and the natural pearling industry. The Institute for Pearls and Gemstones, Danat, was established in 2017 with 'a vision to become the world's preferred institute for natural pearls and gemstones with third party verification services and scientific research'.[16] This revival of traditional industries required the state to embark on an environmental programme to preserve marine and wildlife while promoting eco-tourism. In the nineteenth and early twentieth centuries, innovation in fishing had been stifled by the fear of destroying the seabed. The pearling industry, due to its decentralized operations with limited access to modern pearling techniques, suffered low output and low returns. Pearling operations by foreign companies were discouraged by the British administration. In 1928, and again in 1936, Charles Belgrave estimated that there were 15,000 people employed in Bahrain's pearling industry, while in 1905, there had been 17,633. By 1950, there were only 2,000 divers.[17] Bahrain's dependence on the pearl industry was challenged by the coming of oil. In 1924, the ruler of Bahrain signed an oil concession with the Anglo Persian Oil Company. Bahrain was the first territory in the Gulf to begin production, its first oil well coming on stream in 1931. By 1948–49 it was shipping 7 million tons of oil annually.[18] Only a few pearl merchants survived the decline, and only by diversifying. Yusuf Kanoo had already established an agency representing the Anglo Persian Oil Company and the Persia Steam Navigation Company. He used his experience as a financier for the pearling industry to become a trusted banker in Bombay and Bahrain, financing trade. By the 1940s, the Kanoo brothers and nephews had control over four shipping lines, the Anglo Iranian Oil Company, and Nash Motors. Later they moved into property development, technology, and aircraft services.[19] The merchant houses that retained their relationship with pearls included Ibrahim Al-Fardan of the Al-Fardan family, whose Sitrahad pearl and jewellery shops were found throughout the Gulf states and in Bombay. Hassan Al-Fardan, with interests in real estate and money exchange, also retained the family expertise

[16] Institute for Pearls and Gemstones (Danat), Report, 2018.

[17] Anita L. P. Burdett, *Records of the Persian Gulf Pearl Fisheries 1857–1962* (Gerrards Cross: Archive Editions, 1995), vol. 2, pp. 527, 694.

[18] Burdett, *Records of the Persian Gulf Pearl Fisheries*, p. 694.

[19] Michael Field, *The Merchants: The Big Business Families of Saudi Arabia and the Gulf States* (Woodstock, NY: Overlook Press, 1985), pp. 177–291.

in pearls. Other prominent pearl merchants in Bahrain included Al-Matar, Al-Mannai, and Al-Mahmoud. In an ironic twist, the Mikimoto family of Japan have recently been seeking to revive the traditional pearl industry in Bahrain, a response to the rising competition of cultured pearls from China and South East Asia.[20] Bahrain's initiatives in 2017, through Danat, the Institute for Pearls and Gemstones, sought to revive the pearl industry and to achieve an environmental transformation. Danat is a fully owned subsidiary of Bahrain's Mumtalakat Holding Company, a sovereign wealth fund. In 2018, it produced 3,400 authentication and verification reports.[21] It also organized specialist courses and conferences on natural pearls, collaborating with organizations such as HRD Antwerp and Gem-A.

A major challenge in Bahrain's economic diversification was to attain water security, as rainfall is insecure and ground water close to depletion. Desalination of water was an energy-intensive project and solar-powered desalination plants were installed. Other energy sources for desalination included wind, urban waste, and fermentation of biomass. The focus on the environment involved preserving the seafront, including many of the islands—in detail: the marine and coastal stretches, including coral reefs, mangroves, seagrass beds, saltmarshes, rocky shores, and mudflats; agriculture with palm trees as the main crop; the desert ecosystem where wild mammals, birds, and plants resilient to heat and harsh conditions can survive; and the preservation of freshwater springs and streams that are now depleted owing to overexploitation. In 2016, Bahrain introduced the National Biodiversity Strategy and Action Plan. This was followed by legislation to protect natural reserves in Alareen, Ras Sanad, Tubli Bay, Mashtan Island, Dohat Arad, and Hawar Island. The protected marine areas now account for 21 per cent of Bahrain's total area.[22]

Having outlined the issues relating to the environment, I will now consider a number of case studies, focusing on their competitiveness, collaboration with regional and international corporations, and the extent of government intervention. I will then, encouraged by the work of Robert Shiller, argue that financial instruments, enshrined in Shari'ah, can act as the steward of society's assets, underpin ethical capitalism, protect the environment, and provide welfare security.[23]

---

[20] Robert A. Carter, *Sea of Pearls: Seven Thousand Years of the Industry that Shaped the Gulf* (London: Arabian Publishing, 2012), pp. 281–2.

[21] Danat Report, 2018.

[22] Convention on Biological Diversity, 2016; *Bahrain Human Development Report 2018*, p. 195.

[23] Robert J. Shiller, *Finance and the Good Society* (Princeton, NJ: Princeton University Press, 2012), pp. 19–24, 116, 117, 157, 158, 205.

Renewable Energy and Climate Change Projects: Case Studies

The relationship between economic diversification and a sustainable environment is clear from the projects on alternative sources of energy. As almost all the energy used in Bahrain came from fossil fuels, the administration sought to move to non-fossil sources. With growing electricity and water demands in an arid Bahrain, the increasing CO_2 emissions had to be confronted. Ample solar energy, and to some extent wind energy, can be exploited in Bahrain. Population growth and economic diversification inevitably increased electricity consumption by between 8 and 11 per cent.[24] The Bahrain government introduced several independent water and power projects while privatizing some state-owned electricity and water assets. The first Independent Power Project (IPP), owned by Alazl Power Company, began operations in 2006. By 2009, it accounted for a third of total power-generating capacity.[25] The previously state-owned Al-Had power and water desalination plant was transformed in 2006 into a consortium of private companies, the Al Had Power Company. It produced half the water consumed in Bahrain.[26] In 2008, Bahrain's Electricity and Water Authority awarded a third IPP contract to a joint venture between France's GDF Suez and Kuwait's Gulf Investment Corporation. This US$2.1 billion energy company is located in Al-Dour and, by 2011, would produce 1,200 MW of electricity daily as well as 48 million gallons of desalinated water. Al-Dour IPP would add 50 per cent to Bahrain's electricity capacity in two years. This motivated GE Energy to sign a contract for more than US$500 million to supply advanced power-generating equipment and servicing for 20 years for the Al-Dour plant. This capacity would allow Bahrain, which had been connected to the GCC electricity grid since 2009, to sell surplus power to other GCC countries. It then announced plans to develop a high-tech solar power plant in collaboration with a private company. Bahrain was one of 174 countries to sign the Paris Climate Accord in April 2016. In the same year Bahrain established the National Energy Efficiency Action Plan and the National Renewable Energy Action Plan. This calls for solar panels to be installed on rooftops, wind power projects on land and sea, and solar infrastructure on new residential hubs and on bridges and railways. In 2014, Bahrain signed an agreement with the UNDP to set up a sustainable energy unit to develop alternative energy sources. In August 2017,

---

[24] Ministry of Electricity and Water statistics, available at http://www.mew.gov.bh/default.asp?action=category &id=64.

[25] Bachellerie, *Renewable Energy in the GCC Countries*.

[26] Utilities-Middle East, 'Independents Satisfy Bahraini Needs': http://www.utilities-me.com/article-67-independents-satisfy-bahraini-needs/; US Energy Information Administration, 'Bahrain Analysis Brief': http:www.eia.gov/countries/cab.cfm?fips=BA.

it sought technical and regulatory assistance from the Italian company, Centro Elettrotecnico Sperimentale Italiano, to direct renewable energy into the national electricity grid. The company would also monitor and control the photovoltaic generators. In attracting foreign investment and technology, Bahrain avoided the problems faced by her Gulf neighbours. Foreign multinationals have never been given monopoly or oligopolistic positions in key industries in Bahrain: but collaborative R&D linkages are common in driving the state's economic diversification. The German renewable company JUWI International, cooperating with Fichtner, a global consultancy firm, assisted Bahrain in another solar project in Al-Dour, producing roof panels and wind turbines. Bahrain has an unusually high consumption of electricity, 56 per cent for the residential sector in 2007, 15 per cent for industry, and 28 per cent for the commercial sector. Agriculture consumed only 1 per cent.[27]

In 2014, the Bahrain Petroleum Company, the National Oil and Gas Authority, and the US-based Petra Solar completed Bahrain's first solar power plant, a 5-MW facility that utilized Petra Solar's smart-grid technology to provide energy to BAPCO's Awali township and to the University of Bahrain. The plant was estimated to deliver in excess of 8,000 MWH of energy every year while reducing carbon dioxide emissions by 6900 tonnes each year.[28] Collaborative arrangements may involve foreign alliances and a substantial R&D contribution. The AIG Group, Philips, Capital Impact Partners, Escom, Yellow Door Energy, and Spanish Abenoga, each invested in solar energy projects in Bahrain in 2016–17. For many of these Western companies, Bahrain offered a route into its more conservative but oil-rich neighbours. Bahrain's oil sector is small and relies mainly on the Bahrain and Abu Safa fields, with the latter's revenues being split between Saudi Arabia and Bahrain. Crude oil production from the Bahrain field rose from 35.5 per cent in 2005 to more than 60 per cent in 2015.[29] At the same time, Bahrain also met the challenge of economic diversification away from oil, in part by developing tourism.

The Long Boom and the Pathway to Eco-tourism

Tourism offered a significant area for economic diversification away from Bahrain's dependence on oil. It also helped to intensify Bahrain's integration

---

[27] Bahrain Central Informatics Organization.
[28] 'New Solar Power Projects in Bahrain Add to the Country's Energy Mix', Oxford Business Group, report on Bahrain, 2018, pp. 1–2.
[29] Bahrain National Oil and Gas Authority, Reports, 2005–2015; *Bahrain Human Development Report 2018*, pp. 175–7.

with the GCC nations. Bahrain presented itself as both an exciting historical site and a modern liberated leisure and holiday resort, attracting tourists
from more conservative countries like Saudi Arabia with the charm of great
archaeological sites as well as the pleasures of Manama 'Sin City'. Bahrain
was once known as Dilmun, where the epic hero Gilgamesh searched for the
secret of eternal life. Dilmun's sailors and merchants created a vast network of
trade links to Mesopotamia, the coastal areas of Arabia, Persia, Syria, Turkey,
and the Indus valley in India. Dilmun's prominence as a hub for copper, silver, and tin as well as for pearls, draws modern day tourists. Famous for its
artesian wells, Dilmun had been attracting shipping since ancient times. On
the northern tip of Qal'at-al-Bahrain there are significant archaeological sites,
including a UNESCO World Heritage Site since 2005. It provides insights into
the historical cosmopolitanism that has made a progressive Bahrain unique
in Middle Eastern modernity.[30]

Tourism stimulated a dramatic transformation of transport—road and rail
networks as well as air and shipping facilities—to cope with rising numbers of visitors. In 2015, the Government established the Bahrain Tourism
and Exhibitions Authority (BTEA) and the Bahrain Authority for Culture
Antiquity (BACA). Projects included expanding the number and quality of
beaches, transforming the Hawar Islands into a nature resort, and building
hotels and conference and exhibition facilities. In 2018, BACA, collaborating
with UNESCO on promoting Bahrain as a 'Pearling Testimony of an Island
Economy', presented historical sites in Muharraq as the 'Capital of Islamic
Culture'. There was extensive marketing of Bahrain in the key markets of
China, the UK, Russia, and parts of the MENA region. The King Hamad
Causeway and Rail Bridge, which cost US$5 billion and was opened in 1986,
was essential not just for tourism but also for trade and for labour migration.
It links Bahrain's Khalifa bin Salman Port to the Saudi railway network. It is
a public–private partnership, whose purpose is to secure competition and to
attract capital, technical knowledge, and skills from private entrepreneurs. By
the end of 2018, Gulf Air was expanding its fleet. Bahrain upgraded its international airport to increase capacity by 50 per cent. The state spent US$1
billion on airport improvement and a further Us$10 billion on new luxury
hotels.[31] In 2017, the Economic Development Board reported that Bahrain's
hotel and restaurants had grown by 11.4 per cent and that it was the fastest

[30] O. Al-Ubaydli, 'How Tourism Can Contribute to Sustainable Growth in Bahrain', *Bahrain Human Development Report 2018*, Background Paper, pp. 83–94, in *Bahrain Human Development Report 2018: Pathways to Sustainable Economic Growth in Bahrain* (UNDP Bahrain Center for Strategic International and Energy Studies).

[31] 'Bahrain Upgrades Existing Tourism Infrastructure to Meet Demand', Oxford Business Group on Bahrain, 2018, pp. 1–2.

growing sector of the economy, contributing 3.6 per cent to GDP. Bahrain's National Accounts show that the sector earned US$217.2 million in the third quarter of 2017, up from US$199 million in the third quarter of 2016.

The retail sector, the luxurious shopping malls, draw tourists from Saudi Arabia. A consumption culture based on oil wealth led to the increasing employment of local women. Retailers were challenged to secure the latest goods from the USA, Japan, and India. Increased consumer choice made Bahrain a popular shopping destination for many tourists from the Gulf, competing with Dubai but in a muted cultural manner. Retailing and the wholesale trade accounted for 4.2 per cent of Bahrain's GDP in 2016. Hotels, restaurants, and retail contributed US$2 billion in 2016, up from US$1.9 billion in 2015.[32] In August 2017, Edamah, a subsidiary of Mumtalakat, announced an ambitious programme to create tourist attractions through land reclamation in Muharraq—a promenade, boutiques, restaurants, and an amphitheatre overlooking the bay. This was connected to the city's traditional souq. The development had an eco-tourism underpinning, in the creation of an eco-friendly resort in the North Hawar islands, costing US$928.1 million and creating 3,000 local jobs. The resort included luxurious villas, a renovated Hawar Mosque, and a bird research centre. Mireille Babti, Edamah's chief development officer, announced that Northern Hawar would be developed 'in a holistic manner, promoting sustainability and innovation while preserving the wilderness of the habitat'.[33] But the tourism programme involved large infrastructure projects, an increased airport capacity, a new causeway, and a second bridge for Saudi travellers and traders. In 2016, the Bahrain Airport Company awarded the Dubai-listed Arabtec and Turkey's TAV a US$1.1 billion contract to build a new terminal at the international airport. Bahrain Airport Company is a subsidiary of Mumtalakat, a state holding company. This terminal would increase annual capacity from 10 million to 14 million passengers. The airport modernization is funded by the Abu Dhabi Fund for Development, together with the building of causeways, rail networks, and land reclamation to create marine bays with housing and hotels.[34]

Bahrain's seven shopping malls attracted over 1 million visitors in 2016.[35] The city centre drew in 15 million shoppers, more than 10 times the country's 1.4 million population. The Bahrain Mall in Manama had 2.5 million

---

[32] Economic Development Board data cited in Oxford Business Group, 'Bahrain Upgrades Existing Tourism Infrastructure to Meet Demand', 2018, pp. 2, 8–9.
[33] Economic Development Board data cited in Oxford Business Group, 'Bahrain Upgrades Existing Tourism Infrastructure to Meet Demand', 2018, p. 9.
[34] Oxford Business Group, *Report*, 2018, p. 6.
[35] Directory of the Middle East Council of Shopping Centres, 2017.

visitors, followed by 4.7 million to the Ramli Mall.[36] The majority of these visitors were from Saudi Arabia. This rapid growth is marked by the entry of the retail giant Landmark, which operates in 21 countries and started with one shop in Manama in 1973. By 2018, it had three shopping malls in Bahrain. In the same year, a further 67 outlets were opened in the Juffair area. In 2018, IKEA opened its largest store in the Gulf, in Salmabad. The consumption culture was pursued by Bahrainis but more particularly by visitors from Saudi Arabia and the Gulf, in a striking emulation of the American pattern. Tedlow asserted that America outstripped the world as a nation of consumers.[37] Bahrain also emerged as an important centre for conferences and exhibitions.

Tourism had a considerable impact on the labour market. According to the World Travel and Tourism Council (WTTC), tourism contributed US$1.3 billion to Bahrain's GDP in 2016, 4.1 per cent of the total, and it forecast that the contribution would rise. An important impact of this growth was an increase in employment. It is estimated that 22,500 people were working directly in the sector in 2016, perhaps 54,000 if allied and support activities are included, 9.6 per cent of total employment. WTTC also estimated that travel and tourism investment in 2016 amounted to US$382.9 million.[38] Employment from tourism is higher in Bahrain than anywhere else in the Middle East and comparable to world averages. Higher wages are paid in the public sector because of state subsidies and that might depress employment in tourism.[39] Tourism provided more opportunities for women. It offered new forms of flexible employment.

Employment opportunities for women is an important aspect of the tourism industry. The expansion of the service sector from the 1990s involved growth in clerical and retail activities, and a significant expansion in leisure, tourism, and personal care. Tourism thus drew an unprecedented proportion of women into the labour market. Men were often drawn into better paid government jobs. Traditionally, family and childcare responsibilities limited the employment prospects for women. Yet, paradoxically, this constraint provided opportunities for self-employment, which offered greater flexibility, and as women acquired experience and skills, they moved up the employment ladder. Economic diversification and the growing economy generated

[36] Oxford Business Group, *Report*, 2018, p. 9.
[37] Richard S. Tedlow, *New and Improved: The Story of Mass Marketing in America* (Oxford: Heinemann Professional, 1990); Thorstein Veblen, *The Theory of the Leisure Class: An Economic Study of Institutions* (London: Macmillan, 1924); L. B. Glickman, *Consumer Society in American History: A Reader* (Ithaca, NY: Cornell University Press, 1999).
[38] Oxford Business Group, *Report*, 2018, p. 3.
[39] *Bahrain Human Development Report 2018: Pathways to Sustainable Economic Growth in Bahrain*, pp. 86–7; O. Al-Ubaydli, 'How Tourism Can Contribute to Sustainable Growth in Bahrain', in *Bahrain Human Development Report 2018*, p. 86.

employment opportunities beyond the service sector. Moreover, women had considerable success in politics, for, in 2018, they held 18.8 per cent of parliamentary seats: and 64.2 per cent of adult women had reached secondary level education compared to 57.5 per cent of men. The political landscape has been energized by an elite pool of women. But despite these impressive achievements, there remains a large disparity in the labour market. In 2018, just 44.5 per cent of women found employment compared to 87.3 per cent of men.[40]

A breakdown of the employment structure is available for 2016. It identifies the sectors but does not provide data on gender. However, in a number of areas it provides data on the different levels of local and foreign employment. In hotels and restaurants in 2016, 40,835 were employed, 6.7 per cent of the private sector workforce. Of these, Bahrainis accounted for 3,496, that is 8.6 per cent of those employed in hotels and restaurants. The shopping malls and retail accounted for 23 per cent of the workforce: 14 per cent of the sector's employees were Bahrainis. In other words, foreign labour dominated. Employment levels followed increases or decreases in tourist arrivals.

The total of arrivals in 2005 was 6 million and in 2015, 12 million.[41] As half of the country's residents and a high percentage of workers are expatriates, specifically tourist arrivals may be difficult to determine confidently. But arrivals in Bahrain from the GCC rose from 4.4 million in 2005 to 6.6 million in 2014.[42] Saudi Arabia accounted for almost 87 per cent of tourists in 2015.[43] Saudis could enter Bahrain on their ID cards. In 2012, 45 per cent of GCC arrivals came as tourists, while for non-GCC arrivals the figure was only 16 per cent. Saudis have holiday homes in Bahrain. Cruise liners also brought tourists, and of more diverse nationalities, as many were from Europe. Economic Development Board data for 2016–17 shows that 63 per cent of the European tourists were German. Bahrain's tourism sector benefited from integration within the GCC. In 2015, Saudis accounted for 9,919,617 tourists; other Gulf countries 1,071,226; the Middle East, excluding GCC, 63,782; Asia, 75,008; Europe, 203,848; United States, 48,864; and other countries, 14,761.[44]

Tourism encouraged prostitution in Bahrain's cities, in particular Manama. In 2009, Manama was placed eighth in the top 10 'Sin Cities' of the

[40] *Bahrain Human Development Report 2019*, 'Inequalities in Human Development in the 21st Century: A Briefing Note on the 2019 Human Development Report', pp. 5–6.
[41] Al-Ubaydli, 'How Tourism Can Contribute to Sustainable Growth in Bahrain', p. 86.
[42] World Travel and Tourism Council data 2016.
[43] Al-Ubaydli, 'How Tourism Can Contribute to Sustainable Growth in Bahrain', p. 83.
[44] Data from the Bahrain Tourism and Exhibitions Authority and the World Tourism Organization; the Nationality Passports and Residence Affairs Directorate; and the Ministry of Commerce and Tourism.

world by *Ask Men Magazine*.[45] Though prostitution and related activities were prohibited under the Bahrain Criminal Code, Decree 15 of 1976, the industry flourished. Many of the customers were Saudis, as Saudi Arabia has strict restrictions on alcohol and sex. The high percentage of foreign workers also fuelled prostitution. The Al-Asalah parliamentary bloc sought to halt the granting of visas to Russian, Thai, Ethiopian, and Chinese women in an attempt to curb prostitution in Bahrain but this proposal was rejected. Persians regarded as 'daughters of love' were much in evidence. Bahrain also gained notoriety through sex trafficking. The US State Department monitoring the trafficking of women for sex ranked Bahrain as a tier 1 country.[46] It is perhaps inevitable that rapid economic growth would encourage the exploitation of foreign women for sex. Not least it would attract visitors from conservative Saudi Arabia.

Tourism's demand for transport facilities, including airline services, hotels, even for diverse cuisines, had major implications for economic growth as well as for climate policy. The revival of interest in Bahrain's historical heritage, such as the Dilmun civilization, created demand for modern roads and railways. Tourism also generated new opportunities for women and self-employment, particularly in the service sector. These developments inevitably imposed significant pressures on Bahrain's health, education, and welfare infrastructure.

Economic Diversification: Education, Health, the Environment, and Sustainability

Education and training are crucial for entry into the labour market. Bahrain has the oldest public school in the GCC, established before 1919. Islamic schools existed earlier. In 1926, a second public school was established for boys, followed by a girls' school in 1928. An industrial training institution was established in 1936, a nursing college in 1959, a teachers' institute in 1966, and the Gulf Polytechnic in 1968. In 2018, Bahrain had 210 public schools and 70 private schools with more than 14,000 teachers. The adult literacy rate was 97.5 per cent while enrolment in primary schools was 100 per cent. The dropout rate was less than 0.4 per cent. The educational performance of girls was

---

[45] Susan M. Shaw, Nancy Staton Barbour, Patti Duncan, Kryn Freehling-Burton, and Jane Nichols (ed.), *Women's Lives around the World: A Global Encyclopedia* (Santa Barbara, CA: ABC-CLIO, 2017), p. 26.
[46] 'Bahrain 2018 Trafficking in Persons Report', US Department of State, 29 July 2018.

significantly higher than that of boys at all stages.[47] There is a strong emphasis on gender equality in education.[48] Bahrain's gender inequality in health and life expectancy was just 6 per cent, compared to 18 per cent in the Arab states, while in education, Bahrain's inequality was 19 per cent compared to the Arab states at 33 per cent. In gender development Bahrain outperforms the Arab states by a considerable margin. There is a higher proportion of females in secondary education in Bahrain than in the Arab states and in other developing economies, while female participation in employment too is much higher than in the Arab states, indeed it is almost at the level of the developed world. Women account for 63 per cent of those in tertiary education, men for just 34 per cent. The Arab states, too, record a higher percentage of women in tertiary education compared to men.[49] Bahrain's expenditure on education in 2016 accounted for 2.7 per cent of GDP. Total government expenditure is around 7.6 per cent of GDP, which is lower than in Oman, at 12 per cent. Even though Bahrain spends proportionately less on education than her neighbours, there is an emphasis on mathematics and science, where Bahrain is rated highly by Trends in International Mathematics and Science Study and by the Institute for Progress in International Reading Literacy Study. In the Gulf, only the UAE and Qatar come close to Bahrain's impressive performance in mathematics, science, and in literacy. Bahrain was ranked 24th in quality of education and 31st in mathematics and science education in 2017.[50] Bahrain was aware of a mismatch between education and labour market demands. Bahrain's dependence on foreign skilled workers in engineering projects indicated its failure to produce sufficient graduates in technology, the sciences, and medicine. The National Qualification Framework (NQF), which is the agency for classifying qualifications according to market demands, clearly showed that higher education needed to develop appropriate courses. Subsequently, Bahrain Polytechnic created collaborations with industry, bringing industrial leaders onto its curriculum advisory groups. Bahrain has long been aware of a disparity between qualifications and work replacement. The Labour Market Regulatory Authority and Tamkeen carried out surveys to rectify these imbalances.[51]

A major development was the establishment in 2005 of a comprehensive Information and Technology Institute, involving the creation of King Hamad

[47] *Bahrain Human Development Report 2018*, pp. 106–9.
[48] *Bahrain Human Development Report 2018*, pp. 39, 41; *Bahrain Human Development Report*, 2019, 'Inequalities in Human Development in the 21st Century'.
[49] Data from UNESCO Institute of Statistics.
[50] World Economic Forum, *Global Competition Report*, 2017–18; *Bahrain Human Development Report 2018*; UNDP, *Pathways to Sustainable Development Report*, 2018, pp. 117, 119.
[51] Data have been verified in *Human Development Indices and Indicators*, 2018, 'Statistical Update: Briefing Note for Countries on the 2018 Statistical Update'; *Bahrain Human Development Report*, 2019.

Schools for the Future. These aimed at linking schools to information and communications technology through e-learning and digital education. This educational portal provides online learning and facilitates communication between academics, students, and parents. It also uses different types of software to facilitate IT learning. Bahrain collaborates with the International Society for Technology in Education, which offers professional training. In 2008, the Bahrain Teachers College was established as part of the University of Bahrain to improve technical and vocational education and training. This was a serious issue, as students in technical and vocational education had declined from 33 per cent in 2008 to 14 per cent in 2016.[52] To reverse this decline, in 2017 the government launched a National Strategy for Applied Learning, the impact of which will be considered in the later discussion on FinTech.

Finance, the Evolution of the Green Bond (Sukuk) and the Good Society

The critical component in economic diversification was Bahrain's financial sector, the 'long purse' of state funding. The banking sector was boosted by an expansion in offshore banking, where foreign banks were encouraged to invest by regulatory and tax incentives, and by the growth of Islamic finance and of oil capital inflows from the Gulf states. The regulatory incentives included the absence of capital account restrictions on the banks' international transactions. Offshore banking was also exempt from domestic taxes. Offshore banks were responsible only for an annual licence fee of US$25,000 and were not obliged to meet minimum reserve or liquidity requirements.[53] Bahrain emerged as the most important money market in the Middle East, facilitating the movement of short-term funds between regional banks and foreign exchange transactions in the Gulf, as well as providing trade finance and letters of credit.[54] However, by 1990 Islamic finance was more important than offshore banking. Between 1990 and 2015, the number of Islamic banks and Islamic insurance companies rose from 5 to 25 and from 2 to 11 respectively.[55]

[52] *Bahrain Human Development Report 2018*, p. 122.
[53] A. S. Gerakis and O. Roncesvalles, 'Bahrain's Offshore Banking Center', *Economic Development and Cultural Change*, vol. 31, no. 2 (1983), pp. 271–93.
[54] Rodney Wilson, *Banking and Finance in the Arab Middle East* (London: Macmillan,1983), pp. 110–19.
[55] Central Bank of Bahrain, 2016; Central Bank of Bahrain Register, January 2016. See also Central Bank of Bahrain, *Statistical Bulletin*, 2001–2015.

Islamic commercial objectives can be aligned to the promotion of social good. Maqasid in Islamic finance is directed at the preservation and protection of religion and charities through Sukuk (bonds). Sukuk identifies projects for social and economic investment, in education, housing, social care, and ethical business.[56] This is analogous to Robert Shiller's 'Participation Nonprofit', for example funding a hospital through issuing shares, profits being further invested in non-profit institutions.[57] The investor has a psychological stake akin to ownership. With the dividends, the investor can set up further private foundations and generate more institutions participating in non-profit ventures. Shiller also differentiates between certain types of debt. He identifies the 'salubrious debt', a debt designed for welfare. To avoid mismanagement, regulation and financial innovation would be essential. Shiller also insists that financial contracts should be more 'democratic and nuanced with rights of mankind redefined in more basic terms'. Shiller had earlier shown enthusiasm for Grameen Bank's randomly assigned loans to the poor, which 'increase [the] ability to cope with risk, strengthen community ties and increase access to communal credit'.[58] Shiller further seeks a more imaginative interpretation of contract law. This is particularly needed in Shari'ah, where no human interpretation of the primary sources is required.[59] In Bahrain, one-fifth of government financing is met through Sukuk, for which greater flexibility would provide more effectiveness. Green Sukuk are involved in the following environmental projects: Bahrain PV Park, Al-Dur PV plant and Al-Dur Wind Farm, and Askar Solar PV on a landfill project.[60]

Another Noble Quest about Gas

In gas production and consumption, environmental considerations are hugely important. Bahrain's power generation and water desalination depend on gas. Gas is also consumed by ALBA (Aluminium Bahrain), GPIC (Gulf Petrochemical Industries) and the Bahrain Steel Company. Bahrain has engaged in the integration of the photovoltaic module in producing energy

---

[56] Hatim El-Tahir, 'A New Approach to Jalb Al-Manfa'Ah Through Sustainable Social Inclusion Sukuk', *International Islamic Financial Market (IIFM) Sukuk Report*, 2018, p. 128.

[57] Shiller, *Finance and the Good Society*, pp. 150, 205.

[58] Shiller, *Finance and the Good Society*, p. 44; Dean Karlan and Jonathan Zinman, 'Microcredit in Theory and Practice: Using Randomized Credit Scoring for Impact Evaluation', *Science*, vol. 332 (2011), pp. 1278–84; Abhijit V. Banerjee and Esther Duflo, 'Giving Credit Where it is Due', unpublished paper, Department of Economics, Massachusetts Institute of Technology, 2010.

[59] Richard de Belder, 'The Form over Substance Debate in Islamic Finance: is Aligning Islamic Finance more Proactively with the Ethical Finance Space the Way Forward?', unpublished paper, 2017.

[60] International Renewable Energy Agency, Renewable Energy Market Analysis, GCC, 2019.

from solar radiation. As noted earlier, the pilot project was installed by the American Company Petra Solar at US$25 million. Equally with wind energy and water desalination projects, each is viable as long as finance is secured. Here the issuing of solar Sukuk was an important strategy. Solar Sukuk, which involve risk sharing and are asset-backed, are designed within the Maqasid al-Shari'ah (Objectives of the Shari'ah). This has many elements essential in curbing risk. The first is protection through honour, fulfilment of contracts, preservation of the ties of kinship, honouring the rights of investors, provision of social welfare, and preserving freedom and human dignity. This 'moral economy' has parallels with the 'moral sentiments' of Adam Smith.

Compared to the conventional Sukuk, green Sukuk issuance is small. Conventional Sukuk issuance was US$162 billion in 2019, while the total outstanding debt for green Sukuk amounted to only US$7.9 billion.[61] This reflected pessimism over the prospects for green projects. A clear example is provided by the Gulf Municipality Project for the Gulf Solar Farm. This project sought to improve the grid network through a solar Sukuk structure. But the project involved a complexity of ownerships, responsibilities, and contracts. The asset originator is Gulf Municipality. The project developer is First Gulf Solar, contracted to deliver the final product in two years. The contract is based on istisna (contract of hire, manufacture). But the forward contract is a Forward Ijarah (lease). Gulf Municipality remains powerful within this complex structure. The investors are Sukuk holders and Gulf Solar Sukuk (the Special Purpose Vehicle). Throughout all, the Gulf Electricity and Water Authority has a power purchase agreement for 20 years. The Shari'ah-compliant financing structure includes Murabahah (sale with a mark-up profit), Ijarah (lease), and Mudarabah (an investment partnership), designed to reflect the project's risks and the time required in the different phases to complete. Consequently, the Green Bond is most suitable for financing here, because of the ethical emphasis, while the involvement of Bahrain's First Energy Bank provides financial security despite the formidable challenges.[62]

This blending of the traditional debt-based Sukuk structure, with a commitment to improve the social and environmental impact, is clearly a major advance as Bahrain faces up to its high energy consumption culture. However, certification of a green bond or a climate bond is dependent on a robust legal procedure. Since the bond is highly technical, Shari'ah scholars cannot assume powers of certification. The process requires environmental scientists. This explains why green bonds are less attractive to investors than

---

[61] International Islamic Financial Market, *Annual Sukuk Report 2019*.

[62] International Islamic Financial Market, *A Comprehensive Study of the Global Sukuk Market*, April 2018, pp. 71–93, 125–55.

conventional Islamic bonds. Finally, green Sukuk are debt-based instruments using a conventional interest-rate benchmark, to align it with Maqasid al-Shari'ah. Financing projects that improve the environment and public health are acceptable for Maqasid al-Shari'ah.[63] One advantage of green bonds is that they are embedded in sustainable ownership and responsibility. It is the public authority that commissions innovative programmes with clear environmental objectives and social impacts. However, it is still a niche market. Service providers also benefit from increased flexibility in achieving results. As the outcomes of environmental projects can be difficult to predict, this flexibility is invaluable. Thus, it is often the state and social enterprise organizations with appropriate technical skills that dominate this sector. The investors assume a large part of the risks associated with a project. Green bonds also attract awqaf funding. They can use zakat funds, create Sukuk models, and have access to Qard-al Hasan loans (a charitable interest-free loan). It should be added that microfinance can also be restructured to benefit social and environmental causes through the employment of green Sukuk. The impact of social media can be important here. Another group that could be drawn into supporting green Sukuk are the employees of oil companies, where carbon emissions are huge.[64]

The Search for Global Success: A Case Study of Al Baraka Bank

Globalizing Islamic finance, particularly through Sukuk, brought the Al Baraka Bank to Europe and the USA. This strategic expansion of Islamic finance gave the bank additional ethical and environmental agendas. The Al Baraka Banking Group (ABG) was incorporated on 27 June 2002 and based in Manama. The Group had initially two major shareholders and 10 Islamic banks. But by 2017 there were 12 Islamic banks and one Islamic investment company. An important feature of ABG was the growth in its international links through three strategies of Sukuk investment: a continuously changing mix of investors; geographical distribution in the Middle East and to North Africa, Asia, and Europe; and a sophisticated application of Islamic financial instruments to accord with market demands in each foreign territory, that

---

[63] de Belder, 'The Form over Substance Debate in Islamic Finance'; U. Hyatt, 'Green Bonds: What's Right, What's Wrong', Chartered Financial Analyst Institute, 2015.

[64] S. Denning, 'How Do You Change an Organization Culture?', *Forbes*, vol. 40 (2011); A. Dusuki and S. Bouheraoua, 'The Framework of Maqasid al-Shari'ah [Objectives of Shari'ah] and its Implications for Islamic Finance', *Islam and Civilisational Renewal*, 2011, p. 316; A. Dusuki and A. Abozaid, 'A Critical Appraisal of the Challenges of Realizing Maqasid Al-Shari'ah in Islamic Banking and Finance', IIUM, *Journal of Economics and Management*, vol. 15 (2007); Nicholas H. D. Foster, 'The Financial Sharia as Law and as Ethics: A Suggestion', SOAS, Law of Islamic Finance Working Papers Series No. 10, 2016.

is, the detailed application of Islamic products in specific economic sectors. ABG was listed on the Bahrain Stock Exchange, on NASDAQ, and on the Irish Stock Exchange. It completed the issuance of its first Islamic Sukuk for US$400 million. This was a Perpetual Sukuk, compliant with Basel 111 and Central Bank of Bahrain regulations. It is interesting to note the scale of each of its foreign-based banks within the subsidiaries of the Al Baraka Banking Group (Table 11.1). Through its 675 branches in 16 countries, it offers diverse financing but always in strict compliance with Shari'ah. It provides retail, corporate, treasury, and investment banking. As ABG expanded abroad, its operations in each country reflected a different balance between ownership held directly and owned indirectly within the subsidiaries in that country. The major shareholders are Saudis and Bahrainis. The global performance (in terms of profit) is impressive, both in the Middle East and in Europe. The most common Islamic instruments are Mudarabah, Musharakah, and Ijarah. Tables 11.1a to 11.7 illustrate the multinational character of the Al Baraka Banking Group.

Table 11.1a Subsidiaries of the Al Baraka Banking Group: held directly by the Bank

	Ownership for 2018 (per cent)	Ownership for 2017 (per cent)	Year of incorporation	Country of incorporation	No. of branches, 31 December 2018
Banque Al Baraka D'Algerie	55.90	55.90	1991	Algeria	31
Al Baraka Islamic Bank—Bahrain (AIB)	91.12	91.12	1984	Bahrain	200
Al Baraka Bank Tunis	78.40	78.40	1983	Tunisia	37
Al Baraka Bank Egypt	73.68	73.68	1980	Egypt	32
Al Baraka Bank Lebanon	98.98	98.94	1991	Lebanon	6
Jordan Islamic Bank (JIB)	66.01	66.01	1978	Jordan	105
Al Baraka Turk Participation Bank	56.64	56.64	1985	Turkey	230
Al Baraka Bank Limited (ABL)	64.51	64.51	1989	South Africa	11
Al Baraka Bank Sudan	75.73	75.73	1984	Sudan	28
Al Baraka Bank Syria	23.00	23.00	2009	Syria	13
BTI Bank	49.00	49.00	2017	Morocco	4

Table 11.1b Subsidiaries of the Al Baraka Banking Group: held indirectly by the Bank

	Subsidiary held through	Effective ownership for 2018 (per cent)	Effective ownership for 2017 (per cent)	Year of incorporation	Country of incorporation
Al Baraka Bank (Pakistan)	AIB	53.88	53.88	2010	Pakistan
Itqan Capital	AIB	75.69	75.69	2007	Saudi Arabia
Al-Omariya School Company	JIB	62.31	65.61	1987	Jordan
Al-Samaha Real Estate Company	JIB	62.97	66.01	1998	Jordan
Future Applied Computer Technology Company	JIB	66.01	66.01	1998	Jordan
Sanable Alkhair for Financial Investment	JIB	66.01	66.01	2006	Jordan
Al Baraka Properties (Pty) Limited	ABL	64.51	64.51	1991	South Africa

Globalization facilitated the entry of Islamic states in Asia and Africa into collaboration with ABG. It revealed the opportunities for Bahrain's globalized Islamic finance to transfer overseas advanced methods and technology through partnership agreements. The overseas-based Al Baraka banks constitute an asset for the Bahrain economy. However, despite these international successes and progress in the green Sukuk market, more substantial advances were made by Malaysia. The early success in Malaysia had been through the Shari'ah Supervisory Board at Bank Negara, which worked with the Securities Commission. This helped the issuers reach many investors, while tapping into the sustainable ethical investment base. In addition, Malaysia was not restricted in the issue of certificates for green projects, as, unlike Bahrain, it was not an oil-reliant economy. In 2017, the renewable energy group Tadau Energy issued the first green Sukuk, raising US$59 million to fund a solar power plant in Malaysia. In 2019, Saudi Arabia's Islamic Development Bank initiated a green Sukuk of US$1.12 billion to finance renewable energy, green transportation, and pollution control in GCC member countries.[65] Al Baraka

---

[65] Islamic Development Bank, 28 November 2019: https//www.isdb.org/news/Islamic-development-bank-achieves-new-milestone-with-debut-green-sukuk-worthEuro-1billion-for green-financing-in-its-member-countries.

Table 11.2 Al Baraka Bank: distribution of assets, liabilities, and equity of investment account holders by economic sector, 2017 and 2018

	2018			2017		
	Assets US$ 000	Liabilities US$ 000	IAH US$ 000	Assets US$ 000	Liabilities US$ 000	IAH US$ 000
Manufacturing	3,670,844	100,106	277,065	4,272,944	219,771	202,767
Mining and quarrying	122,771	4,647	21,572	182,855	6,902	27,252
Agriculture	179,627	21,003	4,999	127,190	7,246	7,294
Construction and real estate	2,796,364	21,853	25,271	3,259,085	21,663	36,223
Financial	4,493,331	2,081,910	1,690,425	3,646,634	2,703,293	1,759,254
Trade	1,608,667	254,441	175,776	1,622,738	222,384	161,548
Personal and consumer finance	2,834,613	3,933,665	8,954,660	2,926,192	4,025,988	9,716,539
Government	5,648,272	55,087	70,743	6,177,308	78,584	164,559
Other services	2,476,749	1,980,171	1,901,857	3,238,265	1,774,610	1,806,673
	23,831,238	8,452,883	13,122,368	25,453,211	9,060,441	13,882,109

Table 11.3 Al Baraka Banking Group: consolidated statement of financial position, as of 31 December 2018

	2018 US$ 000	2017 US$ 000
Assets		
Cash and balances with banks	5,008,009	5,430,085
Receivables	10,303,868	12,001,050
Mudarabah and Musharakah financing	2,71,906	2,377,654
Investments	3,067,008	2,888,334
Ijarah Muntahia Bittamleek	1,770,833	1,856,018
Property and equipment	406,564	430,192
Other assets	556,050	469,878
Total Assets	*23,831,238*	*25,453,211*
Liabilities, Equity of Investment Account Holders and Owners' Equity		
Liabilities		
Customer current and other accounts	5,325,924	5,465,433
Due to banks	1,178,758	1,322,470
Long-term financing	976,891	1,236,555
Other liabilities	971,310	1,035,983
Total Liabilities	*8,452,883*	*9,060,441*
Equity of Investment Account Holders	13,122,368	13,882,109
Owners' Equity		
Share capital	1,242,879	1,206,679
Treasury shares	9,203	9,550
Share premium	18,829	18,644
Perpetual tier 1 capital	400,000	400,000
Reserves	165,551	199,282
Cumulative changes in fair values	31,929	40,443
Foreign currency translations	861,313	706,242
Retained earnings	519,587	530,615
Proposed appropriations	37,286	60,334
Equity Attributable to Parent's Shareholders and Sukuk Holders	1,545,545	1,740,205
Non-controlling interest	710,442	770,456
Total Owners' Equity	*2,255,987*	*2,510,661*
TOTAL LIABILITIES, EQUITY OF INVESTMENT ACCOUNT HOLDERS AND OWNERS' EQUITY	*23,831,238*	*25,453,211*

Note: Investment Account Holders, based on the principle of profit and loss sharing. As IAH share profits with the bank, they are required to absorb any losses that could occur.
Sources: Unified Sharia Supervisory Board Report; Report of the Board of Directors; Independent Auditors Report; Consolidated Financial Statements, 31 December 2018.

Table 11.4 Al Baraka Banking Group: structure of ownership—directors' and executive management's direct and indirect interests in bank's shares, 2017 and 2018

Name of director	Position	Nationality	Number of shares, 2017	Number of shares, 2018
Saleh Abdulla Kamel	Chairman	Saudi	660,613,269	680,431,667
Abdulla Ammar Saudi	Vice Chairman	Bahraini	646,942	666,350
Abdulla Saleh Kamel	Vice Chairman	Saudi	328,736	338,598
Mohydin Saleh Kamel	Board Member	Saudi	687,356	707,976
Abdul Elah Sabbahi	Board Member	Saudi	219,320	225,899
Adnan Ahmed Yousif	Board Member (President & Chief Executive)	Bahraini	352	362
Abdulrahman Shehab	Executive Vice President, Head of Operations and Administration	Bahraini	232,274	339,231

Table 11.5a Global performance of Al Baraka Banking Group, I

	2018			2017		
	Assets US$ 000	Liabilities US$ 000	IAH US$ 000	Assets US$ 000	Liabilities US$ 000	IAH US$ 000
Middle East	11,594,671	2,907,485	7,338,507	11,154,872	2,976,028	6,827,712
North Africa	2,743,750	1,429,458	1,042,643	2,691,890	1,355,042	1,042,965
Europe	7,919,036	3,662,996	3,768,663	9,538,495	4,034,513	4,847,691
Others	1,573,781	452,944	972,555	2,067,954	694,858	1,163,741
Total	23,831,238	8,452,883	13,122,368	25,453,211	9,060,441	13,882,109

Bank met rising demand for conventional Sukuk in Western markets, such as the USA and Europe. In these markets there is often a combination of investors seeking Shari'ah-compliant investment with those keen on environmental and social governance priorities. This provides scope for a growing green Sukuk market. In a subtle way, ethics and economics are increasingly linked, and here Bahrain's banks and Malaysian state institutions assisted the emergence of sustainable ethical finance for environmental and public health infrastructures.[66]

[66] 'Quantum Solar Park [Semenanjung] SDN BHD Malaysia Green Sukuk Issuance', in Tahir Ali Sheikh and Mohamed Ayaz Mohamed Ismail, *Selected Sukuk Issuance, International Islamic Financial Market:*

Table 11.5b Global performance of Al Baraka Banking Group, II

	2018			2017		
	Total operating income US$ 000	Net operating income US$ 000	Net income US$ 000	Total operating income US$ 000	Net operating income US$ 000	Net income US$ 000
Middle East	414,924	198,191	114,643	370,546	175,270	101,964
North Africa	132,279	68,822	37,792	103,291	41,437	22,265
Europe	347,782	155,280	48,415	407,474	185,536	60,534
Others	92,834	25,069	15,878	117,379	28,130	22,156
Total	987,819	447,362	216,728	998,690	430,373	206,919

Technology: New Economy, New Opportunities

Bahrain, like its neighbours, often struggled to acquire, adapt, and implement the technology that is essential for sustainable economic development.[67] This, in part, reflects a dense, localized mesh of dependency on oil that is typical of the Gulf states. There are volatile relationships resulting in political upheaval, repressive authoritarianism, chronic economic underdevelopment, mass migration, and war. From the 1970s, Bahrain, faced with dwindling oil wealth, recognized the urgency of economic diversification. As the dominant financial hub of the Middle East, it sought to adopt digital technologies in finance and trade to achieve economic diversification. FinTech, established in October 2017, involved digital innovation based on cryptocurrencies and blockchain (distributed ledger technology), artificial intelligence, machine learning, peer-to-peer lending, equity crowdfunding, and mobile payment systems. These digital innovations relied on expatriate skills but in creating greater decentralization of the economy, enabled SMEs to flourish, along with female entrepreneurship. It revolutionized existing firms, opening up new pathways for digitalization and the democratization of banking and financial services, and even transforming global trade.[68]

Comprehensive Study of the Global Sukuk Market, 2018, pp. 71–93, 125–55; Mark Casson, 'The Economics of Ethical Leadership', in *The Role of Business Ethics in Economic Performance*, edited by Ian Jones and Michael Pollitt (Basingstoke: Palgrave Macmillan, 1998), pp. 31–48.

[67] Omar F. Bizri, *Science, Technology, Innovation and Development in the Arab Countries* (London: Academic Press, 2018).

[68] The integration of the financial and the real economies is considered in detail in Jonathan Ercanbrack, 'The Digital Revolution and the Transformation of Global Trade: The Islamic Financial Paradox', in *Trade Finance: Technology, Innovation and Documentary Credits*, edited by Christopher Hare and Dora Neo

Table 11.6 Al Baraka Banking Group: distribution of specific financial instruments (in US$ 000)

	Cash	Sales receivables	Mudarabah financing	Investment in real estate	Ijarah Muntahia Bittamleek	Investments	Others	Total
Balance at 1 January 2018	33,196	177,793	292,657	48,411	112,345	190,788	48,190	903,380
Deposits	165,784	335,471	256,093	529	59,876	13,421	-	831,174
Withdrawals	168,533	216,196	219,844	937	21,762	54,930	48,190	729,852
Income net of expenses	-	34,160	7,787	465	8,782	2,883	20	54,097
Mudarib's share	-	6,657	1,405	-	107	177	20	8,366
Foreign exchange translations	-	29,570	-	-	-	26,825	-	56,395
Balance at 31 December 2018	*30,447*	*295,001*	*335,288*	*48,468*	*159,134*	*125,700*	*-*	*994,038*
Balance at 1 January 2017	73,558	223,323	286,201	38,150	82,962	157,672	10,177	872,043
Deposits	209,723	235,941	193,416	10,624	48,757	78,964	63,233	840,658
Withdrawals	250,085	299,601	193,622	450	22,081	39,760	26,495	832,094
Income net of expenses	-	30,793	6,662	366	3,321	1,558	233	42,467
Mudarib's share	-	6,790	-	279	614	370	104	8,157
Foreign exchange translations	-	5,873	-	-	-	7,276	1,612	11,537
Balance at 31 December 2017	*33,196*	*177,793*	*292,657*	*48,411*	*112,345*	*190,788*	*48,190*	*903,380*

Table 11.7 Al Baraka Banking Group: alignment with specific banks in the various states

Country	Name	Former Name	Branches
Saudi Arabia	Itqan Capital		1
Jordan	Jordan Islamic Bank		97
Indonesia	Al Baraka Bank Representation		1 Representative Office
Pakistan	Al Baraka Bank		138
Bahrain	Al Baraka Islamic Bank (AIB)	Al Baraka Islamic Investment Bank B.S.C. (E.C.)	19
Turkey	Al Baraka Türk Participation Bank	Albaraka Türk Özel Finas Kurumu A.Ş.	213
Syria	Al Baraka Bank Syria		12
Lebanon	Al Baraka Bank Lebanon		23
Tunisia	Al Baraka Bank Tunisia		22
Algeria	Banque Al Baraka D'Algerie		30
South Africa	Al Baraka Bank Limited		17
Sudan	Al Baraka Bank Sudan		27
Egypt	Al Baraka Bank Egypt	Al Ahram Bank (also formerly known as Egyptian Saudi Finance Bank)	31
Libya	Al Baraka Bank Representation		37
Iraq	Al Baraka Türk Participation Bank		42

Sources: Al Baraka Banking Group Annual Reports, 2015–2019; Central Bank of Bahrain Reports, 2006–2019; Zawya, Bahrain Sukuk Market, 2016–2019; Economic Development Board, Bahrain Financial Service Focus, 2017–18.

The establishment of FinTech, combining conventional and Shari'ah-compliant financial and wider economic instruments at low cost with instant payment, created major opportunities for Islamic finance. It introduced a more transparent, less risky, and more efficient system, as risk is shared between sellers and buyers. FinTech also permeated manufacturing, telecommunications, and government services.[69] In June 2017, the Central Bank of

(Oxford: Oxford University Press, forthcoming); World Trade Organization, *World Trade Report 2018*; Mohamed Hazik and Hassnian Ali, *Blockchain, Fintech and Islamic Finance: Building the Future in the New Islamic Digital Economy* (Berlin: Walter de Gruyter, 2019); Islamic Financial Stability Board, *IFSB Stability Report*, 2017.

[69] Central Bank of Bahrain, *Financial Stability Report*, 2019, chapter 10.

Bahrain launched a regulatory sandbox to enable local and international corporations, financial technology companies, and local banks to test new ideas and create solutions for the financial sector. (The regulatory sandbox facilitates the development of the FinTech sector in a safe space, where innovative products, services, business models, and delivery strategies can be assessed for efficiency and legal governance.) A sandbox has set criteria, allowing for rapid acceptance of applications. Some FinTech solutions, through predefined sandboxes, possess insurance, broking, recognized market operators, and remittance businesses. The Bahrain FinTech Bay (BFB) was launched in February 2018 as a private–public partnership between Bahrain's Economic Development Board and the Singapore-based FinTech Consortium. This partnership was to facilitate innovation, economic organization, and governance. The venture aimed to attract foreign entrepreneurship and expertise to develop local talent and encourage local start-ups. BFB, supported by Tamkeen, had internships for Bahraini students to study at FinTech Bay offices across the world and also at the McDonough Business School at Georgetown University. The overriding ambition of the consortium was to facilitate international links with GCC neighbours. Bahrain's liberal, cosmopolitan reputation in the Gulf states was invaluable here in incubating FinTech initiatives across the Middle East. By August 2018, the consortium provided a licensed capital-market crypto-asset service. The solutions tested in the sandbox ranged from digital banks, crypto platforms, crypto ATMs, and open banking, together with payment services within SMEs for encouraging female entrepreneurs.

The creation of a high-technology financial hub, including the establishment and expansion of FinTech, greatly strengthened Bahrain's economic performance. Between 2014 and 2017 the Bahrain economy grew steadily, 4.4 per cent in 2014, 2.9 per cent in 2015, 3.2 per cent in 2016, and 3.9 per cent in 2017. The main driver was growth in finance. In 2017, financial services accounted for 17 per cent of GDP, while manufacturing accounted for 7 per cent, transport and communications 14 per cent, trading 13 per cent, construction 6 per cent, real estate 6 per cent, and government 7 per cent. The contribution of oil and gas declined from 44 per cent in 2000 to 18 per cent in 2017. The financial sector grew at 3.4 per cent in 2014, 1.7 per cent in 2015, 5.2 per cent in 2016, 5.0 per cent in 2017, and 7.4 per cent in 2018.[70] In 2017, there were some 400 domestic, regional, and international financial institutions in Bahrain, with total assets amounting to US$188.7 billion. Bahrain was the second largest Islamic financial hub in the world, and Islamic finance

---

[70] Central Bank of Bahrain, *Financial Stability Report*, 2019; *Bahrain FinTech Bay Report*, 2018, pp. 31–2.

contributed more than 13 per cent of Bahrain's banking assets. Its bank capital-to-assets ratio is high, at 18.3 per cent: the world ratio is 10.4 per cent and the Basel 111 is 12.5 per cent. Finance was marked by innovation and new technologies, as exemplified in FinTech, launched in October 2017. FinTech and an Innovation Unit were created within the Central Bank. The founding partners of FinTech included banks, corporations, insurance companies, technology companies, specialist IT companies, consultancy groups, Bahrain University, and Bahrain Polytechnic. These founding partners and affiliates of FinTech are mostly based in Manama, with a few based in Kuwait. The diversity of the collaborators and the presence of innovative and research-intensive partners, such as Microsoft and Cork Information Technology, were crucial to the success of FinTech.[71]

In 2019, there were 70 FinTechs in Bahrain, with capital investment amounting to US$22.5 million. The main FinTech verticals were in payments, crypto-assets, and digital banking.[72] In comparison, Singapore had 420 FinTechs, US$30 billion of capital investment, and with FinTech verticals in WealthTech, Payments, and Blockchain.[73] Of course, Singapore had built its financial reputation over many decades. Bahrain was significant in the Gulf but could not match Singapore.

The Economic Organization and Governance of Blockchain

The technological revolution brought by blockchain (distributed ledger technology, or DLT) is highly significant for Islamic finance. Technology has permitted the acceptance of Islamic commercial principles such as Murabahah. While legal and market mechanisms drive the standardization of Islamic finance, it is technology such as blockchain that provides greater

---

[71] The following are the founding partners and affiliated groups: Arab Financial Services, Ahli United Bank, Al Baraka Banking Group, Al Salam Bank, Bahrain Development Bank, Bahrain Polytechnic, American Express Middle East, Arcapita, Batelco, Bank of Bahrain & Kuwait, BENEFIT, BFC Group, Bahrain Insurance Association, A. A. Bin Hindi Group, Bahrain Islamic Bank, BNP Paribas, Cisco, Cork Information Technology, GFH Financial Group, Gulf International Bank, Ibdar Bank, Ithmaar Bank, Investcorp, Kuwait Finance House, Microsoft, National Bank of Bahrain, NEC Payments, PayTabs, Payment International Enterprise, Roland Berger Consultancy, Tap Payments, OIsystems, Mohammed Jalal & Sons, SICO Adsertor, and Murabaha Club. Prominent corporate partners included Takaud Savings and Pensions and Travelex, as associate partners, while supporting partners included the Bahrain Association of Banks, Bahrain Bourse, Economic Development Board, Osool Asset Management, the Central Bank of Bahrain, C5 Accelerate, Rowad, Start-UP Bahrain, and the University of Bahrain.
[72] Central Bank of Bahrain, *Bahrain FinTech Bay Report*, 2019, p. 34.
[73] Data Analytics in the Financial Services Industry, PricewaterhouseCoopers, 2018.

transparency in financial and trading operations.[74] Blockchain is a decentralized database infrastructure for storing data and managing software applications that may facilitate an increase in the transparency of supply chains, accelerate the digitalization of financial and trade transactions, and automate finance and trade contracts. This is particularly valuable for SMEs that must struggle with complex contracts, decide between conflicting legal opinions based on conventional and Islamic financial principles, face severe risk, and may find it difficult to secure capital. Through its automated, transparent systems, blockchain reveals all the players involved in an Islamic financial transaction. It is a consensus-based network that operates only if all parties in the network agree. And it is cryptographically sealed to prevent alterations and protect against fraud. SMEs often face problems in securing credit through banks. Here such complications are eliminated while retaining transparent, risk-free solutions. Economic diversification here is technology driven. Murabahah-based transactions that involve complex contracts, security documents, and legal challenges, are, through blockchain, simplified for SMEs, many of which are run by female entrepreneurs. Blockchain helps to reduce the degree of coordination required of numerous stakeholders in financial and trade transactions. Stakeholders act in silos and in a sequential manner. Records of shippers, export brokers, customs, and banks, when kept separately, are vulnerable to fraud. Blockchain allows an exporter to submit information just once. Agencies involved with the platform would then validate transactions or issue the relevant documents.[75]

Smart contracts are an alternative application of blockchain. Developed through Ethereum, a blockchain-based computing platform, smart contracts oversee online digital agreements between two parties with the exchange of assets executed automatically upon securing a collective agreement. Subsequently, blockchain stores the details of the transaction. This is suitable

[74] Jonathan Ercanbrack, 'The Standardization of Islamic Financial Law: Lawmaking in Modern Financial Markets', *American Journal of Comparative Law*, vol. 67, no. 4 (2019); Hazik and Ali, Blockchain, Fintech and Islamic Finance.
[75] Emmanuelle Ganne, 'Can Blockchain Revolutionize International Trade?', World Trade Organization, 2018, pp. 28–9; V. Buterin, 'Visions Part 1: The Value of Blockchain Technology', https://blog.ethereum.org/2015/04/13/visions-part-1-the-value-of-blockchain-technology/; Sinclair Davidson, Primavera De Filippi, and Jason Potts, 'Economics of Blockchain', https:archives-ouvertes.fr/hal-01382002 submitted 15 October 2016; Richard G. Lipsey, Kenneth I. Carlaw, and Clifford T. Bekar, *Economic Transformations: General Purpose Technologies and Long Term Economic Growth* (Oxford: Oxford University Press, 2005); Elinor Ostrom, 'Beyond Markets and States: Polycentric Governance of Complex Economic Systems', *American Economic Review*, vol. 100, no. 3 (2010), pp. 641–72; M. Pilkington, 'Blockchain Technology: Principles and Applications', in *Research Handbook on Digital Transformations*, edited by F. X. Olleros and M. Zhegu (Cheltenham: Edward Elgar, 2016), available at: http://ssrn.com/abstract=2662660; Aaron Wright and Primavera De Filippi, *Decentralized Blockchain Technology and the Rise of Lex Cryptographia* (New York: Social Science Research Network, 2015).

for Murabahah sales agreements, as the smart contract allows the recording of details of the agency agreement between buyer and seller in relation to the commodity. As Islamic commercial law requires rigorous approval from separate parties, the smart contract, which is self-executing, would contravene Islamic commercial law, and therefore the parties would be required to give consent at each stage without undermining the advantages of the technology.[76] Blockchain has enormous potential, but a robust regulatory framework is essential, particularly with regard to infringement of privacy and the threat of hacking. One important factor here was that the research and development of the application was led by foreign interests. For Bahrain, the network is completely decentralized with easy access to computer networks, validating and using known algorithms, and using cryptocurrencies, contracts, records, or other information vital for its financial hub. The stakeholders gain direct access to the depository, thereby eliminating the need for intermediaries. Blockchain's decentralized network also facilitates global contacts, with its extensive list of investors participating in its automated platform. Above all, talent development was essential for Bahrain. Bahrain's FinTech was regional, and global advances in technologies such as cloud, artificial intelligence, and machine learning, along with data analytics, transformed business and manufacturing operations.[77] In 2017, the University of Bahrain launched a programme called 'Forsati for her', with the aim of training 3,000 women with IT skills and launching 30 start-ups, some in FinTech. This STEM plan increased digital literacy and entrepreneurial participation in innovative projects. Bahrain Polytechnic organized an AI Hackfest with Microsoft for skills training, aimed at high school and university students. Microsoft launched its Azure Skills cloud training, along with programmes aimed at training professionals, politicians, and administrators. The success of blockchain in both Islamic and conventional finance was to transform Bahrain and the Gulf states from state-led oil-dependent economies, thereby increasing economic and social diversity. Ethereum provided a platform, Backfeed, which furnished a paradigmatic case of how blockchain can construct new types of economy built on crypto-economic institutions. The economics of blockchain also reveal the relationship between the economic theories of Ronald Coase (on efficient institutions), F. A. Hayek (on distributed knowledge and private constitutional ordering, including money),

---

[76] Hazik and Ali, *Blockchain, Fintech and Islamic Finance*, p. 145.
[77] Information eGovernment Authority: retrieved from Bahrain Cloud Transformation: Cloud First in eGovernment: http://www.iga.gov.bh/Media/Pdf-Section/Bahrain%20Cloud%20Transformation_Cloud%20First%20in%20eGovernment.pdf.

and James Buchanan (on constitutions and collective action). Blockchain is therefore not just a new technology but a new economy.[78]

The advantages brought by blockchain are clear. First, stakeholders gain direct access to the depository, eliminating the need for intermediaries. Trading procedures are automated on a shared ledger, reducing post-trading operation times. As the financial transactions are recorded, this eliminates the need for a separate trade repository for record keeping. Derivative trading is facilitated, as blockchain's decentralized network connects potential buyers and sellers with updated offers. Smart contracts can also automate derivative contracts on a shared ledger, which reduces operation costs. Syndicated loans are facilitated because borrowers and arrangers can broadcast offers to an extensive list of investors participating in the automated platform. Cross-currency payment is easy as market players are connected automatically, eliminating the need for intermediaries. Finally, a renewed interest in social responsibility in financial technology has been acknowledged through KYC (Know Your Customer).

KYC, a FinTech institution, has customers' credit history and this can be shared between companies in a public but secure ledger. In May 2018, the General Directorate of Traffic planned to develop a blockchain-based vehicle registration system, increasing transparency for all stakeholders and in this way reducing the cost of maintaining the registry. These developments encouraged the Bahrain-based Bank ABC to become the first regional bank to join the R3 distributed ledger consortium, in a bid to access blockchain and improve its digital services.[79] This was also an advantage in making cross-border payments, for Bank ABC operates throughout the Gulf states.[80]

FinTech has led to a significant change in relations between the state and the merchants. Oil, the main agent of urban growth and public welfare, had also changed the relationship between merchants and the state. Intense state-led planning since the 1970s had further changed the dynamics of power between merchants and rulers. Dramatic urbanization in the Gulf states, in particular

---

[78] Davidson, De Filippi, and Potts, 'Economics of Block Chain'.

[79] *Bahrain FinTech Bay Report*, 2018, p. 58.

[80] Michael Casey et al., 'The Impact of Blockchain Technology on Finance: A Catalyst for Change', International Center for Monetary and Banking Studies, Center for Economic Policy Research, 2018; Primavera De Filippi and Aaron Wright, *Blockchain and the Law: The Rule of Code* (Cambridge, MA: Harvard University Press, 2018); Dwaa Osman, 'The State and Innovation: An Analytical Framework', *The Muslim World*, 2017; Bhavin Patel, 'Lowering Barriers to UK-GCC trade', OMFIF, 19 April 2018; Agantino Rizzo, 'Why Knowledge Megaprojects Will Fail to Transform Gulf Countries in Post-carbon Economies: The Case for Qatar', *Journal of Urban Technology*, vol. 24, no. 3 (2017), p. 85.The article by Rizzo lacks empirical data and legal developments. See Rasmus Gjedsso Bertelsen, Neem Noori, and Jean-Marc Rickli (ed.), *Strategies of Knowledge Transfer for Economic Diversification in the Arab States of the Gulf* (Berlin: Gerlach Press, 2018), chapters by Ali A. Alraouf, by Eric Baark, by Isam R. Hamza, and by Ebrahim Radhi.

Qatar and Kuwait, was accompanied by technological change.[81] But FinTech is unique to Bahrain, facilitating the transparent working of financial markets and thereby undermining Arab crony capitalism.

Another important financial instrument creating investment opportunities was the crypto-asset, which Bahrain accepted enthusiastically despite fears of money laundering, the illegal sale of goods and services, the manipulation of exchange rates, and the prospect of financing terrorism. Although the advantages of crypto-assets are clear, not least in increasing opportunities for woman entrepreneurs and for SMEs, disadvantages persist. The advantage of this instrument is that the virtual currencies operate within decentralized core technologies. This avoids a concentration of power that could allow a single person or organization to take control. Moreover, the instrument offers an appearance of greater privacy. That said, economic pressures force it towards accepting a small number of intermediaries, such as currency exchanges and digital wallet services. Hence there are doubts whether digital currencies can grapple with state economic policies. Paul Krugman has suggested that cryptocurrencies may undermine state policies to control inflation and deflation, and he compares the bitcoin economy to the Gold Standard.[82] Singapore also had reservations. Cryptocurrencies are treated in Singapore as a commodity and cannot be accepted as legal tender. The digital tokens Singapore accepts are security tokens, digital currencies, asset-backed tokens, and utility tokens. In November 2018, Singapore introduced a payment services bill that regulated different payment services within cryptocurrencies.[83] This legislation requires cryptocurrency exchanges to be licensed.[84]

[81] Farah Al-Nakib, 'Kuwait City: Urbanization, the Built Environment, and the Urban Experience Before and After Oil, 1716–1986', PhD thesis, University of London, 2011; Madawi Al-Rasheed (ed.), *Transnational Connections and the Arab Gulf* (London: Routledge, 2005).

[82] Paul Krugman, 'Golden Cybervetters', *The New York Times*, 7 September 2011.

[83] Utility tokens are released by a company to provide users with a mechanism to pay for new company products or services, often developed in blockchain technology. Security/Equity tokens work in the same manner as traditional securities. They are also called Equity tokens and act as a stock or share in the company. Reward tokens are special tokens designed to act as a reputation token for a specific blockchain application. Asset tokens are used in buying and selling the assets that they back. This improves the trading of physical assets on digital platforms. Currency tokens act in a similar way to a real currency and are used for payment of purchases. An example is Bitcoin, which is a form of digital currency for buying and selling and can be sent to other users through a digital wallet.

[84] Monetary Authority of Singapore, Crypto-currency Payment Service Regulation Bill 2018; Imtiaz Mohammad Sifat and Azhar Mohamad, 'Revisiting Fiat Regime's Attainability of Shari'ah Objectives and Possible Futuristic Alternatives', *Journal of Muslim Minority Affairs*, vol. 38, no. 1 (2018). This article outlines the merits of cryptocurrencies in achieving Islam's ethical objectives of Maqasid al-Shari'ah. Sherif Ayoub, *Derivatives in Islamic Finance: Examining the Market Risk Management Framework* (Edinburgh: Edinburgh University Press, 2014);Craig R. Nethercott and David M. Eisenberg (ed.), *Islamic Finance: Law and Practice* (Oxford: Oxford University Press, 2012): see chapter by Nethercott, 'Murabaha and Tawarruq', pp. 192–3, 198–9, 200–5 for case studies of the different uses of Murabahah.

Cryptocurrencies and e-Wallets: Economics, Technology, and Governance in Bahrain

In February 2019, cryptocurrencies, a digital currency used in online transactions between parties with no intermediaries, was facing rigorous regulation in Bahrain. The Central Bank of Bahrain issued regulations to license dealing and advisory services on the crypto-assets exchange. The CBB sought to mitigate the risk of financial crime in the use of crypto-assets within or from Bahrain.[85] The CBB licensed specific agents as crypto-asset exchanges, matching pre- and post-trade records, thereby avoiding market manipulation and conflicts of interest. The CBB also controlled the addition of new clients, insisted that no encrypted safe custody accounts of 'wallets' were maintained that cannot be retrieved, and imposed insurance cover. These legal constraints were necessary because of Bahrain's enthusiasm for digital wallets. A considerable number of digital wallets was launched. E-wallet transactions through these digital solutions increased from 165,869 in June 2018 to 1.4 million in June 2019. The value of the transactions increased from BD2.8 million to BD66.0 million over the same period. The volume of transactions through Benefit Pay increased from 11,835 in June 2018 to 806,177 in June 2019, their value from BD0.7 million to BD55.2 million during the same period.[86] There were more than 100 CBB-licensed merchants for mobile wallet applications, including EasyPay (operating within Ithmaar Bank), MaxWallet in Credi Max, and bWallet in Batelco.[87] But there were also reported calamities.[88]

The Risks and the Advantages of Crypto-assets

Crypto-assets play only a marginal role in the new technologically innovative finance. They reduce transaction costs and thereby increase access to finance by SMEs. However, as transactions in cryptocurrencies can be conducted anonymously, they can be misused.[89] This was apparent in the market

---

[85] Central Bank of Bahrain, *Financial Stability Report*, September 2019.

[86] www.batelco.com, www.credimax.com, www.benefit.bh./ www.viva.com.bh, and www.
bfcpayments.comin; Central Bank of Bahrain, *Financial Stability Report*, September 2019; Rainer Bohme, Nicolas Christin, Benjamin Edelman, and Tyler Moore, 'Bitcoin: Economics, Technology, and Governance', *Journal of Economic Perspectives*, vol. 29, no. 2 (2015), pp. 213–38.

[87] *Bahrain FinTech Bay Report*, 2019, p. 35.

[88] Andy Greenberg, 'FBI Says It's Seized $28.5 Million in Bitcoins from Ross Ulbricht, Alleged Owner of Silk Road', *Forbes*, 25 October 2013.

[89] Malte Moser, Rainer Bohme, and Dominic Breuker, 'An Inquiry into Money Laundering Tools in the Bitcoin Ecosystem', Proceedings of APWG eCrime Researchers Summit, San Francisco, 2013; Nakamoto Satoshi, 'Bitcoin: A Peer-to-Peer Electronic Cash System', https://bitcoin.org/bitcoin.pdf, 2008.

reaction after the shutdown of Silk Road, a major digital market for illegal drugs.[90] The Central Bank of Bahrain has sought, through regulation, to curb crime.[91] Increased access is valuable, but it also exposes vulnerable groups. For this reason, the CBB has controlled the addition of new clients on safe 'wallets' by insisting on verification and insurance. Next is the issue of financial stability. But in Bahrain this threat is small as the FinTech institutions are largely separate from the traditional financial system. The global connections of Bahrain's banks provide the essential compatibility with international legal pressures.[92] The Central Bank of Bahrain issues draft directives on digital financial advice.[93] Open banking also plays an important role in Bahrain's technological transformation.

Open Banking

Open banking, which involves data being made accessible to third parties, increases collaboration opportunities between FinTech firms and financial institutions. Consumer data can be protected through the inclusion of unique identifiers, such as fingerprints, facial recognition, and iris scanning. At present, 84 per cent of MENA FinTech start-ups operate in payments, transfers, and remittances.[94] In November 2018, the CBB issued draft regulations on open banking. By December 2019 these were enforced. One impressive development in digital technology for Bahrain was the rapid involvement of the banks. In March 2018, the Bahrain Islamic Bank invested US$10 million to develop its digital infrastructure and, in partnership with PayPal, to provide services through digital channels. The Al Baraka Banking Group launched, through its Turkish subsidiary, the first interest-free digital bank

---

[90] Andy Greenberg, 'FBI Says It's Seized $28.5 Million in Bitcoins from Ross Ulbricht, Alleged Owner of Silk Road', *Forbes*, 25 October 2013; Sophie Song, 'The Rise and Fall of Bitcoin in China: Central Bank Shuts Down all Chinese Bitcoin Exchanges', *International Business Times*, 27 March 2014.

[91] Central Bank of Bahrain, *Financial Stability Report*, September 2019.

[92] Central Bank of Bahrain, 'Fintech and Innovation: Bahrain Economic Development Board', 2019; 'Bahrain Creates History as First Nation to Enact UNCITRAL Model Law on Electronic Transferable Records', retrieved from https://bahrainedb.com/latest-news/bahrain-creates-history-as-first-nation-toenact-uncitral-model-law-on-electronic-transferable-records/; Y. Mersch, 'Virtual or Virtueless? The Evolution of Money in the Digital Age', Official Monetary and Financial Institutions Forum, London, 8 February 2018, available at https://www.ecb.europa.eu/press/key/date/2018/html/ecb.sp180208.en.html

[93] CBB, *Financial Stability Report*, January 2019. See also Maria Demertzis and Guntram B. Wolff, 'The Economic Potential and Risks of Crypto Assets: Is a Regulatory Framework Needed?', *Policy Contribution*, no. 14 (September 2018); Maria Demertzis, Silva Merler, and Guntram Wolff, 'Capital Markets Union and the Fintech Opportunity', *Policy Contribution*, no. 22 (September 2017); Global Legal Research Center, 'Regulation of Cryptocurrency around the World', Law Library of Congress, June 2018; Bank for International Settlements, 'Cryptocurrencies: Looking Beyond the Hype', BIS Annual Economic Report, 2018, Chapter 5.

[94] 'Fin Tech in MENA: Unbundling the Financial Services Industry', Wamda and Payfort, 2017.

in Germany (under the name 'insha') to serve Turkish Muslims in Germany and later all Muslims in Germany. Al Baraka Banking Group, Kuwait Finance House, and Bahrain Development Bank initiated the first global Islamic FinTech consortium. The consortium, ALGO Bahrain, aimed at incorporating 15 FinTech banking platforms by 2022.[95] That incursion into regional markets had a value of US$20 billion in 2017.[96]

Since 2014, the Bahrain Government and the Economic Development Board have been active in supporting entrepreneurial initiatives in the domestic economy through incubators and accelerators. The Bahrain Business Incubator Centre focused on providing administrative support. It provides another supporting platform, the Internet of Things (IoT), with connected hardware, drones, and robotic companies. The C5 Accelerator provided technology investments to promote start-ups through a cloud-computing accelerator programme. Bahrain had adopted a 'Cloud First Policy' by 2019, in which state infrastructure is being moved to the cloud, in order to streamline and simplify processes, reduce costs, and increase the protection of data amid growing cyber-security concerns. The CBB, in partnership with IGA (the Information and eGovernment Authority) and the Benefit Company (national switch), had introduced an advanced Electronic Know-Your-Customer (eKYC) provision that supervised customer boarding information. CH9, another platform, supports start-ups, while Riyadat promotes female-owned start-ups, and Flat6Labs provides seed investment, mentorship, and training in the MENA region, along with Nest, which provides funding for FinTech, Healthcare, and Smart Cities Industries. Rowad assists entrepreneurs to attract investment from wealthy Gulf states, Europe, and the US. Foreign direct investment in 2017 was US$195 million.[97] This growth of foreign investment had structural and strategic implications. It encouraged the proliferation of firms, entrenching patterns of technology distribution and foreign collaborators. The liberal attitude of Bahrain is most evident in FinTech start-ups. Angivest, an investment and consultancy venture, provided seed investment of between US$25,000 and US$100,000. Tenmou, a business group, concentrated on corporate funding, while Tamkeen, established in 2006, was a key agent in these innovative ventures. Tamkeen engaged with microfinance to support SMEs. The Bahrain Development Board, through its Rowad programme, concentrated on training. It launched the Al Waha Fund of US$100 million to support IT initiatives in

[95] *Bahrain FinTech Bay Report*, 2018, pp. 34–5.
[96] Bahrain Economic Development Board, 'Information and Communications Technology', 2018.
[97] 'Bahrain Foreign Direct Investment Trading Economies 2018', in *Bahrain FinTech Bay Report*, 2018, p. 44.

Bahrain and the MENA region.[98] In addition, a large proportion of funds was directed at tourism, real estate, manufacturing, logistics, and financial services.

There were some problems in this form of open banking through digital technology. The FinTech Innovation Unit prepared an Open Banking Study for the CBB in June 2018. This led to the introduction of Open Banking regulations in December 2018. The Open Banking sector had developed two categories of service: Account Information Service Platforms and Payment Initiation Service Platforms. FinTech, as part of these services, sought to support crucial schemes, including financial training programmes and funding schemes.[99] The CBB also created the Bahrain Credit Reference Bureau (Benefit) that stores, analyses, and categorizes credit information. It also provided innovative payment capabilities, enhanced information management, and out-sourcing of services. As digitalization could create problems in communal ties, in February 2019 the CBB introduced, with Benefit and IGA, a national Electronic Know-Your-Client project (National e-KYC). It targeted retail banks, financial services providers, and money exchange networks. Benefit also had the responsibility to secure identity proofs of clients. The increasing drive for financial inclusion and competitiveness led to an international agreement with Abu Dhabi Global Market in November 2018. The Central Bank of Bahrain and Singapore jointly fostered innovation in financial services. The Singapore Monetary Services Authority (MAS) devised an international technology advisory panel, a FinTech Innovation Laboratory, and a Talent Program focused on IT education and training. Bahrain, through MAS, had collaborative agreements with 18 countries, including the US and UK, each based on FinTech-related initiatives.[100] It was claimed by MAS that one in three bank customers in Singapore were on already trialled Open Banking platforms.[101] In June 2017, the CBB introduced the Regulatory Sandbox. The following month, Bahrain issued crowdfunding regulations, followed in August 2017 by a US$20 million investment in global expansion. In 2018, Bahrain saw the launch of e-wallets and the establishment of 'Meem', the first Shari'ah-compliant digital bank in the Gulf, and the launch of the P2P National Payments Service and Benefit-Pay.[102] The flexible processes associated with crowdfunding provided still

---

[98] 'Bahrain Development Bank Launches $100 Million Venture Capital Fund', *Trade Arabia*, 10 May 2018.

[99] CBB, *Financial Stability Report*, September 2019.

[100] *Singapore Business Review*, 18 December 2018, p. 5.

[101] 'Already Trialed Open Banking Platforms', retrieved from https//sbr.com.sg/banking-technology/news/one-in-3 bankcustomers-in Singapore-already-trialed-openbanking-platforms.

[102] *Bahrain FinTech Bay Report*, 2018, p. 36.

more possibilities for women and for SME entrepreneurship, certainly more than traditional Islamic finance.[103]

Crowdfunding and the Power of the People

Crowdfunding is an alternative online fundraising and lending system that individuals can use in a collective effort to secure funding. The funds raised can be used for loans, acquiring property, and for funding a project. Crowdfunding can be divided into four primary categories. First, the funds raised are donations, where the contributors receive no financial return or reward. These funds are primarily for charities. In the second case, contributors did not receive any financial profit but received a reward. These funds, too, were often targeted at Islamic charities. The third category was equity based. Contributors, as equity holders, received financial returns. And the fourth category was lending-based, where firms raised funds through loans with interest payments. Here SMEs were able to raise conventional or Shari'ah-compliant financing through crowdfunding platforms.[104] The World Bank expects global investment in crowdfunding to reach US$93 billion by 2025.[105] Crowdfunding activity in Africa and the Middle East reached US$173 million in 2018.[106] Since 2014 there has been a surge in Islamic crowdfunding, reaching US$173 million in 2018.[107] An important factor here is the pervasiveness of Islamic contracts in crowdfunding, evident in the use of Musharakah in equity-based crowdfunding. In shared-profit crowdfunding, too, Musharakah is evident, while in shared-revenue crowdfunding, the instrument is Musharakah Sukuk, although plain Musharakah is also evident. There is potential for social lending, similar to Qard-al-Hassan within peer-to-peer lending with zero interest. But Shari'ah compliance was often difficult as there are alternative channels for seeking funds, not least because Bahrain is a generous contributor, using the oil wealth flowing in from its neighbours.

---

[103] Charles Tripp, *Islam and the Moral Economy: The Challenge of Capitalism* (Cambridge: Cambridge University Press, 2006), pp. 111, 122, 127, 142; Haider Ala Hamoudi, 'Muhammad's Social Justice or Muslim Cant? Langdellianism and the Failures of Islamic Finance', *Cornell International Law Journal*, vol. 40 (2007), pp. 116–17.
[104] Morrison Julee, 'How Crowdfunding Has Influenced Start-up', *Huffington Post*, 10 February 2017; Omid Torabi and Abbas Mirakhor, *Crowdfunding with Enhanced Reputation Monitoring Mechanism (Fame)* (Oldenbourg: De Gruyter, 2020).
[105] Evan Varamis, 'What Is the Future of Crowdfunding and ICOs?', *Forbes*, 27 March 2018.
[106] Crowdfunding Statista, 2018: www.statista.com.
[107] Central Bank of Bahrain, *Bahrain FinTech Bay Report*, 2019, p. 36; Statista Market Forecast July 2020, based on IMF, World Bank, UN, and Euro Stat. data; World Bank Crowdfunding Report, 2019; World Bank Equity Crowdfunding Statistics, 2018. The most informative source on crowdfunding is 'Crowdfunding Potential for the Developing World', The World Bank, Washington, DC, 2013.

Also, Bahrain seeks to avoid the risk of asymmetric information through collateral intermediaries such as state financial institutions, by the rigorous enforcement of the law and the purchase of insurance to reduce moral hazard. In 2017, Bahrain was the first state in the region to adopt the international standard 'cloud-first policy' for coordinating efficient and low-cost procedures that would secure information and communication technologies through ICT (Information and Communications Technology). Investors and customers felt more secure. In 2019, the cloud system added critical features including an AWS (Amazon Web Services) Infrastructure Region and three Availability Zones as data centres.[108]

Equity-based crowdfunding was commonly used in real estate sales, a response to the reclamation of land for residential and office properties between 2001 and 2017. Between 2001 and 2011, more than 50 square kilometres of land had been reclaimed from the sea. In the years from 1970 to 2000, 70 square kilometres had been reclaimed.[109] The area of Muharraq expanded from 13 square kilometres in 1951 to 56 square kilometres in 2008.[110] Although the major part of land reclamation was through state and large privately listed corporations, building luxurious commercial and private gated communities, a small proportion of the reclaimed land was sought by the less wealthy who used equity crowdfunding to meet part of the costs for building retail, residential, and healthcare properties. Crowdfunding provided a supplementary source of funding.[111] Omar Hesham AlShehabi has argued that the oil boom fuelled the human re-creation of nature along the northern coast of Bahrain, close to Manama and Muharraq. The oil export revenue from the GCC was estimated at US$1.5 trillion between 2000 and 2005.[112] But reclaiming from the sea added to the distress of vulnerable fishermen. An estimated 90 per cent of fishing habitats were either partially or completely destroyed. But as with all projects in Bahrain, legal constraints remained the most powerful check.

The companies seeking crowdfunding had to be licensed under the CBB rule book. Crowdfunding was significant in financing Islamic charities.

---

[108] Information eGovernment Authority: retrieved from Bahrain Cloud Transformation: Cloud First in eGovernment website: http.//www.iga.gov.bh/Media/Pdf-Section/Bahrain. See also Bahrain Economic Development Board, 'Bahrain Creates History as First Nation to Enact UNICTRAL Model Law on Electronic Transferable Records', 16 January 2019.

[109] Al-Sayed, 'Territorial and Coastal Usurpation: Presentation to the Secretariat and Four Associations Forum', 10 November 2005: data compiled from Central Informatics Organization, available at http://www.cio.gov.bh/CIO_ARA/default.aspx.

[110] B. Mohammed, 'Muharraq Grown by Four-fold', Gulf Daily News, 22 June 2010.

[111] Neil Smith, Uneven Development: Nature, Capital, and the Production of Space (Athens, GA: University of Georgia Press, 2008.

[112] Omar AlShehabi, 'Radical Transformations and Radical Contestations: Bahrain's Spatial Demographic Revolution', Middle East Critique, vol. 23, no. 1 (2014), pp. 30, 32.

Crowdfunding regulations covered business-to-business loans and peer-to-business lending. The CBB also issued crowdfunding regulations, putting the minimum capital requirement at BHD25,000, while the total amount raised must not exceed BHD500,000 within a 12-month period, irrespective of the number of projects.[113] Foreign SMEs had to declare their cross-border jurisdiction. Equity crowdfunding was also popular among start-ups in new economic sectors, although they tend to suffer from information asymmetries, which could lead to failure. Frequently, start-ups seek crowdfunding as an additional source and risks are high. With real estate, the market is stable, as state and private corporations see it as a lucrative growth area. Real estate enterprises also attract financial interest from Bahrain's Gulf neighbours. Environmental projects also attract equity crowdfunding. Environmental projects often attract Japanese venture capital and seek equity crowdfunding at a later stage. These projects use equity crowdfunding in order to create media coverage. There are risks involved in having to deal with a multitude of contractual relations but confidence is sustained through an assurance that the venture capital investor or the state will buy out the crowdfunding investor in a crisis. In Bahrain, while the rewards-based model of crowdfunding is philanthropic, being focused on supporting Islamic charities, equity crowdfunding is interested in profits. If an equity crowdfunding initiative is not yielding high returns, it may switch to the lending model.[114] In 2019, the Central Bank of Bahrain invested US$22.5 million in over 70 FinTech units. The real or perceived trust in FinTech drove that investment.

Law and Renaissance in FinTech

The rapid development of digital banking in Bahrain rested on the rigorous application of the law, reinforced by Bahrain's faith in FinTech. In May 2017, the Central Bank of Bahrain, as the financial regulatory authority, introduced the regulatory sandbox and, in August 2017, drew up crowdfunding regulations. In October 2017, Bahrain launched the FinTech and Innovation Unit. In November 2018, the CBB issued draft regulations on open banking,

---

[113] Central Bank of Bahrain, 'FinTech and Innovation', 2019, retrieved from https://www.cbb.gov.bh/fintech/.

[114] Central Bank of Bahrain, *Financial Stability Report*, 2019; *Bahrain Fintech Bay Report*, 2019, pp. 41–5; N. Vulkan, T. Astebro, and M. F. Sierra, 'Equity Crowd-funding: A New Phenomena', *Journal of Business Venturing*, vol. 5 (2016), pp. 37–49; M. Lin, A. R. Prabhala, and S. Viswanathan, 'Judging Borrowers by the Company They Keep: Friendship Networks and Information Asymmetry in Online Peer to Peer Lending', *Management Science*, vol. 59, no. 1 (2013), pp. 17–35; P. Belleflamme, T. Lambert, and A. Schwienbacher, 'Crowdfunding: Tapping the Right Crowd', *Journal of Business Venturing*, vol. 2, no. 5 (2014), pp. 585–609.

collaborating with Gulf financial institutions. May 2018 had seen the introduction of the e-KYC framework, to provide security in identity recognition. In December 2018, draft regulations on crypto-asset and open banking were finalized. In January 2019, the regulations on digital financial advice were introduced, followed in February 2019 by the establishment of a cross-border testing pilot for FinTechs and the finalization of crypto-asset rules.[115]

All crowdfunding platform operators had to comply with the CBB rules on Anti Money Laundering (AML), Combating Financing of Terrorism (CFT), and consumer protection.[116] There is increasing demand for Know-Your-Customer (KYC) solutions to prevent money laundering and fraud. Financial institutions adapt FinTech verticals, such as AI, to support KYC guidelines. AI platforms create algorithms that perform business operations, classifying, directing, and predicting data. Bahrain's AI sector is expected to contribute 8.2 per cent to GDP by 2030.[117]

Bahrain is developing a data protection law. In April 2018, the Finance and Economic Affairs Committee of Bahrain's Shura Council also approved a new bankruptcy law that aims to promote transparency. In the development of digital technology, it was Bahrain's banks, including Bank ABC, Bahrain Islamic Bank, and the Al Baraka Banking Group, that were the drivers. Another significant feature was the provision of education to train local staff. The Bahrain Institute of Banking and Finance provided training courses, together with ICT and Tamkeen. But it is important to ask whether the liberalization of finance through digital technologies allowed conventional and Islamic financial institutions to use shell companies for offshore investment. Does the rapid movement of funds, the speed of transactions, encourage money laundering or support terrorism? Blockchain, a revolutionary instrument for a more inclusive and sustainable global economy, does raise serious governance issues. With its transnational service, lack of formal intermediaries, and decentralized consensus mechanisms, it can descend into illegality and exploitation. On the other hand, the transparency of blockchains inspires trust. Moreover, Bahrain has tight-knit commercial laws, contract laws, and municipal legal structures to deter unlawful trading. In addition, peculiarities arise when Islamic contract law engages with Western contract law. However,

---

[115] Central Bank of Bahrain, *Financial Stability Report*, 2019; *Bahrain FinTech Bay Report*, 2019, pp. 34–5; Gulf Financial Innovation Network 2019, retrieved from http://dfsa.ae/Documents/FinTech/GFIN-Webpage-content-28012019-Final.pdf.
[116] Central Bank of Bahrain, *Financial Stability Report*, 2019; *Bahrain FinTech Bay Report*, 2019, pp. 36, 40.
[117] 'The Potential Impact of Artificial Intelligence in the Middle East', PWC, 2018; 'Spending on Cognitive and Artificial Intelligence Systems to Undergo Sustained Period of Growth in the Middle East & Africa, says IDC', International Data Corporation, 24 October 2017.

in Bahrain, the municipal legal system has shown a willingness to adopt modern usage and compliance, rather than strictly adhere to Islamic tenets. As Ercanbrack has argued, Islamic contract law has progressed from its original sources to become a living law. Indeed, there are similarities as well as differences between Islamic contract law and Western law.[118]

Addendum on Digital Banking

Writing in *The Times* on digital banks in 2020, Katherine Griffiths identified serious weaknesses. FinTechs attract very little capital. She calculates FinTech deposits at £4.8 billion compared to Virgin Money's £64 billion and Metro Bank's £14.5 billion. These figures are presumably for 2020. The volume of FinTech lending is also low, as is the interest earned. Their proportion of bad loans was about the same as for conventional lenders. In Bahrain, Starling has survived through government Bounce Back loans, through which it distributed almost £700 million to small businesses. For Monzo, another FinTech, 23 per cent of its loans involved non-payment and default. Griffiths also raised the issue of the anonymity of customers. In Bahrain, legal measures have been taken to enable FinTech to know its customers. And there has been impressive growth by Revolut, which had attracted 13 million clients by August 2020.[119] Its success lies in its innovative products. The challenge here is to rethink the opportunities that are being created by the presence of digital banks. At the same time, as Milton Friedman argued, 'the social responsibility of business is to increase its profits'.[120] FinTech has engaged in strengthening society and the economy through innovation. FinTech institutions need to maintain social audit and accountability, assisted by the law. The success or failure of FinTech depends on it being persistently alert to the damage caused by weak judgement.

Another compelling story of FinTech is that of Ant. It was established in 2006 and operates the Alipay digital wallet. It provides facilities ranging from insurance, money-lending, credit scoring, and wealth management, and is owned by Jack Ma, the founder of Alibaba. Ma was aware that Chinese consumers mistrusted online payments and therefore created what was perceived to be a more reliable financial system for purchasing goods. Its growth led Jack Ma to separate off Alipay into a distinct FinTech company and he

[118] Jonathan Ercanbrack, *The Transformation of Islamic Law in Global Financial Markets* (Cambridge: Cambridge University Press, 2015), pp. 50–62, 119–29, 277–9, 321–7.

[119] Katherine Griffiths, *The Times*, 19 August 2020, p. 37.

[120] *The New York Times*, 13 September 1970; Milton Friedman, *Capitalism and Freedom* (Chicago, IL: University of Chicago Press, 1962).

named it Ant. He also projected it as an innovative technology business. Ant is soon to be listed on the Hong Kong and Shanghai stock markets. Ant has 1.3 billion active users and accounts for a third of all Chinese electronic payments and moreover is increasing its operations across Asia. Ant is diversifying into wealth management and insurance. Ant earned 21.2 billion Yuan (£2.3 billion) in net profit for the six months to June 2020 on revenues of 72.5 billion Yuan, a net profit of 30 per cent. Net profit in 2017 had been 7 billion Yuan, 0.7 billion in 2018, and 17 billion Yuan in 2019. Many FinTechs are facing losses. Ant's success is built on its huge number of transactions. Its appeal also rests on the fact that the parent company is Alibaba, for this created client contributions through deposits. Digital banks, in accepting deposits from customers, draw them into purchasing other services through the Ant App. Alibaba, popular in China, is utilizing its operating system to promote online activity and therefore boost profits, as Apple does with its iPhone banking app.[121]

This picture of an aggressive accumulation of diverse industries was reinforced when, in November 2020, Ant moved into the fashion market with negotiations to invest US$300 million in Farfetch, an online fashion marketplace. The company, though based in East London, is listed in the United States and is eager to enter China's luxury goods market. Chinese facing travel restrictions seek luxury goods from Alexander McQueen and Prada through online firms. Alibaba, China's dominant online retailer, recently invested US$3.6 billion to acquire a majority holding in the Sun Art Retail Group, listed in Hong Kong.[122] In January 2021, the Ant Group was listed on both the Shanghai and Hong Kong stock exchanges after a decade of success in initiating digital payments. This came after the authorities had forced a withdrawal in November 2020 as Jack Ma was on the point of raising US$34 billion, the world's largest stock market floatation.[123] The regulator now introduced new rules on micro-lending to avoid risk of default. Jack Ma was always a critic of China's financial regulation, calling Chinese banks 'pawnshops' that restrained economic growth. Ant was vital in providing credit to young companies and poor consumers who lacked the collateral necessary to borrow from conventional lenders.

It is important to know precisely why two FinTechs, Currency Cloud and Modular Finance, each of whom received £10 million, failed to meet their targets. British Competition Remedies (BCR), set up to distribute £775 million of semi-public money to boost competition in finance, hit difficulties when

---

[121] Katherine Griffiths, *The Times*, 2 September 2020, p. 37.
[122] Simon Duke, *The Times*, 3 November 2020.
[123] *The Times*, 28 January 2021.

two beneficiaries ignored their commitments. Currency Cloud, a platform founded in 2012 and designed to assist FinTechs to conduct cross-border payments, had committed itself to integrating its platform into three accounting software systems. It abandoned this commitment because of the COVID-19 disruption. But this failure was due more to a lack of strategic orientation and fluctuating competence. Modular Finance, which had raised £18.9 million in May 2020 from private-equity backers, including Highland Europe and Frog Capital, also failed to honour its commitments. It processed £25 billion in payments and included Revolut, Europe's biggest FinTech, as a customer. Modular Finance simply slowed its investment during 2020. It also put back introducing the service that would enable small companies to process payments through their accounting firms. The payment service is now delayed to 2023.[124] BCR has been criticized for both these failures. A lack of transparency and accountability was alluded to. The missed commitments were disclosed in a regulator's report. BCR had allowed both Currency Cloud and Modular to ignore their commitments. British SMEs have been let down by these failures. SMEs need access to business banking. BCR had also faced an accounting scandal in February 2020 when Metro Bank lost £70 million out of a £120 million expansion grant. The Nationwide Building Society had to pay back £50 million after it dropped its plans to push into business banking. Firm corporate governance and a rigorous legal and regulatory framework are clearly crucial.

Cryptocurrencies: Fad or Legitimate?

The global pandemic has hastened the shift towards digital currencies. Serious evidence of this is PayPal's announcement that it will soon allow bitcoin payments.[125] Bitcoin and its equivalents are outside the control of central banks, which poses serious problems. Bitcoin appeals to speculators and their daily movements are highly volatile. The risks are enormous. Oliver Kamm advises against cryptocurrencies, particularly during a crisis. In the COVID-19 crisis, the Bank of England provided liquidity by engaging in asset purchases. In an economy based on bitcoin this would not be possible. In fact, the total number of bitcoins is limited to 21 million and this would discourage consumers and businesses. Better to rely on the economic force of the Central Bank and avoid the cryptocurrencies. 'They are a fad that's best avoided.'[126]

[124] Patrick Hosking, writing in *The Times*, 29 August 2020, p. 49.
[125] Oliver Kamm, *The Times*, 24 October 2020.
[126] *The Times*, 23 October 2020.

The present concentration on digital currency arises because of its benefits during COVID-19. Another factor is the threat from China where expansion of trade through the 'One Belt One Road' initiative provides it with opportunities to bypass the traditional banking system and challenge the American dollar. China has taken 120 patents on blockchain innovations and launched a digital currency pilot in four provinces. This is Xi's challenge and a threat to the rules-based financial trading structure. For Britain and the US there is a real threat from unregulated cryptocurrencies. Sir Mark Lyall Grant, the former National Security Adviser, is urging the UK to seek more control over digital finance.[127]

When bitcoin was launched in 2009 it sought parity with the US dollar. A leaked report from Citigroup expressed fear that bitcoin would increase in importance. This may be categorized as a 'mania', but the threat is open.[128] Bitcoin exists as computer code and has no physical form. Satoshi Nakamoto had intended it to be used as a traditional currency to pay for goods and services. Instead, it has become part of speculative trading. British investors have added to its popularity with trade worth nearly £1 billion in the first seven days of 2021. Its potential volatility has not curbed enthusiasm for it.[129]

Bitcoin expansion has also troubled European Central Bank President Christine Lagarde. Investing in cryptocurrencies on the part of retail investors is risky. Highly sceptical comments by Andrew Bailey, the Governor of the Bank of England, and equally dismissive views from the UK Financial Conduct Authority, ironically followed a threefold rise in bitcoin's price. COVID-19 turbulence and its exploitation by Iran, Russia, China, and other countries facing US financial sanctions, drive such speculative investment. However, the shortage of coin has led to increased mining. Iran faced an enduring power crisis as bitcoin manufacturers expanded mining in industrial areas of Tehran from December 2019. Other nations facing US sanctions were also experimenting with cryptocurrencies. These included Venezuela and Turkey, which triggered a bitcoin mining boom. Investors included Johnny Depp, Kayne West, Ashton Kutcher, and Serena Williams. But there are also growing numbers of conventional international investors. Mass Mutual US insurance group, PayPal, and even J.P. Morgan joined this craze, as well as the philanthropist Jonathan Ruffer.

An Islamic interpretation of the halal and haram of cryptocurrencies could offer a valuable perspective on this new wave. Muslim investors are attracted

---

[127] *The Times*, 25 November 2020.
[128] *The Times*, 25 November 2020.
[129] Patrick Hosking and James Dean, 'Bitcoin Steadies after Wild Weekend', *The Times*, 13 January 2021, p. 34.

to Ethereum, Litecoin, and Golem by recognizing the difference between cryptocurrencies and tokens. Tokens are used in fundraising and are often treated as an asset, like shares in a company.[130] However, religious authorities in Egypt, Turkey, Palestine, and the UK have condemned cryptocurrencies, bitcoin, and blockchain as haram. Use of these currencies in casino gaming is not permissible, as there is gharar (uncertainty) that indicates gambling. Furthermore, the use of cryptocurrency derivatives, as bitcoin futures surged in popularity on the Chicago Mercantile Exchange in December 2017, also disturbed religious groups. But what is impressive is the technology and the increase in clients, in particular women, and that is a liberating phenomenon.

---

[130] Sudais Asif, 'The Halal and Haram Aspect of Cryptocurrencies in Islam', *Journal of Islamic Banking and Finance*, vol. 35, no. 2 (2018), pp. 91–101; Charles W. Evans, 'Bitcoin in Islamic Banking and Finance', *Journal of Islamic Banking and Finance*, vol. 3, no. 1 (2015), pp. 1–11.

12

Ethics of Environment

Climate Crisis in the Age of Market Forces

Bahrain has a total land area of about 780 square km and a coastline of 946 km in length. Bahrain is the main island and is surrounded by a number of smaller islands, some artificially created and some reclaimed land. This number of islands accounts for the long coastline. Land reclamation has created 111 square km of reclaimed land since 1980, and in 2020 it accounted for 15 per cent of the total land area. Bahrain is an arid country with low rainfall, which falls in a brief season, April to October. Bahrain has diverse communities, with urban concentrations in Manama, Muharraq, Rifa, and Hamad Town. The total population in 2019 was 1.5 million, with half of that number comprising expatriates. Agriculture accounts for 0.3 per cent of gross domestic product (GDP) and involves the production of fruit, vegetables, poultry, dairy, and seafood, all for domestic consumption. Agricultural productivity is low, with limited arable land and an arid climate.

Bahrain's own oil production is low, and most comes from Saudi Arabia's Abu Sa'fa oil field. In 2019, Bahrain's production was just under 200,000 barrels a day; that of Saudi Arabia, almost 10 million. In oil, Bahrain is principally a refiner of the oil produced by Saudi Arabia. Bahrain's National Oil and Gas Authority controls a number of subsidiary petroleum companies. In 2017, Bahrain began construction of the Middle East's first natural gas (ING) facility in the Hidd Industrial Area on Muharraq Island, producing natural gas for industrial and urban development. There are also five electric power stations with a combined capacity of 3.9 GW. Electricity consumption is high because of the demand for air conditioning. Bahrain also has a culture of high water consumption. Water is provided at high cost through desalination involving energy-intensive technologies. The marine environment faces high evaporation, creating a serious shortage of fresh water. Bahrain is a high-income economy, with mining and oil and gas operations accounting for 97 per cent of its GDP.[1]

---

[1] Bahrain's Third National Communication under the United Nations Framework Convention on Climate Change, 2020, pp. 1–2.

Islam and Capitalism in the Making of Modern Bahrain. Rajeswary Ampalavanar Brown, Oxford University Press.
© Rajeswary Ampalavanar Brown (2023). DOI: 10.1093/oso/9780192874672.003.0012

Bahrain is a signatory to international agreements on climate, including the UNFCCC, the Kyoto Protocol, the Paris Agreement, the Montreal Protocol on ozone depletion, and the 2013 Beijing Amendment to the Montreal Protocol. Bahrain's own institution is the Sustainable Energy Centre launched in 2014 as a joint project with UNDP (United Nations Development Project). Its concern with energy efficiency and renewable energy led to the National Renewable Energy Action Plan (NREAP) and the National Energy Efficiency Action Plan (NEEAP). In 2006, Bahrain calculated that fossil fuels accounted for 69 per cent of energy needs, while industrial processes accounted for 30 per cent of emissions. Emissions from agriculture and land-use activities were a mere 0.2 per cent of total emissions. Hydrofluorocarbons are the largest components of emissions in Bahrain, accounting for 33 per cent per year. These figures are data from 2007–15.[2]

Bahrain has dense mangrove forests in the Gulf of Tubli. But these are threatened by land reclamation schemes. Extensive land reclamation and illegal dumping of waste has resulted in the loss of a third of the total mangrove area in Tubli Bay by 1992. In 1995, Tubli was declared a protected zone and in 2006, a nature reserve, but the depletion continued. Attempts were made to calculate the economic benefits of mangrove forests, but they are vulnerable to flooding from the sea which threatens eco-tourism. Rising sea levels are a persistent risk, and pose challenges for the population. The seven areas that were particularly vulnerable included Northern Bahrain, Southern Bahrain, Muharraq, Sitra, Nabih Saleh, Umm Al Nassan, and Hawar Islands. Reclaimed land was often less susceptible to rising sea levels, while industrial areas can withstand rising levels if action is taken in planning and construction.

There were also serious threats to municipal water supplies from seawater intrusion. This led to the creation of Water Evaluation and Planning (WEAP) software for the 2015–35 period. A reduction in water usage was sought and leakage was reduced. There was collaboration between Bahrain and Saudi Arabia on groundwater resources and the treatment and storage of waste water.[3] This involved increased efficiency and conservation in the agricultural and industrial sectors.

Greenhouse gas mitigation was at the heart of energy efficiency plans introduced in 2009–13. This was to avoid rising levels of CO_2 emissions. These energy efficiency initiatives created net cost savings estimated at nearly

[2] Bahrain's Third National Communication, p. 3.
[3] Bahrain's Third National Communication, pp. 4–5.

US$41 billion, eight times the savings from renewable energy. The initiatives involved R&D in green technology and climate technologies for SMEs.[4]

As noted earlier, the sectors that are vulnerable to climate change are mangrove forests, coastal areas, and water resources.[5] In Bahrain, dense mangrove forests are located in the Gulf of Tubli, with extensive mudflats between Bahrain Island and Sitra Island. These provide shelter for native species of flora and fauna, and help to reduce seawater turbidity in the bay, as well as feeding sites for commercial shrimp. These areas were safe until extensive land reclamation of the bay from the 1970s and the loss of mangrove areas, particularly after the 2008 global economic crisis. The slurry discharge from the shores led to extensive siltation that damaged the mangrove roots. In addition, waste water was discharged from the Tubli waste water treatment plant, leading to high levels of nitrogen and phosphorus in Tubli Bay. This led to further loss of mangrove areas, from 150 hectares in 1980 to 100 hectares by 1992.[6] In response, Tubli Bay was declared a protected area in 1995, and law 2006/53 designated Tubli Bay a nature reserve. By 2010, only 31 hectares remained, about a fifth of the area in 1980.[7]

The economic value of mangrove is clear in tourism and the associated cultural heritage. In 2016, the Bahrain Tourism and Exhibitions Authority, in collaboration with the Supreme Council for Environment, launched mangrove tourism in Tubli Bay to emphasize its ecological and cultural importance. This involved the protection of commercial fisheries as Tubli Bay has nursery sites for commercial shrimp.

The majority of Bahrain's population live in the northern and southern areas of Bahrain island and in the smaller islands of Muharraq, Sitra, Nabih Saleh Umm Al Nassan, and Hawar, notable for several bird species, small herds of Arabian oryx, and a large population of dugong. Given the acute land scarcity, these coastal areas are essential for economic and social expansion. However, due to land subsidence through oil, gas, and groundwater extraction, a number of IPCC reports have established methods to deal with coastal zone vulnerability in parts of Bahrain.[8] To estimate inundated areas, the IPCC

[4] Bahrain's Third National Communication, p. 8.

[5] M. Abido and S. Al-Jeneid, *Mangrove Vulnerability to Climate Change: Bahrain Case Study* (Bahrain: Arabian Gulf University, 2018); A. El-Kholei, 'Economic Valuation of Mangrove Forest, Kingdom of Bahrain', Arabian Gulf University, Bahrain, Background Paper, March 2018.

[6] FAO, Global Forest Resources Assessment 2005: Thematic Study on Mangroves, Bahrain Country Profile, draft June 2005: http://www.fao.org/forestry/9180-025abb508abb9ae04a45e41c6a5e49c39pdf.

[7] Public Commission for the Protection of Marine Resources, Environment and Wild Life (PCPM-REW2013), Bahrain's Second National Communication under the United Nations Framework Convention on Climate Change, p. 30.

[8] IPCC, 'Good Practice Guidance and Uncertainty Management in National Greenhouse Gas Inventions', 2000; IPCC, Guidelines for National Greenhouse Gas Inventories, 2006.

used land use and land cover maps for each area. The most prominent case was Muharraq with Bahrain International Airport. The IPCC estimated that built-up areas and reclaimed land would lead to a loss of at least 94 per cent of the total area in Muharraq. Of the total sensitive area, only 3 per cent would not be under water.[9] Equally exposed is Sitra, where reclaimed land accounts for 40 per cent of the island's total area. In the Hawar island group, predominantly wetlands, built-up areas account for barely 2 per cent of land area. Here major roads are under threat as well as the population.[10] In 2009, the state introduced building codes in reference to rising sea levels.[11] The ground floor of a new building was to be 1.5 metres above pavement level.[12] Assessment of coastal hazards and the development of emergency strategies is critical, in addition to the identification of no-build zones in vulnerable areas and the regulation of conservation involving coastal protection, that is, the building of dykes, breakwaters, and mangrove plantations.

On Nabih Saleh Island, built-up areas account for 64 per cent of the island's total area. There are no industrial or agricultural vacant areas on the island.[13] Rising sea levels are serious here. On Umm Al-Nassan Island, agriculture accounts for 80 per cent of the land, while just 4 per cent is built-up. Rising sea levels threaten both agriculture and the island's built-up areas.[14] The island's development also involves substantial road construction.

Commanding Heights in Water Resources

As already noted, Bahrain is poorly endowed with fresh water. With a rising population and the push for economic diversification, the shortage is becoming still more acute. It is estimated that, by 2030, there will be less than 50 cubic metres per head per year.[15] In response, the authorities have focused on increasing the supply through seawater desalination. In addition, groundwater resources have deteriorated in quantity and quality. Rising sea levels would have an adverse impact on desalination plants. The challenge is to implement long-term water resource management while

---

[9] IPCC, 'Good Practice Guidance and Uncertainty Management', pp. 39–40.
[10] Bahrain's Third National Communication under United Nations Framework Convention on Climate Change, 2020, p. 34.
[11] IPCC, 'Good Practice Guidance and Uncertainty Management', pp. 41–2.
[12] Kingdom of Bahrain, Prime Ministerial Edict no. 28, Zoning Regulations for Construction, Article 8, section 2.
[13] Kingdom of Bahrain, Supreme Council for Environment, p. 40.
[14] Kingdom of Bahrain, Supreme Council for Environment, p. 41.
[15] W. Zubari, M. Alardi, and A. Al-Shaabani, 'Water Resources Vulnerability and Adaptation to Climate Change in the Kingdom of Bahrain', Climate Change Third Communiqué, Kingdom of Bahrain Project, 2018.

safeguarding the environment. The three main sources of water supply in Bahrain are groundwater, desalinated water, and treated waste water. Desalination has several adverse environmental consequences, including harmful effects on the marine environment. Prior to 1980, the industrial sector relied on groundwater to meet its needs. After 1980, it relied on on-site desalination, which now provides 40 per cent of its requirements.[16] However, around 60 per cent of water consumption is for the municipal sector. In 2016, Bahrain established the National Water Resources Council to promote sustainable water resource management, and notably to reduce the high cost of supplying water to the municipalities. It also sought to protect groundwater resources by establishing cooperation between Bahrain and Saudi Arabia, not least in improving water storage and the treatment of waste water.

Energy Efficiency

The National Energy Efficiency Action Plan (NEEAP) of 2019 initiated a Sustainable Energy Unit which reports directly to the Cabinet and the Minister of Electricity and Water Affairs. The NEEAP sustained consultation with a wide range of stakeholders including the National Oil and Gas Authority, several ministries, the Supreme Council for the Environment, the Bahrain Defence Force, large industrial groups, and academia.[17] Twenty-two initiatives were established to secure a reduction in energy use of 6 per cent by 2025, compared to energy use over the period 2009–13.[18]

Residential and commercial properties account for almost 93 per cent of Bahrain's total building stock. They account for about 87 per cent of annual electricity consumption, largely to power air conditioning. One method to achieve energy reduction is to require efficiency specifications for new buildings and to renovate existing buildings. Another is to make air-conditioning appliances smaller and more efficient.[19] Another initiative was to establish a green building certification programme. These measures could produce savings of up to 52 per cent. Energy management systems were introduced for government buildings and LED lamps were installed for street lighting.

Industrial initiatives to reduce energy consumption were essential as the construction sector contributes over 40 per cent to GDP and in 2014

---

[16] Zubari, Alardi, and Al-Shaabani, 'Water Resources Vulnerability', pp. 47–8; Ministry of Municipalities Affairs and Urban Planning, 1979–2015.
[17] The Sustainable Energy Unit, The Kingdom of Bahrain, the National Renewable Energy Action Plan (NREAP), 2017.
[18] Kingdom of Bahrain, Supreme Council for the Environment, 2018, p. 60.
[19] Kingdom of Bahrain, Supreme Council for the Environment, 2018, p. 62.

employed 16 per cent of the workforce.[20] (The Real Estate Investment Trust and its impact on climate change is covered later in the chapter.) Each of the five major energy users, ALBA (aluminium smelting), GPIC (chemicals), BAPCO (oil refining), TAWEER (oil and gas operations), and Bahrain Steel, in agreements with the Minister of Electricity and Water Affairs, were committed to energy-saving targets. Electricity accounts for half of energy use in Bahrain, growing at 4 per cent per year. To achieve a reduction, supply needs the upgrading of conductors, transformers, and cables. Smart meters are another tool for energy reduction, in that they create an ability to manage daytime consumption peaks through real-time pricing. It is estimated that net savings could be US$135 million. Transport accounts for 31 per cent of primary energy use, growing at 5.3 per cent annually. In Bahrain most people use private cars.

There are also initiatives in renewable energy: solar power, onshore wind, offshore wind, and biogas. Solar power is installed for new housing units, government buildings, and large industrial units. Offshore wind farms are exposed to high humidity and to salt water, making installation and operation challenging.[21]

Biogas initiatives are deployed at the Askar landfill site and the Tubli waste water treatment plant.[22] Technology transfers are pursued through licensing agreements on Trade Related Aspects of Intellectual Property Rights (TRIPS) and opportunities under UNFCC.[23]

The Gulf Cooperation Council encourages the transition to a low-carbon economy through carbon taxes, cap and trade systems, and the promotion of more efficient vehicles. The Economic Vision 2030 emphasizes the reduction of carbon emissions. But Bahrain lacks market-based initiatives and has difficulty in accessing information, knowledge, and skills. The protection of intellectual property rights to provide confidence for investors is slow. A serious impediment arises in Bahrain's tertiary institutions and their lack of expertise. The introduction of solar thermal technologies is expensive and needs the support of industrial corporations and their conversion to

[20] The Sustainable Energy Unit, The Kingdom of Bahrain, the National Renewable Energy Action Plan (NREAP), 2017.
[21] US Energy Information Administration (USEIA), 'Levelized Cost and Levelized Avoided Cost of New Generation Resources in the Annual Cost of New Generation Resources', *The Annual Energy Outlook*, 2019; also The Sustainable Energy Unit, The Kingdom of Bahrain, the National Renewable Energy Action Plan (NREAP), 2017.
[22] Kingdom of Bahrain, Supreme Council for the Environment, 2018, p. 68.
[23] O. Al-Jayyousi, Y. Al-Sultanny, S. Al-Mahamid, A. Mirzal, and A. Bugawa, 'Technology Transfer of Green Technology—Opportunities and Barriers for Technology Transfer to Address Climate Change Risks in Bahrain', 2018; W. Alnaser, N. Alnaser, and I. Batarseh, 'Bahrain's BAPCO, 5MWp PV Grid-Connected Solar Project, *International Journal of Power and Renewable Energy Systems*, vol. 1 (2014).

clean energy technologies, especially in aluminium production. Regulatory reforms are crucial as is support through the GCC. Another challenge is to integrate green strategies with economic diversification.[24]

Predicting Economic and Political Insecurity with Human Vulnerability

Policy debates acquire greater complexity as a result of international climate change agreements. In April 2007, the UN Security Council began to focus on climate change, identifying threats emerging from rapid urbanization and economic diversification. In February 2009, the World Meteorological Organization (WMO) warned that even a five-centimetre rise in sea levels would have major consequences for marine life and human survival. It pointed out that desalination plants meet between 85 and 99 per cent of water requirements in Bahrain and its Gulf neighbours. This introduced fears of contamination of regional water supplies. The WMO further identified the prospect for social breakdown, and fragmentation along class, ethnic, and religious lines, aggravated by refugees fighting for access to energy supplies.[25]

The Gulf is projected to warm by between 3.0 and 5.9 degrees Celsius in the twenty-first century.[26]

Climate Change Challenges: Bahrain's Gulf Neighbours

A major challenge for Bahrain is the high carbon emissions of its neighbours. Energy consumption per capita in the GCC region is estimated at 2.5 times that in the EU, making it the highest in the world.[27] The low cost of energy and government subsidies, as well as the abundance of fossil fuel

---

[24] A. Abahussain, A. El-Kholei, and M. al'Aatim, *Assessing the Level of Knowledge and Awareness of the Climate Change Phenomenon in the Kingdom of Bahrain: Proposed Awareness Plan* (Bahrain: Arabian Gulf University, 2018); Al-Jayyousi et al., 'Technology Transfer of Green Technology'.

[25] R. Eckersley, 'Environmental Security, Climate Change and Globalizing Terrorism', in *Rethinking Insecurity, War and Violence*, edited by D. Grenfell and P. James (London: Routledge, 2008); M. A. Raouf, 'Climate Change Threats, Opportunities and the GCC Countries', Middle East Institute Policy Brief no.12, Washington, DC, 2008; M. A. Raouf, 'Water Issues in the Gulf: Time for Action', Middle East Institute Policy Brief no. 22, Washington, DC, 2009.

[26] T. Mitchell and M. Hulme, 'A Country-by-Country Analysis of Past and Future Warming Rates', Tyndall Centre Working Paper No. 1, University of East Anglia, Norwich, 2000; Kristian Coates Ulrichsen, 'Gulf Security: Changing Internal and External Dynamics', Kuwait Programme on Development, Governance and Globalization in the Gulf States, London School of Economics and Political Science, Working Paper, 2009, pp. 1–39.

[27] J. Lillestam and A. Patt, 'Barriers, Risks, and Policies for Renewables in the Gulf States', *Energies*, 2015; M. Asif, 'Growth and Sustainability Trends in the Building Sector in the GCC Region with Particular Reference to the KSA and UAE', *Renew Sustain Energy Review*, 2016; see also Fahad Radhi Alharbi and

resources, enables excessive consumption, leading to environmental deterioration. Approximately 12 per cent of energy demand in Bahrain is for desalination. Bahrain, like her GCC neighbours, needs clean water production technologies and a shift to renewable energy. But this transition has been slow. Improving efficiency includes the use of steam turbines and combined cycle turbines in power plants for electricity generation. Here the GCC economies need diversification, which the oil-rich economies are more hesitant to pursue, in contrast to Bahrain. Diversification of energy production is within the GCC commitments to reduce hydrocarbon reserves and to move to solar and wind energy.[28] Bahrain has low oil reserves, just 0.12 billion barrels compared to Saudi Arabia's 266 billion barrels. Bahrain's share in gas and oil in revenues was 80 per cent, compared to Saudi Arabia's 90 per cent and Kuwait's 94 per cent.[29]

However, Bahrain can develop alternative energy sources, in particular solar energy. A mean of nearly 2180 kWh/m for annual solar radiation was recorded in Bahrain in 2018.[30] There is also considerable potential for wind energy: indeed, most GCC countries possess significant offshore wind potential, although with different wind speed performances.[31] The most suitable sites for wind energy application are in Saudi Arabia, the only GCC country located on the Red Sea.

However, despite such substantial solar and wind energy resources being available, the use of them is very low. A 2019 International Renewable Energy Agency (IRENA) report revealed that solar and wind energy accounted for only 0.6 per cent of energy generation in the GCC.[32] Power consumption in the GCC has risen at an average annual rate of 8 per cent, higher than any other world region.[33] The critical issues in this search

Denes Csala, 'Gulf Cooperation Council Countries' Climate Change Mitigation Challenges and Exploration of Solar and Wind Energy Resource Potential', *Applied Sciences* MDPI, 2021: https://doi.org/10.3390/app11062648.

[28] H. M. Al-Maamary, H. A. Kazem, and M. T. Chaichan, 'The Impact of Oil Price Fluctuations on Common Renewable Energies in GCC countries', *Renew Sustain Energy Review*, 2017; Alharbi and Csala, 'Gulf Cooperation Council Countries' Climate Change Mitigation Challenges'.

[29] B. Fattouh and L. El-Katiri, *Energy and Arab Economic Development* (New York: United Nations Development Programme, 2012); Secretariat General of the Gulf Cooperation Council: The Cooperation Council for the Arab States of the Gulf, available online: http://www.gcc-sg.org/en-us/Cooperation and Achievements/Pages/Home.aspx.

[30] W. Alnaser and N. Alnaser, 'The Status of Renewable Energy in the GCC Countries', *Renew Sustain Energy Review*, 2011.

[31] W. A-Nassar, S. Neelamani, K. Al-Salem, and H. Al-Dashti, 'Feasibility of Offshore Wind Energy as an Alternative Source for the State of Kuwait', *Energy*, 2019.

[32] International Renewable Energy Agency, *Renewable Energy Market Analysis* (Abu Dhabi: IREA, 2019).

[33] A. Elrahmani, J. Hannun, F. Eljack, and M. Kazi, 'Status of Renewable Energy in the GCC Region and Future Opportunities', *Current Opinion Chemical Engineering*, 2021; R. Praveen, V. Keloth, A. G. Abo-Khalil, A. S. Alghamdi, A. M. Eltamaly, and I. Tlili, 'An Insight to the Energy Policy of GCC Countries to Meet Renewable Energy Targets of 2030', *Energy Policy*, 2020.

for renewable energy alternatives include economic diversification, urban growth, increased energy consumption, and falling solar and wind energy costs.[34]

The impact of cloud and dust often produces severe fog, said to be worse in winter. Deserts carry huge amounts of dust, transported through the Arabian Peninsula (see Figure 12.1), including dust from the deserts of Iraq. The lowest amount of dust recorded in Qatar was 50–113 tons per square km. Bahrain's figure was 64–114 tons per square km.

Action against climate change must revolve around innovative and sustainable strategies and practices. Laws are crucial and must comply with the Paris Agreement under the United Nations Framework Convention on Climate Change. Local carbon taxes on organizations and companies that produce high rates of CO_2 emissions will encourage solar energy production. The GCC region has a huge amount of solar and wind resources compared to the global average.[35]

Environmental Advocacy Coalition and the Law in Bahrain, 1980–2021

The Bahrain Emiri Decree No7/1980 established the Environmental Protection Committee and the Environmental Protection Technical Secretariat. The EPC was affiliated to the Office of the Prime Minister through the Office of the Health Minister and Chairman of EPC. In 1996, the EPC came under the Housing, Municipalities and Environment Ministry, as rising emissions were related to increased housing.

Action through International Law

Under the United Nations Framework Convention on Climate Change (UNFCCC), founded in June 1992 and effective from 1994, litigation is driven both through an obligations strategy and a rights strategy. Environmental

[34] C. M. A. Yip, U. B. Gunturu, and G. L. Stenchikov, 'Wind Resource Characterization in the Arabian Peninsula', *Applied Energy*, 2016.
[35] Alharbi and Csala, 'Gulf Cooperation Council Countries' Climate Change Mitigation Challenges', p. 19; W. E. Alnaser and N. W. Alnaser, 'The Impact of the Rise of Using Solar Energy in GCC Countries', *Renew Energy Environment Sustain*, 2019, pp. 4, 7; B. L. Almutairi, 'Investigating the Feasibility and Soil-Structure Integrity of Onshore Wind Turbine Systems in Kuwait', PhD thesis, Loughborough University, Loughborough, 2017; Elrahmani, Hannun, Eljack, and Kazi, 'Status of Renewable Energy in the GCC Region';W. N. Adger, 'Scales of Governance and Environmental Justice for Adaptation and Mitigation of Climate Change', *Journal of International Development*, 2001.

claims are transformed into human rights claims.[36] This raises serious issues for oil-producing and oil-consuming countries. Limon has described this tension during the negotiations over climate change.[37] The UN was conscious of the overlap between climate change and human rights, but was also aware of states' responsibility for violating human rights because limiting emissions would prove difficult.[38] The UNFCC established the legal framework to limit greenhouse gases in 1992 and this was adopted in the Kyoto Protocol in December 2008. The protection of human rights was evident in the 2014 report.

This obligation to reduce emissions was established under the Kyoto Protocol, Article 3 specified six gases to be reduced 5 per cent below the 1990 level during the period 2008–12, and a further seven specified gases under the Doha amendment.[39] Redesigning the obligations for the state to reduce emissions as part of human rights is creating a dual structure within the UNFCCC, with separable obligations and inseparable obligations. This represents a transformation of the legal architecture of international law from the top-down approach in the Kyoto Protocol to a bottom-up approach in the Paris Agreement. The top-down obligation involved the introduction of timetables and adherence to international law, while the bottom-up approach preserved the autonomy of states in shaping their response to climate change. These are held within UNFCCC legal documents.[40]

In Bahrain, and indeed across the Middle East, infrastructural expansion, changing consumption patterns, and the estrangement of significant sectors of the population made a reduced dependence on fossil fuels extremely challenging. The revolutionary demands inevitably required heavy investment. To protect the poor and vulnerable while pursuing measures to combat climate change is highly complex.[41] Moreover, action against climate change is a shared responsibility involving all states, but this is difficult to achieve

---

[36] Maiko Meguro, 'Litigating Climate Change through International Law: Obligations Strategy and Rights Strategy', *Leiden Journal of International Law*, vol. 33, no. 4 (2020), pp. 933–51.

[37] M. Limon, 'Human Rights and Climate Change: Constructing a Case for Political Action', *Harvard Environmental Law Review*, vol. 33 (2009).

[38] Office of the UN High Commissioner for Human Rights (OHCHR), *Report of the Office of the UN High Commissioner for Human Rights on the Relationship between Human Rights and Climate Change*, UN Doc.A/HRC/10/61 (2009), paragraph 18; OHCHR individual report on human rights and climate change (2014) under HRC resolution 19/10.

[39] The Doha amendment is available at: unfccc.int/files/kyoto protocol/application/pdf/kp doha amendment english.pdf. See also Art. 4.1[b] UNFCCC.

[40] Lavanya Rajamani, 'Ambition and Differentiation in the 2015 Paris Agreement: Interpretative Possibilities and Underlying Politics', *International and Comparative Law Quarterly*, vol. 65, no. 2 (2016); Daniel Bodansky, 'The Paris Climate Change Agreement: A New Hope?', *American Journal of International Law*, vol. 110, no. 2 (2016), pp. 291–2.

[41] Kelly Levin, Benjamin Cashore, Steven Bernstein, and Graeme Auld, 'Overcoming the Tragedy of Super Wicked Problems: Constraining Our Future Selves to Ameliorate Global Climate Change', *Policy Sciences*, vol. 45 (2012), pp. 123–52.

in the Gulf. The transition to a green economy requires not only substantial investment but also careful calculations by each country as to its interests. Collective commitment may well impose unfair obligations and responsibilities on some. To address these issues, COP21 put the emphasis on finance and technology, as well as the mobilization of 100 billion dollars a year by 2020 to assist developing economies. But despite the uncertainty, the UNFCCC emerged as a powerful legal institution. There persists a shared sense of urgency in dealing with climate change. The body of law within the UNFCCC can develop at multiple government levels.[42]

Legal Responses by the Bahrain Government towards Climate Issues

In Bahrain, concern with environmental change was signalled from the 1980s through the protection of land, a broad interest in reducing marine and air pollution, and in the disposal of waste. There also arose interest in the protection of animals and their habitat. International treaties and institutions produced some of the sharpest critiques of environmental behaviour in Bahrain. Bahrain's response included a recasting of economic structures, notably the use of financial bonds in Islamic finance, and an encouragement of stricter ethical behaviour directed towards the over-consumption culture that permeated most of the Gulf states.

The Bahrain Emiri Decree No. 7 of 1980 established the Environmental Protection Committee (EPC) and the Environmental Protection Technical Secretariat (EPTS). The EPC was attached to the Office of the Prime Minister and the Office of the Health Minister and Chairman of the EPC. The Bahrain Decree No. 21/1996 established the Environmental Affairs Agency (EA) which was monitored by the Ministry of Housing, Municipalities, and the Environment. The EA had two Directorates, one the Directorate of Assessment and Planning, the other the Directorate of Environmental Control. But despite these initiatives, local and global capitalism made strategies to protect the environment hazardous.

Since the early 1980s, considerable attention has been paid in Bahrain to the prevention of marine pollution, principally to protect the livelihood of fishermen and to protect wildlife. This led to collaboration with Japan in 2004.

---

[42] Thijs Etty, Veerle Heyvaert, Cinnamon Carlarne, Dan Farber, Jolene Lin, and Joanne Scott, 'Transnational Dimensions of Climate Governance', *Transnational Environmental Law*, vol. 1, no. 2 (2012), pp. 235–43; D. Bodansky, 'Climate Change: Transnational Legal Order or Disorder?', in *Transnational Legal Orders*, edited by Terence C. Halliday and Gregory Shaffer (Cambridge: Cambridge University Press, 2015), p. 287.

Marine monitoring programmes, established since 1983, focused on seawater and fish samples to trace nutrients, heavy metals, chlorinated pesticides, organic matter, and hydrocarbons. Further guidelines were introduced in 1996 to control pollutants. Bahrain signed the Protocol for Protection of the Environment against Pollution from Land-based Sources and the Protocol Concerning Marine Pollution Resulting from Exploration and Exploitation of the Continental Shelf.[43] In 1996, there was legislation protecting land, as Bahrain had become dependent on Africa for agricultural products. The protection of land included concern over chemicals as well as soil conservation.

Industrial and economic diversification had serious repercussions for air pollution. In 1996, a Ministerial Order introduced the monitoring of pollution by motor vehicles. This monitoring was at four locations. A 'fume watch' programme had been introduced in 1994, reporting on polluting vehicles. Chemical pollutants were measured daily, weekly, and monthly, and recorded in annual reports.[44]

Government engagement with the habitats of flora and fauna was striking for a nation deluged with oil wealth and oil-processing industries. Significant here was the National Committee for the Protection of Wildlife attached to the Crown Prince's court. Local studies showed how reclamation had an adverse impact on the habitats of animals, as well as encouraging the growth of damaging invasive species. The UNDP assisted in identifying, minimizing, and mitigating the negative consequences of the rapid development of the coastal areas. There was also a tightening of waste disposal regulations. Waste management practices improved with Bahrain's participation in the UN Conference on Environment and Development (UNCED) held in Rio de Janeiro in June 1992. A national committee, the Environmentally Sound Management of Waste and Chemicals, was established. This committee had members representing BATELCO, the Al-Zamil Coating Factory, Bahrain Aluminium (ALBA), the Environmental Health Directorate, the Bahrain Chemical Society, the Bahrain Ministry of Commerce, and the Bahrain Centre for Studies and Research. Seeking to promote a green environment increased trust within the UN in Bahrain's compliance. This UN connection remained vital for the control of chemical waste, the reduction of waste through recycling, and the creation of sites for industrial waste. Bahrain's close liaison with Saudi Arabia was behind the UN initiatives led by Bahrain, which in 1992 ratified the Basel Convention on Control of Trans-boundary

---

[43] Bahrain Emir Decree No. 9/1990.
[44] All the above on law and the environment are from Government of Bahrain data sources and accessed through https://www.stalawfirm.com/en/blogs/view/environment-2020.html.

Movement of Hazardous Waste and its Disposal, which was implemented in 1993. The GCC countries also complied with industrial waste regulation. Although Bahrain has no nuclear power installations, it formulated the 1996 Environment Law, recognizing protection from radioactive waste created by neighbouring states. This also involved the reporting of environmental accidents, a social responsibility that established Bahrain at the centre of the UN's engagement on environment with the Gulf states.[45]

The Regulation of Energy Efficiency

Bahrain's engagement with international treaties and agreements, although implemented domestically in a fragmentary manner, was nevertheless strong, as shown in its compliance with the Energy Charter Treaty, an international agreement concerned with fossil fuel and established in 1994. In March 2019, in accordance with Bahrain's Vision 2030, the Works, Municipality Affairs and Urban Planning Ministry introduced a law regulating energy efficiency in buildings through a green building and sustainability programme. The Energy Efficiency Action Plan set a national target on energy use and savings. This involved buildings being regulated for energy use and fuel prices, requiring the training of staff in environmental aspects of energy security. In December 2015, the 21st Conference of the Parties of the UN Framework Convention on Climate Change in Paris introduced a programme for survival, that included keeping the rise in global temperature below 2 degrees. Bahrain signed the Paris agreement on 22 April 2016.

Can Islamic Endowments (Waqf) and Obligatory Charitable Contributions (Zakat) Define Spiritual Responsibility for the Environment?

The mobilization of Islamic finance through Green Sukuk targets climate change, agriculture, education, and poverty alleviation. The use of Islamic contracts, wakala, musharka, mudaraba, and ijava provides innovation targeted at specific financing, despite increased transaction costs. In addition, National Green Participative Banks create public–private partnerships that enable the accumulation of expertise for strategic projects. Zakat,

---

[45] Richard C. Warren, *Corporate Governance and Accountability* (Bromborough: Liverpool Academic Press, 2000), pp. 80–109.

alms-giving, contributes to micro-finance for renewable energy projects.[46] Here Islamic financial principles converge with international, European, and American positions on the environment. Shari'ah is an infallible guardian of socially responsible behaviour, providing both financial support, through public–private partnerships, and personal support. Legislative defence of the environment invoked religious principles in the Gulf states, including oil-rich Qatar and Kuwait as well as Bahrain. Undoubtedly, South East Asia had an advantage over the MENA nations, who were dependent on a single natural resource, oil.[47] Bahrain achieved economic growth through the processing of oil and the global provision of Islamic finance.

The waqf embraces economic systems as well as business behaviour, managing land, water resources, urban planning, and the protection of animals.[48] For Bahrain the sustainability of the sea, water, and energy was linked with economic diversification, the growth of cities, and with ambitions of global transition to offset its declining natural resource, oil. The protection of the planet became a dominant feature.[49]

However, in the actual implementation of law there was a diversion, as commercial law, urban planning, and environmental law were often influenced by English law.[50] Waqf foundations often collaborated with environmental NGOs. The Kuwait Awqaf was prominent in environmental activities and it created a waqf corporation, providing funds for environment protection.[51]

There were institutional gaps between the religious endowments and the state departments responsible for environment issues, specifically over funds for mosques and religious schools, as the MENA countries were slow to respond to ecological programmes. However, the South East Asian countries of Malaysia and Indonesia were embracing Shari'ah for environmental

[46] Dalal Aassouli, 'Mobilizing and Leveraging Islamic Climate Finance in the MENA Region: The Potential Role of National Green Participative Banks', in *Climate Change Law and Policy in the Middle East and North Africa Region*, edited by Damilola S. Olawuyi (London: Routledge, 2022).

[47] UN Environment Programme, 'Faith for Earth Dialogue Synthesis Report', 8 May 2019; S. Ramlan, 'Religious Law for the Environment: Comparative Islamic Environmental Law in Singapore, Malaysia and Indonesia', National University of Singapore, Centre for Asian Legal Studies, Working Paper No. 19/03, 2019.

[48] Samira Idllalène, *Rediscovery and Revival in Islamic Environmental Law: Back to the Future of Nature's Trust* (Cambridge: Cambridge University Press, 2021).

[49] Mohammad Abdullah, 'Waqf, Sustainable Development Goals (SDGs) and Maqasid-al-Shariah', *International Journal of Social Economics*, vol. 45, no. 1 (2018), pp. 158–72.

[50] Damilola S. Olawuyi, 'Human Rights and the Environment in Middle East and North African (MENA) Regions: Trends, Limitations and Opportunities', in *Encyclopaedia of Human Rights and the Environment, Indivisibility, Dignity, and Legality*, edited by J. May and E. Daly (Cheltenham: Edward Elgar, 2018).

[51] Samira Idllalène, 'The Role of Environmental Waqf in Addressing Climate Change in the MENA Region: A Comparative Law Analysis', in *Climate Change Law and Policy in the Middle East and North Africa Region*, edited by Damilola S. Olawuyi (Abingdon: Routledge, 2022), pp. 43–62.

programmes. From 2006 to 2016, Majlis Ulamas Indonesia (MUI) issued six fatwas (legal opinions) on environmental matters. These were requests to state and private companies and to religious groups and citizens to engage in environmental matters. These pressures were less pervasive in the MENA countries. This has also resulted in fewer scientific research programmes, although Bahrain and Kuwait did engage in scientific research. Green Finance was notable through Islamic banks. The Green Mosque concept, articulated in the Istanbul Declaration of 2015, stated: 'the earth is green and beautiful and Allah has appointed you his stewards over it'. Mosques were required to become energy efficient, water was to be used more sparingly, and trees were to be planted. The last was strongly supported by the Kanoos in Bahrain. The concept was applied in Malaysia and Morocco.[52] The UN Faith for Earth Initiative was aimed to 'Encourage, Empower and Engage with Faith Based Organizations as partners to achieve Sustainable Development Goals and thereby fulfil Agenda 2030'.[53]

There is also a renewed interest in religious circles in exploiting Islamic finance in three aspects: prohibition of interest, prohibition of contract ambiguity, and prohibition of speculation. Climate financing also ensures the sharing of profit and loss in environmental laws. Equally vital within Shari'ah are instruments such as mudarabah and green sukuk bonds. This has another advantage in attracting international producers of greenhouse gas, notably the Gulf states and the MENA countries, as major oil producers. Islamic financing also enables tax reductions. It is important here to note the convergence of green finance with banking, insurance, and commercial law.[54]

Financing through green bonds and a search for new markets, especially in Europe and America, had been initiated by the World Bank and the European Investment Bank in 2007. The central focus was on the creation of bonds and securities attractive for environment organizations. This Climate Bonds Initiative (CBI) reported success from 2008 to 2018, raising US$521 billion in green bonds. In the first half of 2019 the green bonds issued amounted to US$100 billion globally, and the Environment + Energy Leader proudly forecast a rise to US$250 billion. The architect of this scheme, Kenneth Lay, manager of Rock Creek, had earlier, as Treasurer of the World Bank, developed the first green bonds specifically for environmental projects. The

[52] O. S. Syamimi, I. N. Hanim, M. Zulhaili, and B. Ruwaidah, 'Green Mosque: A Living Nexus', *Environment-Behaviour Proceedings Journal*, vol. 3 (2018), pp. 53–63.
[53] UN Environment Programme, 'Faith for Earth Dialogue Synthesis Report', 8 May 2019.
[54] F. Khalid, 'Islam and the Environment: Ethics and Practice: An Assessment', *Religion Compass*, vol. 4, no. 11 (2010), pp. 707–16.

shaping of robust transparency and understanding to guide investors was a challenge. In 2010, the CBI published the Climate Bonds Standard Certification Scheme. In this radical challenge it was assisted by the International Capital Markets Association in establishing scientific and ethical standards in the issuance of green bonds. External reviews of these instruments were sought through leading firms, CICERO and Sustainalytics, which examined the efficacy of green bonds through a global case study of 5,000 bonds: 88 per cent were labelled as green by the Climate Bonds Initiative (CBI).[55]

The overarching purpose here was to expose the dubious intruders in climate change institutions and investments. Clarification by ICMA (International Capital Market Association) and CBI (Climate Bonds Initiative) exposed the complexity and diversity of green bonds. The Global Sustainable Investment Alliance estimated that US$30.7 trillion in institutional assets globally were utilized to address climate issues. Australia, Canada, Europe, Japan, New Zealand, and the US were involved in this institution from 2018. Islam was challenging the Western values of capitalism while Europe and the US were also seriously addressing the future of the planet, particularly after environmental crises in the 1980s and 1990s.[56] By 2018, the attractiveness of green bonds was further enhanced by their performance in comparison to traditional bonds. Climate-resilient assets appear to be less risky and earn high returns.[57]

It is important to add here that China's 'Clean Coal' project in May 2017 was detected as fraud and removed from the Climate Change indexes, which are compiled by the international organizations noted earlier, only four years later.[58] China maintained its own coal-fired expansion from 2005 to 2017 and even in 2021 it was still expanding the burning of coal.[59] Spurious green bonds were sold by the Spanish oil company Repsol in 2017 but in June 2021 they were excluded from the indexes. The backlash led to greater legal rigour in the certification of green bonds. While all acknowledged the importance of wealth-creating capitalism, the threat from climate change was clearly seen.

[55] Afsaneh Beschloss and Mina Mashayekhi (Rock Creek), 'A Greener Future for Finance: Green Bonds Offer Lessons for Sustainable Finance', *Finance and Development: The Economics of Climate*, IMF F&D, December 2019, pp. 60–1.

[56] David Jeremy, 'Ethics, Religion, and Business in Twentieth Century Britain', *Business in Britain in the Twentieth Century*, edited by Richard Coopey and Peter Lyth (Oxford: Oxford University Press, 2009), pp. 356–84.

[57] Beschloss and Mashayekhi, 'A Greener Future for Finance', p. 61.

[58] A list of the international organizations, 2003–18, is provided in Aassouli, 'Mobilizing and Leveraging Climate Finance in the MENA Region', p. 207: the list draws on World Bank sources and the United Nations Environment Program, *The UNEP Global Litigation Report: 2020 Status Review*, 2020, pp. 8–10.

[59] China is responsible for 27 per cent of global greenhouse emissions: BBC News, 7 May 2021.

Financing a Climate-Resilient Infrastructure through Blockchain Technology: Is It a Solution or a Problem?

Important in seeking a resilient infrastructure in climate change projects was the use of innovative financial instruments supported by digitalization involving blockchain technology. An effective installation of blockchain technology posed serious legal and institutional challenges, despite the enthusiasm for new technologies. Blockchain could also improve existing financial public and private partnerships. The threat of declining material resources in the MENA countries was accompanied by a rising population, expected to reach 600 million by 2050.[60] More than 280 million live in the region's cities, a figure expected to double by 2040, creating food scarcities and, above all, water scarcity as the region is dependent on desalinated water which increases energy consumption. Being located near the coast, the cities face rising water levels. Some parts of the MENA region are also affected by earthquakes. The people are high consumers of electricity because of the increasing use of air conditioners as temperatures rise, although costs are held down by generous state subsidies. It is clear that climate change is a great threat to the MENA region. Vast disparities in living standards adds to the energy crisis. GDP per capita ranges from US$1,000 in Yemen to more than US$20,000 in the Gulf Cooperation Council countries. This wide disparity in wealth adds to transportation and infrastructure costs to meet the consumption demands of the rich. The rich lead a luxurious life while food riots among the poor are inevitable.[61]

Policy debates on the environment acquire greater complexity with the finance managed by the state with little private sector investment. Innovative financial instruments, supported by blockchain technology, can introduce greater transparency and secure lower costs, a more effective allocation of projects, and rigorous monitoring of transactions across networks. The blocks are linked and secured using cryptography. Blockchain technology goes beyond cryptocurrencies and financial transactions and creates a decentralized but secure network structure that can be applied to smart contracts and simplified supply chains. It can integrate stakeholders involved in the value chains and those regulating them, including producers, intermediaries, consumers, and governments. It also supports the implementation of the

[60] World Bank, 'Population Total: Middle East and North Africa', 2019: https://data.worldbank.org/indicator/SP.POP.TOTL.?Locations=ZQ>.

[61] M. Abouelnaga, 'Why the MENA Region Needs to Better Prepare for Climate Change', Atlantic Council Blog, 7 May 2019: www.atlanticcouncil.org/blogs/menasource/why-the-mena-region-needs-to-better-prepare-for-climate-change/.

United Nations 2030 Agenda to achieve sustainable development. It can be used in climate infrastructure projects implemented through public/private partnerships.[62]

Fintech may help trade industry to utilize Islamic finance and reduce commercial risks in climate change projects. Artificial intelligence enables machines to perform cognitive functions normally dependent on humans. This reduces costs. Robots direct warehouse storage, machines package products, and corporations derive data to determine customer preferences and reduce costs. This also leads to a cost-effective transition to globalization. The smart contract works within the blockchain network, thereby eliminating field services embedded in the previous trading structure. It also maintains record keeping and reduces financial costs. The World Food Programme in Jordan reduced administration costs by 98 per cent through blockchain, making accounting processes faster and cheaper.[63]

The technology also reduces the use of foreign technicians and costs. Blockchain working on a single ledger provides privacy for important transactions while increasing efficiency, and thus lowers costs for environmental projects. Digitalization of real-world assets or financial instruments exploiting blockchain technology is essential in MENA countries, increasing transparency and reducing corruption. Data in blockchain cannot be altered.[64]

Blockchain intervention in public/private enterprise reduces costs and produces open contracts, eliminating the prospect of legal confusion. In the MENA countries the technology is used by development agencies. The United Nations Office for the Coordination of Humanitarian Affairs (UNOCHA), the United Nations Office for Project Services (UNOPS), and the United Nations Development Programme (UNDP) use blockchain for transparency, security verification, and resilience. These agencies can collaborate with local PPPs without fear of intransigence. Thus, technology has assisted in securing additional funds and talent for specific projects. The technology also assists in promoting new economic projects.

---

[62] N. Saidi and A. Prasad, 'Background Note: Trends in Trade and Investment Policies in the MENA Region', MENA-OECD Competitiveness Programme, MENA-OECD Working Group on Investment and Trade, 27–28 November 2018, p. 23; United Nations General Assembly, 'Transforming Our World: The 2030 Agenda for Sustainable Development', 21 October 2015, UNDoc.A/RES/70/1, 29; United Nations Development Programme (UNDP), 'The Future is Decentralised Block Chains, Distributed Ledgers, and the Future of Sustainable Development', 2018: www.undp. org/content/dam/undp/library/innovation/The-Future-is -Decentralised.pdf.

[63] K. Dodgson and D. Genc, 'Blockchain for Humanity', Humanitarian Practice Network, 29 November 2017: https://odihpn.org/blog/blockchain-for-humanity/.

[64] D. Uzsoki, 'Tokenization of Infrastructure: A Blockchain-Based Solution to Financing Sustainable Infrastructure', International Institute for Sustainable Development, MAVA, January 2019: www.iisd.org/sites/default/files/publications/tokenization-infrastructure-blockchain-solution.pdf.

Gaps persist in technological ambitions and legal policy. Under the 'Lex cryptographica', self-executing smart contracts and decentralized autonomous organizations enforced quasi-autonomous technological systems.[65] Lessig's coordination of 'code as law' involves a strategic evolution of technology with state law in the context of market forces and social norms.[66] There are weaknesses in blockchain. But the use of smart contracts provides precision, although it is inadequate in preserving contractual autonomy. Smart contracts have their limitations, with reference to execution that requires confidentiality, and Lessing relates this to decentralized control which decreases the power of government. Blockchain through smart contracts can reduce risk, particularly when blockchain operates with public and private collaborators, and that enhances transparency and improves liquidity through increased funding.[67] Blockchain technology has the capacity to make changes to the law, but it is difficult for the law to change blockchain code properties. This constrains legal applications by both the state and regulatory authorities.[68]

However, legal recognition can be achieved through specific provisions in blockchain-based smart contracts. Another option is to avoid introducing specific provisions and seek recognition through a judicial investigation on a case-by-case basis. Alternatively, smart contracts can impose 'hybrid agreements' in cases where it is impossible to achieve consistency, but this complicates the use of smart contracts and affects the transparency of blockchain technology. Tony Prosser proposes that although 'regulation may be needed, it is portrayed as a second best choice for social organization; in principle free markets giving us economic freedom and consumer choices should be preferred whenever possible. Regulation is thus an always regrettable means of correcting market failure ... regulation is part of economic management'.[69]

Would blockchain technology, as a digitalized infrastructure to assist the public sector in improving the environment, be sustainable? Only if

---

[65] Lex cryptographica refers to rules administered through self-executing smart contracts and decentralized, autonomous technological systems. Aaron Wright and Primavera De Filippi, Decentralized Blockchain Technology and the Rise of Lex Cryptographia (New York: Social Science Research Network, 2015): https://ssm.com/abstract=2580664.

[66] L. Lessig, *Code: And Other Laws of Cyber Space* (New York: Basic Books, 1999); P. Tasca and R. Piselli, 'The Blockchain Paradox', in *Regulating Blockchain: Techno-Social and Legal Challenges*, edited by I. Lianos, P. Hacker, S. Eich, and G. Dimitropoulos (Oxford: Oxford University Press, 2019), p. 28.

[67] World Economic Forum and OECD, 'Blended Finance Vol. 1: A Primer for Development Finance and Philanthropic Funders', WEF, September 2015.

[68] Roxana A. Mastor and Ioannis Papageorgiou, 'Financing Climate Resilient Infrastructure in the MENA Region: Potentials and Challenges of Blockchain Technology', in *Climate Change Law and Policy in the Middle East and North Africa Region*, edited by Damilola S. Olawuyi (Abingdon: Routledge, 2022), p. 279.

[69] Tony Prosser, *The Regulatory Enterprise* (Oxford: Oxford University Press, 2010), p. 1. Also R. Herian, *Regulating Blockchain: Critical Perspectives in Law and Technology* (Abingdon: Routledge, 2019), p. 3.

blockchain were collaborating with a dynamic state and private sector, and with international organizations such as UNDP or any UN organization, could blockchain and smart contracts secure economic growth without debilitating losses. Superior technology has to be coordinated with patenting or copyright within the market, and has to adopt a branding that provides some control over intellectual property rights. As with blockchain and smart contracts, market-based learning encroaches into the idiosyncratic firm. Blockchain's attractiveness to criminal activity is discussed in the section on money laundering.

In a 2019 report on global trade-management system software, Gartner listed the various networks developed for cross-border trade technologies using blockchain: 'Universal Trade Network' develops standards for various financial blockchain operators; 'Marco Polo Network' combines an R3 enterprise blockchain platform with 'Trade 1X' blockchain trade finance solutions; while 'Voltron' offers a blockchain-based digital letter of credit service. Blockchain in 'Transport Alliance' (BiTA) uses blockchain for logistics, freight transportation, and software industries. 'Trade Lens' was developed by IBM and Maersk with over 100 corporations participating. The Global Shipping Business Network developed 'CargoSmart' in alliance with nine ocean carriers and terminal operators.[70] Gartner warns in his Report: 'despite the recent advancements, use caution when considering blockchain. Right now it should be viewed as a potential complementary technology, not as a wholesale replacement.'[71]

A number of entrepreneurs were sceptical about blockchain, comparing it to the excitement generated by the dot-com bubble.[72] Greater acceptance and accreditation of the instrument was found in Howard Fosdick's thesis, popularized by Gartner, where the technology occurs within a 'hype cycle' divided into five phases: technology trigger, peak of inflated expectations, trough of disillusionment, slope of enlightenment, plateau of productivity.[73]

Although the rapid spread of blockchain has created cynicism, one important issue is that it is sustained by the spillover effects of cryptocurrencies.[74]

---

[70] William McNeill and Oscar Sanchez Duran, 'Market Guide for Global Trade Management Software', Gartner Report, 10 July 2019.

[71] McNeill and Duran, 'Market Guide for Global Trade Management Software'.

[72] For example, Ben Dickson, 'Are We in a Blockchain Winter', PC Magazine, 6 April 2019: https:sea.pcmag.com/opinion/32222/are-we-in-a-blockchain-winter.

[73] Howard Fosdick, 'The Sociology of Technology Adoption', Enterprise Systems Journal, September 1992; David Furlonger and Rajesh Kandaswamy, 'Hype Cycle for Blockchain Technologies', Gartner Report, 25 July 2018.

[74] Michael J. Casey, 'Crypto Winter is Here and We Only Have Ourselves to Blame', Coindesk.com, 3 December 2018: https://www.coindesk.com/thecrypto-winter-is-here-and-we-only-have-ourselves-to-blame.

The use of these currencies is built within the blockchain, making regulation straightforward, as many are fearful of cryptocurrencies. Inevitably there is always a mismatch between technology promise and legal constraints, but smart contracts are used in developing global trade and in locating supply-chain finance solutions. During the coronavirus pandemic, the harnessing of these technologies in international trade increased, especially blockchain with smart contracts to provide legal acceptance.[75]

The Integration of Blockchain with Smart Contracts: A Classic Form of Decentralized Finance from Maturity to Renaissance through Public–Private Partnerships

Smart contracts can assume responsibilities through their trust-based, open, and accessible financial system. If regulation demands access restrictions, as with security tokens, these are implemented through the token contracts without compromising the decentralized properties. While the traditional financial system is trust-based and dependent on centralized institutions, a decentralized financial system can operate safely with smart contracts. This increases transfer speeds and provides solutions through state and other networks. This therefore strengthens the interaction with private entrepreneurs with an ability to develop and modernize collaboration. Bahrain, and even Dubai with its falling hydrocarbon revenues, use the private sector in their renewable energy targets.[76] Global economic shocks in 2008–09, the oil price collapse of 2014, and the COVID-19 pandemic created energy transition urgency through technology and collaboration with private enterprise.[77]

The advantage of decentralized financial institutions is that trust is secured in smart contracts, resulting in faster transfers of finance. There is, in addition, a transparency with smart contracts, often essential when collaborating with private entrepreneurs. Operational security is increased by the addition of protocols, where risk is mitigated and the concentration of power

---

[75] Nicky Morris, 'Trade Finance Blockchain Race is About to Start', *Ledger Insights*, June 2018; Jonathan Ercanbrack, 'Islamic Trade Law and the Smart Contract Revolution', in *Trade Finance: Technology, Innovation and Documentary Credits*, edited by Christopher Hare and Dora Neo (Oxford: Oxford University Press, 2021), pp. 308–34.

[76] Bahrain National Vision 2030: www.bahrainedb.com/en/about/Pages/economic%20vision%202,030.aspx.

[77] Damilola S. Olawuyi, 'Advancing Innovations in Renewable Energy Technologies as Alternatives to Fossil Fuel Use in the Middle East: Trends, Limitations and Ways Forward', in *Innovation in Energy Law and Technology: Dynamic Solutions for Energy Transitions*, edited by D. Zillman, M. Roggenkamp, L. Paddock, and L. Godden (Oxford University Press, 2018), pp. 354–70.

reduced. However, illicit activity cannot always be prevented and it is therefore essential that smart contracts should manage the decentralized system through upgrades and even emergency shutdown.[78] Shari'ah is an internationally recognized structure but even smart contracts need help. Risks in construction and in the maintenance of solar projects can disrupt state and private entrepreneurs. Kuwait, the UAE, and Bahrain have seen success in projects through public/private collaboration.[79] It is perhaps reasonable to conclude that weak legal structures, a lack of standardized contracts, and inadequate institutional constraints have made it difficult to secure international standards. However, on a decentralized base, smart contracts do assist to a degree.[80]

Cryptocurrencies and Blockchain: From a Solution to a Problem?

The anonymity that is embedded in cryptocurrencies, where regulation is vague, adds to their potential illegitimacy. The currencies can be exploited for money laundering and criminal use by jihadis, as well as creating opportunities for tax evasion in many economies. One of the most successful virtual currencies is bitcoin, which interacts with the conventional financial system and the real economy. The bitcoin network supports a wide range of smart contracts using its powerful scripting language, Script. Script allows users to establish criteria for their bitcoin to be spent, and bitcoin transactions lock specific amounts to these scripts. The most important innovation in bitcoin compared to other forms of cryptographic cash or virtual currencies is its decentralized core technologies.[81] This decentralization avoids concentration of power and is essential for those seeking capital to finance climate change projects. However, economic pressures push for concentration among a small group of intermediaries within the bitcoin system, such as currency exchanges, digital wallet services, and other intermediary groups. Many users rely on digital wallet services that maintain files on sharers with access to phone-based apps. As bitcoins are created through the solution of a mathematical problem, this curbs financial power. There is also a fear of insertion of false transactions and manipulations, for example in the trade in narcotics

---

[78] Fabian Schar, 'Decentralised Finance: On Blockchain and Smart Contract-Based Financial Markets', *Federal Reserve Bank of St. Louis Review*, Second Quarter 2021, pp. 153–74.

[79] M. Brown, 'Projects into 2020: PPP Leads the Way', ALTamimi & Company, 31 January 2020, p. 49.

[80] Ercanbrack, 'Islamic Trade Law and the Smart Contract Revolution'.

[81] Rainer Bohme, Nicolas Christin, Benjamin Edelman, and Tyler Moore, 'Bitcoin: Economics, Technology, and Governance, *Journal of Economic Perspectives*, vol. 29, no. 2 (2015), p. 219.

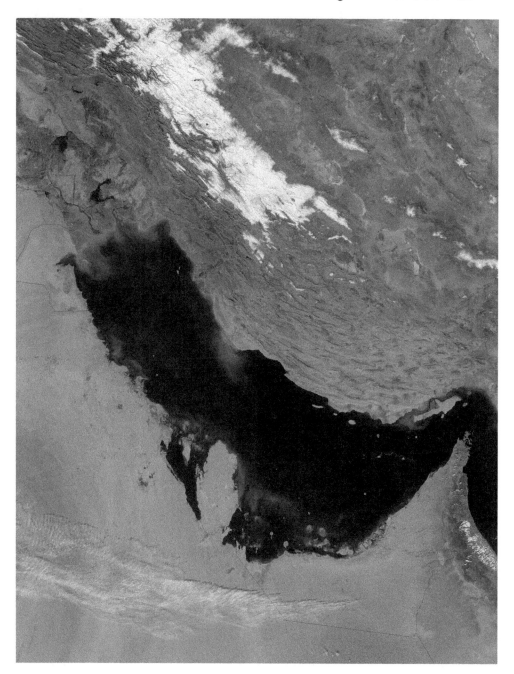

Figure 12.1 Satellite image of the Arabian Peninsula, 2000

Note: Bahrain is the small island in the centre of the image, adjacent to the larger peninsula of Qatar.
Source: SeaWiFS Project, NASA/Goddard Space Flight Center and ORBIMAGE.

and on gambling sites receiving funds from dubious sources. The most popular bitcoin gambling game is Satoshi Dice, one that yields huge earnings. Also, bitcoin can be exploited by those avoiding international capital controls. In December 2013, the People's Bank of China banned Chinese banks from relationships with bitcoin exchanges, a response to prevent the transfer of Yuan overseas through bitcoin routes. Blockchain also imposes barriers to the use of bitcoin without clear information on transactions. But easy transfers are made through the Internet, and this is useful for rapid implementation of responses to climate crises such as floods.[82]

Bitcoin poses several risks to financial markets, including fluctuations in the exchange rate between bitcoin and other currencies. Furthermore, bitcoin users experience shallow market problems when bitcoin affects the market price. Errors in bitcoin transactions cannot be resolved until they are within the blockchain. There is also the risk of theft.[83] There are also vulnerabilities within technologies and exposure to those seeking control of the system, a threat that is evident when bitcoin uses many intermediaries. Bitcoin also raises privacy issues when personal names of operators are revealed. Then bitcoin is exposed to legal and regulatory risks and outrage. Therefore, regulation is important to tackle money laundering, attacks on the currency, and theft.

In March 2013, the US Financial Crimes Enforcement Network issued guidance on virtual currency through registration, reporting, and record keeping. Bitcoin's record keeping allows money to be recovered. But taxation remains a vexatious issue in addition to privacy and anonymity. Bitcoin has implemented a form of Milton Friedman's 'k-per cent rule', which is a proposal to set the annual growth in the money supply to a fixed rate of growth. But what happens if the bitcoin economy grows faster than the supply of bitcoins?[84] In 2011, Krugman, when comparing the bitcoin economy to the Gold Standard, argued that the risks of inflation and deflation were inevitable.[85] Such fears have not stopped the rise of competing virtual currencies, such as Litecoin. But through its decentralization, bitcoin is offering financial opportunities to avert a climate crisis, if used with reasonable caution.

[82] Ron Dorit and Adi Shamir, 'Quantitative Analysis of the Full Bitcoin Transaction Graph', *Financial Cryptography and Data Security*, vol. 7859 of Lecture Notes in Computer Science, 2013, pp. 6–24.
[83] Danny Bradbury, 'Anti-Theft Bitcoin Tracking Proposals Divide Bitcoin Community', *Coindesk*, 15 November 2013.
[84] Milton Friedman, *A Program for Monetary Stability* (New York: Fordham University Press, 1960).
[85] Paul Krugman, 'Golden Cybervetters', *The New York Times*, 7 September 2011.

13

Conclusion

Bahrain the Aspiring Hegemon in the Infernal Middle East

Nelida Fuccaro's path-breaking studies have drawn out the links to tribal and regional associations within Bahrain from the fifteenth century onwards, as well as the increasingly important diasporic capitalism.[1] Tribalism enmeshed with increasing urbanism was central for the development of modern economic and sociopolitical ties. In the fifteenth century, the islands of Bahrain were ruled by the al-Jabr family from Najd, with powerful links to Hormuz, then under Portuguese rule. By the eighteenth century, the al-Madkhur family from Oman governed Bahrain as a dependency of Iran. In 1783, Utub tribes from the Arabian peninsula occupied these islands and this ended Iranian power. Subsequently, within the Utub confederation, the Al-Khalifah family became identified with an increasingly important British presence. There soon evolved a modern state under the British. These political changes took place alongside a vibrant commercial culture, a booming trade in Gulf pearls, and then, in the nineteenth century, the exploitation of oil. Until the last decades of the nineteenth century, British interests in Bahrain were mainly economic, and Manama was the commercial centre. By agreements in 1880 and in 1892, Bahrain became an informal British colony. British interference in the affairs of Bahrain intensified, creating a power struggle between the Al-Khalifah rulers and the British. An important legacy of this contest was the creation of Manama as a powerful mercantile city under British control.

This commercial development was further driven by the rise of oil-rich Gulf neighbours: Saudi Arabia, Kuwait, Qatar, Oman, and, by 1930, the UAE. In recent decades, Bahrain's own oil reserves have greatly declined, and it has responded by creating an innovative, competitive financial sector to serve Bahrain's oil-rich neighbours. Bahrain now flourishes as a financial centre, a powerful hub of Islamic finance. In this it has been assisted by the huge flow of oil wealth from the Gulf producers. Gulf oil revenues drove the urbanization and financial development of Bahrain. In the 1980s, Bahrain, using its

[1] Nelida Fuccaro, 'Understanding the Urban History of Bahrain', *Critique: Critical Middle Eastern Studies*, vol. 17 (2000), pp. 49–81.

Islam and Capitalism in the Making of Modern Bahrain. Rajeswary Ampalavanar Brown, Oxford University Press.
© Rajeswary Ampalavanar Brown (2023). DOI: 10.1093/oso/9780192874672.003.0013

offshore banking sector, transferred Gulf financial surpluses into US treasury and North American securities. Important here were the Al-Baraka Banking Group, an investment bank that is both an Islamic bank and a conventional bank, Gulf Finance House, and Ahli United Bank. The ruling families are pervasive in business, while private sector conglomerates are frequently represented in the state apparatus.

Bahrain's aluminium conglomerate ALBA is owned by the Bahrain Mumtalakat Holding Company and Saudi SABIC. In telecommunications, Viva Bahrain is a subsidiary of Saudi telecom but Batelco is fully owned by Bahrain. By 2015, four Gulf telecommunications firms, including Batelco, Zain Ooredoo, and Etisalat, earned 60 per cent of their revenues outside their domestic markets.[2] Many of their international markets were in Arab countries, although Asia and Africa are also targeted. Bahrain's BMMI Group, in food and agriculture, operates supermarkets in Saudi Arabia.

Among the financial institutions, a pan-GCC ownership structure marks Bahrain's offshore banking sector. Gulf capital is mostly drawn from Saudi Arabia and Kuwait. Oil wealth flows into the GCC banks, as they are mainly state-owned and are therefore secure. Banks are closely interlocked through shared directorships. In addition, they often own non-banking subsidiaries, for example in construction, retail, and telecommunications. The Kuwait Government owns 18.1 per cent of Bahrain's Ahli United Bank, 10.1 per cent being held by the Bahrain Government. Interlocking directorships are significant, for example tying together the Bahrain Petroleum Company, the Bahrain Stock Exchange, Ahli United Bank, the Tamdeen Real Estate Company, and Global Omani Development and Investment. The Al-Baraka Banking Group had a stake in the Dallah al Barakh Group.[3] The ABC Islamic Bank and the Ahli United Bank have interlocking directors. Investment banks such as the Al-Baraka Banking Group operate in both Islamic and conventional finance.

Management has often been exercised through Gulf private equity firms. In 2015, these firms raised US$1 billion and most were based in the GCC, with owners and board directors drawn from across the Gulf.[4] These private equity firms also had ownership outside the GCC. The rapid growth of private equity firms from the 1990s is related to oil wealth and spillovers from Saudi Arabia, Kuwait, and the UAE. The most powerful firm is UAE-based Abraaj

---

[2] Adam Hanieh, *Money, Markets, and Monarchies: The Gulf Cooperation Council and the Political Economy of the Contemporary Middle East* (Cambridge: Cambridge University Press, 2018), p. 89.

[3] Hanieh, *Money, Markets, and Monarchies*, p. 107.

[4] Adam Hanieh, *Capitalism and Class in the Gulf Arab States* (New York: Palgrave Macmillan, 2011), pp. 140–5; Hanieh, *Money, Markets, and Monarchies*, p. 109.

Capital, worth an estimated US$9 billion. In 2007, it raised US$6 billion but in 2009 it experienced some distress.[5]

How does the GCC link all these regional and global interactions? First, the Arab–Persian hybridity of merchant families, Safars and Kanoos, and their transnationalism through the nineteenth and twentieth centuries, were joined in the 1990s by powerful groups from Saudi Arabia and the UAE, al-Kharafi, Olayan, Al Rajhi, Ghurair, Al Futtaim, and Al Shaya, in close networks within the authoritarian states of the GCC. Saudi Arabia and the UAE form the apex. Kuwait and Qatar were autonomous zones of capital accumulation, while Oman and Bahrain were dependent on their wealthy neighbours. However, Bahrain outranked these states with its outstanding success in emerging as a financial hub with a liberal interpretation of Islamic Finance Law. The benefits brought by oil capital flows transformed the economy, in particular banking, creating a globalized economy through international partnerships. The state, employing sovereign wealth funds and its commercial agencies, formed cartels with a compliant merchant class. This is evident in the petrochemical corporations producing and refining oil, real estate developers, telecommunications corporations, and the banks. However, despite a deep devotion to joint management by state and family and to existing business networks, Bahrain employed professionally intermediated finance both at home and abroad. Overall, the separation between private and public control is vague, as ruling families are major shareholders. But cross-border mergers and listing on stock markets in the USA and Ireland provided forms of internationalization in GCC capital markets. FDI brought crucial forms of liberal economic behaviour, and thus the GCC possessed dynamic concentrations of industrial clusters in aluminium and cement production and oil refining, but also reshaped food production, water, electric power, telecommunications, and transport, particularly air transport.

A Hereditary Monarchy and Constitutional Legitimacy

In addition to customary law, state power in Bahrain is institutionalized through the creation of a constitution; the first was written in 1973 after independence from Britain in 1971, which provided for a National Assembly, in which half the members were either appointed by the Amir or were cabinet members. This weakness of popular sovereignty was further accentuated by

[5] MENA Private Equity Association, 2015, p. 5; E. McBride, 'The Story Behind Abraaj Group's Stunning Rise in Global Private Equity', 4 November 2015, cited in Hanieh, *Money, Markets, and Monarchies*, p. 194.

restrictions on voter eligibility with respect to age, natural origin, and gender (naturalized citizens and women were excluded). The 1973 constitution also reaffirmed the principle of a hereditary regime and gave the Amir extensive powers in instigating legislation and appointing members.[6]

This constitution was abrogated in 1975 by Shaikh Isa bin Salman Al-Khalifa under emergency laws that persisted from 1975 to 2002. The stated reason for suspending the partially elected National Assembly was its refusal to pass a security law.[7] The succession of Shaikh Hamad bin Isa Al-Khalifa after his father's death in 1999 led to democratic reform, including a return to constitutional rule, in an attempt to dampen the resentment following the 1990s protests. Hamad introduced a new constitution in 2002, which initiated limited top-down political reforms with the clear aim of containing the opposition while consolidating political power.[8] While easing restrictions, he called for a national dialogue and created a National Action Charter to initiate political reforms. The charter promised a constitutional monarchy with an elected parliament. The king also appointed a human rights commission within the existing Consultative Council to examine human rights abuses. But he also reaffirmed that Bahrain was a hereditary kingdom, and that the monarch had the power to amend the constitution and create a bicameral parliament with an appointed upper house to limit the legislative power of the elected lower house. In fact, the new constitution provided less accountability and reduced representation. Inevitably it was rejected by the opposition. And rising opposition further entrenched the patronage structures supported by local elites. The opposition participated in the 2006 elections, but there was discrimination against the Shi'a who constituted 70 per cent of the population. The opposition boycotted the 2010 elections.

The regime resisted the calls for a justly elected unicameral assembly. Following the suppression of the Arab Spring protests, there were demands for a constitution that protected rights and ended corruption. The response of the state was to use the military of Saudi Arabia and of the Emirate to quell the protests. The use of foreign soldiers undermined Hamad's position, although

---

[6] Omar Hesham AlShehabi, 'Divide and Rule in Bahrain and the Elusive Pursuit for a United Front: The Experience of the Constitutive Committee and the 1972 Uprising'; see also Emile A. Nakhleh, *Bahrain: Political Development in a Modernizing Society* (Lexington, MA: Lexington Books, 1976); Nimer Sultany, *Law and Revolution: Legitimacy and Constitutionalism after the Arab Spring* (Oxford: Oxford University Press, 2017), pp. 273–7.

[7] Michael Hudson, *Arab Politics: The Search for Legitimacy* (New Haven CT: Yale University Press, 1977); M. C. Hudson, 'Arab Politics after the Uprising: Still Searching for Legitimacy', in *Routledge Handbook of the Arab Spring: Rethinking Democratization*, edited by Larbi Sadiki (Abingdon: Routledge, 2014).

[8] Neil Quilliam, 'Political Reform in Bahrain: The Turning Tide', in *Reform in the Middle East Oil Monarchies*, edited by Anoushiravan Ehteshami (Ithaca, NY: Ithaca Press, 2007), pp. 81–2.

the legitimacy of the hereditary monarchy and the bicameral structure remained in place. The powerful upper house secured the monarchy's control, and the quest for democracy remained stunted. Constitutional amendments in 2012 did not weaken the king's power, thus curbing equality and freedom. The Constitutional Court, established in 2002, had little power; in fact it was limited to the judicial review of legislation, and even then could be blocked by the Chief Justice. The constitutional amendments did not constrain the power of the monarchy.[9]

Constitutional and Legal Foundations of Authoritarianism

Arab political and constitutional practices are not idealized versions of the liberal constitutions found in the United States and across Europe, but rather are dictated by the state without genuine popular involvement. They are often a façade to combat populist demands. Nimer Sultany describes them as the practice of 'strategic constitutionalism', designed to serve but not to limit the power of the state.[10] Nathan Brown, too, asserts that Arab constitutions were primarily used to stabilize the state.[11] Thus, as noted earlier, King Hamad introduced a new constitution in 2002 to appease mass protests by Shi'ites and youthful populists, and indeed it did secure the political-legal order. The 1973 Constitution was abrogated in 1975 by Shaikh Isa but the new constitution under King Hamad in 2002 involved a bicameral legislature packed with royalists and loyalists. In other words, constitutions may be employed to empower autocratic rulers.

Authoritarian states are generally highly centralized, but in the case of Bahrain, municipal institutions had legal autonomy because they were mainly in Shi'ite areas and practised Jafari jurisprudence. There was further religious legitimation through the charities of waqf and ma'tam. At the same time, the process of bureaucratization and the centralization of state power was driven by the enlargement of the Bahrain military through the addition of recruits from Saudi Arabia. In Bahrain, constitutionalism has not threatened the authoritarian state. But it has secured liberal Islamist institutions, in particular in Islamic finance, and has underpinned stability even after the Arab Spring of 2011. The monarchy remains secure in the face of rising populism.

---

[9] Sultany, *Law and Revolution*, pp. 273–7.
[10] Sultany, *Law and Revolution*, chapters 2–3.
[11] Nathan J. Brown, *Constitutions in a Non-constitutional World: Arab Basic Laws and the Prospects for Accountable Government* (Albany, NY: SUNY Press, 2001), pp. xiv, 9–10.

Bahrain exhibited an inclusive authoritarian constitutionalism and liberalized global Islamic finance, while politically Islamizing such institutions as the moderate Muslim Brotherhood, and providing political preferences to Shi'ites, merchants, and youth populists.

Law and the Relevance for a Cosmopolitan Liberalism in an Authoritarian State

How do we reconcile Bahraini modernity and authoritarian state control? A sharper understanding of jurisdictional uncertainties would help. In pre-colonial times, limited commercial activity required only simple legal institutions, first with rulers' courts settling social disputes, then tribal arbitration involving both intra-tribal processes and a broader conciliation process. There were also specialized tribunals that settled disputes between merchants. And finally, there were Shari'ah courts that specialized in family law and dispute settlement procedures.[12] In comparison with the desultory nature of legal institutions in Saudi Arabia at that time, Bahrain, from 1930, possessed legal independence, despite its strong cultural and commercial links with its Gulf neighbours.

E. P. Thompson famously and controversially saw the rule of law as 'a cultural achievement of universal significance'.[13] This study of Bahrain illustrates Thompson's argument: the colonial state modernized Bahrain through legal change. The British in Bahrain introduced administrative reforms to secure political control, civil society, and popular participation. Ironically, these reforms may also have contributed to a rise in political conflict. But overall, local tribal hegemony in Bahrain permitted negotiation between Shi'ite leaders and tribal chiefs, a process that secured more moderate Shi'ite leaders and powerful Shi'ite businessmen, collaborating with forms of associated state capitalism.

In 1820, under the rule of the Khalifahs, Bahrain signed an abstention from piracy treaty with the East India Company. Extra-territorial British jurisdiction was in force in 1913, and this created vibrant commercial relationships, which in turn had an impact on the legal system. Unique again for Bahrain, as compared to other Trucial States, was the emergence of a form of legal

---

[12] Nathan Brown, *The Rule of Law in the Arab World: Courts in Egypt and the Gulf* (Cambridge: Cambridge University Press, 1997), p. 130.

[13] E. P. Thompson, *Whigs and Hunters: The Origins of the Black Act* (New York: Pantheon Books, 1975), p. 67. He then stepped back: 'I do not lay any claim to the abstract, extraterritorial impartiality of these rules' (p. 266). See also Ranajit Guha, *Dominance Without Hegemony: History and Power in Colonial India* (Cambridge, MA: Harvard University Press, 1997), pp. 85, 66–7.

pluralism with, first, the jurisdiction of the British Crown and second, juris-diction of local rulers' courts.[14] Hence, British legal influence was strong in Bahrain.[15]

The British Advisor, Charles Belgrave, was involved in the development of the Bahraini legal system and also acted as a judge. Bahrain agreed with the Trucial States (six sheikdoms that were British protectorates, Abu Dhabi, Ajman, Dabas, Ras al-Khaima, Sharjah, and Umm al-Quwain) to introduce mixed courts that employed both English and local judges to investigate cases involving locals and foreigners. By 1955–57, with the introduction of special laws for English courts in regions of Bahrain, William Ballantyne urged the British Government to further encourage the modernization of the region's legal system to secure London's commercial involvement after the withdrawal of Britain. Bahrain thus undertook the translation of some English codes into Arabic to maintain the British legal heritage. In contrast, the other Gulf states reverted back to Shari'ah.[16] However, undermining Ballantyne's position was the supremacy of tribal power insisted on by Belgrave, for it imposed limits on each community and emphasized tribal hegemony.[17]

Rulers historically functioned as judges. Regional rulers were hostile to the principle of an independent judiciary, and this hostility delayed the emer-gence of an efficient, structured legal system. Rulers regarded legal, and particularly judicial development, to be a threat to their inherited author-ity. Hence, the British withdrawal left a major legal gap, and the discovery of oil and soaring commercial activity undermined the immature legal system. Following the failure of the British to impose a successful Anglo-Saxon legal model in the Gulf, the regional rulers, except in Saudi Arabia, opted for the Egyptian-French model.[18]

Modern-Day Transformation: Liberalism and Cosmopolitanism

After 2002, Bahrain underwent further dramatic change when it became a kingdom and adopted a new constitution. The constitution was confirmed in

---

[14] George N. S. Feir, *Modernization of the Law in Arab States: An Investigation into Current Civil, Crim-inal and Constitutional Law in the Arab World* (San Francisco, CA: Austin and Winfield Publications, 1998), p. 47.

[15] William Ballantyne, *Legal Development in Arabia* (London: Graham and Trotman, 1980), p. 8.

[16] Ballantyne, *Legal Development in Arabia*, p. 10.

[17] Mansoor Al-Jamri, 'Conclusion: Birth of a New Legal System—Anglo-Muhammadan Law'. Middle East Studies Association, 32nd Annual Meeting, Chicago, 6 December 1998.

[18] Fahad Al-Zumai, 'Protection of Investors in Gulf Cooperation Council Stock Markets: a Case Study of Kuwait, Bahrain and United Arab Emirates', PhD thesis, University of London, 2006, pp. 54–6.

a referendum that took place in February 2001. The constitution states that there are other sources of law in addition to Shari'ah. The influence of Islamic law is manifested in the civil codes, but overall in Bahrain, Islamic law is less influential than in Kuwait and the UAE.[19] The new Civil Code organizes the sources of law as follows: first is the civil code, then custom, then Islamic law, and finally natural and equity law.[20] This hierarchy can be linked to British influence, as seen in Article 12, Section 3 in the Bahrain Order.

Commercial law in Bahrain is less observant of Shari'ah than the civil codes. Indeed, commercial codes may contradict Islamic principles, such as in permitting riba.[21] The legal gaps in customary commercial law had to be filled by Western law. Unlike jurisdictional politics in other former British colonies, Bahrain rarely determined commercial disputes itself, but instead sought resolution through the London courts.[22]

New Land Clusters: A Vanguard of Royal Absolutism, 1970s to the Present

In Bahrain land ownership and use has been, and remains, a source of tension between the various interests in the kingdom.[23] Important here is the extent to which the state, and by extension the ruling family, has acquired land.[24] Accusations were made that the ruling family had embarked on a programme of land appropriation, in effect denying Shia access to land. Moreover, there exists the belief that land being acquired by the state and royal family is being used to attract foreign investment and tourism. Certainly, a number of the recent major foreign investments have involved land deals, although it should also be pointed out that four new townships, with a total of 250,000 new homes, have also been built. Even where land is registered to the state, its leasing and development agreements with private contractors deny any

---

[19] Al-Zumai, 'Protection of Investors in Gulf Cooperation Council Stock Markets', p. 56.

[20] Article 1, Civil Code No. 19/2001.

[21] Article 1, Bahraini Commercial Law No. 7/1987.

[22] Jonathan Ercanbrack, *The Transformation of Islamic Law in Global Financial Markets* (Cambridge: Cambridge University Press, 2015), pp. 236, 326.

[23] The BICI Report of 2011 identified the lack of affordable housing as a major cause of the civil unrest.

[24] The ruling family have been criticized for undertaking a systematic 'land grab' in Bahrain, which made the family the largest landowner in the kingdom. *Middle East Report*, No. 40, 6 May 2005, p. p. 9, draws attention to the fact that tens of thousands of poor Shi'ites are forced to live in poor quarters, while the royal family owns more land than it uses, as well as prime real estate. For further discussion on the land ownership of the ruling family, see Eric Hooglund, 'Bahrain', in *Persian Gulf States: Country Studies*, edited by Helen C. Metz (Washington, DC: U.S. Government Printing Office, 1994), p. 123; Fuad I. Khuri, *Tribe and State in Bahrain: The Transformation of Social and Political Authority in an Arab State* (Chicago, IL: Chicago University Press, 1980), pp. 35–41.

benefit to the general population and are driven by personal enrichment.[25] It is also argued that the underdevelopment of Shia waqf and the use of state laws to restrict investment in waqf property are means by which the ruling family oppress the Shia. The state's involvement in waqf land came about with the establishment of a state institution. Up until late 1926 or early 1927, the management of waqf property was in the hands of the nazir. However, following a number of high-profile misappropriations of funds, the Department for Waqfs was established. Even so, this presented a problem, in that much waqf property was under Shia ownership and the authorities were predominantly Sunni. The state sought to overcome this problem by creating waqf boards for both Sunni (entrusted to three Sunni Qadis) and Shia (entrusted to a Shia Qadi). The boards then embarked on a process of registration and authentication in the management of waqf land and property. However, ultimate responsibility for land and its use rested with the Al-Khalifah family. The state has been repeatedly accused of the acquisition of land used predominantly by the Shia community for housing developments in the two major cities of Muharraq and Manama. It is seen as an instrument to crush social unrest through intimidation.[26] With the oil boom from the 1990s, luxury residential and commercial centres and shopping malls were constructed for the local rich as well as Gulf citizens, in particular those from Saudi Arabia and Qatar. And infrastructural developments including roads, airports, and telecommunications facilities assisted the creation of Bahrain as a financial hub for the oil-wealthy Gulf states. Adam Hanieh views the 'state as an institutional form [that] articulates and intermediates the power and interests of the capitalist class itself'. Bahrain is 'not a neutral or parasitic institution severed from the social relations of production and accumulation or one that "crowds out" the private sector'.[27] It facilitates the business operations of select groups while alienating the local poor, who are excluded from employment and from their land. The seizure of agrarian and urban lands was driven by the ruling family and their business elites, and by the UAE and Saudi Arabia who were dominant in finance, building, and construction in Bahrain.

The 2011 BICI report established that recently 28 Shia places of worship had been demolished on the orders of the state. The orders involved the

---

[25] The issue has been raised in parliament and has resulted in heated debates, see http://gulfnews.com/news/gulf/bahrain/bahrain-parliament-wants-solution-to-land-reclamation-issue-1.567052; see also http://www.thenational.ae/news/world/middle-east/bahraini-public-lands-sold-and-rented-to-private-investors

[26] Also important as an instrument of intimidation was the destruction of religious structures belonging to Shia. Various websites host photos or bear testament to such destruction. See, for example: http://www.mcclatchydc.com/2011/05/08/113839/while-bahrain-demolishes-mosques.html.

[27] Hanieh, *Money, Markets, and Monarchies*, p. 67.

arbitrary use of laws pertaining to land ownership and to the requirements for building permits. Moreover, state sanction was required for the rejuvenation, rebuilding, or establishment of religious buildings. The legal justification for the destruction orders rested on Council of Ministers Decree No. 2105-05 of 2011, as read in conjunction with Building Regulation Law No. 13 of 1977. The essence of this legislation is that the authorities would apply for a demolition order where an 'administrative violation' had been committed in the construction or reconstruction of a religious property. It was contended in the majority of the 28 demolitions that such an administrative violation had been committed. The law stated that the owner or custodian of a property being condemned had the opportunity to appeal through an administrative hearing. But this did not occur. Where a religious structure was authorized by the Jafari Waqf Board, it too was to be notified, except where there was an immediate danger to life. That also did not occur. The Sunni royal family was, thus again, accused of intimidating the Shia population.

Keeping the State at a Distance from Land Grabs

There is a clear requirement in Bahrain that all land must be registered and that any request to build on land must be authorized through the issuance of a building permit.[28] Registration is completed on receipt from the Royal Court of a royal deed of ownership, usually secured through the Registration Department of the Survey and Registration Bureau.[29] The registration certificate establishes the legal owner and the borders of the land. However, this is not necessarily the position of land subject to a waqf, and despite registration being introduced in the late 1920s it remains the case that not all waqf land has been registered.[30] A waqf that expired from lack of beneficiaries, or was simply abandoned, inevitably fell into disrepair. However, all land deemed to be abandoned or without legal owner becomes the property of the King (Royal Decree Law No. 19 of 2002). In addition, the King remains the supreme authority in allocating public lands for future use, fuelling the belief

[28] This falls under a number of pieces of legislation depending on the building type, although the predominant legislation is Decree Law no. 2 for 1994 and Decree Law no. 3 for 1994.
[29] This is a requirement under law. The Land Registration Act 1979, Chapter V, Article 48, states that registration of an owned property shall result in the issuance of a title deed. Article 1 of the Land Registration Law of 1979 states that the Land Registration Directorate shall undertake the functions of land registration.
[30] However, the Land Registration Law of 1979 under Chapter 6, Article 69 permits the registration of waqf through which a certificate of endowment is issued, although this is only possible after being fully attested before the competent Shari'ah Court.

that the state can simply appropriate land for its own use.[31] Moreover, the area of land in Bahrain has been increased through land reclamation, that land being state-owned and thus put to uses decided by the state.[32] This further feeds the perception that the state controls all land. That control extends to the construction of affordable housing, a powerful instrument that can be used to discourage the rural poor from moving to the urban centres and which might, through higher levels of economic growth, provide them with new employment opportunities.

One possible response here would be to make more effective use of the waqf to secure social benefit.[33] In recent times, the waqf has been used with some success to protect land ownership and to expand access to land.[34] This removes the land from the direct control of the state, although it is accepted that the semi-state body overseeing the land, Jafari Waqf, would need to be further empowered and that tighter control by the authorities would be required. Nonetheless, effective and sustainable use of waqf property presents a major way through which social and economic demands could be further met. But this would require a systematic approach to investment, construction, and the rejuvenation of waqf property. However, given the religious nature of the institution, there are restrictions that may inhibit rejuvenation, notably the laws of perpetuity. Historically, the waqf had a pivotal role in Islamic society not just socially but also economically, especially in economies dominated by agriculture and with limited urbanization. Village communities were often reliant on waqf to provide access to water for irrigation, for example.

---

[31] The state also has the power to take possession of land under a 'Public Benefit Repossession', by which, under a special order, the Land Registry Bureau amends the title of ownership to reflect the property as belonging to the Bahrain government. However, this should be read in conjunction with Article 9 of the Constitution, paragraph (c) which states that 'private ownership is protected. No one shall be disposed of his property except for the public good in the cases specified and the manner stated by law and provided that the landowner is fairly compensated.' See Decree Law no. 8 for 1970 pertaining to the acquisition of lands for public purposes, amended by Decree Law no. 24 for 1975 and Decree Law no. 7 (1984).

[32] The transfer of land titles by the ruling family to Sunni tribal leaders was historically a further way in which wealth and land ownership was structured to the detriment of the Shia. For an overview, see Fred H. Lawson, *Bahrain: The Modernization of Autocracy* (Boulder, CO: Westview Press, 1989), p. 68.

[33] There already exists a procedure by which royal endowments are registered, albeit on a personal level. This is through the Land Registration Bureau, and the process involves the beneficiary presenting the endowment letter, signed by His Majesty the King, together with the CPR/ID card and passport to initiate the registration process. The entry is numbered for registration in the name of the beneficiary for a fee of BD1. The registration number is issued, the documents are prepared, and the beneficiary is contacted to collect the official ownership deeds.

[34] This would require an effective legal framework. If the framework were too restrictive, it would limit the use of the property, a criticism often made in India: see http://articles.timesofindia.indiatimes.com/2011-10-21/hyderabad/30305902_1_wakf-act-wakf-land-wakf-institutions; also Siraj Sait and Hilary Lim, *Land, Law and Islam: Property and Human Rights in the Muslim World* (London: Zed Books, 2006), notably pp. 170–3.

The flow of oil wealth has led to state involvement in waqf, and specifically in waqf property.[35] In Bahrain, the state, through systematic programmes of land appropriation, sought to put that land to better use through redistribution. More than this, waqf land that was subject to a public purpose, or in some way served the community, more often than not fell under the control of the state.

In many ways, some of the private waqf in Bahrain have become 'locked out' properties, in that perpetuity and descendent inheritance have created a large number of actual or potential beneficiaries.[36] As Mustapha Ben Hamouche has pointed out, this has often led to the degradation or even abandonment of a property due to a lack of consensus between beneficiaries.[37] Thus, the laws of waqf pertaining to perpetuity and ownership of the property form a major obstacle to the regeneration of waqf land.[38] In the attempt to protect waqf property and its pious benefits, the laws have the opposite effect and often leave the land abandoned and failing to meet its charitable purpose. This provides the state with legitimate reasons for intervention. However, the ultimate beneficiaries of such intervention may be the ruling family and its capitalist friends. That has meant the economic and political marginalization of the poor, and in turn nurtured major uprisings against the monarchy, as in 2011.

The ruling family's dependence on Saudi oil and arms was dramatically shown in the Saudi-led military intervention in Bahrain during the Arab Spring uprising of 2011. The Arab Spring protesters were mainly young, hit hard by the lack of economic opportunities which had left them marginalized. The youth protests were non-religious and non-sectarian. They opposed the repressive Al-Khalifah monarchy and the substantial immigration into Bahrain from its Gulf neighbours, which further denied the protesters employment opportunities. The next section will consider the land

---

[35] Some commentators have suggested that both public and private waqf were subject to maladministration, and that this ultimately contributed to the decline of the waqf as an institution.

[36] For the purpose of this chapter, perpetuity is taken to be the requirement that once a property is dedicated, it remains waqf forever. In the same way, the conditions stipulated by the founder tie the use of the property to the originating condition. The nature of waqf lends itself more to the donation of land and buildings than to other objects, although there have been waqf of, for example, livestock and books. It should be added that while the question of waqf ownership is a matter of debate among scholars, it is generally accepted that it does not rest with the management or the beneficiaries, with notable exceptions. Uncertain ownership can make it difficult to deal with waqf property, although in limited circumstances there can be judicial involvement to settle ownership or use.

[37] Mustapha Ben Hamouche, 'Manama: The Metamorphosis of a Gulf City', in *The Evolving Arab City: Tradition, Modernity and Urban Development*, edited by Yasser Elsheshtawy (London: Routledge, 2008).

[38] The nature of a waqf, being a voluntary giving of property, permits the founder to stipulate its purpose and management, from which there must be no deviation. Revenues generated by the waqf had to be used exclusively for the originating purpose stipulated by the founder, of course on condition that that purpose is Shari'ah compliant.

reclamation in Bahrain that further deprived farmers and fishermen, the majority of whom were Shi'ite, of their livelihood.

Land Reclamation on Bahrain's Seafront

Land reclamation, which could well involve creating land where previously there was sea, presented serious problems for many in Bahrain, concentrated in villages and cities along the coast. It affected those engaged in pearl diving, agriculture, and fishing. Pearl diving had declined, but fishing and agriculture remained essential sources of employment and food security. The newly created islands had a devastating impact on both occupations. Annual fish catches declined from 16,000 tons to 6,000 tons between 2006 and 2010. It was estimated that 90 per cent of fishing grounds had been either partially or completely destroyed. This brought serious deprivation to Sunnis, although Shi'ites were the most affected group.[39] The collapse of fish stocks led growing numbers to abandon fishing. Bahrain's Fishermen Protection Society had campaigned for a GCC law to facilitate fishing outside Bahrain's borders. Further pressure was exerted by the UN Food and Agriculture Organization, which called for a halt to reclamation, dredging, and the destruction of the reef in order to protect the livelihood of fishermen.[40] A further pernicious development involved illegal reclamation by unlicensed individuals. In September 2012, the Manama Municipal Council reported that nine separate reclamation projects had been carried out in Manama and Karbabad in violation of environmental laws.[41]

Reclamation projects focus on luxury real estate and tourism development. Reclaimed lands include Diyar al-Muharraq, a residential and tourism development of twelve square kilometres; Dilmunia Health Island, 1.25 square kilometres; and Amwaj Island, a mixed residential and tourism project, 2.8 square kilometres. The Northern City, one of the new islands allocated for government-funded housing, occupied 7.4 square kilometres. More prestigious projects include Bahrain Bay, Reef Island, and Bahrain Financial Harbour.[42] On Bahrain's southern tip, the Durrat Al Bahrain reclamation includes six atolls and five petal-shaped islands spread over 21 square

[39] S. Al-Halwachi, 'Land Reclamation Shrinks Fish Production in Bahrain', *Al-Wasat*, 20 November 2010; A. al-Maskati, Al-Wasat, 14 June 2010; Ali Al-Jabal, 2002: cited in Omar AlShehabi, 'Radical Transformations and Radical Contestations: Bahrain's Spatial Demographic Revolution', *Middle East Critique*, vol. 23, no. 1 (2014), p. 32.

[40] 'New GCC Bid to Tackle Territorial Waters Row', *Gulf Daily News*, 24 May 2010.

[41] Al-Aali, 'Reclamation Halted?', *Gulf Daily News*, 27 September 2012.

[42] Elham Fakhro, 'Land Reclamation in the Arabian Gulf: Security, Environment, and Legal Issues', *Journal of Arabian Studies*, vol. 3, no. 1 (2013), pp. 36–52.

kilometres. Another major development was in Muharraq, traditional home of the royal family, which had quadrupled in land area since 1950 through the constant reclamation of land.[43] A further ambitious state project involved the creation of a 40-kilometre-long bridge between Bahrain and Qatar that involved the construction of a road on reclaimed land. Qatar's commitment was driven by the glamour project of hosting the FIFA World Cup in 2022.[44] But at the same time, Qatar was arresting Bahraini fishermen. In 2010, Qatar seized 260 fishermen, while one was killed by a Qatari coast guard patrol. Arrests continued into 2011. There had long been tension between Bahrain and Qatar, for example over coral reefs and islands, but now Qatar was seeking to challenge Bahrain's increasing power and her alignment with Saudi Arabia.[45]

This reclamation of land also involved the transfer of land to private interests associated with the Al-Khalifah family. In 2010, the Investigative Committee of the State Public and Private Properties in the Bahrain Chamber of Deputies provided evidence of the transfer of public lands to private entrepreneurs. It estimated that 90 per cent of reclaimed land was now privately owned, with plans for prestigious real estate and infrastructure projects.[46]

Natives, Expatriates, and Naturalized Citizens

Land reclamation had particularly significant consequences for agriculturalists and fishermen. Since the mid-1990s, more than 70 square kilometres of seafront have been reclaimed, 50 square kilometres between 2001 and 2011.[47] In 2008, 13 square kilometres of sea were reclaimed. The reclamations were concentrated around the northern coast of Bahrain, increasing the land area by 10 per cent. The city area of Muharraq expanded four times between 1951 and 2008, principally through reclamation from the sea.[48] Much of the

---

[43] Mohammed Basma, 'Reclamation Costs Bahrain Millions', Gulf Daily News, 7 March 2009; Mohammed Basma, 'Muharraq Grows by Four Fold', Gulf Daily News, 22 June 2010.
[44] Lidstone Digby, 'Qatar-Bahrain Causeway: A Bridge between Two Cultures', Financial Times, 18 November 2009; Benjamin Millington, 'KBR Awarded Qatar-Bahrain Construction Contract', Construction Week Online, 16 November 2008.
[45] Robert Meyer and Henry Tuttle, 'Bahrain Shuts Al-Jazeera Television Channel as Tensions Flare with Oil Rich Qatar', Bloomberg, 19 May 2010.
[46] M. Mahdi, 'Bahrain Public Lands Sold to Private Investors', The National, 25 March 2010; H. Al-Madhoob, 'National Properties Committee: The Struggle Will Continue until Retrieval of Citizen's Lands', Al-Wasat, 12 May 2010.
[47] Data compiled from Central Informatics Organization website available at http://www.cio.gov.bh/CIO-ARA/default.aspx accessed on 10 April 2012, cited in Omar AlShehabi, 'Radical Transformations and Radical Contestations: Bahrain's Spatial Demographic Revolution', p. 29.
[48] Mohammed Basma, 'Muharraq Grows by Four Fold', Gulf Daily News, 22 June 2010.

reclaimed land was for commercial projects and housing. Real estate and construction accounted for 9.8 per cent of GDP in 2007, with an annual growth rate of 7.1 per cent; they ultimately accounted for 33 per cent of domestic banks loans.[49] In addition Bahrain was the location for prestigious building projects undertaken by UAE real estate corporations.[50]

That commercial and real estate development was intended for wealthy entrepreneurs, both local and from the GCC. It was not intended for the inhabitants who had been displaced, the poor farmers and fishermen. By 2008, more than 20 large gated-housing projects had been built, providing 60,000 new residential units with commercial and office facilities.[51] The development was driven by the oil boom and the rise in oil prices.

The emergence of Bahrain as the financial hub of the Gulf also attracted funds from GCC investors for real estate development. From 2006, liberal property laws allowed GCC nationals to base their construction corporations in Bahrain. In 2007, the largest contractor in Bahrain was from the UAE.[52]

The huge inflow of oil wealth accelerated the pace of land reclamation on the northern coast of the island and in parts of Muharraq and Manama, involving the construction of roads and real estate. By 2010, 65 square kilometres of reclaimed land were valued at US$40 billion, and the combined value of the projects under construction there were valued at US$28.6 billion.[53] The projects including the construction of a Formula 1 track at US$300 million, the Financial Harbour at US$1.3 billion, and the Bahrain airport expansion, costing US$200 million.[54] Bahrain also became involved in projects in the UAE. In 2007, a Cebarco subsidiary was heavily committed to building the infrastructure for the Abu Dhabi Grand Prix. In 2009, there were six large building construction projects within the GCC being carried out by Bahrain companies, compared to seven for companies from Saudi Arabia, three for Kuwait, two for Oman, thirteen for the UAE, and nine for Qatar. That interdependence was a major dynamic in the regional economy.[55]

---

[49] P. Devaux, 'Oil Bonanza and Banking Activity in the GCC Countries', Conjuncture (Economic Research-BNP Paribas), December 2006; Global Investment House, 'GCC Real Estate Sector—Changing Times!', February 2009.

[50] Hanieh, *Capitalism and Class in the Gulf Arab States*, pp. 104–6, 114–16.

[51] DTZ Middle East Market Update Series, Bahrain, September 2008.

[52] B. Redfern, 'Private Developers Drive Boom', *Middle East Economic Digest*, 1 February 2008; Global Investment House, 'GCC Real Estate Sector—Changing Times!', February 2009; Shereef Ellaboudy, 'The Global Financial Crisis: Economic Impact on GCC Countries and Policy Implications', *International Research Journal of Finance and Economics*, no. 41 (2010), pp. 180–94. See also Hanieh, *Capitalism and Class in the Gulf Arab States*, p. 105.

[53] 'A Steady Approach Benefits Bahraini Property and Tourism Sector', *Middle East Economic Digest*, 29 October 2009.

[54] AME info, 'Bahrain Boosts Infrastructure Expenditure', 7 March 2009, cited in AlShehabi, 'Radical Transformations and Radical Contestations', pp. 32–3.

[55] Hanieh, *Capitalism and Class in the Gulf Arab States*, pp. 122–3.

Bahrain's interests were held by long-established business tycoons such as Yusef Kanoo and other members of the Kanoo family. The reclamation projects also greatly strengthened private entrepreneurs with links to the royal family. The reclamation divided the population into expatriates and locals, the rich expatriates living in gated estates on reclaimed land and divided, too, between religious sect and class. Division inevitably increased the power of an entrenched royal absolutism.

Demographic Transformation through Sectarianism, Nationalism, and Royal Absolutism

From the 1980s and 1990s, land reclamation strengthened the position of the rich with powerful ties to the state. An increase in private ownership of land accelerated that trend. The division of the population on sectarian and ethnic grounds and by class and region was long pursued by local rulers to counter political opposition.[56] The rulers also sought to condemn any protest as a Shi'ite attempt to undermine the country and threaten the regime. The oil boom brought in two classes of expatriate: managers and professionals, living in luxurious homes built on reclaimed land; and migrant labour, largely Indians, living in labour camps. In 1941, there were 16,000 expatriates out of a population of 90,000 and they worked mainly in the oil industry. By 1957, there were 24,401 expatriates out of a population of 143,145.[57] By 1975, the number of expatriates had tripled to 60,000, accounting for 22.9 per cent of the population and 37 per cent of the workforce. By 2000, this number had almost quadrupled to 261,000, accounting for 40 per cent of the population and 63 per cent of the workforce. In 2008, expatriates became the majority, 570,000, accounting for 51 per cent of the population and 78 per cent of the workforce.[58]

The 2010 census recorded that out of a total of 666,000 non-citizens, 54 per cent of the population, 562,000 were Asians, of whom an estimated 300,000 were Indians. Arabs, including GCC nationals, accounted for less than 67,000. North Americans and Europeans numbered 16,000. The majority of the expatriate labour force, 307,000 in 2009, were unskilled workers. The construction industry accounted for 32.8 per cent of total employment and within this, foreign workers accounted for close to 89.8 per cent of workers in

---

[56] AlShehabi, 'Radical Transformations and Radical Contestations', p. 34.
[57] TNA FO 371/149151, Population Census of Bahrain, 31 December 1955.
[58] M. Baldwin-Edwards, 'Immigration and Labour Markets in the GCC Countries: National Patterns and Trends, Kuwait', Programme on Development, Governance and Globalization in the Gulf States, London School of Economics, Working Paper No. 15, 2011.

that sector. Wholesale and retail accounted for 17.9 per cent of total employ-ment, with foreign workers accounting for 81.6 per cent of employment in the sector. Foreign workers accounted for 75.1 per cent in manufacturing and 87.9 per cent in domestic service.[59] Illegal workers were estimated to account for 10 per cent of the total workforce.[60]

There was clearly a vast gulf between the North American and European expatriates and the labourer expatriates, mainly Indians, although there was also a substantial number of middle-class expatriates from Asia. The Western expatriates, managers and professionals, lived in private villas and flats while the low-skilled foreign workers lived in labour camps. The low-pay labour-ers from South Asia faced considerable brutality. Underpinning this flow of cheap labour was the historic kafala system of indentured labour, present since the pearling era.[61] In the oil era it introduced a pernicious binary divide, leading to violence against foreign labour. The steady decline in the number of Arab workers since the 1970s, as Bahrain sought to prevent the entry of Pan Arab revolutionary sentiments, may have strengthened local Shi'ite labour. Arabs from poorer nations in the Middle East, largely Shi'ites, were feared, as the Bahrain state was engineering a Sunni dominance by offering foreign Sunnis lucrative jobs and residence with local citizenship. These Sunni were largely Bedouin Arabs from Jordan, Saudi Arabia, Syria, and Yemen, and included Baluchis from Baluchistan in Pakistan. Between 2001 and 2007, some 61,000 were selected to become naturalized citizens, increasing the local citizen population by 15 per cent. They were employed in security and defence services. This strategy of using 'safe' persons from 'safe' states for defence, depriving existing locals on sectarian lines, is reminiscent of the British policy in the nineteenth century of recruiting soldiers from Baluchis-tan and parts of India with a martial tradition. In independent Bahrain, it became an effective strategy to strengthen the minority Sunni authoritar-ian state. Exploiting Indian labour while creating citizens from neighbouring Sunni enclaves strengthened Sunni loyalty and confidence. The Al-Khalifahs therefore faced the Arab Spring confident that the protests could be sup-pressed. Immigrant labour was, and still is, extremely marginalized through the labour camps while Western expatriates were rewarded with lucrative jobs and posh homes. Overarching this was solidarity within the GCC. While Syria declined into chaos, tightly controlled Bahrain rose as a major hub of Islamic and international finance.

[59] Baldwin-Edwards, 'Immigration and Labour Markets in the GCC Countries'.
[60] Omar AlShehabi, 'Radical Transformations and Radical Contestations', p. 35.
[61] Andrew M. Gardner, *City of Strangers: Gulf Migration and the Indian Community in Bahrain* (Ithaca, NY: Cornell University Press, 2010), chapter 2.

Urban Zones of Concentrated Power

In summary, a modern Bahrain was created that secured the power and wealth of the state and its ruler. The oil boom from 1973 brought in huge numbers of foreigners requiring vastly different housing and employment facilities. As Charles Tilly has noted, before the later nineteenth century, in European cities such as Berlin and Madrid, rulers fed the inhabitants at great effort and at great cost to their hinterlands, principally because transportation costs were high.[62] In Bahrain, housing for citizens and expatriates has recently grown at a phenomenal rate. Those on the outskirts of the main cities accounted for 54,983 out of the total of 93,653 households in Bahrain.[63] The inhabitants in this semi-urban sprawl received benefits from the government that included free healthcare, education, and subsidized housing. Between 1975 and 2002, 61,509 families received housing loans.[64] Such subsidies secured political allegiance. The building of Isa Town in the late 1990s exemplified a state 'imagining', replacing a history of semi-statelessness with the presence of a powerful ruler.

But for the local population, the crucial reality was that they were being pushed out of both jobs and housing, as old districts were rebuilt with shopping malls and hotels, catering for tourism. Saudis and other GCC nationals flooded in at weekends, seeking sex, gambling, and alcohol. Major features of this transformation were a new architecture and changing employment patterns. Overlooking the old city centres of Muharraq and Manama were the twin towers of the World Trade Centre and the twin towers of Bahrain's Financial Harbour, both built on reclaimed land. The old architecture, the palm grove, and the coastline were obscured or simply disappeared. Centuries-old, dilapidated buildings confronted new skyscrapers. The Government, palms greased with oil money, grabbed public lands, in particular on the coast, and pushed aside the poor. The rising politics of exclusion translated into resistance. The Arab nationalism and leftist opposition, which had been present in the 1950s and 1970s, gave way to a politics based on religion and sect. Haq, which attracted both Shi'ites and secular members, opposed the 2002 constitution, which allowed only limited political participation The secular leftist organizations, Wa'ad and Al-Menbar, declined

[62] Charles Tilly, 'War Making and State Making as Organized Crime', in *Bringing the State Back In*, edited by Peter Evans, Dietrich Rueschmeyer, and Theda Skocpol (Cambridge: Cambridge University Press, 1985), p. 178.

[63] O. Al Hassan, 2007, 'Khalifa bin Salman: He Chose Achievements, so the Prize Chose Him', *Bahrain News Agency*, 28 April 2007.

[64] M. Saeed, 'Al-Dhahrani Refuses to Ratify MPs' Letter Demanding the Lands' Master Plan from the Political Leadership', *Al-Wasat*, 18 June 2008.

after the 1970s. Sunni religious organizations, the Muslim Brotherhood, the Al-Menbar Islamic Society, and the Salafist Al Asala, were largely supportive of the state.[65]

But it was the issues of public land and the naturalization of foreigners to secure the political hegemony of the Al-Khalifah that created the most serious resistance. The limited availability of land, coupled with rapid population growth, created a dramatic need for housing. The waiting list for government assisted housing exceeded 45,000 households and was increasing by 7,000 each year. It was estimated that BD2.25 billion of government expenditure would be required to meet that housing need.[66] There was anger that new, luxurious developments were being built on stolen lands. Two parliamentary enquiries were launched, one to investigate the theft of public lands and the other, land reclamation. A loose coalition of environmentalists, fishermen, politicians, and local councillors organized meetings and demonstrations against land reclamations. A major focus concerned the Lulu project, built on reclaimed land and overlooking the reclaimed shoreline. On one side was Al Lulu Towers, a real estate project on reclaimed land. On the other side were the Shia villages of Burhama, Sanabis, Jedhafs, and Daih, close to the shoreline. Eventually Lulu was abandoned because protestors had camped there. Al Fateh, the National Unity Gathering, accused the protesters of treason. But it was the issue of political naturalization that, in 2009, drew the biggest demonstration, leading to clashes between local youths and the recently naturalized immigrants.[67] The foundations were laid for the Arab Spring protests of 2011.[68]

The Last Wave for the Great Divergence Theory

Much of the recent literature on the politics and economy of the Middle East has focused on an alleged decline compared to the advance of Europe from the seventeenth century. For example, Timur Kuran persists in identifying legal obstacles rooted in Islamic law as the cause for decline.[69] My

---

[65] Chibli Mallat and J. Gelbort, 'Constitutional Options for Bahrain', *Virginia Journal of International Law*, vol. 2, no. 1 (2011), pp. 1–16; K. Katzman, 'Bahrain: Reform, Security and US Policy', *Congressional Research Service*, 2 March 2011.

[66] N. Zain, '2.25 Billion Dinars Needed to Meet the Demand for Housing', Al-Waqt, 17 April 2010.

[67] M. Abdulla, 'A Huge March Demands the Cessation of Political Naturalization', *Al-Wasat*, 31 January 2009.

[68] *Reuters*, 'Sectarian Clashes Erupt in Bahrain', 3 March 2011; O. H. AlShehabi, 'The Community at Pearl Roundabout Is at the Centre', *The National*, 1 March 2011; Amal Khalaf, 'Squaring the Circle: Bahrain's Pearl Roundabout', *Middle East Critique*, vol. 22, no. 3 (2013).

[69] Timur Kuran, *The Long Divergence: How Islamic Law Held Back the Middle East* (Princeton, NJ: Princeton University Press, 2011).

position is that 'the decline' in the Middle East countries has been greatly exaggerated, indeed recent decades have seen substantial growth, particularly in Islamic finance and in industrialization. Moreover, merchant families of the seventeenth century, notably the Safar and Kanoo, have retained and indeed expanded their power. It is unlikely that Arab entrepreneurs could have matched the achievements of the Europeans over the past three centuries. But that is not decline, for it obscures the achievements of the Arabian peninsula in, for example, pearling, and in an expansive Indian ocean trade in food and silk, built in part on commercial contracts with the Europeans.

Shari'ah: The Developmental Enigma

The oft-repeated argument that Shari'ah has had a constraining influence on capitalism, and is thus responsible for economic decline in the Middle East, is challenged by the long histories of powerful transnational merchant families, the Safar and Kanoos, spread over Bahrain, Iran, Iraq, Oman, Yemen, India, Europe, and America from the late eighteenth century to the present.[70] In a similar way, the Weberian connection of Protestant ethics to the spirit of capitalism—alluding to Shari'ah's alleged aversion to capitalist innovation—can no longer be sustained. The Cairo Geniza records, which document Middle Eastern civilization between the tenth and sixteenth centuries, demonstrate that the Arabs developed complex credit systems before the Europeans.[71] However, Patricia Crone has argued that Arab trade in this period concentrated on domestic needs and not on the surrounding empires.[72]

An important adjustment of Shari'ah involves Hiyal, a legal device that avoids strict observance of Shari'ah law. At the present time Islamic finance uses Hiyal to defend its modern practices and to achieve aims forbidden by Shari'a. Hiyal was employed by the Hanafi leaders Abu Yusuf (d. 798) and al-Khassaf (d. 874). It focuses on matters of worldly interest, to sanction external forms of words and behaviour. Hiyal is utilized in contract law. For

---

[70] John George Lorimer, *The Gazetteer of the Persian Gulf, Oman and Central Arabia, Vol. 2* (Calcutta: Office of the Superintendent Government Printing, 1908; republished by Gregg International, Farnborough, 1970), pp. 754–5; James Onley, *The Arabian Frontier of the British Raj: Merchants, Rulers, and the British in the Nineteenth-century Gulf* (Oxford: Oxford University Press, 2007); Laleh Khalili, *Sinews of War and Trade: Shipping and Capitalism in the Arabian Peninsula* (London: Verso, 2020).

[71] Abraham L. Udovitch, 'Reflections on the Institutions of Credits and Banking in the Medieval Islamic Near East', *Studia Islamica*, vol. 5, no. 2 (1975); Abraham L. Udovitch, *Partnership and Profit in Medieval Islam* (Princeton, NJ: Princeton University Press, 1970), p. 175.

[72] Patricia Crone, *Meccan Trade and the Rise of Islam* (Oxford: Basil Blackwell, 1987). See also Ercanbrack, The Transformation of Islamic Law in Global Financial Markets, pp. 50–86.

example, to prevent a lessee from seeking to cancel a lease on false grounds, the contract demands that a major part of the total rent be paid in the first period, followed by low rents. Hiyal was also used to circumvent the prohibition of riba. Worldly interest justified its acceptance. The Hanafi school was the most relaxed in this respect.[73] Although riba was prohibited, mudarabah (an investment partnership) was used as a specific form of investment, being economically superior to interest-bearing loans as well as ethical. This illustrates how Islamic commercial law introduced investment ethics into trade practices of Muslim and non-Muslim traders in the Middle East. The cash waqf proliferated in the Ottoman empire through the use of Hiyal, using low interest rates and avoiding moral censure.[74] In addition, Islamic financial instruments were often modified to assist the poor, but also some states, for example Iran, had special loans for the underprivileged (Qard al Hasan loans). Such manipulation had serious implications when it was exploited by the Ayatollahs.

Islamic Capitalism 1300 to 1800: Renaissance and Inertia, Illusions and Realities

The roots of an alleged disappointing economic growth in the Middle East have been avidly sought by Timur Kuran.[75] His central observation is that the Middle East was performing well in the medieval period, and yet by the nineteenth and twentieth centuries it had declined. His persistent focus is on Islamic institutions, especially Shari'ah, with their abhorrence of riba seen as a severe constraint on the conduct of business. A further economic curse was the weakness of Islamic economic partnerships because the inheritance system resulted in the fragmentation of property and capital. Here Kuran points to the Islamic charitable endowments, the awqaf, that suffered legal rigidities. However, my analysis of waqf and Islamic finance portrays these ethical projects as diversifying Islamic capitalism and appropriating financial advantages from conservative wealthy neighbours such as Saudi Arabia. In his study of the Mamluks of eighteenth-century Egypt, Daniel Crecelius

---

[73] Frank F. Vogel, 'The Contract Law of Islam and of Arab Middle East', in *International Encyclopedia of Comparative Law, Vol. VII* (Leiden: Brill, 2006), pp. 1–162; Horii Satoe, 'Reconsideration of Legal Devices (Hiyal) in Islamic Jurisprudence: The Hanafis and their "Exits" (Makharij)', *Islamic Law and Society*, vol. 9, no. 3 (2002), pp. 312–57; Muhammed Imran Ismail, 'Legal Stratagems [Hiyal] and Usury in Islamic Commercial Law', PhD thesis, University of Birmingham, 2010.

[74] Murat Cizakca, *Islamic Capitalism and Finance: Origins, Evolution and the Future* (Cheltenham: Edward Elgar, 2011), pp. 80–134, 245–6.

[75] Timur Kuran, *Islam and Mammon: The Economic Predicaments of Islamism* (Princeton, NJ: Princeton University Press, 2004); Kuran, *The Long Divergence*.

450 Islam and Capitalism in the Making of Modern Bahrain

shows how they transformed waqf property into a commercial commodity despite the legal provisions that forbade that transformation. It involved a deviation from Shari'ah rules on permanent ownership of waqf properties, a deviation arising from changed circumstances.[76] And Carl Petry shows how Mamluk Sultans manipulated the waqf to cover their tax payments.[77]

A further obstacle to economic growth, according to Kuran, was the absence in Islamic law of provisions for corporations and banking, with the result that business partnerships were weak. But this ignores the powerful trans-national merchants, the Kanoos and Safars, operating in the Middle East, India, and even Europe, and with links to Western corporations. These links were not shaped by religion but by material conditions, their ties with Arab and Indian rulers and Jewish and Christian merchants. The Middle East was marked by trade and cosmopolitan port cities.

Fernand Braudel traces the trans-oceanic networks of merchants bound by ties of kinship and community, merchants, soldiers, adventurers, and pilgrims, trading between East Africa, Arabia, India, and South East Asia long before the Portuguese, Dutch, French, and the British East India Company.[78] These networks traded precious metals, spices, timber, and aromatics, carried aboard cargo ships and dhows. Europeans later collaborated with these powerful merchants until the rise of European colonialism from the sixteenth century.[79] This rise nurtured close economic relationships between traders and powerful state autocrats.

Continuity and Change

It is useful here to identify the merits of Islamic banking and to demonstrate how Shari'ah can be reconciled with its modern practices. The dominant features of Islamic banking are that the impact of external shocks to assets can be passed on to depositors; and that Islamic banking often pursues conservative practices because of the need to provide stable and adequate returns to investors. Investors are keen to exercise strict discipline since all share the risks. Islamic banks often hold a large share of assets in reserve accounts with the central banks.

[76] Daniel Crecelius, 'The Waqf of Muhammad Bey Abu Al-Dhahab in Historical Perspective', *International Journal of Middle East Studies*, vol. 23, no. 1 (1991), pp. 57–81.
[77] Carl F. Petry, 'Fractionalized Estates in a Centralized Regime: The Holdings of Al-Ashraf Qaythay and Qansuh Al-Ghawri According to their Waqf Deeds', *Journal of the Economic and Social History of the Orient*, vol. 41, no. 1 (1998), pp. 96–117.
[78] Fernand Braudel, *Civilization and Capitalism, 15th–18th Century, Volume 2: The Wheels of Commerce* (Berkeley, CA: University of California Press, 1992).
[79] Khalili, *Sinews of War and Trade*, chapter 1.

Western economists, including Adam Smith, Friedrich Hayek, and John Maynard Keynes, were concerned with interest rates, which they saw as responsible for economic fluctuations. The advantage of Islamic banking is that the profit-sharing contract makes the return to capital dependent on productivity, while the allocation of funds is determined by the viability of the enterprise. Thus, the volume of investment will increase because of this risk-averse accountability. Islamic finance can also reduce speculation in financial markets while secondary markets insist on profit-sharing principles. Islamic finance can be less inflationary because the supply of money is not allowed to exceed the supply of goods. One is therefore tempted to conclude that Islamic finance is less vulnerable in terms of external shocks and liquidity and insolvency risks than are conventional banks. However, this is difficult to state beyond doubt because most often Islamic finance and conventional banking co-exist within an economy.

There are also risks in Islamic finance, the most severe being the use of special vehicles in offshore accounts, the off-the-balance-sheet nature of many transactions and the link to terrorism, and fears of money laundering. There is also weakness in the regulation of Islamic banking. The Shari'ah boards are funded by the same banks that they monitor, and widespread insider dealing can therefore occur. In addition, these financial boards include ill-trained Shari'ah scholars and financial 'experts'. Often, they comprise relatives who own the corporations and governance is weak. Compliance is rarely embedded. The IMF is often too obsequious when appraising the efficiency of Shari'ah.

Challenging the Divergence Debate

Adam Smith's enquiry into the wealth of nations has been reconfigured by Thomas Picketty's *Capital in the Twenty-First Century*.[80] But it is possible that local histories, such as the history of Bahrain, can contribute to the far wider debates stimulated by Smith and Picketty. Bahrain's history and economy can provide an understanding of how economic progress on a global scale is achieved. This volume has focused on the Bahrain state and its legal frameworks that shaped corporations, commercial and financial institutions, and property rights, while highlighting the differences and similarities with its neighbours, who are often ravaged by violence. No comparison has been

---

[80] Adam Smith, *The Wealth of Nations* (London: Penguin, 1986); Thomas Piketty, *Capital in the Twenty-First Century* (Cambridge, MA: Belknap Press of Harvard University Press, 2014).

attempted with Western Europe, no attempt made to engage in the arguments over global economic convergence or divergence.[81]

An important context for the local history of Bahrain, however, has been the work of Braudel.[82] His focus was on sea-borne trade, merchant networks, and the rise of commercial empires, including notably the British East India Company. At the same time, Immanuel Wallerstein identified the importance of labour divisions, surplus appropriation, and the redistribution of gains from trade that enabled Europe to dominate the world from the sixteenth century.[83] However the 'world system' has been criticized for being Eurocentric. Andre Gunder Frank had observed that China had dominated the world economy for much longer than Europe.[84] And this encouraged the view that capitalism had been global and interconnected since the 1600s.[85] The view that modern economic growth arose from the capitalist interconnectedness that emerged in the seventeenth century was challenged by the institutional economic history of the 1980s. Douglas North and others argued the importance of law in creating the economic institutions of capitalism. The West established secure property rights and contractual law in the seventeenth and eighteenth centuries through processes that were uniquely European.[86] In 2002, Kenneth Pomeranz argued that European expansion changed the course of the world economy by giving Europeans access to land and minerals across the world. For Bahrain and the Gulf states, European expansion built on their long-worked trading networks.[87]

The huge expansion of trade brought economic specialization for Bahrain, first in oil and later in Islamic finance and in industrialization (notably in

[81] Angus Maddison, *The World Economy: A Millennial Perspective* (Paris: OECD, Development Studies Centre, 2001); Angus Maddison, *The World Economy: Historical Statistics* (Paris: OECD, Development Studies Centre, 2003); Deepak Lal, 'The World Economy at the End of the Millennium', Department of Economics, University of California, Los Angeles, Working Paper No. 786, September 1998.

[82] Fernand Braudel, *The Perspective of the World: Civilization and Capitalism, 15th to 18th Century* (New York: HarperCollins, 1986).

[83] Immanuel Wallerstein, *The Capitalist World Economy* (Cambridge: Cambridge University Press, 1979); Immanuel Wallerstein, *The Modern World System*, vols. 1–4 (Berkeley, CA: University of California Press).

[84] Andre Gunder Frank, *Reorient: Global Economy in the Asian Age* (Berkeley, CA: University of California Press, 1998).

[85] C. A. Bayly, *The Birth of the Modern World, 1780–1914* (Oxford: Blackwell, 2004). See also Sanjay Subrahmanyam, 'Connected Histories: Notes Towards a Reconfiguration of Early Modern Eurasia', *Modern Asian Studies*, vol. 31, no. 3 (1997), pp. 735–62.

[86] D. C. North, *Structure and Change in Economic History* (New York: Norton, 1981); D. C. North and R. P. Thomas, *The Rise of the Western World: A New Economic History* (New York: Cambridge University Press, 1973).

[87] Kenneth Pomeranz, *The Great Divergence: China, Europe and the Making of the Modern World Economy* (Princeton, NJ: Princeton University Press, 2001); Parasannan Parthasarathi, *Why Europe Grew Rich and Asia Did Not: Global Economic Divergence,1600–1850* (Cambridge: Cambridge University Press, 2012).

cement and aluminium).[88] Here it supplied the Gulf states but also Western markets. In this way, global interconnectedness profoundly shaped the economies of the oil-rich states, and in that respect created economic convergence. And important in that economic convergence—global interconnectedness—has been technological advance.[89] This is clearly seen in Bahrain, first in the extraction and refining of oil and then, in modern times in industrial diversification and in the expansion of FinTech.[90]

Flynn and Giraldez have argued that the expansion of the world economy in the seventeenth century was driven by the European discovery of silver in the Americas.[91] This is also a central theme in *Global Economic History* edited by Tirthankar Roy and Giorgio Riello.[92] It remains important, however, to set local histories within the global analysis, to seek out the particular, and that is the primary aim here. The next section focuses on the role of law and institutions in the creation of the specialized economy of Bahrain, drawing on the work of North, Wallis, and Weingast in emphasizing the importance of the legal incorporation of business firms in underpinning development and growth.[93]

Many of the questions raised on the authoritarian state need further exploration from intellectual sources outside the Middle East and from different disciplines that would enable us to move from narrow, often facile narratives on the state, authoritarianism, and violence. So here I attempt a sharp understanding of India in contrast to the Middle East, not all the states there but a few that have been included in different chapters. A serious comparison with Indian states and behaviour, and their changes too after independence, elicits how diverse institutions contribute to a more stable state. Hopefully

---

[88] For the close connection between expanding trade and economic specialization, see Kevin O'Rourke and Jeffrey Williamson, *Globalization and History: The Evolution of a Nineteenth Century Atlantic Economy* (Cambridge, MA: MIT Press, 2001).

[89] Joel Mokyr, *The Lever of Riches: Technological Creativity and Economic Progress* (Oxford: Oxford University Press, 1990); Joel Mokyr, *The Gifts of Athena: Historical Origins of the Knowledge Economy* (Princeton, NJ: Princeton University Press, 2002); Joel Mokyr, *A Culture of Growth: The Origins of the Modern Economy* (Princeton, NJ: Princeton University Press, 2017).

[90] Umar A. Oseni and S. Nazim Ali (ed.), *Fintech in Islamic Finance: Theory and Practice* (Abingdon: Routledge, 2019); Roger Owen, 'Globalization at the Beginnings of the Twentieth and Twenty-first Centuries', in *Globalization and the Gulf*, edited by John W. Fox, Nada Mourtada-Sabbah, and Mohammed al-Mutawa (Abingdon: Routledge, 2006), pp. 78–89.

[91] D. O. Flynn and A. Giraldez (ed.), *Metals and Monies in an Emerging Global Economy* (Aldershot: Ashgate, 1997); D. O. Flynn and A. Giraldez (ed.), *Global Connections and Monetary History, 1470–1800* (Aldershot: Ashgate, 2003).

[92] Tirthankar Roy and Giorgio Riello (ed.), *Global Economic History* (London: Bloomsbury Academic, 2019).

[93] D. C. North, *Institutions, Institutional Change and Economic Performance* (Cambridge: Cambridge University Press, 1990); D. C. North, J. J. Wallis, and B. R. Weingast, *Violence and Social Orders: A Conceptual Framework for Interpreting Recorded Human History* (Cambridge: Cambridge University Press, 2009). See also Maya Shatzmiller, 'Economic Performance and Economic Growth in the Early Islamic World', *Journal of the Economic and Social History of the Orient*, vol. 54 (2011), pp. 132–84.

this draws a sharp distinction on diverse sources of authoritarianism. A combination of both qualitative, quantitative, and above all the rise of different religions, culture, and science and philosophy may provide a serious understanding of why the Middle East confronts more episodes of authoritarian abuse and violence. Does stakeholding of different ethnic, religious groups in Bahrain with Sunni rulers and Shi'ite autonomy allow a powerful tool to advance stability, growth, and globalization? This also embodies a moderate, cosmopolitan attitude to Shari'ah.

A further factor favouring stability in Bahrain is the presence of Shi'ite moderate behaviour and diverse sources of authority within Shi'ism.

Unique Subtle Forms of Sectarianism Nourished by Historical Lines of Shiite Mercantile Traditions from the Sixteenth Century to the Present

Legal institutionalism poses the qualitative difference between custom, Shari'ah, and state power, and the distinction between the complicated adoption of English Common Law can be investigated through judicial independence: this independence matters in authoritarian states.[94] The special focus here is on the use of law and municipal courts for Shi'as, thereby providing legal autonomy for those who constituted a majority group in Bahrain and helped to preserve their rituals, such as Ashura. Ironically this is also a weapon of the state for social control, centralizing power, and legitimation. Law is usually a powerful tool for rulers seeking social control, but it can also be wielded by the subjects of the state. Municipal courts with links to local ulama are also significant in asserting power, particularly where the use of Ja'fari jurisprudence is essential.[95] Citizens do display legal claims and only descend into street protests like the Arab Spring when important issues such as employment, land security, and educational opportunities are threatened.

These forms of legal resistance, on definite issues that contravene the livelihood of Shi'a, provide a useful insight into how the Shi'a in Bahrain are not dragged into deep destruction as in Lebanon, Palestine, and Syria. Here Bahrain's institutions also provide strength and stability against state

[94] Kureshi Yasser, 'When Judges Defy Dictators: An Audience-Based Framework to Explain the Emergence of Judicial Assertiveness Against Authoritarian Regimes', *Comparative Politics*, vol. 53, no. 2 (2021), pp. 233–57.
[95] Mark Massouud, *Law's Fragile State: Colonial Authoritarianism and Humanitarian Legacies in Sudan* (Cambridge: Cambridge University Press, 2013); James Rosberg, 'Roads to the Rule of Law: the Emergence of an Independent Judiciary in Contemporary Egypt', PhD thesis, Massachusetts Institute of Technology, 1995; Charles Tilly and Sidney Tarrow, *Contentious Politics* (New York: Oxford University Press, 2015), pp. 7–8.

repressiveness and judicial authoritativeness, while powerful networks of Shi'ite merchants, united by class and religious identity, had emerged spontaneously and achieved maturity and renaissance in the trade and commerce of the eighteenth century. This was briefly stymied in the post-1970s independent era when they faced the economic power of the state and economic diversification, augmented by the mounting economic and welfare grievances faced by rural Shi'a. What is clear is that judicial independence for a segmented Shi'a population provides a mutually strengthening challenge to state violations and abuse.[96]

Thus law, though broadly constructed, draws from custom and involves an institutionalized judiciary and legislative apparatus. Here, with state intervention, it shapes modern capitalism. Commerce operates through clan and family ties, religion, ethnicity, bureaucratic co-option, and corruption, and this, in modern Bahrain law, has serious implications for contracts, property relations, and the structure of corporations. A sharp understanding of legal institutionalism can demonstrate how Shari'ah is comfortably positioned with the application of Common Law and Civil Law. Radical ideas that shaped business legitimacy, ownership, structure, and innovation, with market-oriented global ambitions, emerged with legal pluralism. In Bahrain, the state is dominant but strengthened by the real growth of oil capital flows from its Gulf neighbours and the globalization of finance. North, Wallis, and Weingast emphasized this role of law and the legal incorporation underpinning economic development and growth.[97]

A central theme running through the earlier chapters is the globalization of Bahrain and in particular Bahrain's emergence as the financial hub of the Middle East, next only in importance to Malaysia. Bahrain's globalization meshes with traditionalism while seeking liberalism and cosmopolitanism, even within Shari'ah boundaries, when it uses courts in London, the republic of Ireland, and the US to achieve compromises in religion over commercial contracts. The legal pluralistic context in which Shari'ah are transformed into dynamic power relations overlapping tradition are vital in global initiatives. This is globalization that is unique to Bahrain and Dubai. This is a form of de-territorializing supranational character, a form of global arbitration that reveals its significance in achieving neoliberal interactions of global Islamic

---

[96] Asef Bayat, *Life as Politics: How Ordinary People Change the Middle East* (Stanford, CA: Stanford University Press 2010); Asef Bayat, 'Plebeians of the Arab Spring', *Current Anthropology*, vol. 56 (2015), pp. 33–43; Nathan J. Brown, *The Rule of Law in the Arab World: Courts in Egypt and the Gulf* (New York: Cambridge University Press, 1997); Steven D. Schaaf, 'Contentious Politics in the Courthouse: Law as a Tool for Resisting Authoritarian States in the Middle East', *Law & Society Review*, vol. 55, no. 1 (2021), pp. 139–76.

[97] North, Wallis, and Weingast, *Violence and Social Orders*.

finance, and thus there is the global spread of Al-Baraka Banking group throughout the Middle East including Turkey into Europe and the USA.

This economic globalization is not new to Bahrain. Its transnational trading networks achieved liberalism in economic growth as well as within tribal groups and among foreign traders. This is apparent in the historical trading networks from the seventeenth century to the international business networks of such capitalists as the Kanoos and Safars. Though market-mediated culture prevails, it is within state dominance.

Though ambivalence in the use of migrant labour persists, it still constitutes global interaction in the workplace. Bahrain's population grew from 116,000 in 1950 to 620,000 in 1997; in 1997, the expatriate population was 236,000, 39 per cent of that total.[98]

But recently, the most significant form of globalization has been through FinTech and digital technology. This liberates women and removes, to a degree, class and wealth barriers in finance, while sustaining international connections with Microsoft, with Singapore and other global national links, and to global neoliberalism.

The next core theme focuses on the advancing position of Bahraini women in employment. Labour force participation trends between the 1970s and 1990s indicate where the labour market first restricted women's access to paid work but where opportunities then opened up. In Bahrain, the share of young female workers in the labour force rose from 18 per cent in 1980 to 31 per cent in 2000, the highest in the MENA countries. The largest cohort increase was in the 15–24 age group.[99] However, female labour participation rates increased among all age groups, attributed to declining fertility rates, higher educational attainment, and a trend towards female emancipation. However, the large increase in female participation rates during the 1990s also produced high rates of unemployment among young females. In 2001, male youth unemployment was at 17 per cent while for women it was 27 per cent.[100] In Bahrain in 2000, unemployment among young females was 50 per cent higher than for young males. The causes of the higher rates of unemployment among women are diverse. Women work in particular occupations and face different challenges in entry. They also face different family requirements: marriage and children cause a quarter of the gender difference.

[98] BH/CSO,1980–1996; BH/Central Informatics Organization, 2000–18; Statistical Abstracts, Central Informatics Organization; Economic Development Board, Reforming Bahrain's Labour Market, 2004; Andrzej Kapiszewski, 'Population, Labor and Education Dilemmas Facing GCC States at the Turn of the Century', Paper presented at the Conference, Crossroads of the New Millennium, Abu Dhabi, 9 April 2000.
[99] World Development Indicators, 2004, World Bank, Washington, DC.
[100] ILO, LABORSTA, 2004 Global Employment Trends for Youth.

Cultural traditions may also explain gender differences in labour participation rates. The labour market segmentation between males and females is also shaped by the transition from rural to urban employment as well as by the increasing opportunities for women in self-employment. David Blanchflower notes that 'self-employment is the simplest kind of entrepreneurship'.[101] A notable feature of women's involvement in work was the extensive reliance on technology. Technology allows for outsourcing, downscaling, deconcentration, and the subcontracting of labour-intensive service jobs, each stimulating self-employment.[102] Ironically, Geert Hofstede's index on individualism, masculinity, power-distance, and risk-taking reflects the position of women in employment in the Middle East.[103]

Women and Greater Visibility

Female participation in public sector employment rose from 5 per cent in 1971 to 46 per cent in 2011.[104] Latterly, this coincided with an increase in migrant labour during the oil boom and an expansion in the non-oil economic sectors. The increase in foreign direct investment accounted for the expansion in Bahraini female employment but ironically was followed by an increase in Bahraini youth unemployment. Public sector expansion also increased the female labour participation rate. Bahraini women comprised 65 per cent of the female workforce at the end of 2010.[105] This was part of the government initiative to nationalize the labour force. The labour and economic reforms of 2006 further stimulated job creation, including in the private sector, through the provision of technical training for Bahrainis and reductions in the salary differentials between nationals and foreigners. The 2009 revision of the Kafala system, giving foreign employees freedom to change employer, increased opportunities for Bahrainis in the private sector.[106]

---

[101] David G. Blanchflower, 'Self-employment in OECD Countries', NBER Working Paper 7486, Cambridge, MA, 2000, p. 3.

[102] Ferry de Goey, 'Economic Structure and Self-employment during the Twentieth Century', Paper for 8th EBHA Conference, 16–18 September 2004, Barcelona.

[103] Geert Hofstede, *Culture's Consequences: International Differences in Work-Related Values* (London: Sage Publications, 1980); Geert Hofstede, *Cultures and Organizations: Intercultural Cooperation and Its Importance for Survival* (New York: McGraw Hill, 2010).

[104] Bahrain, Central Informatics Organization, *Statistical Abstract*: www.cio.gov.bh, 2011

[105] Bahrain, Central Informatics Organization, *Report*, 2011.

[106] Sharon Nagy, 'Bahraini and Non-Bahraini Women in Bahrain's Workforce: Gender, Work and Nationality', Arabian Humanities: International Journal of Archaeology and Social Sciences in the Arabian Peninsula, 2013, p. 4: https://journals.openedition.org/cy/2144

Bahraini women were largely employed in education, healthcare, and childcare. Oil revenues increased from the 1980s, drawing in foreign female workers from poorer Arab countries and from Asia. They concentrated in domestic employment.[107] Gulf Air recruited Bahraini and European women as flight attendants, and there was an influx of foreign women into the leisure and sex industries.[108] In domestic jobs there was recruitment from Indonesia, the Philippines, and South Asia. The expansion in regional tourism and increased consumerism drove the construction of shopping centres, amusement parks, hotels, and restaurants, each of which recruited foreign workers.[109] The retail sector employed Bahrainis in sales and clerical positions working alongside foreign colleagues. But the entertainment and personal service sectors remain, together with domestic employment, dominated by foreign women and men. Foreign labour remained in the unskilled, low-paid, private sector, while Bahraini women were manoeuvring themselves into the teaching sector, into public schools. Teaching in Bahrain's public schools, which had opened for girls in 1928, was popular for foreign women. Many also worked in foreign firms as clerks and secretaries. Healthcare shifted away from its reliance on foreign labour but at a slower pace than education.[110] Paying greater attention to gender and ethnicity is important for increasing female entry into diverse jobs and acquiring education and skills. The areas encompassing domestic work and healthcare remain dominant spaces for South Asian and South East Asian females, while Bahraini women are increasingly employed in clerical work, healthcare, and for the national airline Gulf Air, besides being self-employed in SMEs.[111] The rise of private entrepreneurship and self-employment among Bahraini women is not difficult to understand, as they are often better educated than Bahraini men. Structural change in the economy through outsourcing increased opportunities for women in private business and in self-employment. A woman would face less public exposure by being self-employed and working from home.

---

[107] Michele Ruth Gamburd, *The Kitchen Spoon's Handle: Transnationalism and Sri Lanka's Migrant Housemaids* (Ithaca, NY: Cornell University Press, 2000); Caitrin Lynch, 'The Good Girls of Sri Lankan Modernity: Moral Orders of Nationalism and Capitalism', *Identities*, vol. 6, no. 1 (1999), pp. 55–89.

[108] Gulf Air Site, 'Gulf Air Celebrates First All-Bahraini Female Cabin Crew Graduation with Tamkeen Support', 2 August 2010: http://www.gulfair.com/English/aboutgulfair/Pages/News.aspx?newsno=180.

[109] Staci Strobl, 'Policing Housemaids: The Criminalization of Domestic Workers in Bahrain', *British Journal of Criminology*, vol. 49, no. 2 (2009), pp. 165–83.

[110] Nagy, 'Bahraini and Non-Bahraini Women in Bahrain's Workforce', pp. 11–12.

[111] S. Al-Najjar, 'Women Migrant Domestic Workers in Bahrain', International Migration Papers, 47, International Migration Programme, International Labour Office, Geneva, 2002.

New Economy–New Opportunities for Women

Reducing the gender gap has been made possible by the expansion of digital financial services, which offers significant opportunities for women. Moreover, FinTech has built trust and attracted savings from domestic workers. Digitalized services provide flexibility, security, and transparency. Financial networks attract female agents responsible for e-payment, for example through Fawry in Egypt and Dinarak in Jordan, to reach female customers. Migrant workers, both men and women, have access to universal digital provision. More than 50 per cent of workers in Bahrain are of foreign origin but digital access provides them with stability in their financial transactions. It is important to emphasize that, for example, the Hawiyati platform developed by Making Cents International has provided migrant women with an entry point to build their credit rating and history, and so acquire personal or business loans. These financial institutions are of immense value in a society that still discriminates against women, although Bahrain and Oman are more progressive than their Gulf neighbours. The inclusive financial structure is even more critical for lower-income workers, both local and foreign.[112] In March 2016, Bahrain launched a US$100 million fund to support female entrepreneurs, supported by the Bahrain Women Development Fund, the Supreme Council of Women, Tamkeen (with an emphasis on education), and the Bahrain Development Bank. This was solely for Bahrainis and had no impact on migrant workers. In contrast, the Arab Women's Enterprise Fund (AWEF), a five-year project funded by the then British Department for International Development (DFID) and established in 2015, had an immense impact in the MENA countries, including in Bahrain. AWEF's Practitioner Learning Brief offered courses to women through DFS (Digital Finance Services) on innovative digital finance. AWEF also encouraged e-payments to assist foreign female workers. But it is perhaps ironic that while advances in technology and education empowered women, Bahrain's youth experienced high unemployment.

Tourism involved prostitution in Bahrain's cities, in particular Manama. In 2009, Manama was placed eighth in the top 10 'Sin Cities' of the world by *Ask Men Magazine*.[113] Though prostitution and related activities were

---

[112] Chloe Gueguen, Sabal AI Majali, and Julia Hakspiel, 'Making Digital Finance Work for Women in the MENA Region: 8 Lessons from the field', ICT Works.

[113] Susan M. Shaw, Nancy Staton Barbour, Patti Duncan, Kryn Freehling-Burton, and Jane Nichols (ed.), *Women's Lives around the World: A Global Encyclopedia* (Santa Barbara, CA: ABC-CLIO, 2017), p. 26.

prohibited under the Bahrain Criminal Code, Decree 15 of 1976, the industry still flourished. Many of the customers are Saudis as Saudi Arabia has
strict restrictions on alcohol and sex. The high percentage of foreign workers also fuelled prostitution. The Al-Asalah parliamentary bloc sought to halt
the granting of visas to Russian, Thai, Ethiopian, and Chinese women in an
attempt to curb prostitution in Bahrain but this proposal was rejected. Persians regarded as 'daughters of love' were much in evidence. Bahrain also
gained notoriety through sex trafficking. The US State Department monitoring the trafficking of sex slaves ranked Bahrain as a tier 1 country.[114] It
is perhaps inevitable that the rapid economic growth since the 1990s would
encourage the exploitation of foreign women for sex. Not least it would attract
visitors from conservative Saudi Arabia.

The following and final section of this conclusion provides an examination of economic and financial change in modern Dubai because Dubai
offers an insightful comparison with Bahrain. In brief, Bahrain has been cautious, focusing on the law and on the stability of institutions. No less driven
to achieve economic diversification and financial expansion, since the 2008
financial crisis, Dubai has been more fractured and potentially unstable.

Dubai: Islamic Finance and the Legal System

Dubai is a constituent of the United Arab Emirates (UAE), a federation of
seven emirates formed in 1971. Defense policy, foreign policy, and the banking system are each coordinated at the federal level. However, Dubai retains
autonomy over its economy, debt issues, law, and over land and natural
resources.

The legal system in the UAE is based on the civil code and Shari'ah law. But
Dubai and its Dubai International Financial Centre, DIFC, operate under
common law and in English, in contrast to the UAE which operates under
civil law and in Arabic. Dubai's DIFC also provides for the use of the law
of England and Wales. This has facilitated the use of sophisticated commercial law while incorporating the use of Shari'ah. There is no separate
Shari'ah legislation in the UAE specifically for commercial transactions. In
the UAE, commercial and banking laws are codified but seek compliance
with Shari'ah principles. However, Islamic banking and financial institutions
operate under Federal law No. 6, 15 December 1985. Also, the Dubai Financial Services Authority, an independent body, regulates the DIFC. Moreover,

---

[114] 'Bahrain 2018 Trafficking in Persons Report', US Department of State, 29 July 2018.

the Securities and Commodities Authority regulates the Dubai Financial Market, while insurance is supervised by the Insurance Commission in the Ministry of Economy, in business relating to Islamic finance. This regulatory structure favours global ambitions.[115] But it also appears to be somewhat chaotic, in contrast to Bahrain where the Central Bank of Bahrain secures regulatory coordination. This may explain why Bahrain signed a memorandum of understanding with the Dubai International Financial Centre on liquidation procedures. Bahrain's central bank maintains strict regulatory control.

The Dubai International Financial Centre was set up as the core financial authority, with a jurisdiction separate from the UAE and with its own common law courts. The DIFC investigates alleged breaches of rules within the Financial Free Zone, which has the autonomy to apply its own regulations and hence is exempt from the regulations of the UAE union.[116]

One relatively consistent factor in the pursuit of Dubai's global ambitions has been the use of legal transplants in Islamic finance.[117] Legal convergence through globalization would result in regulatory systems that are efficient and competitive. But often legal transplants occur that are dependent on political or social factors. One approach has been to model regulations on UK regulations. Bahrain has coordinated its regulation through the Accounting and Auditing Organization for Islamic Financial Institutions (AAOIFI) and the Islamic Financial Stability Board (IFSB). Dubai, in contrast, emulates the UK and EU legal systems.[118] Convergence is particularly strong in securities regulations that are not always rigid in their observance of Islamic law. Consequently, international issuances are attracted by legal transplants that are familiar with Western rules and regulatory frameworks. As with Bahrain, Dubai is attracted to Western investments.[119] It should be added that Malaysia succeeds in Islamic finance with less recourse to legal convergence as it has effective Islamic financial institutions supported by a large domestic market. Dubai and Bahrain, with their low local populations, are dictated by

---

[115] Harun Kapetanovic, 'Islamic Finance and Economic Development: The Case of Dubai', PhD thesis, Department of Middle Eastern Studies, Kings College, London 2017), pp. 172, 175.

[116] UAE Const., Art. 121, Const. Amend. 1 of 2004, translation available at https: www.defc.ae files 5714/5449/7479, constitutional amendment 1 of 2004, English pdf, cited in Paul Lee, 'The Regulation of Securities and Islamic Finance in Dubai: Implications for Models of Shariah', *Journal of Islamic and Near Middle East*, vol. 15 (2016), p. 4.

[117] Alan Watson, *Legal Transplants: An Approach to Comparative Law* (Athens, GA: University of Georgia Press, 1974).

[118] Lee, 'The Regulation of Securities and Islamic Finance in Dubai', p. 29.

[119] Rafael La Porta, Florencio Lopez-de-Silanes, Andrei Schleifer, and Robert Vishny, 'Legal Determinants of External Finance', *Journal of Finance*, vol. 52, no. 3 (1997). See also Howell E. Jackson and Eric J. Pan, 'Regulatory Competition in International Securities Markets', *Business*, vol. 1, no. 653(2001). As people choose high-disclosure regimes and not low-disclosure regimes, the UK and the US are favoured: Lee, 'The Regulation of Securities and Islamic Finance in Dubai', p. 31.

global markets seeking international investors in utilizing Islamic financial instruments.

There are significant differences between the Emirates, not least in ethical behaviour in Islamic finance. Abu Dhabi is the wealthiest, with 95 per cent of UAE hydrocarbon wealth, and it wields significant influence.[120] Although accounting for 35 per cent of the UAE's GDP, Dubai is weakened by the fact that a major part of UAE debt is located within its institutions, its corporations, finance houses, and investment firms. Furthermore, Dubai lacks effective financial stability laws, which was exposed in the 2008 financial crisis. In contrast, Bahrain and Kuwait both possessed resilient legal systems that secured stability. Dubai's high dependence on UAE oil revenues and its high debt exposure added to its fragility, until the introduction of liquidity support facilities in September 2008, in the midst of the 2008 Global Financial Crisis, followed by further intervention by the UAE in September 2009, to improve the capital adequacy ratio of Dubai banks. Regulation had not been rigorously applied. In addition, Dubai was unable to cope with the complexity of global financial markets. The UAE and Dubai lacked accounting and auditing laws except for those firms incorporated in the DIFC. SMEs are particularly vulnerable because of the absence of accounting rules. Despite the creation of the Al Etihad Credit Bureau, vested with responsibility for collecting credit profiles, the lack of transparency was undermining Dubai's position as an Islamic financial hub, as the 2008 financial crisis demonstrated.

Important for Dubai is the regulation of securities and the creation of legal transplants to establish stability and secure Shari'ah compliance.[121] Dubai is second only to Abu Dhabi in economic performance and global reputation, staging prestigious social, cultural, and sporting events. In 2013, it announced its aim to become a global Islamic financial hub, with the creation of the Dubai Islamic Financial City through its Islamic Economy Development Centre. This has required the reinterpretation of Shari'ah in economic and stock market operations.

The major issue is Shari'ah compliance. The Shari'ah Supervisory Board is a committee of Islamic jurists who decide on compliance. To ease this compliance, the DIFC recognizes Islamic funds approved by Malaysia as being legal, as Malaysia is a Shari'ah-compliant jurisdiction. In other words, Dubai is securing Shari'ah compliance through the Securities Commission of Malaysia. In fact, Malaysia and Dubai signed a pact to allow the cross-border

[120] Kapetanovic, 'Islamic Finance and Economic Development: The Case of Dubai', pp. 2, 20.
[121] Lee, 'The Regulation of Securities and Islamic Finance in Dubai', p. 4.

flow of Islamic funds.[122] In addition, Dubai uses the regulatory systems of Malaysia, the US, and the UK to establish forms of Shari'ah compliance in its local legislation. Thus, local legislation within the DIFC involves a hybrid structure that partially codifies the common law and imports the remainder, together with residual English statute law without reference to individual English statutes.[123] There is much further manipulation.[124]

In contrast, Bahrain, Kuwait, and even the UAE are distinct from the DIFC in that they have national Shari'ah authorities in addition to the Shari'ah Supervisory Board (SSB). The UAE has adopted English Common Law on a flexible basis but English Statute Law is applied only to a limited extent and at a fixed date. The Bahrain and Kuwait position gives flexibility and is attractive to foreign clients. It also provides information on Shari'ah compliance. Moreover, it affords significant adaptation to diverse legal, cultural, and religious environments. It is receptive to English Common Law, is passively obedient to Saudi Arabia, is minimalist in its approach to GCC countries, and proactive in its approach to Malaysia. Overall Dubai does endure a complicated, uneasy situation. In contrast Bahrain often uses UK and US regulatory frameworks and courts to promote parity between conventional and Islamic finance.[125]

No substantial quantitative data exists for Dubai to determine its success in securing Shari'ah compliance. Legal amendments in the US and the UK make Islamic finance contracts permissible, as with ijarah and murabahah financing within Islamic and conventional banks. A murabahah-based transaction allows a bankrupt debtor to exit bankruptcy. This was the case with Arcapita Bank.[126]

Overall, the UK has been more receptive than the US to Islamic finance and has passed several specific Islamic finance amendments. However, UK courts, taking the position that Islamic finance introduces considerable uncertainty, insist that Shari'ah contracts are invalid in the UK. This undermines confidence in Shari'ah finance. In the US, the position is different across different states. Securing Shari'ah compliance increases costs, and this encourages Shari'ah scholars to be innovative in customizing Islamic financial instruments to be compliant.[127] When faced with difficulties in

---

[122] Securities Commission, 27 March 2007, cited in Lee, 'The Regulation of Securities and Islamic Finance in Dubai', p. 10.

[123] The hybrid system is revealed in the following local legislation. Contract Law, DIFC Law No. 6, 2004; Law of Security 2005, in DIFC Law No. 8, 2005; Personal Property Law, in DIFC Law No. 9, 2005; and Trust Law, in DIFC Law No. 11, 2005.

[124] David Russell and Gabor Bognar, 'The Application of English Law in the Financial Free Zones of the United Arab Emirates', *Trusts and Trustees*, vol. 23, no. 5 (2017), pp. 480–9.

[125] Lee, 'The Regulation of Securities and Islamic Finance in Dubai', p. 18.

[126] Lee, 'The Regulation of Securities and Islamic Finance in Dubai', p. 19.

[127] Lee, 'The Regulation of Securities and Islamic Finance in Dubai', pp. 22, 23.

interpreting Shari'ah principles, Bahrain and Dubai often chose to use tawar-ruq (a sale and re-sale transaction used to generate liquidity), a controversial transaction in Islamic finance although used widely in Malaysia.[128] Commodity Murabahah was essentially based on tawarruq.[129]

Through international bodies such as IOSCO (International Organiza-tion of Securities Commissions), IFSB (Islamic Financial Services Board), AAOIFI (Accounting and Auditing Organization for Islamic Financial Insti-tutions), Islamic finance works to strict governance, although with a degree of adaptation and compromise to local circumstances.

Dubai's Strategic Growth: New Opportunities through Globalization

Dubai has been transformed from a small island economy with trading links spanning the Indian Ocean, South East Asia, and the east coast of Africa in the 1800s, to a global service hub. The most recent stage in the trans-formation involved a move from oil dependence to a diversified economy from the 1990s. The economy has undergone great change in establishing a critical infrastructure in electricity, communications, roads, and airport and shipping facilities. There has also occurred growth in commerce, logistics, tourism, finance, real estate, and construction, involving the creation of major complexes: The Palm Jumeirah, Burj Khalifa, Dubai Internet City, Dubai Media City, and the Dubai International Financial Centre.[130] This transfor-mation was earlier funded by revenues from oil accumulated since 1966. But those revenues declined dramatically after the 1980s, with oil accounting for less than 5 per cent of GDP by 2006.[131] Growth from the 1990s was funded by foreign direct investment, which increased from US$16.7 billion in 2007 to US$33.7 billion in 2011. FDI increased from 22 per cent of GDP in 2007 to 41 per cent in 2011. Foreign trade grew from US$30.5 billion in 2001 to US$336.5 billion in 2012.[132] Prominent in this economic diversification was

---

[128] Nikan Firoozye, 'Shari'ah Risk or Banking Conundrum?', Opalesque, 3 July 2009. See also Bank Negara Malaysia, *Shari'a Resolutions in Islamic Finance*, 2nd. ed., 2010, p. 96; Ercanbrack, *The Trans-formation of Islamic Law in Global Financial Markets* (Cambridge: Cambridge University Press, 2015), pp. 17, 125, 156.

[129] Azmat Rafique, 'Oman, the Dawn of Islamic Banking', in *The Islamic Finance Handbook: A Practi-tioner's Guide to the Global Markets* (New York: Wiley, 2014), p. 382.

[130] W. Coombe and J. Melki, 'Global Media and Brand Dubai', *Place Branding and Public Diplomacy*, vol. 8, no. 1 (2012), pp. 58–71; Nada Saleh Al Shama, 'Sustainability of the Dubai Model of Economic Development', PhD thesis, Manchester Business School, 2014, p. 15.

[131] Dubai Statistics Centre 2012, National Accounts Reports.

[132] Dubai Statistics Centre, 2007, and Dubai Statistics Centre, 2012; Martin Hvidt, 'The Dubai Model: An Outline of Key Development-process Elements in Dubai', *International Journal of Middle East Studies*, vol. 41, no. 3 (2009), pp. 397–418.

collaboration with foreign corporations. This required the adoption of more liberal economic policies, but Dubai's government retained its control of large companies, as is evident in the establishment of Emirates Airlines in 1985. The airline is owned by the government of Dubai but operates as a commercial group, underpinning Dubai's position in aviation, travel, tourism, and the leisure industries. It employs more than 62,000 people and has 170 aircraft, and saw revenue rise from US$2.1 billion in 2001 to US$21.1 billion in 2012.[133] Another major corporation was Dubai World, which became the fourth largest port operator in the world, managing 15 ports in the Middle East, Africa, Asia, Latin America, and Australia. It also acquired Britain's P&O facilities and the US-based CSX International, thereby accumulating a total valuation of US$8 billion. However, despite its success it faced serious problems in the 2008 financial crisis.[134] However, the strongest performing sector was tourism and leisure, which propelled Dubai's spectacular emergence as a global city. A wide range of international events, exhibitions, and conferences stimulated the growth of hotels, restaurants, and shopping and entertainment facilities. The Dubai Shopping Festival was launched in 1996, attracting 1.5 million visitors in 1997 with a total spend of US$845 million, and 3.98 million visitors with a total spend of US$4.1 billion in 2011.[135] The International Film Festival, Jazz Festival, and Desert Rock Festival were a part of this search for social and cultural prominence, but the events also created revenues to fund economic diversification. Moreover, the creation of specialist free zones attracted FDI that sustained specific industries, including information technology, media services, financial services, healthcare, and higher education, each encouraged by tax exemptions, the freedom to repatriate profits, few visa restrictions, and the substantial networking opportunities.

By 2010, Dubai Internet City, established in 2000, had attracted 850 companies including Microsoft and IBM. It provided for the creation of a knowledge economy, engaging local entrepreneurs together with multinationals. The Dubai Knowledge Village, established in 2003, was close to the Media City Zone. Dubai International Academic City, established in 2007, created links with Australian and European universities, which established college campuses in Dubai, including Manchester Business School, Bradford University, and Michigan State University. The Knowledge and

---

[133] The Emirates Group 2013, Emirates Competitiveness Council, 2013, Competitiveness-UAE current standing: cited in Al Shama, 'Sustainability of the Dubai Model of Economic Development', p. 98.

[134] Christopher Davidson, *Dubai: The Vulnerability of Success* (New York: Columbia University Press, 2008).

[135] Dubai Statistics Centre Report 2012, cited in Al Shama, 'Sustainability of the Dubai Model of Economic Development'.

Human Development Authority, established in 2006, monitored the campuses while seeking to raise education standards. But it was the Dubai International Financial Centre, establishing collaborative links both in the UAE and beyond, that posed the most serious challenges to Bahrain. By 2012, it had 912 registered companies, of which 795 were finance-related, including KPMG and Crédit Suisse, and 117 were retailers.[136]

Ethics and the Age of Market Forces

Dubai is an entrepreneurial city, driven by innovative financial capitalism. It is a global city. Unfortunately, in contrast to Bahrain, it suffered during the 2008 financial crisis. Despite the scale and efficiency of the corporations, the errors of rapid growth and undisclosed FDI incursion remained.

The state structure in Dubai exhibits neo-patrimonialism, where the state revolves around the ruler who maintains relations with capitalist elites. The merchants have been integrated into the state structure since the 1940s. The UAE has granted Dubai substantial autonomy through a flexible state constitution, enabling it to pursue internal and global economic investments. The political structure of the UAE involves both federal and local government. Federal authority is embedded in the Federal National Council representing all seven emirates. The Federal Judiciary, an independent authority, oversees the federal laws and their implementation. Its independence is guaranteed under the UAE constitution. The Federal Judiciary includes the Federal Supreme Court and the Courts of First Instance. The Federal Supreme Court comprises five judges who are responsible for new laws and arbitration in cases of dispute.[137]

Within the federal system, each emirate has political and financial autonomy, its own government departments, local municipalities, and sector departments including tourism, economic affairs, and health. Dubai has established the Dubai Chamber of Commerce, the Dubai Municipality, and the Dubai Department of Tourism and Commerce Marketing. The institutional structure and decision-making are centralized in the emirate and this makes possible greater coordination and, in particular, aligns well with government-related organizations.[138] This centralized structure assists in providing infrastructure, electricity power stations, and water.

---

[136] DIFC Authority Annual Review 2012, cited in Al Shama, 'Sustainability of the Dubai Model of Economic Development', p. 102.

[137] Neil Quilliam, 'The States of the Gulf Cooperation Council', in *Good Governance in the Middle East Oil Monarchies*, edited by T. Najem and M. Hetherington (London: Routledge Curzon, 2003), pp. 29–58.

[138] Hvidt, 'The Dubai Model', pp. 402–3.

There are varied explanations for the substantial economic fractures in Dubai from 2008. One arises from the dominance of a group of corporations, financial institutions, and investment groups owned directly by the Government of Dubai under the umbrella of three major holding companies: Dubai Holding, Dubai World, and the Investment Corporation of Dubai. A major focus was on real estate and finance, although there were significant interests in trade and services, including ports, logistics, transportation, and tourism. The real estate bubble burst in 2008, and much of the foreign wealth tied into that sector increased Dubai's debt. However, highly leveraged real estate enterprises were able to reduce their debt with support from the Central Bank. Government involvement raised doubts as to the financial stability of Dubai World and the other holding companies.

The 2008 Global Financial Crisis had serious implications for Dubai because of Dubai's accumulated debt. In November 2009, Dubai World was reported to be facing a debt payment of more than US$20 billion of bonds and was requesting an extension to May 2010.[139] Total Dubai debt was higher than GDP in the same year, US$79.8 billion.[140] The debt tied to the Investment Corporation of Dubai and to Dubai Holding was also extremely high.[141]

This implied serious fragmentation of state and sovereign wealth and an urgent need to diversify the economy. The state-owned holding companies were now wooed by European institutions, particularly Dubai World and its technological companies, as well as Dubai Holding with its interests in healthcare. Local and international financial institutions funded their projects. Most of the funds were short-term loans rather than bonds. Dubai World debts were 55 per cent from international banks. The rest came from Dubai and Abu Dhabi.[142] The generosity of foreign lenders reflected their faith in the Dubai state.

The diversification strategy extended to real estate, including residential and commercial properties, tourism, and entertainment. But Dubai also encouraged expatriates to purchase these properties. Thus, Emaar Properties, formed in 1997, permitted expatriates to hold 99-year leases and this included Burj Khalifa, the world's tallest tower in 2010, and the huge Dubai Shopping Mall. Another iconic project, Palm Island, was also attractive to foreigners and their money, whatever its source. Dubai World owned Dubai Ports, Dubai Dry Dock, and Jebel Ali Free Zone, as well as marine terminals

---

[139] *Gulf News*, 2008, 'Dubai Calms Investor Worries', available at: http://gulfnews.com/business/economy/dubai-calms-investor-worries-1.144809.

[140] *Al Shama*, 'Sustainability of the Dubai Model of Economic Development', pp. 106–7.

[141] *Morgan Stanley Research*, 'Economics—Is Dubai out of the Woods?', 18 October 2010.

[142] *ING Research*, 'Dubai World and Dubai Debt: Getting the Details', 8 April 2010.

across the Middle East, Asia, Africa, South America, and Australia.[143] However, the heavy borrowing, and the boom in the real estate market fuelled by expatriate buying, increased the financial vulnerability of Dubai. This expansion was triggered by the provision of free land to the holding companies in addition to government investment in the companies. There was further inducement in flexible repayment schedules. Projects such as Palm Island were encouraged to borrow from international financiers. The crash came in 2008.[144] Short-term capital flows had destabilized the Dubai economy: moreover, the origins of the foreign loans were often obscure. Such new challenges require pioneers to develop organizational capabilities if they are to remain as leaders in an industrial oligopoly, and this accentuates weak governance. There are rumours of criminal activity but little data to demonstrate this.

The rapid growth in trade and the deregulation of financial sectors enabled criminal organizations to enter. In 2002, Dubai introduced comprehensive AML (Anti-Money Laundering) legislation in response to internal and external concerns over the activities of these unknown interests.[145] In 2004 and 2005, the Dubai government established the International Financial Centre and the International Financial Exchange to improve financial credibility and to align with New York, London, Tokyo, and Hong Kong in establishing financial platforms for banking and wealth management. By 2012, it had 912 registered companies, of which 795 were in finance and 117 were retailers. The finance companies included KPMG, Swiss International Legal, Merrill Lynch, and HSBC.[146] Nassehi argues that the financial liberalization, championed by the IMF and the World Bank since the 1990s, added to Dubai's instability.[147] But a slack culture in the DFSA, weak regulation and institutions, has created serious gaps in governance. The appetite to attract global financiers has attracted Afghan warlords, Russian and Nigerian kleptocrats, Iranian sanctions busters, and East African gold smugglers. Although the

---

[143] *Dubai World*, 'Marine Terminals Overview', 1 December 2013: available at http://web.dpworld.com/marine-terminals/overview 1December2013

[144] *Dubai Statistics Center*, 2009, Statistical Year Book: online at: http://dsc.gov.ae/EN/Publications/Pages/PublicationsList.aspx?Publication 2009; M. Khamis, A. Senhadji, M. Hasan, F. Kumah, A. Prasad, and G. Sensenbrenner, 'Impact of the Global Financial Crisis in the Gulf Cooperation Council Countries and Challenges Ahead', International Monetary Fund: at http://www.imf.org/external/pubs/ft/dp/2010/dp1001.pdf.

[145] Pino Arlacchi, Executive Director of the United Nations Office for Drug Control and Crime Prevention, Address at the United Nations Convention Against Transnational Organized Crime, Palermo, December 2000.

[146] Dubai International Financial Centre, *Annual Review*, 2012.

[147] Ramin Nassehi, 'Haunted by Capital Inflows: How Hot Money from Abroad Fuelled UAE's Financial Crisis', *International Journal of Sustainable Human Development*, vol. 1, no. 2 (2013), pp. 76–83.

UAE had criminalized money laundering as early as 1987, it was only now responding seriously to World Bank requests for financial rules.[148]

Calls from scholars to monitor the FDI into Dubai were ignored in much of the literature as it came from all over the world. Dubai had a high dependence on FDI, in large part short-term loans. As argued above, capital market liberalization, advocated by the IMF and the World Bank since the 1990s, proved to be destabilizing.[149] The unsustainability of Dubai's ambitious plans for globalization in finance, in particular Islamic finance, produced the huge rise in debt and FDI inflows.[150] In December 2010, Morgan Stanley reported that direct government debt was almost 30 per cent of Dubai's GDP.

Dubai's FDI investment in finance rose from US$5,617 million in 2007 to US$12,716 million in 2011. The largest contributor was the United Kingdom at 21 per cent.[151] Dubai developed institutions in biotechnology with foreign firms, including Pfizer and several European and American groups. It established the Dubai Shopping Festival in 1996 and a range of exhibitions and conferences organized at the Dubai World Trade Centre, pushing for global acknowledgement. An IT project in the late 1990s and early 2000s brought Western Internet companies to Dubai.[152] But modernization through technology and industrial innovation attracted foreign flows of capital that were difficult to appraise and sustain in legitimate sectors. Dubai's property market was a magnet for tainted money. Many Russians facing international sanctions exploited the Dubai property market to launder money. But Sheik Maktoum did attempt to maintain business ethics through law, custom, theological understanding, and foreign exemplars, particularly American.

Dubai was one of the world's largest gold centres, dealing in gold from the conflict-riven areas of East and Central Africa. With its lax financial regulations, Dubai became a conduit for illicit financial transactions. Iran, with close commercial ties with Dubai, was often exploited by international criminal activities in the US and UK.[153]

At the same time, it was the governance system of Dubai that allowed economic liberalization. The Al Maktoum family has driven major projects,

---

[148] World Bank Logistic Performance Index, Global Ranking 2016; John A. Cassara, *Trade-based Money Laundering: The Next Frontier in International Money Laundering Enforcement* (New York: Wiley, 2016), pp. 100, 132; John S. Zdanowicz, 'Trade-based Money Laundering and Terrorist Financing', in *Transnational Financial Crime*, edited by Nikos Passas (London: Routledge, 2013).

[149] See also Paul Krugman, 'Dutch Tulips and Emerging Markets', *Foreign Affairs*, 1995, pp. 28–44.

[150] Al Shama, 'Sustainability of the Dubai Model of Economic Development', pp. 110, 198–9.

[151] Al Shama, 'Sustainability of the Dubai Model of Economic Development', p. 96.

[152] E. M. Rusli and V. G. Kopytoff, 'Investing Like it is 1999', *The New York Times*, 27 March 2011.

[153] Tatyana Gibbs, 'An Analysis of the Effectiveness of Anti Money Laundering and Counter Terrorist Funding Legislation and its Administration in the UAE', PhD thesis, Institute of Advanced Legal Studies, School of Advanced Study, University of London, March 2017.

expanding the Creek, building Jebel Ali Port, Dubai Internet City, Dubai Media City, and the Dubai Financial Centre. There was support for education for all, including women. The UAE has a high literacy rate (73.1) but just 43.5 per cent of women were in the labour market as opposed to 92.3 per cent of men. However, women in Dubai hold political positions as well as in the diplomatic services.[154]

Dubai and Its Role in Tackling Climate Change

Dubai is dominant on the eastern side of the Arabian Peninsula. It has a barren coastline and sand dunes and rugged mountains along the border with Oman. It faces a number of natural threats, rising sea levels, increased temperatures, and water scarcity. But Dubai adopted measures pledging direct intervention to reduce emissions through international collaboration and agreements, including the Kyoto Protocol and the Paris Agreement, aiming to produce 27 per cent of its energy from renewable sources by 2021.[155] Dubai is also committed to a reduction of its carbon footprint by 70 per cent and to use renewable energy for the production of 50 per cent of its electricity by 2050.[156]

Federal Law No. 24 of 1999 (Environmental Law) was the major environmental legislation of the UAE. It instituted a command-and-control culture for the implementation of climate change measures within a market-based programme. It employed sanctions and fines for non-compliance with its regulations. Ministerial Decree No. 98 of 2019, relating to the use of refuse-derived fuel, has a list of regulations relating to environmental protection.[157] Dubai has adopted a compulsory code relating to energy, water, waste, and detailed standards for construction material. All construction projects beginning from 2014 are subject to strict surveillance and rules.[158]

---

[154] Gender Inequality Index, 2012, compiled from United Nations Human Development Programme, International Human Development Indicators, 2013.

[155] In accordance with its National Determined Contribution: UAE 'Vision 2021: United Arab Emirates': www.vision2021.ae/en/national-agenda-2021/list/environment circle; UAE, 'Environment in Vision2021', https:// u.ae/en/information-and-services/environment-and-energy/environment-and-government-agenda.

[156] UAE Energy Strategy 2050: https:uae/en/about-the -uae/strategies-initiatives-and-awards/federal-governments-strategies-and-plans/uae-energy-strategy-2050=:text=The %20strategy%20aims%to% 20increase.AED%20700%20biillion%20by%202050.

[157] 'UAE Ministry of Climate Change and Environment: Legislation', in Georgios Dimitropoulos and Almas Lokhandwala, 'Addressing Climate Change in the MENA Region Through Regulatory Design: Instrument Choice Questions', in *Climate Change Law and Policy in the Middle East and North Africa Region*, edited by Damilola S. Olawuyi (Abingdon: Routledge, 2021), p. 71.

[158] Dubai Green Building Regulations: www.dewa.gov.ae/media/Files/Consultants %20and%20 Contractors/Green%20Building/GreenBuilding-Eng.ashx.

Another principle employed by the UAE was acknowledgement of market pressures for environmental regulation. The introduction of subsidies in the agricultural sector to encourage the use of modern technology led to a renaissance in environmental protection (see Figure 13.1). Regionally oriented organizations, such as Mubdala Capital and the Dubai Green Fund, to finance and support clean-tech, renewable energy, and green economy projects, generated dynamic environmental clusters for change. Mubdala Capital also installed Masdar, a 'future energy' company, initiated by Abu Dhabi. Masdar City is a low-carbon city with buildings made with low-carbon cement and 90 per cent of the aluminium is sourced from recycled materials.[159] Masdar has been active in research and design, and in the expansion of clean energy projects in the UAE and the MENA countries. The Energy Efficiency Standardization and Labelling Program (EESL) provides financial incentives for manufacturers of high-performance energy appliances. Utility corporations have been encouraged to reduce waste and reject the overconsumption culture in the UAE. The UAE introduced environmental taxes on lorries carrying mineral resources. Applying this tax solely on lorries is surprising in a country that has so far not imposed taxes on any sector.[160]

The UAE also collaborated with the Behavioural Insights Team (BIT) in the UK to develop its own culture of environmental behaviour and insights. Abu Dhabi introduced the 'Tarsheed' campaign to prompt a reduction in energy and water consumption, through slogans such as 'Power is a Privilege' and 'Water is a Privilege'.[161] Also significant is the EESL programme under which products carry labels of energy efficiency. The Estidama programme assists in developing construction, using three categories of building development: Pearl Community Rating System, the Pearl Building Rating System, and the Pearl Villa Rating System. From 2010, this rating system became mandatory.

---

[159] Masdar, 'The Source of Innovation and Sustainability-Investment and Leasing Opportunities at Masdar City': https://masdar.ae/media/corporate/downloads/media/mas-mc-brochure-2020.pdf.
[160] 'Environmental Tax Enacted for Fujairah Lorries', *The National*, 1 February 2016.
[161] Tarsheed: Rethink: www.tarsheedad.com/en-us/Pages/Homes.aspx.

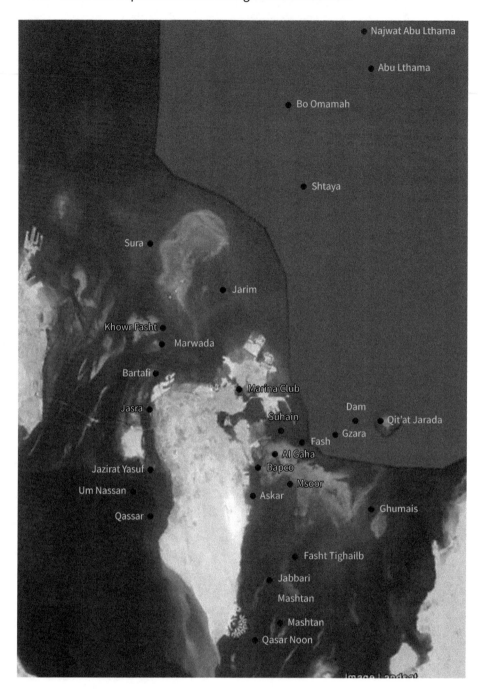

Figure 13.1 Sea sampling sites, 2016

Source: Kingdom of Bahrain, Supreme Council for Environment. The image illustrates the use of technology to determine the response to climate change.

Arabic–English Glossary

Note: The transliteration of Arabic words into the Roman script has followed the Library of Congress transliteration standard. For the sake of simplicity, Arabic words in the singular have been given an English 's' to denote the plural form. Words such as *sukuk*, which are often used in modern financial markets, are used according to custom. Arabic words which, according to the Oxford English Dictionary, have been borrowed into the English language have not been transliterated or italicized.

'ādat at-tujjār: practice of the merchant/trader

Amānah: trust, faithfulness

'Aqd: contract, covenant

arkān: fundamental components (of a contract)

'Arriya: loan

Ashab al-hadith: people of the hadith (traditions). Associated with the Mālikīs

Bāṭil: void (legal)

Bay': sale

Bay' al-'inah: double sale used to circumvent the prohibition of lending with interest

Bay' al-wafah:

Bay' ghai'ib: contract of sale for an absent thing or object

Commenda: an equity partnership (Latin version); similar to the muḍārabah

ḍarūrah: necessity, need

Dayn: debt

Faqīh/Fuqahā': Expert in Islamic jurisprudence (fiqh)

Fāsid: defective (legal)

Fatwa: legal opinion

Fiqh: Islamic jurisprudence

Fitra: the native ability to know of God's existence

Gharar: excessive risk/speculation

Hadith: narration of the words and deeds of the Prophet Muhammad ḥarām: forbidden

ḥawālah: transfer of debt

Hibah: gift

ḥīlah(pl.)/ḥiyal(sg.): legal stratagem

'Ibādāt: sphere of worship

Ibāhah: permissibility

Ijārah: lease

Ijārah muntahia bittamleek: financial lease

'Ijmā': scholarly consensus

Ijtihād: independent reasoning

Ikhtiyār: option

'illah: effective cause. The element utilized in establishing a connection between the
   holy sources, the Quran and Sunna, and a novel case requiring independent juristic
   reasoning (Ijtihād).

Irādah: human will

Istiḥsān: juridical or personal preference

Istiṣlaḥ: public benefit

Istiṣnā': contract of hire

Jāhilīyah: time of ignorance

Jahl: want of knowledge; ignorance

Ju'ālah: reward

Khultah: mixed type of partnership

Kitāb: book

Kitāb al-ḥiyal: book of ḥiyal

Madhhab/Madhāhib: schools of law (Sunni schools of law:Shāfi'i, Mālikī, Ḥanafī, and
   Ḥanbalī)

Makhraj/Makhārij: exit(s), also known as ḥiyal.

Makrūh: reprehensible

Maqāṣid al-sharia: objectives of the sharia

Maṣlaḥah: public interest

Maysir: gambling

Mu'ammalat: transactions

Muḍārabah: an equity partnership. Also known as muqarāḍah and qirāḍ.

Muḍārib: investment agent

Mujtahid: Islamic scholar

Murābaḥah: a sale with a mark-up (profit)

Mushārakah: an equity partnership based on principle of diminishing co-ownership

Naṣṣ: holy text

Nīyah: intention

Qāḍī: Islamic law judge

Qard Hasan: loan, a charitable loan (without interest)

Qaṣd: human intention

Qiyās: analogical reasoning (one of the four sources of Islamic law according to orthodox Sunni Islam)

Rabb al-māl: investor (a partner in the muḍārabah contract)

Ra'y: discretion (legal reasoning)

Ribā: usury, also known as interest

Ribā al-faḍl: ribā of excess

Ribā al-nasi'a: ribā by delay

Ribāwi: ribā-based; illicit

Sabab: cause

Ṣadaqa: voluntary contribution

ṣadd al-dharā'i': blocking the means (legal principle)

ṣaḥīḥ: valid (legal)

Ṣakk: cheque

Ṣakk/Sukuk: Islamic bond; when asset-backed is Islamic investment certificate

Salam: a forward sale

Shahāda: witness; the declaration by which a believer professes her belief in the Islamic faith

Shari'ah: literally, the way; Islamic law

Sharikah al-milk: partnership based on joint ownership

Sharikah al-wujūh: credit partnership

Shirkah/Sharikah: partnership

Shurūṭ: legal formularies; also conditions or appendages to contracts

Sukuk al-ijārah: Islamic securitization based on a lease

Sunna: the living tradition; the sayings and doings of the Prophet Muhammad (holy source)

Sūra: chapter

Takaful: Islamic insurance

Takhayyur: eclectic choice (legal)

Talāq: pronunciation of divorce (by the man)

Talfīq: patching (legal)

Taqlīd: conformity

Tawarruq: commonly used buy-back transaction used to generate cash/liquidity

'Umlah: commission

'urf: custom

Uṣūl al-fiqh: the principles of jurisprudence (methodology)

Wakālah: power of attorney/agency; investment contract in which agent represents investor(s)

Wakīl: agent

Zakāt: obligatory charitable contribution (Islamic law)

Bibliography

Archival Records

British Library, India Office Records (IOR)
Busheri Archive, Manama
Charles D. Belgrave, Personal Diaries, 1926–57
The National Archives (TNA), Kew
University of Exeter, Arab World Documentation Unit

Bahrain Official Publications

Bahrain Central Informatics Organization, 2001–2014
Bahrain Central Informatics Organization, 2011
Bahrain Central Informatics Organization (CIO), *Basic Results: Population, Housing, Buildings and Establishments Census*, 2002
Bahrain Central Informatics Organization, *Household Expenditure and Income Survey*
Bahrain Central Informatics Organization, *Population Statistics*, 2018
Bahrain Central Informatics Organization, *Report for Establishment Survey of Wages Structure and Distribution Survey*, 2006
Bahrain Central Informatics Organization, Results of Census 2010, table 13.08, 2011
Bahrain Centre for Human Rights, 2004
Bahrain Centre for Strategic International and Energy Studies, 'Economic Diversification, Competitiveness and the Role of SMEs: Challenges and Opportunities'
Bahrain Centre for Studies and Research, 2003
Bahrain Economic Development Board, 2011
Bahrain Economic Development Board, *Annual Reports*
Bahrain Economic Development Board, *Islamic Finance Report*, 2015
Bahrain Economic Development Board, Islamic Financial Services Industry, *Stability Report*, 2017, joint publication with World Bank
Bahrain Economic Development Board, 'Report by HE Mr. Khalid Al-Rumaihi', CEO, 2018
Bahrain Government Annual Reports, 1924–70, held in TNA FO 371/132893, cited in Fuccaro, Histories of City and State, pp. 210–11.
Bahrain Human Development Report 2018
Bahrain Independent Commission for Inquiry Report, 10 December 2011
Bahrain Information and Government Authority, 'Cumulative Growth Percentage by Sector of GDP, 2005–2017'
Bahrain, Ministry of Finance and National Economy, *Statistics of the Population Census*
Bahrain Ministry of Industry, Commerce and Tourism, 'SME Contributions in Percentage in Bahrain, 2017'
Bahrain National Museum, *Miscellaneous Archives of the Municipality of Manama, 1938–1963* (Manama)
Bahrain Ministry of Works, *Annual Report*
Bahrain Monetary Authority, *Insider Guidelines*, 2004

Central Bank of Bahrain, *Annual Report*

Central Bank of Bahrain, *Annual Trading Bulletin*

Central Bank of Bahrain, *Financial Sector Overview* (2015)

Central Bank of Bahrain, *Financial Sector Review*

Central Bank of Bahrain, *Financial Stability Report*

Central Bank of Bahrain, *Bahrain FinTech Bay Report*, 2019

Central Bank of Bahrain, *Insurance Market Review*

Central Bank of Bahrain, *Islamic Finance*

Central Bank of Bahrain, *Statistical Bulletin*

Central Bank of Bahrain, *The Review*

Gazette and Land Registration Department, Monthly Statistics, 1980–2009

Information and eGovernment Authority Bahrain, 'FDI Stocks in Bahrain from GCC Countries, 2009–2017'

King's Regulations Order in Council and Bahrain Regulations, 1913–1958 (London: HMSO, 1958)

Labour Market Regulation Authority, *Bahrain Labour Market Indicators*

Ministry of State for Cabinet Affairs, Directorate of Statistics, *The Population of Bahrain: Trends and Prospects* (January 1979)

Ministry of State for Legal Affairs, *Collection of Laws and Proclamations* (1977)

Persian Gulf Administration Reports 1873–1949 (Gerrards Cross: Archive Editions, 1986)

Other Official Publications

Central Bank of Kuwait, *The Kuwait Economy in Ten Years: Economic Report for the Period 1969–79*

FAO Committee on Food Security, *Price Volatility and Food Security: High Level Panel of Experts on Food Security* (Rome, 2011)

FAO, FAOSTAT, *The State of Agricultural Commodity Markets: High Food Prices and the Food Crisis: Experiences and Lessons Learned* (Rome: Food and Agriculture Organization, 2009)

FAO, *Near and Middle East and North Africa: Agriculture towards 2050: Prospects and Challenges* (Rome, 2008)

International Energy Agency, *Electricity Information*

International Energy Agency, *Energy Statistics of Non-OECD Countries*

International Energy Agency, *Natural Gas Information*

International Energy Agency, *Oil Information*

International Labour Organization, 'Women in Business and Management', 2016

International Labour Organization, *World Employment Report*, Geneva, 1998

International Monetary Fund, *Kingdom of Bahrain: Financial Stability Assessment, including Reports on the Observance of Standards and Codes on the Following Topics: Banking Supervision, Insurance Supervision, Securities Regulation, and Anti Money Laundering and Combatting the Financing of Terrorism.* IMF Country Report No. 06/91, March 2006

International Monetary Fund, *Regional Economic Outlook: Middle East and Central Asia*, October 2015

International Monetary Fund, Middle East and Central Asia Department, Washington, DC, 'Impact of the Global Financial Crisis on the Gulf Cooperation Council Countries and Challenges Ahead', 2010, prepared by May Khamis, Abdelhak Senhadji, Maher Hasan, Francis Kumah, Ananthakrishnan Prasad, and Gabriel Sensenbrenner

International Renewable Energy Agency, 'Renewable Energy Market Analysis' (IREA: Abu Dhabi, 2019)

Saudi Arabia Central Department of Statistics, *Social Statistics Labour Force Survey 2002* (Riyadh: Ministry of Economy and Planning, 2003)

Sawt al-Bahrayn: Majallah Adabiyyah wa Ijtima 'iyyah (Beirut: al-Mu'assasah al-'Arabiyyah li al-Dirasat wa al-Nashr, 4 vols., 2003)

UN Data, *National Accounts Main Aggregates Database*

UN High Commissioner for Human Rights (OHCHR), *Report of the Office of the UN High Commissioner for Human Rights on the Relationship between Human Rights and Climate Change*, UN Doc.A/HRC/10/61 (2009)

UNDP, *The Arab Human Development Report*, New York

UNDP, *Pathways to Sustainable Economic Growth in Bahrain*, 2018

UNESCO, *Global Monitoring Report on Education for 2010*, 'General Regional Overview: Arab Countries Path to Equality'

United Nations, *Responding to Globalization: Stock Market Networking for Regional Integration in the ESCWA Region*, 2003

United Nations Economic and Social Commission for Western Asia, *Food Security and Conflict in the ESCWA Region*, New York, 2010

United Nations Population Division, *World Population Prospects: The 2002 Revision* (New York: United Nations, 2003)

United States Department of State, Bureau of Democracy, Human Rights and Labor, *Country Reports on Human Rights Practices* (Washington, DC, 2002)

US Energy Information Administration, *Oil and Gas Journal*

US Geological Survey, *Minerals Yearbook*

World Bank Annual Report 2015 (Washington, DC)

World Bank, *Bahrain Current Economic Position and Prospects*, Report No. 2058, Washington, DC, 1978

World Bank, *Bahrain: The Requirements for Economic Diversification and Sustainability*, Report No. 11281-BH, Washington, DC, 1993

World Bank, *Improving Food Security in Arab Countries*, Washington, DC, 2009

World Bank, *Middle East and North Africa Economic Developments and Prospects: Navigating through the Global Recession* (Washington, DC: 2009)

World Bank, 'Reducing Vulnerability and Increasing Opportunity: Social Protection in the Middle East and North Africa', Washington, DC, 2002

World Bank, 'The Road Not Travelled: Education Reform in the Middle East and North Africa', World Development Indicators, Washington, DC, 2008

World Bank, MENA Development Report, *Gender and Development in the Middle East and North Africa* (Washington, DC, 2004)

World Bank, MENA Development Report, *Unlocking the Employment Potential in the Middle East and North Africa* (Washington, DC, 2004)

Secondary Works

Aassouli, Dalal, 'Mobilizing and Leveraging Islamic Climate Finance in the MENA Region: The Potential Role of National Green Participative Banks', in *Climate Change Law and Policy in the Middle East and North Africa Region*, edited by Damilola S. Olawuyi (London: Routledge, 2022)

Abahussain, A., A. El-Kholei, and M. al'Aatim, *Assessing the Level of Knowledge and Awareness of the Climate Change Phenomenon in the Kingdom of Bahrain: Proposed Awareness Plan* (Bahrain: Arabian Gulf University, 2018)

Abdelbaki, Hisham H., 'An Analysis of Income Inequality and Education Inequality in Bahrain', *Modern Economy*, vol. 3, no. 5 (2012)

Abdelbaki, Hisham Handal, 'Causality Relationship between Macroeconomic Variables and Stock Market Development: Evidence from Bahrain', *International Journal of Business and Finance Research*, vol. 7, no. 1 (2013)

Abdulghaffar, M., O. Al-Ubaydli, and O. Mahmood, 'The Malfunctioning of the Gulf Cooperation Council Single Market: Features, Causes, and Remedies', *Middle Eastern Finance and Economics, no.* 19, pp. 54–67 (2013)

Abdullah, Mohammad, 'Waqf, Sustainable Development Goals (SDGs) and Maqasid-al-Shariah', *International Journal of Social Economics*, vol. 45, no. 1 (2018)

Abido, M., and S. Al-Jeneid, *Mangroves Vulnerability to Climate Change: Bahrain Case Study* (Bahrain: Arabian Gulf University, 2018)

Abouelnaga, M., 'Why the MENA Region Needs to Better Prepare for Climate Change', *Atlantic Council Blog*, 7 May (2019)

Abrahamian, Ervand, 'The Crowd in Iranian Politics 1905–1953', *Past and Present*, vol. 41, no. 1 (1968)

Abrahart, Alan, Iqbal Kaur, and Zafiris Tzannatos, 'Government Employment and Active Labour Market Policies in MENA in a Comparative International Context', in *Employment Creation and Social Protection in the Middle East and North Africa*, edited by Heba Handoussa and Zafiris Tzannatos (Cairo: AUC Press, 2002)

Acemoglu, D., and J. Robinson, 'A Theory of Political Transitions', *American Economic Review*, vol. 91 (2001)

Acemoglu, D., and J. Robinson, *Economic Origins of Dictatorship and Democracy* (New York: Cambridge University Press, 2006)

Adger, W. N., 'Scales of Governance and Environmental Justice for Adaptation and Mitigation of Climate Change', *Journal of International Development*, vol. 13, no. 7, pp. 921–31, (2001)

A-Nassar, W., S. Neelamani, K. Al-Salem, and H. Al-Dashti, 'Feasibility of Offshore Wind Energy as an Alternative Source for the State of Kuwait', *Energy*, vol.169, pp. 783–96, 15 February (2019)

Al-Baharna, Husain M., *British Extra-Territorial Jurisdiction in the Gulf 1913–1971* (Slough: Archive Editions, 1998)

al-Bakir, *Abd al-Rahman, Min al-Bahrayn ila al-manfa* (Beirut: Dar al Kuniz al-Arabiyyah, 2nd edition, 2002)

Al-Hasan, Abdullah, May Khamis and Nada Oulidi, 'A Topography and Analysis of the GCC Banking Systems', IMF Working Paper, forthcoming

Al-Hasan, Hasan T., 'Sectarianism meets the Arab Spring: TGONU a Broad-Based Sunni Movement Emerges in Bahrain', *Arabian Humanities*, vol. 4 (2015)

Al Hassan, O., 'Khalifa bin Salman: He Chose Achievements, so the Prize Chose Him', *Bahrain News Agency*, 28 April 2007

Al-Ikhwan al-Muslimun fi-L-Khalij, *The Muslim Brotherhood in the Gulf* (Dubai: Al-Mesbar Studies and Research Centre, 2014)

Al-Jamri, M., 'Shia and the State in Bahrain: Integration and Tension', *Alternative Politics*, special issue no. 1, pp. 1–24, (November 2010)

Al-Jayyousi, O., Y. Al-Sultanny, S. Al-Mahamid, A. Mirzal, and A. Bugawa, *Technology Transfer of Green Technology—Opportunities and Barriers for Technology Transfer to Address Climate Change Risks in Bahrain*, 2018

Al-Maamary, H. M., H. A. Kazem, and M. T. Chaichan, 'The Impact of Oil Price Fluctuations on Common Renewable Energies in GCC countries', *Renewable and Sustainable Energy Reviews*, vol. 75 (C), pp. 989–1007, (2017)

Al-Mubarak, Muneer Mohamed Saeed, and Allam Mohammed Mousa Hamdan, 'The Impact of Corporate Governance on Market Capitalization: Evidence from Bahrain Bourse', *Corporate Ownership and Control Journal*, vol. 13, no. 3 (2016)

Al-Najjar, S., 'Women Migrant Domestic Workers in Bahrain', International Migration Papers, 47, International Migration Programme, International Labour Office, Geneva, 2002

Al-Rasheed, Madawi (ed.), *Transnational Connections and the Arab Gulf* (London: Routledge, 2005)

Al-Sayed, 'Territorial and Coastal Usurpation: Presentation to the Secretariat and Four Associations Forum', 10 November 2005: data compiled from Central Informatics Organization, available at http://www.cio.gov.bh/CIO_ARA/default.aspx

AlShehabi, Omar, 'Radical Transformations and Radical Contestations: Bahrain's Spatial Demographic Revolution', *Middle East Critique*, vol. 23, no. 1 (2014)

AlShehabi, Omar, 'Rootless Hubs: Migration, Urban Commodification and the "Right to the City" in the GCC', in *Transit States: Labour, Migration and Citizenship in the Gulf*, edited by Abdulhadi Khalaf, Omar AlShehabi, and Adam Hanieh (London: Pluto Press, 2015)

AlShehabi, Omar, 'Contested Modernity: Divided Rule and the Birth of Sectarianism, Nationalism and Absolutism in Bahrain', *British Journal of Middle Eastern Studies*, vol. 44, no. 3 (2017)

Al Tamimi and Company's Corporate Structuring Team, Eman Al Isa, Report, March 2018

Al-Ubaydli, O., and A. Jones, 'GCC Economic Integration: Opportunities and Challenges', *Bahrain National Human Development Report*, Background Paper, 2018

Al-Yousef, A., 'An Evaluation of Bahrain's Major Industries and Their Future Prospects', in *Bahrain and the Gulf*, edited by J. B. Nugent and T. H. Thomas (London: Croom Helm, 1985)

Al-Zumai, Fahad, 'Rentier States and Economic Regulation Infrastructure: Kuwait as a Case Study', *Journal of Law*, vol. 31, no. 3 (2007)

Al-Zumai, Fahad, and Mohammed Al-Wasami, '2008 Financial Crisis and Islamic Finance: An Unrealised Opportunity', *International Journal for the Semiotics of Law*, vol. 29 (2016)

Alharbi, Fahad Radhi, and Denes Csala, 'Gulf Cooperation Council Countries' Climate Change Mitigation Challenges and Exploration of Solar and Wind Energy Resource Potential', *Applied Sciences MDPI*, 2021

Ali, Salman Syed, *Islamic Banking in the MENA Region*, World Bank and Islamic Development Bank, Islamic Research and Training Institute, February 2011

Alnaser, N. W., R. Flanagan, and W. E. Alnaser, 'Potential of Making-over to Sustainable Buildings in the Kingdom of Bahrain', *Energy and Buildings*, vol. 40 (2008)

Alnaser, W. E., and N. W. Alnaser, 'The Status of Renewable Energy in the GCC Countries', *Renewable and Sustainable Energy Reviews*, vol. 15, no. 6, pp. 3074–98, (2011)

Alnaser, W. E., and N. W. Alnaser, 'The Impact of the Rise of Using Solar Energy in GCC Countries', *Renewable Energy and Environmental Sustainability*, vol. 4, no. 7, (2019)

Alnaser, W. E., N. W. Alnaser, and I. Batarseh, 'Bahrain's BAPCO, 5MWp PV Grid-Connected Solar Project', *International Journal of Power and Renewable Energy Systems*, vol. 1 (2014)

Alves, Paulo F., 'The Puzzle of Corporate Control', *International Research Journal of Finance and Economics*, no. 99, pp. 53–63, (2012)

Amihud, Yakov, Haim Mendelson, and Lasse Heje Pedersen, 'Liquidity and Asset Prices', *Foundation and Trends in Finance*, vol. 1, no. 4 (2005)

An-Na'im, 'Abdullahi Aḥmed, *Islam and the Secular State: Negotiating the Future of Shari'a* (Cambridge, MA: Harvard University Press, 2009)

Andersen, Roy R., Robert F. Seibert, Jon G. Wagner, *Politics and Change in the Middle East: Sources of Conflict and Accommodation* (Hoboken, NJ: Prentice Hall, 6th edition, 2001)

Anderson, Lisa, 'Absolutism and the Resilience of Monarchy in the Middle East', *Political Science Quarterly*, vol. 106, no. 1 (1991)

Annual Report of Mumtalakat, 2010 to December 2014, pp. 108–9

Ansani, A., and V. Daniele, 'About a Revolution: The Economic Motivations of the Arab Spring', *International Journal of Development and Conflict*, vol. 3, no. 3 (2012)

Appadurai, Arjun, *Modernity at Large: Cultural Dimensions of Globalization* (Minneapolis, MN: Minneapolis University Press, 2005)

Archer, Simon, and Brandon Davies, 'Islamic Collective Investment Schemes', in *Islamic Capital Markets and Products: Managing Capital and Liquidity Requirements under Basel III*, edited by Simon Archer and Rifaat Ahmed Abdel Karim (Chichester: Wiley, 2018)

Archer, Simon, and Rifaat Ahmed Abdel Karim, 'Liquidity Risk Management and High Liquid Assets', in *Islamic Capital Markets and Products: Managing Capital and Liquidity Requirements under Basel III*, edited by Simon Archer and Rifaat Ahmed Abdel Karim (Chichester: Wiley, 2018)

Archer, Simon, Brandon Davies, and Rifaat Ahmed Abdel Karim, 'Overview of the Islamic Capital Market', in *Islamic Capital Markets and Products: Managing Capital and Liquidity Requirements under Basel III*, edited by Simon Archer and Rifaat Ahmed Abdel Karim (Chichester: Wiley, 2018)

Arezki, R., and M. Bruckner, 'Food Prices, Conflict, and Democratic Change', University of Adelaide, Department of Economics, Research Paper no. 2011-04, 2011

Ariffin, Noraini Mohd, and Salina Hj. Kassim, 'Liquidity Risk Management and Financial Performance of Islamic Banks: Empirical Evidence', in *Islamic Banking and Financial Crisis: Reputation, Stability, and Risks*, edited by Habib Ahmed, Mehmet Asutay, and Rodney Wilson (Edinburgh: Edinburgh University Press, 2014)

Arjomand, Said Amir, *The Turban for the Crown* (New York: Oxford University Press, 1988)

Asif, M., 'Growth and Sustainability Trends in the Building Sector in the GCC Region with Particular Reference to the KSA and UAE', *Renewable and Sustainable Energy Reviews*, vol. 55, pp. 1267–73, (2016)

Asif, Sudais, 'The Halal and Haram Aspect of Cryptocurrencies in Islam', *Journal of Islamic Banking and Finance*, vol. 35, no. 2 (2018)

Asiri, Batool K., and Mohamed A. Abdalla, 'Economic Growth and Stock Market Development in Bahrain', *Journal of Applied Finance and Banking*, vol. 5, no. 2 (2015)

A-Tajir, Mahdi Abdalla, *Bahrain 1920–45: Britain, the Shaykh and the Administration* (London: Croom Helm, 1987), pp. 8, 80–3

Ayoub, Sherif, *Derivatives in Islamic Finance: Examining the Market Risk Management Framework* (Edinburgh: Edinburgh University Press, 2014)

Ayres, Ian, and Jonathan R. Macey, 'Institutional and Evolutionary Failure and Economic Development in the Middle East', *Yale Journal of International Law*, vol. 30 (2005)

Aziz, Talib, 'The Role of Muhammad Baqir al-Sadr in Shii Political Activism in Iraq from 1958 to 1980', *International Journal of Middle East Studies*, vol. 25, no. 2 (1993)

Bacha, Obiyathulla Ismath, and Daud Vicary Abdullah, 'Malaysia's Islamic Capital Markets—a Case Study', in *Islamic Capital Markets and Products: Managing Capital and Liquidity Requirements under Basel III*, edited by Simon Archer and Rifaat Ahmed Abdel Karim (Chichester: Wiley, 2018)

Bachellerie, Imen Jeridi, *Renewable Energy in the GCC Countries: Resources, Potential and Prospects* (Jeddah: Gulf Research Center, 2012)

Baer, Gabriel, *Studies in the Social History of Modern Egypt* (Chicago, IL: Chicago University Press, 1969)

'Bahrain 2018 Trafficking in Persons Report', US Department of State, 29 July 2018

Bahrain Central Informatics Organization, 2011, results of census, 2010

Bahrain, 'Sukuk Perceptions and Forecast Study, 2017', p. 25

Bahrain Bourse report 2010

Bahrain Bourse Report, December 2016

'Bahrain Development Bank Launches $100 Million Venture Capital Fund', *Trade Arabia*, 10 May 2018

Bahrain Economic Development Board, 'Bahrain Creates History as First Nation to Enact UNICTRAL Model Law on Electronic Transferable Records', 16 January 2019

Bahrain Economic Development Board, 'Information and Communications Technology', 2018

Bahrain Family Business Association, *Assessment of Family Business Enterprises in the Kingdom of Bahrain*, 2010

Bahrain FinTech Bay Report, 2018

Bahrain Human Development Report 2019, 'Inequalities in Human Development in the 21st Century: A Briefing Note on the 2019 Human Development Report', pp. 5–6.

Bahrain Ministry of Labour and Bahrain Centre for Studies and Research, Report, 2004

Bahrain Ministry of Labour and Bahrain Centre for Studies and Research, *Labour Force Survey*, November 2004

Bahrain National Oil and Gas Authority, Reports, 2005–2015

Bahrain National Vision 2030: www.bahrainedb.com/en/about/Pages/economic%20 vision%202,030.aspx.

Bahrain Petroleum Company, *The BAPCO Story* (Manama, n.d.)

Bahrain Tourism and Exhibitions Authority and the World Tourism Organization; the Nationality Passports and Residence Affairs Directorate

'Bahrain Upgrades Existing Tourism Infrastructure to Meet Demand', Oxford Business Group on Bahrain, 2018, pp. 1–2.

Bahrain's Second National Communication under the United Nations Framework Convention on Climate Change, p. 30

Bahrain's Third National Communication under the United Nations Framework Convention on Climate Change, 2020, pp. 1–2

Bahri, Luayy, 'The Opposition in Bahrain: A Bellwether for the Gulf', *Middle East Policy*, vol. 5, no. 2 (1997)

Bahri, Luayy, 'The Socio-Economic Foundations of the Shi'ite Opposition in Bahrain', *Mediterranean Quarterly*, vol. 11, no. 3 (2000)

Baldwin-Edwards, M., 'Immigration and Labour Markets in the GCC Countries: National Patterns and Trends, Kuwait', Working Paper No. 15, Programme on Development, Governance and Globalization in the Gulf States, London School of Economics, 2011

Bales, Kevin, *Disposable People: New Slavery in the Global Economy* (Berkeley, CA: University of California Press, 2004)

Bales, Kevin, *Understanding Global Slavery: A Reader* (Berkeley, CA: University of California Press, 2005)

Ballantyne, William, *Legal Development in Arabia* (London: Graham and Trotman, 1980)

Balli, F. S. A., and R. Louis, 'Sectoral Equity Returns and Portfolio Diversification Opportunities across the GCC Region', *Journal of International Financial Markets, Institutions and Money*, vol. 25 (2013)

Balz, Killian, 'Shari'a Risk? How Islamic Finance has Transformed Islamic Contract Law', Islamic Legal Studies Program, Harvard Law School, Occasional Publications 9, September 2008.

Bank for International Settlements, 'Cryptocurrencies: Looking Beyond the Hype', BIS Annual Economic Report, 2018

Barberis, Nicholas, Ming Huang and Tano Santos, 'Prospect Theory and Asset Prices', *Quarterly Journal of Economics*, vol. 116 (2001)

Barro, Robert, and Jong-Wha Lee, 'International Data on Educational Attainment: Updates and Implications', Centre for International Development, Working Paper No. 42, Harvard University, 2000

Barro, Robert, and Jong-Wha Lee, 'A New Dataset of Educational Attainment in the World, 1950–2010', NBER Working Paper No. 15902, 2010

Bartlett, Christopher, and Sumantra Ghoshal, *Managing Across Borders: The Transnational Solution* (Cambridge, MA: Harvard University Press, 1989)

Basher, Syed Abul, and Perry Sadorsky, 'Hedging Emerging Market Stock Prices with Oil, Gold, VIX and Bonds: A Comparison between DCC, ADCC, and Go-Garch', *Energy Economics*, vol. 54 (2016)

Baskin, Jonathan Barron, 'The Development of Corporate Financial Markets in Britain and the US 1600–1914: Overcoming Asymmetric Information', *Business History Review*, vol. 62, no. 2 (1988)

Bayat, Asef, *Life as Politics: How Ordinary People Change the Middle East* (Stanford, CA: Stanford University Press 2010)

Bayat, Asef, 'Plebeians of the Arab Spring', *Current Anthropology*, vol. 56 (2015)

Bayly, C. A., *The Birth of the Modern World, 1780–1914* (Oxford: Blackwell, 2004)

Beck, Thorsten, Asli Demirgüç-Kunt, and Ouarda Merrouche, 'Islamic Banking vs. Conventional Banking: Business Model, Efficiency and Stability', World Bank Policy Research Working Paper No. WPS5446, 2010

Beiling, W. A., 'Recent Developments in Labor Relations in Bahrayn', *Middle East Journal*, vol. 13, no. 2 (1959)

Bel-Air, Francoise De, 'Demography, Migration and the Labour Market in Bahrain', Gulf Research Center and Migration Policy Centre, European University Institute, GLMM-EN-No. 6, 2015

Belgrave, C. D., *Personal Column* (London: Hutchinson, 1960)

Belgrave, J. H. D., *Welcome to Bahrain*, 3rd edition (London: Augustan Press, 1957); 5th edition (London: Augustan Press, 1965)

Belleflamme, P., T. Lambert, and A. Schwienbacher, 'Crowdfunding: Tapping the Right Crowd', *Journal of Business Venturing*, vol. 2, no. 5 (2014)

Bellin, E., 'The Robustness of Authoritarianism in the Middle East: Exceptionalism in Comparative Perspective', *Comparative Politics*, vol. 36, no. 2 (2004)

Benton, Laura, *Law and Colonial Cultures: Legal Regimes in World History, 1400–1900* (Cambridge: Cambridge University Press, 2002)

Beny, N. L., 'A Comparative Empirical Investigation of Agency and Market Theories of Insider Trading', University of Michigan Legal Working Paper Series, 2004

Berkowitz, D., K. Pistor, and J. F. Richard, 'Economic Development, Legality and the Transplant Effect', *European Economic Review*, vol. 47 (2003)

Bertelsen, Rasmus Gjedsso, Neem Noori, and Jean-Marc Rickli (ed.), *Strategies of Knowledge Transfer for Economic Diversification in the Arab States of the Gulf* (Berlin: Gerlach Press, 2018)

Beschloss, Afsaneh, and Mina Mashayekhi (Rock Creek), 'A Greener Future for Finance: Green Bonds Offer Lessons for Sustainable Finance', *Finance and Development: The Economics of Climate*, IMF F&D, December 2019

BH/CIO 2011, *Results of Census 2010*

Bhide, A., 'The Hidden Costs of Stock Market Liquidity', *Journal of Financial Economics*, vol. 34 (1993)

Bi, Farmida, 'AAOIFI Statement on Sukuk and Its Implications', Norton Rose Fulbright, (September 2008)

BIS Consolidated Banking Assets

Bizri, Omar F., *Science, Technology, Innovation and Development in the Arab Countries* (London: Academic Press, 2018)

Black, F., and M. Scholes, 'The Pricing of Options and Corporate Liabilities', *Journal of Political Economy*, vol. 81, no. 3, pp. 637–54, (1973)

Blackaby, Nigel, Constantine Partasides, Alan Redfern, and Martin Hunter, *Redfern and Hunter on International Arbitration* (Oxford: Oxford University Press, 2015)

Blanchflower, David G., 'Self-employment in OECD Countries', NBER Working Paper No. 7486, Cambridge, MA, 2000

Blaydes, Lisa, *Elections and Distributive Politics in Mubarak's Egypt* (Cambridge: Cambridge University Press, 2011)

Bodansky, Daniel, 'Climate Change: Transnational Legal Order or Disorder?', in *Transnational Legal Orders*, edited by Terence C. Halliday and Gregory Shaffer (Cambridge: Cambridge University Press, 2015)

Bodansky, Daniel, 'The Paris Climate Change Agreement: A New Hope?', *American Journal of International Law*, vol. 110, no. 2 (2016)

Bohme, Rainer, Nicolas Christin, Benjamin Edelman, and Tyler Moore, 'Bitcoin: Economics, Technology, and Governance', *Journal of Economic Perspectives*, vol. 29, no. 2 (2015)

Bolton, P., and E. L. Von Thadden, 'Blocks, Liquidity, and Corporate Control', *Journal of Finance*, vol. 53, no. 1 (1998)

Bouri, Elie, 'Oil Volatility Shocks and the Stock Markets of Oil Importing MENA Economies: A Tale from the Financial Crisis', *Energy Economics*, vol. 51 (2015)

Bowen, John R., 'How Could English Courts Recognize Shariah', *University of St Thomas Law Journal*, vol. 7, no. 3, pp. 411–35, (2010)

Bradbury, Danny, 'Anti-Theft Bitcoin Tracking Proposals Divide Bitcoin Community', *Coindesk*, 15 November 2013

Bratton Jr., W., 'The Nexus of Contracts Corporation: A Critical Appraisal', *Cornell Law Review*, vol. 74 (1989)

Braudel, Fernand, *The Perspective of the World: Civilization and Capitalism, 15th to 18th Century* (New York: HarperCollins, 1986)

Braudel, Fernand, *Civilization and Capitalism, 15th–18th Century, Volume 2: The Wheels of Commerce* (Berkeley, CA: University of California Press, 1992)

Braverman, H., *Labour and Monopoly Capital: The Degradation of Work in the Twentieth Century* (New York: Monthly Review Press, 1974)

Breisinger, Clemens, Olivier Ecker, Perrihan Al-Riffai, Yu Bingxin, *Beyond the Arab Awakening: Policies and Investments for Poverty Reduction and Food Security* (Washington, DC: IFPRI, 2012)

'A Brief Introduction to Comparative Law', SOAS website 2018

Brioschi, F., L. Buzzacchi, and M. Colombo, 'Risk Capital Financing and the Separation of Ownership and Control in Business Groups', *Journal of Banking and Finance*, vol. 13 (1989)

Brockman, P., and D. Y. Chung, 'Investor Protection and Firm Liquidity', *Journal of Finance*, vol. 58, no. 2 (2003)

Brown, Ian, *A Colonial Economy in Crisis: Burma's Rice Cultivators and the World Depression of the 1930s* (Abingdon: Routledge, 2005)

Brown, Ian, *Burma's Economy in the Twentieth Century* (Cambridge: Cambridge University Press, 2013)

Brown, M., 'Projects into 2020: PPP Leads the Way', ALTamimi & Company, 31 January 2020, p. 49

Brown, Nathan J., *The Rule of Law in the Arab World: Courts in Egypt and the Gulf* (New York: Cambridge University Press, 1997)

Brown, Nathan J., *Constitutions in a Non-constitutional World: Arab Basic Laws and the Prospects for Accountable Government* (Albany, NY: SUNY Press, 2001)

Brown, Rajeswary Ampalavanar, 'Capitalism and Islam: Arab Business Groups and Capital Flows in South East Asia', in *Remaking Management: Between Global and Local*, edited by Chris Smith, Brendan McSweeney, and Robert Fitzgerald (Cambridge; New York: Cambridge University Press, 2008)

Brown, Rajeswary Ampalavanar, 'Islamic Endowments and the Land Economy in Singapore: The Genesis of an Ethical Capitalism, 1830–2007', *South East Asia Research*, vol. 16, no. 3 (2008)

Brown, Rajeswary Ampalavanar, *Islam in Modern Thailand: Faith, Philanthropy, and Politics* (London: Routledge, 2014)

Brown, Rajeswary Ampalavanar, *The Chinese and Indian Corporate Economies: A Comparative History of Their Search for Economic Renaissance and Globalization* (Abingdon: Routledge, 2017)

Browser, C. N., and J. K. Sharpe, 'International Arbitration and the Islamic World: The Third Phase', *American Journal of International Law*, vol. 97 (2003)

Brumberg, Daniel, 'The Trap of Liberalized Autocracy', *Journal of Democracy*, vol. 13, no. 4 (2002)

Brumberg, Daniel, 'Transforming the Arab World's Protection-Racket Politics', *Journal of Democracy*, vol. 24, no. 3 (2013)

Brunnermeier, Markus, 'Deciphering the Liquidity and Credit Crunch of 2007–2008', *Journal of Economic Perspectives*, vol. 23, no. 1 (2009)

Brunnermeier, Markus, and L. H. Pedersen, 'Market Liquidity and Funding Liquidity', *Review of Financial Studies*, vol. 22, no. 6 (2009)

Burdett, Anita L. P., *Records of the Persian Gulf Pearl Fisheries 1857–1962* (London: Archive Editions, 1995)

Burke, Edmund, 'Towards a History of Urban Collective Action in the Middle East: Continuities and Change 1750–1980', in *Etat, ville et mouvements sociaux au Magreb et au Moyen-Orient/Urban Crises and Social Movements in the Middle East*, edited by Kenneth Brown, Bernard Hourcade, Michele Jole, Claude Liauzu, Peter Sluglett, Sami Zubalda (Paris: L'Harmattan, 1989)

Buterin, V., 'Visions Part 1: The Value of Blockchain Technology', https:/blog.ethereum.org/2015/04/13/visions-part-1-the-value-of-blockchain-technology/

Campante, Filipe R., and Davin Chor, 'Why was the Arab World Poised for Revolution? Schooling, Economic Opportunities, and the Arab Spring', *Journal of Economic Perspectives*, vol. 26, no. 2 (2012)

Carhart, M. M., 'On Persistence of Mutual Fund Performance', *Journal of Finance*, vol. 52 no. 1 (1997)

Carmichael, J., and M. Pomerleano, *The Development and Regulation of Non-Bank Financial Institutions* (Washington, DC: World Bank, 2002)

Carter, Robert A., *Sea of Pearls: Seven Thousand Years of the Industry that Shaped the Gulf* (London: Arabian Publishing, 2012)

Casey, Michael, Jonah Crane, Gary Gensler, Simon Johnson, and Neha Narula, 'The Impact of Blockchain Technology on Finance: A Catalyst for Change', International Center for Monetary and Banking Studies, Center for Economic Policy Research, 2018

Casey, Michael J., 'Crypto Winter is Here and We Only Have Ourselves to Blame', Coindesk.com, 3 December 2018

Cassara, John A., *Trade-based Money Laundering: The Next Frontier in International Money Laundering Enforcement* (New York: Wiley, 2016)

Casson, Mark, *Enterprise and Competitiveness: A Systems View of International Business* (New York: Oxford University Press, 1990)

Casson, Mark, *The Entrepreneur: An Economic Theory* (Oxford: Oxford University Press, 1991)

Casson, Mark, 'The Economics of Ethical Leadership', in *The Role of Business Ethics in Economic Performance*, edited by Ian Jones and Michael Pollitt (Basingstoke: Palgrave Macmillan, 1998)

Central Bank of Bahrain Rulebook, vol. 2, Islamic Banks, Thomson Reuters (2015)

Chakrabarty, Dipesh, *Rethinking Working-Class History: Bengal 1890–1940* (Princeton, NJ: Princeton University Press, 1989)

Chakrabarty, Dipesh, 'Fifty Years of E. P. Thompson's The Making of the English Working Class', *Economic and Political Weekly*, 21 December 2013

Chandavarkar, Raj, 'The Making of the Working Class: E. P. Thompson and Indian History', in *Mapping Subaltern Studies and the Postcolonial*, edited by Vinayak Chaturvedi (London: Verso, 2000)

Chandler, Alfred D., *Scale and Scope: Dynamics of Industrial Capitalism* (Cambridge, MA: Harvard University Press, 1990)

Chen, X., J. Harford, and L. Kai, 'Monitoring: Which Institutions Matter?', *Journal of Financial Economics*, vol. 86 (2007)

Choi, Stephen J., 'Law, Finance and Path Dependence: Developing Strong Securities Markets', *Texas Law Review*, vol. 80 (2002)

Christelow, Allan, 'The Transformation of the Muslim Court System in Colonial Algeria: Reflections on the Concept of Autonomy', in *Islamic Law: Social and Historical Contexts*, edited by Aziz Al-Azmeh (London: Routledge, 1988)

Cizakca, Murat, 'Awqaf in History and its Implications for Modern Islamic Economics', *Islamic Economic Studies*, vol. 6, no. 1 (1998)

Cizakca, Murat, *A History of Philanthropic Foundations: The Islamic World from the Seventh Century to the Present* (Istanbul: Bogazici University Press, 2000)

Cizakca, Murat, *Islamic Capitalism and Finance: Origins, Evolution and the Future* (Cheltenham: Edward Elgar, 2011)

Cochrane, J. H., 'The Dog that Did Not Bark: A Defense of Return Predictability', *Review of Financial Studies*, vol. 21 (2007)

Coffee Jr., John, 'The Rise of Dispersed Ownership: The Roles of Law and the State in the Separation of Ownership and Control', *Yale Law Journal*, vol. 111 (2001)

Cole, Juan R. I., 'Of Crowds and Empires: Afro Asian Riots and European Expansion 1857–1882', in *States of Violence*, edited by Fernando Coronil and Julie Skurski (Ann Arbor, MI: University of Michigan Press, 2006)

Cole, Juan R. I., 'Rival Empires of Trade and Immami Shi'ism in Eastern Arabia, 1300–1800', *International Journal of Middle East Studies*, vol. 19, no. 3 (1987)

Cole, Juan R. I., *Roots of North India: Shi'ism in Iran and Iraq: Religion and State in Awadh, 1722–1859* (Berkeley, CA: University of California Press, 1980)

Cole, Juan R. I., *Sacred Space and Holy War: The Politics and History of Shi'ite Islam* (London: I. B. Tauris, 2002)

Collins, Lawrence, *Dicey, Morris and Collins on the Conflict of Laws*, Vol. 11 (London: Sweet and Maxwell, 2006)

Commins, David Dean, 'Wahhabis, Sufis and Salafis in Early Twentieth Century Damascus', in *Guardians of Faith in Modern Times: 'Ulama' in the Middle East*, edited by Meir Hatina (Leiden: Brill, 2009)

Convention on Biological Diversity, 2016

Cook, Michael, *Commanding Right and Forbidding Wrong in Islamic Thought* (Cambridge: Cambridge University Press, 2000)

Cooke, P., and K. Morgan, *The Associational Economy: Firms, Regions and Innovation* (Oxford: Oxford University Press, 1998)

Coombe, W., and J. Melki, 'Global Media and Brand Dubai', *Place Branding and Public Diplomacy*, vol. 8, no. 1 (2012)

Cooper, Frederick, 'Work, Class and Empire: An African Historian's Retrospective on E. P. Thompson', *Social History*, vol. 20, no 2 (1995)

Cottrell, Alvin J., C. Edmund Bosworth, R. Michael Burrell, Keith McLachlan, and Roger M. Savory, *The Persian Gulf States: A General Survey* (Baltimore, MD: John Hopkins University Press, 1980)

Crecelius, Daniel, 'The Waqf of Muhammad Bey Abu Al-Dhahab in Historical Perspective', *International Journal of Middle East Studies*, vol. 23, no. 1 (1991)

Crone, Patricia, *Meccan Trade and the Rise of Islam* (Oxford: Basil Blackwell, 1987)

Crystal, Jill, *Oil and Politics in the Gulf: Rulers and Merchants in Kuwait and Qatar* (Cambridge: Cambridge University Press, 1995)

Darwiche, Fida, *The Gulf Stock Exchange Crash: The Rise and Fall of Souq al-Manakh* (London: Croom Helm, 1986)

Davidson, Christopher, *Dubai: The Vulnerability of Success* (New York: Columbia University Press, 2008)

Davidson, Sinclair, Primavera De Filippi, and Jason Potts, 'Economics of Blockchain', https:archives-ouvertes.fr/hal-01382002 submitted 15 October 2016

Davies, Brandon, 'Eligible Capital and Capital Instruments', in *Islamic Capital Markets and Products: Managing Capital and Liquidity Requirements under Basel III*, edited by Simon Archer and Rifaat Ahmed Abdel Karim (Chichester: Wiley, 2018)

Demertzis, Maria, and Guntram B. Wolff, 'The Economic Potential and Risks of Crypto Assets: Is a Regulatory Framework Needed?', *Bruegel Policy Contribution*, no. 14 (September 2018)

Demertzis, Maria, Silva Merler, and Guntram Wolff, 'Capital Markets Union and the Fin Tech Opportunity', *Policy Contribution*, no. 22 (September 2017)

Denning, S., 'How do you Change an Organization Culture', *Forbes*, vol. 40 (2011)

Denton Wilde Sapte, 'Recent Decisions on Islamic Finance Transactions in Bank Briefings', Denton Wilde Sapte Law Office (April 2004)

Deringil, Selim, 'The Struggle against Shi'ism in Hamidian Iraq: A Study in Ottoman Counter-Propaganda', *Die Welt des Islams* (Leiden: Brill, New Series, 1990)

Dessus, Sebastien, 'Human Capital and Growth', Working Paper No. 22, World Bank, Middle East and North Africa, April 2001

Devaux, P., 'Oil Bonanza and Banking Activity in the GCC Countries', *Conjuncture* (Economic Research-BNP Paribas), December 2006

Diaz, Elena Maria, and Fernando Perez de Gracia, 'Oil Price Shocks and Stock Returns of Oil and Gas Corporations', *Finance Research Letters*, vol. 20 (2017)

Dickson, Ben, 'Are We in a Blockchain Winter', *PC Magazine*, 6 April 2019

Dimitropoulos, Georgios, and Almas Lokhandwala, 'Addressing Climate Change in the MENA Region Through Regulatory Design: Instrument Choice Questions', in *Climate Change Law and Policy in the Middle East and North Africa Region*, edited by Damilola S. Olawuyi (Abingdon: Routledge, 2021)

Directory of the Middle East Council of Shopping Centres, 2017

Diwan, Ishac, 'Understanding Revolution in the Middle East: The Central Role of the Middle Class', *Middle East Development Journal*, vol. 5, no. 1 (2013)

Diwan, Kristin Smith, *Kuwait: Finding Balance in a Maximalist Gulf* (Washington, DC: The Arab Gulf States Institute, 2018)

Dodgson, K., and D. Genc, 'Blockchain for Humanity', Humanitarian Practice Network, 29 November 2017

Donald, David C., with contributions by Jiangyu Wang and Jefferson P. Vanderwolk, *A Financial Centre for Two Empires: Hong Kong's Corporate, Securities and Tax Laws in its Transition from Britain to China* (Cambridge: Cambridge University Press, 2014)

Donati, Caroline, 'The Economics of Authoritarian Upgrading in Syria: Liberalization and the Reconfiguration of Economic Networks', in *Middle East Authoritarianisms: Governance, Contestation, and Regime Resilience in Syria and Iran*, edited by Steven Heydemann and Renoud Leenders (Stanford, CA: Stanford University Press, 2013)

Dorit, Ron, and Adi Shamir, 'Quantitative Analysis of the Full Bitcoin Transaction Graph', *Financial Cryptography and Data Security*, vol. 7859 of Lecture Notes in Computer Science, 2013

DTZ Middle East Market Update Series, Bahrain, September 2008

Duan, J. C., A. F. Moreau, C. W. Sealy, 'Fixed-rate Deposit Insurance and Risk Shifting Behaviour at Commercial Banks', *Journal of Banking and Finance*, vol. 16, no. 7 (1992)

Dusuki, A., and A. Abozaid, 'A Critical Appraisal of the Challenges of Realizing Maqasid Al-Shari'ah in Islamic Banking and Finance', IIUM, *Journal of Economics and Management*, vol. 15 (2007)

Dusuki, A., and S. Bouheraoua, 'The Framework of Maqasid al-Shari'ah [Objectives of Shari'ah] and its Implications for Islamic Finance', *Islam and Civilisational Renewal*, vol. 2, no. 2, pp. 316–36, (2011)

Dyer, Paul, 'Human Capital and the Labour Market in Bahrain', in *Bahrain Country Profile: The Road Ahead for Bahrain* (Cairo: Economic Research Forum, 2008)

Dyer, Paul, and Samer Kherfi, 'Gulf Youth and the Labour Market', in *Young Generation Awakening: Economics, Society, and Policy On the Eve of the Arab Spring*, edited by Edward A. Sayre and Tarik M. Yousef (New York: Oxford University Press, 2016)

Eckersley, R., 'Environmental Security, Climate Change and Globalizing Terrorism', in *Rethinking Insecurity, War and Violence*, edited by D. Grenfell and P. James (London: Routledge, 2008)

Economic Development Board Annual Report, 2010–19

El-Chaarani, Hani, 'The Impact of Oil Prices on Stock Markets: New Evidence during and after the Arab Spring in Gulf Cooperation Council Economies', *International Journal of Energy Economics and Policy*, vol. 9, no. 4, pp. 214–23, (2019)

El Gamal, Mahmoud A., *Islamic Finance, Law, Economics and Practice* (Cambridge: Cambridge University Press, 2006)

El-Kholei, A., 'Economic Valuation of Mangrove Forest, Kingdom of Bahrain' (Arabian Gulf University, Background Paper, March 2018.)

El-Meehy, Asya, 'Relative Deprivation and Politics in the Arab Uprisings', research Report, 'Social Justice and Development Policy in the Arab World' programme, Issam Fares Institute for Public Policy and International Affairs, American University of Beirut, 2014

El-Radhi, Yesenn, *Economic Diversification in the Gulf States: Public Expenditure and Non-oil Economic Growth in Bahrain, Oman and Qatar* (Berlin: Gerlach Press, 2018)

El-Tahir, Hatim, 'Bahrain: Threads of Growth Markets in Islamic Finance', in *The Islamic Finance Handbook: A Practitioner's Guide to the Global Markets*, edited by Sasikala Thiagaraja, Andrew Morgan, Andrew Tebbutt, and Geraldine Chan (Singapore: Wiley, 2014)

El-Tahir, Hatim, 'A New Approach to Jalb Al-Manfa'Ah through Sustainable Social Inclusion Sukuk', *International Islamic Financial Market [IIFM] Sukuk Report*, 2018

El-Tahir, Hatim, 'Bahrain's Islamic Capital Markets—a Case Study', in *Islamic Capital Markets and Products: Managing Capital and Liquidity Requirements under Basel III*, edited by Simon Archer and Rifaat Ahmed Abdel Karim (Chichester: Wiley, 2018)

Eliash, Joseph, 'Misconceptions Regarding the Juridical Status of the Iranian "Ulama"', *International Journal of Middle East Studies*, vol. 10, no. 1 (1979)

Ellaboudy, Shereef, 'The Global Financial Crisis: Economic Impact on GCC Countries and Policy Implications', *International Research Journal of Finance and Economics*, no. 41 (2010)

Elrahmani, A., J. Hannun, F. Eljack, and M. Kazi, 'Status of Renewable Energy in the GCC Region and Future Opportunities', *Current Opinion in Chemical Engineering*, vol. 31, (March 2021)

Ercanbrack, Jonathan, 'The Digital Revolution and the Transformation of Global Trade: The Islamic Financial Paradox', in *Trade Finance: Technology, Innovation and Documentary Credits*, edited by Christopher Hare and Dora Neo (Oxford: Oxford University Press, forthcoming)

Ercanbrack, Jonathan, *The Transformation of Islamic Law in Global Financial Markets* (Cambridge: Cambridge University Press, 2015)

Ercanbrack, Jonathan, 'The Standardization of Islamic Financial Law: Lawmaking in Modern Financial Markets', *American Journal of Comparative Law*, vol. 67, no. 4 (2019)

Ercanbrack, Jonathan, 'Islamic Trade Law and the Smart Contract Revolution', in *Trade Finance: Technology, Innovation and Documentary Credits*, edited by Christopher Hare and Dora Neo (Oxford: Oxford University Press, 2021)

Ernst & Young, 'How Will the GCC Close the Skills Gap?', 2015

Ernst & Young, 'Survey on Family Business in the Kingdom of Bahrain, 2009–10'

Etty, Thijs, Veerle Heyvaert, Cinnamon Carlarne, Dan Farber, Jolene Lin, and Joanne Scott, 'Transnational Dimensions of Climate Governance', *Transnational Environmental Law*, vol. 1, no. 2 (2012)

European Centre for Democracy and Human Rights, 'Advocating for Human Rights in the Gulf Region; Bahrain Migrant Workers Rights', Brussels, June 2019

Evans, Charles W., 'Bitcoin in Islamic Banking and Finance', *Journal of Islamic Banking and Finance*, vol. 3, no. 1 (2015)

Fakhro, Elham, 'Land Reclamation in the Arabian Gulf: Security, Environment, and Legal Issues', *Journal of Arabian Studies*, vol. 3, no. 1 (2013)

Fakhro, Munira, 'The Uprising in Bahrain: An Assessment', in *The Persian Gulf at the Millennium: Essays in Politics, Economy, Security, and Religion*, edited by Gary Sick and Lawrence G. Potter (New York: St Martin's Press, 1997)

Falkenstein, Eric G., 'Preferences for Stock Market Characteristics as Revealed by Mutual Fund Portfolio Holdings', *Journal of Finance*, vol. 51, no. 1 (1996)

Fama, E. F., and K. R. French, 'Luck Versus Skill in the Cross Section of Mutual Fund Returns', *Journal of Finance*, vol. 65, no. 5 (2010)

Farah, T. T., *Protection and Politics in Bahrain 1869–1915* (Beirut: The American University of Beirut, 1985)

Fasano, Ugo, and Rishi Goyal, 'Emerging Strains in GCC Labour Markets', Topics in Middle Eastern and North African Economics: Proceedings of the Middle East Economic Association, vol. 6, September 2004

Fattouh, B., and L. El-Katiri, 'Energy and Arab Economic Development', United Nations Development Programme, 2012

Featherstone, David, and Paul Griffin, 'Spatial Relations, Histories from Below and the Makings of Agency: Reflections on The Making of the English Working Class at 50', *Progress in Human Geography*, vol. 40, no. 3 (2016)

Febvre, Lucian, 'La sensibilite et l'histoire: comment reconstituer la vie affective d'autrefois?', *Annales d'histoire sociale*, vol. 3 (1941)

Feener, Michael, *Sharia and Social Engineering: The Implementation of Islamic Law in Contemporary Aceh, Indonesia* (Oxford: Oxford University Press, 2013)

Feir, George N. S., *Modernization of the Law in Arab States: An Investigation into Current Civil, Criminal and Constitutional Law in the Arab World* (San Francisco, CA: Austin and Winfield Publications, 1998)

Field, Michael, *The Merchants: The Big Business Families of Saudi Arabia and the Gulf States* (Woodstock, NY: Overlook Press, 1985)

Filippi, Primavera De, and Aaron Wright, *Blockchain and the Law: The Rule of Code* (Cambridge, MA: Harvard University Press, 2018)

Finnie, D., 'Recruitment and Training of Labor: The Middle East Oil Industry', *Middle East Journal*, vol. 12, no. 2 (1958)

Firoozye, Nikan, 'Shari'ah Risk or Banking Conundrum?', *Opalesque*, 3 July 2009

Fisher, Irving, *The Works of Irving Fisher*, edited by William J. Barber, James Tobin, Robert W Dimand, and Kevin Foster, 14 vols. (London: Pickering and Chatto, 1996)

Floor, W., *The Persian Gulf: A Political and Economic History of Five Port Cities, 1500–1730* (Washington, DC: Mage, 2006)

Flynn, D. O., and A. Giraldez (ed.), *Metals and Monies in an Emerging Global Economy* (Aldershot: Ashgate, 1997)

Flynn, D. O., and A. Giraldez (ed.), *Global Connections and Monetary History, 1470–1800* (Aldershot: Ashgate, 2003)

Forstenlechner, I., and E. Rutledge, 'Unemployment in the Gulf: Time to Update the "Social Contract"', *Middle East Policy*, vol. 17, no. 2 (2010)

Fosdick, Howard, 'The Sociology of Technology Adoption', *Enterprise Systems Journal*, September 1992

Foster, Nicholas H. D., 'Company Law Theory in Comparative Perspective: England and France', *American Journal of Comparative Law*, vol. 48, no. 4 (2000)

Foster, Nicholas H. D., 'Comparative Commercial Law: Rules or Context', in *Comparative Legal Studies: A Handbook*, edited by D. Nelken and E. Orucu (Oxford: Hart Publishing, 2007)

Foster, Nicholas H. D., 'Islamic Finance Law as an Emergent Legal System', *Arab Law Quarterly*, vol. 21, no. 170 (2007)

Foster, Nicholas H. D., 'Using Comparative Commercial Law in the Study of Legal Transformation: Commercial Aspects of the Early Stages of Ottoman Legal Transition', in *Islamic Law Facing the Challenges of the 21st Century*, edited by R. Shaham and A. Layish (Jerusalem: Van Leer Jerusalem Institute, 2011)

Foster, Nicholas H. D., 'The Financial Sharia as Law and as Ethics: A Suggestion', SOAS Working Paper No. 10, Law of Islamic Finance, 2016

Foucault, Michel, *Power/Knowledge: Selected Interviews and Other Writings 1972–1977*, translated and edited by Colin Gordon and Leo Marshall (New York: Pantheon Books, 1980)

Frank, Andre Gunder, *Reorient: Global Economy in the Asian Age* (Berkeley, CA: University of California Press, 1998)

Franklin, Rob, 'Migrant Labor and the Politics of Development in Bahrain', *Middle East Report*, 132 (1985)

Friedman, Milton, *A Program for Monetary Stability* (New York: Fordham University Press, 1960)

Friedman, Milton, *Capitalism and Freedom* (Chicago, IL: University of Chicago Press, 1962)

Friedman, Willa, Michael Kremer, Edward Miguel, and Rebecca Thornton, 'Education as Liberation?', NBER Working Paper No. 16939, 2011

Fry, Maxwell J., *Emancipating the Banking System and Developing Markets for Government Debt* (New York: Routledge, 1997)

Fuccaro, Nelida, 'Islam and Urban Space: Ma'tam in Bahrain before Oil', *Newsletter of the Institute for the Study of Islam in the Modern World*, no. 3 (1999)

Fuccaro, Nelida, 'Understanding the Urban History of Bahrain', *Critique: Critical Middle Eastern Studies*, vol. 17 (2000)

Fuccaro, Nelida, 'Mapping the Transnational Community: Persians and the Space of the City in Bahrain, *c.*1869–1937', in *Transnational Connections in the Arab Gulf*, edited by Madawi al-Rasheed (London: Routledge, 2005)

Fuccaro, Nelida, *Histories of City and State in the Persian Gulf: Manama since 1800* (Cambridge: Cambridge University Press, 2009)

Fuccaro, Nelida, 'Pearl Towns and Early Oil Cities: Migration and Integration in the Arab Coast of the Persian Gulf', in *Migration and the Making of Urban Modernity in the Ottoman Empire and Beyond*, edited by Ulrike Freitag, Malte Fuhrmann, Nora Lafi, and Florian Riedler (London: Routledge, 2010)

Fuccaro, Nelida, 'Shaping the Urban Life of Oil in Bahrain: Consumerism, Leisure and Public Communication in Manama and in the Oil Camps 1932–1960s', *Comparative Studies of South Asia, Africa, and the Middle East*, vol. 33, no. 1 (2013)

Fuccaro, Nelida (ed.), *Violence and the City in the Modern Middle East* (Stanford, CA: Stanford University Press, 2016)

Furedi, Frank, *Politics of Fear* (New York: Continuum, 2005)

Furlonger, David, and Rajesh Kandaswamy, 'Hype Cycle for Blockchain Technologies', Gartner Report, 25 July 2018

Furneaux, Paul, Samer Hijazi, John Lee, and Jamal Fakhro, 'Cross-border Development in Islamic Banking', *Islamic Finance Review, Euromoney Yearbooks* (2008–09), p. 45

Fyzee, Asaf Ali Asghar, *Outlines of Muhammadan Law* (New Delhi: Oxford University Press, 5th edition, 2008)

Gamburd, Michele Ruth, *The Kitchen Spoon's Handle: Transnationalism and Sri Lanka's Migrant Housemaids* (Ithaca, NY: Cornell University Press, 2000)

Ganne, Emmanuelle, 'Can Blockchain Revolutionize International Trade?', World Trade Organization, 2018

Gardner, Andrew M., 'Strategic Transnationalism: The Indian Diasporic Elite in Contemporary Bahrain', *City & Society*, vol. 20, no. 1 (2008)

Gardner, Andrew M., *City of Strangers: Gulf Migration and the Indian Community in Bahrain* (Ithaca, NY: Cornell University Press, 2010)

Gardner, Simon, *An Introduction to the Law of Trusts* (Oxford: Oxford University Press, 2011)

Gas, Dana, 'Dana Gas outlines broad terms for Sukuk discussions', UAE Government, (13 June 2017)

Gaudiosi, Monica M., 'The Influence of the Islamic Law of WAQF on the Development of Trust in England: The case of Merton College', *University of Pennsylvania Law Review*, vol. 136 (1988)

Gause III, F. Gregory, 'Why Middle East Studies Missed the Arab Spring: The Myth of Authoritarian Stability', *Foreign Affairs*, vol. 90, no. 4 (July/August 2011)

Gause III, F. Gregory, *Oil Monarchies: Domestic and Security Challenges in the Arab Gulf States* (New York: Council on Foreign Relations Press, 1994)

Geertz, Clifford, 'Religion as a Cultural System', In *Anthropological Approaches to the Study of Religion*, edited by Michael Banton (London: Tavistock Publications, 1966)

Gengler, Justin, 'Electoral Rules and Threats Cure Bahrain's Sectarian Parliament', The Monkey Cage, 1 December 2014: www.washingtonpost.com/blogs/monkey-cage/wp/2014/12/01/electoral-rules-and-threats-cure-bahrains-sectarian-parliament/

Gengler, Justin, *Group Conflict and Political Mobilization in Bahrain and the Arab Gulf: Rethinking the Rentier State* (Bloomington, IN: Indiana University Press, 2015)

Gerakis, A. S., and O. Roncesvalles, 'Bahrain's Offshore Banking Center', *Economic Development and Cultural Change*, vol. 31, no. 2 (1983)

Ghassan al-Shihabi, 'Al-Ikhwan al-Muslimun fi-I-Bahrain: Tahulat al-"Aqud al-Sab'a"' [The Muslim Brotherhood in Bahrain: the Seven Decades' Transformations], in Al-Ikhwan al-Muslimun fi-L-Khalij, *The Muslim Brotherhood in the Gulf* (Dubai: Al-Mesbar Studies and Research Centre, 2014), p. 163

Gil, M., 'The Earliest Waqf Foundations, *Journal of Near Eastern Studies*, vol. 57, no. 2 (1998)

Gilroy, Paul, *The Black Atlantic: Modernity and Double Consciousness* (London: Verso, 1993)

Glaeser, Edward, Giacomo Ponzetto, and Andrei Shleifer, 'Why Does Democracy Need Education?', *Journal of Economic Growth*, vol. 12, no. 2 (2007)

Glickman, L. B., *Consumer Society in American History: A Reader* (Ithaca, NY: Cornell University Press, 1999)

Global Investment House, 'GCC Real Estate Sector-Changing Times!', February 2009

Global Legal Research Center, 'Regulation of Cryptocurrency around the World', Law Library of Congress, June 2018

Goldstone, J. A., 'Islam, Development and the Middle East: A Comment on Timur Kuran', in *Institutional Barriers to Economic Change: Cases Considered* (Washington, DC: USAID, 2003)

Gompers, Paul A., and Andrew Metrick, 'Institutional Investors and Equity Prices', *Quarterly Journal of Economics*, vol. 116, no. 1 (2001)

Goodwyn, Lawrence, *Democratic Promise: The Populist Moment in America* (New York: Oxford University Press, 1976)

Granovetter, M., 'Problems of Explanation in Economic Sociology', in *Networks and Organizations: Structure, Form and Action*, edited by N. Nohria and R. Eccles (Cambridge, MA: Harvard University Press, 1992)

Gueguen, Chloe, Sabal Al Majali, and Julia Hakspiel, 'Making Digital Finance Work for Women in the MENA Region: 8 Lessons from the Field', Information and Communications Technology

Guha, Ranajit, *Dominance Without Hegemony: History and Power in Colonial India* (Cambridge, MA: Harvard University Press, 1997)

Guha, Ranajit, *Elementary Aspects of Peasant Insurgency in Colonial India* (Durham, NC and London: Duke University Press, 1999)

Gulf Air, *History of Gulf Air*, 2013

Gulf Cooperation Council, 'Labour Market Reforms to Boost Employment and Productivity in the GCC: an Update', 25 October 2014, prepared by IMF staff, pp. 10–13

Gulf Financial Innovation Network 2019, retrieved from http://dfsa.ae/Documents/FinTech/GFIN-Webpage-content-28012019-Final.pdf

Gulf Research Center, 'Renewable Energy in the GCC Countries', 2012

Gutteridge, H. C., *Comparative Law: An Introduction to the Comparative Method of Legal Study and Research* (Cambridge: Cambridge University Press, 1949)

Habermas, Jürgen, *The Structural Transformation of the Public Sphere: Inquiry into a Category of Bourgeois Society* (Cambridge: Polity Press, 1992)

Hall, Catherine, 'The Rule of Difference: Gender, Class and Empire in the Making of the 1832 Reform Act', in *Gendered Nations: Nationalisms and Gender in the Long Nineteenth Century*, edited by Ida Blom, Karen Hagemann, and Catherine Hall (Oxford: Berg, 2000)

Hall, Robert E., 'Why Does the Economy Fall to Pieces after a Financial Crisis?', *Journal of Economic Perspectives*, vol. 24, no. 4 (2010)

Hammoudeh, Shawkat, and Elsa Alesia, 'Relationship between Spot/Futures Prices of Crude Oil and Equity Indices for Oil Producing Economies and Oil Related Industries', *Arab Economic Journal*, vol. 11 (2002)

Hammoudeh, Shawkat, and Elsa Aleisa, 'Dynamic Relationships among GCC Stock Markets and NYMEX Oil Futures', *Contemporary Economic Policy*, vol. 22, no. 2 (2004)

Hammoudeh, Shawkat, Huimin Li, and Bang Jeon, 'Causality and Volatility Spillovers among Petroleum Prices of WTI, Gasoline and Heating Oil in Different Locations', *North American Journal of Economics and Finance*, vol. 14, no. 1 (2003)

Hamon, Jacques, and Edith Ginglinger, 'Ownership, Control and Market Liquidity', *Finance*, vol. 33, no. 2 (2012)

Hamouche, Mustapha Ben, 'Manama: The Metamorphosis of a Gulf City', in *The Evolving Arab City: Tradition, Modernity and Urban Development*, edited by Yasser Elsheshtawy (London: Routledge, 2008)

Hamoudi, Haider Ala, 'Muhammad's Social Justice or Muslim Cant? Langdellianism and the Failures of Islamic Finance', *Cornell International Law Journal*, vol. 40 (2007)

Hamoudi, Haider Ala, 'The Death of Islamic Law', *Georgia Journal of International and Comparative Law*, vol. 38 (2010)

Hamoudi, Haider Ala, 'Repugnancy in the Arab world', *Willamette Law Review*, vol. 48 (2012)

Hanieh, Adam, *Capitalism and Class in the Gulf Arab States* (New York: Palgrave Macmillan, 2011)

Hanieh, Adam, *Money, Markets, and Monarchies: The Gulf Cooperation Council and the Political Economy of the Contemporary Middle East* (Cambridge: Cambridge University Press, 2018)

Hannah, Leslie, 'Strategic Games, Scale, and Efficiency, or Chandler goes to Hollywood', in *Business in Britain in the Twentieth Century: Decline and Renaissance*, edited by Richard Coopey and Peter Lyth (Oxford: Oxford University Press, 2009)

Hansman, Henry, and Ugo Mattei, 'The Functions of Trust law: A Comparative Legal and Economic Analysis', *New York University Law Review*, vol. 73 (1998)

Hanson, Maren, 'The Influence of French Law on the Legal Development of Saudi Arabia', *Arab Law Quarterly*, vol. 2, no. 3 (1987)

Hanushek, E., L. Woessmann, and L. Zhang, 'General Education, Vocational Education and Labour Market Outcomes over the Life Cycle', NBER Working Paper No. 17504, National Bureau of Economic Research, 2011

Harrigan, Jane, *The Political Economy of Arab Food Sovereignty* (Basingstoke: Palgrave Macmillan, 2014)

Harrigan, Jane and Hamed El Said, *Economic Liberalization, Social Capital and Islamic Welfare Provision* (Basingstoke: Palgrave Macmillan, 2009)

Hawaldar, Iqbal Thonase, Babitha Rohit, and Prakash Pinto, 'Testing of Weak Form of Efficient Market Hypothesis: Evidence from the Bahrain Bourse', *Investment Management and Financial Innovations*, vol. 14, 2 (2017)

Hazik, Mohamed, and Hassnian Ali, *Blockchain, Fintech and Islamic Finance: Building the Future in the New Islamic Digital Economy* (Berlin: Walter de Gruyter, 2019)

Herb, Michael, *All in the Family: Absolutism, Revolution, and Liberal Prospects in the Middle East Monarchies* (New York: SUNY Press, 1998)

Herb, Michael, 'Princes and Parliaments in the Arab World', *Middle East Journal*, vol. 58, no. 3 (2004)

Herian, R., *Regulating Blockchain: Critical Perspectives in Law and Technology* (Abingdon: Routledge, 2019)

Hermassi, Hela, 'Tunisian Revolution and Regional Imbalance', *Global Advanced Research Journal of Management and Business Studies*, vol. 2, no. 2 (2013)

Hertog, Steffen, 'Defying the Resource Curse: Explaining Successful State Owned Enterprises in Rentier States', *World Politics*, vol. 62, no. 2 (2010)

Hertog, Steffen, 'A Comparative Assessment of Labour Market Nationalization Policies in the GCC', in *National Employment, Migration and Education in the GCC: The Gulf Region: Economic Development and Diversification*, edited by S. Hertog (Berlin: Gerlach Press, 2013)

Hertog, Steffen, 'Arab Gulf States: An Assessment of Nationalization Policies', Gulf Labour Markets and Migration Programme, Research Paper no. 1, 2014

Heyneman, S., *Islam and Social Policy* (Nashville, TN: Vanderbildt University Press, 2004)

Hibou, Beatrice, *Privatising the State* (London: Hurst, 2004)

Hill, R. L., 'Baladiyya-Arab East', *Encyclopedia of Islam*, 2nd edition, vol. 1, 1976

HMRC, *Impact Assessment of Sukuk [Islamic Bonds] Legislation* (London: HM Revenue & Customs, 2008)

Hobsbawm, E. J., 'Machine Breakers', in *Uncommon People: Resistance, Rebellion and Jazz* (London: Abacus, 1952)

Hobsbawm, E. J., *Primitive Rebels* (Manchester: Manchester University Press, 1984)

Hobsbawm, Eric J., *Worlds of Labour: Further Studies in the History of Labour* (London: Weidenfeld and Nicolson, 1984)

Hodgson, Geoffrey M., 'The Great Crash of 2008 and the Reform of Economics', *Cambridge Journal of Economics*, vol. 33, no. 6 (2009)

Hodgson, Marshall G. S., *The Venture of Islam: Conscience and History in a World Civilization*, vol. 2 (Chicago, IL: Chicago University Press, 1974)

Hoepner, Andreas G. F., Hussain G. Rammal, and Michael Rezec, 'Islamic Mutual Funds' Financial Performance and International Investment Style: Evidence from 20 Countries', *European Journal of Finance*, vol. 17, no. 9–10 (2011)

Hofstadter, Richard, *The Age of Reform: From Bryan to FDR* (New York: Vintage, 1955)

Hofstede, Geert, *Culture's Consequences: International Differences in Work-Related Values* (London: Sage Publications, 1980)

Hofstede, Geert, *Cultures and Organizations: Intercultural Cooperation and its Importance for Survival* (New York: McGraw Hill, 2010)

Hooglund, Eric, 'Bahrain', in *Persian Gulf States: Country Studies*, edited by Helen C. Metz (Washington, DC: US Government Printing Office, 1994)

Hudson, Alastair, *Great Debates in Equity and Trusts* (Basingstoke: Palgrave Macmillan Education, 2014)

Hudson, Michael, *Arab Politics: The Search for Legitimacy* (New Haven, CT: Yale University Press, 1977)

Hudson, M. C., 'Arab Politics after the Uprising: Still Searching for Legitimacy', in *Routledge Handbook of the Arab Spring: Rethinking Democratization*, edited by Larbi Sadiki (Abingdon: Routledge, 2014)

Human Development Indices and Indicators, 2018, 'Statistical Update: Briefing Note for Countries on the 2018 Statistical Update'

Human Rights Watch, 'For a Better Life: Migrant Worker Abuse in Bahrain and the Government Reform Agenda', HRW, 30 September 2012

Huntington, Samuel P., *Political Order in Changing Societies* (New Haven, CT: Yale University Press, 1968)

Hussain, Saleh H., and Chris Mallin, 'The Dynamics of Corporate Governance in Bahrain: Structure, Responsibilities and Operations of Corporate Boards', *Corporate Governance Journal*, vol. 11, no. 3 (2003)

Hvidt, Martin, 'The Dubai Model: An Outline of Key Development-process Elements in Dubai', *International Journal of Middle East Studies*, vol. 41, no. 3 (2009)

Hyatt, U., 'Green Bonds: What's Right, What's Wrong', Chartered Financial Analyst Institute, 2015

Idllalène, Samira, *Rediscovery and Revival in Islamic Environmental Law: Back to the Future of Nature's Trust* (Cambridge: Cambridge University Press, 2021)

Idllalène, Samira, 'The Role of Environmental Waqf in Addressing Climate Change in the MENA Region: A Comparative Law Analysis', in *Climate Change Law and Policy in the*

Middle East and North Africa Region, edited by Damilola S. Olawuyi (Abingdon: Routledge, 2022)

ILO, 'International Labour Migration: A Rights-based Approach', Geneva, 2010

ILO LABORSTA 2004

IMF, 'Labour Market Reforms to Boost Employment and Productivity in the GCC: An Update', 25 October 2014, p. 29

ILO, October 2011, 'Economically Active Population, Estimates and Projections', 6th ed.: http://laborsta.ilo.org/applv8/data/EAPEP/eapep_E.html

IMF World Economic Outlook, 2010

IMF World Economic Outlook Database, April 2011

Imtiaz Uddin Ahmad in *JKAU: Islamic Economics*, vol. 10 (1418/1998), pp. 57–9

Institute for Pearls and Gemstones (Danat), Report, 2018

International Crisis Group, 'Bahrain's Sectarian Challenge', *Middle East Report*, no. 40 (2005), p. 15

International Monetary Fund, 'Gulf Cooperation Council Countries: Enhancing Economic Outcomes in an Uncertain Global Economy', Washington, DC, 2011

International Crisis Group, Tentative Jihad: Syria's Fundamentalist Opposition', *Middle East Report*, no. 131, 12 October 2012

International Organization of Securities Commission, *IOSCO Principles for Collective Investment Schemes*, 1995

International Trade Union Confederation, 'Countries at Risk: Violations of Trade Union Rights', 2013, p. 36

IPCC, 'Good Practice Guidance and Uncertainty Management in National Greenhouse Gas Inventions', 2000; IPCC, Guidelines for National Greenhouse Gas Inventories, 2006

Iqbal, F., *Sustaining Gains in Poverty Reduction and Human Development in the Middle East and North Africa* (Washington, DC: World Bank, 2006)

'Islamic Trade Law and the Smart Contract Revolution', in Trade Finance: Technology, Innovation and Documentary Credits, edited by Christopher Hare and Dora Neo (Oxford: Oxford University Press, 2021)

Jackson, Howell E., and Eric J. Pan, 'Regulatory Competition in International Securities Markets', *Business*, 1, 653, 2001

Jalal, Ayesha, 'Exploding Communalism: The Politics of Muslim Identity in South Asia', in *Nationalism, Democracy and Development: State and Politics in India*, edited by Sugata Bose and Ayesha Jalal (Delhi: Oxford University Press, 1997)

Jensen, M. C., 'The Performance of Mutual Funds in the Period 1945–64', *Journal of Finance*, vol. 23, no. 2 (1968), pp. 389–416.

Jensen, Michael C., 'Eclipse of the Public Corporation', *Harvard Business Review*, 1989

Jensen, M. C., and W. Meckling, 'Theory of the Firm: Managerial Behavior, Agency Costs and Ownership Structure', *Journal of Financial Economics*, vol. 4, no. 3 (1976)

Jeremy, David, 'Ethics, Religion, and Business in Twentieth Century Britain', *Business in Britain in the Twentieth Century*, edited by Richard Coopey and Peter Lyth (Oxford: Oxford University Press, 2009)

Jobst, Andreas, et al., 'Islamic Bond Issuance—What Sovereign Debt Managers Need to Know', International Monetary Fund, (July 2008)

Jones, Charles M., and Gautam Kaul, 'Oil and the Stock Markets', *Journal of Finance*, vol. 11, no. 2 (1996)

Jones, Marc Owen, *Political Repression in Bahrain* (Cambridge: Cambridge University Press, 2020)

Jones, Toby, 'We Know What Happened in Bahrain: Now What?', *Carnegie Endowment for International Peace*, 1 December 2011

Jones, Toby, 'Bahrain's Revolutionaries Speak: An Exclusive Interview with Bahrain's Coalition of February 14th Youth', *Jadaliyya*, 22 March 2012

Jones, T. C., and A. Shehabi, 'Bahrain's Revolutionaries', *Foreign Policy*, 2 January 2012

Joyce, Miriam, *Ruling Shaikhs and Her Majesty's Government, 1960–1969* (London and Portland, OR: Frank Cass, 2003)

Juhmani, Omar, 'Corporate Governance and the Level of Bahraini Corporate Compliance with IFRS Disclosure', *Journal of Applied Accounting Research*, vol. 18, no. 1 (2017)

Julee, Morrison, 'How Crowdfunding Has Influenced Start-up', *Huffington Post*, 10 February 2017

Kabbani, Nader, and Ekta Kothari, 'Youth Employment in the MENA Region: A Situational Assessment', Special Protection Paper No 0534, September 2005

Kahn-Freund, Otto, 'On Uses and Misuses of Comparative Law', *Modern Law Review*, vol. 37 (1974)

Kahneman, Daniel, *Thinking Fast and Slow* (New York: Penguin Random House, 2011)

Kahneman, Daniel, and Richard H. Thaler, 'Anomalies, Utility maximization and Experienced Utility', *Journal of Economic Perspectives*, vol. 20, no. 1 (2006)

Kahneman, Daniel, and Amos Tversky, 'Prospect Theory: An Analysis of Decision under Risk', *Econometrica*, vol. 47 (1979)

Kahneman, Daniel, and Amos Tversky (ed.), *Choices, Values, and Frames* (Cambridge: Cambridge University Press, 2000)

Kaiser, Ross M. K., and N. Mazaheri, 'The Resource Curse in MENA: Political Transitions, Resource Wealth, Economic Shocks and Conflict Risk', World Bank Policy Research Working Paper No. 5742, Washington, DC, 2011

Kamba, W. J., 'Comparative Law: A Theoretical Framework', *International and Comparative Law Quarterly*, vol. 23 (1974)

Kamrava, Mehran, *Politics and Society in the Third World* (London: Routledge, 1993)

Kamrava, Mehran (ed.), *Gateways to the World: Port Cities in the Persian Gulf* (London: Hurst, 2016)

Kandil, Hazem, 'Why Did the Egyptian Middle-Class March to Tahrir Square?', *Mediterranean Politics*, vol. 17, no. 2 (2012)

Kanoo, Khalid M., *The House of Kanoo: A Century of an Arabian Family Business* (London: London Centre of Arabian Studies, 1997)

Karlan, Dean, and Jonathan Zinman, 'Microcredit in Theory and Practice: Using Randomized Credit Scoring for Impact Evaluation', *Science*, vol. 332 (2011)

Karstedt, Suzanne, 'Democracy, Values, and Violence: Paradoxes, Tensions and Comparative Advantages of Liberal Inclusion', *The Annals of the American Academy of Political and Social Science*, 605, 1 (May 2006)

Kaufmann, Daniel, Aart Kraay, and Massimo Mastruzzi, 'Governance Matters 111: Governance Indicators for 1996–2002', World Bank Policy Research Working Paper No. 3106, Washington, DC, 2003

Kawabe, N., 'The Development of Distribution Systems in Japan before World War II', *Business and Economic History*, vol. 18 (1989)

Kazin, Michael, The *Populist Persuasion: An American History* (Ithaca, NY and London: Cornell University Press, 1998)

Kemball A. B., 'Statistical and Miscellaneous Information Connected with the Possessions, Revenues, Families of the Ruler of Bahrain', *Bombay Selections*, vol. 24, p. 291

Kempf, Alexander, and Stefan Ruenzi, 'Status Quo Bias and the Number of Alternatives: An Empirical Illustration from the Mutual Fund Industry', *Journal of Behavioral Finance*, vol. 7, no. 4 (2006)

Kerr, Cortni, and Toby Jones, 'A Revolution Paused in Bahrain', in *The Arab Revolts: Dispatches on Militant Democracy in the Middle East*, edited by David McMurray and Amanda Ufheil-Somers (Bloomington, IN: Indiana University Press, 2013)

Khalaf, Abdulhadi, 'Labour Movements in Bahrain', MERIP Reports, 132, 1985

Khalaf, Abdulhadi, *Unfinished Business: Contentious Politics and State-Building in Bahrain*, Research Report in Sociology 1, Lund University, 2000

Khalaf, Amal, 'Squaring the Circle: Bahrain's Pearl Roundabout', *Middle East Critique*, vol. 22, no. 3 (2013)

Khalid, F., 'Islam and the Environment: Ethics and Practice: An Assessment', *Religion Compass*, vol. 4, no. 11 (2010)

Khalili, Laleh, *Sinews of War and Trade: Shipping and Capitalism in the Arabian Peninsula* (London: Verso, 2020)

Khuri, Fuad I., *From Village to Suburb: Order and Change in Greater Beirut* (Chicago, IL: University of Chicago Press, 1975).

Khuri, Fuad I., *Tribe and State in Bahrain: The Transformation of Social and Political Authority in an Arab State* (Chicago, IL: Chicago University Press, 1980)

Kilborn, Jason J., 'Foundations of Forgiveness in Islamic Bankruptcy Law: Sources, Methodology, Diversity', *American Bankruptcy Law Journal*, vol. 85 (2011)

Kilian, L., 'Not all Oil Price Shocks Are Alike: Disentangling Demand and Supply Shocks in the Crude Oil Market', *American Economic Review*, vol. 19 (2009)

King, Anthony D., *Colonial Urban Development: Culture, Social Power and Environment* (London: Routledge and Kegan Paul, 1976)

Kirzner, Israel M., *Competition and Entrepreneurship* (Chicago, IL: University of Chicago Press, 1973)

Kostiner, Joseph (ed.), *Middle East Monarchies: The Challenge of Modernity* (Boulder, CO: Lynne Rienner, 2000)

Kotb, H., 'Protest Movements in Bahrain: Developments in Bahrain's Political Society', in *Protest Movements in the Arab Nation*, edited by Amr Al Shobky (Beirut: Center for Arab Unity Studies, 2011)

Kotilaine, J., 'Turning Entrepreneurship into a Growth Driver', Bahrain National Human Development Report Background Paper, 2018

Kraetzschmar, H., 'Mapping Opposition Cooperation in the Arab World: From Single-Issue Coalitions to Transnational Networks', *British Journal of Middle Eastern Studies*, vol. 38, no. 3 (2011)

Kramer, Martin, *Ivory Towers on Sand: The Failure of Middle Eastern Studies in America* (Washington, DC: Washington Institute for Near East Policy, 2001)

Kropf, Annika, *Oil Export Economies: New Comparative Perspectives on the Arab Gulf States* (Berlin: Gerlach Press, 2016)

Krugman, Paul, 'Dutch Tulips and Emerging Markets', *Foreign Affairs*, 1995

Kullab, Yarob, and Chen Yan Dongbei, 'The Impact of Institutional Ownership on Income Accounting Strategy: Evidence from Bahrain', *Academy of Accounting and Financial Studies Journal*, vol. 22, no. 1 (2018)

Kuran, Timur, 'Islamic Economics and the Islamic Sub-economy', *Journal of Economic Perspectives*, vol. 9, no. 4 (1995)

Kuran, Timur, *Islam and Mammon: The Economic Predicaments of Islamism* (Princeton, NJ: Princeton University Press, 2004)

Kuran, Timur, 'Why the Middle East is Economically Underdeveloped: Historical Mechanisms of Institutional Stagnation', *Journal of Economic Perspectives*, vol. 18 (2004)

Kuran, Timur, 'The Scale of Entrepreneurship in Middle Eastern History: Inhibitive Roles of Islamic Institutions', Working Paper No. 10, Economic Research Initiatives at Duke, (2008)

Kuran, Timur, *The Long Divergence: How Islamic Law Held Back the Middle East* (Princeton, NJ: Princeton University Press, 2011)

Kuran, Timur, 'Legal Roots of Authoritarian Rule in the Middle East: Civic Legacies of the Islamic Waqf', *American Journal of Comparative Law*, vol. 64, no. 2 (2016)

Kurzman, Charles, 'Organizational Opportunity and Social Movement Mobilization: A Comparative Analysis of Four Religious Movements', *Mobilization*, vol. 3, no. 1 (1998)

Kuznets, Simon, 'Quantitative Aspects of the Economic Growth of Nations: Industrial Distribution of National Product and Labor Force', *Economic Development and Cultural Change*, vol. 5, no. 4, Supplement, 1957

La Porta, Rafael, Florencio Lopez-de-Silanes, Andrei Schleifer, and Robert Vishny, 'Legal Determinants of External Finance', *Journal of Finance*, vol. 52, no. 3 (1997)

La Porta, Rafael, Florencio Lopez-de-Silanes, Andrei Schleifer, and Robert Vishny, 'Investor Protection and Corporate Governance', *Journal of Financial Economics*, vol. 58 (2000)

La Porta, Rafael, Florencio Lopez-de-Silanes, Andrei Schleifer, and Robert Vishny, 'Investor Protection and Corporate Valuation', *Journal of Finance*, vol. 57, no. 3 (2002)

Lacroix, Stephane, *Awakening Islam: The Politics of Religious Dissent in Contemporary Saudi Arabia* (Cambridge, MA: Harvard University Press, 2011)

Lal, Deepak 'The World Economy at the End of the Millennium', Department of Economics Working Paper No. 786, University of California, Los Angeles, September 1998

Landes, David, *The Unbound Prometheus: Technological Change and Industrial Development in Western Europe from 1750 to the Present*, 2nd edn. (Cambridge: Cambridge University Press, 2003)

Lawson, Fred H., *Bahrain: The Modernization of Autocracy* (Boulder, CO: Westview Press, 1989)

Lawson, Fred H., 'Repertoires of Contention in Contemporary Bahrain', in *Islamic Activism: A Social Movement Theory Approach*, edited by Quintan Wiktorowicz (Bloomington, IN: Indiana University Press, 2004)

Layish, Aharon, 'The Muslim Waqf in Israel', *Hamizrah Hehadash: The New East, Quarterly of the Israel Oriental Society*, vol. XV, no. 1–2 (1965)

Lee, Paul, 'The Regulation of Securities and Islamic Finance in Dubai: Implications for Models of Shariah', *Journal of Islamic and Near Middle East*, vol. 15 (2016)

Lehman, Bruce N., and David M. Modest, 'Trading and Liquidity on the Tokyo Stock Exchange: A Bird's Eye View', *Journal of Finance*, vol. 49, no. 3 (1994)

Lessig, L., *Code: And Other Laws of Cyber Space* (New York: Basic Books, 1999)

Levin, Kelly, Benjamin Cashore, Steven Bernstein, and Graeme Auld, 'Overcoming the Tragedy of Super Wicked Problems: Constraining our Future Selves to Ameliorate Global Climate Change', *Policy Sciences*, vol. 45 (2012)

Lidstone, D., 'Sector Regaining its Confidence after the Shock of Crisis', *The Financial Times*, (10 November 2009)

Lillestam, J., and A. Patt, 'Barriers, Risks, and Policies for Renewables in the Gulf States', *Energies*, vol. 8, no. 8, pp.8263–85, (2015)

Limon, M., 'Human Rights and Climate Change: Constructing a Case for Political Action', *Harvard Environmental Law Review*, vol. 33 (2009)

Lin, M., A. R. Prabhala, and S. Viswanathan, 'Judging Borrowers by the Company they Keep: Friendship Networks and Information Asymmetry in Online Peer to Peer Lending', *Management Science*, vol. 59, no. 1 (2013)

Lipset, Seymour Martin, 'Some Social Requisites of Democracy: Economic Development and Political Legitimacy', *American Political Science Review*, vol. 53, no. 1 (1959)

Lipsey, Richard G., Kenneth I. Carlaw, and Clifford T. Bekar, *Economic Transformations: General Purpose Technologies and Long Term Economic Growth* (Oxford: Oxford University Press, 2005)

Lofgren, H., and A. Richards, *Food Security, Poverty and Economic Policy in the Middle East and North Africa* (Washington, DC: IFPRI, 2003)

Longrigg, S. H., *Oil in the Middle East: Its Discovery and Development* (London: Oxford University Press, 1968)

Longva, Anh, *Walls Built on Sand: Migration, Exclusion and Society in Kuwait* (Boulder, CO: Westview Press, 1997)

Longva, Anh, 'Keeping Migrant Workers in Check: The Kafala System in the Gulf', *Middle East Report*, no. 211, pp. 20–22, (Summer 1999)

Looney, R. E., 'An Economic Assessment of Bahrain's Attempts at Industrial Diversification', Industrial Bank of Kuwait Papers, 1989

Looney, R. E., *Manpower Policies and Development in the Persian Gulf Region* (Westport, CT: Praeger, 1994)

Lorimer, John George, *The Gazetteer of the Persian Gulf, Oman and Central Arabia* (Calcutta: Office of the Superintendent Government Printing, 1908; republished by Farnborough: Gregg International, 1970), vol. 2

Louer, Laurence, 'The Political Impact of Labour Migration in Bahrain', *City & Society*, vol. 20, no. 1 (2008)

Louer, Laurence, *Transnational Shia Politics: Religious and Political Networks in the Gulf* (London: Hurst, 2011)

Louer, Laurence, 'Sectarianism and Coup-Proofing Strategies in Bahrain', *Journal of Strategic Studies*, vol. 36, no. 2 (2013)

Lund, Aron, 'Syria's Salafi Insurgents: The Rise of the Syrian Islamic Front', Swedish Institute for International Affairs, UI Brief 17, 17 March 2013

Lynch, Caitrin, 'The Good Girls of Sri Lankan Modernity: Moral Orders of Nationalism and Capitalism', *Identities*, vol. 6, no. 1 (1999)

Macko, William, and Diego Sourrouille, *Investment Funds in MENA* (Washington, DC: World Bank 2010)

Maddison, Angus, *The World Economy: A Millennial Perspective* (Paris: OECD, Development Studies Centre, 2001)

Maddison, Angus, *The World Economy: Historical Statistics* (Paris: OECD, Development Studies Centre, 2003)

Maita, Aida, 'Arbitration of Islamic Financial Disputes', *Annual Survey of International and Comparative Law*, vol. 20, no. 1, article 7 (2014)

Makdisi, G., *Islamic Institutions of Learning in Islam and the West* (Edinburgh: Edinburgh University Press, 1981)

Maki, Uskali (ed.), *Fact and Fiction in Economics: Models, Realism, and Social Construction* (Cambridge: Cambridge University Press, 2002)

Malaeb, Hanan, N., 'The "Kafala System" and Human Rights: Time for a Decision', *Arab Law Quarterly*, vol. 29 (2015)

Mallat, Chibli, 'Commercial Law in the Middle East: Between Classical Transactions and Modern Business', *American Journal of Comparative Law*, vol. 48, no. 1 (2000)

Mallat, Chibli, and J. Gelbort, 'Constitutional Options for Bahrain', *Virginia Journal of International Law*, vol. 2, no. 1 (2011)

Mapp, H. V., *Leave Well Alone! Where Oil Shapes Dynasties and Destinies* (Southend: Prittle Brook, 1994)

Marglin, S. A., 'What Do Bosses Do? The Origins and Functions of Hierarchy in Capitalist Production', *Radical Review of Political Economics*, vol. 6, no. 2 (1974)

Marx, Karl, *Capital: A Critique of Political Economy*, vol. 1 (London: Lawrence & Wishart, 1972)

Massouud, Mark, *Law's Fragile State: Colonial Authoritarianism and Humanitarian Legacies in Sudan* (Cambridge: Cambridge University Press, 2013)

Mastor, Roxana A., and Ioannis Papageorgiou, 'Financing Climate Resilient Infrastructure in the MENA Region: Potentials and Challenges of Blockchain Technology', in *Climate Change Law and Policy in the Middle East and North Africa Region*, edited by Damilola S. Olawuyi (Abingdon: Routledge, 2022)

Mathiesen, Toby, *Sectarian Gulf: Bahrain, Saudi Arabia and the Arab Spring that wasn't* (Stanford, CA: Stanford University Press, 2013)

Mattar, Noor, 'Bahrain's Shia Muslims Tense as Politicians and Preachers Pledge Allegiance to ISIS', *Global Voices*, 24 July 2014: https://globalvoices.org/2014/07/24/bahrains-shia-muslims-tense-as-politicians-andpreachers-pledge-allegiance-to-isis/

Mayer, A. E., 'The Shariah: A Methodology or a Body of Substantive Rules?', in *Islamic Law and Jurisprudence*, edited by N. Heer (Seattle, WA: University of Washington Press, 1990)

McCarthy, Nolan, Keith Poole, and Howard Rosenthal, *Polarized America: The Dance of Ideology and Unequal Riches* (Cambridge, MA: MIT Press, 2008)

McCraw, Thomas K., *Prophet of Innovation: Joseph Schumpeter and Creative Destruction* (Cambridge, MA: Harvard University Press, 2007)

McMillen, Michael J. T., 'The Arcapita Group Bankruptcy: A Restructuring Case Study', International Shari'ah Research Academy for Islamic Finance and the Thomson Reuters Report, 8 November 2015

McNeill, William, and Oscar Sanchez Duran, 'Market Guide for Global Trade Management Software', Gartner Report, 10 July 2019

Meguro, Maiko, 'Litigating Climate Change through International Law: Obligations Strategy and Rights Strategy', *Leiden Journal of International Law*, vol. 33, no. 4 (2020)

Merryman, John Henry, 'Ownership and Estate (Variations on a Theme by Lawson)', *Tulane Law Review*, vol. 48 (1974)

Mersch, Y., 'About the Role of Central Bank in Financial Stability and Prudential Liquidity Supervision and the Attractiveness of Islamic Finance', IFSB Public Lecture on Financial Policy and Stability, Kuala Lumpur, Islamic Financial Services Lecture, 2009

Mersch, Y., 'Virtual or Virtueless? The Evolution of Money in the Digital Age', Official Monetary and Financial Institutions Forum, London, 8 February 2018

Merton, R. C., 'An Analytic Derivation of the Cost of Deposit Insurance and Loan Guarantees: An Application of Modern Option Pricing Theory', *Journal of Banking and Finance*, vol. 1, no. 1 (1977)

Metcalf, Barbara Daly, *Making Muslim Space in North America and Europe: Comparative Studies in Muslim Societies* (Berkeley, CA: University of California Press, 1992)

Millington, Benjamin, 'KBR Awarded Qatar-Bahrain Construction Contract', *Construction Week Online*, 16 November 2008

Minsky, Hyman, *Stabilizing an Unstable Economy* (New York: McGraw-Hill Professional, 2008)

Mirakhor, Abbas, 'Islamic Finance and Globalization: A Convergence?', *Journal of Islamic Economics, Banking and Finance*, vol. 3, no. 2 (2007)

Mirakhor, Abbas, 'Epistemology of Finance: Misreading Smith', *Islamic Finance Review*, vol. 1 (2011)

Mirakhor, Abbas, and Hossein Askari, *Islam and the Path to Human and Economic Development* (New York: Palgrave Macmillan, 2010)

Mirakhor, Abbas, and Noureddine Krichenne, 'The Recent Crisis: Lessons for Islamic Finance', IFSB Public Lecture on Financial Policy and Stability, Kuala Lumpur, Islamic Finance Services Board, 2009

Mirakhor, Abbas, and Iqbal Zaidi, 'Profit and Loss Sharing Contracts', in *Handbook of Islamic Banking*, edited by M. Kabir Hassan and Mervyn K. Lewis, (Cheltenham: Edward Elgar, 2007)

Mishra, A., 'International Investment Patterns: Evidence Using a New Dataset', *Research in International Business and Finance*, vol. 21, no. 2 (2007)

Mitchell, T., and M. Hulme 'A Country-by-Country Analysis of Past and Future Warming Rates', Tyndall Centre Working Paper No. 1, University of East Anglia, 2000

Mokyr, Joel, *The Lever of Riches: Technological Creativity and Economic Progress* (Oxford: Oxford University Press, 1990)

Mokyr, Joel, *The Gifts of Athena: Historical Origins of the Knowledge Economy* (Princeton, NJ: Princeton University Press, 2002)

Mokyr, Joel, *A Culture of Growth: The Origins of the Modern Economy* (Princeton, NJ: Princeton University Press, 2017)

Momani, B., 'Gulf Cooperation Council Oil Exporters and the Future of the Dollar', *New Political Economy*, vol. 13, no. 3 (2008)

Momen, Moojan, *An Introduction to Shi'i Islam: The History and Doctrines of Twelver Shi'ism* (New Haven, CT: Yale University Press, 1985)

Monetary Authority of Singapore, Crypto-currency Payment Service Regulation Bill 2018

Moody's Investors Service, 'Sukuk Issuance Surges, Dominated by Government Related Issuers', press release (10 November 2009)

Morck, Randall, 'On the Economics of Concentrated Ownership', *Canadian Business Law Journal*, vol. 26 (1996)

Morck, Randall, Andrei Schleifer, and Robert W. Vishny, 'Do Managerial Objectives Drive Bad Acquisitions?', *Journal of Finance*, vol. 45, no. 1 (1990)

Morck, Randall, Andrei Schleifer, and Robert W. Vishny, 'The Stock Market and Investment: Is the Market a Sideshow?', *Brookings Papers on Economic Activity*, vol. 21, no. 2 (1990)

Morgan, Kevin, and Philip Cooke, *The Associational Economy: Firms, Regions and Innovation* (Oxford: Oxford University Press, 1998)

Moritz, Jessie, 'Rents, Start-ups, and Obstacles to SME Entrepreneurialism in Oman, Bahrain and Qatar', in *Employment and Career Motivation in the Arab Gulf States: The Rentier Mentality Revisited*, edited by Annika Kropf and Mohamed A. Ramady (Berlin: Gerlach Press, 2015)

Morris, Nicky, 'Trade Finance Blockchain Race is About to Start', *Ledger Insights*, June 2018

Muranaga, J., and M. Ohsawa, 'Measurement of Liquidity Risk in the Context of Market Risk Calculation', in *The Measurement of Aggregate Market Risk* (Basel: Bank for International Settlements, 1997)

Myers, S. C., and N. S. Majluf, 'Corporate Financing and Investment Decisions when Firms have Information that Investors do not have', *Journal of Financial Economics*, vo. 13, no. 2 (1984)

Nadar, Aisha, 'Islamic Finance: Potential Implications for Dispute Resolution', *Arbitration*, vol. 75, no. 3 (2009)

Naeem, Muhammad Abubakr, Fiza Qureshi, Muhammad Arif, and Faruk Balli, 'Asymmetric Relationship between Gold and Islamic Stocks in Bearish, Normal, and Bullish Market Conditions', *Resources Policy*, vol. 72 (2021)

Nagy, Sharon, 'Bahraini and Non-Bahraini Women in Bahrain's Workforce: Gender, Work and Nationality', *Arabian Humanities: International Journal of Archaeology and Social Sciences in the Arabian Peninsula*, vol. 1 (2013)

Naifar, Nader, and Mohammed Salah Al Dohaiman, 'Nonlinear Analysis among Crude Oil Prices, Stock Markets' Return and Macro-Economic Variables', *International Review of Economics and Finance*, vol. 27 (2013)

Najjar, Naser J., 'Can Financial Ratios Reliably Measure the Performance of Banks in Bahrain?', *International Journal of Economics and Finance*, vol. 5, no. 3 (2013)

Nakhleh, Emile A., *Bahrain: Political Development in a Modernizing Society* (Lexington, MA: Lexington Books, 1976)

Naon, Grigera, 'The Role of International Commercial Arbitration', *Arbitration*, vol. 65 (1999)

Nassehi, Ramin, 'Haunted by Capital Inflows: How Hot Money from Abroad Fuelled UAE's Financial Crisis', *International Journal of Sustainable Human Development*, vol. 1, no. 2 (2013)

Nekhili, Ramzi, Saad Darwish, and Marwan Mohamed Abdeldayem, 'Impact of Education Tourism on Bahrain's Economic Growth: A Perspective', International Journal of Learning and Development', 9, 2 (2019).

Nelken, David, 'Eugen Erlich, Living Law and Plural Legalities', *Theoretical Inquiries in Law*, vol. 9, no. 2 (2008)

Nethercott, Craig R., and David M. Eisenberg (ed.), *Islamic Finance: Law and Practice* (Oxford: Oxford University Press, 2012)

Neumark, David, and Donna Rothstein, 'School-to-Career Programs and Transitions to Employment and Higher Education', NBER Working Paper No. 10060, Cambridge, MA, 2003

Niethammer, Katya, 'Voices in Parliament, Debates in Majilis, and Banners on Streets: Avenues of Political Participation in Bahrain', EUI Working Paper No. 27, Robert Schuman Centre for Advanced Studies, Florence, 2006

Nili, Farhad, 'Iran: Islamic Banking and Finance', in *The Islamic Finance Handbook: A Practitioner's Guide to the Global Markets*, edited by Sasikala Thiagaraja, Andrew Morgan, Andrew Tebbutt, and Geraldine Chan (Singapore: Wiley, 2014)

Noland, Marcus, and Howard Pack, *The Arab Economies in a Changing World* (Washington, DC: Peterson Institute, 2007)

North, D. C., *Structure and Change in Economic History* (New York: Norton, 1981)

North, D. C., *Institutions, Institutional Change and Economic Performance* (Cambridge: Cambridge University Press, 1990)

North, D. C., and R. P. Thomas, *The Rise of the Western World: A New Economic History* (New York: Cambridge University Press, 1973)

North, D. C., J. J. Wallis, and B. R. Weingast, *Violence and Social Orders: A Conceptual Framework for Interpreting Recorded Human History* (Cambridge: Cambridge University Press, 2009)

Nugent, Jeffrey B., 'Does Labor Law Reform Offer an Opportunity for Reducing Arab Youth Unemployment', in *Young Generation Awakening: Economics, Society, and Policy on the Eve of the Arab Spring*, edited by Edward A. Sayre and Tarik M. Yousef (Oxford: Oxford University Press, 2016)

Nusair, Salah A., 'The Effects of Oil Price Shocks on the Economies of Gulf Cooperation Council Countries: Nonlinear Analysis', *Energy Policy*, vol. 91 (2016)

Nusair, Salah A., and Jamal A. Al-Khasawneh, 'Oil Price Shocks and Stock Market Returns of the GCC Countries: Empirical Evidence from Quantile Regression Analysis', *Economic Change and Restructuring*, vol. 51, no. 4 (2018)

O'Connor, F. A., B. M. Lucey, J. A. Batten, and D. G. Baur, 'The Financial Economics of Gold—a Survey', *International Review of Financial Analysis*, vol. 41 (2015)

OECD, 'Due Diligence for Responsibility Supply Chains of Minerals from Conflict and High Risk Areas', (2019)

Oh, Won Yong, Young Kyun Chang and Aleksey Martynov, 'The Effect of Ownership Structure on Corporate Social Responsibility: Empirical Evidence from Korea', *Journal of Business Ethics*, 104 (2011)

Olawuyi, Damilola S., 'Advancing Innovations in Renewable Energy Technologies as Alternatives to Fossil Fuel Use in the Middle East: Trends, Limitations and Ways Forward', in *Innovation in Energy Law and Technology: Dynamic Solutions for Energy Transitions*, edited by D. Zillman, M. Roggenkamp, L. Paddock, and L. Godden (Oxford: Oxford University Press, 2018)

Olawuyi, Damilola S., 'Human Rights and the Environment in Middle East and North African (MENA) Regions: Trends, Limitations and Opportunities', in *Encyclopaedia of Human Rights and the Environment, Indivisibility, Dignity, and Legality*, edited by J. May and E. Daly (Cheltenham: Edward Elgar, 2018)

Omar al Shehbai, 'The Community at Pearl Roundabout Is at the Centre', The National (1 March 2011)

Onley, James, *The Arabian Frontier of the British Raj: Merchants, Rulers, and the British in the Nineteenth-century Gulf* (Oxford: Oxford University Press, 2007)

Onley, James, 'Transnational Merchant Families in the Nineteenth and Twentieth Century Gulf', in *The Gulf Family: Kinship Policies and Modernity*, edited by Alanoud Alsharekh (London: SAQI in association with London Middle East Institute SOAS, 2007)

O'Rourke, Kevin, and Jeffrey Williamson, *Globalization and History: The Evolution of a Nineteenth Century Atlantic Economy* (Cambridge, MA: MIT Press, 2001)

Oseni, Umar A., and S. Nazim Ali (ed.), *Fintech in Islamic Finance: Theory and Practice* (Abingdon: Routledge, 2019)

Osman, Dwaa, 'The State and Innovation: An Analytical Framework', *The Muslim World*, 2017

Osmani, N.M., and M. F. Abdullah, 'Mushrakak Mutanagisch Home Financing: A Review of Literatures and Practices of Islamic Banks in Malaysia', *International Review of Business Research Papers*, vol. 6, no. 2 (2010)

Ostrom, Elinor, 'Beyond Markets and States: Polycentric Governance of Complex Economic Systems', *American Economic Review*, vol. 100, no. 3 (2010)

Owen, Roderic, *The Golden Bubble: Arabian Gulf Documentary* (London: Collins, 1957)

Owen, Roger, *The Middle East in the World Economy 1800–1914* (London: I. B. Tauris, 1981)

Owen, Roger, 'Globalization at the Beginnings of the Twentieth and Twenty-first Centuries', in *Globalization and the Gulf*, edited by John W. Fox, Nada Mourtada-Sabbah, and Mohammed Al-mutawa (Abingdon: Routledge, 2006)

Oxford Business Group, 'Bahrain Upgrades Existing Tourism Infrastructure to Meet Demand', 2018, pp. 2, 8–9.

Oxford Economics, 'The Impact of Inflation and Deflation on the Case for Gold', (July 2011)

Ozbek, Nadir, 'Philanthropic Activity, Ottoman Patriotism and the Hamidian Regime 1876–1909', *International Journal of Middle Eastern Studies*, vol. 37 (2005)

Palgrave, William Gifford, *Narrative of a Year's Journey through Central and Eastern Arabia, 1862–1863*, 2 vols. (London: Macmillan, 1865, reproduced by Gregg Publishing, 1969)

Pandya, Sophia, 'Women's Shi'i Ma'atim in Bahrain', *Journal of Middle East Women's Studies*, vol. 6, no. 2 (2010)

Parthasarathi, Parasannan, *Why Europe Grew Rich and Asia Did Not: Global Economic Divergence, 1600–1850* (Cambridge: Cambridge University Press, 2012)

Patel, Bhavin, 'Lowering Barriers to UK-GCC trade', OMFIF, 19 April 2018

Paul, Ryan, 'The School-to-Work Transition: A Cross-National Perspective', *Journal of Economic Literature*, vol. 39 (2001)

Peters, S., 'Waqf in Classical Islamic Law', in *The Encyclopaedia of Islam*, edited by P. J. Bearman, T. H. Bianquis, C. E. Bosworth, E. van Donzel, W. P. Heinrichs (Leiden: Brill, 2000)

Peterson, J. E., *The Arab Gulf States: Steps towards Political Participation* (New York: Praeger, 1988)

Petry, Carl F., 'Fractionalized Estates in a Centralized Regime: The Holdings of Al-Ashraf Qaythay and Qansuh Al-Ghawri According to Their Waqf Deeds', *Journal of the Economic and Social History of the Orient*, vol. 41, no. 1 (1998)

Pettigrew, A. M., and E. Fenton (ed.), *The Innovating Organization* (London: Sage, 2000)

Pierret, Thomas, 'Les oulémas: une hégémonie religieuse ébranlée par la revolution', in *Pas de printémps pour la Syrie*, edited by Francois Burgat and Bruno Paoli (Paris: La Découverte, 2013)

Pierret, Thomas, *Religion and State in Syria: Sunni Ulama from Coup to Revolution* (Cambridge: Cambridge University Press, 2013)

Pierret, Thomas, 'State Management of Religion in Syria: The End of Indirect Rule?', in *Middle East Authoritarianisms: Governance, Contestation, and Regime Resilience in Syria and Iran*, edited by Steven Heydemann and Reinoud Leenders (Stanford, CA: Stanford University Press, 2013)

Pierret, Thomas, 'The Syrian Baath Party and Sunni Islam: Conflicts and Connivance', *Middle East Brief*, no. 77 (2014)

Pierret, Thomas, 'Merchant Background, Bourgeois Ethics: The Syrian Ulama and Economic Liberalization', in *Syria from Reform to Revolt: Culture, Society and Religion*, edited by Christa Salamandra and Leif Stenberg (Syracuse, NY: Syracuse University Press, 2015)

Pierret, Thomas, and Kjetil Selvik, 'Limits of Authoritarian Upgrading in Syria: Private Welfare, Islamic Charities, and the Rise of the Zayd Movement', *International Journal of Middle East Studies*, vol. 41, no. 4 (2009)

Piketty, Thomas, *Capital in the Twenty-First Century* (Cambridge, MA: Belknap Press of Harvard University Press, 2014)

Pilkington, M., 'Blockchain Technology: Principles and Applications', in *Research Handbook on Digital Transformations*, edited by F. X. Olleros and M. Zhegu (Cheltenham: Edward Elgar, 2016)

Pioppi, S., 'From Religious Charity to the Welfare State and Back: The Case of Islamic Endowments (waqfs) Revival in Egypt', EU Working Papers, RCAS No. 2004/34

Piore, M., and C. Sabel, *The Second Industrial Divide: Possibilities for Prosperity* (New York: Basic Books, 1984)

Pitelis, C. N., *Market and Non-Market Hierarchies: Theory of Institutional Failure* (Oxford: Blackwell, 1993)

Polanyi, Karl, *The Great Transformation: The Political and Economic Origins of our Time* (Boston, MA: Beacon Books, 1957)

Pomeranz, Kenneth, *The Great Divergence: China, Europe and the Making of the Modern World Economy* (Princeton, NJ: Princeton University Press, 2001)

Popp, Andrew, and John Wilson, 'Business in the Regions: From "Old" Districts to "New" Clusters?', *Business in Britain in the Twentieth Century*, edited by Richard Coopey and Peter Lyth (Oxford: Oxford University Press, 2009)

Porter, Michael, 'Capital Disadvantage: America's Failing Capital Investment System', *Harvard Business Review*, vol. 70, no. 5 (1992)

Postel, Charles, *The Populist Vision* (Oxford and New York: Oxford University Press, 2007)

'The Potential Impact of Artificial Intelligence in the Middle East', PWC, 2018

Powers, David S., 'The Islamic Family Endowment [waqf]', *Vanderbilt Journal of Transitional Law*, vol. 32, no. 4 (1999)

Praveen, R., V. Keloth, A. G. Abo-Khalil, A. S. Alghamdi, A. M. Eltamaly, and I. Tlili, 'An Insight to the Energy Policy of GCC Countries to Meet Renewable Energy Targets of 2030', *Energy Policy*, vol. 147 (December 2020)

PricewaterhouseCoopers, 2018

Pritchett, Lant, 'Has Education had a Growth Payoff in the MENA Region?', World Bank, Middle East and North Africa Working Paper No. 18, December 1999

Prosser, Tony, *The Regulatory Enterprise* (Oxford: Oxford University Press, 2010)

Public Commission for the Protection of Marine Resources, Environment and Wild Life (PCPMREW2013)

Qubain, Fahim I., 'Social Classes and Tensions in Bahrain', *Middle East Journal*, vol. 9, no. 3 (1955)

Quilliam, Neil, 'The States of the Gulf Cooperation Council', in *Good Governance in the Middle East Oil Monarchies*, edited by T. Najem and M. Hetherington (London: Routledge Curzon, 2003)

Quilliam, Neil, 'Political Reform in Bahrain: The Turning Tide', in *Reform in the Middle East Oil Monarchies*, edited by Anoushiravan Ehteshami (Ithaca, NY: Ithaca Press, 2007)

Radhi, Hassan Ali, *Judiciary and Arbitration in Bahrain* (Leiden: Kluwer Law International, 2003)

Rafique, Azmat, 'Oman, the Dawn of Islamic Banking', in *The Islamic Finance Handbook: A Practitioner's Guide to the Global Markets* (New York: Wiley, 2014)

Rajamani, Lavanya, 'Ambition and Differentiation in the 2015 Paris Agreement: Interpretative Possibilities and Underlying Politics', *International and Comparative Law Quarterly*, vol. 65, no. 2 (2016)

Rajan, Raghuram G., *Fault Lines: How Hidden Fractures Still Threaten the World Economy* (Princeton, NJ: Princeton University Press, 2010)

Rajeswary Ampalavanar Brown, review of Ercanbrack, 'The Transformation of Islamic Law', in *Modern Law Review*, vol. 81, no. 3 (2018), pp. 563–6

Ramlan, S., 'Religious Law for the Environment: Comparative Islamic Environmental Law in Singapore, Malaysia and Indonesia', National University of Singapore, Working Paper No. 19/03, Centre for Asian Legal Studies, 2019

Raouf, M. A., 'Climate Change Threats, Opportunities and the GCC Countries', Middle East Institute Policy Brief No.12, Washington, DC, 2008

Raouf, M. A., 'Water Issues in the Gulf: Time for Action', Middle East Institute Policy Brief No. 22, Washington, DC, 2009

Ratner, David L., 'Corporations and the Constitutions', *University of San Francisco Law Review*, vol. 15 (1981)

Read R. A., 'Report on Strikes and Riots in Bahrain', 12 March 1956, TNA, FO 371/120545

Redfern, B., 'Private Developers Drive Boom', *Middle East Economic Digest*, 1 February 2008

Richards, A., and J. Waterbury, *A Political Economy of the Middle East* (Oxford: Westview, 2006)

Ridge, N., *Education and the Reverse Gender Divide in the Gulf States: Embracing the Global, Ignoring the Local* (New York: Teachers College Press, 2014)

Rioja, Felix, and Neven Valev, 'Stock Markets, Banks and the Sources of Economic Growth in Low and High Income Countries', *Journal of Economic Finance*, vol. 38 (2014)

Rizzo, Agantino, 'Why Knowledge Megaprojects will Fail to Transform Gulf Countries in Post-carbon Economies: The Case for Qatar', *Journal of Urban Technology*, vol. 24, no. 3 (2017)

Rojewski, J. W. (ed.), *International Perspectives on Workforce Education and Development* (Greenwich, CT: Information Age Publishing, 2004)

Rosenthal, Leonard, *The Kingdom of the Pearl* (London: Nisbet & Co, 1920, reprinted 1984)

Rothschild, Michael, and Joseph Stiglitz, 'Equilibrium in Competitive Insurance Markets: An Essay in the Economics of Imperfect Information', *Quarterly Journal of Economics*, vol. 90, no. 4 (1976)

Rotundo, G., and A. M. D'Arcangelis, 'Ownership and Control in Shareholding Networks', *Journal of Economic Interaction and Coordination*, vol. 5 (2010)

Roy, Tirthankar, and Giorgio Riello (ed.), *Global Economic History* (London: Bloomsbury Academic, 2019)

Rumaihi, M. G., *Bahrain: Social and Political Change Since the First World War* (London: Bowker, 1976)

Russell, David, and Gabor Bognar, 'The Application of English Law in the Financial Free Zones of the United Arab Emirates', *Trusts and Trustees*, vol. 23, no. 5 (2017)

Sabel, C., and J. Zeitlin, 'Historical Alternatives to Mass Production: Politics, Markets and Technology in Nineteenth-century Industrialization', *Past and Present*, no. 108, pp. 133–76 (August 1985)

Sabit, Mohammad Tahir, and Mar Iman Abdul Hamid, 'Obstacles of the Current Concept of Waqf to the Development of Waqf Properties and the Recommended Alternative', *Malaysian Journal of Real Estate*, vol. 1, no. 1 (2006)

Sachs, Jeffrey D., and Andrew M. Warner, 'Natural Resource Abundance and Economic Growth', National Bureau of Economic Research, Working Paper No. 5398, Cambridge, MA, 1995

Sadique, M. A., 'Development of Dormant Waqf Properties: Application of Traditional and Contemporary Modes of Financing', *International Islamic University of Malaysia Law Journal*, vol. 18 (2010)

Sahlman, William A., 'The Structure and Governance of Venture Capital Organizations', *Journal of Financial Economics*, vol. 27 (1990)

Said, Edward, *Orientalism* (New York: Vintage, 1979)

Saidi N., and A. Prasad, 'Background Note: Trends in Trade and Investment Policies in the MENA Region', MENA-OECD Competitiveness Programme, MENA-OECD Working Group on Investment and Trade, 27–28 November 2018, p. 23

Sait, Siraj, and Hilary Lim, *Land, Law and Islam: Property and Human Rights in the Muslim World* (London: Zed Books, 2006)

Sakai, Keiko, 'Modernity and Tradition and the Islamic Movements in Iraq: Continuity and Discontinuity in the Role of the Ulama', *Arab Studies Quarterly*, vol. 23, no. 1 (2001)

Salahi-Isfahani, D., and N. Dhillon, 'Stalled Youth Transitions in the Middle East: A Framework for Policy Reform', Middle East Youth Initiative, Working Paper No. 8, Wolfensohn Center for Development, Brookings Institution, Washington, DC, 2008

Salem, Rania Abdelfattah, and Ahmed Mohamed Badreldin, 'Assessing Resilience of Islamic Banks: An Empirical Analysis', in *Islamic Banking and Financial Crisis: Reputation, Stability, and Risks*, edited by Habib Ahmed, Mehmet Asutay, and Rodney Wilson (Edinburgh: Edinburgh University Press, 2014)

Salih, S. A., *The Challenges of Poverty Alleviation in IDB Member Countries* (Jeddah: Islamic Development Bank, 1999)

Santen, Emma van, 'Islamic Banking and Finance Regulation in Malaysia: Between State, Shari'a, the Courts and Islamic Moral Economy', *Company Lawyer*, vol. 38, no. 1 (2018)

Santos, Andre Oliveira, 'Integrated Ownership and Control in GCC Corporate Sector', IMF Working Paper, 2015

Sarin, A., K. A. Shastri, and K. Shastri, 'Ownership Structure and Stock market Liquidity', Working Paper, Santa Clara University, 2000

Satoe, Horii, 'Reconsideration of Legal Devices (Hiyal) in Islamic Jurisprudence: The Hanafis and Their "Exits" (Makharij)', *Islamic Law and Society*, vol. 9, no. 3 (2002), 312–57

Satoshi, Nakamoto, 'Bitcoin: A Peer-to-Peer Electronic Cash System', https://bitcoin.org/bitcoin.pdf, 2008.

Schaaf, Steven D., 'Contentious Politics in the Courthouse: Law as a Tool for Resisting Authoritarian States in the Middle East', *Law & Society Review*, vol. 55, no. 1 (2021)

Schar, Fabian, 'Decentralised Finance: On Blockchain and Smart Contract-Based Financial Markets', *Federal Reserve Bank of St. Louis Review*, Second Quarter 2021

Schechter, Relli, 'Reading Advertisements in Colonial /Development Context: Cigarettes Advertising and Identity Politics in Egypt c.1919–1939', *Journal of Social History*, vol. 39, no. 2 (2005)

Schechter, Relli, 'Global Conservatism: How Marketing Articulated a Neotraditional Saudi Arabian Society during the First Oil Boom, c.1974–1984', *Journal of Macromarketing*, vol. 31, no. 4 (2011)

Schumpeter, J., *The Theory of Economic Development* (Cambridge, MA: Harvard University Press, 1911)

Scott, James C., *The Moral Economy of the Peasant: Rebellion and Subsistence in Southeast Asia* (New Haven, CT: Yale University Press, 1976)

Scott, James C., *Weapons of the Weak: Everyday Forms of Peasant Resistance* (New Haven, CT: Yale University Press, 1985)

Scott, James C., *Domination and the Arts of Resistance: Hidden Transcripts* (New Haven, CT: Yale University Press, 1990)

Scott, James C., *The Art of Not Being Governed: An Anarchist History of Upland Southeast Asia* (New Haven, CT: Yale University Press, 2009)

Secombe, Ian, and Richard Lawless, 'Foreign Worker Dependence in the Gulf and the International Oil Companies 1910–50', *International Migration Review*, vol. 20, no. 3 (1986)

Selim, Hoda, and Chahir Zaki, 'The Institutional Curse of Natural Resources in the Arab World', in *Understanding and Avoiding the Oil Curse in Resource-rich Arab Economies*, edited by Ibrahim Elbadawi and Hoda Selim (Cambridge: Cambridge University Press, 2016)

Sen, Amartya, *Poverty and Famines: An Essay on Entitlement and Deprivation* (Oxford: Clarendon Press, 1981)

Setser, B., and R. Ziemba, 'GCC Sovereign Funds: Reversal of Fortune', Council of Foreign Relations, January 2009

Sewell, William, 'Toward a Post-Materialist Rhetoric for Labor History', in *Rethinking Labor History: Essays on Discourse and Class Analysis*, edited by Lenard R. Berlanstein (Champaign, IL: University of Illinois Press, 1993)

Sharabi, Hisham, *Neopatriarchy* (Oxford: Oxford University Press, 1988)

Shatzmiller, Maya, 'Economic Performance and Economic Growth in the Early Islamic World', *Journal of the Economic and Social History of the Orient*, vol. 54 (2011)

Shaw, Susan M., Nancy Staton Barbour, Patti Duncan, Kryn Freehling-Burton, Jane Nichols (ed.), *Women's Lives around the World: A Global Encyclopedia* (Santa Barbara, CA: ABC-CLIO, 2017)

Sheikh, Tahir Ali, and Mohamed Ayaz Mohamed Ismail, *Selected Sukuk Issuance, International Islamic Financial Market: Comprehensive Study of the Global Sukuk Market*, 2018, pp. 71–93, 125–55

Sheng, Andrew, *From Asian to Global Financial Crisis: An Asian Regulator's View of Unfettered Finance in the 1990s and 2000s* (Cambridge: Cambridge University Press, 2009)

Sherman, Eugene J., 'Gold: A Conservative Prudent Diversifier: Gold has Lowered Volatility and Improves Returns in almost all Environments', *Journal of Portfolio Management*, vol. 8, no. 3 (1982)

Shiller, Robert J., 'The Use of Volatility Measures in Assessing Market Efficiency', *Journal of Finance*, vol. 36, no. 2 (1981)

Shiller, Robert J., 'Stock Prices and Social Dynamics', Carnegie Rochester Conference Series on Public Policy, 1984

Shiller, Robert J., *Finance and the Good Society* (Princeton, NJ: Princeton University Press, 2012)

Shiller, Robert J., 'Investor Behavior in the 1987 Stock Market Crash: Survey Evidence', NBER Working Paper No. 2446 (November 1987)

Shiller, Robert J., and J. Pound, 'Survey Evidence on Diffusion of Interest and Information among Investors', *Journal of Economic Behavior and Organization*, vol. 12 (1989)

Shleifer, Andrei, and Robert W. Vishny, 'A Survey of Corporate Governance', *Journal of Finance*, vol. 52, no. 2 (1997)

Sifat, Imtiaz Mohammad, and Azhar Mohamad, 'Revisiting Fiat Regime's Attainability of Shari'ah Objectives and Possible Futuristic Alternatives', *Journal of Muslim Minority Affairs*, vol. 38, no. 1 (2018)

Singer, Amy, 'A Note on Land and Identity: From Zeamet to Waqf', in *New Perspectives on Property and Land in the Middle East*, edited by Roger Owen (Cambridge, MA: Harvard University Press, 2001)

Sirri, Erik R., and Peter Tufano, 'Costly Search and Mutual Fund Flows', *Journal of Finance*, vol. 53, no. 5 (1998)

Smith, Adam, *The Wealth of Nations* (London: Penguin, 1986)

Smith, Neil, *Uneven Development: Nature, Capital, and the Production of Space* (Athens, GA: University of Georgia Press, 2008

'Spending on Cognitive and Artificial Intelligence Systems to Undergo Sustained Period of Growth in the Middle East & Africa, says IDC', International Data Corporation, 24 October 2017

Springborg, Robert, 'The Precarious Economics of Arab Springs', *Survival: Geopolitics and Strategy*, vol. 53, no. 6 (2011)

Staber, U., N. Schaefer, and B. Sharma (ed.), *Business Networks: Prospects for Regional Development* (Berlin: de Gruyter, 1996)

Standard and Poor, 'Sukuk Market Has Continued to Progress to 2009, Despite Some Roadblocks', press release (September 2009)

Standing Committee for Economic and Commercial Cooperation of the Organization of Islamic Cooperation (COMEC), *The Diversification of Islamic Financial Instruments: Case Study Bahrain*, edited by Alaa Alabed (COMEC, 2017)

Stearns, Peter N., and Carol Z. Stearns, 'Emotionology: Clarifying the History of Emotions and Emotional Standards', *American Historical Review*, vol. 90, no. 4 (1988)

Stibbard, Paul, David Russell and Blake Bromley, 'Understanding the Waqf in the World of the Trust', *Trust and Trustees*, vol. 18 (2012)

Stigler, George, *The Organization of Industry* (Homewood, IL: R. D. Irwin, 1968)

Stork, Joe, 'Bahrain Crisis Worsens', *Middle East Report*, No. 204 (July–September 1997)

Stork, Joe, *Routine Abuse, Routine Denial: Civil Rights and the Political Crisis in Bahrain* (New York: Human Rights Watch, 1997)

Strobl, Staci, 'Policing Housemaids: The Criminalization of Domestic Workers in Bahrain', *British Journal of Criminology*, vol. 49, no. 2 (2009)

Subrahmanyam, Sanjay, 'Connected Histories: Notes towards a Reconfiguration of Early Modern Eurasia', *Modern Asian Studies*, vol. 31, no. 3 (1997)

Sultany, Nimer, *Law and Revolution: Legitimacy and Constitutionalism after the Arab Spring* (Oxford: Oxford University Press, 2017)

The Sustainable Energy Unit, The Kingdom of Bahrain, the National Renewable Energy Action Plan (NREAP), 2017

Syamimi, O. S., I. N. Hanim, M. Zulhaili, and B. Ruwaidah, 'Green Mosque: A Living Nexus', *Environment-Behaviour Proceedings Journal*, vol. 3 (2018)

Tasca, P., and R. Piselli, 'The Blockchain Paradox', in *Regulating Blockchain: Techno-Social and Legal Challenges*, edited by I. Lianos, P. Hacker, S. Eich, and G. Dimitropoulos (Oxford: Oxford University Press, 2019)

Tedlow, Richard S., *New and Improved: The Story of Mass Marketing in America* (Oxford: Heinemann Professional, 1990)

Teubner, Gunther, 'Legal Irritants: Good Faith in British Law or How Unifying Law Ends up in New Divergences', *Modern Law Review*, vol. 61, no. 1 (1998)

Thaler, R. H., 'Mental Accounting and Consumer choice', *Marketing Science*, vol. 4 (1985)

Thel, Steve, '$850,000 in Six Minutes: The Mechanics of Securities Manipulation', *Cornell Law Review*, vol. 79 (1994)

Thomas, K., 'Kingdom Takes on Gulf Shipping Giants', *Middle East Economic Digest*, vol. 53, no. 16 (2009)

Thomas, Vinod, Yan Wang, and Xibo Fan, 'Measuring Education Inequality: Gini Coefficient of Education', World Bank Research Paper No. 2525 (Washington, DC: World Bank, 2001)

Thompson, E. P., 'The Moral Economy of the English Crowd in the Eighteenth Century', *Past and Present*, vol. 50, no. 1 (1971)

Thompson, E. P., *Whigs and Hunters: The Origins of the Black Act* (New York: Pantheon Books, 1975)

Thompson, E. P., *The Making of the English Working Class* (Harmondsworth: Penguin, 1991)

Tilly, Charles, 'War Making and State Making as Organized Crime', in *Bringing the State Back In*, edited by Peter Evans, Dietrich Rueschmeyer, and Theda Skocpol (Cambridge: Cambridge University Press, 1985)

Tilly, Charles, *Durable Inequality* (Berkeley, CA: University of California Press, 1998)

Tilly, Charles, and Sidney Tarrow, *Contentious Politics* (New York: Oxford University Press, 2015)

Torabi, Omid, and Abbas Mirakhor, *Crowdfunding with Enhanced Reputation Monitoring Mechanism (Fame)* (Oldenbourg: De Gruyter, 2020)

Torabi, Omid, and Sahul Haeed bin Muhammad Ibrahim, 'Qard al-Hasan Loans in Iran', Working Paper, Kuala Lumpur, INCEIF, The Global University in Islamic Finance, 2012

Trantino, Gustavo Crespi, 'Computation, Estimation and Prediction Using the Key Indicators of the Labour Market (KILM) data set', Employment Strategy Paper, 2004/16, International Labour Organization, Employment Strategy Department, Geneva

Trentmann, Frank, 'Beyond Consumerism: New Historical Perspectives on Consumption', *Journal of Contemporary History*, vol. 39, no. 3 (2004)

Tripp, Charles, *Islam and the Moral Economy: The Challenge of Capitalism* (Cambridge: Cambridge University Press, 2006)

Tripp, Charles, *The Power and the People: Paths of Resistance in the Middle East* (Cambridge: Cambridge University Press, 2013)

Turen, Seref, 'Performance and Risk Analysis of Islamic Banks: The Case of Bahrain Islamic Bank', *Journal of King Abdulaziz University: Islamic Economics*, vol. 7 (1415/1995)

Turk, Austin T., *Political Criminality: The Defiance and Defence of Authority* (Beverly Hills, CA: Sage Publications, 1982)

Udovitch, Abraham L., *Partnership and Profit in Medieval Islam* (Princeton, NJ: Princeton University Press, 1970)

Udovitch, Abraham L., 'Reflections on the Institutions of Credits and Banking in the Medieval Islamic Near East', *Studia Islamica*, vol. 5, no. 2 (1975)

Ulrichsen, Kristian Coates, 'Gulf Security: Changing Internal and External Dynamics', Working Paper, Kuwait Programme on Development, Governance and Globalization in the Gulf States, London School of Economics and Political Science, 2009

Ulrichsen, Kristian Coates, 'The GCC States and the Shifting Balance of Global Power', Center for International and Regional Studies, Georgetown University, Occasional Paper 6, 2010

UN Environment Programme, 'Faith for Earth Dialogue Synthesis Report', 8 May 2019

Unger, Roberto Mangabeira, *Knowledge and Politics* (New York: Free Press, 1976)

Unger, Roberto Mangabeira, 'The Critical Legal Studies Movement', *Harvard Law Review*, vol. 96, no. 3 (1983)

United Nations Development Programme (UNDP), 'The Future is Decentralised Block Chains, Distributed Ledgers, and the Future of Sustainable Development', 2018

United Nations, Economic and Social Affairs, Population Division, '2013 World Population Prospects: The 2012 Revision', DVD ed.

United Nations Educational, Scientific & Cultural Organization, 2004

United Nations General Assembly, 'Transforming Our World: The 2030 Agenda for Sustainable Development', 21 October 2015, UNDoc.A/RES/70/1, 29

United Nations Statistics Division, National Accounts Main Aggregates Database

Urdal, Henrik, 'A Clash of Generations? Youth Bulges and Political Violence', *International Studies Quarterly*, vol. 5, no. 3 (2006)

Usmani, Shaykh Muhammad Taqi, 'Post-crisis Reforms: Some Points to Ponder', in World Economic Forum, *Faith and the Global Agenda: Values for the Post Crisis Economy* (Geneva: World Economic Forum, 2010)

Uzi, Rabi and Joseph Kostiner, 'The Shi'is in Bahrain: Class and Religious Protest', in *Minorities and the State in the Arab World*, edited by Ofra Bengio and Gabriel Ben-Dor (Boulder, CO: Lynne Rienner, 1999)

Uzsoki, D., 'Tokenization of Infrastructure: A Blockchain-Based Solution to Financing Sustainable Infrastructure', International Institute for Sustainable Development, MAVA, January 2019

Valeri, Marc, 'Contentious Politics in Bahrain: Opposition Cooperation between Regime Manipulation and Youth Radicalization', in *Opposition Cooperation in the Arab World: Contentious Politics in the Time of Change*, edited by Hendrik Kraetzschmar (London: Routledge, 2012)

Valeri, Marc, 'Oligarchy vs. Oligarchy: Business and Politics of Reform in Bahrain and Oman', in *Business Politics in the Middle East*, edited by Stephen Hertog, Giacomo Luciani, and Marc Valeri (London: Hurst, 2013)

Valeri, Marc, 'Islamist Political Societies in Bahrain: Collateral Victims of the 2011 Popular Uprising', in *Islamists and the Politics of the Arab Uprisings*, edited by Hendrik Kraetzchmar and Paolo Rivetti (Edinburgh: Edinburgh University Press, 2018)

Veblen, Thorstein, *The Theory of the Leisure Class: An Economic Study of Institutions* (London: Macmillan, 1924)

Veneroso, Frank, 'Memories of the Souk Al Manakh', see http://www.dfm.co.ac/dfm/main/main.htm

Villiers, Alan, *Sons of Sinbad: An Account of Sailing with the Arabs in Their Dhows*. Introduction By W. Facey, Y. Al-Hijji and G. Pundyk (London: Arabian Publishing, 2006)

Vogel, Frank E., 'The Contract Law of Islam and of Arab Middle East', in *International Encyclopedia of Comparative Law* (Leiden: Brill), vol. VII (2006)

Vogel, F. E., and S. L. Hayes, *Islamic Law and Finance: Religion, Risk and Return* (The Hague: Kluwer International Law Publishers, 1998)

Vulkan, N., T. Astebro, and M. F. Sierra, 'Equity Crowd-funding: A New Phenomena', *Journal of Business Venturing*, vol. 5 (2016)

Walbridge, Linda S., 'Introduction: Shi'ism and Authority', in *The Most Learned of the Shi'a: The Institution of the Marja' Taqlid*, edited by Linda S. Walbridge (New York: Oxford University Press, 2001)

Wallerstein, Immanuel, *The Capitalist World Economy* (Cambridge: Cambridge University Press, 1979)

Wallerstein, Immanuel, *The Modern World System, Vols. 1–4* (Berkeley, CA: University of California Press, 2011)

Warde, Ibrahim, *Islamic Finance in the Global Economy* (Edinburgh: Edinburgh University Press, 2010)

Warren, Richard C., *Corporate Governance and Accountability* (Bromborough: Liverpool Academic Press, 2000)

Watson, Alan, *Legal Transplants: An Approach to Comparative Law* (Athens, GA: University of Georgia Press, 1974)

Weber, Max, *Economy and Society: An Outline of Interpretive Sociology* (Berkeley, CA: University of California Press, 1978)

Wedderburn-Day, A. Roger, 'Sovereign Sukuk: Adaptation and Innovation', *Law and Contemporary Problems*, vol. 73, no. 4 (2010)

Weiss, Max, *In the Shadow of Sectarianism: Law, Shi'ism and the Making of Modern Lebanon* (Cambridge, MA: Harvard University Press, 2010)

Weiss, Max, 'Fear and its Opposites in the History of Emotions', in *Facing Fear: The History of an Emotion in Global Perspective*, edited by Michael Laffan and Max Weiss (Princeton, NJ: Princeton University Press, 2012)

Wilson, Rodney, *Banking and Finance in the Arab Middle East* (London: Macmillan, 1983)

Wilson, Rodney, with Abdullah Al-Salamah, Monica Malik, and Ahmed Al-Rajhi, *Economic Development in Saudi Arabia* (London: Routledge Curzon, 2004)

Woertz, Eckart, *Oil for Food: The Global Food Crisis and the Middle East* (Oxford: Oxford University Press, 2013)

World Bank Database, 2011

World Bank Database, 2014

World Bank, Washington DC

World Development Indicators (WDI) 2004, World Bank, Washington, DC

World Economic Forum, *Global Competition Report*, 2017–18

World Economic Forum and OECD, 'Blended Finance Vol. 1: A Primer for Development Finance and Philanthropic Funders', WEF, September 2015

World Economic Forum, *Global Gender Gap Report* (Geneva: World Economic Forum, 2015)

World Food Programme 2009 Operations, 'Targeted Food Support to Vulnerable Groups Affected by High Food Prices'

World Gold Council, 'The Relevance of Gold as a Strategic Asset, Individual Investors', World Gold Council: https://www.gold.org/goldhub/research/relevance-ofgold-as-a-strategic-asset-2020-individual

Wright, Aaron, and Primavera De Filippi, *Decentralized Blockchain Technology and the Rise of Lex Cryptographia* (New York: Social Science Research Network, 2015)

Xiong, Wei, and Jialin Yu, 'The Chinese Warrants Bubble', *American Economic Review*, 101 (2011)

Yasser, Kureshi, 'When Judges Defy Dictators: An Audience-Based Framework to Explain the Emergence of Judicial Assertiveness against Authoritarian Regimes', *Comparative Politics*, vol. 53, no. 2 (2021)

Yesenn El-Radhi, Economic Diversification in the Gulf States. Public Expenditure and Non-oil Economic Growth in Bahrain, Oman, and Qatar. Bahrain Sectoral Employment Shares Bahraini and Non-Bahraini Nationals 1971–2010, p. 151

Yip, C. M. A., U. B. Gunturu, and G. L. Stenchikov, 'Wind Resource Characterization in the Arabian Peninsula', *Applied Energy*, vol. 164, pp. 826–36 (15 February 2016)

Young, K., and T. Al-Hashmi, 'Women's Economic Inclusion in Bahrain', Bahrain National Human Development Report, Background Paper, 2018

Zartman, I. W., 'Opposition as Support of the State', in *Beyond Coercion: The Durability of the Arab State*, edited by A. Dawisha and I. W. Zartman (London: Croom Helm, 1988)

Zawya Sukuk Database, *Bahrain as a Centre for Islamic Banking*, 2005.

Zdanowicz, John S., 'Trade-based Money Laundering and Terrorist Financing', in *Transnational Financial Crime*, edited by Nikos Passas (London: Routledge, 2013)

Zubari, W., M. Alardi, and A. Al-Shaabani, 'Water Resources Vulnerability', pp. 47–8; Ministry of Municipalities Affairs and Urban Planning, 1979–2015

Zubari, W., M. Alardi, and A. Al-Shaabani, 'Water Resources Vulnerability and Adaptation to Climate Change in the Kingdom of Bahrain', Climate Change Third Communiqué, Kingdom of Bahrain Project, 2018

Zweigert, Konrad, and H. Kotz, *An Introduction to Comparative Law*, trans. Tony Weis (Oxford: Oxford University Press, 3rd edition, 1988)

Newspapers

Akhbar Al Khaleej
Al-Ayam
Al-Waqt
Al-Wasat
Bahrain News Agency
Daily Star (Beirut)
Financial Times
Forbes
Global Voices
The Guardian
Gulf Daily News
Gulf Mirror
Huffington Post
International Business Times
Los Angeles Times
McClatchy Newspapers
The National
The New York Times
Reuters
Singapore Business Review
Trade Arabia
Wall Street Journal
Washington Post

Non-governmental Reports

AAOIFI, *Accounting, Auditing, and Governance Standards for Islamic Financial Institutions: Financial Accounting Standards* (2010)

Bahrain Centre for Islamic Banking Report

Bankscope, *Islamic Finance Reports*

Committee for Economic and Commercial Cooperation of the Organization of Islamic Coop-
    eration (COMCEC), Standing Coordination Office, 'Diversification of Islamic Financial
    Instruments', October 2017, prepared by Alaa Alaabed
Containerisation International, *Containerisation International Yearbook*
Credit Suisse Research Institute, *Emerging Consumer Survey*, 2011
Deloitte Research and Analysis, *Global Impact Report*, 2012
Deloitte Research and Analysis, 'Sustainable Finance: Can Sukuk Become a Driver of Solar
    and Green Energy Growth?', 2018
Deloitte & Touche, Middle East, 'The Global Gold Investment Market: Traits for Shari'ah-based
    Investment Solutions', 2021
GOVERN, 'What Role for Institutional Investors in Corporate Governance in the Middle East
    and North Africa?', Report issued by GOVERN, the Economic and Corporate Governance
    Centre, in joint collaboration with Bogazici University, Centre for Research in Corporate
    Governance and Financial Regulation, coordinated by Alissa Amico, Vedat Akgiray and
    Zeynep Ozcelik, October 2016
ICD-Thomson Reuters, *Islamic Finance Development Report*
International Crisis Group, 'Popular Protests in North Africa and the Middle East [111]: The
    Bahrain Revolt', *Middle East /North Africa Report* 105, 6 April 2011
International Islamic Financial Market, *A Comprehensive Study of the Global Sukuk Market*,
    April 2018
International Islamic Financial Market, *IIFM Sukuk Report*
Islamic Financial Services Board, *Annual Stability Report*
Middle East Economic Digest
Middle East Economic Review
Middle East Report (Washington State: Tacoma)
Moody's Global Corporate Finance, 'Gulf Corporates: The Flip Side of Globalization', June 2009
NCB Capital, 'The Rise of Institutional Investors', 2010
NYSE Corporate Accountability and Listing Standards Committee Report, June 2002
OECD, 'Investment Governance and the Integration of Environmental, Social, and Gover-
    nance Factors', 2017
Oxford Business Group, *A Developing Market in Equities in Bahrain*, 2017
Oxford Business Group, 'New Solar Power Projects in Bahrain add to the Country's Energy
    Mix', 2017
Oxford Business Group, *Report Bahrain*, 2013, 2020
Oxford Business Group, 'Several Innovations in the Pipeline to Deepen Bahrain's Capital
    Markets', *Bahrain Report*, 2017
Oxford Business Group, *The Report: Bahrain* 2019
Standard & Poor's Global Stock Markets Factbook, 2012
Standard & Poor, *Islamic Finance Outlook Thomson Reuters Report*
Zawya, MENA *Mutual Funds Quarterly Bulletin*

Commercial Reports

Al Baraka Banking Group
Bahrain Petroleum Company (Manama)
Gulf Finance House
Gulf Petrochemical Industries Company
Investcorp
Majlis Ugama Islam Singapore

Mumtalakat
Temasek Holdings
Warees Investments

Unpublished Work

Abdelbaki, Hisham H., 'The Impact of Macroeconomic Policies on Income Distribution: An Empirical Study of Egypt', PhD, Development and Project Planning Centre, Bradford University, 2001

Al-Ansari, Fuad, 'Public Open Space on the Transforming Urban Waterfront of Bahrain: The Case of Manama City', PhD thesis, Newcastle University, 2009

Al-Jamri, Mansoor, 'Conclusion: Birth of a New Legal System—Anglo-Muhammadan Law', Middle East Studies Association, 32nd Annual Meeting, Chicago, 6 December 1998

Al-Nakib, Farah, 'Kuwait City: Urbanization, the Built Environment and the Urban Experience Before and After Oil, 1786–1986', PhD thesis, University of London, 2011

Al-Ramahi, Aseel, 'Competing Rationalities: The Evolution of Arbitration in Commercial Disputes in Modern Jordan', PhD thesis, University of London, 2008

Al Shama, Nada Saleh, 'Sustainability of the Dubai Model of Economic Development', PhD thesis, Manchester Business School, 2014

Al Sultan, Fawzi, 'Averting Financial Crisis—Kuwait', World Bank Working Paper No. 243, 1989

Al-Zumai, Fahad, 'Protection of Investors in Gulf Cooperation Council Stock Markets: A Case Study of Kuwait, Bahrain and United Arab Emirates', PhD thesis, University of London, 2006

Al-Zumai, Fahad, 'The Evolution of Corporate Law in the Arab World: The Everlasting Grip of the State', unpublished paper, Kuwait University, no date

Alaabed, Alaa, 'Risk Shifting and Islamic Banking', PhD thesis, INCEIF, the Global University of Islamic Finance, Kuala Lumpur, Malaysia, 2016

Almutairi, B. L., 'Investigating the Feasibility and Soil-Structure Integrity of Onshore Wind Turbine Systems in Kuwait', PhD thesis, Loughborough University, 2017

Alotaibi, Abdullah R., 'Financial Integration in the Gulf Region', PhD thesis, School of Business, University of Western Sydney, 2014

Banerjee, Abhijit V., and Esther Duflo, 'Giving Credit Where it is Due', unpublished paper, Department of Economics, Massachusetts Institute of Technology, Cambridge, MA, 2010

Bean, William, 'The Contemporary Financial Development of Kuwait and Bahrain: A Study of Contrasts', PhD thesis, Princeton University, 1988

Belder, Richard de, 'The Form over Substance Debate in Islamic Finance: Is Aligning Islamic Finance more Proactively with the Ethical Finance Space the Way Forward?', unpublished paper, 2017

Bushehri, A. A., 'Struggle of [sic] National Identity', unpublished typescript, 1995

Deloitte Chartered Institute for Securities and Investment, 'Islamic Finance Scalable and Sustainable Funding Source for Social Infrastructure', March 2018

El-Meehy, Aysa, 'Rewriting the Social Contract: The Social Fund and Egypt's Politics of Hidden Retrenchment', University of Toronto dissertation, 2009

El-Meehy, Aysa, 'Welfare Restructuring in Rentier Arab States: The Case of Bahrain', Paper presented at Gulf Research meeting, Cambridge, July 2011

Ercanbrack, Jonathan, 'Challenging Shari'ah Compliance of Islamic Finance Products: A Few Discussion Points', Working Paper for conference on Shari'ah and Compliance of Islamic Finance, School of Oriental and African Studies, London, 22 February 2018

Gibbs, Tatyana, 'An Analysis of the Effectiveness of Anti Money Laundering and Counter Terrorist Funding Legislation and its Administration in the UAE', PhD thesis, Institute of Advanced Legal Studies, School of Advanced Study, University of London, March 2017

Goey, Ferry de, 'Economic Structure and Self-employment during the Twentieth Century', Paper for 8th EBHA conference, 16–18 September 2004, Barcelona

Gornall, John, 'Some Memories of BAPCO', typescript, Awali, Bahrain, May 1965

Hamza, Manaf Yousuf, 'Land Registration in Bahrain: Its Past, Present and Future within an Integrated GIS Environment', PhD dissertation, University of East London, 2003

Harrigan, Jane, 'Did Food Prices Plant the Seeds of the Arab Spring?', Inaugural Lecture, School of Oriental and African Studies, 28 April 2011

Hayashi, Masami, 'Financial Crisis Prevention: A Psychological Approach from Behavioral Science', MPhil dissertation, Institute of Development Studies, University of Sussex, 2001

Herb, Michael, 'Islamist Movements and the Problem of Democracy in the Arab World', Paper delivered to the MESA Annual Conference, November 2005

Ismail, Muhammed Imran, 'Legal Stratagems [Hiyal] and Usury in Islamic Commercial Law', PhD thesis, University of Birmingham, 2010

Juma, Mandeel Fa'eq, 'Planning Regulations for the Traditional Arab-Islamic Built Environment in Bahrain', MA dissertation, University of Newcastle, 1992

Kahf, M., 'Towards the Revival of Awaqf: A Few Fiqhi Issues to Reconsider', Paper presented at the Harvard Forum of Islamic Finance and Economics 1999

Kapetanovic, Harun, 'Islamic Finance and Economic Development: The Case of Dubai', PhD thesis, Department of Middle Eastern Studies, Kings College, London 2017

Kapiszewski, Andrzej, 'Population, Labor and Education Dilemmas Facing GCC States at the Turn of the Century', Paper presented at the conference, Crossroads of the New Millennium, Abu Dhabi, 9 April 2000

Lane, Philip R., and Gian Maria Milessi-Ferretti, 'Oil Shocks and External Balances', IMF Annual Research Conference, 3–4 November 2016, pp. 1–2

Maynard, Brian P., 'The Role of the Ulama in Shi'ite Social Movements: Bahrain, Lebanon and Iraq', MA thesis, Main National Security Affairs, Naval Postgraduate School, 2005

Moser, Malte, Rainer Bohme, and Dominic Breuker, 'An Inquiry into Money Laundering Tools in the Bitcoin Ecosystem', Proceedings of APWG eCrime Researchers Summit, San Francisco, CA, 2013

Muranaga, J., and T. Shimizu, 'Market Microstructure and Market Liquidity', mimeo, 1999

Pierret, Thomas, 'The Charitable Sector in Syria under the Ba'th: The Irrelevance of Law', unpublished paper

Razavian, Mohammad Taghi, 'Iranian Communities of the Persian Gulf: A Geographical Analysis', PhD thesis, University of London, 1975

Rosberg, James, 'Roads to the Rule of Law: The Emergence of an Independent Judiciary in Contemporary Egypt', PhD thesis, Massachusetts Institute of Technology, Cambridge, MA, 1995

Schumacher, Ilsa Amelia, 'Ritual Devotion among Shi'i in Bahrain', PhD dissertation, University of London, 1987

Torabi, Omid, 'Using Reputation (Fame) to Reduce Information Asymmetry in Islamic Risk-Sharing Crowd Funding Models: A Game Theory Approach', PhD dissertation, International Centre for Education in Islamic Finance (INCEIF), 2017

Index